DATE DUE		
MAR 1 4 2000		
NOV 2 1 2001		
FEB - 4 2002		
FEB 2 7 2002		
OCT 3 0 2002		

	APR 1 2 1997
OCT 2 6 1994	MAY 2 9 1997
NOV 2 8 1994	FEB 1 2 1998
FEB - 2 1995	FEB 2 1 1998
FEB 17 1995	Mar 8
MAR - 3 1995	22
APR - 3 1995	APR - 6 1998

BRODART   Cat. No. 23-221

Panic Disorder and Agoraphobia

A Comprehensive Guide for the Practitioner

Panic Disorder and Agoraphobia

A Comprehensive Guide for the Practitioner

EDITORS: JOHN R. WALKER, G. RON NORTON, AND COLIN A. ROSS
University of Manitoba

BROOKS/COLE PUBLISHING COMPANY
PACIFIC GROVE, CALIFORNIA

Consulting Editor: *C. Eugene Walker, University of Oklahoma*

Brooks/Cole Publishing Company
A Division of Wadsworth, Inc.

Printed in the United States of America

10 9 8 7 6 5 4 3 2 1

Library of Congress Cataloging-in-Publication Data

Panic disorder and agoraphobia: a comprehensive guide for the
   practitioner/edited by John R. Walker, G. Ron Norton, and Colin A.
   Ross.
        p. cm.
   Includes index.
   ISBN 0-534-11286-2
   1. Panic disorders. 2. Agoraphobia. I. Walker, John R., [date]–
   II. Norton, G. Ron, [date]–   . III. Ross, Colin A.
   [DNLM: 1. Agoraphobia. 2. Fear. WM 178 P1912]
RC535.P355 1990
616.85'223--dc20
DNLM/DLC
for Library of Congress   90-2284
                                                                     CIP

Sponsoring Editor: *Claire Verduin*
Editorial Associate: *Gay C. Bond*
Production Coordinator: *Marlene Thom*
Manuscript Editor: *Pamela Evans*
Permissions Editor: *Marie Dubois*
Interior and Cover Design: *Vernon T. Boes*
Art Coordinator: *Cloyce J. Wall*
Interior Illustration: *Fog Press*
Typesetting: *Fog Press*
Printing and Binding: *Arcata Graphics/Martinsburg*

We would like to dedicate this book to the researchers and practitioners in the area of panic disorder and agoraphobia and to our wives.

J. R. W.
G. R. N.
C. A. R.

Contributors

Marty M. Antony, B.Sc. Anxiety Disorders Clinic, Department of Psychiatry, Toronto General Hospital, Toronto, Canada

David H. Barlow, Ph.D. Professor and Director, Phobia and Anxiety Disorders Clinic, Center for Stress and Anxiety Disorders, State University of New York at Albany, Albany, NY

T. K. Bouman, Ph.D. Research Clinical Psychologist, Department of Clinical Psychology, Academic Hospital, University of Groningen, Groningen, The Netherlands

P. M. G. Emmelkamp, Ph.D. Professor of Clinical Psychology and Psychotherapy, Department of Clinical Psychology, Academic Hospital, University of Groningen, Groningen, The Netherlands

Cecilia A. Essau, M.A., Dipl.-Psych. Staff Scientist, Department of Evaluation Research, Max-Planck-Institute of Psychiatry, Munich, West Germany

Rejean Fontaine, M.D. Associate Professor of Research, University of Montreal; Assistant Professor, Department of Psychiatry, McGill University, Montreal, Canada

Abby J. Fyer, M.D. Associate Clinical Professor of Psychiatry, College of Physicians and Surgeons of Columbia University, Co-Director, Anxiety Disorders Clinic, New York State Psychiatric Institute, New York, NY

George N. M. Gurguis, M.D. Visiting Medical Staff Fellow, Unit on Anxiety and Affective Disorders, Biological Psychiatry Branch, National Institute of Mental Health, Bethesda, MD

Richard S. Hallam, M.Sc., Ph.D., Dipl.-Psych. Senior Lecturer in Psychology, University College and Middlesex Hospital Medical School, University of London

Jeffrey E. Hecker, Ph.D. Director of Psychological Services, Department of Psychology, University of Maine, Orono, ME

Rolf G. Jacob, M.D. Associate Professor, Department of Psychiatry, University of Pittsburgh School of Medicine, Pittsburgh, PA

Donald F. Klein, M.D. Professor of Psychiatry, College of Physicians and Surgeons of Columbia University, Director of Research, New York State Psychiatric Institute, New York, NY

Klaus Kuch, M.D. Assistant Professor, Department of Psychiatry, University of Toronto, Toronto, Canada

Malcolm Lader, M.D., Ph.D. Professor of Clinical Psychopharmacology, Institute of Psychiatry, University of London

Scott O. Lilienfeld, M.A. Graduate Student, Clinical Psychology, Department of Psychology, University of Minnesota, Minneapolis, MN

G. Ron Norton, Ph.D. Professor and Chair, Department of Psychology, University of Winnipeg, Winnipeg, Canada

B. Ashok Raj, M.D. Associate Professor, Department of Psychiatry and Behavioral Medicine, University of South Florida College of Medicine, Tampa, FL

Ronald M. Rapee, Ph.D. Lecturer, Department of Psychology, University of Queensland, Australia

Colin A. Ross, M.D. Associate Professor, Department of Psychiatry, University of Manitoba, Winnipeg, Canada

Diana Sandberg, M.D. Assistant Clinical Professor of Psychiatry, College of Physicians and Surgeons of Columbia University, New York, NY

M. Katherine Shear, M.D. Director, Anxiety Disorders Clinic, Payne Whitney Psychiatric Clinic, The New York Hospital, New York, NY

David V. Sheehan, M.B., B.Ch., B.A.O. Professor, Department of Psychiatry and Behavioral Medicine, University of South Florida College of Medicine, Tampa, FL

Richard P. Swinson, M.D. Professor, Department of Psychiatry, University of Toronto, Toronto, Canada

Geoffrey L. Thorpe, Ph.D. Associate Professor, Department of Psychology, University of Maine, Orono, ME

Thomas W. Uhde, M.D. Chief, Unit on Anxiety and Affective Disorders, Biological Psychiatry Branch, National Institute of Mental Health, Bethesda, MD

John R. Walker, Ph.D. Associate Professor, Department of Psychiatry, University of Manitoba, Winnipeg, Canada

Hans-Ulrich Wittchen, M.D., Dipl.-Psych. Head, Department of Evaluation Research, Max-Planck-Institute of Psychiatry, Munich, West Germany; Head, Department of Clinical Psychology, University of Mannheim, Mannheim, West Germany

Preface

The idea for this book germinated during the planning for a regional conference on anxiety disorders titled Anxiety and Panic Disorders: The Long-Range View, held in Winnipeg, Canada, in March 1987 by the Department of Psychiatry at the University of Manitoba. With the support of the Royal College of Physicians and Surgeons of Canada and the National Health Research and Development Program of Health and Welfare Canada, it was possible to arrange for some of the preeminent researchers in the field to attend. Additional support for the conference was provided by Bristol Laboratories, Cyanamid Pharmaceuticals, Hoffmann-La Roche Ltd., Lederle Pharmaceutical Products, Parke-Davis Canada Inc., Pfizer Canada Inc., Squibb Canada Inc., and Upjohn Co. of Canada. We would like to express our appreciation to these organizations for their support of the conference.

The presentations at the conference and, more importantly, the response from attending practitioners convinced us to expand the scope of the book to focus on practitioners' concerns. Many books on anxiety disorders have focused on the researcher's concerns and left many practitioners' questions unanswered. These books have also tended to be written either from the biological or the psychological point of view, when the practitioner must in fact be knowledgeable about both approaches to answer patients' questions and make well-informed recommendations for treatment. We decided, therefore, that the most appropriate target audience for the book was the practitioner or student in psychiatry, psychology, or other mental health profession who is called upon to treat individuals with panic disorder and who would prefer to do so from a sound scientific base. Long-term management and outcome were emphasized, as these are particularly important considerations for the practitioner. Where research was not yet available to answer questions important to the practitioner, we asked contributors to draw on their extensive clinical experience to make practical recommendations. We included two chapters focusing on management of the difficult case—something not always considered in descriptions of treatment approaches.

Our approach—asking contributors to conform to a standard outline for their chapters—was more demanding than the usual task faced by contributors, and we appreciate their cooperation and patience as we worked to ensure parallel formats among the chapters. We would also like to thank the publishers and authors who allowed us to reproduce tables, figures, and instruments from other sources.

Acknowledgments

It is not possible to complete a book like this without the encouragement and assistance of a great many people. We would particularly like to thank Philip Katz, Nady el-Guebaly, and Lorne Sexton for their administrative support, for both the conference and the book. Garry Martin and David Barlow provided assistance in the book's planning stages. Outstanding secretarial support was provided by Renée Frenette, Nancy Clark, and Donna Fontaine. Barry Mallin was of great help in carrying out the challenging task of translation among computer systems and word processing programs. Our research assistant, Susan Ness, did an excellent job of checking the manuscripts and ensuring a consistent style throughout the book. Pat Hebert provided important library and research support at every stage of the project. Our publisher, Brooks/Cole, offered valuable assistance; we would especially like to thank Pamela Evans and Marlene Thom for their diligent and helpful editorial work.

A number of our colleagues and students helped us by reviewing the outlines and some of the chapters and by providing feedback from the practitioner's point of view: Dennis Dyck, Gloria Eldridge, Patricia Furer, Andrea Hazen, Steve Holborn, Jaye Miles, Dave Ness, Jack O'Riordan, Vincent Paul, Joe Rallo, Linda Rhodes, Lynne Robinson, Gary Rockman, Katherine Schultz, Rick Shore, Razzaque Siddiqui, Laine Torgrud, Nancy Wightman, and Keith Wilson. Gloria Eldridge deserves special mention for her feedback on early drafts of Chapters 1 and 15. Gayle Beck offered many helpful comments as well. To these individuals and the many others who provided their generous assistance we would like to extend our sincere thanks. Finally, we would especially like to thank our families for their support, encouragement, and patience as we took time away from our usual work and home routines to finish this book.

John R. Walker
G. Ron Norton
Colin A. Ross

Contents

CHAPTER 3

The Epidemiology of Panic Attacks, Panic Disorder, and Agoraphobia

103

HANS-ULRICH WITTCHEN AND CECILIA A. ESSAU

CHAPTER 4
The Biology Of Panic Disorder: A Long-term View and Critique   150
MALCOLM LADER

CHAPTER 5
Psychosocial Aspects of Panic Disorder   175
GEOFFREY L. THORPE AND JEFFREY E. HECKER

PART 2
TREATMENT   209

CHAPTER 6

The Pharmacologic Treatment of
Panic Disorder and Agoraphobia   – 211

ABBY J. FYER, DIANA SANDBERG, AND DONALD F. KLEIN

CHAPTER 9

The Psychodynamic Approach in the Treatment of Panic Disorder   335

M. KATHERINE SHEAR

CHAPTER 10

The Role of The Primary Care Physician in the Treatment of Panic Disorder   352

REJEAN FONTAINE

PART 3
FUTURE DIRECTIONS IN
RESEARCH, ASSESSMENT, AND TREATMENT   431

Panic Disorder and Agoraphobia

A Comprehensive Guide for the Practitioner

BASIC
CONCEPTS

PART 1

CHAPTER 1

Panic Disorder and Agoraphobia: An Introduction

G. RON NORTON, JOHN R. WALKER, AND COLIN A. ROSS

Panic disorder is a common problem frequently seen in general and mental health settings. Wittchen and Essau (Chapter 3), in reviewing epidemiological studies, suggest that approximately 5% of the population will have agoraphobia at some time in their life and another 2% will have panic disorder without agoraphobia. They report a remarkable consistency in the lifetime prevalence of panic disorder found by researchers using similar methodology in different locations (for example, the United States, Germany, Canada, and Puerto Rico) and in different cultural and racial groups. Community studies suggest that women have problems with panic attacks and agoraphobia approximately twice as often as men, although the ratio for panic disorder without agoraphobia is nearly equal for males and females. Age of onset is typically between 20 and 30 years of age (Wittchen & Essau, Chapter 3).

Many more people experience panic attacks that never develop into the full-blown disorder. Studies in nonclinical populations suggest that one-third or more of young adults experience infrequent panic attacks (Norton, Dorward, & Cox, 1986). Although these individuals do not seek treatment as frequently as do those with the full-blown disorder, they do experience higher levels of general anxiety and depression than individuals without panic attacks. It is likely that some proportion of these individuals will go on to experience the full-blown disorder, and that early intervention may enable them to avoid its most negative effects.

Panic disorder and agoraphobia present in many different ways and are often associated with other mental health problems such as major depression and chemical dependency. The problem may develop very rapidly and can be very disabling. It is not uncommon for individuals to seek help who have long and productive work histories but who are now on the verge of losing a job or who are already on sick leave. The problem also interferes with an individual's ability to function in the family. Studies of health care utilization (reviewed by Wittchen and Essau in Chapter 3) indicate that individuals with panic disorder are heavy users of health services, actually using mental health services more often than individuals with other serious mental health problems, including schizophrenia, major affective disorder, and somatization disorder (Boyd, 1986). Both the disability produced by panic disorder and the heavy utilization of health services suggests that there are significant economic consequences of effective — or ineffective — treatment.

In the past 20 years, researchers and clinicians have developed treatment procedures that provide marked relief to most people who experience panic disorder. Fyer, Sandberg, and Klein (Chapter 6) maintain that approximately 85% of patients receiving pharmacological treatment will be panic free once the treatment is adjusted to an adequate level. Similarly, Rapee and Barlow (Chapter 7) claim that approximately 80% of panic disorder patients with minimal phobic avoidance will be panic free following cognitive-behavioral therapy. Although these results are impressive, our understanding of the causes and treatment of panic disorder is still incomplete and demands more and better research. However, the practitioner faced with distressed patients cannot wait until treatment procedures have been perfected. Therefore, *Panic Disorder and Agoraphobia: A Comprehensive Guide for the Practitioner* has two major goals: first, to provide the practitioner with up-to-date information about the etiology and treatment of panic disorder, and second, to address what needs to be done in the future to improve our understanding of panic disorder. There has been a tendency in the past for most practitioners to work from either a primarily biological or psychological point of view in addressing these problems. In this book we hope to present both views through the eyes of practitioner/researchers who have worked in this area for many years. We feel that even though most practitioners specialize in one or the other of these approaches, it is important that they be knowledgeable about both in order to make informed choices in assessment and treatment and to help their patients make informed choices.

What Is Panic Disorder?

Case Examples

Panic disorder has a core set of symptoms, but its presentation may vary along several important dimensions. Three case histories are included here to illustrate the commonalities and differences in presentation.

> Karen was a 33-year-old part-time office worker seen by one of the authors. She described her problem as starting when she was in a dental office having several fillings. She was not particularly anxious about seeing the dentist, but after 40 minutes in the chair she suddenly noticed that her heart was racing, she was soaked with perspiration, she had difficulty catching her breath, and she had "pins and needles" feelings in her hands and feet. She became very panicky and felt that she had to get out of the situation and get some fresh air. The dentist said that it wasn't safe for her to walk alone, gave her oxygen, and called an ambulance. The ambulance attendants recognized that she was hyperventilating, removed the oxygen mask, and had her breathe into a paper bag. Whenever she tried to tell them what had happened, she would start to breathe very rapidly again and they would have her stop talking and breathe into a paper bag.

At the local hospital she had an ECG; the emergency room physician told her that nothing was wrong and that she could go home. She could recall no other specific advice. She felt extremely unsteady and was shocked that they were sending her home when she was feeling so badly. The next day she had to return, accompanied by her mother, to the dentist's office to have the fillings finished. It was all she could manage to tolerate 5 minutes in the chair while the work was finished.

Later in the interview she recalled that at the time of the panic attack in the dentist's chair she was awaiting another dental procedure with a specialist that would involve cutting the gum, treating an area of gum disease, and then stitching the gum. The procedure had been demonstrated to her weeks earlier with a model and she found it very frightening. She recalled thinking just before she had the panic attack that she would have to be in the chair even longer for the dental surgery. After the experience in her own dentist's office, she canceled the periodontal procedure.

Following the first panic attack Karen was very worried about having another, partly because she did not know what had happened to her. She was so anxious that she began to have difficulty eating, feeling that she would be unable to swallow the food and might choke. Her distress was compounded by what she felt was an unsympathetic response from her family physician. He suggested that the problem was just "nerves" and that she take an analgesic when she went in for dental surgery. He also provided a prescription for diazepam, to take as needed.

Over the next few weeks Karen's problem with anxiety was accompanied by increasing feelings of depression; she found herself crying frequently and unable to deal with her regular routine. She struggled to hide this from her friends and family, but eventually they found out and were very supportive. At the time of the first interview, Karen reported that she had been contemplating suicide to escape from her distress and to lift the burden from her family. She had difficulty staying alone at home because of her feelings of anxiety and depression. She had lost 12 pounds since the onset of the problem. Her breathing was fast and irregular during the interview, and she felt so unsteady that it was difficult to walk without the assistance of her husband, who accompanied her.

Detailed questioning in the second interview revealed that Karen had actually had difficulty with anxiety, at least intermittently, since young adulthood. She preferred to avoid closed-in situations—such as small rooms, some restaurants, and large social gatherings—where she would have difficulty leaving to get fresh air if she felt unwell. She had experienced episodes of shakiness, tingling, and paleness in response to these situations and to stressful life events. Over the years she had occasionally used diazepam. Her father had had a similar problem since he was about 35 years old.

Other patients present with long-standing problems with panic disorder and agoraphobia but with less severe current distress.

Nancy was a 36-year-old homemaker who presented requesting help for a long-standing problem with agoraphobia. She had been in individual psychotherapy for 3 years and had seen little improvement. She reported that her first panic attack had occurred 4 or 5 years previously in a large department store at about the time her parents were separating. She suddenly felt faint and dizzy and had difficulty focusing her eyes. She then noticed that her heart was thumping, her chest was tight, and she was nauseated. She felt panicky and left for home immediately. At home she gradually started feeling better. The next time she went downtown she had a similar experience, and it was not long before she was avoiding a great many such situations.

At the time she came to the clinic, she had difficulty walking more than a few houses from her home unless accompanied by a family member or friend. She continued to have panic attacks in unfamiliar situations, whether accompanied or alone, and in situations from which she felt escape was difficult. She also had occasional attacks alone at home. She had a great deal of anticipatory anxiety when she had to enter difficult situations. Panic attacks were very frightening experiences for her; when she was having one she thought she was likely to faint and perhaps even die. She had intense migraine headaches at times and worried about having an undiagnosed brain tumor. Only her immediate family knew of her problem.

The history revealed that Nancy was the only child of an affectionate father who had a problem with alcoholism and an extremely rejecting mother who threatened to leave her and her father many times while she was growing up.

Men as well as women experience panic disorder. The man discussed in the following example developed panic disorder following a serious illness.

George was a 45-year-old manager who consulted the Anxiety Disorders Clinic following his recovery from a heart attack. He had an intense fear of having another heart attack and perhaps dying from it. His initial problem was with sleep-onset insomnia, starting in the hospital and continuing when he returned home. He was worried that he might have a heart attack during his sleep and be unable to call for help. He was receiving a minor tranquilizer at bedtime and found that this helped him sleep, but he did not want to continue on this medication indefinitely.

As we explored his sleeping pattern, George also revealed that he often woke during the night in intense anxiety. He found it extremely difficult to get back to sleep at these times. His heart attack had been marked by symptoms of moderate severity, including tingling in his left arm, difficulty breathing, and a heavy feeling in his chest. The symptoms he experienced when he woke during the night were similar: a tingling arm, shortness of breath, chest heaviness, and a feeling of intense anxiety and fear of death. On one occasion he had his wife take him to the emergency department of a local hospital during the night when he thought he was having another heart attack (he was not). He noted that on at least some of the occasions when he awoke during the night he was sleeping on his left side, as had been his habit before the heart attack. This could have caused the tingling in his arm; he mentioned also that he tended to avoid sleeping on his side following the heart attack because he found these sensations unpleasant.

He experienced similar but less intense feelings when he entered the basement workroom where he first experienced symptoms of the heart attack, so he avoided entering the basement. He also tended to avoid situations in which his heart rate increased, even though his cardiologist had recommended participation in a closely supervised rehabilitation exercise program when he left the hospital. The cardiologist and his personal physician had told him that the damage to his heart muscle in the attack was minimal and that he should gradually resume normal activities.

These patients demonstrate part of the range of problems seen in individuals with panic disorder and agoraphobia. Karen was having much more severe distress at the time she came for treatment, and in fact there was a serious risk of suicide. Nancy, on the other hand, though quite disabled, was in a fairly stable situation with a somewhat less urgent need to initiate treatment. Both had factors in their family background to suggest a family history of mental health problems (panic disorder or alcoholism). Karen had a happy childhood and early development, whereas Nancy had a traumatic and stressful upbringing. George had no family history of mental health problems and a generally happy childhood with one traumatic accident in young adulthood in which some friends were killed. In George's case the life situation that preceded the onset of panic attacks was clearly traumatic; adjustment disorder with anxious mood and post–traumatic stress disorder could be considered as alternative diagnoses. There were many other important biological and psychological factors in these case examples, but those factors will be dealt with thoroughly in the following chapters.

Experiences with the Health Care System

One fairly typical feature in the cases we've described was Karen's and Nancy's experience in obtaining treatment. Both presented to a variety of health service providers in an attempt to find adequate treatment. Both experienced a good deal of frustration in obtaining treatment that they found helpful. It is common to talk to patients who have seen a wide range of practitioners and who have undergone a truly impressive battery of medical tests searching for the cause of their distress. The reactions of service providers range from the sympathetic and helpful to the response that the patient "just has anxiety" and is putting unreasonable demands on expensive health care services. Many patients in our Anxiety Disorders Clinic report that they first found a thorough explanation of their problem through an article in a newspaper or popular magazine or through seeing the problem presented on a television program. Many of those who have some information about the range of treatments available have obtained this information through the self-help books that are increasingly available in bookstores and public libraries.

Typically, the most accessible services are those of a general or family physician. These service providers generally use modest doses of the minor tranquilizers to treat panic disorder. They vary in experience with this problem from being very able to provide appropriate pharmacological treatment and make referrals to being relatively uninformed about panic disorder. Modest doses of minor tranquilizers may produce temporary relief for some; however, a good deal of disability and distress usually remains, and often patients develop additional problems—such as phobic avoidance, excessive dependency, and chemical dependency—in their attempt to cope with the disorder.

Recently the authors carried out a study of patients presenting with anxiety problems such as panic disorder in local immediate care health facilities: the emergency department of a large teaching hospital and a walk-in clinic (Ross, Walker, Norton, & Neufeld, 1988). Patients who emphasized somatic symptoms in their presentation received diagnostic tests, focusing primarily on cardiac or thyroid problems. Those who emphasized anxiety as a primary complaint tended not to be sent for diagnostic tests; instead they were given minor tranquilizers and referred back to their own physicians or to psychiatric services when they were accessible. These findings were similar to those of Katon and his co-workers (Katon, 1984; Katon, Vitaliano, Russo, Jones, & Anderson, 1987), who found that most people with panic disorder seen in primary care settings initially present with somatic problems and consequently are not diagnosed as having an anxiety disorder. Katon (1984) found that the three most common presentations were cardiac symptoms (chest pain, tachycardia, irregular heart beat), gastrointestinal symptoms (especially epigastric distress), and neurologic symptoms (headache, dizziness/vertigo, syncope, or parasthesias), and that 81% of the patients he saw in consultation had pain as a presenting complaint.

As most persons with anxiety problems will obtain service in the general health and mental health services sector, rather than in specialized anxiety clinics, it is important that practitioners in those settings be familiar with panic disorder and its treatment. Our experience has been that both practitioners and consumers are gradually becoming more sophisticated in their understanding of panic disorder, although it continues to be difficult to obtain access to specialized services when they are necessary.

Diagnosis

Most practitioners in North America use the criteria published by the American Psychiatric Association in the *Diagnostic and Statistical Manual of Mental Disorders* (DSM-III-R) (American Psychiatric Association, 1987) in making formal diagnoses. The diagnoses are discussed briefly here to familiarize the reader with the terminology that will be used in this chapter and the remainder of the book. The terms and criteria are described in detail by Jacob and Lilienfeld in Chapter 2, which covers diagnosis and medical and psychological evaluation, and the reader is encouraged to refer to that chapter for a thorough discussion.

Within the DSM-III-R framework, a *panic attack* is defined as a period of intense fear or discomfort in which the person experiences at least four of the following symptoms: shortness of breath or smothering sensations; dizziness, unsteady feelings, or faintness; palpitations or accelerated heart rate;

trembling or shaking; sweating; choking; nausea or abdominal distress; depersonalization or derealization; numbness or tingling sensations; flushes (hot flashes) or chills; chest pain or discomfort; fear of dying; and fear of going crazy or doing something uncontrolled. (Attacks with fewer than four of these symptoms are defined as *limited symptom attacks*.)

For a diagnosis of *panic disorder* to be assigned, the person must meet several criteria. First, at one time during the disturbance one or more panic attacks must have occurred that were unexpected (did not occur immediately before or after exposure to a situation that almost always caused anxiety) and that were not triggered by situations in which the person was the focus of others' attention. Second, *either* four attacks must have occurred in a 4-week period at some point *or* one or more attacks must have been followed by at least a month of persistent fear of having another. Third, during at least some of the attacks at least four of the listed symptoms must have developed suddenly and increased in intensity within 10 minutes of the beginning of the first symptom noticed in the attack. And finally, it cannot be established that an organic factor initiated and maintained the disturbance. Once the presence of panic disorder is established, the next step is to evaluate the extent of related phobic avoidance. In *panic disorder with agoraphobia* the person has a

> fear of being in places or situations from which escape might be difficult or embarrassing or in which help might not be available in the event of a panic attack . . . . As a result of this fear, the person either restricts travel or needs a companion when away from home, or else endures agoraphobic situations despite intense anxiety . . . . Common agoraphobic situations include being outside the home alone, being in a crowd or standing in a line, being on a bridge, and traveling in a bus, train, or car [APA, 1987, pp. 238–239].

Panic disorder without agoraphobia is the diagnosis assigned in cases that meet the criteria for panic disorder but in which there is not even mild agoraphobic avoidance. *Agoraphobia without history of panic disorder* is the diagnosis assigned in cases in which there is agoraphobic avoidance but no history of panic disorder. In these cases there are frequently limited-symptom attacks. There is some controversy about the frequency of occurrence of this last disorder; this is discussed in more detail by Wittchen and Essau in Chapter 3.

Jacob and Lilienfeld (Chapter 2) point out that the differential diagnosis of panic disorder and agoraphobia requires a thorough understanding not only of the characteristics of these disorders but also of related psychiatric and medical disorders. People with a variety of mental health problems including major depression, psychoses, and other anxiety disorders also experience panic attacks. People with medical disorders such as thyroid and cardiac disease may experience symptoms similar to panic attacks. Frequently individuals present with more than one fully developed medical or psychiatric disorder and with related psychosocial problems, so that thorough assessment and treatment planning may be quite challenging. Jacob and Lilienfeld as well as others (Rapee & Barlow, Chapter 7; Sheehan & Raj, Chapter 11) stress the importance of using reliable and valid assessment instruments that provide specific diagnoses of anxiety and other disorders, including a quantitative assessment of the problem that may be used in evaluation of outcome. Chapter 2 provides an extensive review of structured interviews and other assessment devices that are of value in diagnosis.

History of the Concepts of
Panic Disorder and Agoraphobia

One of the earliest accounts of what was probably panic disorder in the formal medical literature was Da Costa's (1871) description of "irritable heart." He reported on a large number of cases of irritable heart seen in the army during and after the U.S. Civil War, but noted that this problem was also very common in private practice in both peacetime and wartime. He described irritable heart as a functional cardiac problem involving symptoms in other systems as well. The most common symptoms were palpitation, cardiac pain, rapid pulse, shortness of breath, digestive problems, and nervous disorders such as giddiness (dizziness), disturbed sleep, and headache. The reader will recognize that many of these symptoms overlap with those of present-day panic disorder. Da Costa indicated that irritable heart was often seen in otherwise healthy young men and related the causes to

> ... quick and long marches, heavy work, producing the affection [sic], or even slight exertion in those whose constitution has been impaired by insufficient or indigestible food, or whose strength has suffered, or condition of the heart has been disturbed by diarrhea or fever .... It seems to me the most likely that the heart has become irritable, from its over-action and frequent excitement, and that disordered innervation keeps it so [p. 40].

Similar syndromes were described by Oppenheim (1918) and by Cohen and White (1950) as "neurocirculatory asthenia."

Agoraphobia was also described in the medical literature at about this time. Mathews, Gelder, and Johnston (1981) describe the early work published in German:

> Westphal suggested the name agoraphobia for a condition in which the most striking symptom was anxiety that appeared when one was walking across open spaces or through empty streets. Westphal was not the only person to have noticed the condition at that time, for there is an earlier description by Benedikt (1870) in the previous year. However, Benedikt thought that the central feature was dizziness rather than anxiety, and he accordingly suggested the name *Platzschwindel* ("dizziness in public places"), which has not survived [p. 1].

Shear (Chapter 9) points out that in the early 1900s Freud described "anxiety neurosis," one of the features of which was the "anxiety attack," a term used before the term *panic attack*. Unfortunately Freud's later writings, which greatly influenced the development of the concept of anxiety neurosis, focused on unconscious psychosexual components that may have directed researchers and clinicians away from more fundamental physiological and psychological factors in the anxiety disorders.

In the early 1960s, while evaluating a new drug for treatment of psychiatric disorders (imipramine), Klein and his colleagues made the unexpected observation that it was useful in suppressing panic attacks experienced by patients with anxiety neurosis but that it had little effect on the less extreme generalized anxiety experienced by these patients. He followed this observation with a number of clinical reports (Klein & Fink, 1962; Klein, 1964) that suggested that imipramine had a specific effect in suppressing panic attacks, whereas other drugs—such as diazepam—were effective in reducing generalized anxiety. This "pharmacological dissection" of the components of anxiety neurosis initiated a change in research focus that was as dramatic as it was productive, stimulating research into treatment, nosology, epidemiology, and the basic biological and psychological mechanisms in anxiety disorders. Although Klein's work fundamentally changed our approach to understanding anxiety disorders, his initial findings may have been partly an artifact of the specific drugs and dose levels used. Recent studies show that patients with panic disorder respond positively to high-potency triazolobenzodiazepines, such as alprazolam (Fyer, Sandberg, & Klein, Chapter 6), and to high doses of diazepam (Noyes et al., 1984). If patients with panic disorder respond to both antidepressants and benzodiazepines, it is possible that panic disorder and generalized anxiety disorder may not be qualitatively different, as Klein and his colleagues suggested they were. The differences might instead be mainly of degree or of severity or might reflect a more complex interaction between biological events, learned behavior patterns, and current environmental forces.

Phobic anxiety disorders were one of the earliest areas of focus of the behavior therapies as they developed in the late 1950s and through the 1960s. Mathews et al. (1981), who participated in many of the developments in this area, provide an interesting description of the development of treatment approaches for agoraphobia. Early approaches to treatment involved "graded retraining" in which patients "were first taught to relax and then they were exposed gradually to increasingly fearful situations, while they attempted to remain as relaxed as possible" (Mathews et al., 1981, p. 71). The therapist accompanied the patient into the feared situation and the treatment required large amounts of therapist time (often on the order of 50 to 100 sessions with inpatients with agoraphobia) to produce modest progress. The procedure was so expensive and produced such modest results that it was seen to be of limited practical utility. Wolpe's (1958) work on systematic desensitization was very influential in the field, and this procedure was used with agoraphobia. Work with outpatients suggested that systematic desensitization, carried out in the imagination with instructions to practice exposure in real life between sessions, was more effective than traditional individual or group psychotherapy in treating outpatients with agoraphobia.

As long as the work emphasized keeping anxiety at low levels, as is traditionally done in systematic desensitization, progress was relatively slow. A number of studies of "flooding," which emphasized facing high-anxiety situations and then allowing anxiety to decrease with exposure, suggested that the technique overcame phobic avoidance much more rapidly. At first studies of flooding emphasized imaginal exposure, but soon studies incorporated real-life exposure after or instead of imaginal exposure. The success of flooding approaches created a resurgence of interest in in vivo or real-life exposure to feared situations, as there was less concern with maintaining anxiety at low levels. Mathews et al. (1981) suggest that in many cases the exposure the patient attempts between treatment sessions has the greatest effect on reduction of phobic avoidance. This view has led to studies of treatment in which homework assignments in the natural environment between sessions are seen as important components of treatment. These studies resulted in more rapid and less expensive treatments for agoraphobic avoidance.

Because behavioral treatments concentrated on the reduction of phobic avoidance, there was initially little focus on assessment and treatment of the panic attacks that were typically a part of this problem. As Thorpe and Hecker (Chapter 5) indicate, early behavioral research was based on simple conditioning models that did not adequately accommodate cognitive and physiological factors within their explanatory systems.

As the early pharmacological and behavioral studies were being carried out, dramatic improvements in research methodology made it more feasible to isolate the active components of treatment and to compare alternative treatments. Encouraging treatment studies did a great deal to stimulate basic biological and psychological research on panic disorder and agoraphobia.

Influenced by Klein's work highlighting the importance of panic attacks, in 1980 the American Psychiatric Association published the third edition of the *Diagnostic and Statistical Manual of Mental Disorders* (American Psychiatric Association, 1980). The DSM-III, as it was known, represented a major change in the way in which anxiety disorders were conceptualized. The presence of spontaneous panic attacks became a major feature in the differential diagnosis of anxiety disorders. This change from earlier editions of the DSM was based largely on the success of the Research Diagnostic Criteria (RDC) developed by Spitzer, Endicott, and Robins (1978). The RDC were, for the most part, empirically derived from signs and symptoms specific to particular psychiatric disorders. The revised version of the *Diagnostic and Statistical Manual of Mental Disorders* (DSM-III-R) (American Psychiatric Association, 1987), has placed even more emphasis on the presence of spontaneous panic attacks. For example, the DSM-III grouped agoraphobia with panic attacks along with other phobic disorders. The revised version places panic disorder in a separate category that varies on several continua: (1) the amount of avoidance, (2) the number of symptoms experienced during a panic attack, and (3) the overall severity of the disorder. These continua represent important dimensions in planning a treatment program. For example, many researchers and clinicians (such as Rapee & Barlow, Chapter 7) believe that panic attacks and avoidance represent distinct aspects of panic disorder and require different treatment approaches.

Organization of the Book

Following this introductory chapter, in Chapter 2 Jacob and Lilienfeld provide a comprehensive description of diagnostic and assessment procedures useful in developing a differential diagnosis and assessment of panic disorder. Chapter 3, written by Wittchen and Essau, provides background on the epidemiology of panic attacks, panic disorder, and agoraphobia, drawing on research carried out in several countries in North America and Western Europe. These authors also offer information on the different diagnostic systems for anxiety disorders used in North America and in Europe. In Chapter 4, Malcolm Lader describes the biological factors in panic disorder and critiques some of the models that have been used by biological practitioners and researchers. Similarly, Thorpe and Hecker in Chapter 5 review psychological models of panic disorder and agoraphobia and then critically review the evidence that has been gathered to evaluate those models.

Part 2 examines the most widely used treatments for panic disorder and agoraphobia as well as the most commonly encountered problems in treatment. In Chapter 6, Fyer, Sandberg, and Klein describe the pharmacological treatment of panic disorder and agoraphobia, and in Chapter 7, Rapee and Barlow provide a detailed description of the cognitive-behavioral treatment of panic attacks and agoraphobic avoidance. Many individuals with panic disorder receive both pharmacological and psychological treatment. In Chapter 8, Swinson, Kuch, and Antony review the practical and research issues to consider when deciding whether to combine pharmacological and cognitive-behavorial treatments. Emphasizing integration with cognitive-behavioral or pharmacological treatment, Shear describes in Chapter 9 how panic disorder may be approached from a psychodynamic point of view. Fontaine (Chapter 10) discusses the role of the primary care physician and makes recommendations for an approach to panic disorder in primary care medical settings.

Often individuals presenting for treatment of panic disorder have other medical or psychological problems or difficult life situations that may not be considered in works describing treatment of the "typical" patient. The last two chapters in the treatment section address treatment of the "difficult" or harder-to-treat patient. Many of these situations (such as chemical dependency, marital difficulty, and medical problems) come up so frequently that most practitioners should be familiar with them. As only a limited amount of research is available to guide us in this area, it is helpful to have the views of practitioner/researchers with a wide range of clinical experience. Sheehan and Raj (Chapter 11) discuss the pharmacological treatment of the difficult case, and Emmelkamp and Bouman (Chapter 12) consider the psychological treatment of patients with similar problems.

In Part 3, the final three chapters of the book focus on future directions in research, assessment, and treatment. In Chapter 13, Gurguis and Uhde review research on the neurotransmitter systems that may be involved in the anxiety disorders and consider new directions for research. In Chapter 14, Hallam speculates on future directions for psychosocial research and the integration of biological and psychological factors. In the last chapter, we have a "final word" of commentary on some of the important questions raised by earlier chapters. Although we have come a long way in our understanding and treatment of panic disorder, there is a great deal of work still to be done.

Our chapter contributors bring a variety of different practical and theoretical considerations to their work and often display differences of opinion about how to manage particular treatment situations. Where research was not yet available to assist us in dealing with important clinical questions, we asked our contributors to draw on their own extensive clinical experience to make practical recommendations. We hope that this will help practitioners develop their own approach to challenging treatment situations.

References

American Psychiatric Association. (1980). *Diagnostic and statistical manual of mental disorders* (3rd ed.). Washington, DC: Author.

American Psychiatric Association. (1987). *Diagnostic and statistical manual of mental disorders* (3rd ed., rev.). Washington, DC: Author.

Benedikt, V. (1870). "Über Platzschwindel." *Allgemeine Wiener Medizinische Zeitung, 15,* 488.

Boyd, J. H. (1986). Use of mental health services for the treatment of panic disorder. *American Journal of Psychiatry, 143,* 1569–1574.

Cohen, M. E., & White, P. D. (1950). Life situations, emotions and neurocirculatory asthenia (anxiety neurosis, neurasthenia, effort syndrome). In H. G. Wolff (Ed.), *Life stress and bodily disease* (Nervous and Mental Disease, Research Publication No. 29). Baltimore: Williams & Wilkins.

Da Costa, J. M. (1871). On irritable heart: A clinical study of a form of functional cardiac disorder and its consequences. *American Journal of the Medical Sciences, 61,* 17–52.

Katon, W. (1984). Panic disorder and somatization: Review of 55 cases. *The American Journal of Medicine, 77,* 101–106.

Katon, W., Vitaliano, P. P., Russo, J., Jones, M., & Anderson, K. (1987). Panic disorder: Spectrum of severity and somatization. *Journal of Nervous and Mental Disease, 175,* 12–19.

Klein, D. F. (1964). Delineation of two drug responsive anxiety syndromes. *Psychopharmacologia, 5,* 397–408.

Klein, D. F., & Fink, M. (1962). Psychiatric reaction pattern to imipramine. *American Journal of Psychiatry, 119,* 438.

Mathews, A. M., Gelder, M. G., & Johnston, D. W. (1981). *Agoraphobia: Nature and treatment*. New York: Guilford Press.

Norton, G. R., Dorward, J., & Cox, B. J. (1986). Factors associated with panic attacks in nonclinical subjects. *Behavior Therapy, 17,* 239–252.

Noyes, R., Jr., Anderson, D. J., Clancy, J., Crowe, R. R., Slymen, D. J., Ghoneim, M. M., & Hindrichs, J. V. (1984). Diazepam and propranolol in panic disorder and agoraphobia. *Archives of General Psychiatry, 41,* 287–292.

Oppenheim, B. S. (1918). Report on neurocirculatory asthenia and its management. *Military Surgeon, 42,* 711–744.

Ross, C. A., Walker, J. R., Norton, G. R., & Neufeld, K. (1988). Management of anxiety and panic attacks in immediate care facilities. *General Hospital Psychiatry, 10,* 129–131.

Spitzer, R. L., Endicott, J., & Robins, E. (1978). Research diagnostic criteria: Rationale and reliability. *Archives of General Psychiatry, 36,* 773–782.

Wolpe, J. (1958). *Psychotherapy by reciprocal inhibition*. Stanford, CA: Stanford University Press.

CHAPTER 2

Panic Disorder: Diagnosis, Medical Assessment, and Psychological Assessment

ROLF G. JACOB AND SCOTT O. LILIENFELD

In this chapter we describe the assessment of patients with panic disorder. The chapter is organized according to the typical sequence of steps that new patients might undergo when they enter an anxiety disorders program: initial evaluation, medical evaluation, and secondary evaluation.

The initial evaluation is a general psychiatric interview covering all potential problem areas. The patient is asked to supply basic demographic and social data, and a "psychiatric review of systems" is done. This review includes questions not only about anxiety symptoms but also about history of depression, suicidal behavior, mania, psychosis, alcohol use, antisocial behavior, drug abuse, medical problems, and prescribed medications.

Conducting the initial interview and making the preliminary diagnosis requires familiarity not only with basic symptoms of anxiety but also with the diagnostic criteria for psychiatric disorders. Therefore, in the first main section of this chapter, we describe the diagnostic criteria for panic disorder, briefly describe the characteristics of other anxiety disorders, and discuss the main psychiatric differential diagnostic considerations.

The medical evaluation is done by a medically trained person and includes eliciting the medical history, a review of systems, and physical and laboratory examinations. If the patient is well known by a community physician and was examined recently, this step may be omitted, provided that the community physician can supply the appropriate information. Even though the medical evaluation may be completed by a person other than the patient's therapist, the therapist should be conversant with the medical differential diagnosis of panic disorder. Hence, we discuss the medical differential diagnosis in the second main section.

The purpose of the secondary evaluation is to confirm the diagnosis, to quantify aspects of the disorder, and to make a behavioral assessment. The secondary evaluation is typically done by the program or the therapist actually treating the patient. The clinician reviews information obtained in the initial evaluation and the medical evaluation, and conducts more detailed and focused interviews and tests. The secondary evaluation may also include a psychophysiological assessment and may require several sessions, particularly if the treatment program is conducting research.

In the third main section, we consider the type of assessments that would usually be done during the secondary evaluation, such as psychological tests or structured interviews, and behavioral and psychophysiological tests. In this

16

last section, we will evaluate the reliability and validity of the most commonly used tests. Chapter 7 provides further examples of secondary assessments as well as practical details on how to conduct the behavioral assessment.

The Initial Evaluation

The initial evaluation requires knowledge of the terms used to describe different types of anxiety seen in patients and of the diagnostic criteria for diagnosing various anxiety disorders. Therefore, we will first define the basic terms *fear*, *phobia*, *anxiety*, and *panic*. Then we will describe the diagnostic criteria for panic disorder according to the revised third edition of the *Diagnostic and Statistical Manual of Mental Disorders* (American Psychiatric Association, 1987). Finally, we will consider the differential diagnosis of panic disorder with respect to psychiatric disorders.

Basic Concepts

Definitions of Fear and Phobia

Dorland's Medical Dictionary defines the term *fear* as a "normal emotional response to consciously recognized and external sources of danger. This response is manifested by alarm, apprehension, or disquiet" (*Dorland's Illustrated Medical Dictionary*, 1979). From a linguistic point of view, the word *fear* is derived from the Old English word for "danger" (Marks, 1969; compare the Swedish *fara* or German *Gefahr* meaning "danger"). Thus, the stimulus of the fear, or the danger, is semantically embedded in the word *fear*. In other words, we do not simply have fear; we always have *a* fear of *something*.

The term *phobia* means a pathological degree of fear. Derived from the Greek word *phobos* (meaning "flight" or "terror"), phobias are special kinds of fear that are (1) out of proportion to the demands of the situation, (2) cannot be explained or reasoned away by the patient, (3) are beyond voluntary control, and (4) lead to avoidance behaviors of the feared situations (Marks, 1987). Like fears, phobias are always linked to specific danger stimuli. Long lists of names of phobias can be created by simply adding the suffix *phobia* to the Greek word for the feared stimulus, such as acrophobia, meaning fear of heights; claustrophobia, meaning fear of enclosed spaces; and agoraphobia, meaning fear of open places. The emotional response to a phobic stimulus is sometimes called *phobic anxiety*.

Anxiety and Panic

Although the feared stimulus is always known in fears or phobias, this is not necessarily true with respect to anxiety. *Anxiety* is defined as "a feeling of apprehension, uncertainty, and fear, without apparent stimulus and associated with physiological changes (tachycardia, sweating, tremor, etc.)" (*Dorland's Illustrated Medical Dictionary*, 1979). Thus, the term *anxiety* is commonly used to describe apprehension without apparent cause. The term *free-floating anxiety* is sometimes used to further highlight the apparent lack of cause for the anxiety. In actuality, however, anxiety is often accompanied by cognitive activities, such as worries or anticipation of bodily harm (Beck, Laude, & Bohnert, 1974). Judging from the content of cognitive activities accompanying anxiety, it often seems related to anticipated future unpleasant, dangerous, or uncontrollable events (Barlow, 1988; Melges, 1982). If the anxiety is about an expected event involving exposure to a phobic situation, the term *anticipatory anxiety* is often used.

The definition of anxiety just given includes two parts: (1) a feeling of apprehension and (2) physiological symptoms, such as tachycardia, tremors, sweating, and dizziness. From this description, one can infer that anxiety may have two components, a cognitive and a somatic. Indeed, Barrett (1972) indicated that anxiety responses could be classified into two major subtypes, one involving awareness of unpleasant feelings about oneself and the other awareness of somatic changes such as blushing or rapid heartbeat. Hamilton (1959) and Buss (1962) reported similar subsets of anxiety in their analyses of self-ratings of anxiety. They found that two components, psychic and somatic, accounted for the major proportion of the variance in anxiety measures.

Cognitive anxiety refers to the cognitive activities, such as worrying, that accompany anxiety. Anxious cognitions can often be identified semantically by virtue of their beginning with the words *What if . . .* (Emery & Tracy, 1987), such as What if I faint? or What if I have a heart attack?

Somatic anxiety is characterized by somatic symptoms such as heart palpitations, sweating, and trembling. Some of the somatic sensations appear to be similar to symptoms induced by hyperventilation, whereas others are similar to those induced by high autonomic arousal (Jacob & Rapport, 1984). The somatic anxiety symptoms related to hyperventilation include shortness of breath, dizziness, numbness or tingling sensations, and chest pain or discomfort. The symptoms of autonomic arousal include heart palpitations, trembling, shaking, sweating, choking, and flushes or chills.

A type of anxiety that has been a significant focus of research and clinical attention is panic. *Panic* is defined as a "sudden surge of acute and intense terror" (Marks, 1969). Thus, panic is a form of anxiety characterized by sudden onset and high intensity. *Panic attacks*, furthermore, are marked by a high degree of somatic anxiety symptoms. Somatic symptoms during panic include shortness of breath, heart palpitations, tremors, and sweating, among others. Panic attacks are also usually accompanied by cognitive symptoms of fears of impending bodily harm, such as fear of having a heart attack or seizure, and often lead to frantic efforts to leave the situation.

The word *panic* is derived from the name of the Greek rural deity, Pan, who was associated not only with pastoral scenes and delightful music, but also with sudden, inexplicable terror (Marks, 1969). It is currently debated whether panic represents an emotional state qualitatively different from anxiety, or whether panic is "merely" an extreme form of anxiety (Turner, Beidel, & Jacob, 1988).

Panic attacks can be of two varieties: "unexpected" or "expected." Although the symptoms of the two types of panic are probably identical (Margraf, Taylor, Ehlers, Roth, & Agras, 1987), the distinction between expected and unexpected panic is important in the current guidelines for the diagnosis of different anxiety disorders. Unexpected or spontaneous panic attacks come as a total surprise to the patient, who often describes the event as "coming from out of the blue." Expected panic attacks, on the other hand, occur only in specific phobic situations. Conceptually, expected panic attacks would be equivalent to extreme degrees of phobic anxiety of sudden onset.

Diagnosis of Panic Disorder

Panic Disorder Without Agoraphobia

In the preceding section, we discussed the basic terms used to describe different kinds of fears and anxiety. In this section we'll discuss the diagnostic criteria for panic disorder according to the DSM-III-R.

The essential feature of panic disorder is the experience of recurrent panic attacks. Initially in the development of the disorder these attacks are "unexpected," but later they may become "expected" because victims are conditioned to situations in which attacks occurred previously and that they may begin to avoid. These avoidance behaviors herald the onset of a more severe form of panic disorder, agoraphobia with panic.

Table 2.1 lists the diagnostic criteria for panic disorder. Criterion A states that at some time during the disorder the panic attacks were of the unexpected variety. Criterion A also clarifies that unexpected panic attacks do *not* include those that occur immediately before or on exposure to a situation that almost always caused anxiety (such as animals, in the case of simple animal phobia). The criterion further states that panic attacks triggered by being the focus of others' attention do not qualify for a diagnosis of panic disorder. Thus, if a patient has panic attacks only in social situations, the diagnosis would be social phobia rather than panic disorder. We will discuss further the differences between panic disorder and social phobia.

Even though by definition at least some of the panic attacks in panic disorder are spontaneous, in actuality many are not spontaneous but are related to the patient's anticipating or being in specific feared situations. Margraf et al. (1987), using self-monitoring techniques over 6 consecutive days, studied the incidence of both spontaneous and situational attacks in 27 panic disorder patients. Spontaneous attacks were defined as having sudden onset with little or no provocation; situational panic attacks were defined as surges of panic in feared situations. Furthermore, minor attacks and episodes of anticipatory anxiety were also recorded; these were defined by their smaller

TABLE 2.1 Diagnostic Criteria for Panic Disorder

A. At some time during the disturbance, one or more panic attacks (discrete periods of intense fear or discomfort) have occurred that were (1) unexpected, i.e., did not occur immediately before or on exposure to a situation that almost always caused anxiety, and (2) not triggered by situations in which the person was the focus of others' attention.

B. Either four attacks, as defined in criterion A, have occurred within a four-week period, or one or more attacks have been followed by a period of at least a month of persistent fear of having another attack.

C. At least four of the following symptoms developed during at least one of the attacks:
1. shortness of breath (dyspnea) or smothering sensations
2. dizziness, unsteady feelings, or faintness
3. palpitations or accelerated heart rate (tachycardia)
4. trembling or shaking
5. sweating
6. choking
7. nausea or abdominal distress
8. depersonalization or derealization
9. numbness or tingling sensations (paresthesias)
10. flushes (hot flashes) or chills
11. chest pain or discomfort
12. fear of dying
13. fear of going crazy or of doing something uncontrolled
Note: Attacks involving four or more symptoms are panic attacks; attacks involving fewer than four symptoms are limited symptom attacks (see Agoraphobia without History of Panic Disorder).

D. During at least some of the attacks, at least four of the C symptoms developed suddenly and increased in intensity within ten minutes of the beginning of the first C symptom noticed in the attack.

E. It cannot be established that an organic factor initiated and maintained the disturbance, e.g., amphetamine or caffeine intoxication, hyperthyroidism.

Note: Mitral valve prolapse may be an associated condition, but does not preclude a diagnosis of panic disorder.

Reprinted with permission from the *Diagnostic and Statistical Manual of Mental Disorders. Third Edition, Revised.* Copyright 1987 American Psychiatric Association.

number of specific panic symptoms (see Criterion C). The 27 patients had a total of 175 panic attacks over a 6-day period. Spontaneous and situational attacks occurred with about equal frequency; thus only half of the attacks in these patients were "spontaneous." There was an interesting difference between the two types of attacks with respect to distribution over the 24 hours of the day: whereas situational attacks occurred primarily during the daytime hours, spontaneous attacks were more evenly distributed over the day and night. Some spontaneous attacks even occurred in the middle of the night. Furthermore, most situational attacks occurred while driving (31%), whereas spontaneous attacks occurred at home (39%), especially when the patient was alone.

Criterion B is the frequency criterion for panic. Either 4 attacks over a 4-week period or at least one attack followed by persistent fears of having another attack for at least 1 month is required. As we discuss later, the frequency of panic determines the severity of the disorder. Margraf et al. (1987) found that in approximately half of their patients, the average frequency of spontaneous attacks (panic or minor attacks) was less than 2 per week; in one-third of the patients, the frequency was between 2 and 5.9 attacks per week; one-ninth of the patients had more than 6 per week.

Infrequently occurring panic attacks,—that is, panic attacks occurring at a frequency less than 4 times per week, have been reported to occur in as many as 34% of college students (Norton, Harrison, Hauch, & Rhodes, 1985) and in 14.1% of residents in the greater Houston area selected for phone interviews on a random basis (Salge, Beck, & Logan, 1988). It would be interesting to study how many of these individuals also have persistent fears of further panic.

Criterion C states that at least 4 of 13 specific anxiety symptoms must be present during at least one of the attacks. In the Margraf et al. study, the most common symptom in spontaneous panic attacks was heart palpitations (73%), followed by dizziness (61%), dyspnea (37%), trembling or shaking (37%), sweating (37%), and nausea or abdominal distress (32%). Furthermore, fear of going crazy or doing something uncontrolled and hot flashes or cold chills occurred in 24% of the attacks, chest pain in 17%, faintness in 15%, and parasthesias in 10%. Interestingly, although the complaint of palpitations was highly prevalent for all types of attacks, only the situational panic attacks were associated with actual increases in heart rate. Thus, the complaint of palpitations does not necessarily correspond with actual physiological change in heart rate.

Attacks in which fewer than four symptoms are present are recognized as a panic equivalent and are called *limited symptom attacks*. In the Margraf et al. (1987) study, these were called "minor" panic attacks. Of the 175 attacks recorded in this study, about half were full-blown panic attacks, and half were minor attacks. The number of symptoms in the panic attack was related to the intensity of the attack. The symptom pattern, however, did not differ among different types of attacks.

Criterion D, the "sudden onset" criterion, states that at least some of the attacks show a sudden crescendo pattern within the course of 10 minutes. The average duration of the attack is about 30 minutes for a full-blown attack and 20 minutes for a minor attack (Margraf et al., 1987). Durations of several hours are rare. We have seen patients complaining of "all-day panics," but in such patients a diagnosis of agitated depression or personality disorder should be considered.

Finally, Criterion E states that the panic cannot be caused by organic factors, such as hyperthyroidism or caffeine intoxication. However, it is permissible to diagnose panic disorder in the presence of mitral valve prolapse, a valvular abnormality of the heart that may be associated with panic disorder (see medical differential diagnosis section). This criterion points to the medical differential diagnosis of panic disorder. Patients in whom medical disorders are causing the panic are given the diagnosis of organic anxiety syndrome.

Once the diagnosis of panic disorder has been made, the severity of the disorder is rated. Panic disorder is either "mild," "moderate," "severe," "in partial remission," or "in full remission." Severe panic disorder is characterized by at least eight panic attacks during the past month; mild panic disorder, by either limited symptom attacks or no more than one full-blown attack during the past month. A moderate severity rating is made if the severity is between "mild" and "severe." In full remission, there have been no panic or limited symptom attacks during the past month and in partial remission, there is a condition falling in between "mild" and "in full remission."

Panic Disorder with Agoraphobia

The DSM-III-R recognizes two forms of agoraphobia: *panic disorder with agoraphobia* and *agoraphobia without history of panic disorder*. Table 2.2 lists the diagnostic criteria for panic disorder with agoraphobia. Patients with agoraphobia are considered to have a more advanced form of panic disorder (Klein, Ross, & Cohen, 1987). These patients avoid situations in which panic attacks might occur and situations from which they cannot easily escape. For a diagnosis of panic disorder with agoraphobia, patients must not only qualify for a diagnosis of panic disorder as defined previously, but also have at least mild degrees of agoraphobic avoidance (see Criterion A).

Criterion B describes the pattern of avoidance in panic disorder with agoraphobia: "places or situations from which escape might be difficult ... or in which help might not be available in the event of a panic attack." Indeed, whenever these patients go into a new situation, they quickly scan for possible escape routes and then place themselves strategically to minimize escape time. Situations most commonly avoided include driving, stores, crowds, lines, being alone, elevators, and social gatherings (Vittone & Uhde, 1985).

The degree of agoraphobic avoidance can be "mild," "moderate," or "severe"; this should be specified in the diagnosis. Some patients develop quite extreme degrees of agoraphobic avoidance and do not leave their homes; for others even their home may not be safe if they have to stay there alone, resulting in frequent calls to the therapist or significant others at work.

TABLE 2.2 Diagnostic Criteria for Panic Disorder with Agoraphobia

A. Meets the criteria for panic disorder.

B. Agoraphobia: Fear of being in places or situations from which escape might be difficult (or embarrassing) or in which help might not be available in the event of a panic attack. (Include cases in which persistent avoidance behavior originated during an active phase of panic disorder, even if the person does not attribute the avoidance behavior to fear of having a panic attack.) As a result of this fear, the person either restricts travel or needs a companion when away from home, or else endures agoraphobic situations despite intense anxiety. Common agoraphobic situations include being outside the home alone, being in a crowd or standing in a line, being on a bridge, and traveling in a bus, train, or car.

Specify current severity of agoraphobic avoidance:

Mild: Some avoidance (or endurance with distress), but relatively normal lifestyle, e.g., travels unaccompanied when necessary, such as to work or to shop; otherwise avoids traveling alone.

Moderate: Avoidance results in constricted lifestyle, e.g., the person is able to leave the house alone, but not to go more than a few miles unaccompanied.

Severe: Avoidance results in being nearly or completely housebound or unable to leave the house unaccompanied.

In Partial Remission: No current agoraphobic avoidance, but some agoraphobic avoidance during the past 6 months.

In Full Remission: No current agoraphobic avoidance and none during the past 6 months.

Specify current severity of panic attacks:

Mild: During the past month, either all attacks have been limited symptom attacks (i.e., fewer than four symptoms), or there has been no more than one panic attack.

Moderate: During the past month attacks have been intermediate between "Mild" and "Severe."

In Partial Remission: The condition has been intermediate between "In Full Remission" and "Mild."

In Full Remission: During the past 6 months, there have been no panic or limited symptom attacks.

Reprinted with permission from the *Diagnostic and Statistical Manual of Mental Disorders. Third Edition, Revised.* Copyright 1987 American Psychiatric Association.

Psychiatric Differential Diagnosis

The psychiatric differential diagnosis of panic disorder includes two possibilities: (1) the panic attacks were caused by a disorder different from panic disorder and the patient is therefore given a diagnosis of the other disorder only, or (2) the patient has panic disorder coexisting with other psychiatric symptoms. In the second case, there are two options with respect to diagnosis: (a) the patient is given a diagnosis of panic disorder, as well as that of another psychiatric disorder, or (b) the patient is given only a diagnosis of panic disorder.

Deciding which of these possibilities applies depends on specific "hierarchical rules" in the DSM-III-R. For example, if the panic attacks were considered to be caused by or maintained by organic factors such as amphetamine intoxication or hyperthyroidism, the diagnosis would not be panic disorder but rather amphetamine intoxication or organic anxiety syndrome, respectively (Option 1). On the other hand, if a patient fulfills criteria for both depression and panic disorder, both diagnoses are given (Option 2a). Finally, if the patient fulfills most symptomatic criteria for generalized anxiety disorder or hypochondriasis, but the symptoms exclusively involve fear of panic attacks or their possible medical significance, only the diagnosis of panic disorder is given (Option 2b).

In this section, we first consider the differential diagnosis between panic disorder and other anxiety disorders. Then we consider the diagnosis of other psychiatric disorders.

Anxiety Disorders

In addition to panic disorder, the anxiety disorder category of the DSM-III-R includes simple and social phobia, generalized anxiety disorder, agoraphobia without history of panic disorder, obsessive-compulsive disorder, and post–traumatic stress disorder. We briefly describe each of these disorders and then discuss the differential diagnosis between the disorder and panic disorder. Adjustment disorder with anxious mood, although not strictly an anxiety disorder, is also included in this section.

Social Phobia

Social phobia is characterized by a fear of situations in which the person is exposed to possible scrutiny by others, according to the DSM-III-R. Socially phobic patients fear that their performance in the social situation will lead to negative evaluation by others. In social situations, these individuals frequently experience symptoms of somatic anxiety, such as palpitations, trembling, blushing, sweating, and feeling a lump in their throats—symptoms that may be indistinguishable from the somatic sensations of panic. One source of the fear of negative evaluation in social phobia is the possibility that these symptoms may be noticed by others. Thus, like patients with panic disorder, socially phobic patients fear their own anxiety symptoms.

Whereas the symptoms of social phobia can resemble those of panic disorder, certain anxiety symptoms may be more common to panic disorder, others to social phobia. Patients with panic disorder tend to have more symptoms of weakness, difficulty in breathing, dizziness, fainting, and tinnitus but fewer symptoms of blushing (Amies, Gelder, & Shaw, 1983). Another difference can be found in the cognitive element: in social phobia the fear is of embarrassment or humiliation because of inadequate performance, whereas in panic disorder the fear is often of bodily harm (Turner & Beidel, 1989). Furthermore, the goal of escape may differentiate social phobia from panic disorder: panic patients seek out trusted others, whereas socially phobic patients prefer to be left alone.

In addition, certain associated features differentiate panic disorder from social phobia: in social phobia, the onset usually is during adolescence, whereas the peak onset of panic disorder is the middle twenties (Amies et al., 1983; Öst, 1987). In social phobia, a history of a conditioning event (e.g., major embarrassment during a high school speech) is often elicited, whereas, according to our experience, such events are not as common in panic disorder. In panic disorder with agoraphobia, the sex distribution is predominantly female, whereas social phobia tends to be evenly distributed across the sexes (Amies et al., 1983). Finally, panic disorder patients tend to be extroverts, whereas socially phobic patients tend to be introverts.

Despite these several differences between panic disorder and social phobia, there is also considerable overlap. In patients who have both panic attacks and social fears, therefore, the differential diagnosis between panic disorder and social phobia can be difficult. Depending on the specific pattern of panic, fear, and avoidance, patients with panic and social fears could have (1) panic disorder and social phobia combined, (2) panic disorder only, or (3) social phobia only.

One criterion for social phobia in the DSM-III-R specifies that if a patient has panic disorder as well as social fears, *the social fears should not be related only to a fear of having panic attacks*. Thus, if a patient has panic attacks both in and out of social situations and the patient fears the social situation primarily because of anticipated panic, or anticipated difficulty in leaving the social situation in case of panic, the diagnosis is panic disorder but not social phobia.

Conversely, Criterion A of panic disorder states that the *panic attacks in panic disorder should not be triggered only by situations in which the person was the focus of others' attention*. Thus, if a patient throughout the course of his or her disorder only had panic attacks in social situations the diagnosis is social phobia. However, in cases with predominantly social avoidance, a concomitant panic disorder may be missed because a history of spontaneous panic attacks outside of the social situation was overlooked or not reported. For example, one of our patients initially reported that he had panic attacks only in social situations and consequently was diagnosed as having social phobia. Later during treatment, it became apparent that he had panic attacks in nonsocial situations as well. For this reason and also because his main concern when in the social situation was the possibility of a panic attack, this patient was rediagnosed as having panic disorder.

To complicate things further, a patient may have *both* panic disorder and social phobia. For both disorders to be diagnosed, the social fear should not be merely a consequence of fear of panic. Thus, the dual diagnosis is appropriate if the patient has panic attacks in several situations, but the social anxiety concerns fear of negative evaluation related to performance, not only to fear of having a panic attack. Many of these distinctions between social phobia and panic disorder may seem academic in nature. Nevertheless, they may have implications for treatment, particularly if the treatment is expected to work for one but not the other disorder.

Simple Phobia

Simple phobia is characterized by fears of specific, circumscribed stimuli other than panic attacks or social situations; exposure to the feared situation almost invariably provokes an immediate anxiety response, per the DSM-III-R. Thus, in simple phobia, the anxiety response occurs regularly and immediately upon exposure to or in anticipation of the feared situation. The fear-eliciting stimuli of different simple phobias include animals (such as snakes, spiders, dogs, or mice) or specific situations (for example, thunderstorms, heights, or enclosed spaces such as elevators).

The situations avoided by individuals with simple phobia overlap in part with those of patients with panic disorder. For example, fear of elevators may be an expression of panic disorder or of simple phobia. If the specific fear is part of a larger pattern of fears characteristic of panic disorder or agoraphobia without panic, a diagnosis of simple phobia is not made.

The anxiety reactions in simple phobia can be so intense that they intensify into panic attacks. Claustrophobic anxiety reactions have been used as an experimental analogue to panic (Rachman, 1988). The question is whether there might be differences in the attributes of the panic attacks of a person with panic disorder who is going into a feared situation and those of a person with simple phobia. One answer, according to the DSM-III-R, is found in the *unpredictable* nature of some of the panic attacks in panic disorder. Panic attacks in panic disorder are not limited to one specific phobic situation. Furthermore, unlike phobic anxiety, which should occur at the beginning or in anticipation of each exposure to the phobic stimulus, unpredictable panic attacks can occur at any time during an exposure, or not at all. However, the latter distinction seems to oversimplify matters: unpredictable panic occurs also in claustrophobia (Rachman, 1988). Nevertheless, if the patient reports that sometimes the panic occurs late in the feared situation or not at all, the patient may have had unpredictable panic. In this case, to confirm the diagnosis of panic disorder, one should look for unpredictable panic attacks in situations other than that of the primary phobia.

Agoraphobia Without History of Panic Disorder

If a patient has agoraphobia but does not have panic attacks that qualify for a diagnosis of panic disorder—that is, if the patient avoids public places but for reasons unrelated to fear of panic attacks—the diagnosis is agoraphobia without panic. The latter condition may occur with or without limited symptom attacks, and the presence or absence of limited symptom attacks should be specified. Patients having agoraphobia without panic seen at our clinic typically avoided situations in which there was no easy access to a bathroom, because of their fear of losing control of their bladder or bowels.

Among clinical cases with anxiety disorders, agoraphobia without history of panic is reported to be very rare (Spitzer, 1988). However, in the community, the prevalence of agoraphobia without history of panic disorder may be as high as or even higher than panic disorder (Weissman, 1988).

Generalized Anxiety Disorder

Generalized anxiety disorder is characterized by excessive worry. Worry is excessive when it is unrealistic and when it is focused on too many different things. The worries are accompanied by somatic anxiety symptoms, but these are not as intense as those of panic attacks and furthermore do not necessarily have the sudden onset characteristic of panic. For a DSM-III-R diagnosis of generalized anxiety disorder, a patient must have excessive anxiety or apprehensive expectation about two or more life circumstances. Furthermore, the focus of these worries is unrelated to panic disorder, social phobia, obsessive-compulsive disorder, or anorexia nervosa. For example, the worries cannot be merely about having a panic attack. Generalized anxiety disorder is a chronic disorder; according to DSM-III-R, the minimum duration is 6 months.

Panic attacks may occur in generalized anxiety disorder (Barlow et al., 1985). If criteria for both disorders are fulfilled, both diagnoses are given. Thus, generalized anxiety disorder may coexist with panic disorder. Patients with the dual diagnosis would be expected to have not only panic attacks and worry about future panic but also chronic feelings of anxiety and worry about matters unrelated to panic (such as finances or their children's performance in school).

Post–Traumatic Stress Disorder

Post–traumatic stress disorder is defined by characteristic symptoms that follow catastrophic events; that is, events that are outside the range of usual human experience, such as battlefield experiences, earthquakes, rapes, assaults, torture, and car accidents with serious physical injury. These characteristic symptoms involve recurrent intrusive recollections or dreams of the event, at times including dissociative "flashback" experiences. Patients with post–traumatic stress disorder often experience intense psychological distress in situations that remind them of the traumatic event. For example, one World War II veteran known to one of us had a history of crawling under the bed whenever he heard a propeller airplane fly over his house. These patients often will avoid situations that arouse recollections of the trauma and therefore may show avoidance behaviors that are similar to those displayed by patients with phobias, including agoraphobia. Thus, a symptom that looks like phobic avoidance may actually be a manifestation of post–traumatic stress disorder. Because of the distinctiveness of the associated features as well as the history of traumatic events, it should not be hard to differentiate post–traumatic stress disorder from panic disorder—provided, of course, that this information is elicited during assessment.

Obsessive–Compulsive Disorder

Obsessive-compulsive disorder is a severe anxiety disorder characterized by frequent and incapacitating obsessive thoughts or compulsive rituals—or both—that the patient recognizes as being irrational (Jacob, Ford, & Turner, 1987). The time spent in the grip of these behaviors typically exceeds 1 hour per day.

Patients with obsessive-compulsive disorder may develop avoidance behaviors related to the content of their obsessive ideation. Furthermore, they may have panic attacks; for example, when the rules that they impose on themselves or others have been broken, or when they are actively experiencing an obsession. These panic attacks would probably be of the "predictable" sort; therefore, it should not be necessary to give a concomitant diagnosis of panic disorder. It is possible, however, for panic disorder and obsessive-compulsive disorder to coexist. The DSM-III-R does not give much guidance, but in the latter case the patient would be expected to have had panic attacks independent of obsessions or compulsions.

Obsessive-compulsive symptoms of insufficient severity to qualify for a diagnosis of obsessive-compulsive disorder often occur in panic disorder. Fava, Zielenzny, Luria, and Canestrari (1988) found that patients with agoraphobia had higher scores on a compulsion checklist than control subjects. These scores improved with behavioral treatment of agoraphobia. Mellman and Uhde (1987) found that 19 of 70 patients (27%) with panic disorder also had obsessive-compulsive symptoms. Panic patients with obsessive-compulsive symptoms had a higher prevalence of concomitant depression and alcohol or drug abuse. After completed treatment, these patients also had more remaining panic attacks and more generalized anxiety. Thus, panic patients with coexisting obsessive-compulsive symptoms may have a less favorable prognosis than those without such symptoms.

Adjustment Disorder with Anxious Mood

It is important to recognize that not all individuals with panic attacks or anxiety complaints have an anxiety disorder. Some of these individuals may have adjustment disorder with anxious mood. The essential feature of adjustment disorder, per the DSM-III-R, is a maladaptive pattern of overreaction to an identifiable psychosocial stressor that began within 3 months after the stressor but did not persist for more than 6 months. Furthermore, there is an expectation that when the stressor ceases, the adjustment disorder will remit.

There are various kinds of adjustment disorders: adjustment disorder with depressed mood, adjustment disorder with physical complaints, and so forth. Adjustment disorder with anxious mood resembles generalized anxiety disorder, although panic attacks also can occur. It would be interesting to study whether some of the respondents with infrequent panics described by Norton et al. (1985) or Salge et al. (1988) would qualify for a diagnosis of an adjustment disorder.

Summary: Recapitulation of Anxiety Disorders Diagnosis

We have now acquired the basic tools to be able to diagnose the different anxiety disorders. To recapitulate, the classification of anxiety disorders is based on (1) the presence or absence of unexpected panic attacks or fear of further panic attacks, (2) the presence or absence of avoidance behavior, and (3) the presence or absence of specific symptoms such as (a) obsessions or compulsions, and (b) intrusive memories of traumatic events.

TABLE 2.3 Overview of Anxiety Disorders Diagnosis

		Avoidance	
		+	−
Unexpected panic and fear of panic as core symptom	+	Panic disorder with agoraphobia	Panic disorder
	−	Simple phobia Social phobia Agoraphobia without panic	Generalized anxiety disorder
Obsessions or compulsions		Obsessive-compulsive disorder	
Recollections of trauma		Post–traumatic stress disorder	

The answers to the panic and avoidance questions determine the diagnosis according to the "basic two-by-two" of the anxiety disorders depicted in Table 2.3. If panic disorder (as defined previously) is present and avoidance behaviors are absent, the diagnosis is likely to be panic disorder without agoraphobia. If, on the other hand, both panic and avoidance are present, the diagnosis would be panic disorder with agoraphobia.

If unexpected panic is absent, but avoidance is present, the diagnosis is either simple phobia, social phobia, or agoraphobia without panic, depending on the nature of the fear. Finally, if the patient presents with anxiety but panic is not the central disturbance, the diagnosis may be generalized anxiety disorder. The diagnosis may also be adjustment disorder with anxious mood, depending on the duration of the disorder and the presence of specific stressors.

The presence of certain symptoms supersedes the basic two-by-two anxiety table: Anxiety-producing recollections of traumatic events form the basis for the diagnosis of post–traumatic stress disorder, and the presence of obsessions or compulsions constitutes a basis for the diagnosis of obsessive-compulsive disorder.

Psychiatric Disorders Other Than Anxiety Disorders

Panic disorder can coexist with most of the other mental disorders listed in the DSM-III-R. Therefore, all patients with panic disorder should have a full psychiatric evaluation, with questions aimed at ruling out major psychiatric disorders such as depression, substance abuse, and organic mental disorders.

Depression

Much has been written about the relationship between depression and anxiety. For a review of the earlier literature, see Roth and Mountjoy (1982) and Winokur (1988). When evaluating patients with a complaint of panic attacks, it is important to be alert to the possibility of a concomitant depression. Depression, according to the DMS-III-R, is characterized by pervasive feelings of sadness or lack of interest or pleasure, combined with symptoms of decreased or increased appetite with weight loss or weight gain, insomnia or hypersomnia, psychomotor retardation or agitation, fatigue or loss of energy, feelings of worthlessness or inappropriate guilt, diminished ability to think or concentrate, and recurrent thoughts of death or suicide.

The differential diagnosis between anxiety and depression has been simplified in the DSM-III-R in that if both panic disorder and depression are present, both the depression and panic disorder are diagnosed. It is clinically useful to assess which of the two disorders is the "primary" condition. The determination of the primary disorder can be made according to several different criteria, including which came first temporally, or which is the more "massive and preponderant" (Winokur, 1988). We recommend using a combination of these criteria and establishing which condition has occurred with and without the other in the patient's history. If episodes of depression have occurred without panic attacks, but episodes of panic occurred only during episodes of depression, the panic disorder is the secondary disorder. Conversely, if depression occurred only during parts of panic disorder episodes, whereas panic disorder occurred without depression, the depression is the secondary disorder.

Thus, there are four possible combinations: (1) "pure" depression (without panic), (2) depression with secondary panic disorder, (3) panic disorder with secondary depression, and (4) "pure" panic disorder. In the case of panic disorder with secondary depression, the depression is the less preponderant disorder and occurs only during episodes of panic disorder, possibly as a consequence of the social incapacitation that develops as the panic disorder progresses. In the case of depression with secondary panic, depression is the more preponderant disorder and the panic attacks occur only during episodes of depression. Depression with secondary panic may be a marker of severe agitated depression (Coryell et al., 1988).

In a study focusing on outpatients with anxiety disorders, Barlow, DiNardo, Vermilyea, Vermilyea, and Blanchard (1986) diagnosed major affective disorder in 15% of 41 agoraphobic patients and 12% of 17 patients with panic disorder without agoraphobia. In addition, dysthymic disorder was diagnosed in 24% of the agoraphobic patients and 23% of the patients with panic disorder. In a more recent study, Lesser et al. (1988) found that, in a sample of panic patients from which patients with primary depression had been excluded, the prevalence of secondary depression was 31% (23% of patients with uncomplicated panic disorder, 25% of patients with limited phobic avoidance, and 33% of patients with agoraphobia). Thus, secondary depression is quite common in panic disorder. On a lifetime basis, the incidence of depression in panic patients may be even higher. In a study using the lifetime version of the Schedule for Affective Disorders supplemented by a special section on anxiety disorders (Fayer & Endicott, 1984), Breier, Charney, and Heninger (1986) found that 70% of 60 patients had an episode of major depressive disorder at some time in their lives; in 43% of these, however, the onset of depression was *before* the first panic attacks.

The studies just mentioned concerned the prevalence of depression in anxiety disorder clinic populations. In a study in which the focus was on a sample of 307 patients with affective disorders, on the other hand, Coryell et al. (1988) found that 80% had depression only (D), 17% had depression with panic attacks (DP), and only 3.6% had depression secondary to panic attacks (PD). Comparing D with DP, the authors found that the depressions of DP had been longer, more often were of the endogenous or agitated type, and were characterized by guilt, early morning awakening, terminal insomnia, anorexia, anhedonia, lack of reactivity, difficulty concentrating, and fatigue. DP also had poorer prognosis than D. Importantly, there was no difference between D and DP in the incidence of anxiety disorders in first-degree relatives of the patient. Such a finding is consistent with DP being a more severe form of D. On the other hand, comparing PD with DP, PD had less family history of depression and a higher incidence of anxiety disorders in first-degree relatives. These latter findings suggest that DP and PD are etiologically distinct disorders.

From a clinical standpoint, it is important to recognize severe forms of depression, particularly if depression is primary. Such patients may not be able to complete behavioral programs for panic disorder or agoraphobia. They may also be at risk for suicide. Weight loss, significant difficulties concentrating, and sleep disturbance are symptoms that suggest the need to treat depression. On the other hand, most secondary mild depressions will remit with treatment of the panic disorder (Lesser et al., 1988).

Substance Abuse Disorders

Alcohol is a frequent problem in panic disorder. Bibb and Chambless (1986) reported that alcohol dependence was characteristic of 12% of agoraphobic patients, and Thyer et al. (1986) reported that 27% of agoraphobic patients and 8% of panic disorder patients scored in the problem drinking range on the Michigan Alcoholism Screening Test.

Conversely, alcoholic patients frequently have panic attacks. Cox, Norton, Dorward, and Fergusson (1989) found that 31% of alcoholic inpatients fulfilled diagnostic criteria for panic disorder and 13% reported being treated previously for panic attacks. The panic attacks preceded the onset of alcoholism in 40% of the cases. Most of the alcoholic panic patients reported that they used alcohol to relieve panic.

Other forms of drug abuse that may contribute to the development of panic disorder include marijuana abuse (Moran, 1986), caffeine abuse (Boulenger, Uhde, Wolff, & Post, 1984), and cocaine abuse (Aronson & Craig, 1986). Increased anxiety or panic commonly occurs during withdrawal from minor tranquilizers (whether prescribed or "abused") and has been described as occurring as a result of abrupt withdrawal from amitriptyline (Gawin & Markoff, 1981).

Based on these data, substance abuse should always be a consideration when evaluating patients with panic disorder. In some cases, according to our clinical experience, drug abuse was a problem at the onset of the panic disorder, but the panic attacks continued even though the patients stopped their drug use. The possibility of caffeine-induced panic appears to be another important consideration, as panic patients appear to have an increased sensitivity to caffeine (Boulenger et al., 1984).

Personality Disorders

Patients with panic disorder or agoraphobia or both have frequently been noted to possess long-standing maladaptive personality attributes. Most writers have focused on characteristics such as dependency and unassertiveness (Andrews, 1966) and hysteroid tendencies (Chambless & Mason, 1986). Nevertheless, the extent to which these factors predispose to, rather than result from, the disorder is unclear. The systematic assessment of personality disorders in panic disorder patients may be useful for two reasons in clinical practice. First, it provides the clinician with valuable information regarding personality traits that may impede therapeutic progress. For example, individuals with a dependent personality may have particular difficulty carrying out programmed practice assignments; those with passive-aggressive personality may attempt to subtly undermine treatment. Second, personality issues may be important foci for treatment after panic attacks and agoraphobic avoidance have abated.

Only a few investigators have examined the prevalence of Axis II disorders among patients with panic disorder. Reich, Noyes, and Troughton (1987) compared three groups of panic patients varying in the severity of their agoraphobic avoidance (none, limited, and extensive). They found that, compared with patients showing no avoidance, patients with agoraphobic avoidance had a higher prevalence of dependent personality disorder and a higher prevalence of disorders in the anxious-fearful cluster (dependent, avoidant, compulsive, and passive-aggressive personality disorders).

Friedman, Shear, and Frances (1987) administered the SCID-II (an instrument to measure personality disorders) to a sample of 26 panic patients, and found that 15 (58%) satisfied criteria for at least one personality disorder. The prevalence of personality disorders was greater among patients with extensive avoidance than those with limited avoidance. Diagnoses were divided approximately equally between the anxious-fearful cluster of personality disorders (such as avoidant and compulsive personality disorder) and the dramatic-emotional cluster (such as histrionic personality disorder). Only one patient fulfilled criteria for dependent personality disorder, and no patients had diagnoses in the odd-eccentric cluster (such as schizotypal personality disorder or paranoid personality disorder). Again, however, no comparison group was included.

There is clearly a need for controlled studies of the prevalence of personality disorders among patients with panic disorder. Nevertheless, the extant literature suggests that this prevalence may be elevated over chance levels. The extent to which these personality features are affected by the treatment of panic attacks and agoraphobia is unclear, although Mavissakalian and Hamann (1986) reported that behavioral treatment of agoraphobics led to a reduction in dependent personality features. Despite these uncertainties, it is likely that the systematic assessment of personality disorders can greatly assist the clinician in the planning of interventions for panic disorder and agoraphobia.

Summary: Conducting the Initial Evaluation

In the foregoing sections we provided a background on the material that needs to be gathered during the initial assessment. However, we did not discuss the assessment itself; that is, the interactions between the clinician and the patient. The initial assessment's main purpose is to obtain a broad spectrum of information necessary for the psychiatric diagnosis. To obtain all the necessary information, the patient should be scheduled for a 90-minute interview. Eliciting this information requires (1) extensive knowledge of psychopathology and (2) all the clinical skills that the clinician has acquired during his or her training, such as appropriate interview techniques and the ability to determine mental status. In addition, special adjustments may be required because of the high anxiety levels of the patients. The initial assessment involves the following steps: (1) pre-interview observations, (2) getting to know the patient, (3) exploration of the presenting problem, (4) the psychiatric review of systems, (5) the social and family history, and (6) termination of interview. Furthermore, the assessment may be supplemented by a number of short, screening pencil-and-paper tests.

Pre-interview Observations

Prior to the initial interview, the clinician collects any preliminary information available on the patient. For example, is this patient known to the clinic from prior episodes? What information is available from the original phone contact during which the patient made the appointment? Such information will usually give the clinician a preliminary idea of why the patient is seeking treatment.

The clinical assessment begins with observations of the patient's waiting room behavior. For example, did the patient arrive accompanied or unaccompanied? Does the patient "look" anxious? The initial handshake will yield further information: a cold and sweaty hand is highly characteristic of patients with anxiety disorders and indicates a high degree of physiological arousal. Hand tremor could mean even higher anxiety levels or the presence of other conditions, such as alcohol withdrawal or hyperthyroidism.

Taking the patient from the waiting room into the office may require further deliberations. Should the significant other accompanying the patient be asked to come along? In our view, for reasons of confidentiality the patient should be seen alone, at least during part of the interview. However, the significant other can be asked to provide additional information during some part of the session. Some agoraphobic patients are so anxious that they insist the significant other be present during the entire interview, or at least that the door of the office remain open. In such cases it is better to accommodate the patient's needs rather than insist on a private session. Observations of this kind say more than any verbal description about the severity of the patient's problem.

Getting to Know the Patient

For patients with severe anxiety disorders, the act of coming in for an appointment may have been a major undertaking in itself. It is useful to allow the patient to ventilate and share this information. The clinician might begin the interview by asking what it was like to come in for the interview today. Besides putting the patient at ease, this approach will yield information on travel restrictions, fear of medical settings, ability to function alone, and so forth.

The next step is to obtain a rudimentary knowledge of the patient's background: age, marital and occupational status, number of children, and who lives in the patient's household.

The Presenting Problem

The next question concerns the problem for which the patient is seeking help. This question and further probing should provide information on the presence and extent of panic attacks, avoidance behavior, generalized anxiety, and interference with the patient's social functioning.

The interviewer then focuses on the historical development of the problem. It is useful to ask about the first panic attack, the symptoms experienced, and how the attack was handled. Often the patient will remember this attack vividly. In conjunction with the onset, what was going on in the patient's life? We frequently see onset of panic disorder after a major shift of the patient's attachment pattern, such as death of a parent, pregnancy (in self, wife, or girlfriend), childbirth, divorce, engagement, or marriage. Possible conditioning events such as traffic accidents should be explored. The development of avoidance behavior should be probed in some detail. As the patient allows the history of the panic disorder to unfold, the clinician should take note of the possible episodic nature of the problem and of past treatment attempts, including attempts at self-help, helpful advice from others, and psychological or psychopharmacological treatments.

The Psychiatric Review of Systems

The next set of questions constitutes a psychiatric review of systems. As mentioned earlier, the psychiatric review of systems surveys mental functioning over a broad spectrum of psychopathology. It requires that the interviewer be highly conversant with basic psychopathology, including the DSM-III-R criteria for various disorders. This material should be covered fairly early in the interview; otherwise the therapist may develop premature hypotheses about the patient's problem. Indeed, the most common mistake inexperienced clinicians make during their assessments is to spend too much time on the presenting problem, causing them to prematurely commit themselves to a particular line of action or diagnosis. Further details of the presenting problem can be obtained during the secondary assessment or during the final phase of the initial assessment.

The order in which the information for the psychiatric review of systems is elicited is irrelevant, as long as all the areas are covered by the end of the interview. On completion of this review, the clinician should be able to make a diagnosis according to DSM-III-R. The DSM-III-R requires that the clinician provide ratings on five different axes: Axis I (psychiatric disorders), Axis II (personality disorders), Axis III (physical disorders), Axis IV (severity of psychosocial stressors), and Axis V (global assessment of functioning).

The specific areas of the psychiatric review of systems are as follows.

1. *Other anxiety disorders.* The patient is asked about social fears, other specific fears, generalized anxiety, obsessions or compulsions, and post–traumatic stress experiences.

2. *Depression.* As mentioned earlier, it is important to identify those cases in which the panic attacks are secondary to a primary depressive disorder, because depression with panic appears to be a particularly severe form of depression requiring aggressive therapy, including inpatient treatment in some cases. Sleep difficulties—particularly early morning awakening—appetite disturbance (eating too little or too much) with weight loss or gain, difficulties concentrating that interfere with work performance, and marked decrease in interest or generalized loss of pleasure from most activities are useful screening behaviors. If the patient has a history of depression, the specific episodes of the disorder have to be elicited as well as their temporal relationship to panic. An assessment of whether the depression is primary or secondary is made.

3. *Suicidal behavior.* Questions about past or present suicidal ideation (including passive death wishes, recurrent fantasies, actual plan, choice of

method, suicide notes, actual attempts) are a routine part of the exploration of depressive episodes. It is included here as a separate heading to highlight the importance of this area of inquiry.

4. *Mania*. In some depressive patients, the depression represents a phase in a bipolar disorder. Manic phases are elicited by questions about decreased need for sleep, feeling unusually good, spending sprees, thoughts racing, increase in activity, and pressure of speech.

5. *Psychosis*. Panic attacks can occur in psychotic states (Kahn, Puertollano, Schane, & Klein, 1988; Winokur, 1988). Exploration of potential psychosis elicits any experiences of hallucinations, irrational beliefs, or irrational speech or behavior. Because panic patients frequently fear that they are "going crazy," this content area has to be approached with considerable tact. Patients may be reassured that "these are questions we ask everybody, for our records." A good lead-in question for paranoia is "Have you ever had a feeling that people deliberately held you back or tried to give you a hard time?" followed by asking whether the patient has had the feeling that people were taking special notice of him or her. Patients are asked about any unusual experiences such as telepathy, dreams coming true, hearing voices when no one was around, visions, or speaking in ways that others could not understand. Psychotic patients are often quite evasive, so if the clinician suspects that the patient is suppressing such information a collaborate interview with a significant other is important. After answering these questions, the patient may need to be reassured that patients with panic disorder rarely if ever become psychotic.

6. *Physical disorders and prescribed medication*. The patients are asked about their history of physical disorders, current and past medical or surgical treatments, and names and addresses of their physicians. All currently prescribed medication should be listed in detail.

7. *Nicotine, caffeine, alcohol, and substance abuse*. Patients tend to feel less defensive about their smoking and coffee intake, so we usually ask about the amount of current and past intake of these substances first. Panic patients are known to have an increased sensitivity to caffeine. With respect to alcohol, the patient is asked to give the average number of drinks per day, as well as whether alcohol is used to relieve anxiety. Follow-up questions include whether the patient was ever told that he or she had problems with alcohol, whether there has been a history of drinking in the morning hours, whether the patient has had withdrawal symptoms ("shakes") or blackouts, and whether the patient has received treatment for alcoholism. It is important to remember that patients frequently underreport their use of alcohol.

With respect to other substance abuse, the present and past use of specific drugs should be probed, including marijuana, psychedelic drugs (for example, LSD), stimulants ("uppers" such as amphetamine, Ritalin, and diet pills), barbiturates and minor tranquilizers ("downers" such as meprobamate and valium), pain medication, and opioids. Furthermore, patients should be asked if they have ever used drugs intravenously.

8. *Antisocial behavior*. It is often difficult to get the patient to provide this information willingly. Nevertheless, we routinely ask whether the patient has any history of legal problems, violence, or poor impulse control.

9. *Personality disorders*. A diagnosis of personality disorder emerges as the patient's life history becomes known. Diagnosing personality disorders with any degree of certainty often requires several contacts. Nevertheless, preliminary observations can be made during the initial interview. Important clues to the presence of personality disorders are provided by the patient's mood, affect, and style of discourse. For example, is the patient extroverted or introverted? Is the style of discourse global or detailed? We recommend the book *Neurotic Styles* by Shapiro (1965) to sensitize the clinician to these different cognitive styles.

To elicit specific information relevant to a personality diagnosis, patients can be asked to compare their personalities with those of their parents or siblings. For example, which one of the two parents does the patient resemble the most? How would people who know the patient well describe the patient as a person? After such initial general questions, the patients can be asked more specifically to rate themselves on particular personality traits. For example, do they consider themselves to be perfectionistic, a workaholic, sensitive to criticism, easily bored, needing attention from others, prone to form intense relationships, or uncomfortable when alone?

To know what information to elicit, the clinician needs to be familiar with the personality disorder criteria in the DSM-III-R. The most important ones to consider with regard to panic disorder are borderline personality disorder (impulsive acts, feelings of emptiness, self-mutilatory behavior); histrionic personality disorder (impressionistic style of speech lacking in detail, dramatic expression of emotions, seductiveness, impatience with details); compulsive personality disorder (detail-oriented, restricted expression of affect, perfectionism); dependent personality disorder (allows others to make his or her life decisions); avoidant personality disorder (avoids almost all relationships out of fear of rejection); and passive-aggressive personality disorder (sulky, argumentative, sabotaging).

10. *Current stressors*. This information is necessary for the diagnosis on Axis IV of the DSM-III-R. The patient is asked about life stresses during the past year that may have led to the onset, recurrence, or exacerbation of the disorder. The following areas are covered: significant others (engagement, marriage, divorce); parenting (becoming a parent, illness of child); other interpersonal stressors (friends, neighbors); and occupational, financial, legal, and developmental (phase-of-life) problems. In the DSM-III-R these problems are rated on a 6-point scale from "none" to "catastrophic." Furthermore, the clinician should specify whether the stressor is acute (duration of less than 6 months) or enduring (more than 6 months).

At this time, the clinician asks if the patient is pursuing litigation—for example, to obtain worker's compensation or as a party in a civil suit for damages after a traffic accident. Such legal issues may drastically alter the contingencies for the patient to get better. It may even be advisable to defer treatment until after the legal matters have been settled.

11. *Global assessment of functioning.* This information is necessary for the diagnosis on Axis V of the DSM-III-R. This rating is done once for current functioning, and once for highest level of functioning during the past year. The ratings are done on a 0-to-90-point scale (90 = highest level of functioning) and form a composite of psychological, social, and occupational functioning. For specific definitions of anchor points see DSM-III-R, page 12.

Social History and Family History

The social history tracks the patient's life from birth to the day of the interview. Questions include educational status, marital history, children, and so forth. Some of this information will already have been elicited at the beginning of the interview (see "Getting to Know the Patient"). For patients with anxiety disorders, it is important to ask about history of childhood anxiety problems, such as separation anxiety and shyness.

The family history involves drawing a family tree starting with the grandparents and including all of their descendants. Include information on anxiety disorders in family members, as well as other psychiatric disorders such as alcoholism, depression, psychosis, or chronic medical disorders. Finally, specify the cause of death for each deceased family member.

Terminating the Interview

Before ending the interview, patients are asked whether any important information has been overlooked. Furthermore, it is important at this point to elicit the patient's understanding of the problem. Treatment goals and expectations should be discussed, as well as how these fit into overall life goals. At this point, the clinician provides feedback and discusses the treatment alternatives, along with the further assessments that are necessary.

Aids for the Initial Interview

In our setting, the information elicited in the initial interview is recorded in the Initial Evaluation Form (IEF) (Mezzich, Dow, Rich, Costello, & Himmelhoch, 1981). The IEF consists of an unstructured section in which reasons for referral, history of present illness, past psychiatric problems, family history, medical history, social history, and the mental status are recorded. The mental status section includes the following items: (1) general appearance and behavior; (2) speech and thought rate and pattern; (3) mood and affect; (4) thought content and perception; and (5) sensorium, orientation, intellectual functions, and insight. The IEF has a structured section in which 64 specific psychiatric symptoms are recorded for the current episode of illness as well as for the past. Brief checklists are also included eliciting specific information on family history, social history, and medical history.

The Hamilton Anxiety Rating Scale (Hamilton, 1959) and the Hamilton Rating Scale for Depression (Hamilton, 1960) are interview-based scales for assessment of general anxiety and depression. Unfortunately, though these scales provide a numerical value related to the degree of anxiety and depression, they do not differentiate well between the two conditions. More recently, Riskind, Beck, Brown, and Steer (1987) have used factor analysis to modify the scoring of the two scales to better discriminate between anxiety and depression. With this modification, these two scales may become even more useful as an aid in initial assessment. The two Hamilton scales are also included in the Anxiety Disorders Interview Schedule (ADIS), to be described in a later section.

A number of brief pencil-and-paper instruments can be employed to aid in the initial assessment of the patient. One of the most useful ones is the Chambless Mobility Inventory, which provides a concurrent overview of the patient's avoidance pattern. (A description of this instrument is provided later in this chapter.) The Symptom Questionnaire (also described later in this chapter) is useful for identifying specific somatic sensations during and between panic attacks. The Beck Depression Inventory (Beck, Rush, Shaw, & Emery, 1979; Beck, Steer, & Garbin, 1988) can assist in the identification of depression. Although not yet tested extensively, the Cognitions Checklist, recently published to differentiate between the cognitions of depression and anxiety, may become helpful in making this distinction (Beck, Brown, Eidelson, Steer, & Riskind, 1987).

The Cornell Medical Index (Brodman, Erdmann, & Wolff, 1949) is a useful checklist of physical and mental symptoms that can be employed for a preliminary review of physical and psychiatric symptoms. Finally, the SCL-90 is a relatively brief inventory measuring psychopathology on a number of scales, including somatization, obsessive-compulsive features, interpersonal sensitivity, depression, anxiety, hostility, phobic anxiety, paranoid ideation, and psychoticism (Derogatis, Rickels, & Rock, 1976). The SCL-90 is useful for confirming or alerting the clinician to the presence of psychopathology, whether related to anxiety or not.

After the initial evaluation is completed, the patient is given an appointment for the next visit. Arrangements are also made to obtain the patient's medical records from community physicians. Unless the patient is already under the regular care of a physician, an appointment is also made for a physical examination.

The Medical Evaluation

It is well known that patients with psychiatric disorders have a high likelihood of having a medical disorder (Koryani, 1980). When medically evaluating patients with panic disorder, one is confronted with two partially conflicting tasks. The first and overriding task is not to miss any significant medical disorder. The second is to be alert to the hypochondriacal tendencies for which patients with panic disorder are notorious and not further aggravate them (Jacob & Turner, 1988). As mentioned earlier, the medical examination includes a review of systems and a physical and laboratory examination. The review of systems and physical examination should be done by a medically trained person who can check for symptoms of diseases within specific organ systems. Laboratory examinations are done for general screening purposes, and further tests are added if a specific medical disorder is suspected.

Table 2.4 lists the medical disorders that can present with anxiety or symptoms that are similar to those of panic disorder. It's immediately obvious that the possibilities are numerous. In general, panic attacks beginning after age 40 should prompt suspicions of an underlying medical disorder. If the attacks are judged to be caused by an underlying medical disorder, the psychiatric diagnosis would be organic anxiety disorder, rather than panic disorder.

TABLE 2.4 Differential Diagnosis of Panic Disorder

Main symptoms	Condition suspected	Differentiating symptoms	Confirming test
Tremor, sweating, pallor, dizziness	Reactive hypoglycemia	Symptoms 2–4 hours after meal	5-hr glucose-tolerance tests
	Insulin-secreting tumors		Fasting blood-glucose and blood-insulin levels
Palpitations	Paroxysmal atrial tachycardia, ventricular extrasystoles	Sudden onset of rapid heart rate	24-hr electrocardiographic monitoring, event recording
	Mitral valve prolapse	Systolic click or late systolic murmur	Echocardiogram
Dizziness	Orthostatic hypotension, anemia	Worse upon arising and exercise	Blood pressure and pulse, standing vs. sitting or lying down, blood count
	Benign positional vertigo	Triggered by rotation of head, jogging, stooping	Barany maneuver, otoneurological examination

Main symptoms	Condition suspected	Differentiating symptoms	Confirming test
Dyspnea, hyperventilation	Congestive heart failure	Rapid shallow breathing	Chest x-ray, EKG
	Pneumonia, pleuritis	Fever	Chest x-ray
	Asthma	Wheezing on expiration	Pulmonary function tests
	Chronic obstructive pulmonary disease	Precipitated by smoking	
	Alcohol withdrawal	History of alcohol use	
Chest pain	Angina pectoris	Precipitated by physical exercise, emotions, or heavy meals	Electrocardiogram, exercise electrocardiogram
	Myocardial infarction	Prolonged severe pain	Electrocardiogram, cardiac enzymes
	Costal chondritis	Tender spots in costochondral junctions	Normal cardiologic evaluation
	Pleuritis, pneumonia	Fever	Chest x-ray
Feelings of unreality	Temporal lobe epilepsy	Micropsia, macropsia, perceptual distortions, hallucinations	EEG with nasopharyngeal leads
	Psychedelic use or "flashback"	History of use	
Hot and cold flashes	Carcinoid syndrome		5-HIAA in 24-hr urine
	Menopause	Female sex, appropriate age	
Weakness	Multiple sclerosis	Age <40, fluctuating symptoms	Neurologic evaluation
	Transient ischemic attacks	Age >40, paralysis	

(continued)

TABLE 2.4 (continued)

Main symptoms	Condition suspected	Differentiating symptoms	Confirming test
Miscella-neous	Hyperthyroidism	Rapid heart rate, warm sweaty hands	Thyroid function tests
	Hypothyroidism	Voice changes	
	Hyperpara-thyroidism	Varied psychiatric symptoms	Blood calcium levels
	Hypopara-thyroidism	Tetany, increased sensitivity to hyperventilation	
	Pheochromo-cytoma	High blood pressure	Catecholamines in 24-hr urine
	Acute intermittent porphyria	History of barbiturate intake	Urine porphobilino-gen during attack
Drug use	Amphetamine intoxication	Paranoid feelings	Drug screen
	Hallucinogen abuse	"Flashbacks"	
	Withdrawal from barbiturates or minor tranquilizers	Agitation	
	Withdrawal from opioids	Pain, general malaise	
	Alcohol withdrawal	History of alcohol use	
	Amitriptyline withdrawal	History of amitriptyline use	

SOURCE: Jacob, R. G., & Rapport, M. D. (1984). Panic disorder: Medical and psychological parameters. In S. M. Turner (Ed.), *Behavioral theories and treatment of anxiety*. New York: Plenum. Reprinted with permission.

Besides suffering from medical disorders that cause paniclike symptoms, panic patients may also be at increased risk for medical disorders symptomatically unrelated to panic. Vittone and Udhe (1985) found that 58% of their panic patients had previously unrecognized medical disorders. (This figure appears higher, however, than what our clinical experience evaluating anxiety disorders would indicate.) The illnesses discovered by Vittone and Uhde included not only mild conditions, such as iron deficiency anemia, but also serious illnesses, such as multiple endocrine adenomas, cerebrovascular accidents, and brain venous malformations. Hall, Popkin, Devaul, Faillace, and

Stickney (1978) found that a wide variety of conditions could result in anxiety symptoms: pneumonia, thyroid and parathyroid disorders, paroxysmal atrial tachycardia, hypochromic anemia, ulcerative colitis, and scabies, to name a few. Hall (1980) highlighted the prominence of neurological disorders, including transient ischemic attacks and head injuries.

Besides current illnesses, panic patients may also be at increased risk for medical illnesses in the future. Noyes, Clancy, Hoenk, and Slymen (1978), in a 6-year follow-up study, reported that patients with anxiety neurosis, compared with surgical controls, had more illness during follow-up, including peptic ulcer disease (31% versus 14%), hypertension (27% versus 11%), and heart disease (17% versus 4%). However, because the study was completed before the DSM-III was formulated, we do not know if these patients had panic disorder. Male patients with panic disorder may also be at increased risk of developing cardiac disorders later in life, although the literature (to be discussed further later) is not consistent in this regard.

In the sections that follow we will selectively discuss the most common differential diagnostic considerations; that is, only a selection of those disorders listed in Table 2.4. These disorders include endocrine and metabolic disorders, neurological disorders, and cardiac disorders. It should be noted that the empirical data linking panic disorder to different medical conditions are often sketchy. The sample sizes of the relevant studies have often been small, making it difficult to identify rare conditions. In our view, even if a particular medical condition is rare statistically speaking, depending on the severity or treatability of the disorder, even one missed diagnosis could have significant consequences.

Endocrine and Metabolic Disorders

In this section we will discuss thyroid disorders, hypoglycemia, and pheochromocytoma. Other possible conditions that won't be discussed include hypo- or hyperparathyroidism, Cushing's syndrome, and the carcinoid syndrome (see Table 2.4).

Thyroid Disorders

Patients with hyperthyroidism can have varied psychiatric symptoms, including anxiety and phobia. In 115 patients with hyperthyroidism, Ficarra and Nelson (1947) found various types of phobias, including claustrophobia, fear of being alone, fear of crowds, and fear of heights. Most of the phobic patients were women. Similarly, Trzepacz, McCue, Klein, Levey, and Greenhouse (1988a) examined the psychiatric symptoms of thirteen patients with hyperthyroidism. The most common condition was major depression, occurring in nine of the thirteen patients. In addition, agoraphobia occurred in one, panic disorder in four, and generalized anxiety in eight of the patients. Three of the patients had hypomania. Treatment of the thyroid disorder resulted in significant decreases in measures of anxiety as well as depression (Trzepacz, McCue, Klein, Greenhouse, & Levey, 1988b).

Kathol, Turner, and Delahunt (1986) assessed the symptoms of 29 patients with hyperthyroidism and found that 23 (79%) would have fulfilled diagnostic criteria for generalized anxiety disorder. Fully 21 of these 23 patients experienced a resolution of their symptoms when the thyroid disorder was treated. In addition, 9 of the 29 patients met the DSM-III criteria for depression. In another report, Kathol and Delahunt (1986) indicated that 13 of 32 hyperthyroid patients had somatic symptoms consistent with panic attacks, except that the symptoms in hyperthyroidism did not occur in discrete attacks. The high prevalence of anxiety may be a reflection of symptomatic overlap between hyperthyroidism and anxiety.

Conversely, thyroid disorders have been observed in panic disorder and phobia, although not consistently so across studies. Lindemann, Zitrin, and Klein (1984) examined 295 phobic patients for history of hyper- or hypothyroidism. The prevalence of thyroid disorder histories was 11.7% in panic disorder, 8.3% in mixed phobias, and 4.9% in simple phobias. The thyroid disorders included both hyper- and hypothyroidism in about equal proportions. It should be noted, however, that no thyroid function tests were actually obtained in this study, which raises concerns about generalizing these findings to newly screened panic disorder patients.

Another study yielding a high prevalence of thyroid abnormalities in panic disorder was conducted by Matuzas, Al-Sadir, Uhlenhuth, and Glass (1987), who examined thyroid function in 55 patients. Of the 55, 3 had a history of thyroid illness and treatment, 4 had elevations in thyroid function screening tests, and 7 tested positive for microsomal antibodies. Overall, 11 of the 42 women (26%) and 1 of the 13 men showed abnormalities in thyroid function. The authors felt that the prevalence of thyroid abnormalities in panic patients was higher than in the general population but did not actually include a nonpanic comparison group in their study.

In contrast, other studies suggest that thyroid disorders are of little concern in panic disorder. Fishman, Sheehan, and Carr (1985) determined T3, T4, and TSH levels in 82 patients with panic disorder, some of whom were receiving treatment. In none of the patients did the thyroid function tests indicate a thyroid disorder, but an unusually high proportion of the patients had undetectable levels of TSH; the implication of the latter finding is unclear. Furthermore, Stein and Uhde (1988), in the only study that included a control group, compared 26 panic patients with 26 controls on various thyroid indices and found no difference between the two groups. However, patients or normal subjects with previously documented thyroid disease were excluded from the study. Therefore, the authors concluded that the results of the study could not be taken as evidence that thyroid screening tests were unnecessary for panic patients.

In conclusion, thyroid disorders frequently present with anxiety or affective symptoms. Conversely, some studies with panic disorder patients suggest abnormalities in thyroid function, but with one exception none of these studies has been well controlled. Moreover, the study that was controlled had excluded patients with histories of thyroid disorders. Since thyroid disorders require specific treatments, routine screening of panic patients for thyroid abnormalities would seem to be indicated, even though the number of new cases of thyroid disorders discovered may be low.

Idiopathic Postprandial Hypoglycemia

Reactive or postprandial hypoglycemia is thought to be caused by an excessively high secretion of insulin after ingesting carbohydrates, resulting in a rapid decline of blood sugar to hypoglycemic blood levels and compensatory secretions of catecholamines and other hormones. The symptoms of hypoglycemia occur 2 to 4 hours after meals and include headache, mental dullness, fatigue, confusion, anxiety, irritability, sweating, palpitations, tremor, and hunger sensations (Permutt, 1976). The diagnosis of hypoglycemia is made with the aid of the 5-hour glucose tolerance test. Reactive hypoglycemia can be an initial sign of diabetes and may also occur with liver disease, alcoholism, and after gastrectomy, but it is primarily an idiopathic condition. Reactive hypoglycemia should be differentiated from fasting hypoglycemia, which is usually a sign of clinically significant underlying illness.

Reactive hypoglycemia used to be an overdiagnosed condition that was employed as a convenient explanation for almost any ill-defined symptom (Yager & Young, 1979). For example, Permutt (1980) estimated that "non-hypoglycemia" was at least five times as common as verified hypoglycemia. Similarly, Ford, Bray, and Swerdloff (1976) verified the diagnosis of hypoglycemia in only 4 of 30 patients previously so diagnosed. In recent practice, however, hypoglycemia seems to be diagnosed infrequently and reluctantly.

Uhde, Vittone, and Post (1984) found that seven of nine patients with panic disorder had hypoglycemic responses to the oral glucose tolerance test. The patients became symptomatic (hunger, lightheadedness, diaphoresis, and palpitations) around the time of glucose nadir (at 210 to 300 minutes) and experienced an increase in generalized or "free-floating" anxiety; however, they did not experience panic attacks. Nevertheless, the prevalence of symptomatic hypoglycemia seems quite high.

Schweizer, Winokur, and Rickels (1986) subjected ten panic patients to experimentally induced hypoglycemia by means of insulin infusions. The patients reported symptoms such as palpitations, sweating, tremulousness, and hot and cold flashes, but again no panic attacks. Because panic attacks did not occur in either of the latter two studies, it is often concluded that hypoglycemia is not a factor in panic disorder. However, both studies involved small sample sizes, and hypoglycemia was actually common in the Uhde et al. (1984) study. It thus might be possible that hypoglycemia is a factor in a relatively small number of panic patients, although the causal relationship between hypoglycemia and panic may be unclear in these patients.

From the studies discussed, it would appear that reactive hypoglycemia is not a very important consideration in panic disorder. Nevertheless, it would seem prudent to remain alert to the possibility of hypoglycemia in a few cases, especially in patients who report symptoms related to meals, panic attacks accompanied by sensations of hunger, or in patients with gastric surgery (Raj & Sheehan, 1987).

Pheochromocytoma

Pheochromocytomas are tumors of catecholamine-secreting tissues. Most pheochromocytomas (90%) are located in the adrenal medulla, but they can also develop at other sites, such as in the ganglia of the sympathetic chain (Manger & Gifford, 1982). Pheochromocytomas occur at a rate of 0.1% in patients with persistent diastolic hypertension. They occur at any age and in both sexes, but most commonly in women between 40 and 50 years of age.

The symptoms of pheochromocytomas are related to the secretion of excessive amounts of adrenaline and noradrenalin. The symptoms occur in episodes or paroxysms persisting from a few minutes to as long as a week (Manger & Gifford, 1982). The most common symptom is severe headache, occurring in 70% to 90% of pheochromocytoma patients, followed by excessive sweating, palpitations, and anxiety, nervousness, or panic. Ninety percent of the patients have hypertension, which is episodic or paroxysmal in nature in 40% of the cases. Anxiety appeared to be particularly common in the variety with paroxysmal hypertension. In patients with pheochromocytoma and paroxysmal hypertension, anxiety symptoms occurred in 60%; among patients with sustained hypertension, anxiety or panic occurred in 28%.

In a recently reported series of 17 patients with pheochromocytoma, diagnosable anxiety disorders were reported to be relatively rare (Starkman, Zelnik, Nesse, & Cameron, 1985). Two patients fulfilled the DSM-III diagnostic criteria for generalized anxiety disorder, two had "possible" generalized anxiety disorder, and one had "possible" panic disorder. Nevertheless, five out of seventeen patients with possible or definite anxiety disorder (29%) seems higher than one would expect in the general population. Specific psychological symptoms included feeling that something terrible might happen (five patients) and fears of dying (four patients). However, ten patients reported no psychological symptoms. As a group, pheochromocytoma patients scored lower than anxiety disorder patients on a number of anxiety-related symptoms.

Since pheochromocytomas are quite rare, and because panic does not occur in all patients with pheochromocytoma, it is unlikely that many pheochromocytoma patients exist in the panic disorder population. Nevertheless, because the condition is a serious one that requires surgery, patients in whom panic occurs with severe headaches, sweating, or flushing should be referred for further evaluation (which involves obtaining measures of plasma and urine catecholamines and radiological examinations).

Neurological and Otoneurological Conditions

Vestibular Dysfunction

Dizziness is one of the somatic symptoms of panic. It is also often a consequence of hyperventilation, particularly if the dizziness is described as "light-headedness." Many panic patients also report symptoms of imbalance, such as veering toward one side or another. A few have histories of vertigo, particularly at the onset of the panic disorder (Jacob, Lilienfeld, Furman, Durrant, & Turner, 1988). The latter type of symptoms also occur in vestibular dysfunction (Jacob, 1988). Furthermore, patients with vestibular dysfunction often show increased anxiety and "pseudoagoraphobic" symptoms, such as intolerance of driving on wide roads or over crests of hills and trouble looking up and down supermarket aisles (Jacob, 1988).

In a study of 21 panic patients, selected because they had symptoms of imbalance during or dizziness between panic attacks, we found a high prevalence of abnormalities on clinical vestibular tests (Jacob, Moller, Turner, & Wall, 1985). Vestibular dysfunction, as measured by vestibular function tests, can occur in disorders of the peripheral vestibular organ as well as the central nervous system. Neurological and otological examinations of the patients did not identify any specific neurological disorders that might have caused the dysfunction. Nevertheless, these findings, as well as those of earlier studies (Hallpike, Harrison, & Slater, 1951; Pratt & McKenzie, 1958), suggest that vestibular dysfunction occurs in a subgroup of patients with panic disorder.

We do not know at this time, however, what the prevalence of vestibular dysfunction would be in panic patients not specifically selected for vestibular-type symptoms. We also do not know whether vestibular dysfunction is more common in panic disorder than in other anxiety disorders. Our current estimate is that the prevalence of vestibular dysfunction in panic disorder may be as high as one in every six or seven unselected patients.

The causal direction of the relationship of panic and vestibular dysfunction is unclear. Increased arousal and hyperventilation can increase the sensitivity of the vestibular system (Theunissen, Huygen, & Folgering, 1986). It is possible, therefore, that the effect of vestibular dysfunction is potentiated by anxiety. Because of the uncertain status of vestibular dysfunction in panic, for clinical practice we do not recommend routine vestibular testing of all patients with panic disorder, but reserve such tests for patients with vestibular or ear-related symptoms, such as intolerance of motion (compare with space phobia, discussed presently), sensations of imbalance, and ear pressure.

Besides vestibular dysfunction, imbalance in agoraphobia may be related to neurological disorders, including strokes. A pseudoagoraphobic syndrome involving balance dysfunction labeled *space phobia* was described by Marks and Bebbington (1976) and by Marks (1981). The space-phobic patients were afraid of falling and of open spaces lacking visuospatial support for orientation in space, such as driving over crests of hills. Many of these patients had difficulty walking. The average age of onset was 55 years. These patients had vestibular dysfunction or various neurological disorders, such as cerebellar defects, cerebral atrophy, and strokes.

Seizure Disorders

Anxiety, panic, or fear can be a manifestation of seizure disorders, particularly temporal lobe epilepsy (Brodsky, Zuniga, Casenas, Ernstoff, & Sachdev, 1983; Taylor & Lochery, 1987). Anxiety or panic is particularly common if the seizure activity involves the limbic system, especially the amygdala. In an interesting paper, Gloor, Olivier, Quesney, Andermann, and Horowitz (1982) studied the symptoms of patients with intractable temporal lobe epilepsy in whom intracerebral depth electrodes had been implanted at various locations. The symptoms were elicited either as a result of naturally occurring seizure activity or as a consequence of brain stimulation. Fear was the most commonly observed symptom, occurring in 7 of the 35 patients. Other common experiences included complex visual hallucinations (5 patients), memory recall (5 patients), and familiarity or déjà vu (4 patients). Of interest is that there were individual differences in responses to hippocampal stimulation based in part on the past experiences of the individual. The individual nature of the responses to hippocampal stimulation may explain why fear was not observed in all the patients.

If panic can be a symptom of temporal lobe epilepsy, the question arises whether panic disorder and temporal lobe epilepsy can be differentiated on symptomatic grounds. Harper and Roth (1962) compared the symptoms of 30 patients with temporal lobe epilepsy and 30 patients with the "phobic anxiety–depersonalization syndrome," a condition that appears to be similar to severe panic disorder (one or more attacks per day) with perhaps added features of severe personality disorder. This is the only study directly comparing the symptoms of temporal lobe epilepsy with an anxiety disorder equivalent. Harper and Roth found that episodic anxiety attacks with autonomic changes such as palpitations, sweating, and gastric discomfort occurred in both phobic anxiety–depersonalization syndrome and temporal lobe epilepsy. Similarly, "temporal lobe" symptoms such as depersonalization, déjà vu sensations, and perceptual distortions, including olfactory hallucinations, were found in both conditions (although the latter symptom should be less common in pure panic disorder than in the phobic anxiety–depersonalization syndrome). On the other hand, there were important differences between temporal lobe epilepsy and phobic anxiety–depersonalization syndrome. The patient with temporal lobe epilepsy had more automatic behavior, episodic disturbances of speech, self-injury during attacks, fecal or urinary incontinence, and difficulty recalling the attack. They had less persistent anxiety, depression, feelings of unsteadiness, and derealization, and fewer phobias. The temporal lobe attacks typically ended abruptly, whereas panic attacks ended gradually.

More recent studies of panic in seizure disorders have been at the level of case reports without contrasting them with nonseizure anxiety groups. Two cases reported by Volkow, Harper, and Swann (1986) were characterized by associated symptoms that were atypical for panic disorder, such as a history of motor seizures, sleepwalking, and poor impulse control in one case, and auditory hallucinations and poor impulse control in the other case. Other clinicians similarly have reported associated features in seizure disorders that included severe derealization, irritability, disinhibited and aggressive behavior, hallucinations, and a relative absence of phobic avoidance (Brodsky et al., 1983; Edlund, Swann, & Clothier, 1987). In one case, neurological examination revealed a right temporal lobe meningioma (Ghadirian, Gauthier, & Bertrand, 1986).

The only study attempting to address the prevalence of seizure disorder in a group of patients with panic disorder was conducted by Stein, Mellman, Roy-Byrne, Post, and Uhde (1988). Among 35 panic patients evaluated by sleep-deprived EEG with nasopharyngeal leads, a very low prevalence of EEG abnormalities was found. Similarly, treatment of panic disorder with carbamazepine, an antiseizure drug, revealed that 40% showed cessation of panic attacks, but 50% showed an increase; overall, the improvement rate was quite low (Uhde, Stein, & Post, 1988).

The relationship between panic disorder and seizure disorders is complex and includes possibilities other than a seizure disorder causing panic. The other possibilities are that the panic and seizure disorders coexist without being causally related, or that treatment of panic disorder reactivates a preexisting seizure disorder. Variations such as these are illustrated in three cases reported by Weilburg, Bear, and Sachs (1987). In the first case, the panic appeared to be directly related to the seizure activity; the clinical presentation was one of panic disorder. Workup for epilepsy was prompted by subtle neurological findings such as clumsiness in one hand, attention deficits, and hypokinesia in part of the face. The panic attacks did not respond to imipramine but responded to antiseizure medication. In the second case, panic appeared related to an interictal behavior syndrome. The panic attacks abated with change of the antiseizure medication. In the third case, epilepsy and panic were independent, but the seizure disorder was reactivated by treatment of the panic disorder with phenelzine.

To summarize, panic attacks can be a manifestation of an underlying seizure disorder. However, among patients seeking help for panic disorder, seizure disorders are probably quite rare and therefore of relatively little concern. Another possibility to keep in mind, however, is that a coexisting but symptomatically unrelated seizure disorder may become activated by pharmacological treatment of panic.

An underlying seizure disorder should be suspected if there are characteristic associated symptoms or signs, as exemplified in the preceding clinical descriptions. Routine EEGs or neurological referrals should not be necessary in patients with panic disorder, unless the associated features make a diagnosis of seizure disorder more likely. Since routine EEGs do not always pick up the seizure focus (Weilburg, Pollack, Murray, & Garber, 1986), the diagnosis of epilepsy can be quite difficult.

Exposure to Organic Solvents or Toxic Chemicals

Exposure to solvents can result in dose-related psychological symptoms including disorientation, lightheadedness, headaches, nausea, and decreasing levels of consciousness (Dager, Holland, Cowley, & Dunner, 1987). In addition, panic attacks can occur as an idiosyncratic reaction that is not dose related. Dager et al. reported three cases in whom panic disorder appeared to have been precipitated by exposure to organic solvents. In each of the cases, the panic attacks continued even in the absence of solvent exposure.

Increased anxiety has also been reported as a result of exposure to organophosphate compounds used as insecticides. Levin, Rodnitzky, and Mick (1976) found that commercial sprayers of these compounds, compared with unexposed farmers, had increased levels of pervasive anxiety, restlessness, and sleep disturbance.

Exposure to organic solvents or toxic chemicals is probably an infrequent cause of panic. It should be quite feasible to identify such cases merely by routinely asking about history of such exposure in the review of systems.

Heart Disease

Ever since the description of Da Costa's syndrome more than 100 years ago, the cardiovascular system has been a particular focus of studies on anxiety. Therefore, the literature in this field is quite extensive.

There is conflicting evidence that patients with panic disorder, particularly males, may be at increased risk for developing heart disease. For example, Noyes et al. (1978), in the follow-up study described earlier, found an increased prevalence of hypertension and heart disease in panic patients compared with controls. In a retrospective follow-up study on former inpatients with panic disorder, Coryell, Noyes, and Clancy (1982) found an increased risk for death from cardiovascular causes in male patients; this finding was partially replicated in a later study on outpatients (Coryell et al., 1986). However, the increase of risk for heart disease was minimal, and other similar studies have produced negative results (Margraf, Ehlers, & Roth, 1988).

An important recent prospective population-based study involving 1500 white men aged 40 to 64 years showed that phobic anxiety, as measured by the Crown-Crisp Experiential Index, was strongly related to future ischemic heart disease, particularly fatal events (Haines, Dimeson, & Meade, 1987). During the follow-up period, 105 subjects had an ischemic heart disease episode during the next 6 to 7 years. Those scoring approximately in the uppermost quartile on the phobic anxiety subscale had a relative risk of ischemic heart disease that was two times higher than those scoring in the lowest quartile; for fatal ischemic events, the relative risk was over three times higher. These data suggest a relationship between phobic anxiety and increased risk for heart disease in men aged 40 or above. It is not clear, however, whether these findings can be generalized to clinical phobias or to females aged 20 to 30—that is, the "typical" panic patient.

The reasons the risk for heart disease would be greater for patients with anxiety disorders are unclear. One possibility might be that the risk would be mediated via the development of high blood pressure (Noyes et al., 1978). However, in a recent study employing ambulatory 24-hour blood pressure monitoring (Shear et al., unpublished), no elevations in 24-hour blood pressure were found in panic patients. Another mechanism might be decreased cardiac perfusion caused by hyperventilation. Hyperventilation can lead to electrocardiographic changes consistent with coronary artery spasm or myocardial ischemia (e.g., Freeman & Nixon, 1985; Lary & Goldschlager, 1974). For example, in a study in which coronary blood flow was actually measured during cardiac catheterization, Neill and Hattenhauer (1975) reported that hyperventilation decreased coronary blood flow in nine out of ten patients undergoing cardiac catheterization for evaluation of ischemic coronary artery disease.

Aside from whether panic disorder patients are at increased risk for developing cardiac disease, the question is whether there are specific cardiac conditions that should be ruled out when the panic disorder is diagnosed. Cardiac conditions that have been discussed in the literature include mitral valve prolapse and cardiac arrhythmias. Of these, mitral valve prolapse has received the most attention, and we will discuss this condition first. We will also discuss congestive heart failure as a differential diagnosis and conclude this section by discussing a newly identified population of panic patients: patients in cardiology clinics with nonanginal chest pain.

Mitral Valve Prolapse

Mitral valve prolapse (MVP) involves an alteration in the connective tissue of the mitral valve with dissolution of the collagen and secondary proliferation of myxomatous tissue, resulting in the mitral valve leaflets becoming stretched and elongated and bulging into the atrium (Devereux, 1985). MVP is diagnosed by a combination of characteristic auscultatory (stethoscope) findings and echocardiography. Two forms of MVP are recognized: primary and secondary. The secondary form occurs in diverse conditions, such as connective tissue disorders, papillary muscle dysfunction, and rheumatic carditis (Sevin, 1987).

The base rate of MVP in the general population is 4% to 7% (Devereux, 1985). MVP tends to cluster in families. The base rate is higher in women than in men. In women the prevalence rate also appears to be a function of age. In the third decade, the prevalence in women can be as high as 17%, whereas in the ninth decade, the prevalence is 1% (Sevin, 1987).

MVP has few adverse consequences for the afflicted person's health. However, male sex and age above 40 appear to predict adverse consequences from MVP (Shear, 1988). Some individuals with pronounced MVP are at increased risk for complications such as supraventricular tachycardia and other arrhythmias as well as for endocarditis. Furthermore, severe cases can develop mitral regurgitation, ventricular arrhythmias, and sudden death.

The diagnosis of MVP usually has few implications for the patient's care. To prevent the development of endocarditis, patients with MVP may need prophylactic antibiotic therapy before childbirth or before anticipated surgery, including dental extractions. The management of panic disorder with MVP does not differ from the management of panic disorder without MVP; thus MVP is not a contraindication for any of the pharmacological or behavioral treatments used for panic disorder (Crowe, 1985).

An association between MVP and panic was first reported by Pariser, Pinta, and Jones (1978) in a case study of a 25-year-old woman with MVP who fulfilled diagnostic criteria for panic disorder. Studies comparing groups of panic patients with normal subjects published shortly thereafter showed an increased prevalence of MVP in patients with panic attacks compared with controls (Kantor, Zitrin, & Zeldis, 1980; Venkatesh et al., 1980). Similarly, a number of more recent studies describe a high prevalence of MVP. Liberthson, Sheehan, King, and Weyman (1986) reported a prevalence of MVP, diagnosed by *either* auscultation *or* echocardiography, of 34% in 131 patients with panic disorder; 17% met *both* clinical and echocardiographic criteria for MVP. Matuzas et al. (1987) reported that 50% of 65 panic patients had MVP; the rate was independent of whether the patients had uncomplicated panic disorder, panic disorder with agoraphobia, or panic attacks as part of another disorder. The latter finding suggests that MVP might cluster with panic as a symptom, rather than with panic disorder as a diagnostic entity. Consistent with this, Dager, Cowley, and Dunner (1987) found that anxious patients with a history of panic attacks had a higher prevalence of MVP than anxious patients without panic attacks. There was no correlation between the presence or absence of symptoms such as tachycardia, chest pain, or dyspnea and MVP; panic patients with MVP tended to respond better to a placebo than did patients without MVP.

In contrast to the high prevalence rates of MVP found in the latter studies, Shear, Devereux, Kramer-Fox, Mann, and Frances (1984) found MVP in only 2 of 25 patients with panic disorder (8%), a prevalence similar to that in the general population. Similarly, Mavissakalian, Salerni, Thompson, and Michelson (1983) found that the prevalence of MVP was no higher than would be expected in the general population. Overall, then, different studies have found highly variable prevalence of MVP in panic disorder, ranging between 0% and 50% (Margraf et al., 1988 and studies just reviewed). Furthermore, the type of MVP found in panic patients may be the mildest variety. Gorman et al. (1988)

found that 39% of 36 panic patients had MVP, compared with 18% in normal controls; the MVP in almost all the positive cases, however, was considered mild.

Because MVP can occur in other psychiatric disorders besides panic disorder, MVP does not seem to be specifically related to panic disorder. In a study on bipolar affective disorder, Giannini et al. (1984) found auscultatory and echocardiographic evidence for MVP in 9 of 32 bipolar patients compared with 2 of 16 unipolar patients. Similarly, Chaleby and Ziady (1988) reported a high prevalence of MVP in social phobia.

If there is an association between MVP and panic, then one should find increased prevalence of panic disorder among individuals diagnosed as having MVP. It is often thought that MVP is associated with symptoms such as palpitations, chest pain, dyspnea, and panic. However, many of these associations may be spurious ones caused by symptomatic patients selecting themselves for cardiological evaluation. In a recent study in which relatives of patients with MVP were recruited for evaluation, 81 of the relatives also had MVP but 172 did not (Devereux et al., 1986). Comparing the symptoms and signs in the relatives with and without MVP, the differentiating findings were palpitations (40% versus 24%) and various minor chest deformities (41% versus 16%) such as pectus excavatum, decreased anteroposterior chest diameter, straight back, and scoliosis occurring more commonly in relatives with MVP. On the other hand, repolarization abnormalities, chest pain, and dyspnea were equally common in both groups. Importantly, there was no difference between the two groups with respect to anxiety and panic symptoms. Thus, among individuals with MVP who were not self-selected because they sought cardiac evaluations, there was no increased prevalence of panic compared with non-MVP controls.

In a similar study, Hartman, Kramer, Brown, and Devereux (1982) found a 16% prevalence of panic disorder among 141 patients with mitral valve prolapse, but only 1 of 33 relatives had panic attacks. The high prevalence rate in the patients again appears to have been a result of the selection of highly symptomatic individuals for echocardiographic evaluation. Finally, Mazza, Martin, Spacavento, Jacobsen, and Gibbs (1986) compared the prevalence of anxiety disorders in a group of 48 MVP patients referred from primary care, medicine, and cardiology clinics with a group of normal volunteers; in this study, no increased prevalence rate of anxiety disorders was found.

To summarize, the literature relating MVP to panic is confusing and inconsistent. One reason for the inconsistency may be the poor reliability of the diagnosis of MVP (Margraf et al., 1988). The criteria for diagnosing MVP differ depending on the cardiologist interpreting the findings. Gorman, Shear, Devereux, King, and Klein (1986) arranged for 15 panic disorder patients to be diagnosed by two different cardiologists: one diagnosed MVP in 9 of the patients (60%); the other found MVP in none. To resolve the relationship of MVP to panic, future studies should (1) include normal controls as well as psychiatric patients with other mental disorders, with controls matched for age and sex; and (2) use blind methodology in the diagnosis of MVP (Gorman et al., 1988). With the exception of the need for prophylactic antibiotic treatment in some cases, the presence or absence of MVP does not affect treatment choice or prognosis. Therefore, routine testing of panic disorder patients for MVP does not seem indicated.

Cardiac Arrhythmias

The symptoms of palpitations in panic disorder could be related to cardiac arrhythmias of various kinds. Clearly, heart rate can increase markedly during panic attacks (see section on ambulatory heart rate monitoring). Furthermore, during the behavioral avoidance test (during which, as we discuss later, patients are taken into the very situations that they fear), heart rates may exceed 150 beats per minute. Such elevations of heart rate, however, do not constitute true (that is, pathological) cardiac arrhythmias.

The diagnosis of clinically significant cardiac arrhythmias is greatly aided by the use of ambulatory electrocardiographic monitoring. Shear et al. (1987) had 23 patients with panic disorder undergo such monitoring for a 24-hour period. Five of the patients had full-blown panic attacks during the recording day. All five also had increased rates of premature ventricular contractions (PVCs) which tended to occur more frequently during the panic attacks. In addition, periods of nonpanic anxiety occurred in 16 patients; during these periods PVCs as well as atrial premature complexes and slow atrial tachycardia were noted. Overall, except for the occurrence of PVC couplets in two cases, none of the arrhythmias were judged to be clinically important.

Although the Shear et al. study indicated that clinically significant cardiac arrhythmias did not occur in a large proportion of cases, the clinician nevertheless needs to be concerned about the rare cases in which they might occur. For example, panic related to ventricular tachycardia has been reported by Brown and Kemble (1981), and we also know of a patient referred for panic disorder in whom episodes of ventricular tachycardia were documented. Heart rates exceeding 160 to 180 beats per minute while not exercising or exposed to phobic situations, attacks of tachycardia that terminate suddenly rather than gradually, arrhythmias of very brief duration, significant clouding of consciousness or syncope (loss of consciousness), and a history of past or current heart disease are indications for immediate medical attention (Sokolow & Massie, 1988).

Angina Pectoris and Congestive Heart Failure

The symptoms of angina pectoris include attacks of chest pain of short duration. Angina pectoris is most commonly precipitated by exertion such as lifting and walking, after heavy meals, in cold weather, or after emotional stress. The pain is acute and commonly described as a constricting feeling or sensation of pressure. It is commonly located in the center of the chest or slightly to the left, and at times radiates to one or both arms (Levine, 1980). The pain is relieved after 1 to 5 minutes of rest or by nitroglycerin.

In a study on 72 cases undergoing coronary angiography, Costa et al. (1985) found that coronary artery disease was positively correlated with age, occupational status, and education. Chest pain while walking was the one symptom that was most consistently related to coronary artery disease, whereas chest pain during sleep, concomitant symptoms of dizziness and sighs, pain radiation to the right lower chest, and lack of relief of pain by rest were negatively correlated with coronary disease.

Congestive heart failure is a condition characterized by the inadequate pumping action of the heart. As a result, fluid accumulation occurs in the peripheral organs, manifesting as edema. If fluid accumulation occurs in the lungs, breathing difficulties can occur that can mimic those of panic attacks. Patients with congestive heart failure often become more symptomatic upon assuming the supine position. For example, they frequently need to use several pillows while sleeping or assume a semireclining position. One symptom of congestive heart failure is paroxysmal nocturnal dyspnea: the patient wakes up suddenly in the middle of the night with extreme air hunger. Such symptoms may unwittingly be labeled panic attacks, especially in patients with a prior history of anxiety or affective disorders.

Angina pectoris and congestive heart failure occur in older patients and so are rare in patients at ages typical for the onset of panic disorder. Furthermore, the characteristics of the symptoms should be sufficient to direct attention to the possibility of heart disease in the affected patients. However, in older patients, it may be difficult to make the differentiation unless further medical evaluations are made. For example, a patient was recently referred to us from a medical inpatient unit with a referral diagnosis of panic disorder with nocturnal panic attacks. Chest x-rays showed this patient to have pulmonary congestion caused by heart failure. Treatment of congestive heart failure resulted in remission of the nocturnal "panic." The patient had had one past episode of panic attacks and also had a "difficult" temperament characterized by frequent confrontations with the medical staff. It is possible that the cardiac origin of her "panic" attacks had been missed because of these associated psychiatric features.

Panic Disorder in Cardiology Clinics

The advent of coronary angiography has led clinicians to recognize that a great number of the patients presenting for cardiological examination because of chest pain do not have impaired coronary arteries. Psychiatric studies of patients with chest pain and normal coronary arteries often reveal a high prevalence of psychiatric morbidity. In a study of 99 patients evaluated by coronary arteriography, 31 were found to have no coronary artery disease, 15 had slight coronary artery disease with less than 50% obstruction, whereas the remaining had significant obstructive disease (Bass & Wade, 1984). The patients without coronary artery disease had significantly higher psychiatric morbidity than those with abnormal coronary arteries and tended to be younger (with an average age of 44 years compared with 51 years) and more often female (54% versus 23%). Anxiety neurosis was a particularly common diagnosis in this group, occurring in nine cases (30%). The symptoms of breathlessness at rest, faintness, palpitations, paresthesias, sweating, and suffocation occurred more commonly in the group with normal coronary arteries than in the other groups.

Beitman and his co-workers (Beitman et al., 1987a, 1987b; Beitman et al., in press) examined 104 of 195 patients with nonanginal chest pain with the Structured Clinical Interview for the DSM-III-R (SCID). Of these patients, 30 had a history of coronary artery disease, and of them, 59% fit criteria for panic disorder. The remaining 74 patients were judged to have no history of coronary artery disease; of them, 51% fit diagnostic criteria for current panic disorder and another 11% had had panic disorder in the past. Only a small proportion of patients with panic disorder had phobic avoidance, and of those that did, many reported discomfort rather than fear, a finding considered to be evidence for the existence of "nonfearful panic disorder." The treatment effect of alprazolam was tested in a group of ten patients with "nonfearful" panic disorder; seven experienced a reduction in panic frequency, but two dropped out because of an increase in symptoms (Beitman et al., 1988).

Thus, patients with panic disorder may have cardiac problems. However, in cardiology clinics, many patients with cardiologic complaints may actually have panic disorder. The latter patients constitute a new area for potential psychological or psychiatric intervention.

Summary of Medical Differential Diagnosis

Psychiatric patients in general have a greater prevalence of physical symptoms than do normal controls (Koryani, 1980), and panic disorder is probably no exception. Therefore, all panic patients should receive a thorough medical history, review of systems, physical examination, and screening laboratory tests. The screening laboratory examination includes a complete blood count, serum electrolytes, calcium, phosphate, thyroid function tests, liver function tests, electrocardiogram, urine analysis, and possibly a urine drug screen (Raj & Sheehan, 1987; Stein, 1986). The liver function tests are included as a marker for advanced alcoholism in addition to screening for symptomatically unrelated medical conditions. Further tests can be ordered as suggested by the history and physical findings.

If the patient has a personal physician, most of the necessary data to rule out significant medical disorders should already be on file. If these data can be obtained, it should not be necessary to duplicate the personal physician's evaluation.

A question being actively investigated is whether certain medical disorders are related to panic disorder, either by triggering panic attacks or by mimicking the symptoms of panic. To test for such specificity, one would need to examine the prevalence of medical disorders in panic patients compared with nonpanic psychiatric controls, such as patients with depression. Few such studies have been done.

In the preceding sections we described some medical conditions that could mimic the symptoms of panic disorder; Table 2.4 provides further examples of such disorders. In order of frequency, mitral valve prolapse and vestibular dysfunction may be the most commonly found conditions in panic patients. These conditions are usually benign. Informing patients with vestibular dysfunction about their condition may reduce their fear.

More serious medical conditions mimicking panic are probably rare, especially in young patients between the ages of 20 and 30. Many of these conditions, however, are more likely to be found in patients who are more than 35 or 40 years old at the onset of panic disorder. Because many of these conditions are treatable, one should energetically pursue clues leading to their discovery. These conditions include cardiac disorders such as cardiac arrhythmias, angina pectoris, and congestive heart failure; neurological disorders such as seizure disorders; and endocrine or metabolic disorders including thyroid disorders, parathyroid disorders, hypoglycemia, and pheochromocytoma.

Most of the medical disorders mimicking panic provide symptomatic clues that should increase the degree of suspicion for the disorder. For example, the following symptoms, if present during panic, should prompt further investigation. Loss of consciousness, hallucinations, falling, and "cosmic" feelings suggest seizure disorders. Imbalance, ear pressure, and intolerance of certain movements of the head or the visual surround suggest vestibular dysfunction. Panic associated with hunger suggests hypoglycemia, and panic associated with severe headaches and elevations of blood pressure suggests pheochromocytoma. Panic attacks that are very brief or that have a sudden offset suggest seizure disorders or a cardiac arrythmia such as paroxysmal atrial tachycardia.

Furthermore, organic disorders are of greater concern if the patient displays impulsive, aggressive, and interictal behavior (seizure disorder); if the patient shows persistent tachycardia, warm, sweaty hands, and intolerance of warm environments (hyperthyroidism); if the patient has crushing chest pain (angina, myocardial infarction); or if there is a relative absence of avoidance behavior or anticipatory anxiety.

The Secondary Evaluation

The secondary evaluation is conducted to add further detail to the report of the initial one. It is usually conducted by the therapist, clinic, or program actually responsible for treating the patients. The approaches chosen depend on the purpose of the program. Generally, secondary assessment has two broad aims: (1) confirming the diagnosis and (2) quantifying the extent or severity of the disorder. The distinction between these two aims is similar to that between the "molar" and "molecular" assessments discussed by Hersen (1988). The molar approach focuses on commonalities among patients with different psychiatric disorders for the purpose of classification. The molecular approach follows the molar approach and involves a more refined assessment focusing on differences among patients belonging to the same diagnostic class.

Confirming the diagnosis may require a structured interview that considers psychiatric symptoms relevant to a large number of psychiatric disorders. Quantifying the severity of panic disorder is a more refined assessment to derive quantitative estimates of the main aspects of the problem. This is done to examine differences between patients of the same diagnostic class (Wolpe, 1986, cited by Hersen, 1988). This information is used to further plan the treatment intervention or to assess treatment outcome.

Anxiety or panic, like any emotion, can be conceptualized as composed of responses in three response systems: verbal report, overt acts, and expressive physiology (Lang, 1968; Lang, 1984). Unfortunately, these systems are only loosely interconnected; hence, for a complete picture, assessments of all three are necessary. Therefore, assessment instruments include measures based on self-report, behavioral tests such as the behavioral avoidance test, and physiological assessments. Of these, the latter are technically the most difficult and of least relevance for clinical practice.

In the next sections, we will first consider instruments suitable for making psychiatric diagnoses, including assessment instruments of personality disorders. We also include a section on the assessment of marital adjustment. We will then consider instruments suitable for the quantification of panic disorder. These instruments tap into the three main channels of emotional expression: verbal behavior, overt behavior, and physiological expression. When choosing an instrument for inclusion in the secondary assessment battery, an important consideration is the reliability and validity of the instrument. Therefore, we will discuss concepts of reliability and validity in the next section and keep them in mind when describing the actual instruments in the sections that follow.

Reliability and Validity

Reliability

The reliability of an assessment instrument refers to its consistency or stability—that is, its ability to yield similar scores across a series of measurements. In classical test theory, reliability refers to the degree to which a test's variance is "true" variance (Anastasi, 1982). In other words, the variability of scores on a highly reliable test reflects primarily genuine differences rather than errors of measurement. Three major types of reliability are relevant for our purposes: (1) test-retest reliability, (2) internal reliability, and (3) interrater reliability. Unfortunately, these three types of reliability overlap considerably less, conceptually, than is commonly supposed (Loevinger, 1957).

Test-retest reliability refers to the extent to which a measure provides similar scores on different occasions. It must be noted, however, that a low test-retest reliability coefficient may reflect genuine instability in the phenomenon being measured and thus may not indicate low reliability in the sense of classical test theory. For example, an index of the frequency of panic attacks among patients with panic disorder may exhibit low test-retest reliability; nevertheless, this may reflect the test's sensitivity to genuine variability in the frequency of panic attacks among individuals, rather than measurement error. Test-retest reliability is an inadequate measure of reliability in this case.

Internal reliability refers to the homogeneity of a test's items; a test with high internal reliability possesses items that appear to be tapping the same trait. Internal reliability is typically given by Cronbach's alpha (Cronbach, 1960), which is mathematically equivalent to the mean of a test's total possible split-half reliability coefficients (a split-half reliability coefficient is simply the correlation between any two halves of a test, such as all odd and all even items).

Finally, interrater reliability refers to the extent to which different observers agree on the trait being measured.

Validity

Validity is generally defined as the extent to which a test or instrument measures what it is purported to measure. It is well known that the reliability of an instrument constrains its validity; that is, a test cannot be valid unless it is reliable. What is less well known, however, is that the validity of an instrument is limited not by its reliability per se but by its square root (Cronbach, 1960). This is because the proportion of true variance in test scores is the *index of reliability*, which is equivalent to the square root of the reliability coefficient (Anastasi, 1982). Thus, a test's validity may theoretically exceed its reliability, although this rarely occurs (Meehl, 1986). Of course, an instrument may possess extremely high reliability but negligible or zero validity; an index of height employed as a measure of intelligence is but one frequently cited, albeit fanciful, example. Nevertheless, reliability and validity are best viewed not as conceptually distinct psychometric properties, but rather as lying along a continuum. Thus, reliability may be thought of as the correspondence between two attempts to measure a trait via maximally similar methods, whereas validity may be thought of as the correspondence between two attempts to measure a trait via maximally dissimilar methods (Campbell & Fiske, 1959). We can distinguish among four major types of validity: (1) predictive validity, (2) concurrent validity, (3) content validity, and (4) construct validity.

Predictive validity refers to an instrument's ability to predict a criterion that is measured well after the individual takes the test. An example of predictive validity would be the relationship of a trait anxiety measure to future psychological adjustment.

Concurrent validity, sometimes referred to as convergent validity, differs from predictive validity only in that the criterion is measured at essentially the same time as the instrument being validated. Content validity refers to the extent to which an instrument's items represent an adequate sample of the domain to be measured. For instance, a test of state anxiety containing many depression items would be said to possess low content validity.

Finally, construct validity refers to the extent to which a test can be said to measure a hypothetical entity—that is, one that is not operationally defined (Cronbach & Meehl, 1955). As construct validity is considerably more complex than the other forms of validity and subsumes them in many cases, it warrants a fuller discussion.

In their seminal article, Cronbach and Meehl (1955) argue that the validity of a test purporting to measure a hypothetical entity, or construct, may be established through several indirect means. These include demonstrating a test's (1) concurrent and predictive validity with other psychometric measures of the same construct, (2) sensitivity to the effects of treatment (or, in some cases, insensitivity to the effects of treatment, depending on the investigator's conceptualization of the construct), (3) ability to distinguish among criterion groups, and (4) factorial validity, —that is, the extent to which a test's factor structure conforms with that predicted on the basis of the investigator's understanding of the construct. Also relevant to construct validity is what Campbell and Fiske (1959) called discriminant validity: an instrument's ability to correlate negligibly with variables that are theoretically unrelated to the construct purportedly measured by the instrument. Ideally, the investigator begins the process of construct validation by formulating a "nomological network" of predictions flowing from his or her hypotheses regarding the construct. As these predictions are progressively confirmed, the evidence for the instrument's construct validity accumulates. Because many of the self-report inventories discussed in the following sections were designed to assess hypothetical, internal states or traits (for example, cognitions of impending danger, fears of specific stimuli, or anxiety proneness), we shall have occasion to return to these considerations of construct validity throughout our review of these instruments.

Diagnosis with Structured Clinical Interviews

Several structured clinical interviews are currently available to increase the reliability of diagnosis. These include the Anxiety Disorders Interview Schedule, the Structured Interview for the DSM-III, and the NIMH Diagnostic Interview Schedule.

The Anxiety Disorders Interview Schedule (ADIS)

The ADIS is a structured interview that includes the Hamilton Anxiety and Depression scales, as well as specific questions concerning the presence or absence of DSM-III criteria for each of the anxiety disorders and affective disorders (DiNardo, O'Brien, Barlow, Waddell, & Blanchard, 1983). The reliability for discriminating between anxiety disorders and other disorders was kappa = .70. For specific anxiety disorders, kappa was .65 for panic disorder, .85 for agoraphobia with panic, and .57 for generalized anxiety disorder (Barlow, 1985). A revised version has been developed for DSM-III-R criteria (DiNardo & Barlow, 1988); in this version, the reliability for generalized anxiety disorder is improved (D. H. Barlow, personal communication, September, 1986).

The Structured Clinical Interview for the DSM-III (SCID)

The SCID (Spitzer, Williams, & Gibbon, 1988) constitutes a systematic evaluation of DSM-III-R criteria for all psychiatric disorders. It exists in a patient and nonpatient version; there is also a version specifically for the personality disorders (see "Diagnosis of Personality Disorders"). The SCID has the potential of becoming the "gold standard" of psychiatric diagnosis; however, data on the reliability of the SCID are only now forthcoming. Riskind, Beck, Berchick, Brown, and Steer (1987) evaluated the interrater reliability of the differential diagnosis of depression versus generalized anxiety disorder versus other disorders, using the SCID supplemented by a manual describing diagnostic difficulties arising in the differential diagnosis of depression and generalized anxiety disorder. The reliability raters observed the SCID interview on videotape. The reliability, as measured by Cohen's kappa, was .74 for overall diagnosis, .72 for depression versus other disorders, and .79 for generalized anxiety disorder versus other diagnoses.

The NIMH Diagnostic Interview Schedule (DIS)

The DIS is a structured diagnostic interview designed to be administered by lay interviewers (Robins, Helzer, Croughan, & Ratcliff, 1987). The instrument has been employed to assess the prevalence of various psychiatric conditions in the NIMH Epidemiologic Catchment Area Program (Regier et al., 1984). German and Spanish versions of the DIS are available (Canino et al., 1987; Wittchen, Semler, & von Zerssen, 1985).

Given the importance of the data that have been accumulated with the DIS, it is important to determine the reliability and validity of the DIS with respect to anxiety disorders. Helzer et al. (1985) determined the reliability and validity of DIS diagnosis by having the DIS readministered by a physician, who also departed from the DIS and asked further questions to follow up on clinical hunches. During the DIS interview, the physicians also completed a checklist of DSM-III criteria. Reliability and validity of the DIS were determined in several ways. First, reliability was determined by comparing the results of the DIS administered by the layperson and the DIS administered by the physician. The test-retest kappas were .34 for panic disorder, .49 for agoraphobia, .38 for social phobia, .34 for simple phobia, and .24 for obsessive-compulsive disorder. Second, concurrent validity was assessed as the agreement between the physician DIS and the physician DSM-III checklist. The kappas for this comparison were uniformly high: .86 for panic disorder, .97 for agoraphobia with panic, .91 for social phobia, .91 for simple phobia, and .63 for obsessive-compulsive disorder. These high correlations no doubt reflect the fact that the same person did both assessments. The second validity assessment was a comparison between lay DIS and physician DSM-III checklists. This time, the agreement was fairly low: .42 for panic disorder, .46 for agoraphobia, .40 for social phobia, .31 for simple phobia, and .12 for obsessive-compulsive disorder.

Boyd (1986) reviewed seven studies (including the one by Helzer reviewed above) that assessed the validity of the DIS for panic disorder. For four studies involving community samples, sensitivity was 0%, 33%, 50%, and 80% and specificity 100%, 100%, 92%, and 92%. Kappas ranged between −.02 and .89. For three studies involving patients, sensitivities were 25%, 27%, and 44%, and specificities 88%, 93%, and 93%. The kappa reliabilities ranged between .14 and .40.

Recently, Erdman et al. (1987) examined 220 patients of a Veterans Administration Hospital, most of whom were inpatients, with the DIS administered by lay interviewers, and compared the results of the DIS with clinical diagnosis based on information in the patient's chart. The kappas of current DIS diagnosis compared with clinical diagnosis was .00 for panic disorder, .10 for simple phobia, −.03 for social phobia, and .22 for agoraphobia. The DIS tended to overdiagnose phobias by a large amount: 14 versus 1 for social phobia and 18 versus 1 for simple phobia.

Thus, the validity of the DIS has varied across different studies. Its lack of consistent validity in the clinical setting may be related to differences in implicit hierarchical rules for making a diagnosis. Another shortcoming in the DIS is that "panic attacks" are covered by only one screening question concerning sudden anxiety and one follow-up question concerning somatic symptoms of panic (contingent on answering "yes" to the previous question). Adding four additional somatically oriented questions increased the prevalence of diagnosed panic disorders in a primary care setting by 19% (Katon, Vitaliano, Russo, Jones, & Anderson, 1987).

The DIS was designed to be implemented on a large scale in the community setting and to diagnose a broad spectrum of mental disorders. Because of the lack of extensive coverage of the panic/phobia spectrum and its low validity in the clinical setting, however, we consider the DIS to be an unsuitable instrument for clinical use.

Diagnosis of Personality Disorders

Assessment instruments for personality disorders include both self-report instruments and structured interviews. The psychometric properties of these instruments have been thoroughly discussed by Widiger and Frances (1987).

Among the semistructured and structured interview schedules available for the assessment of personality disorders are the personality disorders version of the Structured Clinical Interview for the DSM-III (SCID-II), (Spitzer et al., 1988); the Structured Interview for the DSM-III Personality Disorders (SIDP) (Pfohl, Stangl, & Zimmerman, 1983); the Diagnostic Interview for Personality Disorders (DIPD) (Zanarini, Frankenburg, Chauncey, & Gunderson, 1987); and the Personality Disorder Examination (PDE) (Loranger, Sussman, Oldham, & Russakoff, 1985).

To our knowledge, no reliability data have appeared as yet on the SCID-II. The SIDP, on the other hand, appears to have adequate interrater reliability for most diagnoses, although, as Widiger and Frances (1987) observe, these reliabilities were generally not calculated on the basis of independent interviews. The interrater reliabilities of the PDE appear to be highly promising (Widiger & Frances, 1987), although again these values are based on joint interviews. The PDE is being revised to allow for greater interviewer probing of specific behavioral examples (A. Loranger, personal communication, 1987). Finally, for the DIPD, interrater reliability (based on the same interview being observed by several raters) ranged from kappa = .52 (narcissistic personality disorder) to 1.00 (avoidant personality disorder, antisocial personality disorder). Test-retest reliability (based on a group of patients who were interviewed twice) ranged from kappa = .46 (passive-aggressive personality disorder) to .85 (borderline personality disorder).

Several omnibus self-report questionnaires exist for the diagnosis of personality disorders. Unfortunately, none of them has received sufficient empirical support to warrant its routine use in clinical practice. The Millon Clinical Multiaxial Inventory (MCMI) (Millon, 1983) is a 175-item, true/false inventory that yields scores on 11 personality disorders, each given their corresponding DSM-III names. Millon's conceptualization of several of these disorders (such as antisocial, passive-aggressive), however, differs considerably from that of the DSM-III, meaning that the clinician and researcher should exercise caution in extrapolating from the MCMI to DSM-III. The MCMI has been harshly criticized for extensive item overlap in its personality disorder scales, which may create artifactual covariation among several personality disorders (Widiger & Frances, 1987). This item overlap is also probably responsible at least in part for the relatively poor discriminant validity of the MCMI personality disorder scales (Widiger & Sanderson, 1987). The evidence for the convergent validity of several of the MCMI scales appears promising but is relatively preliminary (Widiger & Frances, 1987).

The Personality Diagnostic Questionnaire (PDQ) (Hyler, Rieder, Spitzer, & Williams, 1982) adheres more strictly to the DSM-III conceptualization of

Axis II disorders. Unfortunately, the PDQ possesses low test-retest reliabilities for many of its scales and appears to be contaminated by social desirability response biases (Widiger & Frances, 1987). Little evidence regarding the construct validity of the PDQ scales is available.

The Assessment of Marital Adjustment

The preceding sections all pertained to the assessments of the patient with panic disorder. However, patients do not live in a vacuum; their lives are significantly influenced by factors in their social environments. One such factor is the stress from significant life events (see "The Initial Interview"). Another factor, the focus of this section, is the marital relationship of the patient. Two recent studies have indicated that the marriages of agoraphobics are not particularly distressed (Arrindell & Emmelkamp, 1986; Fisher & Wilson, 1985), although marital factors have long been implicated in the etiology of agoraphobia by some writers (Fry, 1962; Vandereycken, 1983). The marital relationship may be important to consider when planning and implementing treatment, but again, little actual data is available. Thus, the predictive validity of marital dysfunction for agoraphobic treatment outcome is a significant area for further study. At this point, because of numerous ambiguities in the research literature, we recommend that the clinician assessing marital functioning among panic disorder patients interpret the results with caution, since they have no clear treatment implications.

The practitioner or researcher has a wide variety of instruments to choose from in measuring marital adjustment. Unfortunately, this wide variety has led in part to considerable inconsistency in the procedures employed by different researchers, making comparisons across studies difficult or impossible (Vandereycken, 1983). The three most useful self-report measures of marital adjustment are the Locke-Wallace Marital Adjustment Scale (Locke & Wallace, 1959), the Dyadic Adjustment Scale (Spanier, 1979), and the Marital Satisfaction Inventory (Snyder, Wills, & Keiser, 1981).

The Locke-Wallace Marital Adjustment Scale was the most frequently used measure of marital satisfaction for many years following its publication (Sharpley & Cross, 1982), and it is still commonly used today. It is a 15-item, rationally derived test with good internal reliability (split-half reliability = .90). It possesses concurrent validity with other marital satisfaction measures and distinguishes between well-adjusted and poorly adjusted marital criterion groups (Locke & Wallace, 1959).

The Dyadic Adjustment Scale (DAS) is a 32-item measure that shares a number of items with the Locke-Wallace Marital Adjustment Scale. It was developed using a combination of empirical (ability to distinguish between married and divorced samples) and factor-analytic approaches. The DAS has also been adapted as an interview schedule. The internal reliability of the DAS is excellent (Cronbach's alpha = .96; Spanier & Thompson, 1982). Spanier

(1979) reports that the DAS comprises four major factors: consensus, satisfaction, cohesion, and affectional expression subscales. This factor structure was replicated using maximum-likelihood confirmatory factor analysis by Spanier and Thompson (1982). Unfortunately, a study with a smaller, perhaps inadequate, sample (Sharpley & Cross, 1982) did not replicate this factor structure. Construct validity data on the DAS is gradually accumulating (Spanier & Lewis, 1980).

The Marital Satisfaction Inventory (MSI) is a 280-item instrument constructed by combining rational and item-analytic procedures. Its scales have adequate internal (mean alpha = .88) and test-retest reliability (mean = .89). The MSI consists of one validity scale, one global affective scale, and nine clinical scales, including affective communication, sexual dissatisfaction, quality and quantity of leisure time spent together, problem-solving communication, and dissatisfaction with children. Scores on these eleven scales can be converted into T-scores to yield an MMPI-like profile. The MSI distinguishes between couples with marital distress and couples with sexual dysfunction, and its scales appear to exhibit convergent and discriminant validity with a number of clinical correlates, including spousal interaction, psychiatric and physical distress, and interaction regarding children (Snyder, Wills, & Keiser, 1981).

Finally, the interested reader may wish to examine the Positive Feelings Questionnaire (O'Leary, Fincham, & Turkewitz, 1983), which measures positive affect toward a marital partner, and the Areas of Change Questionnaire (AC) (Margolin, Talovic, & Weinstein, 1983), which assesses partners' primary presenting complaints. The AC yields data on three major domains: (1) each partner's areas of desired change, (2) perceived change—that is, each partner's perception of the areas of change desired by the other—and (3) perceptual accuracy, that is, the degree to which each partner is aware of the areas of change desired by the other.

Although self-report indices are useful for assessing marital dysfunction, their validity is constrained by the inability or unwillingness of some partners to report truthfully on significant aspects of marital conflict and dissatisfaction. An alternative to self-report instruments that circumvents these limitations is the use of observational methods (Cromwell, Olson, & Fournier, 1976). Observers may watch the marital interaction via cameras or one-way mirrors or may become part of the interaction itself. A number of coding systems have been developed to quantify important aspects of the marital interaction (Weiss & Margolin, 1986). For the clinician, however, the assessment of marital function through structured observations may not be feasible or may not have high priority until more scientific information has accumulated about the role of the marital relationship in panic disorder. Informal observations, however, can be made if the spouses are interviewed in a joint session. Furthermore, one of the shorter inventories described previously might be used in routine clinical practice.

The Quantification of Panic Disorder

The quantification of panic disorder follows the traditional "triple-response measurement" of anxiety. As mentioned earlier, the three response channels measured include verbal behavior, overt behavior, and physiological expression of anxiety or panic. Of these three measures, those based on self-report have by far the greatest use in clinical practice. Therefore, we will begin this section by reviewing the most common self-report instruments and then proceed to behavioral assessment and finally, to psychophysiological assessment. There are gray areas: for example, self-monitoring of avoidance or of exposure to feared situations involves patients monitoring their own behavior, but self-report rather than direct observation of behavior is used.

Self-Report Instruments

The self-report instruments that are used in the assessment of panic disorder fall into two basic categories: (1) those measuring various aspects of panic disorder phenomenology and (2) those measuring the intensity of more general anxiety. The former are used specifically with patients with panic disorder or perhaps other phobias, whereas the latter have a more general use, including assessing anxiety levels in normal subjects. As noted earlier, these measures primarily provide quantitative estimates of the severity of aspects of panic disorder. As a result, they tend to be more sensitive to treatment effects than are instruments designed to establish the presence or absence of a diagnosis (for example, structured clinical interviews). Indeed, Agras and Jacob (1981) found self-report inventories to be among the most sensitive measures of improvement over the course of treatment.

A number of self-report inventories have been developed to aid in the assessment of various features of panic disorder. These instruments may be divided into those measuring (1) elicitors of panic and anxiety, including the situations producing agoraphobic avoidance, (2) the phenomenology of panic and anxiety, (3) cognitive aspects of panic, and finally (4) state anxiety.

Measures of Elicitors of Panic or Anxiety

FEAR SURVEY SCHEDULE

Several questionnaires have been designed to assess stimuli that trigger panic or anxiety in patients with panic disorder. The Fear Survey Schedule (FSS) (Wolpe & Lang, 1964) is a general index of fearfulness that can be employed both as a quantitative measure and as a device to ascertain a client's pattern of fears. It consists of 72 items in 6 different categories of fear: animal, social/interpersonal, tissue damage/illness and death, noises, classical phobias (such as fears of high places, deep water, darkness, or lightning), and miscellaneous (such as falling, making mistakes, failure, or strange places). The respondent rates each item on a 5-point Likert-type scale, thus providing the clinician with a measure of the severity of each fear. The authors report no factor or cluster analysis, however, to justify their subdivision of these items into six subgroups. Factor analyses by other investigators have not consistently confirmed the six-factor structure posited by Wolpe and Lang (Hersen, 1973). Although several of the fears assessed by the FSS are among those typically found among panic disorder patients (for instance, being in an elevator, being alone, or being in large open spaces), agoraphobic fears appear to be underrepresented. Thus, the FSS is not an ideal instrument for assessing agoraphobic avoidance. Factor-analytic studies have found a replicable but small agoraphobia factor in the FSS (Arrindell & Emmelkamp, 1986; Hafner & Ross, 1984; Oei, Cavallo, & Evans, 1987). The test-retest reliability of the FSS is excellent; Michelson and Mavissakalian (1983) reported a coefficient of .90 over a 3- to 16-week interval.

The FSS exhibits adequate convergent validity with other measures of anxiety. Hersen (1973) reports moderate to high correlations (range .27 to .60) between the FSS and other anxiety indices, including the Taylor Manifest Anxiety Scale, across 15 studies. The FSS has been reported to be sensitive to the effects of treatment for agoraphobia and to distinguish between consonantly and nonconsonantly treated subjects (Michelson, 1986). Moreover, the social/interpersonal and tissue damage/illness and death subscales significantly differentiate agoraphobics from both nonphobic psychiatric patients and normal subjects (Arrindell & Emmelkamp, 1986), and discriminant functions derived from factor scores discriminate between agoraphobic patients and patients with other anxiety disorders (Oei et al., 1987). Thus, there is suggestive evidence for the construct validity of the FSS. The reader should consult Hersen (1973) for a more comprehensive review of the reliability and validity of the FSS and similar inventories, including Geer's (1965) empirically derived Fear Survey Schedule II.

FEAR QUESTIONNAIRE

The briefer Fear Questionnaire (FQ) (Marks & Mathews, 1979) consists of 23 items to be rated by the respondent on an 8-point Likert-type scale with respect to avoidance. The FQ yields scores on three factor-analytically derived subscales—agoraphobia, blood-injury, and social phobia—as well as a total phobia score. In spite of their brevity, the agoraphobia subscale and total score have both been reported to have test-retest reliabilities of between .80 and .90, which are clearly adequate for clinical purposes. The correlations between the FQ agoraphobia subscale and the other two subscales are positive but relatively low (Mavissakalian, 1986), suggesting good discriminant validity for the former subscale. The agoraphobia subscale exhibits good convergent validity with behavioral avoidance tests (BATs), described later, and self-rated subjective anxiety during BATs, particularly at posttreatment (Mavissakalian & Hamann, 1986). Like the FSS, the FQ has been demonstrated to be sensitive to treatment effects (Marks & Mathews, 1979; Mavissakalian, 1986). Moreover, its responsiveness to the effects of treatment for agoraphobia is relatively specific to the agoraphobia subscale (Mavissakalian, 1986). Patients with agoraphobia have been reported to score higher and improve more on the FQ than patients with social or other phobias (Marks & Mathews, 1979), although the latter finding may represent a regression to the mean artifact (in other words, the tendency of extreme scores on an imperfectly reliable test to approach the mean upon retest). Finally, scores on the FQ agoraphobia subscale are consistently higher among women than men (Mizes & Crawford, 1986), which corresponds to known sex differences in the prevalence of the disorder. In sum, these findings provide preliminary, although promising, support for the construct validity of the FQ and suggest that its agoraphobia subscale may prove useful as a dependent measure of treatment outcome in agoraphobia. A sample of the Fear Questionnaire is provided in this book's appendix.

MOBILITY INVENTORY

An instrument that more specifically assesses agoraphobic avoidance is the Mobility Inventory (MI) (Chambless, Caputo, Jasin, Gracely, & Williams, 1985), a recent instrument that is rapidly coming into widespread use. Unlike the FSS and the FQ, the MI generates independent measures of *avoidance alone* (AAL) and *avoidance accompanied* (AAC). This feature is likely to make the MI more sensitive to agoraphobic avoidance than the FSS or FQ, because many agoraphobic patients avoid situations when alone that they readily confront in the presence of a trusted companion. An additional advantage of the MI is its more comprehensive coverage of agoraphobic situations, making it more useful both for the assessment of the severity of agoraphobic avoidance and for the planning of interventions (such as designing hierarchies for in vivo exposure). The MI also contains a single item asking respondents to estimate the number of panic attacks experienced during the previous week.

The test-retest reliabilities of the AAL and AAC scales were reasonably good over a 31-day interval (with a range of .75 to .90). Internal consistencies, as assessed by Cronbach's alpha, were excellent for both scales (with a range of .91 to .97). The test-retest reliability of the index of panic frequency, however, was lower and more inconsistent (with a range of .56 to .62), probably because of variability in the frequency of patients' panic attacks. As noted earlier, low test-retest reliability may reflect a test's sensitivity to changes in psychological phenomena over time. This suggests that future measures of panic frequency should be based on ratings over a longer period of time to minimize daily fluctuations in the occurrence of attacks. Self-monitoring of attacks (see "Self-monitoring Techniques") may be one method of accomplishing this reliably.

There is also solid evidence for the convergent and discriminant validity of the MI avoidance subscales. For example, the AAL and AAC scales correlate highly with the FQ agoraphobia subscale, providing evidence for the convergent validity of both instruments. The AAL and AAC scales also correlate with measures of trait anxiety (the Spielberger trait anxiety scale) as predicted by the hypothesized association of agoraphobia with anticipatory anxiety. It also correlates with the Beck Depression Inventory, which may be related to the fact that depression often develops secondary to the constriction of activities in agoraphobia. The discriminant validity of the two avoidance scales is demonstrated by their negligible correlations with the Psychoticism scale of the Eysenck Personality Questionnaire, indicating that their high correlations with the other scales discussed above is not caused solely by method covariance, a correlation between two tests produced by their shared method of assessment (Campbell & Fiske, 1959).

Moreover, agoraphobic patients typically score much higher on the AAL scale than on the AAC scale, which is consistent with the modal pattern of agoraphobic avoidance. In addition, both the avoidance scales and the index of panic frequency are sensitive to agoraphobia treatment by in vivo exposure over a 6-month period (Chambless et al., 1985).

The MI has also had success distinguishing between diagnostically defined criterion groups. Patients with agoraphobia have been found to have higher scores than both normal control subjects and patients with social phobia (Chambless et al., 1985). Craske, Rachman, and Tallman (1986) compared MI scores across five comparison groups: agoraphobia patients, social phobia patients, senior citizens, students, and students' relatives. They found a general pattern of decreasing agoraphobic avoidance across the five groups in the order listed, confirming the relative specificity of the MI avoidance scales to agoraphobia. Agoraphobic patients also scored significantly higher on the panic frequency measure compared with the other four comparison groups. Finally, panic frequency was weakly, but significantly, correlated with both the AAL and AAC scales, as expected. The low magnitude of these correlations may be explained by the low reliability of the panic frequency measure, as discussed previously. A sample copy of the MI is provided in this book's appendix.

RATINGS OF AVOIDANCE OF SPECIFIC SITUATIONS

Researchers have had agoraphobic patients rate their avoidance of a specific situation by means of single items. Williams and Rappoport (1983), for example, correlated self-ratings of avoidance on the item "driving alone" with behavioral tests of driving alone. They reported an average correlation of only −.18. This and similar studies are reviewed by Williams (1984), who notes that investigators have consistently found very weak or zero correlations between self-rated fear or avoidance on individual items and behavioral performance. He points out that such results are caused in part by the global and imprecise nature of these items. For instance, the meaning of "driving alone" may range from driving a car one block on a deserted road to the nearby grocery to driving a car several hundred miles in heavy traffic on a cross-country trip.

An alternative way of making this same point in psychometric terms is that individual items tend to be unreliable since they contain a large component of measurement error. This problem is well known and was probably the principal villain in the controversy regarding the cross-situational consistency of personality (Mischel, 1968). Williams (1984) suggests circumventing this difficulty by replacing global self-ratings with ratings of precise, specific behaviors (for instance, driving a car alone 10 miles on a moderately crowded highway). This does not really solve the problem, however, because such individual items contain a high component of "situational uniqueness" (Epstein, 1979), that severely limits their generalizability and validity (recall that high reliability does not ensure, and in some cases may lower, validity). A more satisfactory solution would be to obtain multiple self-ratings of the kind of precise, specific behaviors that Williams suggests, and then to aggregate those items to obtain a composite measure that possesses both good reliability and good content validity (in other words, sufficiently broad coverage of the phobic domain). To our knowledge, this approach has never been adopted for the assessment of specific fears.

SITUATIONAL CHARACTERISTICS QUESTIONNAIRE

In the course of treating panic disorder patients at our Anxiety Disorders Clinic at Western Psychiatric Institute and Clinic in Pittsburgh, we (Jacob, Lilienfeld, Furman, Durrant, & Turner, 1988) have become intrigued by a rather unique class of phobic elicitors in a subset of these patients—those with vestibular dysfunction. In discussing the common eliciting stimuli of anxiety and panic with these patients, we discovered that their attacks appeared to be preceded by one of three classes of stimuli. One of them consisted of classic agoraphobic stimuli (for example, sitting in the middle of a crowded church or leaving one's home alone). The other two, however, consisted of situations characterized by (1) an absence or paucity of visual support for orientation in space or (2) head movements. The former class of stimuli had already been recognized in the space-phobic neurological patients with agoraphobialike symptoms of Marks and Bebbington (1976). We have elected to coin the term *motion phobia* to describe the anxiety resulting from exposure to the second class of elicitors among panic patients with vestibular disorders.

To systematically assess these latter two classes of atypical elicitors of panic, we have recently developed the Situational Characteristics Questionnaire, a 38-item self-report measure. The items were culled from three sources: (1) stimuli described by Marks (1981) and by Marks and Bebbington (1976) in their description of space phobia, (2) conversations with our panic patients with vestibular disorders, and (3) our clinical intuitions regarding stimuli likely to produce space or motion phobia or both. The questionnaire is still under development and consists of two parts. Part I inquires which dimensions of a particular phobic situation create the most discomfort: for example, being in a stationary versus a moving elevator, looking at the end of a tunnel versus lights on the side of the tunnel, driving on smooth versus bumpy roads. In each case, the space- or motion-phobic elicitor is paired with a nonspace- and nonmotion-phobic alternative (in the three examples above, the space- or motion-phobic elicitor is listed second). This paired format was utilized to control for the fact that many of the situations (such as being in an elevator) elicit panic attacks or anxiety in many panic patients and thus would not be specific to panic patients with vestibular dysfunction. The order of these two alternatives was counterbalanced across items to minimize response bias. Part II of the questionnaire consists of several situations that have no clear opposite—for example, riding on a roller coaster or aerobic exercise.

Preliminary reliability and construct validity data for the Situational Characteristics Questionnaire are currently being collected, and we intend to revise it by contrasting the responses of panic patients with vestibular dysfunction with those of panic patients without vestibular dysfunction. In addition, we plan to perform a factor analysis on a large sample to provide factorial validity (Cronbach & Meehl, 1955) for our theoretically based distinction between space and motion phobia. The current version of the questionnaire is included in this book's appendix.

Assessment of Panic Symptoms

ACUTE PANIC INVENTORY

Several self-report inventories are available to the clinician and researcher for assessing the symptoms of panic attacks. The Acute Panic Inventory (API) consists of 17 items measuring panic symptoms (feeling faint, fear of dying, being generally fearful, heart palpitations, difficulty breathing, and so on), which are rated on a 4-point scale. Dillon, Gorman, Liebowitz, Fyer, and Klein (1987) reported on the use of this instrument in 89 patients with panic disorder who underwent lactate infusion. The criterion measure of panic during these infusions was a psychiatrist's rating of panic based on the observation of abrupt escalation of fear and distress accompanied by somatic sensations of panic. The psychiatrist was not blind to whether the lactate or a placebo was infused. The presence of panic during the first 10 minutes of infusion ("early panic") resulted in significant increases in the API index, such that a score of greater than 20 or an increase by more than 13 points completely separated early panickers from those who did not panic. Nevertheless, by these criteria 6 of 30 patients who had not yet panicked but would go on to panic during the second half of the infusion ("late panic") were misclassified as early panic. Furthermore, the API identified only 18 of 30 late panickers by these criteria.

Both the profile of API symptoms and the total API score can also be employed to compare the phenomenology of experimentally induced panic with the patient's "usual" panic attacks. The total score of lactate-induced panic approached that of the patient's usual panic (Liebowitz et al., 1984). Seven of the 17 API symptoms differentiated lactate-induced panic from usual panic (Liebowitz et al., 1984). Usual panic had higher "fear of dying," "confusion," "sense of unreality," "difficulty concentrating," and "sweating" but lower "urgency to urinate" and "twitching." The sensitivity of the API to lactate infusion and its ability to distinguish lactate-induced from usual panic suggests that it is valid for some purposes. Nevertheless, because to our knowledge there is no published reliability data on the API, it should be used with caution (although the presence of positive validity findings implies that a test has at least some reliability).

SYMPTOM QUESTIONNAIRE

A measure of panic phenomenology that we have found useful in assessing panic disorder patients is our Symptom Questionnaire (Jacob & Beidel, 1988). This inventory contains 25 items measuring the frequency of a variety of symptoms of panic disorder, including all the major somatic symptoms in the DSM-III-R, and additionally inquires in particular detail regarding symptoms that are potential correlates of vestibular dysfunction (dizziness, vertigo, spinning sensations in the head, tinnitus, and so on). The frequency of each symptom is rated on a 4-point scale from "never or hardly ever" to "very often or almost constantly," and is elicited for both panic attacks and periods between attacks. A version for normal subjects inquires about the same symptoms without reference to anxiety.

We administered the Symptom Questionnaire to 325 college students, 47 agoraphobic patients, and 10 socially phobic patients. A dizziness subscale was derived a priori consisting of 10 items measuring dizziness and light-headedness. Its test-retest reliability (Spearman-rank correlations were employed as nonparametric measures of bivariate association) was $r = .64$ in college students, .89 in agoraphobic patients between attacks, and .83 in agoraphobic patients during attacks (Jacob & Beidel, 1988). With respect to criterion validity, agoraphobic patients had significantly higher scores on the dizziness scale between attacks than did college students. They also had significantly higher dizziness scores than socially phobic patients, a finding replicating that of Amies et al. (1983). A copy of the Symptom Questionnaire appears in this book's appendix.

Measures of Cognition

A number of authors (see, for instance, Beck & Emery, 1985) have focused on the role of cognitive factors in the etiology of panic disorder and agoraphobia. In particular, it has been proposed (Goldstein & Chambless, 1978) that agoraphobic avoidance results primarily from the fear of having another panic attack, the so-called fear-of-fear cycle. As conceptualized by these writers, this secondary fear derives from irrational cognitions regarding catastrophic consequences that might result from the panic attack and an exaggerated reaction to somatic sensations potentially signaling anxiety (Chambless, Caputo, Bright, & Gallagher, 1984). Beck and Emery (1985), Clark (1986), and others have similarly argued that most if not all panic attacks result from the catastrophic misinterpretation of unexplained interoceptive stimuli. Chambless et al. (1984) have developed two widely used companion questionnaires, the Agoraphobic Cognitions Questionnaire (ACQ) and the Body Sensations Questionnaire (BSQ) to assess these cognitive factors in panic disorder. Reiss, Peterson, Gursky, and McNally (1986) developed a scale designed to measure beliefs of danger associated with bodily symptoms. Other checklists designed to measure specific cognitions include the Automatic Thoughts Questionnaire (Ganellen, Matuzas, Uhlenhuth, Glass, & Easton, 1986) and the recently developed Cognitions Checklist, an instrument suitable for the assessment of "automatic thoughts" differentiating anxiety from depression (Beck et al., 1987).

AGORAPHOBIC COGNITIONS QUESTIONNAIRE

The ACQ is a 14-item questionnaire measuring cognitions regarding catastrophic consequences of experiencing panic. Items were developed from reports of patients and therapists concerning the patient's fear-provoking thoughts during occurrences of intense anxiety. Examples of its items are "I am going to go crazy," "I will have a heart attack," "I will not be able to control myself," "I must have a brain tumor," and "I am going to act foolish." The respondent is required to rate each item on a 5-point Likert-type scale for the frequency with which each thought occurs during periods of anxiety. Based on the overt content of these items, Chambless et al. (1984) hypothesized that the ACQ contained two major factors, one corresponding to fear of disastrous physical consequences and one to fear of disastrous behavioral or social consequences.

Chambless et al. (1984) reported the test-retest reliability of the ACQ to be .86 and an internal consistency of alpha = .80, which are good values, particularly for a brief scale. As predicted, a factor analysis revealed two major factors that accounted for approximately half of the common variance of the items. These factors corresponded well with those described above. The ACQ was found to exhibit good convergent validity with several psychometric measures: the AAL scale and panic frequency scales of the MI (data on the AAC scale were not reported), the Beck Depression Inventory, and the Neuroticism scale of the Eysenck Personality Inventory, which correlates highly with measures of anxiety. A negligible correlation was found between the ACQ and the Eysenck Psychoticism Scale, which provides some evidence for discriminant validity. It was also demonstrated to be sensitive to in vivo exposure treatment and to discriminate between patients with agoraphobia and normal subjects (Chambless et al., 1984). The specificity of the ACQ to agoraphobia, rather than to anxiety disorders in general, however, remains to be determined. Indeed, Craske et al. (1986) found that the ACQ did not distinguish significantly between agoraphobia patients and social phobia patients, although the difference was in the predicted direction. The lack of a significant difference may, however, reflect the association between social fears and extent of agoraphobic avoidance (see Chapter 7).

Rachman, Lopatka, and Levitt (1988) recently administered the ACQ to a sample of panic disorder patients who were asked to complete behavioral tests that would substantially increase the likelihood of their panicking. These tests were selected on the basis of prior knowledge concerning situations that induced panic attacks in each patient (such as entering a supermarket alone). Rachman et al. reported that ACQ scores were much higher on trials during which patients panicked than on trials during which patients did not panic, confirming the predicted relationship between panic attacks and fearful cognitions. The most frequently endorsed cognitions were fears of passing out, acting foolishly, and losing control. Moreover, panic attacks accompanied by the endorsement of ACQ items (in other words, accompanied by fears of disastrous consequences) were associated with more somatic symptoms than were panic attacks unaccompanied by the endorsement of ACQ items. Although the direction of causality is unclear, this indicates that the presence of cognitions of catastrophic harm may be associated with greater severity of panic. A copy of the ACQ is included in this book's appendix.

BODY SENSATIONS QUESTIONNAIRE

The Body Sensations Questionnaire (BSQ) (Chambless et al., 1984) consists of 17 items regarding fear of somatic sensations that typically occur during a panic attack, such as heart palpitations, paresthesias, sweating, and nausea. The primary difference between the BSQ and the API or Symptom Questionnaire discussed earlier is that the BSQ asks subjects to rate their *fear* of these sensations (on a 5-point scale). The test-retest reliability of the BSQ is .67, which is rather low, probably because of the variability in the severity of panic attacks. Internal consistency, however, was excellent (alpha = .87). The BSQ exhibited a similar pattern of convergent validity with measures of psychopathology (see previously), as did the ACQ, although all correlations were lower. Discriminant validity was again found with the Eysenck Psychoticism scale, as was sensitivity to the effects of in vivo exposure and ability to distinguish between agoraphobic and normal subjects. Once again, however, the specificity of these findings to agoraphobia remains unascertained. A sample of the BSQ is included in this book's appendix.

ANXIETY SENSITIVITY INDEX

Reiss et al. (1986) have recently developed the Anxiety Sensitivity Index (ASI) to assess individual differences in "anxiety sensitivity"—that is, expectations regarding the adverse consequences of anxiety. In other words, a person scoring high on the ASI presumably believes that anxiety leads to negative outcomes such as illness, embarrassment, or social anxiety (Reiss et al., 1986). The ASI consists of 16 items rated by the subject on a 5-point scale. Examples of items include "When my stomach is upset, I worry that I might be seriously ill," "When I am nervous, I worry that I might be mentally ill," "It scares me when my heart beats rapidly," and "It scares me when I become short of breath." Inspection of the item content of the ASI suggests that most of the items (including the last two mentioned above) measure fear of anxiety symptoms, rather than beliefs regarding the negative consequences of anxiety, as argued by the authors. This distinction is significant, because Reiss et al. argue that their hypothesis of anxiety sensitivity provides a more complete explanation for the etiology of panic attacks than does that of Chambless and her colleagues who, as discussed earlier, view panic attacks as arising solely from the fear of having further attacks. Although a factor analysis of the ASI reassuringly revealed a single factor with high loadings on 13 out of the 16 items, it is not at all clear that the authors' interpretation of this factor as "anxiety sensitivity," rather than the more parsimonious "fear-of-fear" proposed by Chambless and her colleagues, is appropriate.

Reiss et al. reported the test-retest reliability of the ASI to be .75, which although adequate is far from excellent. Cronbach's alpha, however, was .88 (Peterson & Heilbronner, 1987). Reiss et al. also found that patients with agoraphobia and patients with mixed anxiety disorders scored higher than college students, with agoraphobic patients obtaining the highest scores. In addition, using hierarchical multiple regression, they found that the ASI accounted for variance in Geer's (1965) Fear Survey Schedule over and above the Taylor Manifest Anxiety Scale (1953) and a specially constructed scale measuring the frequency of anxiety symptoms. As they point out, this suggests that the ASI possesses incremental validity relative to measures of trait anxiety.

Several interesting more recent papers provide further evidence for the construct validity of the ASI. The ASI is sensitive to the effects of cognitive-behavioral treatment of agoraphobia. McNally and Lorenz (1987) found the posttreatment ASI scores of agoraphobic patients to be indistinguishable from those of normal subjects. Lyons, Talano, Gitter, Martin, and Singer (cited in Holloway & McNally, 1987) discovered that ASI behaved as a moderator variable (Anastasi, 1982) in the controversial relationship between panic disorder and mitral valve prolapse syndrome; only those mitral valve prolapse patients with high ASI scores developed panic attacks. Finally, Holloway and McNally (1987) reported that patients with high ASI scores experienced more anxiety and hyperventilatory sensations following 5 minutes of hyperventilation than did subjects with low ASI scores. High ASI scorers also tended to report more nonspecific bodily sensations during hyperventilation than low ASI scorers. Although the results of these studies are impressive, it remains to be demonstrated that the ASI measures cognitions regarding adverse consequences of anxiety, rather than simply fear of the somatic and psychic concomitants of anxiety. Moreover, the results of most of the studies on the ASI, including those just cited, appear to be equally consistent with the more parsimonious hypothesis that the ASI simply measures trait anxiety. Unfortunately, few investigations of the construct validity of the ASI have included trait anxiety measures. Further work will be required to clarify the extent to which the ASI assesses a disposition distinct from trait anxiety.

OTHER MEASURES OF COGNITIONS OR AUTOMATIC THOUGHTS

As cognitive theories of anxiety have become more refined, assessment instruments have been developed to measure specific aspects of cognitions. For example, Ganellen et al. (1986) developed a 22-item self-report instrument, the Anxious Thoughts and Tendencies Scale (AT&T), which included the following subscales: catastrophizing, selective abstraction, and intrusive thoughts. The internal consistency of these subscales was high: Cronbach's alpha = .90, .82, and .83, respectively. However, the correlations between the subscales, particularly between catastrophizing and selective abstraction, were also high, indicating that the scales may not measure independent phenomena. Agoraphobic patients scored significantly higher on the sum of the three scales than did patients with panic disorder without agoraphobia. The AT&T scores showed significant correlations with depression and general anxiety but were unrelated to panic frequency.

A checklist developed to differentiate the cognitions seen in anxiety disorders from those of depression is the Cognitions Checklist (CCL) developed by Beck et al. (1987). This 43-item instrument consists of an anxiety and depression subscale. Cronbach's alpha was .90 for anxiety and .92 for depression. Test-retest reliabilities for the two subscales were .79 and .76. The intercorrelation between the two scales was .57, reflecting a high degree of covariation between anxious and depressive cognitions.

In a cross-validation sample, the correlation between the anxiety subscale and the Hamilton Anxiety and Depression scales, respectively, were .54 and .36; for the depression subscale, these correlations were .37 and .62, respectively. Thus, discriminant validity is evident from the larger correlation between the CCL subscale and the same-affect Hamilton scale. A discriminant function correctly classified 79% of anxious patients and 83% of depressed patients.

Measures of State Anxiety

For our purposes, measures of anxiety may be subdivided into two broad categories: state anxiety and trait anxiety measures. The former measures provide an index of momentary anxiety, the latter of anxiety-proneness. Measures of state anxiety are more relevant for the assessment of panic disorder, as they may be useful as therapy outcome measures. Since anticipatory anxiety is a necessary DSM-III-R criterion for the diagnosis of panic disorder, improvement in panic disorder symptoms should be reflected by a decrease in state anxiety. Consequently, we focus our discussion primarily on state anxiety instruments. Although trait anxiety measures may be predictive of treatment response or relapse among panic patients, research will be necessary to confirm those relationships.

A measure of state anxiety that is frequently employed during exposure to a phobic stimulus is Walk's (1956) Fear Thermometer (FT). The FT is simply a 10-point scale on which the subject rates his or her current anxiety level during exposure to the feared situation. Thus, an agoraphobic patient might be asked to make FT ratings of several phobic stimuli, such as crowds, elevators, and malls, during both pre- and posttreatment Behavioral Avoidance Tests (see later section for a description of the Behavioral Avoidance Test). The FT has adequate test-retest reliability and correlates highly with therapist ratings of fear (Bernstein, Borkovec, & Coles, 1986). The FT has also been found to predict behavioral performance ratings and training program completion among parachute jumpers (Walk, 1956).

Most state anxiety measures, however, are designed to assess subjects' current level of anxiety in typical life circumstances, rather than their fear during confrontation with a feared stimulus. A multitude of such measures have been constructed, and our review of them will necessarily be highly selective. The Zung Self-Rating Anxiety Scale (SAS) (Zung, 1971) was developed by selecting consensual diagnostic criteria for anxiety from major sources in the literature. The SAS also comes in a clinician-administered form, the Anxiety Status Inventory (ASI). Closely related to the ASI is the Hamilton Anxiety Scale (HAS), another clinician-administered instrument. These forms are virtually identical in their item content, with the exception that the ASI contains items assessing panic and "mental disintegration," and the HAS contains items assessing phobias, concentration difficulty, depressed mood, and interview behavior. Zung (1979) reports the correlation between the SAS and HAS to be .75. Both Zung's and Hamilton's measures are highly reliable and have been extensively validated (Zung, 1979).

As its name implies, the State-Trait Anxiety Inventory (STAI) (Spielberger, Gorsuch, & Lushene, 1970) assesses both state and trait anxiety. Both the state and trait forms of the STAI have good reliability (Kleinknecht, 1986). Auerbach (1973) found that, as predicted, the trait scale of the STAI remained stable throughout surgery, whereas the state scale scores were highest prior to surgery and progressively dropped following surgery. Moreover, patients with high trait anxiety scores also had higher presurgery state anxiety scores, suggesting that the trait anxiety scale may measure a predisposition to become anxious in the presence of environmental stressors. A child version of the STAI, the STAIC, has also been developed (Spielberger, Edwards, Luchene, Montuori, & Platzek, 1973).

Another measure of anxiety is the Taylor Manifest Anxiety Scale (TMAS) (Taylor, 1953). Derived from the MMPI, this scale was originally conceptualized as a trait anxiety scale to be used for selection of experimental subjects with high or low anxiety. However, the scale has been used in treatment outcome research for agoraphobia and shown to be sensitive to treatment effects (Michelson, 1987). The test-retest reliability after 4 weeks was .88. The scale discriminated well between normal subjects and psychiatric patients.

Another frequently used measure of state anxiety is Zuckerman's (1960) Multiple Affect Adjective Checklist (MAACL). The MAACL consists of 21 adjectives to be checked off by subjects based on how they feel today (the "today" form) and how they generally feel (the "general" form). The former is essentially a measure of state anxiety, the latter of trait anxiety. These 21 adjectives were selected from a large adjective pool based on their ability to empirically differentiate (1) high- and low-anxiety subjects as identified by a psychiatric interview, and (2) subjects in a hypnotically induced anxiety condition from control subjects. The today form of the MAACL has good internal reliability (alpha = .85) but low test-retest reliability over a 1-week interval (.31). The latter is probably a result of the substantial fluctuations in state anxiety over time.

In a study of college students, Zuckerman (1960) found scores on the today form to rise on examination days relative to nonexamination days; moreover, students who received high scores on examinations exhibited a significantly smaller rise in today scores than did students who received low scores. The today form of the MAACL has also been found to be sensitive to several treatment interventions, although little is known regarding its relationship to other state anxiety measures (Bernstein et al., 1986). Unfortunately, adjective checklists such as the MAACL are susceptible to an unwanted response set, namely individual differences in the propensity to make check marks. Thus, it is generally best to use true/false or Likert-type scales, which compel all subjects to mark all items (Tellegen, 1985).

Finally, the Anxiety Differential (AD) (Husek & Alexander, 1963) utilizes Osgood's semantic differential technique to assess various components of state anxiety. The subject is required to rate a series of target words (for example, "me," "fingers," "breathing," and "dreams") on a series of 7-point bipolar adjective scales reflecting different dimensions of anxiety. For example, the subject is asked to rate "hands" on a scale of wet/dry, and is asked to rate "me" on a scale of calm/jittery. The AD has been reported to possess adequate internal and test-retest reliability, and to distinguish anxiety from nonanxiety states, both between and within subjects (Bernstein et al., 1986). Husek and Alexander (1963), for example, found the AD to be sensitive to the effects of examinations among students. They also reported that only a small minority of subjects was able to identify the purpose of the inventory, and that these subjects had scores identical to those who could not identify the purpose of the inventory. This low face validity may make the AD less subject to response sets, such as social desirability, than other state anxiety inventories.

In summary, there are a number of self-report inventories available to both the clinician and the researcher for the assessment of state anxiety. These measures may be useful both for the assessment of anxiety for diagnostic purposes (for instance, in the assessment of anticipatory anxiety in patients with panic disorder) and for treatment outcome in patients with anxiety disorders, including panic disorder. For a more detailed review and discussion of state anxiety measures, see Bernstein et al. (1986).

Self-monitoring Techniques

One of the potential drawbacks of self-report measures of panic and agoraphobic avoidance is their reliance on retrospective estimates, rendering them susceptible to inaccuracies resulting from memory loss and unintentional distortion (Tellegen, 1985). This shortcoming can be redressed through the use of self-monitoring techniques, which ask the subject to record ongoing subjective states or behaviors. A study comparing self-monitored panic with retrospective measures (from a questionnaire or interview) of panic was published by Margraf et al. (1987). Retrospective reports of panic identified a greater number of symptoms than self-monitored panic, particularly the symptoms of fear of going crazy, faintness, trembling or shaking, and fear of dying. Nevertheless, the rank order of symptom frequency was similar for the two methods (with a Spearman rank correlation of .61).

As noted by Rapee and Barlow in Chapter 7, frequent self-monitoring appears to be more reliable and valid than only occasional monitoring. This increment in reliability and validity probably results from the increased number of observations, resulting in a reduction of measurement error following aggregation (Epstein, 1979).

Self-monitoring is not, however, without its limitations. For example, self-monitoring may have reactive effects (Bellack & Lombardo, 1984). In other words, patients' behaviors or internal states may change solely as a function of self-observation. For example, agoraphobic patients monitoring their daily behaviors may realize that their activities have become far more constricted than they had previously thought, leading them to increase their self-exposure to feared situations. Although to our knowledge self-monitoring has not been demonstrated to have reactive effects in panic or agoraphobia patients, this possibility should be considered whenever self-monitoring methods are employed.

A further problem with self-monitoring in some patients is compliance (O'Brien & Barlow, 1984). Many patients fail to complete self-monitoring assignments, particularly when recording is to be done frequently. Noncompliance may be reduced somewhat by providing patients with detailed instructions regarding the technique and rationale of self-monitoring, and by meeting with patients on a regular basis to discuss the assignments (O'Brien & Barlow, 1984). A variety of self-monitoring procedures are available to assess dependent variables among patients with panic disorder and agoraphobia. Patients may simply be asked to provide frequency counts of panic attacks, cognitions, or other subjective events over a specified time interval, or to record the amount of time spent performing agoraphobia-relevant behaviors (for example, doing things outside of the house or shopping at a mall). A technique that to our knowledge is not yet employed in panic disorder research is the quasirandom sampling of subjective anxiety levels or cognitions. This procedure requires subjects to carry a signal device that sounds at irregular intervals, informing them when to record specified variables (Klinger, 1978).

Barlow and his colleagues have constructed two useful self-monitoring instruments, the Self-Monitoring of Activities Form (Barlow, O'Brien, & Last, 1984) and the Self-Monitoring of Anxiety Form (Waddell, Barlow, & O'Brien, 1984). The former elicits daily ratings on total time away from the home, total time away from the home alone, total time spent engaged in programmed practice, and other pertinent behavioral variables. The latter elicits ratings of anxiety on an 8-point Likert-type scale four times daily. Subjects are also asked to record every instance of anxiety that exceeds a scale value of 4 and to report whether these were panic attacks. See Himadi, Boice, and Barlow (1986) for a more detailed description of these two forms, and Rapee and Barlow (in Chapter 7) for an example of an actual self-monitoring form currently used in their clinic.

Patients may also be asked to keep diaries detailing such variables as level of subjective anxiety, frequency of panic attacks, cognitions, medication-taking, and avoidance behaviors. Ganellen et al. (1986), for example, employed a panic attack diary with the following categories: (1) spontaneous major attacks (full-blown panic attacks without apparent cause), (2) spontaneous minor attacks (less than three DSM-III symptoms), and (3) situational attacks (panic). Each attack was rated by the patient for intensity (on a 10-point scale) and duration. Comparing panic patients with and without agoraphobia, they found significantly more spontaneous major attacks in the pure panic disorder patients (5.8 per week versus 2.4 per week), but no differences in the other types of attacks. No differences in intensity were found. In addition to their utility as treatment outcome measures, diaries can also be employed to obtain manipulation checks on programmed practice assignments (O'Brien & Barlow, 1984).

In our opinion, self-monitoring should be included in the assessment of panic disorder whenever possible. For routine clinical practice, the self-monitoring form described in Chapter 7 and an alternative form in this book's appendix are useful. More specialized research questions will require that investigators design their own monitoring forms.

Behavioral Avoidance Tests

The measures discussed thus far have relied on the patient's self-report. The Behavioral Avoidance Test (BAT) was originally designed to constitute a direct behavioral measure of phobia; that is, the second channel of the "tripartite" assessment of panic disorder.

Currently, however, the BAT is actually a self-contained example of triple response measurements. Thus, the BAT is not necessarily limited to actual performance measures (such as the number of phobic situations mastered) but may also include self-report measures of anxiety and cognitive activities, as well as physiological measures, particularly heart rate. For example, the fear thermometer discussed previously or similar measures are often administered during the behavioral avoidance test. In this section we will only describe the behavioral and self-report aspects of the BAT and leave the physiological assessments for the next section.

The BAT was first employed in research by Lang and Lazovik (1963), who measured fear among snake-phobic subjects by instructing subjects to approach and eventually touch and handle a live snake. In the BAT, the subject is instructed to ascend a hierarchy of increasingly anxiety-provoking stimuli in vivo. These stimuli are arranged either in discrete steps—or more commonly—along a continuous dimension such as time or distance. For example, an agoraphobic patient might be asked to sit alone in a crowded restaurant for as long as possible, or to walk alone as long as possible in the downtown area of a busy city. The patient's score on the BAT is either simply the highest point attained in the hierarchy, or a more complex weighted score of anxiety levels and avoidance combined. The interrater reliability of the BAT is generally nearly perfect (Bernstein et al., 1986). Moreover, the BAT has consistently proven to be sensitive to the effects of treatment. Nevertheless, the methodological issues involved in the selection and interpretation of the BAT are often underestimated (Williams, 1984).

One of the principal problems associated with the use of the BAT is its reactivity to demand characteristics (Orne, 1962). In other words, patients may approach or remain in situations that they would ordinarily avoid or escape from because of their beliefs regarding what the therapist expects of their performance. Sources of demand characteristics include "evaluation apprehension" (Rosenberg, 1965), a desire to please or not disappoint the therapist, and patient expectations regarding the beneficial effects of treatment on performance. Some or all of these factors may compromise the ecological validity of the BAT (that is, its generalizability to the outside world). They may also explain the low diagnostic sensitivity of the BAT. In one study (Mavissakalian & Hamann, 1986), more than half of the agoraphobic patients completed four out of five BAT items prior to treatment, even though these items were specifically tailored to each patient's primary agoraphobic fears (see the following pages). Clearly, this limits the utility of the BAT as a therapy outcome measure, because of pretreatment ceiling effects.

Unfortunately, there is no satisfactory solution to the problem of demand characteristics, although having the therapist observe the patient unobtrusively rather than directly may minimize it. Alternatively, the patient may report on his or her progress during the BAT with a measure that can subsequently be verified by the therapist objectively. For example, the patient can report on certain landmarks during a standardized "behavioral walk." These indirect techniques may also minimize the objection that agoraphobic patients are more likely to confront and remain in phobic situations when in the presence of another individual (Himadi et al., 1986). An additional possibility for research purposes might be to have the BAT administered by a research assistant who conceals his or her involvement with the treatment program and leads the patient to believe he or she is conducting the assessment as part of a different study. Although this technique entails deception, it has been used successfully in social psychological research to evaluate the role of demand characteristics in the forced compliance paradigm (Tedeschi & Lindskold, 1976).

Other methodological decisions involved in the use of the BAT have been reviewed by Williams (1984). He contends that it is important not to set limits on how anxious subjects may become during the test, because this will restrict the range of subjects' performance and confound the behavioral and subjective components of anxiety. Consequently, the investigator will be unable to examine the relationship between behavior and self-reported anxiety. Although we agree, we should point out that the use of a behavioral criterion for termination of the BAT may exacerbate the problem of demand characteristics just discussed. The ideal solution, as Williams points out, is simply to measure subjective anxiety at regular intervals during the BAT. This has been accomplished by having subjects report their anxiety levels to the therapist or, more ideally, record their levels with a small portable tape recorder (O'Brien & Barlow, 1984).

Williams also urges that treatment elements be removed from the BAT to as great an extent as possible. Baseline assessment of claustrophobia, for example, has been demonstrated to have therapeutic effects (Leitenberg, Agras, Edwards, Thomson, & Wincze, 1970). Thus, Williams advised that exposure to phobic stimuli be minimized by allowing subjects only a brief period of time to confront each situation. Unfortunately, this practice may introduce an unwanted element of artificiality into the BAT, thereby limiting its ecological validity. Of course, the use of comparably treated comparison groups should obviate the problem that Williams addresses.

Two major types of BAT have been employed in agoraphobia research: the Standardized Behavioral Avoidance Test (SBAT) and the Individualized Behavioral Avoidance Test (IBAT; Himadi et al., 1986). The SBAT consists of a single test that is identical for all subjects. For instance, agoraphobic subjects may be asked to complete a "behavioral walk" through a standardized course divided into roughly equal intervals and told to note a particular landmark or place a mark at the farthest point reached (Williams, 1984). As another example, Williams and Rappoport (1983) had all subjects drive a car along an increasingly anxiety-provoking route. The primary disadvantage of the SBAT is that it is not equally difficult for all subjects because of the heterogeneity of feared situations among patients (Williams, 1984).

The IBAT, in contrast, contains items that are selected on the basis of each patient's idiosyncratic profile of agoraphobic fears (Mathews, Gelder, & Johnston, 1981). Mathews and his colleagues, for example, develop an equal-interval hierarchy of 15 fears for each patient, based on the latter's estimates of fear in each situation. Rather than attempt all items in the hierarchy, the patient attempts only enough for a "ceiling" to be estimated. There are at least two major drawbacks to this method (Williams, 1984). First, it assumes that subjects are capable of arranging fear-provoking items into a Guttman scale (that is, one that is perfectly cumulative). This assumption is highly questionable given the low correlation between self-reported fear and actual behavior on individual items discussed earlier.

A second problem, which is applicable to IBATs in general, is that scores are essentially ipsative; that is, they take into account the relative, rather than absolute, standing of behaviors within subjects. Indeed, the IBAT of Mathews and colleagues is constructed so that all patients achieve essentially the same initial score and are thus inappropriate for nomothetic (or across-subject) comparisons. Nevertheless, they can be quite useful for within-subject assessments. See Chapter 7 for Rapee and Barlow's excellent description of the construction of an IBAT.

Recently, methods have been developed to self-monitor *cognitions* during the behavioral avoidance test. Schwartz and Michelson (1987) employed a technique in which agoraphobic subjects reported their thoughts into a portable tape recorder while they were undergoing a behavioral avoidance test. During scoring, these statements were classified into (1) negative, self-defeating statements (for example, "my legs are weak and shaky"), (2) positive, coping statements ("I am going to make it"), and (3) task-irrelevant statements. The reliability of the classification of the self-statements was high; kappa = .87. A "state-of-mind" score was derived by dividing positive statements by the sum of positive and negative statements (thus discarding the neutral statements). Before treatment, the state-of-mind score was .4, indicating a negative bias. After treatment the score changed to .7, indicating a more positive state of mind.

To summarize, the BAT is a technically complicated test. Because by definition patients with panic disorder without agoraphobia exhibit little avoidance, the BAT is not useful for them. Because of these limitations, the BAT is not essential to the clinical management of agoraphobia; however, it is likely to continue as a component in the research assessment of agoraphobia.

Physiological Measures

Psychophysiological assessment has traditionally constituted the third and final channel in the "tripartite" assessment of anxiety. In this chapter we will limit ourselves to a cursory discussion of issues that are either clinically relevant or being discussed frequently in the current literature.

In clinical practice, physiological measures are particularly useful for monitoring therapeutic procedures requiring the patient to be exposed to fearful scenes, such as flooding or systematic desensitization. A second use of physiological measures is as an outcome measure, or as a laboratory measure to test specific hypotheses concerning the autonomic nervous system. Of the different possible physiological measures, heart rate and skin conductance are the most commonly employed.

Skin Conductance

Sweaty and cold hands are consistent attributes of many patients with anxiety disorders. It is therefore not surprising that skin conductance measures have been employed to characterize patients with anxiety disorders and their response to sedative drugs (Lader & Wing, 1966). Skin conductance is highly responsive to environmental and behavioral stimuli; therefore, for it to be a reliable measure, the environment has to be highly standardized. Typically, a sound-attenuated booth is employed. To facilitate comparisons among different laboratories, standardized procedures have been established (Fowles et al., 1981).

Measures of skin conductance probably have little clinical use in the assessment of panic disorder. However, in the laboratory, skin conductance is a sensitive measure of sympathetic arousal and can be used to test specific hypotheses concerning arousal levels and the response to stress in panic disorder patients. In a recent study, for example, Roth et al. (1986) examined whether panic disorder patients had (1) elevated levels of tonic arousal and (2) increased reactivity to stress. To answer these questions, the authors compared skin conductance and heart rate responses of 37 agoraphobic patients with those of normal controls under baseline, habituation, and startle conditions. They found that agoraphobic patients had significantly higher average skin conductance levels and more nonspecific fluctuations. Furthermore, habituation occurred at a slower rate in the phobic patients. However, there were no differences with respect to the magnitude of skin conductance responses to specific stimuli. Thus, the agoraphobic patients were no more reactive than the normal subjects but had higher arousal levels and habituated more slowly. Similarly, with respect to heart rate, agoraphobic patients showed higher counts but did not show increased reactivity to the stimuli presented. Thus, these findings indicated that agoraphobic patients had higher levels of physiological "activation" but did not have higher "reactivity" to behavioral stimuli.

Heart Rate

Like skin conductance, heart rate measurements are commonly employed in the laboratory to assess anxiety responses. The study by Roth et al. (1986) discussed in the preceding section is an example of such an application. Another use of heart rate measures is to assess anxiety levels or panic attacks in the freely moving individual, using ambulatory heart rate measurements. Ambulatory heart rate measurements became possible as a result of the availability of lightweight physiological monitors that patients can carry during regular daily activities. They have been employed in two ways: (1) to measure naturally occurring panic on a 24-hour basis and (2) to measure "fear" or arousal in the behavioral avoidance test.

AMBULATORY HEART RATE

During panic attacks, there is often a substantial increase in heart rate. This was confirmed by two reports on patients who developed panic attacks while they were undergoing physiological assessments (Cohen, Barlow, & Blanchard, 1985; Lader & Mathews, 1970). It would seem enticing, then, to measure naturally occurring panic attacks with 24-hour ambulatory recordings of heart rate. Indeed, Freedman, Ianni, Ettedgui, Pohl, and Rainey (1984) found that seven of eight patients experienced increases in heart rate coinciding with panic episodes.

However, Taylor, Telch, and Hawick (1983) found that only three of eight self-reported panic episodes were accompanied by heart rate increases, and Taylor et al. (1986) found that only 58% of self-reported panic episodes were accompanied by increases in heart rate. Conversely, only four of fourteen heart rate episodes identified by the heart rate monitor as signifying panic actually were accompanied by subjective panic. Furthermore, in a later similar study by Margraf et al. (1987), based on a larger number of panic attacks, the heart rate increases observed with panic attacks were limited to situational panic attacks; spontaneous panic attacks were not associated with higher heart rates. The low sensitivity and specificity of ambulatory heart rate and its inability to register panic attacks of the "spontaneous" variety significantly limit the use of this measure in the clinical assessment of panic.

HEART RATE DURING THE BEHAVIORAL AVOIDANCE TEST

Heart rate has been employed as a measure of fear in agoraphobic patients during the behavioral avoidance test. The heart rate response to the feared stimulus (for example, walking downtown) can be calculated as the difference between a baseline heart rate level and the "stress" level during the test itself. To control for the effect of physical activity and anticipatory baseline, it is desirable to obtain a "walking baseline"; that is, to measure heart rates while the subject is walking in a situation not involving feared stimuli. This walking baseline, however, may be affected by anticipatory anxiety. For this reason it is advantageous to schedule the walking baseline *after* the behavioral walk has been completed. To factor out possible differences in heart rate caused by physical activity, such activity may be measured via an activity monitor or as the speed at which the patient completed the behavioral avoidance test.

Although heart rate measures during a behavioral avoidance test have been employed as an outcome measure of behavioral treatment of agoraphobia (Michelson, Mavissakalian, & Marchione, 1985), they are probably less useful as measures of treatment with antidepressant medication, because of the effect that these drugs have on heart rate.

If heart rate is a measure of fear during completion of a behavioral avoidance test, then agoraphobic patients should have higher heart rate responses to this test than do normal subjects. A detailed account of ambulatory heart rate changes during the behavioral avoidance test has been provided by Holden and Barlow (1986). Ambulatory heart rate was measured in ten agoraphobic patients and ten nonphobic controls during seven behavioral avoidance tests requiring a 1-mile walk into downtown Albany. The walk was subdivided into a number of "stations" at which the subjects recorded their anxiety levels in SUDs (Subjective Units of Distress, a rating of anxiety levels). Heart rates were calculated for the 15-second periods preceding and following each station. After the walk, a "walking baseline" was obtained to control for differences in heart rate caused by factors other than anxiety or anticipatory anxiety. Three of these walks occurred before treatment for agoraphobia, one after 6 weeks of treatment, and three after completion of the 12-week treatment program.

A number of measures of heart rate were presented, including the mean heart rate for the entire walk, the differences between heart rates during the behavioral avoidance test and the subsequent walking baseline, and a measure of between-walk variability. It was found that the agoraphobic patients had generally higher heart rates than the nonphobic subjects. As treatment progressed, heart rate decreased for the phobic patients, as expected; surprisingly, however, heart rate decreased for the controls as well. Furthermore, the change of heart rate from test to the posttest walking baseline (heart rate responses) did not differentiate agoraphobic patients from controls.

Test-retest reliability of heart rate for the phobic patients was .63 for the three pretreatment walks and .54 for the three posttreatment walks. For heart rate *responses*, the test-retest reliability was .48 pretreatment and .29 posttreatment. For the controls, the reliability of heart rate responses was .34 pretreatment and .001 posttreatment. Thus, the reliability of heart rate responses was low.

The lack of ability of heart rate responses to discriminate between agoraphobic patients and normal subjects in the behavioral avoidance test was confirmed by Roth et al. (1986), who also reported (in the study described under "Skin Conductance") ambulatory heart rate data during a behavioral avoidance test. As did Holden and Barlow (1986), Roth et al. found increased tonic heart rates in agoraphobic patients compared with controls, but heart rate reactivity, as measured by the difference between sitting heart rates and heart rates during the behavioral avoidance test, did not differentiate between the groups. The lack of specificity of the response measure may be related to higher baseline heart rates in agoraphobic patients caused by anticipatory anxiety.

Ambulatory heart rate measurements during BATs require a high degree of technical and statistical sophistication. Although there is a place for such measures in the research assessment of panic disorder, their clinical use seems limited. For this reason, we recommend against using heart rate measures in routine clinical practice.

Synchrony, Concordance, and Response Profiles

Until now, we have discussed the different measurement channels of self-report, overt behavior, and physiological expression of anxiety in isolation. However, if these channels are measuring different aspects of the same phenomenon—anxiety or panic—then measures across these channels should be interrelated. Research has shown, however, that the responses on the three systems are only loosely correlated at best (Lang, 1968). Rachman and Hodgson (1974) discussed how fear and avoidance at times can vary independently or even inversely. Consequently, researchers have shifted their attention to the discrepancies between physiological and other measures of anxiety. The terms *synchrony* versus *desynchrony, concordance* versus *discordance, consonance* versus *nonconsonance,* and *reactivity patterns* have been employed with respect to different aspects of these discrepancies. When a patient undergoes treatment for anxiety while being monitored for physiological reactivity (such as heart rate) and phobic avoidance—for example, during a behavioral avoidance test—one would expect that the reduction in fear would manifest as both a decrease in phobic avoidance and a decrease in heart rate. This pattern, a parallel change in heart rate and phobic avoidance, is called synchrony.

Conversely, if phobic avoidance decreases while heart rate increases, we would have a case of desynchrony. However, the term *desynchrony* also applies to cases in which phobic avoidance increases while the heart rate decreases, and *synchrony* to cases in which both phobic avoidance and heart rate increase. These two synchrony or desynchrony conditions are probably separate phenomena (Mavissakalian, 1987). Mavissakalian and Michelson (1982) reported that desynchrony was more common early in treatment, if measured over shorter periods of time (for example, 1 month versus 2 months), and is related to the generally slower pace at which heart rate responded to treatment compared with avoidance behavior. Similar findings were obtained in social phobia by Öst, Jerremalm, and Jansson (1984). The effect of synchrony versus desynchrony on treatment outcome was studied by Vermilyea, Boice, and Barlow (1984) and by Mavissakalian (1987). In both studies there were tendencies for the patients with desynchronous changes to have poorer overall outcome than those with synchronous changes, but in neither study were the differences between "synchronizers" and "desynchronizers" statistically significant. The sample sizes in these studies, however, were too small for adequate statistical power.

If the treatment effects are measured repeatedly (e.g., pretreatment, midtreatment, posttreatment, follow-up), the possible permutations of synchrony/desynchrony increase in exponential fashion (L. Michelson, personal communication, June 20, 1988). A simpler way of looking at the pattern among response channels is to use a posttest-only approach, in which the responses of patients at posttreatment are compared with those of other patients rather than with their own pretreatment values. In other words, a reactivity profile is established for each patient relative to that of other patients. Terms used to describe different response profiles include *concordance* and *disconcordance*. A concordant subject is one who is below specific cutoff points for each of the three channels; those who are above the cutoff on at least one channel are disconcordant or discordant.

A third possible use of response profiles across the three channels of assessment is to classify patients at pretreatment. The purpose of such a classification is to aid in assigning patients to treatments that specifically address the channel showing the "excessive" response. The interaction between reactor type and effect of different treatments was evaluated for social phobia by Öst, Jerremalm, and Johansson (1981). Forty socially phobic subjects underwent a speech test, based on which 16 "behavioral reactors" and 16 "physiological reactors" were identified. Among patients assigned to social skills training, behavioral reactors did better than physiological reactors on some of the measures; among patients assigned to applied relaxation, physiological reactors did better than behavioral reactors. In a later study, Öst, Jerremalm, and Jansson (1984) applied the same paradigm to agoraphobia; behavioral reactors or physiological reactors were assigned to one of two treatments: exposure (a "behavioral" treatment) and applied relaxation (a "physiological" treatment). In this study, however, no differential effect of reactor status on treatment outcome was found. Michelson (1986), on the other hand, reported that "cognitive," "physiological," and "behavioral" reactors assigned to the consonant treatment (that is, relaxation for the physiological reactors, graduated exposure for the behavioral reactors, and paradoxical intention for the cognitive reactors) had better long-term outcome than those assigned to a nonconsonant treatment. Further research is needed to establish the utility of these interrelationships for clinical practice.

Summary

In this chapter we provided an overview of the assessment of patients with panic disorder. We did so by following a patient from the initial contact with the clinic and the initial evaluation through the medical assessment and finally through the secondary assessment. The entire assessment program requires several sessions.

In the initial evaluation, a preliminary diagnosis and differential diagnosis are made. In the differential diagnosis, other anxiety disorders as well as other psychiatric disorders are considered. Among the anxiety disorders, differentiation between panic disorder and other disorders is largely based on the history of unexpected panic attacks. Other psychiatric disorders presenting with panic attacks include depression and substance abuse disorders and, more rarely, psychotic states. It is particularly important to identify patients in whom panic attacks are secondary to depression because of the potentially serious consequences, which may include suicide, if a primary depression is not receiving adequate attention in the treatment program. Among the substance abuse disorders, alcoholism is the most important consideration, and the possibility of excessive caffeine intake should not be overlooked.

The medical evaluation of panic disorder is similar to that done for any patient: it includes a medical history, review of symptoms from specific organ systems, and a physical and laboratory examination. The role of different medical disorders in panic has often been overstated; nevertheless, the therapist should be aware that certain medical conditions can present with anxiety symptoms, including panic. These conditions include metabolic and endocrine disorders, such as hyperthyroidism, hypothyroidism, and hypoglycemia; neurological and otoneurological conditions, such as vestibular dysfunction and seizure disorders; and finally cardiac disorders, such as cardiac arrhythmias, angina pectoris, and congestive heart failure. The role of mitral valve prolapse in panic is unclear but probably has been overemphasized in the literature. We propose that all patients undergo a basic physical and laboratory screening, with further examinations as suggested by specific aspects of the symptom picture. The index of suspicion for organic anxiety syndromes is increased significantly if the panic disorder begins after age 40, if the panic attacks are associated with certain symptoms such as hunger or headaches, or if the panic attacks are of very brief duration or stop abruptly.

The secondary evaluation is conducted for two purposes: to confirm the diagnosis and to quantify relevant aspects of the disorder. Instruments for diagnosis may include various diagnostic interview schedules for the diagnosis of Axis I disorders as well as the assessment of personality disorders. Quantification of panic disorder is necessary to measure treatment effects and to identify subtypes of panic patients. The expression of panic and anxiety occurs in three main channels that are only loosely correlated: verbal report, overt behavior, and physiological response. Most of the instruments used in the clinical assessment of panic are based on self-report. These include measures of panic-eliciting stimuli, measures of panic phenomenology, measures of cognitions, and measures of state anxiety. Such measures frequently involve retrospective patient reports. These should be supplemented by self-monitoring for the purpose of obtaining a prospective assessment of panic symptoms and behavior. Finally, the behavioral dimension of panic may be assessed by the behavioral avoidance test and in the physiological dimension by various measures such as heart rate. The behavioral and physiological measures are technically difficult to obtain and are not mandatory for routine clinical assessment.

We hope that this chapter has provided the reader with a useful background for the assessment of panic disorder. We have attempted to highlight potential pitfalls in the course of the assessment, as well as to provide a selection of assessment instruments. Chapter 7, by Rapee and Barlow, will provide additional details of practical use for the clinician.

References

Agras, W. S., & Jacob, R. G. (1981). Phobia: Nature and measurement. In M. Mavissakalian & D. H. Barlow (Eds.), *Phobia: Psychological and pharmacological treatment*. New York: Guilford Press.

American Psychiatric Association. (1987). *Diagnostic and statistical manual of mental disorders* (3rd ed., rev.). Washington, DC: Author.

Amies, P. L., Gelder, M. G., & Shaw, P. M. (1983). Social phobia: A comparative clinical study. *British Journal of Psychiatry, 142*, 174–179.

Anastasi, A. (1982). *Psychological testing* (5th ed.). New York: Macmillan.

Andrews, J. D. W. (1966). Psychotherapy of phobias. *Psychological Bulletin, 66*, 455–480.

Aronson, T. A., & Craig, T. J. (1986). Cocaine precipitation of panic disorder. *American Journal of Psychiatry, 143*(5), 643–645.

Arrindell, W. A., & Emmelkamp, P. M. G. (1986). Marital adjustment, intimacy and needs in female agoraphobics and their partners: A controlled study. *British Journal of Psychiatry, 149*, 592–602.

Auerbach, S. M. (1973). Trait-state anxiety and adjustment to surgery. *Journal of Consulting and Clinical Psychology, 40*, 264–271.

Barlow, D. H. (1985). The dimensions of anxiety disorders. In H. A. Tuma & F. J. Maser (Eds.), *Anxiety and the anxiety disorders*. Hillsdale, NJ: Lawrence Erlbaum.

Barlow, D. H. (1988). Current models of panic disorder and a view from emotion theory. In A. J. Frances & R. E. Hales (Eds.), *American Psychiatric Press review of psychiatry* (Vol. 7). Washington, DC: American Psychiatric Press.

Barlow, D. H., DiNardo, P. A., Vermilyea, B. A., Vermilyea, J., & Blanchard, E. B. (1986). Co-morbidity and depression among the anxiety disorders. *Journal of Nervous and Mental Disease, 174,* 63–72.

Barlow, D. H., O'Brien, G. T., & Last, C. G. (1984). Couples treatment of agoraphobia. *Behavior Therapy, 15,* 41–58.

Barlow, D. H., Vermilyea, J., Blanchard E. B., Vermilyea B. B., DiNardo, P. A., & Cerny, J. A. (1985). The phenomenon of panic. *Journal of Abnormal Psychology, 94,* 320–328.

Barrett, E. S. (1972). Anxiety and impulsiveness: Toward a neuropsychological model. In C. D. Spielberger (Ed.), *Anxiety: Current trends in theory and research* (Vol. 1, pp. 195–222). New York: Academic Press.

Bass, C., & Wade, C. (1984). Chest pain with normal coronary arteries: A comparative study of psychiatric and social morbidity. *Psychological Medicine, 14,* 51–61.

Beck, A. T., Brown, G., Eidelson, J. I., Steer, R. A., & Riskind, J. H. (1987). Differentiating anxiety and depression: A test of the cognitive content-specificity hypothesis. *Journal of Abnormal Psychology, 96,* 179–183.

Beck, A., & Emery, E. (1985). *Anxiety disorders and phobias: A cognitive perspective*. New York: Basic Books.

Beck, A. T., Laude, R., & Bohnert, M. (1974). Ideational components of anxiety neurosis. *Archives of General Psychiatry, 31,* 319–325.

Beck, A. T., Rush, A. J., Shaw, B. F., & Emery, G. (1979). *Cognitive therapy of depression*. New York: Guilford Press.

Beck, A. T., Steer, R. A., & Garbin, M. S. (1988). Psychometric properties of the Beck Depression Inventory: Twenty-five years of evaluation. *Clinical Psychology Review, 8,* 77–100.

Beitman, B. D., Basha, I., Flaker, G., DeRosear, L., Mukerji, V., & Lamberti, J. (1987a). Major depression in cardiology chest pain patients without coronary artery disease and with panic disorder. *Journal of Affective Disorders, 13,* 51–59.

Beitman, B. D., Basha, I., Flaker, G., DeRosear, L., Mukerji, V., & Lamberti, J. (1987b). Non-fearful panic disorder: Panic attacks without fear. *Behaviour Research and Therapy, 25,* 487–492.

Beitman, B. D., Basha, I., Flaker, G., DeRosear, L., Mukerji, V., Trombka, L., & Katon, W. (in press). Atypical or non-anginal chest pain: Panic disorder or coronary artery disease? *Archives of Internal Medicine.*

Beitman, B. D., Basha, I. M., Trombka, L. H., Jayaratna, M. A., Russel, B. D., & Tarr, S. K. (1988). Alprazolam in the treatment of cardiology patients with atypical chest pain and panic disorder. *Journal of Clinical Psychopharmacology, 8,* 127–130.

Bellack, A. S., & Lombardo, T. W. (1984). Measurement of anxiety. In S. M. Turner (Ed.), *Behavioral theories and treatment of anxiety*. New York: Plenum Press.

Bernstein, D. A., Borkovec, T. D., & Coles, M. G. H. (1986). Assessment of anxiety. In A. R. Ciminero, K. S. Calhoun, & H. E. Adams (Eds.), *Handbook of behavioral assessment* (2nd ed.). New York: Wiley.

Bibb, J. L., & Chambless, D. L. (1986). Alcohol use and abuse among diagnosed agoraphobics. *Behaviour Research and Therapy, 24,* 49–58.

Boulenger, J.-P., Uhde, T. W., Wolff, E. A., & Post, R. M. (1984). Increased sensitivity to caffeine in patients with panic disorders. *Archives of General Psychiatry, 41*(11), 1067–1071.

Boyd, J. H. (1986). Use of mental health services for the treatment of panic disorder. *American Journal of Psychiatry, 143*(12), 1569–1574.

Breier, A., Charney, D. S., & Heninger, R. (1986). Agoraphobia with panic attacks: Development, diagnostic stability and course of illness. *Archives of General Psychiatry, 43,* 1029–1036.

Brodman, K., Erdmann, A., & Wolff, H. G. (1949). *Cornell Medical Index Health Questionnaire.* Ithaca, NY: Cornell University Medical College.

Brodsky, L., Zuniga, J. S., Casenas, E. R., Ernstoff, R., & Sachdev, H. S. (1983). Refractory anxiety: A masked epileptiform disorder? *Psychiatric Journal of the University of Ottawa, 8*(1), 42–45.

Brown, H. N., & Kemble, S. B. (1981). Episodic anxiety and cardiac arrhythmias. *Psychosomatics, 22,* 907–925.

Buss, A. H. (1962). Two anxiety factors in psychiatric patients. *Journal of Abnormal and Social Psychology, 65,* 426–427.

Campbell, D. T., & Fiske, D. (1959). Convergent and discriminant validity by the multitrait-multimethod matrix. *Psychological Bulletin, 56,* 81–105.

Canino, G. J., Bird, H. R., Shrout, P. E., Rubio-Stipec, M., Bravo, M., Martinez, R., Sesman, M., Guzman, A., Guevara, L. M., & Costas, H. (1987). The Spanish Diagnostic Interview Schedule: Reliability and concordance with clinical diagnoses in Puerto Rico. *Archives of General Psychiatry, 44,* 720–726.

Chaleby, K., & Ziady, G. (1988). Mitral valve prolapse and social phobia. *British Journal of Psychiatry, 152,* 280–281.

Chambless, D. L., Caputo, G. C., Bright, P., & Gallagher, R. (1984). Assessment of fear of fear in agoraphobics: The Body Sensations Questionnaire and the Agoraphobic Cognitions Questionnaire. *Journal of Consulting and Clinical Psychology, 52,* 1090–1097.

Chambless, D. L., Caputo, G. C., Jasin, S. E., Gracely, E. J., & Williams, C. (1985). The Mobility Inventory for Agoraphobia. *Behaviour Research and Therapy, 23,* 35–44.

Chambless, D. L., & Mason, J. (1986). Sex, sex role stereotyping, and agoraphobia. *Behaviour Research and Therapy, 24,* 231–235.

Clark, D. M. (1986). A cognitive approach to panic. *Behaviour Research and Therapy, 24,* 461–470.

Cohen, A. S., Barlow, D. H., & Blanchard, E. B. (1985). Psychophysiology of relaxation-associated panic attacks. *Journal of Abnormal Psychology, 94,* 96–101.

Coryell, W., Endicott, J., Andreasen, N. C., Keller, M. B., Clayton, P. J., Hirschfeld, R. M. A., Scheftner, W. A., & Winokur, G. (1988). Depression and panic attacks: The significance of overlap as reflected in follow-up and family study data. *American Journal of Psychiatry, 145*(3), 293–300.

Coryell, W., Noyes, R., & Clancy, J. (1982). Excess mortality in panic disorder: A comparison with primary unipolar depression. *Archives of General Psychiatry, 39,* 701–703.

Coryell, W., Noyes, R., & House, J. D. (1986). Mortality among outpatients with panic disorder. *American Journal of Psychiatry, 143,* 508–510.

Costa, P. T., Zonderman, A. B., Engel, B. T., Baile, W. F., Brimlow, D. L., & Brinker, J. (1985). The relation of chest pain symptoms to angiographic findings of coronary artery stenosis and neuroticism. *Psychosomatic Medicine, 47*(3), 285–293.

Cox, B. J., Norton, G. R., Dorward, J., & Fergusson, P. (1989). The relationship between panic attacks and chemical dependencies. *Addictive Behaviors, 14*, 53–60.

Craske, M. G., Rachman, S. J., & Tallman, K. (1986). Mobility, cognitions, and panic. *Journal of Psychopathology and Behavioral Assessment, 8*, 199–210.

Cromwell, R. E., Olson, D. H., & Fournier, D. G. (1976). Tools and techniques for diagnosis and evaluation in marital and family therapy. *Family Process, 15*, 1–49.

Cronbach, L. J. (1960). *Essentials of psychological testing* (2nd ed.). New York: Harper & Row.

Cronbach, L. J., & Meehl, P. E. (1955). Construct validity in psychological tests. *Psychological Bulletin, 52*, 281–302.

Crowe, R. R. (1985). Mitral valve prolapse and panic disorder. *Psychiatric Clinics of North America, 8*, 63–71.

Dager, S. R., Cowley, D. S., & Dunner, D. L. (1987). Biological markers in panic states: Lactate-induced panic and mitral valve prolapse. *Biological Psychiatry, 22*, 339–359.

Dager, S. R., Holland, J. P., Cowley, D. S., & Dunner, D. L. (1987). Panic disorder precipitated by exposure to organic solvents in the work place. *American Journal of Psychiatry, 144*(8), 1056–1058.

Derogatis, L. R., Rickels, K., & Rock, A. F. (1976). The SCL-90 and the MMPI: A step in the validation of a new self-report scale. *British Journal of Psychiatry, 128*, 280–289.

Devereux, R. B. (1985). Mitral valve prolapse. *Primary Care, 12*, 39–54.

Devereux, R. B., Kramer-Fox, R., Brown, W. T., Shear, K., Hartman, N., Kligfield, P., Lutas, E. M., Spitzer, M. C., & Litwin, S. D. (1986). Relation between clinical features of the mitral prolapse syndrome and echocardiographically documented mitral valve prolapse. *Journal of the American College of Cardiology, 8*, 763–772.

Dillon, D., Gorman, J. M., Liebowitz, M. R., Fyer, A. J., & Klein, D. F. (1987). Measurement of lactate-induced panic and anxiety. *Psychiatry Research, 20*, 97–105.

DiNardo, P. A., & Barlow, D. H. (1988). Anxiety Disorders Interview Schedule, Revised. Phobia and Anxiety Disorders Clinic, 1535 Western Avenue Albany, New York, 12203.

DiNardo, P. A., O'Brien, G. T., Barlow, D. H., Waddell, M. T., & Blanchard, E. B. (1983). Reliability of DSM-III anxiety disorder categories using a new structured interview. *Archives of General Psychiatry, 40*, 1070–1074.

Edlund, M. J., Swann, A. C., & Clothier, J. (1987). Patients with panic attacks and abnormal EEG results. *American Journal of Psychiatry, 144*(4), 508–509.

Emery, G., & Tracy, N. L. (1987). Theoretical issues in the cognitive-behavioral treatment of anxiety disorders. In L. Michelson & L. M. Ascher (Eds.), *Anxiety and stress disorders: Cognitive-behavioral assessment and treatment*. New York: Guilford Press.

Epstein, S. (1979). The stability of behavior: I. On predicting more of the people more of the time. *Journal of Personality and Social Psychology, 37*, 1097–1126.

Erdman, H. P., Klein, M. H., Greist, J. H., Bass, S. M., Bires, J. K., & Machtinger, P. E. (1987). A comparison of the Diagnostic Interview Schedule and clinical diagnosis. *American Journal of Psychiatry, 144*(11), 1477–1480.

Fava, G. A., Zielenzny, M., Luria, E., & Canestrari, R. (1988). Obsessive-compulsive symptoms in agoraphobia: Changes with treatment. *Psychiatry Research, 23*, 57–63.

Fayer, A., & Endicott, J. (1984). *The Schedule for Affective Disorder and Schizophrenia—Lifetime version modified for Study of Anxiety Disorders*. New York: New York State Psychiatric Institute.

Ficarra, B. J., & Nelson, R. A. (1947). Phobia as a symptom in hyperthyroidism. *American Journal of Psychiatry, 103*, 831–832.

Fisher, L. M., & Wilson, G. T. (1985). A study of the psychology of agoraphobia. *Behaviour Research and Therapy, 23,* 97–107.

Fishman, S. M., Sheehan, D. V., & Carr, D. B. (1985). Thyroid indices in panic disorder. *Journal of Clinical Psychiatry, 46,* 432–433.

Ford, C. V., Bray, G. A., & Swerdloff, R. S. (1976). A psychiatric study of patients referred with a diagnosis of hypoglycemia. *American Journal of Psychiatry, 133*(3), 290–294.

Fowles, D. C., Christie, M. J., Edelberg, R., Grings, W. W., Lykken, D. T., & Venables, P. H. (1981). Publication recommendations for electrodermal measures. *Psychophysiology, 18,* 232–239.

Freedman, R. R., Ianni, P., Ettedgui, E., Pohl, R., & Rainey, J. M. (1984). Psychophysiological factors in panic disorder. *Psychopathology, 17*(Suppl. 1), 66–73.

Freeman, L., & Nixon, P. G. F. (1985). Are coronary artery spasm and progressive damage to the heart associated with the hyperventilation syndrome? *British Medical Journal, 291,* 851–852.

Friedman, C. J., Shear, M. K., & Frances, A. (1987). DSM-III personality disorders in panic patients. *Journal of Personality Disorders, 1,* 132–135.

Fry, W. F. (1962). The marital context of an anxiety syndrome. *Family Process, 4,* 245–252.

Ganellen, R. J., Matuzas, W., Uhlenhuth, E. H., Glass, R., & Easton, C. R. (1986). Panic disorder, agoraphobia, and anxiety-relevant cognitive style. *Journal of Affective Disorders, 11,* 219–225.

Gawin, F. H., & Markoff, R. A. (1981). Panic anxiety after abrupt discontinuation of amitriptyline. *American Journal of Psychiatry, 138*(1), 117–18.

Geer, J. H. (1965). The development of a scale to measure fear. *Behaviour Research and Therapy, 3,* 45–53.

Ghadirian, A. M., Gauthier, S., & Bertrand, S. (1986). Anxiety attacks in a patient with a right temporal lobe meningioma. *Journal of Clinical Psychiatry, 47*(5), 270–271.

Giannini, A. J., Price, W. A., & Loisell, R. H. (1984). Prevalence of mitral valve prolapse in bipolar affective disorder. *American Journal of Psychiatry, 141,* 991–992.

Gloor, P., Olivier, A., Quesney, L. F., Andermann, F., & Horowitz, S. (1982). The role of the limbic system in experiential phenomena of temporal lobe epilepsy. *Annals of Neurology, 12,* 129–144.

Goldstein, A. J., & Chambless, D. L. (1978). A reanalysis of agoraphobia. *Behavior Therapy, 9,* 47–59.

Gorman, J. M., Goetz, R. R., Myer, M., King, D. I., Fyer, A. J., Liebowitz, M. R., & Klein, D. F. (1988). The mitral valve prolapse—panic disorder connection. *Psychosomatic Medicine, 50,* 114–122.

Gorman, J. M., Shear, K., Devereux, R. B., King, D. L., & Klein, D. F. (1986). Prevalence of mitral valve prolapse in panic disorder: Effect of echocardiographic criteria. *Psychosomatic Medicine, 48,* 167–171.

Hafner, R. J., & Ross, M. W. (1984). Agoraphobia in women: Factor analysis of symptoms and personality correlates of factor scores in a clinical population. *Behaviour Research and Therapy, 22,* 441–444.

Haines, A. P., Dimeson, J. D., & Meade, T. W. (1987). Phobic anxiety and ischemic heart disease. *British Medical Journal, 295,* 297–299.

Hall, R. C. W. (1980). Somatopsychic disorders. In R. C. W. Hall (Ed.), *Psychiatric presentations of medical illness.* New York: S. P. Medical and Scientific Books.

Hall, R. C. W., Popkin, M. K., Devaul, R. A., Faillace, L. A., & Stickney, S. K. (1978). Physical illness presenting as psychiatric disease. *Archives of General Psychiatry, 35,* 1315–1320.

Hallpike, C. S., Harrison, M. S., & Slater, E. (1951). Abnormalities of the caloric test results in certain varieties of mental disorders. *Acta Oto-Laryngologica, 39,* 151.

Hamilton, M. (1959). The assessment of anxiety states by rating. *British Journal of Medical Psychology, 32,* 50–55.

Hamilton, M. (1960). A rating scale for depression. *Journal of Neurology, Neurosurgery and Psychiatry, 23,* 57–61.

Harper, M., & Roth, M. (1962). Temporal lobe epilepsy and the phobia-anxiety-depersonalization syndrome. *Comprehensive Psychiatry, 3,* 129–151.

Hartman, N., Kramer, R., Brown, T., & Devereux, R. B. (1982). Panic disorder in patients with mitral valve prolapse. *American Journal of Psychiatry, 139*(5), 669–670.

Helzer, J. E., Robins, L. N., McEvoy, L. T., Spitznagel, E. L., Stoltzman, R. K., Farmer, A., & Brockington, I. F. (1985). A comparison of clinical and Diagnostic Interview Schedule diagnoses: Physician reexamination of lay-interviewed cases in the general population. *Archives of General Psychiatry, 42,* 657–666.

Hersen, M. (1973). Self-assessment of fear. *Behavior Therapy, 4,* 241–257.

Hersen, M. (1988). Behavioral assessment and psychiatric diagnosis. *Behavioral Assessment, 10,* 107–121.

Himadi, W. G., Boice, R., & Barlow, D. H. (1986). Assessment of agoraphobia—II. Measurement of clinical change. *Behaviour Research and Therapy, 24,* 321–332.

Holden, A. E., & Barlow, D. H. (1986). Heart rate and heart rate variability recorded *in vivo* in agoraphobics and nonphobics. *Behavior Therapy, 17,* 26–42.

Holloway, W., & McNally, R. J. (1987). Effects of anxiety sensitivity on the response to hyperventilation. *Journal of Abnormal Psychology, 96,* 330–334.

Husek, T. R., & Alexander, S. (1963). The effectiveness of the anxiety differential in examination stress situations. *Educational and Psychological Measurement, 23,* 309–318.

Hyler, S., Rieder, R., Spitzer, R., & Williams, J. (1982). *The Personality Diagnostic Questionnaire (PDQ).* New York: New York State Psychiatric Institute.

Jacob, R. G. (1988). Panic disorder and the vestibular system. *Psychiatric Clinics of North America, 11,* 361–374.

Jacob, R. G., & Beidel, D. C. (1988). *The Symptom Questionnaire.* Manuscript in preparation.

Jacob, R. G., Ford, R., & Turner, S. M. (1987). Obsessive compulsive disorder. In M. Hersen (Ed.), *Practice of inpatient behavior therapy: A clinical guide.* New York: Grune & Stratton.

Jacob, R. G., Lilienfeld, S. O., Furman, J., Durrant, J., & Turner, S. M. (1988). *Space and motion phobia in panic disorder with vestibular dysfunction.* Manuscript submitted for publication.

Jacob, R. G., Moller, M. B., Turner, S. M., & Wall, C. (1985). Otoneurological examination in panic disorder and agoraphobia with panic attacks: A pilot study. *American Journal of Psychiatry, 142*(6), 715–720.

Jacob, R. G., & Rapport, M. D. (1984). Panic disorder. In S. M. Turner (Ed.), *Behavioral theories and treatment of anxiety.* New York: Plenum.

Jacob, R. G., & Turner, S. M. (1988). Panic disorder: Diagnosis and assessment. In A. J. Frances & R. E. Hales (Eds.), *American Psychiatric Press review of psychiatry* (Vol. 7). Washington, DC: American Psychiatric Press.

Kahn, J. P., Puertollano, M. A., Schane, M. D., & Klein, D. F. (1988). Adjunctive alprazolam for schizophrenia with panic anxiety: Clinical observation and pathogenetic implications. *American Journal of Psychiatry, 145*(6), 742–744.

Kantor, J. S., Zitrin, C. M., & Zeldis, S. M. (1980). Mitral valve prolapse syndrome in agoraphobic patients. *American Journal of Psychiatry, 137*(4), 467–469.

Kathol, R. G., & Delahunt, J. W. (1986). The relationship of anxiety and depression to symptoms of hyperthyroidism using operational criteria. *General Hospital Psychiatry, 8,* 23–28.

Kathol, R. G., Turner, R., & Delahunt, J. (1986). Depression and anxiety associated with hyperthyroidism: Response to antithyroid therapy. *Psychosomatics, 27,* 501–505.

Katon, W., Vitaliano, P. P., Russo, J., Jones, M., & Anderson, K. (1987). Panic disorder: Spectrum of severity and somatization. *Journal of Nervous and Mental Disease, 175,* 12–18.

Klein, D. F., Ross, D. C., & Cohen, P. (1987). Panic and avoidance in agoraphobia. *Archives of General Psychiatry, 44*(4), 377–385.

Kleinknecht, R. A. (1986). *The anxious self: Diagnosis and treatment of fears and phobias.* New York: Human Sciences Press.

Klinger, E. (1978). Dimensions of thought and imagery in normal waking states. *Journal of Altered States of Consciousness, 4,* 97–113.

Koryani, E. K. (1980). Somatic illness in psychiatric patients. *Psychosomatics, 21,* 887–891.

Lader, M. H., & Mathews, A. (1970). Physiological changes during spontaneous panic attacks. *Journal of Psychosomatic Research, 14,* 377–382.

Lader, M. H., & Wing, L. (1966). *Physiological measures, sedative drugs, and morbid anxiety.* London: Oxford University Press.

Lang, P. J. (1968). Fear reduction and fear behavior: Problems in treating a construct. In J. M. Shlien (Ed.), *Research in psychotherapy* (Vol. 3). Washington, DC: American Psychological Association.

Lang, P. J. (1984). Cognition in emotion: Concept and action. In C. Izard, J. Kagan, & R. Zajonc (Eds.), *Emotions, cognition, and behavior.* New York: Cambridge University Press.

Lang, P. J., & Lazovik, A. D. (1963). The experimental desensitization of a phobia. *Journal of Abnormal and Social Psychology, 66,* 519–525.

Lary, D., & Goldschlager, N. (1974). Electrocardiogram changes during hyperventilation resembling myocardial ischemia in patients with normal coronary arteriograms. *American Heart Journal, 87,* 383–390.

Leitenberg, H., Agras, S., Edwards, J. A., Thomson, L. E., & Wincze, J. P. (1970). Practice as a psychotherapeutic variable: An experimental analysis within single cases. *Journal of Psychiatric Research, 7,* 215–225.

Lesser, I. M., Rubin, R. T., Pecknold, J. C., Rifkin, A., Swinson, R. P., Lydiard, R. B., Burrows, G. D., Noyes, R., & DuPont, R. L. (1988). Secondary depression in panic disorder and agoraphobia. *Archives of General Psychiatry, 45,* 437–443.

Levin, H. S., Rodnitzky, R. L., & Mick, D. L. (1976). Anxiety associated with exposure to organophosphate compounds. *Archives of General Psychiatry, 33,* 225–228.

Levine, H. J. (1980). Difficult problems in the diagnosis of chest pain. *American Heart Journal, 100,* 108–118.

Liberthson, R., Sheehan, D. V., King, M. E., & Weyman, A. E. (1986). The prevalence of mitral valve prolapse in patients with panic disorder. *American Journal of Psychiatry, 143*(4), 511–515.

Liebowitz, M. R., Fyer, A. J., Gorman, J. M., Dillon, D., Appleby, I. L., Levy, G., Anderson, S., Levitt, M., Palij, M., Davies, S. O., & Klein, D. F. (1984). Lactate provocation of panic attacks. I. Clinical and behavioral findings. *Archives of General Psychiatry, 41,* 764–770.

Lindemann, C. G., Zitrin, C. M., & Klein, D. F. (1984). Thyroid dysfunction in phobic patients. *Psychosomatics, 25,* 603–606.

Locke, H. J., & Wallace, K. M. (1959). Marital-adjustment and prediction tests: Their reliability and validity. *Marriage and Family Living, 21,* 251–255.

Loevinger, J. (1957). Objective tests as instruments of psychological theory. *Psychological Reports, 3,* 635–694.

Loranger, A., Sussman, V., Oldham, J., & Russakoff, L. M. (1985). *Personality Disorder Examination (PDE): Directions.* Unpublished manuscript. New York Hospital-Cornell Medical Center, White Plains, NY.

McNally, R. J., & Lorenz, M. (1987). Anxiety sensitivity in agoraphobics. *Journal of Behavior Therapy and Experimental Psychiatry, 18,* 3–11.

Manger, W. M., & Gifford, R. W. (1982). Hypertension secondary to pheochromocytoma. *Bulletin of the New York Academy of Medicine, 58,* 139–158.

Margolin, G., Talovic, S., & Weinstein, C. D. (1983). Areas of Change Questionnaire: A practical approach to marital assessment. *Journal of Consulting and Clinical Psychology, 51,* 920–931.

Margraf, J., Ehlers, A., & Roth, W. T. (1988). Mitral valve prolapse and panic disorder: A review of their relationship. *Psychosomatic Medicine, 50,* 93–113.

Margraf, J., Taylor, C. B., Ehlers, A., Roth, W. T., & Agras, W. S. (1987). Panic attacks in the natural environment. *Journal of Nervous and Mental Disease, 175,* 558–565.

Marks, I. (1969). *Fears and phobias.* New York: Academic Press.

Marks, I. (1981). Space "phobia": A pseudoagoraphobic syndrome. *Journal of Neurology, Neurosurgery and Psychiatry, 44,* 387–391.

Marks, I. (1987). *Fears, phobias, and rituals.* New York: Oxford University Press.

Marks, I. M., & Bebbington, P. (1976). Space phobia: Syndrome or agoraphobic variant? *British Medical Journal, 2,* 345–347.

Marks, I. M., & Mathews, A. M. (1979). Brief standard self-rating for phobic patients. *Behaviour Research and Therapy, 17,* 263–267.

Mathews, A. M., Gelder, M. G., & Johnston, D. W. (1981). *Agoraphobia: Nature and treatment.* New York: Guilford Press.

Matuzas, W., Al-Sadir, J., Uhlenhuth, E. H., & Glass, R. M. (1987). Mitral valve prolapse and thyroid abnormalities in patients with panic attacks. *American Journal of Psychiatry, 144,* 493–496.

Mavissakalian, M. (1986). The fear questionnaire: A validity study. *Behaviour Research and Therapy, 24,* 83–85.

Mavissakalian, M. (1987). Trimodal assessment in agoraphobia research: Further observations on heart rate and synchrony/desynchrony. *Journal of Psychopathology and Behavioral Assessment, 9*(1), 89–98.

Mavissakalian, M., & Hamann, M. S. (1986). Assessment and significance of behavioral avoidance in agoraphobia. *Journal of Psychopathology and Behavioral Assessment, 8,* 317–327.

Mavissakalian, M., & Michelson, L. (1982). Patterns of psychophysiological change in the treatment of agoraphobia. *Behaviour Research and Therapy, 20,* 347–356.

Mavissakalian, M., Salerni, R., Thompson, M. E., & Michelson, L. (1983). Mitral valve prolapse and agoraphobia. *American Journal of Psychiatry, 140*(12), 1612–1614.

Mazza, D. L., Martin, D., Spacavento, L., Jacobsen, J., & Gibbs, H. (1986). Prevalence of anxiety disorders in patients with mitral valve prolapse. *American Journal of Psychiatry, 143*(3), 349–352.

Meehl, P. E. (1986). Diagnostic taxa as open concepts: Meta-theoretical and statistical questions about reliability and construct validity in the grand strategy of nosological revision. In T. Millon and G. L. Klerman (Eds.), *Contemporary directions in psychopathology: Toward the DSM-IV*. New York: Guilford Press.

Melges, F. T. (1982). *Time and inner future: A temporal approach to psychiatric disorders*. New York: Wiley.

Mellman, T. A., & Uhde, T. W. (1987). Obsessive-compulsive symptoms in panic disorder. *American Journal of Psychiatry, 144*(12), 1573–1576.

Mezzich, J. E., Dow, J. T., Rich, C. L., Costello, A. J., & Himmelhoch, J. M. (1981). Developing an efficient clinical information system for a comprehensive psychiatric institute: II. Initial Evaluation Form. *Behavior Research Methods and Instrumentation, 13*, 464–478.

Michelson, L. (1986). Treatment consonance and response profiles in agoraphobia: The role of individual differences in cognitive, behavioral and physiological treatments. *Behaviour Research and Therapy, 24*, 263–275.

Michelson, L. (1987). Cognitive-behavioral assessment and treatment of agoraphobia. In L. Michelson & L. M. Ascher (Eds.), *Anxiety and stress disorders: Cognitive-behavioral assessment and treatment*. New York: Guilford Press.

Michelson, L., & Mavissakalian, M. (1983). Temporal stability of self-report measures in agoraphobia research. *Behaviour Research and Therapy, 21*, 695–698.

Michelson, L., Mavissakalian, M., & Marchione, K. (1985). Cognitive and behavioral treatments of agoraphobia: Clinical, behavioral and psychophysiological outcomes. *Journal of Consulting and Clinical Psychology, 53*, 913–925.

Millon, T. (1983). *Millon Clinical Multiaxial Inventory manual* (3rd ed.). Minneapolis, MN: National Computer Service.

Mischel, W. (1968). *Personality assessment*. New York: Wiley.

Mizes, J. S., & Crawford, J. (1986). Normative values on the Marks and Mathews Fear Questionnaire: A comparison as a function of age and sex. *Journal of Psychopathology and Behavioral Assessment, 8*, 253–262.

Moran, C. (1986). Depersonalization and agoraphobia associated with marijuana use. *British Journal of Medical Psychology, 589*, 187–196.

Neill, W. A., & Hattenhauer, M. (1975). Impairment of myocardial O_2 supply due to hyperventilation. *Circulation, 52*, 854–858.

Norton, G. R., Harrison, B., Hauch, J., & Rhodes, L. (1985). Characteristics of people with infrequent panic attacks. *Journal of Abnormal Psychology, 94*, 216–221.

Noyes, R., Clancy, J., Hoenk, P. R., & Slymen, D. J. (1978). Anxiety neurosis and physical illness. *Comprehensive Psychiatry, 19*, 407–413.

O'Brien, G. T., & Barlow, D. H. (1984). Agoraphobia. In S. M. Turner (Ed.), *Behavioral theories and treatment of anxiety*. New York: Plenum.

Oei, T. P., Cavallo, G., & Evans, L. (1987). Utility of Fear Survey Schedule with an Australian sample of anxiety disorders patients. *Journal of Behavior Therapy and Experimental Psychiatry, 18*, 329–336.

O'Leary, K. D., Fincham, F., & Turkewitz, H. (1983). Assessment of positive feelings toward spouse. *Journal of Consulting and Clinical Psychology, 51*, 949–951.

Orne, M. T. (1962). On the social psychology of the psychological experiment: With particular reference to demand characteristics and their implications. *American Psychologist, 17*, 776–783.

Öst, L. G. (1987). Age of onset in different phobias. *Journal of Abnormal Psychology, 96*, 223–229.

Öst, L. G., Jerremalm, A., & Jansson, L. (1984). Individual response patterns and the effects of different behavioral methods in the treatment of agoraphobia. *Behaviour Research and Therapy, 22,* 697–707.

Öst, L. G., Jerremalm, A., & Johansson, J. (1981). Individual response patterns and the effects of different behavioral methods in the treatment of social phobia. *Behaviour Research and Therapy, 19,* 1–16.

Pariser, S. F., Jones, B. A., Pinta, E. R., Young, E. A., & Fontana, M. E. (1979). Panic attacks: Diagnostic evaluations of 17 patients. *American Journal of Psychiatry, 136*(1), 105–106.

Pariser, S. F., Pinta, E. R., & Jones, B. A. (1978). Mitral valve prolapse syndrome and anxiety neurosis/panic disorder. *American Journal of Psychiatry, 135*(2), 246–247.

Permutt, M. A. (1976). Postprandial hypoglycemia. *Diabetes, 25,* 719–733.

Permutt, M. A. (1980). Is it really hypoglycemia? If so, what should you do? *Medical Times, 108,* 35–43.

Peterson, R. A., & Heilbronner, R. L. (1987). The Anxiety Sensitivity Index: Construct validity and factor analytic structure. *Journal of Anxiety Disorders, 1,* 117–121.

Pfohl, B., Stangl, D., & Zimmerman, M. (1983). *Structured Interview for DSM-III Personality Disorders, SIDP* (2nd ed.). Unpublished manual, University of Iowa College of Medicine, Iowa City, IA.

Pratt, R. T. C., & McKenzie, W. (1958). Anxiety states following vestibular disorders. *Lancet, 2,* 347–349.

Rachman, S. (1988). Panics and their consequences: A review and prospect. In S. Rachman & J. D. Maser (Eds.), *Panic: Psychological perspectives.* Hillsdale, NJ: Lawrence Erlbaum.

Rachman, S., & Hodgson, R. (1974). I. Synchrony and desynchrony in fear and avoidance. *Behaviour Research and Therapy, 12,* 311–318.

Rachman, S., Lopatka, C., & Levitt, K. (1988). Experimental analyses of panic—II. Panic patients. *Behaviour Research and Therapy, 26,* 33–40.

Raj, A., & Sheehan, D. V. (1987). Medical evaluation of panic attacks. *Journal of Clinical Psychiatry, 48,* 309–313.

Regier, D. A., Myers, J. K., Kramer, M., Robins, L. N., Blazer, D. G., Hough, R. L., Eaton, W. W., & Locke, B. Z. (1984). The NIMH epidemiologic catchment area program: Historical context, major objectives, and study population characteristics. *Archives of General Psychiatry, 41,* 934–941.

Reich, J., Noyes, R., Jr., & Troughton, E. (1987). Dependent personality disorder associated with phobic avoidance in patients with panic disorder. *American Journal of Psychiatry, 144*(3), 323–326.

Reiss, S., Peterson, R. A., Gursky, D. M., & McNally, R. J. (1986). Anxiety sensitivity, anxiety frequency, and the prediction of fearfulness. *Behaviour Research and Therapy, 24,* 1–8.

Riskind, J. H., Beck, A. T., Berchick, R. J., Brown, G., & Steer, R. A. (1987). Reliability of DSM-III diagnoses for major depression and generalized anxiety disorder using the structured clinical interview for DSM-III. *Archives of General Psychiatry, 44,* 817–820.

Riskind, J. H., Beck, A. T., Brown, G., & Steer, R. A. (1987). Taking the measure of anxiety and depression. Validity of the Reconstructed Hamilton Scales. *The Journal of Nervous and Mental Disease, 175*(8), 474–479.

Robins, L. N., Helzer, J. E., Croughan, J., & Ratcliff, K. S. (1987). National Institute of Mental Health Diagnostic Interview Schedule: Its history, characteristics and validity. *Archives of General Psychiatry, 38*, 381–389.

Rosenberg, M. J. (1965). When dissonance fails: On eliminating evaluation apprehension from attitude measurement. *Journal of Personality and Social Psychology, 1*, 28–42.

Roth, M., & Mountjoy, C. Q. (1982). The distinction between anxiety states and depressive disorders. In E. S. Paykel, *Handbook of affective disorders* (pp. 70–91). New York: Guilford Press.

Roth, W. T., Telch, M. J., Taylor, C. B., Sanchitano, J. A., Gallen, C. C., Kopell, M. L., McClenahan, K. L., Agras, W. S., & Pfefferbaum, A. (1986). Autonomic characteristics of agoraphobia with panic attacks. *Biological Psychiatry, 21*, 1133–1154.

Salge, R. A., Beck, J. G., & Logan, A. C. (1988). A community survey of panic. *Journal of Anxiety Disorders, 2*, 157–167.

Schwartz, R. M., & Michelson, L. (1987). State-of-mind model: Cognitive balance in the treatment of agoraphobia. *Journal of Consulting and Clinical Psychology, 4*, 557–565.

Schweizer, E., Winokur, A., & Rickels, K. (1986). Insulin-induced hypoglycemia and panic attacks. *American Journal of Psychiatry, 143*(5), 654–655.

Sevin, B. H. (1987). Mitral valve prolapse, panic states, and anxiety. A dilemma in perspective. *Psychiatric Clinics of North America, 10*, 141–150.

Shapiro, D. (1965). *Neurotic Styles*. New York: Basic Books.

Sharpley, C. F., & Cross, D. G. (1982). A psychometric evaluation of the Spanier Dyadic Adjustment Scale. *Journal of Marriage and the Family, 44*, 739–741.

Shear, M. K. (1988, June). *Panic disorder and mitral valve prolapse*. Paper presented at the scientific session of the Academy for Behavioral Medicine Research, Hidden Valley, PA.

Shear, M. K., Devereux, R. B., Kramer-Fox, R., Mann, J. J., & Frances, A. (1984). Low prevalence of mitral valve prolapse in patients with panic disorder. *American Journal of Psychiatry, 141*(2), 302–303.

Shear, M. K., Kligfield, P., Harshfield, G., Devereux, R. B., Polan, J. J., Mann, J. J., Pickering, T., & Frances, A. J. (1987). Cardiac rate and rhythm in panic patients. *American Journal of Psychiatry, 144*(5), 633–637.

Shear, M. K., Polan, J. J., Harshfield, G., Pickering, T., Mann, J. J., Frances, A., & James, G. *Ambulatory monitoring of blood pressure and heart rate in panic patients*. Unpublished manuscript.

Snyder, D. K., Wills, R. M., & Keiser, T. W. (1981). Empirical validation of the Marital Satisfaction Inventory: An actuarial approach. *Journal of Consulting and Clinical Psychology, 49*, 262–268.

Sokolow, M., & Massie, B. (1988). Heart and great vessels. In S. A. Schroeder, M. A. Krupp, L. M. Tierny et al. (Eds.), *Current medical diagnosis and treatment, 1988*. Norwalk, CT: Appleton & Lange.

Spanier, G. B. (1979). The measurement of marital quality. *Journal of Sex and Marital Therapy, 5*, 288–300.

Spanier, G. B., & Lewis, R. A. (1980). Marital quality: A review of the seventies. *Journal of Marriage and the Family, 42*, 825–839.

Spanier, G. B., & Thompson, L. (1982). A confirmatory analysis of the Dyadic Adjustment Scale. *Journal of Marriage and the Family, 44*, 731–738.

Spielberger, C. D., Edwards, C. D., Luchene, R. E., Montuori, J., & Platzek, D. (1973). *State-Trait Anxiety Inventory for Children*. Palo Alto, CA: Consulting Psychologists Press.

Spielberger, C. D., Gorsuch, R. R., & Lushene, R. E. (1970). *State-Trait Anxiety Inventory test manual for form X*. Palo Alto, CA: Consulting Psychologists Press.

Spitzer, R. L. (1988, May). *The diagnosis of panic disorder*. Paper presented at the 141st Annual Meeting of the American Psychiatric Association, Montreal, Canada (Symposium IS11).

Spitzer, R. L., Williams, J. B. W., & Gibbon, M. (1988). *Structured Clinical Interview for DSM-III-R*. Biometrics Research Department, New York State Psychiatric Institute, 722 West 168th Street, New York, NY 10032.

Starkman, M. N., Zelnik, T. C., Nesse, R. M., & Cameron, O. G. (1985). Anxiety in patients with pheochromocytomas. *Archives of Internal Medicine, 145*, 248–252.

Stein, M. B. (1986). Panic disorder and medical illness. *Psychosomatics, 27*, 833–838.

Stein, M. B., Mellman, T. A., Roy-Byrne, P. P., Post, R. M., & Uhde, T. W. (1988, May). *EEG abnormalities in panic disorder*. Paper presented at the Biological Psychiatry Meeting, Montreal, Canada.

Stein, M. B., & Uhde, T. W. (1988). Thyroid indices in panic disorder. *American Journal of Psychiatry, 145*, 745–747.

Taylor, C. B., Sheikh, J., Agras, W. S., Roth, W. T., Margraf, J., Ehlers, A., Maddock, R. J., & Gossard, D. (1986). Ambulatory heart rate changes in patients with panic attacks. *American Journal of Psychiatry, 143*(4), 478–482.

Taylor, C. B., Telch, M. J., & Hawick, D. (1983). Ambulatory heart rate changes during panic attacks. *Journal of Psychiatry Research, 17*, 261–266.

Taylor, D. C., & Lochery, M. (1987). Temporal lobe epilepsy: Origin and significance of simple and complex auras. *Journal of Neurology, Neurosurgery, and Psychiatry, 50*, 673–681.

Taylor, J. A. (1953). A personality scale of manifest anxiety. *Journal of Abnormal and Social Psychology, 48*, 285–290.

Tedeschi, J. T., & Lindskold, S. (1976). *Social psychology: Interdependence, interaction, and influence*. New York: Wiley.

Tellegen, A. (1985). Structures of mood and personality and their relevance to assessing anxiety, with an emphasis on self-report. In A. H. Tuma & J. D. Maser (Eds.), *Anxiety and the anxiety disorders*. Hillsdale, NJ: Lawrence Erlbaum.

Theunissen, E. M. J., Huygen, P. L. M., & Folgering, H. T. (1986). Vestibular hyperreactivity and hyperventilation. *Clinical Otolaryngology, 11*(3), 161–169.

Thyer, B. A., Parrish, R. T., Himle, J., Cameron, O. G., Curtis, G. C., & Nesse, R. M. (1986). Alcohol abuse among clinically anxious patients. *Behaviour Research and Therapy, 24*(3), 357–359.

Trzepacz, P. T., McCue, M., Klein, I., Levey, G. S., & Greenhouse, J. A. (1988a). Psychiatric and neuropsychological study of patients with untreated Graves' disease. *General Hospital Psychiatry, 10*, 49–55.

Trzepacz, P. T., McCue, M., Klein, I., Greenhouse, J., & Levey, G. S. (1988b). Psychiatric and neuropsychological response to propranolol in Graves' disease. *Biological Psychiatry, 23*, 678–688.

Turner, S. M., & Beidel, D. C. (1989). Social phobia: Clinical syndrome, diagnosis and co-morbidity. *Clinical Psychology Review, 9*, 3–18.

Turner, S. M., Beidel, D. C., & Jacob, R. G. (1988). Assessment of panic. In S. Rachman & J. Maser (Eds.), *Panic: Psychological perspectives*. Hillsdale, NJ: Lawrence Erlbaum.

Uhde, T. W., Stein, M. B., & Post, R. M. (1988). Lack of efficacy of carbamazepine in the treatment of panic disorder. *American Journal of Psychiatry, 145*, 1104–1109.

Uhde, T. W., Vittone, B. J., & Post, R. M. (1984). Glucose tolerance testing in panic disorder. *American Journal of Psychiatry, 141*(11), 1461–1463.

Vandereycken, W. (1983). Agoraphobia and marital relationship: Theory, treatment, and research. *Clinical Psychology Review, 3*, 317–338.

Venkatesh, A., Pauls, D., Crow, R., Noyes, R., Van Valkenburg, C., Martins, J. B., & Kerber, R. E. (1980). Mitral valve prolapse in anxiety neurosis. *American Heart Journal, 100*, 302–305.

Vermilyea, J. A., Boice, R., & Barlow, D. H. (1984). Rachman and Hodgson (1974) a decade later: How do desynchronous response systems relate to the treatment of agoraphobia? *Behaviour Research and Therapy, 22*, 615–621.

Vittone, B. J., & Uhde, T. (1985). Differential diagnosis and treatment of panic disorder: A medical model perspective. *Australian and New Zealand Journal of Psychiatry, 19*, 330–341.

Volkow, N. D., Harper, A., & Swann, A. C. (1986). Temporal lobe abnormalities and panic attacks. *American Journal of Psychiatry, 143*(11), 1484–1485.

Waddell, M. T., Barlow, D. H., & O'Brien, G. T. (1984). A preliminary investigation of cognitive and relaxation treatment of panic disorder: Effects of intense anxiety vs. 'background' anxiety. *Behaviour Research and Therapy, 22*, 393–402.

Walk, R. D. (1956). Self-ratings of fear in fear-evoking situations. *Journal of Abnormal and Social Psychology, 52*, 171–178.

Weilburg, J. B., Bear, D. M., & Sachs, G. (1987). Three patients with concomitant panic attacks and seizure disorder: Possible clues to the neurology of anxiety. *American Journal of Psychiatry, 144*(8), 1053–1056.

Weilburg, J. B., Pollack, M., Murray, G. B., & Garber, H. J. (1986). On panic attacks and neurologic problems. *American Journal of Psychiatry, 143*(12), 1626–1627.

Weiss, R. L., & Margolin, G. (1986). Assessment of marital conflict and accord. In A. R. Ciminero, K. S. Calhoun, & H. E. Adams (Eds.), *Handbook of behavioral assessment* (2nd ed.). New York: Wiley.

Weissman, M. M. (1988, May). *The epidemiology of panic disorder and agoraphobia*. Paper presented at the 141st Annual Meeting of the American Psychiatric Association, Montreal, Canada.

Widiger, T. A., & Frances, A. (1987). Interviews and inventories for the measurement of personality disorders. *Clinical Psychology Review, 7*, 49–75.

Widiger, T. A., & Sanderson, C. (1987). The convergent and discriminant validity of the MCMI as a measure of the DSM-III personality disorders. *Journal of Personality Assessment, 51*, 228–242.

Williams, S. L. (1984). On the nature and measurement of agoraphobia. In M. Hersen, R. Eisler, & P. M. Miller (Eds.), *Progress in behavior modification*. New York: Academic Press.

Williams, S. L., & Rappoport, J. A. (1983). Cognitive treatment in the natural environment for agoraphobics. *Behavior Therapy, 14*, 299–313.

Winokur, G. W. (1988). Anxiety disorders: Relationship to other psychiatric illness. *Psychiatric Clinics of North America, 11*, 287–294.

Wittchen, H.-U., Semler, G., von Zerssen, D. (1985). A comparison of two diagnostic methods: Clinical ICD diagnoses vs. DSM-III and Research Diagnostic Criteria using the Diagnostic Interview Schedule (Version 2). *Archives of General Psychiatry, 42,* 677–684.

Wolpe, J., & Lang, P. S. (1964). A fear survey schedule for use in behaviour therapy. *Behaviour Research and Therapy, 2,* 27–30.

Yager, J., & Young, R. J. (1979). Nonhypoglycemia is an epidemic condition. *New England Journal of Medicine, 291,* 907–908.

Zanarini, M. C., Frankenburg, F. R., Chauncey, D. L., & Gunderson, J. G. (1987). The diagnostic interview for personality disorders: Inter-rater and test-retest reliability. *Comprehensive Psychiatry, 28,* 467–480.

Zuckerman, M. (1960). The development of an affect adjective checklist for the measurement of anxiety. *Journal of Consulting and Clinical Psychology, 24,* 457–462.

Zung, W. W. K. (1971). A rating instrument for anxiety disorders. *Psychosomatics, 12,* 371–379.

Zung, W. W. K. (1979). Assessment of anxiety disorder: Qualitative and quantitative approaches. In W. E. Fann, I. Karacan, A. D. Pokorny, & R. L. Williams (Eds.), *Phenomenology and treatment of anxiety.* New York: Spectrum.

CHAPTER 3

The Epidemiology of Panic Attacks, Panic Disorder, and Agoraphobia

HANS-ULRICH WITTCHEN AND CECILIA A. ESSAU

The Contribution of Epidemiological Data to Our Understanding of Panic Disorder

Epidemiology is the field of research that estimates the frequency of a disorder and studies its distribution in populations. Epidemiological data permit the analysis of factors, including risk factors, that determine the distribution of a disorder in different populations. These data can also be used to test specific hypotheses about the etiology of a disorder and its relationship to other mental and physical disorders. Prominent issues in the epidemiology of panic disorder include how specific certain symptoms are to the development of this disorder and how specific characteristics are related to its course and outcome.

The importance of epidemiology is particularly evident when we consider that only a fraction of persons affected by anxiety disorders are actually seen and treated in mental health settings. These treated samples are generally not representative of the entire population with anxiety disorders, because clinical services have specific selection processes for patients. In addition, patients in clinical settings tend to differ in their help-seeking behavior and in the symptomatology, chronicity, and comorbidity of their disorder. If we rely exclusively on studies in clinical settings, then our understanding of the disorder may be biased or severely limited. Epidemiological studies should be by definition representative and include both treated and untreated persons to obtain a true estimate of the prevalence of a disorder and to provide a comprehensive understanding of it.

Basic Concepts and Definitions in Epidemiology

Some basic epidemiologic concepts such as case, risk factor, and population at risk must be mastered to understand epidemiological data (Weissman, 1987). The term *case* denotes a disease, disorder, or symptom pertaining to a person within a defined population. Any condition that increases a person's likelihood of developing the disorder is termed a *risk factor. Population at risk* means the number of persons in the reference group who have a greater chance of experiencing the pathology being studied.

The quantitative unit that measures the frequency of a disorder and its association with other variables is termed the *rate*, which is the number of cases divided by the number of persons in the pool from which the cases are derived and the time within which the cases are obtained (Weissman, 1987). The *prevalence* of a disorder is the proportion of individuals ill in a given population. There are several types of prevalence; the most common are point, period, 6-month, and lifetime. *Point prevalence* is the proportion of individuals ill in a population at a given point in time. It helps to identify groups at high risk for having a disorder—whether because they have a higher rate of incidence, a greater chronicity, or both (Eaton et al., 1985). *Period prevalence* is the proportion of the population ill during a specific period of time. The concept is particularly useful for studying psychiatric disorders when the onset and termination of an episode are difficult to ascertain. *Six-month prevalence* specifies the presence of certain mental disorders within 6 months preceding the assessment period. *Lifetime prevalence* refers to the proportion of individuals in the population who have or have ever had the disorder up to the point of examination. *Incidence* is the rate of new cases of a disorder in the population during a specified period of time. *Morbid risk* is defined as the individual's lifetime risk of having a first episode of the disorder under study.

Special attention has to be paid to the definition of a case with a specific anxiety disorder and what diagnostic strategy seems most appropriate in establishing the presence of a disorder.

What Is a Case?

Epidemiological Considerations

A reliable assessment of symptoms and a reliable classification of the disorder to be assessed is a prerequisite for any clinical research. This is even more important—but also more difficult—in epidemiological research, because we frequently deal with less severe cases than are found in treated samples. Thus, it is more difficult to draw clear boundaries between "healthy" and "sick" individuals and between the disorder studied and other disorders. The need for reliable diagnostic criteria has become even more imperative with the development of pharmacological and psychological treatment methods that claim to be specific for different anxiety disorders (see Chapters 6 and 7). As Jablensky (1985) and Wittchen (1986) point out, clear and reliable diagnoses are difficult to make because the classification of anxiety disorders is still evolving. Furthermore, a number of studies have shown basic problems in the reliable assessment of anxiety disorders (Wittchen & Semler, 1986). These problems are reflected in the epidemiological literature, making the picture somewhat confusing at first sight.

A review of the literature on epidemiology reveals three approaches to classifying an anxiety disorder case. Broadly speaking, these approaches are

(1) the assignment of a *clinical diagnosis* to a subject by a psychiatrist (the clinical approach); (2) the use of a self-report questionnaire or interview to assess well-being or distress as well as symptoms or syndromes of anxiety (the dimensional approach); and (3) the administration of a standardized diagnostic interview (the categorical approach).

1.   The *clinical approach* has been used most frequently in European epidemiological studies (see, for example, Essen-Möller, 1956; Helgason, 1964). In these studies either the psychiatrist personally interviewed subjects in a population or a summary of interview responses was given to a psychiatrist, who subsequently assigned diagnoses.

2.   The *dimensional approach* is another method of surveying mental disorders in a general population that was frequently used before the 1980s. Items from self-administered pencil-and-paper tests (such as the Minnesota Multiphasic Personality Inventory or the SCL-90) or from general interviews or checklists (such as the Health Opinion Survey, the Health Interview Survey, and parts of the Psychiatric Epidemiological Research Interview) are used to assess symptomatology. These dimensional instruments are frequently designed for self-report or use by lay interviewers to save money and allow the accumulation of large samples. Many items and questions in these schedules are aimed at eliciting the symptomatology of broad classes of disorders (for example, anxiety or depression), whereas others are designed to elicit a general sense of distress and lack of well-being. Individuals reporting a high level of personal distress would be considered "cases." This method, however, does not allow the assignment of a clinical diagnosis. Consequently it does not permit us to answer specific questions about panic disorder or other anxiety diagnoses.

3.   The *categorical approach* favors standardization and the elimination of bias. As has been emphasized by many authors (for example, Regier et al., 1984), epidemiological data should be collected with instruments that can provide a specific set of criteria with a high degree of reliability and that allow the delineation of specific diagnoses. The development of these instruments in psychiatry is strongly linked to the recent introduction of specific diagnostic criteria and operationalized diagnoses. Several such instruments have been developed; they are based on either the Feighner Criteria (Feighner et al., 1972), the Research Diagnostic Criteria (RDC) (Spitzer, Endicott, & Robins, 1978), or the third edition of the Diagnostic and Statistical Manual of Mental Disorders (DSM-III) (American Psychiatric Association, 1980). Standard interviews used in the study of panic attacks and panic disorder are the structured Schedule for Affective Disorders and Schizophrenia (SADS) and, more recently, the fully structured Diagnostic Interview Schedule (DIS) (Robins, Helzer, Ratcliff, & Seyfried, 1982) as well as the Structured Clinical Interview (SCID) for the revised version of the DSM-III (DSM-III-R) (Spitzer & Williams, 1983). These interviews can considerably reduce the observer, information, and criterion variance that may result from using less standardized diagnostic

instruments. Furthermore, these newer methods promise to allow comparisons of results across different clinical and epidemiological studies when clinical interviewers are carefully trained and experienced in applying the instrument (Helzer et al., 1985; Wittchen, Semler, & von Zerssen, 1985). The assessment of panic attacks, panic disorder, and other phobic disorders (according to the DSM-III criteria) with these structured interviews has generally produced results with good reliability.

As the epidemiologic studies of anxiety disorders and panic attacks based on the DIS are reported repeatedly throughout this paper, we will give parts of the most relevant DIS questions to demonstrate the specificity of this approach (see Table 3.1). A major advantage of using the DIS in epidemiological settings is that it is highly structured and consequently may be administered by nonclinicians as well as clinicians (Helzer et al., 1985; Robins et al., 1982). This is important, because clinicians are both expensive and scarce when samples are large.

TABLE 3.1 "Operationalization" of Panic Disorder: Related Questions in the Diagnostic Interview Schedule

---

62. Have you ever had a spell or attack in which you suddenly felt frightened, anxious, or very uneasy in situations in which most people would not be afraid?
    A. Could you tell me about one spell or attack like that?
    B. Did a spell ever seem to come on for no particular reason—without anything having happened that seemed to explain it?
       RECENCY: When was the last time you had a spell that came on for no reason?
    C. Have you ever had such a bad spell that you had to do something about it—such as telephoning someone or leaving the room or house?
       RECENCY: When was the last time you had a spell that bad?
63. During one of your worst spells of suddenly feeling frightened or anxious or uneasy, did you ever notice that you had any of the following problems? During this spell,
    A. were you short of breath—having trouble catching your breath?
    B. did your heart pound?
    C. were you dizzy or lightheaded?
    D. did your fingers or feet tingle?
    E. did you have tightness or pain in your chest?
    F. did you feel as if you were choking or smothering?
    G. did you feel faint?
    H. did you sweat?
    I. did you tremble or shake?
    J. did you feel hot or cold flashes?
    K. did things around you seem unreal?
    L. were you afraid either that you might die or that you might act in a crazy way?
       RECENCY: When was the last time you (had/were SYMPTOM) during an attack or spell of feeling frightened or anxious?
64. How old were you the first time you had one of these sudden spells of feeling frightened or anxious?

65. Have you ever had three spells like this close together—say within a 3-week period?

RECENCY: Have you had three spells in 3 weeks since (MONTH/YEAR)?

SOURCE: Modified from Robins, L. N., Helzer, J. E., Croughan, J. et al. (1981). NIMH Diagnostic Interview Schedule, Version III. St. Louis, MO: Washington University School of Medicine.

Definition of Panic Attacks and Panic Disorder

An additional problem in the epidemiological literature arises from significant changes in the classification systems in the last decade that make it difficult to generalize findings across various studies unless the same diagnostic systems and instruments are used. For example, recent British or European studies typically use the ninth revision of the International Classification of Disease (ICD-9) (World Health Organization, 1978), but U.S. studies typically use the DSM-III and DSM-III-R. Because it seems unwise to discard all the old literature on this topic, it is important to clarify the concepts used in anxiety research "*before* the DSM-III burst on the world" (Marks, 1986, p. v). A review of the literature since 1920 reveals two heterogeneous groups of clinical syndromes and definitions for anxiety disorders. The first refers to a great variety of so-called phobias, phobic disorders, or phobic neuroses. Phobias (ICD-9, 300.2) are characterized by "external triggers" for the anxiety and avoidance behavior. The second group of anxiety problems can be characterized by the predominance of autonomic symptoms, as well as "anxiety-response-features" with an apparent lack of anxiety-provoking "external triggers." Disorders of this group have been described using terms such as *cardiac neurosis, effort syndrome, nervous exhaustion, neurasthenia,* or *neurocirculatory asthenia,* and are classified as anxiety neurosis in the ICD-9 (300.0). These terms describe the recurrent but chronic anxiety states that are characterized by symptoms such as dyspnea, palpitations, fatigue, and preoccupation with somatic states. This heterogeneous group of disorders includes features of DSM-III panic disorder and generalized anxiety disorder. Although a few authors discussed sub-typing (see Marks, 1986), further classification of anxiety disorders was not addressed in the major systems before 1980. The more differentiated classification of anxiety disorders has been addressed by the RDC (Spitzer et al., 1978), the DSM-III and the DSM-III-R (American Psychiatric Association, 1987). In addition, there is still considerable controversy (Jablensky, 1985; Hand & Wittchen, 1986) over whether agoraphobia with panic attacks is most appropriately classified with panic disorder, as suggested by the DSM-III-R, or with agoraphobia without a history of panic attacks.

Strongly influenced by the work of Klein (1967) and Sheehan (1982) on patients with recurrent anxiety states, the DSM-III-R broadly classifies anxiety disorders as *anxiety states* or *phobic disorders*. Anxiety states include specific definitions for panic disorder with or without agoraphobia, generalized anxiety disorder, obsessive-compulsive disorder, and post–traumatic stress disor-

der. Phobic disorder has specific definitions for agoraphobia without a history
of panic disorder, social phobia, and simple phobia (see Chapter 2). Table 3.2
summarizes the changes in the classification systems from ICD-8/9 to the
DSM-III and DSM-III-R.

TABLE 3.2 Changes in the Classification Systems from the ICD-8/9 to the DSM-III and
DSM-III-R

ICD-8/9	DSM-III	DSM-III-R
Anxiety neurosis (300.0)	Panic disorder	Panic disorder without agoraphobia
	Generalized anxiety disorder	Generalized anxiety disorder
Phobia (300.2)	Agoraphobia with panic attacks	Panic disorder with agoraphobia
	Agoraphobia without panic attacks	Agoraphobia without history of panic disorder[a]
	Simple phobia	Simple phobia
	Social phobia	Social phobia

[a] Subtype classification is possible.

An important change took place between the publication of the DSM-III
and the DSM-III-R. In the latter, the concept of panic disorder was enlarged
by including those disorders that were classified in DSM-III under agoraphobia *with* panic attacks. Thus, the diagnosis of agoraphobia is now almost solely
a residual category for those cases who have never experienced a panic
attack–related anticipatory anxiety reaction. This decision was based on the
assumption that agoraphobic symptoms are frequently only a secondary
complication of panic attacks. This typical course of the disorder is reflected
in the DSM-III-R classification, in which different degrees of phobic avoidance
are grouped as subtypes of panic disorder. Cases of agoraphobia that do not
develop agoraphobia secondary to panic disorder are diagnosed as agoraphobia without history of panic disorder.

The "symptom progression model" (Klein, 1981; Goldberg, 1982), which
emphasized the importance of the initial occurrence of spontaneous panic
attacks in the development of agoraphobia, has not been clearly supported by
recent epidemiological data. Studies by Weissman, Leaf, Holzer, and
Merikangas (1985) and by Wittchen (1986) could only partially confirm that
hypothesis. Basing their evidence on the DIS age-of-onset question, these
authors found that only a small proportion of the subjects who had at least
one panic attack *and* agoraphobia reported the occurrence of panic attacks
before the onset of agoraphobia. In addition, the key role of panic as a "tracer
condition" for agoraphobia was not confirmed, because 50% of all subjects
with agoraphobia had never experienced either panic attack–like states or the
full-blown panic disorder. These data were interpreted as supporting the view

that agoraphobia is a distinct entity that should not be subsumed under panic disorder.

How Prevalent Are Panic Disorder and Panic Attacks in the Population?

Prevalence of Panic Disorder and Other Anxiety Disorders

When considering *all* studies of anxiety disorders—both older and more recent ones—it seems at first glance that there is considerable variation in the prevalence of anxiety disorders in general and of panic disorder in particular (see Table 3.3). However, a closer examination reveals a surprisingly high concordance. Differences in the studies' designs, settings, and methodologies account for most of the variation. As can be seen from Table 3.3, (1) the more recent findings display less variation than earlier ones, and (2) the 6-month and lifetime prevalence rates in the more recent studies are consistently higher. As most of the more recent epidemiological studies on panic attacks and panic disorder have used the DIS as a case-finding instrument, we would like to discuss the findings revealed by it in more detail.

The largest study of its kind ever conducted was the Epidemiological Catchment Area (ECA) Study using the DIS. The ECA survey was conducted in five sites in the United States (New Haven, Baltimore, St. Louis, Durham, and Los Angeles) to investigate the prevalence and incidence of specific disorders in the general population. In each site, adults aged 18 and older were sampled according to a complex survey design. The total sample size for the ECA Study was 18,572, the sample at each site ranging from 3004 to 5035 subjects. Published results on anxiety disorders from four (New Haven, Baltimore, St. Louis, and Los Angeles) of the five sites showed surprisingly similar rates for panic disorder, with lifetime prevalence rates ranging between 1.4% and 1.5% (Karno et al., 1987; Robins et al., 1984). The prevalence rates for phobic disorder (including agoraphobia, social phobia, and simple phobia) were also rather similar across the sites, except in Baltimore, where a much higher rate was found. No clear explanation has been provided for Baltimore's higher rate of phobic disorder. As were the lifetime rates, the 6-month rates for each specific anxiety disorder were rather evenly distributed across the four sites—excepting again phobic disorder in Baltimore (Burnam et al., 1987; Myers et al., 1984). The prevalence rates of each anxiety disorder across the ECA sites are presented in Table 3.3. The Munich Follow-Up Study (MFS), a study comparable to the ECA study though much smaller (N = 1366), was conducted in 1981 (Wittchen & von Zerssen, 1988). In the MFS, a community survey across West Germany, the lifetime prevalence of DIS/DSM-III anxiety disorders found in adults between the ages of 24 and 64 years was 13.9%. The lifetime rate for panic disorder was 2.4%; for agoraphobia, 5.7%; for simple phobia, 8.0%; and for obsessive-compulsive disorder, 2.0%

TABLE 3.3 Prevalence of Anxiety Disorders and Syndromes in the Community

	Agras et al.	Weismann & Myers	Dean et al.	Costello	Bebbington et al.	Uhlenhuth	Angst & Dobler-Mikola	Wittchen et al.	ECA				Wittchen	Canino et al.	Bland et al.
									St. Louis	Balti-more	New Haven	Los Angeles			
	1969	1980[b]	1983[c]	1982[c]	1982	1983[c]	1985[e]	1988					1986	1987	1988
Prevalence period	Point	Point	1-mth	1-yr	1-mth	1-yr	1-yr	6-mth (life)	6-mth (life)	6-mth (life)	6-mth (life)	6-mth (life)	6-mth (life)	6-mth (life)	6-mth (life)
N	325	511	576	449	800	3161	456	115 (131)	3004	3481	3058	3125	1504	1513	3258
Methods		RDC	RDC	PSE	PSE	DSM-III	DSM-III	ICD-9	DIS	DIS	DIS	DIS	DIS	DIS	DIS
G.A.D.		2.5	2.6		7.6[d]	6.4	5.2								
Panic disorder		0.4	0.7				3.1		0.9 (1.5)	1.0 (1.4)	0.6 (1.4)	0.9 (1.5)	1.1 (2.4)	1.1 (1.7)	0.7 (1.2)
Phobic disorder	7.7[a]	1.4		19.0a				4.8 (6.4)	5.4 (9.4)	13.4 (23.3)	5.9 (7.8)	6.3 (11.7)		6.3 (12.2)	5.1 (8.9)
Agoraphobia +/− panic	0.6				0.2	1.2	2.5		2.7 (3.9)	5.8	2.8 (3.5)		3.6 (5.7)	3.9 (6.9)	(2.9)
Social phobia							1.1		1.2	2.2				1.1 (1.6)	(1.7)
Simple phobia							3.7		4.5 (7.7)	11.8	4.7 (6.2)		4.1 (8.0)	4.4 (8.6)	(7.2)
Other phobia						2.3	1.2								1.6
Obsessive-compulsive disorder					0.0			0.5 (1.1)	1.3 (1.9)	2.0 (3.0)	1.4 (2.6)	0.7 (2.1)	1.8 (2.0)	1.8 (3.2)	(3.0)
Anxiety neurosis								1.3 (2.5)							

Note: Rates are given as percentages; numbers in brackets are lifetime prevalence rates. a = phobic symptoms, b = definite and probable diagnoses are combined in these rates, c = women only, d= including mild symptoms, e = syndromes. Methods used: RDC = Research Diagnostic Criteria, PSE = Present State Examination, ICD-9 = International Classification of Disease—9th rev, DSM-III = Diagnostic and Statistical Manual of Mental Disorders—3rd ed., DIS = Diagnostic Interview Schedule

(Wittchen, 1986). The 6-month prevalence for anxiety disorders was slightly lower than the lifetime rates. Wittchen's findings (1986) for anxiety disorders and panic disorder specifically were not significantly different from those of the ECA, both before and after adjusting for some minor age differences and controlling for race distribution (Wittchen & Burke, in preparation). The adjusted ECA overall results (New Haven, Baltimore, St. Louis, Durham, and Los Angeles) for the lifetime rate of anxiety disorders was 15.1%; of panic disorder, 2.1%; of simple phobia, 9.3%; of agoraphobia, 4.8%; and of obsessive-compulsive disorder, 3.1%. In addition, no differences were found between the MFS and the adjusted ECA for 6-month prevalence.

A study similar to these two was carried out in Edmonton, Canada. The lifetime prevalence of panic disorder, which was also assessed by the DIS, was 1.2%; of agoraphobia, 2.9%; of social phobia, 1.7%; and of simple phobia, 7.2% (Bland, Orn, & Newman, 1988). The 6-month rates for panic and phobic disorders were 0.7% and 5.1%, respectively (Bland, Newman, & Orn, 1988b).

Similar findings with regard to the frequency of panic disorder were reported for Hispanic populations in Puerto Rico and for a subsample of the ECA, the Los Angeles site. The Puerto Rico study (Canino et al., 1987) was conducted during the spring and fall of 1984, using a Spanish translation of the DIS. In this study, which involved 1513 subjects, aged 18 to 64 years, Canino et al. reported the lifetime prevalence of anxiety disorders to be 13.6%. Of all the phobic disorders, simple phobia had the highest rate (4.4%), followed by agoraphobia (3.9%). The lifetime rate for panic disorder was 1.7%, and the 6-month rate was 1.1%. The 6-month rates for phobic disorders resembled the lifetime rates in that simple phobia had the highest rate, followed by agoraphobia (6.9%).

In summary, a high consistency in prevalence rates has been found not only across sites in the same culture, but also across different cultures among studies that used proper epidemiological sampling procedures and the same case-finding instrument. Panic disorder occurs in adults with a lifetime prevalence of about 2% and with a 6-month prevalence of about 1.2%. Agoraphobia, which is conceptually and clinically linked to panic disorder, is more common, with a lifetime prevalence of about 5% and a 6-month prevalence of approximately 4%.

The purpose of the rest of this section is to compare the foregoing findings (using the DIS) with those of studies that were based on other case-finding methods or on the ICD-9 class of anxiety neurosis.

In a much-cited earlier interview survey of a general population in Greater Burlington, Vermont, the overall prevalence of phobias was 7.7% (Agras, Sylvester, & Oliveau, 1969). Subjects who had high scores on a Fear Inventory were then reinterviewed by a psychiatrist, who made a diagnosis for phobic neurosis based on the DSM-I criteria. Of the cases with a diagnosis of phobia (7.7% prevalence), most were considered to have a mildly disabling illness (7.5%); very few were regarded as severely disabled (0.2%). Common types of phobias reported by these subjects included illness or injury, storm, and animal phobias. The rate for agoraphobia was 0.6%. However, no specific prevalence for panic disorder or panic attacks was reported.

Another interesting group of studies used the Present State Examination (PSE) (Wing, Cooper, & Sartorious, 1974). The PSE allows us to define a symptom index that can be used in conjunction with a severity index (index of definition) as a case-finding method. Thus, it permits us to relate the resulting syndrome profile to the ICD-9 diagnostic classification. Several studies use this approach (Bebbington, Contractor, Hurry, & Tennant, 1982; Costello, 1982; Dean, Surtees, & Sashidharan, 1983).

In a community survey of 800 residents of Camberwell, London, Bebbington et al. (1982) reported that the 1-month prevalence of anxiety disorders was 2.9%. However, the rate for general anxiety symptoms (including symptoms of a panic attack) was higher: 7.6%. Severe agoraphobia with avoidance was found in only 0.2% and agoraphobic symptoms in 17.4%. Although the authors did not find any social phobia with avoidance, social unease was found in 16.3%. Likewise, no case of severe obsessive-compulsive disorder with avoidance was identified, but obsessive-compulsive symptoms were found in 10.8%.

Costello (1982) examined the prevalence of fears and phobias among 449 Canadian women between the ages of 18 and 65. All were interviewed using the shortened form of the ninth edition of the PSE. Costello found the overall prevalence for phobic symptoms to be 19%. The total prevalence of mild fear was 0.64%; of mild fear plus avoidance, 0.36%; of intense fear, 0.24%; and of intense fear plus avoidance, 0.19%. The prevalence of various types of fear, regardless of their intensity, were as follows: separation anxiety, 0.13%; fear of animals, 0.43%; fear of mutilation, 0.21%; social anxiety, 0.29%, and fear of nature, 0.41%.

Dean and colleagues (1983) compared the prevalence of anxiety disorders using four different diagnostic systems (Catego/ICD-8, RDC, Bedford College Checklist, and Feighner Criteria) in a community sample in Edinburgh. In this study 576 women between the ages of 18 and 65 were interviewed. The prevalence of anxiety neurosis according to the Catego/ICD-8 was 0.5% and that of phobic neurosis 2.3%. Based on the RDC, the rate for generalized anxiety disorder was 2.6% and for panic disorder, 0.7%.

Epidemiological data on anxiety disorders, based on either RDC or DSM-III criteria, are available from two community studies conducted in the United States (the New Haven Survey and the National Survey of Psychotherapeutic Drug Use) and from Zurich, Switzerland (the Zurich Study).

The New Haven Survey was a community survey of persons living in the New Haven, Connecticut, area in 1975 and 1976. A total of 511 adults were interviewed by clinically trained persons using the SADS—lifetime version (Weissman & Myers, 1980) which is a structured interview guide that records information on the subjects' functioning and symptomatology. The *current* prevalence for generalized anxiety was 2.5%; for phobic disorder, 1.4%; and for panic disorder, 0.4%. Another important finding of this study was that, according to the RDC, anxiety disorders overlapped among themselves and also with depression (Weissman & Merikangas, 1986). Over 80% of the subjects who received the diagnosis of generalized anxiety disorder have had at least one other anxiety disorder. Of all those with phobias, 30% had experienced panic disorder at some time in their life. With respect to the comorbidity between anxiety disorders and major depression, 7% of those with generalized anxiety disorder, 2% with panic disorder, and 4% with phobia had had major depression at least once in their lifetime.

The National Survey of Psychotherapeutic Drug Use took place in 1979, primarily to investigate the prevalence and patterns of psychotherapeutic prescription drug use among noninstitutionalized American adults aged 18 to 79 years (Uhlenhuth, Balter, Mellinger, Cisin, & Clinthorpe, 1983). The survey elicited a variety of common psychological symptoms, using a modified version of the Hopkins Symptom Checklist. The checklist has a number of scales, including scales for anxious mood and panic phobia. Diagnoses were assigned, using algorithms, that were similar to the DSM-III criteria for several mutually exclusive diagnostic groups. The overall 1-year prevalence of the agoraphobia-panic syndrome was 1.2%, women's rates being more than three times higher than men's. The prevalence of this syndrome increased slightly with age. The prevalence of other phobic syndromes was 2.3%, again with higher rates for females than for males. Furthermore, these phobic syndromes tended to be most predominant among subjects under 35 years old. The rate for generalized anxiety was 6.4%.

The Zurich Study was conducted in Switzerland in 1978 and included a sample of 2201 males and 2346 females, 19 and 20 years of age (Angst & Dobler-Mikola, 1985). Of these subjects, about 50% completed the SCL-90. Based on their total scores on the SCL-90 (either high or low scores), 10% of the total sample was chosen to participate in a prospective interview study. The DSM-III diagnoses were derived from both the checklist and the structured interview. Within a year of screening, a total of 220 males and 236 females participated in a structured interview. The 1-year prevalence of various anxiety syndromes was general anxiety, 5.2%; panic, 3.1%; simple phobia, 3.7%; social phobia, 1.1%; and agoraphobia, 2.5%.

Epidemiological studies based on the ICD-9 category of anxiety neurosis generally are consistent with the findings of the prevalence of panic disorder. Two examples of such studies include the MFS (Wittchen et al., 1988) and the so-called Traunstein study (Dilling & Weyerer, 1984), both of which took place in Germany. Within the 7-year MFS that is also reported in Table 3.3 for the DIS/DSM-III findings, Wittchen et al. (1988) reported that the lifetime prevalence of anxiety neurosis was 2.5% and the 6-month prevalence was 1.3%. The lifetime rate for phobic neurosis was 6.4% and the 6-month rate was 4.8%. The diagnosis for anxiety neurosis was based on ICD-9, applied by a clinical psychiatrist using a structured checklist (Wittchen et al., 1985). Among the subjects of Upper Bavaria (the Traunstein study), Dilling and Weyerer (1984) reported a 6-month prevalence rate of anxiety neurosis of 2.1% in the first wave of the study.

So far no clear evidence of the frequency of panic disorder and agoraphobia in clinical settings, such as in general practitioners' offices and medical institutions, can be reported. However, based on the earlier studies reviewed by Marks (1986), it can be expected that a two- to fivefold higher prevalence of panic disorder can be found in primary care settings or in more specialized settings where patients with cardiac complaints come for advice and help.

Prevalence of Panic Attacks

Although there is convincing evidence that panic disorder is rather rare (lifetime prevalence 2%, current 1%), at least according to the DSM-III, there is a general consensus that *panic attacks* are common. Nevertheless, under the new definition of panic disorder (based on the DSM-III-R) this prevalence would change, because all subjects previously classified as having agoraphobia with panic attacks would be reclassified under panic disorder; this change would increase the lifetime prevalence to about 4% and the current prevalence to about 2%. Recent research has shown that panic attacks are not specific to panic disorder, because they occur across a wide range of other psychological disorders and in nonclinical populations (Margraf & Ehlers, 1988). Barlow et al. (1985), for example, found in a study of 108 patients with different anxiety and affective disorders that about 80% reported having had at least one panic attack. Although the frequency of attacks varied across diagnoses, only a few differences in symptom patterns associated with the attacks were found. Furthermore, symptom severity was similar for patients with situational and spontaneous attacks.

Comparable results were found by Wittchen and Burke (in preparation) in a study of the specificity of panic attacks in a wide range of former psychiatric inpatients with diagnoses of psychotic disorder (N = 58), affective disorders (N = 60), and neurotic disorders (N = 76). In all groups panic attacks were rather frequent, with rates ranging from 48% (affective disorders) to 80% (schizoaffective disorder, N = 26). Although the context in which panic attacks occur in other mental disorders and their severity *seems* to be different, the specific characteristics of panic attacks in other disorders has not yet been explored sufficiently to draw any conclusions. If panic attacks are not specific to individuals with panic disorder, it is important to study the distribution of this phenomenon in the general population. Only a few detailed attempts to do so have been made. One is the study by Von Korff, Eaton, and Keyl (1983). Based on the ECA data, they found panic attacks to be quite common, with a 6-month prevalence rate of 3%, somewhat more than 1.5% of whom reported severe and recurrent attacks. The 6-month prevalence of DSM-III panic disorder varied from 0.6% to 1.0%.

Another approach to studying the distribution of panic attacks in the general population is to use questionnaire screening methods. Norton and his colleagues (Norton, Harrison, Hauch, & Rhodes, 1985; Norton, Dorward, & Cox, 1986) in Winnipeg, Canada, initiated this line of research. In their first study, Norton et al. (1985) had 186 undergraduate students complete two self-report questionnaires, the Hopkins Symptom Checklist and a specially designed Anxiety Questionnaire. The Anxiety Questionnaire asked subjects to give information about their current levels of anxiety as well as the frequency and symptoms of any panic attacks. An unexpected finding was that 34.4% of the students reported having had one or more panic attacks in the past year; 2.2% reported having had a minimum of three attacks in the past 3 weeks. In a second study (Norton et al., 1986), 35.9% of the 256 undergraduate students reported experiencing at least one panic attack in the past year and 3.1% at least three attacks in the past 3 weeks. In addition, some of the subjects with nonclinical panic attacks reported experiencing some of the same symptoms found in patients with well-defined panic disorder or agoraphobia with panic attacks. The authors concluded from the findings of these two studies that panic attacks occur rather frequently in presumably normal people.

In a series of experiments that examined the characteristics of "nonclinical panickers," Margraf and Ehlers (1988) found results similar to Norton et al. (1985, 1986). They used the German translation of the Panic Attack Questionnaire (PAQ) designed by Norton et al. (1986). In their first study, Margraf and Ehlers found that 46% of their 170 undergraduates reported experiencing at least one panic attack in the previous year. In the second study, the figure was 59%. A total of 2% (Study 1) and 1% (Study 2) of the students reported having had at least three attacks in the previous 3 weeks. Another aspect of Margraf and Ehlers's study was to compare nonclinical panickers identified by the PAQ with controls (those who reported no attacks or anxiety symptoms on the PAQ). The most consistent differences found between nonclinical panickers and controls were tonically elevated levels of self-reported anxiety and symptoms. Physiological reactivity to laboratory stressors differentiated only poorly between these groups, and cardiovascular measures did not differentiate these groups at all. Furthermore, several characteristics of the nonclinical panickers had previously been described in clinical panic disorder patients: phobophobia, somatization, general anxiousness, and depression. Margraf and Ehlers concluded that the results of studies of nonclinical panickers are consistent with many of the psychophysiological, cognitive, and psychological models of panic (e.g., Barlow, 1986; van den Hout, 1988) that suggest a number of causal factors in the development of panic (such as fear of anxiety symptoms, or an anxiety response to hyperventilation). These results, however, are difficult to reconcile with the hypothesis (discussed later in this chapter) that separation anxiety or active avoidance behavior is an essential antecedent of panic attacks.

We are only beginning the fascinating study of the phenomenon of panic attacks. Prospective studies are needed to determine how subjects with nonclinical and infrequent panic attacks differ from others in the population, and to examine which of those subjects go on to develop full-blown panic disorder, with or without agoraphobia. Such studies are also essential for investigating whether panic attacks and panic disorder represent a heterogeneous phenomenon with a large number of underlying causes.

Risk Factors

Risk factors can be broadly defined as conditions that increase an individual's chance of developing the disorder under study. An examination of general risk factors such as sex, age, marital status, and race can be useful for investigating etiological hypotheses, as several psychiatric disorders (for example, depression and alcohol abuse) have been found to have different risk factors.

Sex

Almost all epidemiological studies report higher rates of psychiatric disorders in females than in males. This preponderance of women is especially marked in anxiety disorders, and particulary with regard to phobias; indeed, agoraphobia has often been called a "woman's syndrome" (Fodor, 1974). This finding seems to be supported equally by earlier and more recent studies. In their review of five population studies done in the United States, the United Kingdom, and Sweden between 1943 and 1966, Marks and Lader (1973) found the highest prevalence of anxiety states in women, especially those between the ages of 16 and 40.

The Zurich Study (Angst & Dobler-Mikola, 1985) found higher rates in female subjects for panic syndrome, simple phobia, social phobia, and generalized anxiety. With regard to agoraphobia, a reverse finding was found: females had a slightly lower rate than males (see Table 3.4).

Results from the ECA survey indicated a higher lifetime prevalence of panic disorder among females than males in New Haven, Baltimore, and St. Louis. Similar rates were obtained in the MFS (Wittchen, 1986) and the Edmonton study (Bland, Orn; & Newman; 1988). It is important to note, however, that although females in the ECA study showed a consistently higher lifetime rate of panic disorders than males, the only statistically significant sex difference was found in St. Louis. Furthermore, the rates for Puerto Rico (Canino et al., 1987) were almost equal, and the survey by Weissman, Myers, and Harding (1978), using the SADS, even showed a reverse relationship for the RDC criteria (see Table 3.4).

With regard to symptoms of panic attacks, the female preponderance is more pronounced than on the level of diagnosis. Wittchen (1986) reported a two-fold higher rate of panic symptoms for females as compared to males. But he also noted that this finding was related to age. Whereas a higher rate of

TABLE 3.4 Sex and the Prevalence of Anxiety Disorders

	New Haven 1978	Zurich[a] 1985	ECA (1984) New Haven	ECA (1984) Baltimore	ECA (1984) St. Louis	MFS 1986	Puerto Rico 1987	Edmonton 1988
Prevalence period	point	1-yr	6-mth (life)	6-mth (life)	6-mth (life)	6-mth (life)	6-mth (life)	6-mth (life)
Panic disorder								
Male	0.5	0.8	0.3 (0.6)	0.8 (1.2)	0.7 (0.9)	(1.7)	1.2 (1.6)	0.4 (0.8)
Female	0.3	4.9	0.9 (2.1)	1.2 (1.6)	1.0 (2.0)	(2.9)	0.9 (1.9)	1.0 (1.7)
Agoraphobia								
Male		3.1	1.1 (1.5)	3.4 (5.2)	0.9 (1.5)	(2.9)	2.4 (4.9)	(1.5)
Female		2.0	4.2 (5.3)	7.8 (12.5)	4.3 (6.4)	(9.3)	5.4 (8.7)	(4.3)
Social phobia								
Male		0.3		1.7	0.9		1.1 (1.5)	(1.4)
Female		1.8		2.6	1.5		1.1 (1.6)	(2.0)
Simple phobia								
Male		3.1	3.2 (3.8)	7.3 (14.5)	2.3 (4.0)		3.4 (7.6)	(4.6)
Female		4.2	6.0 (8.5)	15.7 (25.9)	6.5 (9.4)		5.3 (9.6)	(9.8)
Obsessive-compulsive disorder								
Male			(2.0)	(2.6)	(1.1)		1.3 (3.3)	1.6 (2.8)
Female			(3.1)	(3.3)	(2.6)		2.3 (3.1)	1.6 (3.1)
Phobic disorder								
Male	0.9							
Female	1.7							
Generalized anxiety disorder								
Male	1.8	2.2						
Female	3.1	7.8						

Note: Rates are given as percentages.
[a] syndrome

panic symptoms was reported in women under 30 years of age, no significant difference was found between males and females in older age groups.

Unlike the findings for panic disorder, the sex differences in other anxiety disorders (such as agoraphobia and other phobias) reach a statistically significant level in the majority of studies. For example, the lifetime prevalence for agoraphobia was significantly higher for women than for men in all three ECA sites, with rates ranging from 5.3% to 12.5% for women and from 1.5% to 5.2% for men. Similarly, a preponderance of females was found having simple phobia. The 6-month rates for agoraphobia, social phobia, and simple phobia were all significantly higher in females than in males across the ECA sites.

Using the ECA data from five sites (New Haven, East Baltimore, St. Louis, Durham, and Los Angeles), Bourdon and his colleagues (Bourdon et al., 1988) found significant sex differences for agoraphobia and simple phobia at all the sites. Although females also had a higher prevalence for social phobia, the difference was not significant. The ratios of females to males for anxiety diagnoses were as follows: agoraphobia, 2.7 : 1; simple phobia, 1.9 : 1; and social phobia, 1.4 : 1. Thus, the preponderance of females can be summarized as being less marked for panic disorder than for agoraphobia or other phobias.

Currently there are no convincing explanations for the sex differences found in panic disorder and agoraphobia aside from those used to explain the generally higher psychiatric morbidity of females: hormonal factors such as the menstrual cycle and the disadvantageous socioeconomic factors reflecting the current social role of females (Weissman & Klerman, 1977).

Age

There is a strong relationship between age and the prevalence rates of agoraphobia and panic disorder. The frequency of agoraphobia in most samples is highest in the age group of 30 years and less—usually with an age of onset under 26—whereas consistently lower prevalence rates are reported for subjects 45 years and older. The ECA study found that the group with the highest lifetime rate of panic disorder was between 25 and 44 years of age; the lowest rate was found in those 65 and older (Robins et al., 1984). Subjects in the 65-years-and-older group also had the lowest lifetime rate for agoraphobia and simple phobia, a finding that was consistent across the three ECA sites.

Von Korff et al. (1983) supported the findings of Robins et al. (1984) in a more differentiated analysis of a subsample of the ECA data. They found that age was strongly linked to the prevalence of simple panic attacks (those that failed to meet the DSM-III frequency criterion for panic disorder), recurrent and severe attacks, and DSM-III panic disorder. Across all sites, the highest prevalence of simple panic attacks, recurrent and severe attacks, and DSM-III panic disorder was found in the age group between 25 and 44 years; subjects 65 years and older had a substantially lower prevalence of panic attacks than did other age groups. Further support was provided by Bland, Orn, and Newman (1988). These authors divided their subjects into six different age groups: 18 to 24 years, and then by 10-year increments to 65 and older. The highest lifetime rate of panic disorder was obtained among those in the age group of 25 to 34 years (2.1%), and the lowest rate in the 65-and-over age group (0.3%). The lifetime prevalence rates for agoraphobia, social phobia, and simple phobia were evenly distributed across age groups.

Other findings suggest that the age of highest risk for having panic disorder may be more variable. Wittchen (1986), for example, found a slightly higher lifetime rate for panic disorder in the age group of 45 to 64 years (2.9%) than in that of 25 to 44 years (2.1%). No difference was found for agoraphobia (25-to-44 age group = 5.9%, 45-to-64 age group = 5.7%). The effect of age on simple phobia was consistent with previous findings, in that a higher rate was obtained in the younger age group (25-to-44 age group = 9.7%, 45-to-64 age group = 6.5%). These findings may have been influenced by a cohort effect, because the MFS (Wittchen, 1986) was based on a follow-up sample. Among Puerto Ricans, the 6-month and lifetime prevalence rates for panic disorder, agoraphobia, social phobia, and simple phobia tend to get progressively higher with age. For example, the lifetime rates for panic disorder in the three age groups were 18 to 24 years = 0.6%, 25 to 44 years = 2.0%, and 45 to 64 years = 2.2%. The 6-month rates for panic disorder were 18 to 24 years = 0.6%, 25 to 44 years = 1.0%, and 45 to 64 years = 1.4%. The lifetime rates for agoraphobia were 18 to 24 years = 4.9%, 25 to 44 years = 6.3%, 45 to 64 years = 9.7%; the 6-month rates were 18 to 24 years = 3.4%, 25 to 44 years = 3.8%, and 45 to 64 years = 4.7%.

To summarize, there is a general agreement across studies conducted in North America using the DIS that a higher 6-month and lifetime prevalence of agoraphobia and other phobic disorders was found in the younger age group, and that a general drop in the prevalence of agoraphobia was noted among subjects over 50 years of age. One possible explanation for this is the higher exposure to life events (marriage, starting a career, and so on) for younger people than for older. The findings of Canino et al. (1987) and Wittchen (1986) were not in agreement with this, however, which suggests sampling differences. The relationship between age and the prevalence of panic disorder needs to be explored in more detail in future studies. There are also some indications that women may be at greater risk in the younger age groups and males in the older age groups (Wittchen & Burke, in preparation).

Marital Status

One unexpected finding of recent epidemiological studies has been that separated and divorced subjects have higher rates of panic disorder. Similar findings have been reported for affective disorder. With current data it is not possible to conclude whether separation or divorce causes panic disorder, panic disorder causes separation or divorce, or some other factor is causally related to both. Regardless of the sequence, there is some evidence that marital disruption—for example, divorce or separation—is commonly accompanied by a higher prevalence of agoraphobia and panic disorder.

In the ECA study (Von Korff et al., 1983), the highest 6-month prevalence of panic disorder was obtained among separated or divorced subjects. This held true for all three sites (New Haven, East Baltimore, and St. Louis). Rates for recurrent and severe attacks were also consistently highest among the separated or divorced subjects in all three sites. Higher rates of simple panic attacks were also noted among separated or divorced subjects in New Haven and in East Baltimore. Among subjects in St. Louis, the highest rate of simple panic attacks was obtained among those who were never married.

Weissman and Myers (1980) categorized the marital status of their respondents as either "currently married" or "not currently married." They found the point prevalence of panic disorder among currently unmarried respondents to be 1.5%; among currently married respondents, 0.0%. Similar findings were obtained for generalized anxiety disorder (not married = 3.0%, married = 2.4%), but for phobic disorder, a higher rate was obtained among currently married subjects (1.9%) than among the unmarried (0.0%). The relationship between agoraphobia and marital status was not examined in this study.

In the Edmonton study (Bland, Orn, & Newman, 1988), higher lifetime rates of panic disorder, social phobia, and simple phobia were obtained from subjects who were widowed, separated, or divorced than from those who were either married or never married. The 6-month prevalence rates of phobia, panic disorder, and obsessive-compulsive disorder were higher among those who were not cohabiting than among those who were (Bland, Newman, & Orn, 1988b). "Cohabiting" was defined as living with a spouse or living with a mate as though married. The prevalence rates for agoraphobia on this dimension were not reported.

These studies seemed to support the—as yet unexplained—observation that those who are divorced and separated experience a higher prevalence of panic disorder. It remains to be determined in future studies whether this finding is an artifact. As marital status is related to age, future research should examine the relationship between marital status and prevalence in specific age groups. Furthermore, as panic disorder frequently coexists with major depression, this relationship may not be limited to panic disorder. It is also interesting to note that no such relationship with marital status was found for agoraphobia in the majority of studies reviewed by Marks (1987).

Other Risk Factors

Other factors such as education, race, urbanization, and employment status have not proven to be consistent and powerful risk factors for the development of panic attacks, panic disorders, or agoraphobia. It has been reported that British patients with agoraphobia (with and without panic attacks) tend to resemble the general population in intelligence, religious affiliation, and social class (Marks & Herst, 1970; Thorpe & Burns, 1983). Similar findings have also been reported for treated and untreated subjects, and for former inpatients in the MFS (Wittchen & von Zerssen, 1988). Nevertheless, several recent studies that have investigated these traditional risk factors in more detail have produced some conflicting results.

Education

The prevalence of agoraphobia and panic disorder seems to be slightly higher among people with less education. In the ECA survey (Robins et al., 1984), education level was divided between college graduates (n = 839) and "other graduates" (n = 2218). Of all the ECA sites, significant differences in the lifetime rates of panic disorder were obtained only in St. Louis, which had a preponderance of "other graduates." In New Haven and Baltimore, panic disorder was evenly distributed among college and other graduates. But with respect to agoraphobia, the other-graduate group had a significantly higher rate, a finding that was consistent in all three sites.

Von Korff et al. (1983), in a more elaborate analysis of the same ECA data, found the highest rates of panic disorder among those with less than 12 years of education (that is, 8 to 11 years). However, the prevalence rates varied greatly according to education level. For example, rates found among those with 0 to 8 years of education at each site were 2.8% (New Haven), 13.2% (East Baltimore), and 20.7% (St. Louis); among those with 9 to 11 years of education, the rates were 8.9% (New Haven), 14.4% (East Baltimore), and 4.4% (St. Louis). As for simple panic attacks, less consistent patterns were found among educational levels in the three sites. For example, the highest rate of simple panic attacks found in New Haven occurred among those with more than 13 years of education, whereas in East Baltimore and St. Louis, the highest rate was noted among those with 9 to 11 years of education. With regard to recurrent and severe attacks, the highest and the lowest rates were found in subjects with 0 to 8 and with more than 13 years of education, respectively.

Canino and her colleagues (1987) indicated in the Puerto Rico survey that subjects with 7 to 11 years of education had the highest lifetime prevalence of panic disorder; their rate was significantly higher than those at other educational levels. The 6-month rate for panic disorder was also higher among those with 7 to 11 years of education compared to those at other educational levels; however, this difference was not statistically significant. The lifetime rates for agoraphobia and for social and simple phobias decreased progressively with higher levels of education.

Race

With regard to race, Robins et al. (1984) found no significant relationship between black or nonblack racial status and the lifetime diagnosis of panic disorder in any of the ECA sites. With respect to agoraphobia, slightly higher rates were found among blacks across all sites, although the only significant finding was obtained in Baltimore (black = 13.4%, nonblack = 7.2%). However, this finding should be interpreted with great caution, because more blacks were sampled in Baltimore than in either New Haven or St. Louis, and the rates of most anxiety disorders were also considerably higher in Baltimore.

With regard to symptoms of panic, Von Korff et al. (1983) found somewhat higher rates of recurrent and severe attacks among nonwhites in New Haven and East Baltimore and lower rates in St. Louis. Similarly, race differences were noted for simple panic attacks in all three sites, with a higher rate in nonwhites: the rates of simple panic attacks for whites and nonwhites were 13.7% versus 20% in New Haven, 8.8% versus 11.1% in East Baltimore, and 13.6% versus 17.7% in St. Louis. On the other hand, Weissman and Myers (1980) reported higher point prevalences for some anxiety disorders among whites (panic disorder: white = 0.4%, nonwhite = 0.0%; phobic disorder: white = 1.5%, nonwhite = 0.0%).

Urbanization

In an attempt to examine the relationship between urbanization and psychiatric disorder, Robins et al. (1984) divided the area of residence into central city, inner suburb, and small town/rural. Based on these groupings, they found the small town/rural environment in St. Louis to be significantly related to a higher rate of panic disorder than the central city (2.1% versus 1.7%) or inner suburb (0.8%) environments. Rates for agoraphobia tended to be the highest in the central city (4.6%), next highest in the inner suburb (4.3%), and lowest in the small town/rural area (3.7%).

In Puerto Rico (Canino et al., 1987), the lifetime and 6-month prevalence rates of panic disorder, social and simple phobias, and obsessive-compulsive disorder were higher in urban than in rural areas. As for agoraphobia, the lifetime rate was significantly higher in urban (8.2%) than in rural (4.6%) areas.

A community survey (part of the ECA) among 3941 adult residents of Piedmont, North Carolina (Blazer et al., 1985), indicated no significant urban/rural difference in the prevalence of agoraphobia or obsessive-compulsive disorder. No prevalence data for panic disorder without agoraphobia was reported.

Employment Status

To date, very few epidemiologic studies have attempted to examine the relationship between employment status and the prevalence of anxiety disorders. Bland, Stebelsky, Orn, and Newman (1988) reported slightly higher lifetime rates of panic disorder, agoraphobia, social phobia, and simple phobia in unemployed than in employed subjects. These findings were replicated in the MFS, in that higher lifetime and 6-month prevalence rates for anxiety neurosis and phobia (based on ICD-9) were found among unemployed subjects (Essau & Wittchen, in preparation).

To summarize, findings on the relationship between education, race, urbanization, and employment status and the prevalence of anxiety disorders are far from conclusive. More elaborate analyses that take into account some confounding variables such as age and comorbidity with other disorders are needed.

Comorbidity with Other Psychiatric Disorders

It has long been noted in clinical studies that patients with anxiety disorder in general—and panic disorder and agoraphobia in particular—also frequently suffer from generalized anxiety, worry, persistent unpleasant thoughts, depression, and problems with dependency. The overlap of syndromes and disorders is indeed puzzling and remains an unresolved issue in psychopathology and classification. In this context the vexing distinctions between panic disorder and agoraphobia and among depression, generalized anxiety, and panic disorder are the hardest to "tease out" (Marks, 1987, p. 306).

With the advent of explicit diagnostic criteria and operationalized diagnoses, there has been an increased emphasis in the field of epidemiology on studying the relationship among these symptoms, syndromes, and disorders. Such studies have used the lifetime approach and diagnostic instruments that do not employ diagnostic hierarchies for assessing prevalence rates, so that the occurrence and clustering of syndromes and disorders over the whole lifespan of a subject can be determined.

Comorbidity is defined as the co-occurrence of two or more different disorders in the same individual during a specified time period (for example, cross-sectional, 6-month, lifetime). One promising effect of comorbidity studies is that they may allow a better understanding of common etiological mechanisms and types of disorders (Tuma & Maser, 1985). Therefore, we will briefly review the relationship of anxiety disorders to each other and to other psychiatric disorders in some selected epidemiological and family studies.

Comorbidity Among the Anxiety Disorders

The overlap among spontaneous panic attacks, phobic avoidance, and autonomic symptoms with all forms of phobias and other anxiety disorders has been documented for some time (Marks, 1987). However, firm epidemiological evidence has only recently been presented for comorbidity among the anxiety disorders. Based on the ECA data analysis, several authors (for example, Weissman, Leaf, Blazer, Boyd, & Florio, 1986) have pointed out that almost 50% of all subjects with a lifetime anxiety disorder had at least one other anxiety disorder. Comorbidity with panic disorder is quite marked. The majority of cases with a diagnosis of panic disorder also have agoraphobia or simple phobia. This result was confirmed by Wittchen (1988a), who found considerable overlap among the anxiety disorders (DIS lifetime diagnosis). Of all the anxiety cases, only 26 (33.8%) had just one anxiety disorder diagnosis. The most frequent comorbidity patterns involved agoraphobia *and* simple phobia, and either one of those disorders with panic disorder. Furthermore, 40% of all cases with either simple phobia or agoraphobia also fulfilled the DSM-III diagnostic criteria for panic disorder—or at least the criteria for one severe panic attack. These findings agree with a number of other clinical studies as well as the traditional dimensional model of anxiety that put more emphasis on the features common to all anxiety disorders (Marks, 1987).

Breier, Charney, and Heninger (1986) found anticipatory anxiety and generalized anxiety in more than 80% of patients having either panic disorder or agoraphobia with panic attacks. Some 30% of the patients reported the onset of a generalized anxiety disorder prior to the occurrence of their first panic attack, and 60% experienced the onset of a generalized anxiety disorder concurrently with panic disorder and agoraphobia. In an attempt to analyze comorbidity patterns, Cottraux, Mollard, and Duinat-Pascal (1988) compared the clinical and psychometric data of 71 patients having agoraphobia plus panic attacks with 54 patients having social phobia. Their patients had been referred to a behavior therapy unit over a 6-year period and diagnosed according to the DSM-III criteria. Of the 54 patients with social phobia, 7% received a secondary diagnosis of agoraphobia and 6% a diagnosis of panic disorder without agoraphobia. Only 12.5% of the 71 patients with agoraphobia had a secondary diagnosis of social phobia. Patients with agoraphobia experienced more panic attacks than those with social phobia. Simple phobia and panic attacks were significantly more common among patients with agoraphobia than those with social phobia. Similar results were reported by Barlow, DiNardo, Vermilyea, Vermilyea, and Blanchard (1986).

The frequent occurrence of panic-related phenomena in other anxiety disorders has also stimulated a closer examination of the etiological hypotheses discussed in the section on definition of panic disorder early in this chapter.

Comorbidity with Depression

The wide body of literature on theoretical, clinical, and statistical aspects of the intimate relationship between anxiety and depression is so confusing that many authors decide to write two separate chapters on these studies: one stressing the similarities and the other the differences between anxiety and depression (Marks, 1987). Epidemiological studies before the introduction of the DSM-III most frequently stressed the shared aspects of anxiety and depression—consistent with the ICD-8 and ICD-9 concept of neurotic disorders, which regarded features of anxiety as legitimate parts of depression and vice versa (Helmchen & Linden, 1986; see also questionnaire literature and factor analytic studies in Marks, 1987).

Some examples might clarify this viewpoint. Tennant, Hurry, and Bebbington (1981) found that 67% of community subjects with psychiatric disorders had anxiety plus depression that could not be differentiated. Likewise, in a primary care population, 96% of those with psychiatric disorder had an anxiety-depression syndrome that could not be subdivided reliably (Cooper & Sylph, 1973). Similar findings were reported by Dilling and Weyerer (1984) and by Jablensky, Sartorious, Gulbinat, and Ernberg (1981).

As part of the Yale Family Study, Leckman et al. (1983) examined the relationship between anxiety and depression in 521 first-degree relatives of 82 normal controls and 810 first-degree relatives of 133 depressed or anxious probands. Of the 133 probands, 77 had the DSM-III anxiety disorders (agoraphobia, panic disorder, and generalized anxiety disorder), and of these, two-thirds had also experienced episodes of depression. The relatives of probands with both major depression *and* panic disorder or generalized anxiety were found to have the highest rates of major depression (20%). This rate compares with 11.5% of the relatives of depressed probands with agoraphobia, 10.7% of the relatives of depressed probands without any anxiety disorder, and 5.6% of the relatives of normal controls. The prevalence of anxiety disorders among relatives of depressed probands with panic disorder was 15.8%, the highest rate among all proband groups and twice the rate of risk for anxiety disorder among relatives of normal controls.

Weissman et al. (1984) extended the findings of an association between depression and panic disorder in the adult relatives of probands to children of some of the Leckman et al. (1983) probands. The subjects consisted of 19 children, aged 6 to 17 years, of 11 probands with depression plus panic disorder. Compared to children of controls and depressed probands with no anxiety disorder, children of probands with depression and panic disorder showed an increased rate for depression (26.3%) and anxiety disorders (36.8%), especially separation anxiety disorder. The rate in normal children was 0.0% for major depression and 2.3% for anxiety disorders. Among children of depressed probands without anxiety disorder, the rates increased to 13.2% for major depression and dropped to 0.0% for anxiety disorder. As in adult relatives, the findings in children supported a close relationship between major depression and panic disorder.

Again, the most convincing epidemiological data were provided by the ECA study as well as the studies by Canino et al. (1987) and Wittchen (1986). Each of these noted that at least 30% of all anxiety disorder cases in the general population sample also fulfilled lifetime diagnostic criteria for major depression and/or dysthymia. A more detailed analysis by Wittchen and Burke (in preparation) that pooled data from all of these studies, as well as the data by Bland et al. (1988a), further confirmed these findings. In addition, it was found that in the majority of cases the onset of anxiety preceded the onset of depression. These findings match the results from a recent collaborative clinical study. As part of the Cross-National Collaborative Panic Study (Lesser et al., 1988) on the efficacy of alprazolam in panic disorder with and without depression, depressive symptomatology in 481 subjects with panic disorder and phobic avoidance was examined. All subjects, aged 18 to 65 years, considered eligible to participate in the study were interviewed using the Structured Clinical Interview for the DSM-III (Upjohn version). Thirty-one percent of the subjects had an episode of major depression following the onset of panic disorder. Subjects who received a diagnosis of either current or past major depression had a significantly longer history of panic disorder, and subjects with current major depression also scored higher on measures of anxiety and depression. Another important finding was that depression and phobic avoidance were correlated with an increased severity of panic attacks.

Comorbidity with Substance Abuse

The fact that individuals use alcohol and/or sedating drugs to relieve symptoms of anxiety has motivated many researchers to explore the possible association between substance abuse and anxiety disorders. Although an abundance of clinical observations and studies have attempted to examine the role of substance abuse in patients with panic disorder or phobic disorder, epidemiologic studies are lacking.

Among patients with agoraphobia (with or without panic attacks), estimates of the frequency of alcohol abuse and alcoholism vary between 14% and 20% (Bibb & Chambless, 1986). Unfortunately, most studies fail to clarify whether alcohol abuse preceded or followed the onset of the anxiety disorder. Two major clinical studies have attempted to explore these issues. Thyer et al. (1986) examined alcohol abuse in 156 patients who met the DSM-III criteria for agoraphobia with panic attacks, panic disorder, simple or social phobia, or generalized anxiety disorder. All subjects completed the Michigan Alcoholism Screening Test (MAST), on which a score of 5 or higher indicates alcoholism. Of all the patients, 17.3% scored in the alcoholic range. The mean MAST scores for the anxiety disorder groups were as follows: agoraphobia with panic attacks = 6.03, panic disorder = 1.16, simple phobia = 2.33, social phobia = 3.36, and generalized anxiety disorder = 1.00. Patients with agoraphobia had a significantly higher score on the MAST than did those with panic disorder or generalized anxiety disorder.

Bibb and Chambless (1986) reported that 22 of their 254 outpatients who met the DSM-III criteria for agoraphobia with panic attacks also met the MAST criterion for alcoholism (5 or more on the MAST). The DSM-III alcoholism rates were similar: 10% of their outpatients with agoraphobia were diagnosed as abusing alcohol, 12% as being dependent on it, and 13%, either or both. Age-of-onset data for agoraphobia and problem drinking were available for 16 of the 22 alcoholic patients. Of the 16, 56% reported that agoraphobia began prior to their alcohol problems, 31% that problem drinking came first, and 13% that the disorders originated concurrently. More alcoholic than nonalcoholic patients with agoraphobia indicated that they used alcohol to self-medicate for phobic symptoms or dysphoria.

Epidemiological data on this relationship have recently been reported by Helzer and Canino (in press). Using the ECA data, they reported a higher rate of alcoholism in subjects with anxiety disorders—particularly those with panic disorder—than in the population in general. Similar results have been reported by Wittchen and Bronish (in press), who found that 14.7% of their subjects with an alcohol diagnosis in the MFS were also diagnosed as having an anxiety disorder—most frequently, agoraphobia and phobic disorders.

There has also been clear evidence showing an excessive prevalence of drug abuse or dependence among those with panic disorder. The only study reporting an increased frequency of abuse of prescribed medication was the recent analysis of the MFS data. Wittchen (1988b) reported that 40% of his subjects with agoraphobia and panic disorder in the general population also had a history of substance abuse (drug and alcohol combined) as defined by the DIS/DSM-III criteria. However, because of the small sample size, further studies are needed to draw firm conclusions about the prevalence of other substance abuse in anxiety patients.

Comorbidity with Separation Anxiety

Klein and Fink (1962) speculated that panic attacks in patients with agoraphobia may be a "mature" expression of the type of distress and panic experienced by some children upon separating from their mothers. Clear epidemiological evidence for this assumption is, however, missing.

The following three areas of clinical research have provided some support for the association of anxiety disorders with separation anxiety.

1. *Family concordance for separation anxiety and agoraphobia.* This line of research indicates that parents of children with separation anxiety display a greater frequency of panic disorder or agoraphobia than do parents of children without separation anxiety. Weissman and her colleagues (1984) examined the family concordance of separation anxiety and adult anxiety in children (aged 6 to 17) of both depressed and normal adults. Based on a structured clinical interview, the adult patients were classified in four groups: depressed without anxiety disorder, depressed plus agoraphobia, depressed plus panic disorder, and depressed plus generalized anxiety disorder. Separation anxiety was diagnosed in 36.8% of the children of the adults with depression plus panic disorder, and in 11.1% of the children of those with depression and

agoraphobia. None of the children whose parents had depression alone—and only 6.3% of those whose parents had depression plus generalized anxiety disorder—reported separation anxiety.

2. *Similarity of drug treatment effects for separation anxiety and agoraphobia.* The finding that imipramine has a positive effect in treating agoraphobia and panic disorders (see, for example, Gittelman & Klein, 1973) led to the suggestion that separation anxiety and agoraphobia/panic disorder represent variants of similar pathology. In a placebo-controlled study of imipramine treatment in 44 school-phobic youngsters, Gittelman and Klein found that 90% of the children receiving imipramine reported feeling much better, compared with only 24% of those on the placebo. Children on imipramine also reported fewer complaints on school days and experienced less distress.

3. *History of childhood separation anxiety in patients with agoraphobia.* Studies of this particular area have indicated that separation anxiety is a common feature in the histories of patients with agoraphobia in comparison with other groups of patients. In Klein's (1964) original observations, about half of his 32 hospitalized patients with agoraphobia reported having had severe separation anxiety as children. Klein reported that this finding was specific to this patient group, compared with patients having schizophrenia or an affective disorder. Some support also came from clinical studies by Raskin, Peeke, Dickman, and Pinsker (1982), although their results conflicted with other studies. Breier et al. (1986), for example, found a markedly lower frequency (18%) of childhood separation anxiety in their patients than did Klein. A study by Buglass, Clarke, Henderson, Kreitman, and Presley (1977) also failed to find an excess of reported childhood separation anxiety among agoraphobic patients.

Studies attempting to explore childhood separation anxiety in patients with agoraphobia have produced conflicting findings. Because patients were asked retrospectively about the presence of separation anxiety in their childhood, the information may include a high proportion of memory lapse errors. Controlled longitudinal epidemiological studies to further clarify the possible link between childhood and adult anxiety disorders have been all too rare because of the cost, effort, and time involved. Yet these will be necessary before definite conclusions can be drawn.

Comorbidity with Somatization Disorder

Epidemiological data showing the comorbidity of agoraphobia and panic disorder with somatization are very rare. One major complication in studying this comorbidity at an epidemiological level is that few cases with somatization disorder can easily be identified, because of the very strict diagnostic criteria of the DSM-III.

In clinical studies King, Margraf, Ehlers, and Maddock (1986), for example, examined the hypothesis that somatization overlaps with panic syndromes in their study of 44 females with either panic disorder or agoraphobia with panic attacks and 27 nonanxious females. All subjects completed a self-report inventory to measure somatization, visceral sensitivity, and nonspecific neurotic symptoms. The authors found a significant overlap of somatization and panic syndromes. Patients with panic disorder not only showed higher average somatization scores than did normal controls but more than a quarter of them also met the DSM-III diagnosis of somatization disorder.

In a recent study of 55 panic disorder patients (using the DSM-III criteria) referred to psychiatric consultation in primary care, Katon (1984) reported that 61% of the women had at least 14 physical symptoms listed on their medical record. Thirty-three percent of the men with panic disorder had cardiac, gastrointestinal, and neurologic symptoms. Many of these frequently reported symptoms (palpitation, chest pain, fainting, and so on) also overlap with symptoms of DSM-III somatization disorder. Another study showing a close relationship between panic disorder and somatization disorder was conducted by Sheehan, Ballenger, and Jacobsen (1980). A high percentage of their patients reported having chest pain (58%), sore muscles (68%), upset stomach or nausea (82%), and headache (86%). The patients also scored very highly on the somatization scale of the SCL-90.

The findings from clinical studies suggest an association between anxiety disorders and somatization; however, more extensive epidemiological studies are needed before conclusions can be drawn.

Summary

To summarize, the frequency of the comorbidity of panic disorder and agoraphobia with depression, somatization, and substance abuse is high. With this in mind, clinicians should carefully check for the presence of additional disorders in their patients. This is particularly important because the combination of these problems may affect treatment response as well as the long-term course of agoraphobia and panic disorder.

As epidemiological data on the comorbidity of personality disorder and physical illness (for example, mitral value prolapse) with panic disorder and agoraphobia are lacking, we have to refer to the available clinical studies, which are discussed in Chapters 2, 5, and 7.

Natural Course

Although anxiety disorders have been reported to be the most common psychiatric disorders in the community (Lepine, 1987; Marks, 1987; Myers et al., 1984; Robins et al., 1984; Wittchen et al., 1988), little is known about their natural course and the frequency of spontaneous remission in untreated cases. This uncertainty is rather surprising, given the number of studies (such as studies on treatment effectiveness, follow-up studies, and prospective long-term epidemiological studies) of these disorders. A closer look reveals a number of deficiencies that hinder exploration of the natural history of untreated anxiety disorders. These deficiencies include the following.

1.   Epidemiological studies on the natural history of untreated anxiety disorder are very rare. The only prospective study known to us is the one conducted by Agras, Chapin, and Oliveau (1972).

2.   Few studies explore the natural course of a differentiated subclassification of anxiety disorders as suggested by the DSM-III or DSM-III-R.

3.   Few studies use the diagnostic instruments with proven reliability, so that findings may be generalized across studies.

4.   Even large epidemiological studies such as the ECA Study have some inherent problems related to the validity of data collected by nonclinicians and the degree to which those data can be generalized to "true" patient populations.

5.   Several methodological challenges are inherent in the evaluation of the long-term course and outcome of anxiety disorders. These challenges include finding an instrument that would specifically assess the long-term course of symptoms, avoidance behavior, and social and psychological aspects, as well as determining what would be appropriate indicators of course and outcome (for example, age of onset, mean duration of illness, severity and psychosocial impairments, development of other psychiatric disorders, and remission rates of symptoms and social impairments).

6.   There is a lack of theoretical models that offer an acceptable framework in which the long-term course of anxiety disorder can be examined. Such models would need in particular to address key aspects such as vulnerability, risk factors, full and partial remission, relapse, rebound phenomena, comorbidity, chronicity, and intervening biological as well as social and psychosocial factors that lack a precise and generally accepted definition. Within this context, several variables (see Table 3.5) that may affect the development, course, and outcome of an anxiety disorder have often been neglected.

Thus, our present knowledge about the natural course of anxiety disorders is dependent on a few retrospective studies (Marks & Herst, 1970) and several treatment studies (Lydiard & Ballenger, 1987; Marks, 1987; Mathews, Gelder, & Johnston, 1981; Sheehan, 1987). These studies, which usually present a length-of-illness history prior to the index treatment as well as follow-up results, cannot be regarded as providing a firm basis for knowledge about the natural history of anxiety disorder because of their methodological problems (for instance, differences in the selection of patients, design, length of follow-up period, nosological concept, diagnostic instruments used, and criteria for improvement) and theoretical considerations. The natural course of a disorder in a stricter sense should be based on representative samples, including

untreated subjects, so that findings can be generalized to nonclinical populations and to different clinical groups.

TABLE 3.5 Variables Affecting the Development, Course, and Outcome of Disorders

---

Social, cultural, and environmental factors (external factors)
    Living conditions and arrangements
    Sociocultural norms
    Social and technical network/integration
    Life events and changes in life conditions
    Environmental strains and stressors (e.g., work)
    Structure of the (mental) health system

Psychological factors
    Individual lifestyle
    Self-perception
    Goals and aspirations in life
    Emotional arousal and stability
    Former experience with anxiety and illness
    Attitudes toward disorder
    Attitudes toward therapy

Biological factors
    Central and autonomic functions
    Internal biological conditioning ("kindling")
    Degrees and duration of biological dysfunctions
    Individual variation in the regeneration capacity of the disturbed functions
    "Spontaneous" remission of biological dysfunction
    Effects of medication and other biological treatments
    Adverse therapy effects (biological)

EXTERNAL FACTORS	+	PSYCHOLOGICAL FACTORS	+	BIOLOGICAL FACTORS	=	OUTCOME

Long-term Course and Outcome

The long-term natural course of untreated agoraphobia and panic disorder
described in a few controlled long-term studies fluctuates, often punctuated
by partial remissions and severe relapses of varying duration (Reich, 1986). In
addition, Marks and Herst (1970) reported that partial rather than full remission is to be expected in the absence of treatment.

Spontaneous panic attacks have been found to correlate highly with
general anxiety and depressed mood (Chambless, 1985; Marks et al., 1983), but
they can also spring "from out of the blue," even during periods without
generally increased anxiety or depression. Spontaneous panic attacks may
strike at any time of the day, although stressful situations and several biological factors may trigger attacks more frequently and intensively. The finding,
in clinical samples (Breier & Charney, 1985), that spontaneous panics seemed
to diminish over time, may simply reflect a less severe illness phase that could

be aggravated at a later date. It may also be explained by an age cohort effect, as panic disorder is found less frequently among those over 50 years. Although differences in course between panic disorder and agoraphobia have been reported by some authors (Marks, 1987; Uhde et al., 1985; Wittchen, 1988a), the course of panic disorder broadly resembles that of agoraphobia.

According to detailed analyses of the MFS data, the natural course of various forms of anxiety disorders can be summarized as follows.

1. The most common pattern of symptom course can be described generally as chronic and persistent. There is a low rate of spontaneous and complete remissions in all groups. Untreated by a specialist, the overall group with anxiety disorders has a 66% chance of developing major depression, dysthymia, substance abuse or dependence, or other disorders after the onset of the anxiety disorder.

2. The majority of cases with simple phobias had a chronic symptom pattern characterized by the persistence of mild rather than severe symptoms of anxiety over decades. Only 16% remitted completely over the follow-up period of 7 years. Among cases with "pure" simple and social phobias, severe and stable psychosocial restrictions were rare or transient. More than one-third of this group had a long-term course of the disorder that was "complicated" by the presence of depression and substance abuse. The onset of depression and substance abuse usually occurred after the first manifestation of the phobia—in most cases, more than 10 years later.

3. Unlike simple and social phobias, panic disorder had a later age of onset (and consequently a significantly shorter illness history), the highest comorbidity rates with other anxiety disorders, the highest number of treated cases, the most severe psychosocial impairments, and the worst outcome. All panic disorders, except for one case, fulfilled DSM-III criteria for other (lifetime) disorders, mostly major depression (71.4%) or alcohol or drug abuse (50%). The course of symptoms was either stable-chronic or chronic with episodic exacerbations. Although these findings should be interpreted with great caution because of the low number of cases (N = 14), some other studies have found similar results. The chronic nature of the condition is supported by some earlier treatment studies (Errera & Coleman, 1963; Marks, 1970; Roberts, 1964) as well as by the more recent report by Breier et al. (1986), who found similar comorbidity rates.

4. Cases with agoraphobia with and without panic attacks were generally more severely impaired and had a markedly higher comorbidity rate for depression than did other phobias. Like other studies (Angst & Dobler-Mikola, 1985, 1986; Weissman et al., 1986), the MFS identified more cases of agoraphobia without history of panic attacks than cases with those features. The dominant pattern of the long-term course was chronic with slightly higher remission rates than cases with panic disorder.

5. The degree of psychosocial impairment in all groups of anxiety disorder was apparently related to the lifetime occurrence of a major depression.

In contrast to the chronic and unremitting course of anxiety symptoms, the course of depression was episodic, with full remissions. Nevertheless, it is remarkable that psychosocial dysfunctions were significantly more severe and frequent in all cases with a depression, even if the depression was fully remitted. This might be an indication of long-lasting psychosocial aftereffects of depression, possibly remitting more slowly than the psychopathological features (Paykel, Weissman, & Prusoff, 1978; Wittchen et al., 1988). On the other hand, it may be that an episode of major depression becomes more likely in cases of serious disability. At present, little information is available on which problem develops first. Help-seeking behavior also seems to be related to the occurrence of depression, especially in cases with panic disorder and agoraphobia.

Age of Onset

Age of onset is defined as the year of the first occurrence of a specific disorder. In addition to improving our understanding of the natural history of a disorder, age-of-onset information is useful in determining particular ages of vulnerability, increasing the possibility of directing services toward such groups. According to the DSM-III-R, the average age of onset for panic disorder is the late 20s. The age of onset for agoraphobia without history of panic disorder varies, though it frequently occurs in the 20s or 30s.

In the National Survey of Agoraphobia, Burns and Thorpe (1977) found the mean age of onset for agoraphobia to be 28.0 years (SD = 10.4). The mean age of onset for females (28.5 years, SD = 10.3) was significantly older than for males (24.3 years, SD = 10.0). Few subjects reported that they developed agoraphobia under the age of 16 (9%) or over the age of 40 (13%). Studying 30 married women with agoraphobia who had been referred to outpatient clinics, Buglass et al. (1977) found the mean age of onset for current agoraphobic symptoms to be 31 years. In a study by Anderson, Noyes, and Crowe (1984), the mean age of onset was 16.1 years for generalized anxiety disorder and 22.8 years for panic disorder.

In a study involving 423 psychiatric outpatients, Thyer, Parrish, Curtis, Nesse, and Cameron (1985) found the mean age of onset to be as follows: simple phobia, 16.1 years (SD = 13.0); social phobia, 15.7 (SD = 8.5); panic disorder, 26.6 (SD = 11.5); agoraphobia with panic attacks, 26.3 (SD = 9.1); agoraphobia without panic attacks, 27.5 (SD = 7.8); generalized anxiety disorder, 22.8 (SD = 12.0). Simple and social phobias had significantly lower ages of onset than any other anxiety disorder except for generalized anxiety. In agoraphobia with panic attacks 49 (51%) of the 95 cases reported an onset by the age of 25, with a range of 3 to 51 years. The age of onset for agoraphobia without panic attacks ranged from 16 to 45; only 5 of the 20 patients said their disorder began before they were 25. The age of onset for patients with panic disorder ranged from 5 to 51, with 29 patients (45%)

experiencing their first panic attack after the age of 30. Cottraux et al. (1988), in a study of 125 behavior therapy patients, found an average age of onset for social phobia of 20 and for agoraphobia with panic attacks of 27.

In the MFS (Wittchen, 1986), the age of onset of anxiety disorders was determined by asking patients the age at which they experienced the full clinical picture of their disorder. Among the 75 subjects with a lifetime panic disorder and/or any other phobic disorder, Wittchen (1986) found the following mean ages of onset: phobic disorder (such as simple and social phobias), 15.3 years; agoraphobia, 29.6; panic disorder, 37.0; panic disorder and agoraphobia, 33.6; agoraphobia plus other phobias, 16.3. In a more differentiated analysis of the MFS, Wittchen (1988a) reported that most (35%) of the cases with panic disorder first experienced it between the ages of 31 and 40 (see Table 3.6). With regard to agoraphobia (with or without panic attack), 24% of the subjects (the highest percentage) had an age of onset between 21 and 30 years; two other peaks of onset were 11 to 20 years (21%) and 41 to 50 years (22%). Simple phobia's peak of onset was less than 10 years of age, and obsessive-compulsive disorder's was between 31 and 40. It is worth noting that the percentage of cases with simple phobia drops steadily as age increases.

The age-of-onset analysis by Von Korff et al. (1983), using the ECA data, showed the highest proportion of subjects having an onset in the 15 to 19-year age range and only rare onset of panic disorder after 40 (Fig. 3.1). In the Edmonton Study, the mean age of onset for panic disorder tended to be slightly higher for females (21.5 years) than for males (19.3 years) (Bland, Newman, & Orn, 1988a). A reverse finding was obtained for phobic disorder: the mean age of onset for females was 9.5 years and for males, 14.1 years. The highest percentages of onset for phobic and panic disorders in females were found in ages 0 to 9 (64%) and 10 to 19 (34%), with a rapid drop in succeeding years. In males, the highest percentages of onset for phobic and panic disorders were between the ages of 10 and 29.

TABLE 3.6 Distribution of Age of Onset for Anxiety Disorders in the Munich Follow-Up Study

	DSM-III diagnoses			
	Panic disorder (N = 14)	Agoraphobia (N = 26)	Simple phobia (N = 32)	Obsessive-compulsive disorder (N = 13)
Distribution of age of onset (years)				
10 and under	0%	16%	36%	10%
11–20	14%	21%	26%	20%
21–30	20%	24%	18%	10%
31–40	35%	18%	11%	40%
41–50	7%	22%	2%	10%
51 and over	20%	0%	2%	10%

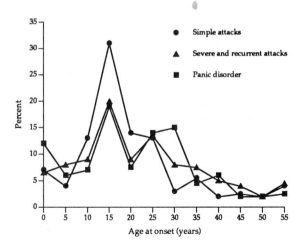

FIGURE 3.1 Percentage Distribution of Age at Onset (Years) for Cases with Simple Panic Attacks, Severe and Recurrent Panic Attacks, and Panic Disorder. (Source: Von Korff, M. R., Eaton, W. W., & Keyl, P. M. (1983) The epidemiology of panic attacks and panic disorder. *American Journal of Epidemiology*, 122: 976. Reprinted by permission.)

There is good clinical and epidemiological evidence that panic disorder most frequently starts in the late 20s and early 30s. However, one must be cautious about generalizing these findings, because data on the age of onset were gathered retrospectively (Wittchen et al., 1989). This method may not be as accurate as those in which new cases are identified close to the time of onset. In retrospective reporting, especially by older subjects, earlier (less severe) phases of the disorder may be missed due to recall problems. In spite of these cautions, as the same reporting method is used for various disorders there is no reason to doubt the magnitude of the age-of-onset differences reported among the disorders. The finding that many subjects had their first panic attack before the age of 20 raises the question of mode of onset and the factors that precipitate the onset of panic attacks and panic disorder.

Mode of Onset and Precipitating Factors

The mode of onset in panic disorder is usually described as sudden—an episode of acute, sustained panic followed by the development of phobic avoidance. Detailed epidemiological evidence for this view is lacking. However, based on the survey of a correspondence club (called the Open Door) of individuals with agoraphobia throughout Great Britain, significant disability was found to begin on an average of 15 months after the onset of agoraphobia. Once the phobia started, 80% were never again completely free of symptoms.

With respect to the precipitating factors, most patients claim vivid recall of their first panic attack and its circumstances. But again, no epidemiological data are available. Aronson and Logue (1987) reported that more than 75% of their patients could identify the precipitants of their first panic attack. Uhde et al. (1985) indicated that 80% of their cases with panic disorder have had one or more stressful life events within 6 months of their first attack. Traumatic events in a strict sense seem to be rare and were reported by only 3% to 8% of agoraphobic patients (Franklin, 1985; Goldstein & Chambless, 1978). Although numerous organic factors (not discussed here) have been proposed as having etiological importance, almost no study is available that allows us to estimate how important they actually are to the development of panic disorder. Alcohol (Lepine, 1987), cocaine (Aronson & Logue, 1987), and excess caffeine intake (Boulenger, Uhde, Wolff, & Post, 1984) can be cited as examples. Most studies have focused on the possible association between panic disorder or agoraphobia and childhood experience, genetic factors, and stressful life events. Because epidemiological studies of these relationships are lacking, some clinical studies will be presented here.

Childhood Experiences and Family Relationships

There have been many studies of the childhood and family relationships of patients with agoraphobia and panic disorder. When the relationship between maternal overprotectiveness and agoraphobia was measured using the Maternal Overprotection Questionnaire, Solyom, Silberfeld, and Solyom (1976) reported that the mothers of 21 patients with agoraphobia scored significantly higher on the "overprotective" scale of this questionnaire than did mothers of normal subjects.

Findings from the National Survey of Agoraphobia (Burns & Thorpe, 1977) also indicated that 37% of their sample reported their mothers to be overprotective, with significantly more females reporting this factor. Another 43% of the cases perceived their fathers as strict and unaffectionate. Describing their relationship with their mothers, 16% characterized it as "distant" or "very distant"—but about 30% described their relationship with their father that way. The suggestion that agoraphobic patients have overprotective mothers was not, however, supported by Parker (1979). In a study of 41 patients with agoraphobia and 40 socially phobic patients, Parker found that agoraphobic patients rated their mothers as less caring and less overprotective than did socially phobic patients.

In a study that examined the relationship between early development and psychiatric disorders, 55 subjects with various diagnoses were interviewed (Raskin et al., 1982). Of the 17 subjects with panic disorder, 8 reported an early maternal separation; of those 8 subjects, 5 were permanently separated. Furthermore, 7 subjects with panic disorder reported repeated physical abuse, and 12 were brought up in a grossly disturbed childhood environment. Similarly, Shafar (1976) found that more than one-third of their subjects with agoraphobia (n = 68) and social phobia (n = 20) reported a very unhappy or disrupted childhood; 12% described it as the most important factor in the onset of their phobia.

In a study by Buglass and colleagues (1977), the familial background of 30 agoraphobic housewives was compared with the history of 30 controls. Earlier attitudes toward parents were assessed in a semistructured interview. On scales measuring positive and negative feelings toward parents, patients could not be distinguished from controls. The two groups did not differ significantly in parental deprivation, parental death in childhood, interparental dominance, parental quarrels, or parental separation. The only familial background factor significantly differentiating the agoraphobic housewives from the controls was the presence of others not biologically related to the family. Stepparents, stepsiblings, or adopted siblings were found to be more common in the childhoods of agoraphobic subjects than those of controls.

There seems to be no general agreement on a definitive association of panic disorder and agoraphobia with childhood experience. Although some studies found mothers of agoraphobic patients to be overprotective, others did not. Many patients with panic or phobic disorders reported an unhappy or disturbed childhood; however, this finding should not be considered conclusive until it is confirmed by large, controlled epidemiological studies.

Familial and Genetic Factors

The genetic role in panic disorder was noted over a century ago. In their review paper, Cohen, Badal, Kilpatrick, Reed, and Whote (1951), for example, found that 19 different reports published between 1869 and 1948 identified a familial predisposition to anxiety disorders. In 1951, in a study involving the systematic collection of family history data, Cohen et al. (1951) reported that two-thirds of the families of their chronically ill patients had at least one affected relative. About 27 years later Noyes, Clancy, Crowe, Hoenk, and Slymen (1978) replicated the work of Cohen et al. (1951), using a sample of anxiety patients and surgical controls. They found an 18% morbidity risk for anxiety neurosis among first-degree relatives of patients with neurosis, compared with only 3% among control relatives. In addition, the risk for female relatives was found to be twice as high as for male relatives.

In a study that used either the DSM-III or the RDC with 278 first-degree relatives of 41 probands with panic disorder and 262 relatives of 41 controls, Crowe, Noyes, Pauls, and Slymen (1983) found that the morbidity risk for panic disorder was 17.3% in patients' relatives and only 1.8% in the control relatives. As in other studies (Noyes et al., 1978), female subjects had twice the risk of panic disorder as male subjects.

Harris, Noyes, Crowe, and Chaudhry (1983) compared the morbid risk for first-degree relatives of patients with agoraphobia or panic disorder with nonanxious controls. The morbidity risk of anxiety disorders in first-degree relatives was 32% for agoraphobia patients, 33% for patients with panic disorder, and 15% for controls. In addition, a higher risk of an alcohol disorder was found in the relatives of agoraphobic patients.

All these studies point to the importance of the family history in panic disorder. Nonetheless, we should be cautious in interpreting these findings, because environmental factors, in addition to genetic variables, may have affected familial patterns. To clarify this point, several twin studies have been conducted.

The principle behind twin studies is that the probability of developing the same illness with a genetic component is higher for monozygotic (MZ) twins than for dizygotic (DZ) twins, because the MZ twins have an identical genetic endowment but DZ twins a more disparate genetic composition. Carey and Gottesman (1981) reviewed studies of anxiety neurosis and reported a concordance of 88% and 38% for phobias in MZ twins and DZ twins, respectively. Likewise, the concordance rate in obsessive-compulsive disorder was 87% for 15 MZ twins and only 47% for 15 DZ twins. In a study of adult same-sexed twin patients in Norway, Torgersen (1983) found that 32 MZ twins had a significantly higher concordance rate for panic disorder or agoraphobia with panic attacks than did 53 DZ twins (31% versus 0%). This finding suggests some genetic predisposition for these disorders.

Stressful Life Events

Life events are defined as experiences that disrupt or threaten to disrupt an individual's usual activities and that may consequently cause readjustment in that person's behavior (Dohrenwend & Dohrenwend, 1974). While many of these events are commonly experienced in the natural life cycle (marriage, divorce, change of job, and so on), some events are more unusual (for instance, natural disaster). For life events that cause major adjustments in behavior and considerable psychological disturbance, the term *stressful life events* is often used.

Several studies have reported that psychiatric patients experience more major life events before the onset of a disorder than do control subjects. This phenomenon has long been recognized in studies of depressed and schizophrenic patients. It was not until recently that researchers began to investigate the etiological importance of stressful life events in anxiety disorders, particularly in panic disorder and agoraphobia.

Finlay-Jones and Brown (1981) studied the effect of life events on psychiatric symptoms in 164 young women attended by a general practitioner. All subjects were interviewed with a structured psychiatric instrument, the Present State Examination, and were asked about the occurrence of major life events in the year before the onset of their symptoms. Patients with anxiety neurosis reported a significantly higher frequency of severe-degree life events than did controls. The cases with depressive disorder were more likely to report events related to severe loss, whereas those with both depression and anxiety frequently reported severe loss or severe danger before the onset of disorder.

Faravelli (1985) compared the life event experience of 23 outpatients treated for panic disorder (using the DSM-III criteria) with the experience of 23 controls. Life events were determined by means of a semistructured interview that explored the occurrence of an event as well as its circumstances. Patients with panic disorder reported significantly more events in the 12 months prior to their first panic attack than did controls, and the events were clustered an average of 2 months prior to the onset of symptoms. As for the quality of the events, 83% of the patients compared with only 48% of the controls reported one or more severe events.

In an uncontrolled study, Katon (1984) reported that 38% of 55 patients with panic disorder had experienced a significant separation from their spouse or family in the year before the onset of their disorder. Another 9% reported the death of a close friend or family member; 16% reported a near-death experience. Likewise, in a study of 60 patients who met the DSM-III criteria for either agoraphobia with panic attacks or panic disorder, Breier et al. (1986) found that 63% reported a stressful life event occurring in the 6 months prior to the first panic attack. The most important of these events was the "threatened or actual separation from an important person."

Last, Barlow, and O'Brien (1984) interviewed 58 patients with agoraphobia to assess whether their disorder was preceded by stressful life events. About 81% reported at least one life event immediately preceded the onset of the disorder. Events related to "interpersonal conflict" (such as marital or familial strife) were most frequently reported, followed by "birth/marriage/hysterectomy," "death/illness of significant others," and "drug reaction." For heuristic purposes, the authors collapsed the reported life events into "conflict events" (marital/familial, death/illness of significant others) versus endocrine-physiological reactions (birth/miscarriage/hysterectomy, drug reaction). Given this dichotomy, 50% reported events related to conflict and 41% reported endocrine or physiological reactions.

Franklin and Andrews (in press) had agoraphobic patients complete the Tennant and Andrews Life Event Inventory to record events experienced before the onset of their disorder. In comparison with the controls, who had been requested to record life events experienced in the past 12 months, the patients reported significantly more life events in the year before the onset of their disorder. In another study, Franklin (cited in Andrews, 1987) compared the number of life events experienced by agoraphobic patients with those of generalized anxiety disorder patients and matched controls. Life events were recorded by either an unstructured interview or a questionnaire. Compared with generalized anxiety disorder patients, agoraphobic patients experienced significantly more events and reported a higher degree of distress about them. Further comparison indicated that patients with these two disorders reported more events than did their matched controls.

Lelliott, Marks, McNammee, and Tobena (1989) found that 22 of 56 patients (42%) having panic disorder with agoraphobia reported a major life event in the month prior to the first panic. Six reported familial or marital arguments; three experienced a threatened or actual separation; four reported an illness in a family member; two experienced the death of a close friend or relative; one had a personal physical illness; two were pregnant or gave birth; one had financial troubles; and three experienced other types of events.

These life event studies, using clinical samples, suggest that the onset of panic disorder and agoraphobia tends to be preceded by stressful life events. Patients with panic disorder and agoraphobia also experience more severe life events compared with those with generalized anxiety disorder or controls. However, all these studies have serious methodological and conceptual deficits. As it is known that genetic (Reich, James, & Morris, 1972), biological (Marks, 1986), and personality factors play a role in the etiology, it seems unlikely that life events by themselves can explain the development of the disorder.

Some support for the critical role played by a combination of factors has fairly recently been presented in a study by Lelliott et al. (1989). They found that the first panic attack reported by their 56 patients having panic disorder with agoraphobia occurred more often in late spring or summer, during warm weather, than it did in winter or cold weather. About 70% of their patients had prodromal depression, anxiety, or avoidance in the month before their first panic. As for the sequence of symptom onset, 23% reported that agoraphobic avoidance preceded their first panic attack. Another 32% reported avoidant behavior within days of their first attack (which came "out of the blue" for 20%). Forty-one percent began avoiding after more than one attack (between 1 week and 11 years later). These findings were explained according to the "integrated model of agoraphobia with panic disorder," which considers the prepotency and preparedness of agoraphobic cues under stress, kindling of panic, and positive feedback loops from panic, avoidance, and somatic and cognitive concomitants.

Health Service Utilization

An important finding in recent epidemiological research is the high utilization rate of medical services by persons with an anxiety disorder. The MFS, for example, indicated a significantly high rate of visits to nonpsychiatric health facilities, especially to general practitioners and internal medicine specialists. The mean number of visits to general health settings by cases with agoraphobia and/or panic disorder was 62 in a 7-year interval, as compared with 28 by a matched (for age, sex, and marital status) control group. Similarly, other investigators (Shapiro et al., 1984) have reported relatively high utilization rates for anxiety disorders in all types of health service, including mental health service and general medical providers. Shapiro et al. found that between 15.4% and 22.8% of those with anxiety or somatoform disorders in New Haven, Baltimore, and St. Louis had made at least one mental health visit to either a general or a mental health provider in the 6 months before the study. In a more elaborate analysis of the ECA data from all five sites, Boyd (1986) reported that in comparison with subjects who had other psychiatric disorders, those with panic disorder had the highest number of mental health visits. Furthermore, they received about three times more mental health treatment than did those with phobia, alcohol abuse or dependence, or drug abuse or dependence, and about twelve times more treatment than those with no DIS disorder. In another analysis of the ECA data from all five sites (see Table 3.7), cases with agoraphobia were found to be higher users of services, particularly in the specialty mental health sector, than those with other phobias (Thompson et al., 1988).

TABLE 3.7 Percentage of Persons with Agoraphobia and Other Phobias Using Services by Sector in the Past 6 Months, All ECA Sites Combined: Weighted Data[a]

Type of phobia	Visit for mental health reason to				Visit for general health reason to general health sector	Visit for any reason to any sector (overall help-seeking)
	Specialty mental health sector	General health sector	Other human services sector	Any sector (overall mental health help-seeking)		
Agoraphobia	12.1% (1.5)	10.7% (1.7)	3.9% (0.9)	26.7% (2.1)	53.3% (2.3)	70.9% (2.0)
Other phobia	6.2% (1.0)	7.1% (0.1)	2.4% (0.6)	15.6% (1.5)	56.7% (2.2)	67.5% (2.0)

[a]Numbers in parentheses are standard errors in percent.
SOURCE: Thompson, J. W., Burns, B. J., Bartko, J., Boyd, J. H., Taube, C. A., & Bourdon, K. H. (1988). The use of ambulatory services by persons with and without phobia. *Medical Care, 26:* 190. Reprinted with permission.

We can summarize the typical treatment of anxiety disorders by paraphrasing Klerman's words about depressive disorders. Anxiety patients in the community are poorly recognized and treated. Most cases who receive no specific psychological or pharmacological intervention (or a combination of both) tend to have a symptom pattern that is persistent and chronic. There is a remarkably high long-term risk for developing psychopathological and psychosocial complications and a low probability of complete remission. It remains to be seen whether we have developed efficient treatment strategies to change the unfavorable pattern of the natural course and outcome, and whether it is possible to make those treatment methods available to those in need of help. Recent long-term follow-up studies of severely impaired inpatient samples (Krieg, Bronisch, Wittchen, & von Zerssen, 1987; Wittchen & von Zerssen, 1988) and the low rate of cases receiving any specific or adequate professional help in the health care system do not justify optimism.

Conclusion

Recent epidemiologic studies indicate that panic disorder (using the DSM-III definition) occurs in adults with a lifetime prevalence of about 2% and a 6-month rate of 1.2%. These studies also indicate that panic disorder frequently coexists with other anxiety disorders and with other psychiatric disorders such as depression and substance abuse. Agoraphobia has been estimated to have a lifetime prevalence rate of about 5% and a 6-month rate of approximately 4%. Using the new DSM-III-R classification, we can conjecture that almost 50% of these agoraphobic subjects would be reclassified as having panic disorder with agoraphobia.

The mean age of onset for various anxiety disorders is generally from the late teens to the mid-20s, with infrequent onset after 40. Anxiety disorders often have a duration of many years, and many individuals, especially those with panic disorder and agoraphobia, are markedly impaired in social functioning. Substance abuse and depression are common complications associated with long-term course and poor outcome, respectively.

Being female and divorced, separated, or widowed is associated with a higher prevalence of panic disorder and agoraphobia. Other risk factors (such as race, urbanization, and education) and various precipitating factors have not proven to be consistently and powerfully related to the development of panic disorder and agoraphobia. More epidemiologic studies exploring these factors and the comorbidity between anxiety disorders and somatization, personality disorder, and physical illness are needed. Further studies should also explore the natural course of these disorders.

References

Agras, W. S., Chapin, N., & Oliveau, D. C. (1972). The natural history of phobia. *Archives of General Psychiatry, 26,* 315–317.

Agras, W. S., Sylvester, D., & Oliveau, D. (1969). The epidemiology of common fear and phobia. *Comprehensive Psychiatry, 10,* 151–156.

American Psychiatric Association. (1980). *Diagnostic and statistical manual of mental disorders,* (3rd. ed.). Washington, DC: Author.

American Psychiatric Association. (1987). *Diagnostic and statistical manual of mental disorders,* (3rd. ed., rev.). Washington, DC: Author.

Anderson, D. J., Noyes, R., & Crowe, R. R. (1984). A comparison of panic disorder and generalized anxiety disorder. *American Journal of Psychiatry, 141,* 572–575.

Andrews, G. (1987). *Stressful life events and anxiety.* Unpublished manuscript.

Angst, J., & Dobler-Mikola, A. (1985). The Zurich study—V. Anxiety and phobia in young adults. *European Archives of Psychiatric Neurological Science, 234,* 408–418.

Angst, J., & Dobler-Mikola, A. (1986). Assoziation und Depression auf syndromaler und diagnostischer Ebene. In H. Helmschen & M. Linden (Eds.), *Die Differnzierung von Angst und Depression.* Heidelberg: Springer.

Aronson, T. A., & Logue, C. M. (1987). On the longitudinal course of panic disorder: Developmental history and predictors of phobic complications. *Comprehensive Psychiatry, 28,* 344–355.

Barlow, D. H. (1986). A psychological model of panic. In B. F. Shaw, F. Cashman, Z. V. Segal, & T. M. Vallis (Eds.), *Anxiety disorders: Theory, diagnosis, and treatment. New York: Plenum.*

Barlow, D. H., DiNardo, P. A., Vermilyea, B. B., Vermilyea, J., & Blanchard, E. (1986). Comorbidity and depression among the anxiety disorders. *Journal of Nervous and Mental Disease, 174,* 63–72.

Barlow, D. H., Vermilyea, J., Blanchard, E. B., Vermilyea, B. B., DiNardo, P. A., & Cerny, J. A. (1985). The phenomenon of panic. *Journal of Abnormal Psychology, 94,* 320–328.

Bebbington, P., Contractor, N., Hurry, J., & Tennant, C. (1982). *Prevalence of anxiety and obsessional symptoms in the Camberwell community.* Unpublished data.

Bibb, J., & Chambless, D. (1986). Alcoholism and alcohol abuse among diagnosed agoraphobics. *Behaviour Research and Therapy, 24,* 49–58.

Bland, R. C., Newman, S. C., & Orn, H. (1988a). Age of onset of psychiatric disorders. *Acta Psychiatrica Scandinavica, 77*(Suppl. 338), 43–49.

Bland, R. C., Newman, S. C., & Orn, H. (1988b). Period prevalence of psychiatric disorders in Edmonton. *Acta Psychiatrica Scandinavica, 77*(Suppl. 338), 33–42.

Bland, R. C., Orn, H., & Newman, S. C. (1988). Lifetime prevalence of psychiatric disorders in Edmonton. *Acta Psychiatrica Scandinavica, 77*(Suppl. 338), 24–32.

Bland, R. C., Stebelsky, H., Orn, H., & Newman, S. C. (1988). Psychiatric disorders and unemployment in Edmonton. *Acta Psychiatrica Scandinavica, 77*(Suppl. 338), 72–80.

Blazer, D., George, L. K., Landerman, R., Pennybacker, M., Melville, M. L., Woodbury, M., Manton, K. G., Jordan, K., & Locke, B. (1985). Psychiatric disorders: A rural/urban comparison. *Archives of General Psychiatry, 42,* 651–656.

Boulenger, J.-P., Uhde, T. W., Wolff, E. A. III, & Post, R. M. (1984). Increased sensitivity to caffeine in patients with panic disorder: Preliminary evidence. *Archives of General Psychiatry, 41,* 1067–1071.

Bourdon, K. H., Boyd, J. H., Rae, D. S., Burns, B. J., Thompson, J. W., & Locke, B. Z. (1988). Gender differences in phobias: Results of the ECA community survey. *Journal of Anxiety Disorders, 2*(3), 227–241.

Boyd, J. F. (1986). Use of mental health services for the treatment of panic disorder. *American Journal of Psychiatry, 143,* 1569–1574.

Breier, A., & Charney, D. S. (1985, May). *The natural course of agoraphobia–panic disorder.* Paper presented at the American Psychiatric Association Convention.

Breier, A., Charney, D. S., & Heninger, G. R. (1986). Agoraphobia with panic attacks: Development, diagnostic stability, and course of illness. *Archives of General Psychiatry, 43,* 1029–1036.

Buglass, D., Clarke, J., Henderson, A. S., Kreitman, N., & Presley, A. S. (1977). A study of agoraphobic housewives. *Psychological Medicine, 7,* 73–86.

Burnam, M. A., Hough, R. L., Escobar, J. I., Karno, M., Timbers, D. M., Telles, C. A., & Locke, B. Z. (1987). Six-month prevalence of specific psychiatric disorders among Mexican Americans and non-Hispanic whites in Los Angeles. *Archives of General Psychiatry, 44,* 687–694.

Burns, L. E., & Thorpe, G. L. (1977). The epidemiology of fears and phobias (with particular reference to the National Survey of Agoraphobics). *Journal of International Medical Research, 5,* 1–7.

Canino, G. J., Bird, H. R., Shrout, P. E., Rubio-Stipec, M., Bravo, M., Martinez, R., Sesman, M., & Guevara, L. M. (1987). The prevalence of specific psychiatric disorders in Puerto Rico. *Archives of General Psychiatry, 44,* 727–735.

Carey, G., & Gottesman, I. I. (1981). Twin and family studies of anxiety, phobia, and obsessive disorder. In D. F. Klein & J. Rabkin (Eds.), *Anxiety: New research and changing concepts.* New York: Raven Press.

Chambless, D. L. (1985). The relationship of severity of agoraphobia to associated psychopathology. *Behaviour Research and Therapy, 23,* 305–310.

Cohen, M. E., Badal, D. W., Kilpatrick, A., Reed, E. W., & Whote, P. D. (1951). The high familial prevalence of neurocirculatory asthenia (anxiety neurosis, effort syndrome). *American Journal of Human Genetics, 3,* 126–158.

Cooper, B., & Sylph, J. (1973). Life events in the onset of neurotic illness: An investigation in general practice. *Psychological Medicine, 3,* 421–435.

Costello, C. G. (1982). Fears and phobias in women: A community study. *Journal of Abnormal Psychology, 91,* 280–286.

Cottraux, J., Mollard, E., & Duinat-Pascal, A. (1988). Agoraphobia with panic attacks and social phobia: A comparative clinical and psychometric study. *Psychiatry and Psychobiology, 3,* 49–56.

Crowe, R. R. Noyes, R., Pauls, D. L., & Slymen, D. (1983). A family study of panic disorder. *Archives of General Psychiatry, 40,* 1065–1069.

Dean, C., Surtees, P. G., & Sashidharan, S. P. (1983). Comparison of research diagnostic systems in an Edinburgh community sample. *British Journal of Psychiatry, 142,* 247–256.

Dilling, H., & Weyerer, S. (1984). Prevalence of mental disorders in the small-town–rural region of Traunstein (Upper Bavaria). *Acta Psychiatrica Scandinavica, 69,* 60–79.

Dohrenwend, B. S., & Dohrenwend, B. P. (1974). Some issues in research on stressful life events. *Journal of Nervous and Mental Disease, 166,* 7–15.

Eaton, W. W., Weissman, M. M., Anthony, J., Robins, L. N., Blazer, D. G., & Karno, M. (1985). Problems in the definition and measurement of prevalence and incidence of psychiatric disorders. In W. W. Eaton & L. Kessler (Eds.), *Epidemiology field methods in psychiatry: The NIMH Epidemiologic Catchment Area Program* (pp. 311–326). New York: Academic Press.

Errera, P., & Coleman, J. V. (1963). A long-term follow-up study of neurotic phobic patients in a psychiatric clinic. *Journal of Nervous and Mental Disease, 136,* 267–271.

Essau, C., & Wittchen, H.-U. (in preparation). *Lifetime and 6-month prevalence of psychiatric disorders (ICD-9) in the Munich Follow-Up Study.*

Essen-Möller, E. (1956). Individual traits and morbidity in a Swedish rural population. *Acta Psychiatrica et Neurologica Scandinavica*(Suppl. 100), 1–160.

Faravelli, C. (1985). Life events preceding the onset of panic disorder. *Journal of Affective Disorders, 9,* 103–105.

Feighner, J. P., Robins, E., Guze, S. B., Woodruff, R. A., Winokur, G., & Munoz, R. (1972). Diagnostic criteria for use in psychiatric research. *Archives of General Psychiatry, 26,* 57–63.

Finlay-Jones, R., & Brown, G. W. (1981). Types of stressful life event and the onset of anxiety and depressive disorders. *Psychological Medicine, 11,* 803–815.

Fodor, I. G. (1974). The phobic syndrome in women: Implications for treatment. In V. Franks & V. Burtle (Eds.), *Women in therapy.* New York: Raven Press.

Franklin, J. A. (1985). *Agoraphobia: Its nature, aetiology, maintainence and treatment.* Unpublished manuscript, Sydney.

Franklin, J. A., & Andrews, G. (in press). Stress and the onset of agoraphobia. *Australian Psychologist.*

Gittelman, R., & Klein, D. F. (1973). School phobia: Diagnostic considerations in the light of imipramine effects. *Journal of Nervous and Mental Disease, 156,* 199–215.

Goldberg, R. J. (1982). *Anxiety: A guide to biobehavioral diagnosis and therapy for physicians and mental health clinicians.* New York: Medical Examination.

Goldstein, A. J., & Chambless, D. L. (1978). A re-analysis of agoraphobia. *Behavior Therapy, 9,* 47–59.

Hand, I., & Wittchen, H.-U. (Eds.). (1986). *Panic and phobias.* Heidelberg: Springer.

Harris, E. L., Noyes, R., Crowe, R. R., & Chaudhry, D. R. (1983). Family study of agoraphobia. *Archives of General Psychiatry, 40,* 1061–1064.

Helgason, T. (1964). Epidemiology of mental disorders in Iceland. *Acta Psychiatrica Scandinavica, 40*(Suppl. 173), 11–176.

Helmchen, H., & Linden, M. (Eds.). (1986). *Die Differenzierung von Angst und Depression.* Heidelberg: Springer.

Helzer, J., & Canino, G. (Eds.). (in press). *Comparison of rates of alcoholism.* Oxford: Oxford University Press.

Helzer, J. E., Stoltzman, R. K., Farmer, A., Brockington, I. F., Plesons, D., Singerman, B., & Works, J. (1985). Comparing the DIS/DSM-III–based physician reevaluation. In E. E. Eaton & L. G. Kessler (Eds.), *Epidemiologic field methods in psychiatry. The NIMH Epidemiologic Catchment Area Program.* New York: Academic Press.

Jablensky, A. (1985). Approaches to the definition and classification of anxiety and related disorders. In A. H. Tuma & J. D. Maser (Eds.), *Anxiety and the anxiety disorders.* Hillsdale, NJ: Lawrence Erlbaum.

Jablensky, A., Sartorius, N., Gulbinat, W., & Ernberg, G. (1981). Depressives contacting psychiatric services in 4 cultures. *Acta Psychiatrica Scandinavica, 63,* 367–383.

Karno, M., Hough, R. L., Burnam, M. A., Escobar, J. I., Timbers, D. M., Santana, F., & Boyd, J. H. (1987). Lifetime prevalence of specific psychiatric disorders among Mexican Americans and non-Hispanic whites in Los Angeles. *Archives of General Psychiatry, 44,* 695–701.

Katon, W. (1984). Panic disorder and somatization: Review of 55 cases. *The American Journal of Medicine, 77,* 101–106.

King, R., Margraf, J., Ehlers, A., & Maddock, R. (1986). Panic disorder—Overlap with symptoms of somatization disorder. In I. Hand & H.-U. Wittchen (Eds.), *Panic and phobias, Vol. 1.* Heidelberg: Springer.

Klein, D. F. (1964). Delineation of two drug-responsive anxiety syndromes. *Psychopharmacologia, 5,* 397–408.

Klein, D. F. (1967). Importance of psychiatric diagnoses in prediction of clinical drug effects. *Archives of General Psychiatry, 16,* 118–126.

Klein, D. F. (1981). Anxiety reconceptualized. In D. F. Klein & J. G. Rabkin (Eds.), *Anxiety: New research and changing concepts.* New York: Raven Press.

Klein, D. F., & Fink, M. (1962). Psychiatric reaction patterns to imipramine. *American Journal of Psychiatry, 119,* 432–438.

Krieg, J. C., Bronisch, T., Wittchen, H.-U., & von Zerssen, D. (1987). Anxiety disorders: A long-term prospective and retrospective follow-up study of former inpatients suffering from an anxiety neurosis or phobia. *Acta Psychiatrica Scandinavica, 76,* 36–47.

Last, C. G., Barlow, D. H., & O'Brien, G. T. (1984). Precipitants of agoraphobia: Role of stressful life events. *Psychological Reports, 54,* 567–570.

Leckman, J. F., Weissman, M. M., Merikangas, K. R., Pauls, D. L., & Prusoff, B. A. (1983). Panic disorder and major depression. *Archives of General Psychiatry, 40,* 1055–1060.

Lelliott, P., Marks, I., McNammee, G., & Tobena, A. (1989). Onset of panic disorder with agoraphobia: Towards an integrated model. *Archives of General Psychiatry, 46,* 1000–1004.

Lepine, J. P. (1987). Epidemiologie des attaques de panique et de l'agoraphobie. In J.-P. Boulenger (Ed.), *L'attaque de panique: Un nouveau concept?* Chateau de Loir: Goureau.

Lesser, I. M., Rubin, R. T., Pecknold, J. C., Rifkin, A., Swinson, R. P., Lydiard, R. B., Burrows, G. D., Noyes, R., Jr., & DuPont, R. L., Jr. (1988). Secondary depression in panic disorder and agoraphobia. *Archives of General Psychiatry, 45,* 437–443.

Lydiard, R. B., & Ballenger, J. C. (1987). Antidepressants in panic disorder and agoraphobia. *Journal of Affective Disorders, 13,* 135–168.

Margraf, J., & Ehlers, A. (1988). Panic attacks in non-clinical subjects. In I. Hand & H.-U. Wittchen (Eds.), *Panic and phobias, Vol. 2.* Heidelberg: Springer.

Marks, I. M. (1970). The classification of phobic disorders. *British Journal of Psychiatry, 116,* 377–386.

Marks, I. M. (1986). Foreward. In I. Hand & H.-U. Wittchen (Eds.), *Panic and phobias, Vol. 1.* Heidelberg: Springer.

Marks, I. M. (1987). *Fear, phobias, and rituals: Panic, anxiety, and their disorders.* Oxford: Oxford University Press.

Marks, I. M., Gray, S., Cohen, D., Hill, R., Mawson, D., Ramm, E., & Stern, R. (1983). Imipramine and brief therapist-aided exposure in agoraphobics having self-exposure homework. *Archives of General Psychiatry, 40,* 153–162.

Marks, I. M., & Herst, E. R. (1970). A survey of 1200 agoraphobics in Britain. *Social Psychiatry, 5,* 16–24.

Marks, I. M., & Lader, M. (1973). Anxiety states (anxiety neurosis): A review. *Journal of Nervous and Mental Disease, 156,* 3–18.

Mathews, A. M., Gelder, G., & Johnston, D. W. (1981). *Agoraphobia: Nature and treatment.* New York: Guilford Press.

Myers, J. K., Weissman, M. M., Tischler, G. L., Holzer, C. E., Leaf, P. J., Orvaschel, H., Anthony, J. C., Boyd, J. H., Burke, J. D., Jr., Kramer, M., & Stoltzman, R. (1984). Six-month prevalence of psychiatric disorders in three communities. *Archives of General Psychiatry, 41,* 959–967.

Norton, G. R., Dorward, J., & Cox, B.J. (1986). Factors associated with panic attacks in non-clinical subjects. *Behavior Therapy, 17,* 239–252.

Norton, G. R., Harrison, B., Hauch, J., & Rhodes, L. (1985). Characteristics of people with infrequent panic attacks. *Journal of Abnormal Psychology, 94,* 216–221.

Noyes, R., Jr., Clancy, J., Crowe, R. R., Hoenk, P. R., & Slymen, D. J. (1978). The familial prevalence of anxiety neurosis. *Archives of General Psychiatry, 35,* 1057–1059.

Parker, G. (1979). Reported parental characteristics of agoraphobics and social phobics. *British Journal of Psychiatry, 135,* 555–560.

Paykel, E. S., Weissman, M. M., & Prusoff, B. A. (1978). Social maladjustment and severity of depression. *Comprehensive Psychiatry, 19,* 121–128.

Raskin, M., Peeke, H. V. S., Dickman, W., & Pinsker, H. (1982). Panic and generalized anxiety disorders. *Archives of General Psychiatry, 39,* 687–689.

Regier, D. A., Meyer, J. K., Kramer, M., Robins, L. N., Blazer, D. G., Hough, R. L., Eaton, W. W., & Locke, B. Z. (1984). The NIMH Epidemiologic Catchment Area (ECA) Program: Historical context, major objective, and study population characteristics. *Archives of General Psychiatry, 41*, 934–941.

Reich, J. (1986). The epidemiology of anxiety. *Journal of Nervous and Mental Disease, 174*, 129–136.

Reich, T., James, J. W., & Morris, C. A. (1972). Multiple thresholds in the transmission of semi-continuous traits. *Annals of Human Genetics, 36*, 163–186.

Roberts, A. H. (1964). Housebound housewives—A follow-up study of a phobic anxiety state. *British Journal of Psychiatry, 110*, 191–197.

Robins, L. N., Helzer, J. E., Ratcliff, K. S., & Seyfried, W. (1982). Validity of the Diagnostic Interview Schedule, Version II: DSM-III diagnoses. *Psychological Medicine, 12*, 855–870.

Robins, L. N., Helzer, J. E., Weissman, M. M., Orvaschel, H., Gruenberg, E., Burke, J. D., Jr., & Regier, D. A. (1984). Lifetime prevalence of psychiatric disorders at three sites. *Archives of General Psychiatry, 41*, 949–959.

Shafar, S. (1976). Aspects of phobic illness—A study of 90 personal cases. *British Journal of Medical Psychology, 49*, 221–236.

Shapiro, S., Skinner, E. A., Kessler, L. G., Von Korff, M., German, P. S., Tischler, G. L., Leaf, P. J., Benham, L., Cottler, L., & Regier, D. A. (1984). Utilization of health and mental health services. *Archives of General Psychiatry, 41*, 971–978.

Sheehan, D. V. (1982). Panic attacks and phobias. *New England Journal of Medicine, 307*, 156–158.

Sheehan, D. V. (1987). Benzodiazepines in panic disorder and agoraphobia. *Journal of Affective Disorders, 13*, 169–181.

Sheehan, D. V., Ballenger, J., & Jacobsen, G. (1980). Treatment of endogenous anxiety with phobic, hysterical, and hypochondriacal symptoms. *Archives of General Psychiatry, 37*, 51–59.

Solyom, L., Silberfeld, M., & Solyom, C. (1976). Maternal overprotection in the etiology of agoraphobia. *Journal of Canadian Psychiatric Association, 21*, 109–113.

Spitzer, R. L., Endicott, J., & Robins, E. (1978). Research diagnostic criteria: Rationale and reliability. *Archives of General Psychiatry, 35*, 773–782.

Spitzer, R. L. & Williams, J. B. W. (1983). *Structured clinical interview for DSM-III (SCID)*. New York: New York Psychiatric Institute.

Tennant, C., Hurry, J., & Bebbington, P. (1981). The short-term outcome of neurotic disorders in the community—Demographic and clinical predictors of remission of neurotic disorders in the community. *Australian and New Zealand Journal of Psychiatry, 15*, 111–116.

Thompson, J. W., Burns, B. J., Bartko, J., Boyd, J. H., Taube, C. A., & Bourdon, K. H. (1988). The use of ambulatory services by persons with and without phobia. *Medical Care, 26*, 183–198.

Thorpe, G. K., & Burns, L. E. (1983). *The agoraphobic syndrome*. New York: Wiley.

Thyer, B. A., Parrish, R. T., Curtis, G. C., Nesse, R. M., & Cameron, O. G. (1985). Age of onset of DSM-III anxiety disorders. *Comprehensive Psychiatry, 26*, 113–122.

Thyer, B. A., Parrish, R. T., Himle, J., Cameron, O. G., Curtis, G. C., & Nesse, R. M. (1986). Alcohol abuse among clinically anxious patients. *Behaviour Research and Therapy, 24*, 357–359.

Torgersen, S. (1983). Genetics of neuroses: The effect of sampling variation upon the twin concordance ratio. *British Journal of Psychiatry, 142*, 126–132.

Tuma, A. H., & Maser, J. D. (Eds.). (1985). *Anxiety and the anxiety disorders.* Hillsdale, NJ: Lawrence Erlbaum.

Uhde, T. W., Boulenger, J.-P., Roy-Byrne, P. P., Geraci, M. F., Vittone, B. J., & Post, R. M. (1985). Longitudinal course of panic disorder: Clinical and biological considerations. *Progress in Neuro-Pharmacology and Biological Psychiatry, 9,* 39–51.

Uhlenhuth, E. H., Balter, M. B., Mellinger, G. G., Cisin, I. H., & Clinthorpe, J. (1983). Symptom checklist syndromes in the general population: Correlations with psychotherapeutic drug use. *Archives of General Psychiatry, 40,* 1167–1173.

van den Hout, M. A. (1988). Panic, perception, and pCO_2. In I. Hand & H.-U. Wittchen (Eds.), *Panic and phobias, Vol. 2.* Heidelberg: Springer.

Von Korff, M., Eaton, W., & Keyl, P. (1983). The epidemiology of panic attacks and panic disorder: Results of three community surveys. *American Journal of Epidemiology, 122,* 970–981.

Weissman, M. M. (1987). Epidemiology overview. In R. E. Hales & A. I. Frances (Eds.), *Annual review of psychiatry, Vol. 6.* Washington, DC: American Psychiatric Press.

Weissman, M. M., & Klerman, G. L. (1977). Sex differences and the epidemiology of depression. *Archives of General Psychiatry, 34,* 98–112.

Weissman, M. M., Leaf, P. J., Blazer, D. G., Boyd, J. H., & Florio, L. P. (1986). Panic disorder: Clinical characteristics, epidemiology, and treatment. *Psychopharmacology Bulletin, 22,* 787–791.

Weissman, M. M., Leaf, P. J., Holzer, C. E., & Merikangas, K. P. (1985). Epidemiology of anxiety disorders. *Psychopharmacology Bulletin, 21,* 538–541.

Weissman, M. M., Leckman, J. F., Merikangas, K. R., Gammon, G. D., & Prusoff, B. A. (1984). Depression and anxiety disorders in parents and children. *Archives of General Psychiatry, 41,* 845–853.

Weissman, M. M., & Merikangas, K. R. (1986). The epidemiology of anxiety and panic disorders: An update. *Journal of Clinical Psychiatry, 47,* 11–17.

Weissman, M. M., & Myers, J. K. (1980). Psychiatric disorders in a U.S. community: The application of Research Diagnostic Criteria to a resurveyed community sample. *Acta Psychiatrica Scandinavica, 62,* 99–111.

Weissman, M. M., Myers, J. K., & Harding, P. S. (1978). Psychiatric disorders in a U.S. urban community. *American Journal of Psychiatry, 135,* 459–462.

Wing, J. K., Cooper, J. E., & Sartorious, N. (1974). *Measurement and classification of psychiatric symptoms.* Cambridge: Cambridge University Press.

Wittchen, H.-U. (1986). Epidemiology of panic attacks and panic disorders. In I. Hand & H.-U. Wittchen (Eds.), *Panic and phobias, Vol. 1.* Heidelberg: Springer.

Wittchen, H.-U. (1988a). Natural course and spontaneous remissions of untreated anxiety disorders: Results of the Munich Follow-Up Study (MFS). In I. Hand & H.-U. Wittchen (Eds.), *Panic and phobias, Vol. 2.* Heidelberg: Springer.

Wittchen, H.-U. (1988b). Zum Spontanverlauf unbehandelter Fälle mit Angststörungen und Depressionen. In H.-U. Wittchen & D. von Zerssen (Eds.), *Verläufe behandelter und unbehandelter Depressionen und Angststörungen.* Heidelberg: Springer.

Wittchen, H.-U., & Bronish, T. (in press). Use, abuse, and dependence of alcohol in West Germany—Lifetime and 6-month prevalence in the Munich Follow-Up Study. In J. Helzer & G. Canino (Eds.), *Comparison of rates of alcoholism.* Oxford: Oxford University Press.

Wittchen, H.-U., & Burke, J. (in preparation). *DIS/DSM-III prevalence rates of mental disorders in the U.S. and Germany.*

Wittchen, H.-U., Burke, J., Semler, G., Pfister, H., von Cranach, M., & Zaudig, M. (1989). Recall and dating reliability of psychiatric symptoms—Test-retest reliability of time related symptom questions in a Standardized Psychiatric Interview (CIDI/DIS). *Archives of General Psychiatry, 46,* 437–443.

Wittchen, H.-U., Hecht, H., Zaudig, M., Vogl, G., Semler, G., & Pfister, H. (1988). Häufigkeiten und Schwere psychischer Störungen in der Bevölkerung—Eine epidemiologische Feldstudie. In H.-U. Wittchen & D. von Zerssen (Eds.), *Verläufe behandelter und unbehandelter Depressionen und Angststörungen in der Bevölkerungen.* Heidelberg: Springer.

Wittchen, H.-U., & Semler, G. (1986). Diagnostic reliability of anxiety disorders. In I. Hand & H.-U. Wittchen (Eds.), *Panic and phobias, Vol. 1.* Heidelberg: Springer.

Wittchen, H.-U., Semler, G., & von Zerssen, D. (1985). A comparison of two diagnostic methods—Clinical ICD diagnosis versus DSM-III and Research Diagnostic Criteria using the Diagnostic Interview Schedule (Version 2). *Archives of General Psychiatry, 42,* 677–684.

Wittchen, H.-U., & von Zerssen, D. (Eds.). (1988). *Verläufe behandelter und unbehandelter Depressionen und Angststörungen in der Bevölkerungen.* Heidelberg: Springer.

World Health Organization. (1978). *Glossary of mental disorders and guide to their classification.* Geneva: Author.

CHAPTER 4

The Biology
of Panic Disorder:
A Long-term View and Critique

MALCOLM LADER

Introduction

Research into what has been dubbed "panic disorder" has burgeoned in the past decade for a variety of reasons. First, there is a cycle of fashion in research, usually reflecting the novelty of concepts or the concatenation of approaches from different disciplines. The advent of new techniques powerfully influences this process; for example, the new imaging techniques have led to a reexamination of many psychiatric syndromes in terms of their morphology and, more recently, function (Herold & Frackowiak, 1986). Ultimately, in fact, advances depend on techniques.

Second, personalities are important. Although concepts and techniques will provide new information, its rate of accrual is dependent on the degree of single-mindedness with which a few individuals pursue the topic. This has been true in the area of panic disorder, in which much of our thinking and, indeed, our practical management of patients has been profoundly influenced by the work and publications of the group of workers in New York directed by Donald Klein. The initial observation was that panic attacks responded to treatment with imipramine whereas background, generalized anxiety did not (Klein, 1964). Klein regarded avoidance behavior as secondary to panic attacks, thus giving paramountcy in this area to panic.

A third and pragmatically important reason is that therapeutic advances have resulted in the reappraisal of panic as a symptom, syndrome, and perhaps disorder. The ineffectiveness of anxiolytic doses of benzodiazepines was recognized early. This more or less coincided with the use, by Klein and by others, of antidepressants in the management of patients complaining of panic. In the United States and Canada tricyclic antidepressants became the standard treatment, and this practice was widely adopted by psychiatrists in continental Europe. In the United Kingdom, although tricyclic antidepressants were favored by some, the monoamine oxidase inhibitor class of antidepressants had their influential advocates, especially where phobic anxiety was marked. When pharmacological treatments are deemed effective for a psychiatric condition, a stimulus is given to biological research. Although few are so unsophisticated as to aver that if a condition is helped by drugs, it must be biological *in origin*, most would accept that biological *mechanisms* are involved in some way. Working out how a drug ameliorates a certain condition will not necessarily tell us much about the etiology or even the pathogenesis—but it might!

The fourth reason for the increased tempo of research reflects powerful and perfectly legitimate commercial interests. The development of newer benzodiazepines with perhaps greater ceiling efficacy has led to a reexamination of one of these drugs, alprazolam, for the treatment of panic disorder. Around the umbra of large-scale but essentially standard clinical trials a penumbra of studies on panic has developed. Many of these studies pertain to biological aspects of the topic. Only a few have been completed and analyzed, but eventually an impressive body of data will become available.

Thus, of the various aspects of panic, the biological have received most emphasis. This reflects the prominent biological features of panic attacks, the presumption of major biological influences in the etiology and pathogenesis of these phenomena, and the possible relationship to physical disorders such as mitral valve prolapse. As a result some of the psychological aspects have been relatively neglected, though some attempts have been made to synthesize the various approaches into a coherent whole.

This chapter will essay a critique of studies on the biological aspects of panic disorder, pointing out both methodological and conceptual shortcomings. The literature will not be reviewed in detail because excellent compendious reviews already exist (for example, Shear, 1986). It is my contention that all of us researching in this area have been guilty at times of allowing our research fervor to outstrip our scientific caution. The most notable example concerns the nosological status of panic disorder and is discussed in the next section. Another example concerns the way genetic data have been interpreted and will be outlined later. The adoption of provocative tests for anxiety has outstripped the establishing of their validity, the lactate story being the best example here. It behooves us to maintain our critical faculties, even to the point of skepticism or at the risk of being dismissed as nihilistic by the enthusiasts. Biological psychiatry is littered with the corpses of overdeveloped hypotheses that failed to take seriously certain inconvenient facts.

I make no apologies for keeping to the critical, perhaps overcritical, side of the continuum between gullible acceptance and obstinate rejection. Time and time again, advances in medicine have been delayed until accepted practice was questioned. Psychiatry has been more guilty of this than most branches of medicine. The vogue for leucotomies in the 1940s and 1950s rightly brought obloquy on their advocates. On a more theoretical level, the concept of hysteria has probably hindered progress in the study of "neurotic disorders" more than it has aided it. Animal models of anxiety are often more to be admired for their ingenuity than applauded for their validity.

For all these reasons, the biological aspects of panic will be discussed in terms of how they help the practitioner, both student and experienced therapist, rather than in terms of their theoretical implications. The long-range view will be adopted whenever feasible.

Diagnostic Considerations

The nosological status of panic attacks and panic disorder is of profound relevance to the whole long-term strategy, if not the short-term tactics, of biological research. If panic constitutes a disorder separate from anxiety disorder, the most powerful epistemiological approach is to seek out qualitative biological differences between the two conditions. If panic is merely a severe form of anxiety disorder, then measures differing quantitatively are of relevance. But, of course, the argument can be turned the other way: qualitative biological differences could be adduced as evidence that panic and anxiety are distinct disorders, quantitative continua as evidence that the two conditions merge; the distinction is a fairly arbitrary one.

But all of this is fairly new, indeed of this decade. Until the publication of the *Diagnostic and Statistical Manual* (American Psychiatric Association, 1980), psychiatrists did not officially recognize panic disorder as a distinct clinical entity. From a European perspective it is astonishing how readily North American psychiatrists have accepted the separability of panic disorder from anxiety disorder. In the United Kingdom, and in much of Europe, the distinction has proved unconvincing (Jablensky, 1985). A 1987 consensus conference concluded that the evidence to date could equally support the interpretation that panic attacks were a symptom-complex of severe anxiety on a continuum from anxiety disorder itself (Consensus Statement, 1987).

The reasoning of the consensus statement is worth elaborating on, as it should sound a note of British caution amid all the transatlantic enthusiasm for a new clinical entity. The onus of proof lies with those who would establish a distinction between panic disorder and generalized anxiety disorder. Have they argued their case successfully?

Historically, the concept of anxiety neurosis was established toward the end of the last century. Among its cardinal features, somatic—especially cardiovascular—symptoms were assigned great significance. Panic originally implied collective and excessive fear reactions, and this meaning persists in the lay sense. Later the term came to have rather different connotations stressing individual psychological responses. Again, cardiovascular elements were afforded great prominence. Distinguishing features of panic were described as the rapid rate of onset of the attack and the feeling of loss of personal control.

The epidemiology of panic attacks and disorders varies according to the sample studied and the criteria used. Wide differences in estimates are found between outpatient investigations, surveys of general practice attenders, and population studies. In one American study (Weissman, Myers, & Harding, 1978), prevalences were panic disorders = 0.4%, phobic disorders = 1.4%, and generalized anxiety disorders = 2.5% of the general population. More useful information is obtained if attempts are made to categorize the severity of the panic attacks. In one unpublished UK study carried out in the vicinity of Leicester, occasional panics were present in 1 in 10 of the general population, whereas frequent disabling panic attacks were reported by only 1 in 50 of the adult population. This was still four times the prevalence of the U.S. study, suggesting that the DSM-III criteria may be too restrictive. The natural history of panic, either as a disorder—that is, a cluster of symptoms occurring alone—or forming part of another psychiatric illness, has not been established.

Community studies show that anxiety neuroses are familial, the tendency to run in families being even more marked when the subject suffers from panic. Other genetic studies, underpinning the biological approach to panic, are discussed in a later section.

The bulk of morbidity in anxiety disorders is encountered in primary care, but current diagnostic schemes, devised mainly by and for psychiatrists, are often unsatisfactory in that context. Patients may present with anxiety, phobia, panic, and depressive symptoms in various combinations. As symptom clusters are not stable over time, changes often evolve in appropriate diagnostic labels. Somatization is so common that patients who experience panic attacks often focus on their bodily rather than their psychological symptoms.

In summary, panic attacks can be regarded as a characteristic cluster of symptoms that can occur alone or as part of another disorder with its own place in the classificatory scheme. The controversy that has arisen concerns the nosological status of disorders in which symptoms of panic occur in conjunction with other disorders such as agoraphobia, generalized anxiety, or depression. In the revised American classification, the DSM-III-R (American Psychiatric Association, 1987), panic attacks are given primacy and are deemed to delineate a separate diagnostic entity called panic disorder. The proposed revision of the ICD uses the terms *panic disorder* or *episodic anxiety* to describe a condition in which panic attacks are the major feature, in the absence of significant anxiety, and are best considered a separate disorder or a more severe form of generalized anxiety.

In descriptive, clinical terms, it is useful to recognize the symptom cluster of panic attacks, which can be defined operationally in terms of features and content. Most patients have generalized anxiety as well, suggesting that panic attacks often represent a severe form of more generalized anxiety. In others, panic attacks occur in the absence of other significant symptoms. No good purpose is served in trying to encompass both patterns of illness under a single rubric.

Thus, for research purposes, which are what concern us here, individual symptom clusters such as panic, phobic anxiety, generalized anxiety, and depression should be categorized separately. They should be rated separately in terms of frequency, duration, and severity, and an open mind should be kept about their interrelationship. In the search for biological antecedents and correlates, it is heuristic to break down clinical syndromes into as many components as have face validity. If no differences are apparent, the groups can be recombined. The basic unit for research purposes, then, is the panic attack itself, which is carefully defined in the DSM-III-R. But this produces an arbitrary dichotomy between panic attacks that satisfy DSM-III-R criteria and lesser attacks that do not but that may still have biological relevance. Sheehan and Sheehan (1983) defined four categories of panic attacks: (1) major spontaneous panic attacks—"devastating anxiety that comes very suddenly"—accompanied by three or more symptoms of panic, (2) minor attacks with one or two symptoms, (3) anticipatory anxiety episodes, and (4) situational panic attacks that include three or more panic attacks and follow an anticipatory anxiety episode. This classification may confound severity with context, but at least it reflects most practitioners' clinical experience.

It is obviously important that clear diagnostic criteria be used in the research laboratory. If an arbitrary distinction is made between patients with panic attacks and nonpanic attacks and only the former are included in studies, the appearance of a clear distinction between panic disorder and anxiety disorder will be perpetuated. By and large, most studies compare patients with panic disorder meeting DSM-III or DSM-III-R criteria with normal controls, find a difference, and conclude that the data support a biological abnormality in a condition called panic disorder. This is a myopic way of conducting scientific enquiry. Studies should be mounted making nosological assumptions. All the clinical data necessary for allocation to a particular category or another should be collected, together with anything else that might be remotely germane. A wide range of patients should be studied, with particular emphasis on those that fall just outside the core categories. A complete spectrum of severity should be included: anxious, panicking, phobic, and depressed patients together with large normal groups. Analysis of the data would be done with respect to individual symptoms, then symptom clusters, then syndromes, and finally diagnostic categories. Biological studies should concentrate on biological features. For example, the symptom of palpitations is probably a better starting point for a cardiovascular investigation than one of hypervigilance.

The Panic Attack

Whatever the nosological status of panic disorder, the criterion for research is the presence of panic attacks. These involve an overwhelming subjective feeling of terror, and usually of impending doom, imminent insanity, or loss of control. They are accompanied by a wide variety of symptoms listed in the DSM-III-R and involve almost every bodily system (Vittone & Uhde, 1985).

Surprisingly few studies have attempted to typify the biological features of spontaneous panic attacks. The first reports of somatic changes accompanying spontaneously occurring panic attacks were reported by Lader and Mathews (1970). During the course of extensive recordings of anxious patients in the laboratory, before and during the presentation of repeated auditory stimuli, three patients developed typical panic attacks. The first experienced panic after about 10 minutes of trying to relax, the second after 50 minutes of laboratory recording, and the third on "coming to" after a period of mild drowsiness. Increases in heart rate were the first physiological changes noted, but these were very closely followed by increased sweat gland activity. Fore-arm extensor muscle activity increase was generally delayed for up to a minute, if it occurred at all. The attacks were self-limiting and subsided within a few minutes without interrupting the recording. That the attacks should have occurred on the basis of a state of relaxation in two of the three subjects is noteworthy. It may suggest that some physiological "dampening mechanism" becomes switched off when the patient is not anxious, resulting in a vulnerability to uncontrolled rises in anxiety. An alternative speculation from a cognitive approach might suggest that relaxation allows disturbing cognitions to intrude suddenly and results in rapid anxiety rises. A psychodynamic explanation would emphasize the return of repressed emotions.

A second report concerned two patients who experienced sudden panic attacks during relaxation sessions (Cohen, Barlow, & Blanchard, 1985). Just before the panic episode, each patient showed a minor reduction in heart rate and EMG. One patient then had an abrupt increase in heart rate from 66 to 100 beats per minute, the other from 66 to 114 beats per minute. Other studies have evaluated physiological changes during exposure to phobic imagery or objects: for example, plasma free MHPG concentrations were elevated 30 minutes after a provoked panic attack (Ko et al., 1983).

Modern technology now allows cardiac and other monitoring of panic patients as they go about their daily business. Thus, the changes during panic attacks can be detailed, antecedent influences identified, and the effects of treatment monitored. Nevertheless, interpretation of the records may not be easy. For example, Freedman, Ianni, Ettedgui, and Puthezhath (1985) noted heart rate increases of 16 to 38 beats per minute in 7 of 8 panic attacks. But as physical activity was not measured simultaneously, it was not possible to ascertain whether the changes were caused by an increased workload on the heart or by psychological influences. A way out of this confounding of physiological and psychological influences lies in the careful selection of psychophysiological measures. Although many such measures have physiological imperatives—for example, the heart must pump blood—a few are believed to provide "purer" measures of behavioral influences. One is electrodermal activity from the palms of the hands or the fingertips. This measures sweat gland activity that, unlike activity elsewhere, is not thermoregulatory but rather reflects the state of psychological vigilance of the individual. A second but more problematical measure is the electroencephalogram, which reflects neuronal activity in a complex way but has no direct physiological function, only an indirect one. Both these measures can be monitored with portable equipment, though not as easily as the heart rate.

Another solution is to monitor physical activity and then to attempt to apportion alterations in heart rate between physiological and psychological factors. A recent study compared 12 female patients with self-reported panic attacks with 12 female control subjects (Taylor et al., 1986). The patients reported 33 panic attacks during the period when they were wearing ambulatory devices measuring both heart rate and physical activity. Of these, 17 were major, 8 minor, and 8 situational; in addition, 8 episodes of anticipatory anxiety were reported. Two-thirds of the major, one-third of the minor, two-thirds of the situational, but none of the anticipatory anxiety attacks were accompanied by unequivocal increases in heart rate. Six of the spontaneous panic attacks awoke the patient from sleep. The time from start to peak of panic averaged 4 minutes; the heart rate increased by a mean of 39 beats per minute, and the episodes lasted on the average 20 minutes. Spontaneous and situational panics were indistinguishable, both before and during the episodes. Background heart rates did not differ between patients and controls.

A comment should be made on the interpretation of the panic attacks that awoke the patients from sleep. They cannot be adduced as evidence that panic has a biological etiology, as the extensive literature on dreaming attests. However, waking in a panic is quite a common symptom and may reflect the sort of lowering of defenses postulated earlier with regard to relaxation.

From these and a few other studies, it would appear that the concordance between subjective and objective changes in panic attacks is not all that high. One might have expected major physiological change to accompany all reports of panic; this was not found. Nor were reports of panic always an accompaniment of episodes of tachycardia. Even allowing for technical difficulties, these discrepancies suggest that other factors must operate in the induction of panic attacks.

Psychological Factors

At this juncture, it is essential to set biological aspects of panic into a wider context, in particular with respect to psychological factors. The latter have been invoked in a succession of hypotheses from James (1884) through Freud (1961a, 1961b, 1961c) to modern behavior theorists.

Most recently, cognitive factors have been examined with respect to panic. One hypothesis emphasizes the "catastrophic" nature of misinterpretations of bodily feelings (Clark, 1986). The sensations misinterpreted are mainly those implicated in normal anxiety reactions such as palpitations, breathlessness, and dizziness. The catastrophic misinterpretation perceives these sensations as signaling much more danger than is justified. For example, palpitations are regarded as evidence of an impending heart attack. The model predicts that in patients with panic disorder, any manipulation that induces bodily sensations—for example, lactate infusion—will be likely to precipitate a panic attack. Biological factors might operate in several ways. Panic patients may be more physiologically labile anyway, and thus more likely to experience bodily sensations. Inhibitory influences such as $alpha_2$-adrenoceptors may be deficient in panic patients (Nutt, 1986), and sudden surges in sympathetic activity might be more likely than in normal subjects. This formulation is a corollary of a similar one for generalized anxiety: indeed, it has been found that anxious patients are more aware of their heart rates than are normal persons (Tyrer, Lee, & Alexander, 1980).

Multifactorial formulations have become increasingly common in biological psychiatry, as attempts to define a simple relationship between a symptom cluster and a biological variable have become obviously fruitless. Both individual physiological and psychological variation may be such as to vitiate any obvious relationship, even before any mediating or confounding variables are taken into account. For example, resting pulse rates vary greatly, and what appears to be normal in one individual might be unusually high in another. Only changes with a provocative procedure would elucidate this.

Adaptation is another important mechanism, on both the psychological and the physiological level. Furthermore, feedback loops may exist in different strengths in different individuals, and critical points may differ. An example is the relationship between activation and adaptation. In many systems it is apparent that adaptation slows down as activation increases. At a critical level of activation, adaptation will cease, and further stimulation will result in a runaway activation. Perhaps this mechanism underlies some panic attacks (Lader & Mathews, 1968). Interruption of this vicious circle may be difficult without using powerful outside influences such as sedative drugs. Again, a wide range of psychological influences may impinge at various points in this circle, dampening it or gearing it even higher.

Genetic Aspects

One anchor point for putative biological influences in a psychiatric disorder is the establishment of a significant genetic influence. Early studies suggested that the incidence of anxiety disorder in first-degree relatives of probands with anxiety disorders was about 15% (Carey & Gottesman, 1981). A more recent study, using interviews of family members, recorded an incidence of 25% of panic disorder in first-degree relatives of panic disorder probands compared with only 2.3% in relatives of normal controls. Such a difference was not found for generalized anxiety disorders (Crowe, Noyes, Pauls, & Slymen, 1983).

Twin studies yield parallel data. Slater and Shields (1969) reported a concordance rate for "anxiety state" in MZ twins of 41% and in DZ twins of only 4%. Torgersen (1983), in Norway, examined 32 MZ and 53 DZ twins and found the concordance rate for anxiety disorders with panic attacks to be substantially higher in MZ than DZ twins (31% versus 0%); no such difference was found for anxiety disorders without panic attacks. On the other hand, other psychiatric disorders were common in the co-twins of anxiety disorder probands, suggesting the possible heterogeneity of this disorder.

Such genetic data have been adduced as evidence that panic attacks constitute a disorder separate from generalized anxiety disorder. But these data could equally well mean that panic attacks represent a more severe form of anxiety and that a predisposition to such severe forms is what is genetically determined. In any case, the influence of genetic factors in panic attacks is undoubted, though the high number of discordant MZ pairs even in the panic disorder group (69%) also demonstrates the importance of environmental factors.

As Torgersen (1983) asks, what is inherited? It might be a predisposition to a biological deficiency—for example, less-than-average activity of GABA-ergic mechanisms, allowing the release of neuronal activity under marked internal or external stimulation to the point of panic. This would fit with a polygenic model. Less likely is a single gene abnormality with variable penetrance; for example, the absence of some useful but not essential inhibitory pathway. Looking for such an abnormality would be extremely difficult unless a highly specific marker for panic disorder were discovered.

The whole twin study approach is, of course, open to the objection that MZ twins are not treated by their families, or by their environment in general, in exactly the same manner as the members of DZ twin pairs. Parents tend to emphasize the differences between DZ twins and minimize the distinctions between MZ twins. Two types of genetic studies may avoid this drawback. The first is the adopted-away twin investigation, in which twins removed from their biological families at an early age and raised in adoptive families are traced and examined and their concordance rates calculated. The practical difficulties of such a study are apparent but have been successfully overcome in studies of some psychiatric conditions such as schizophrenia. There are a few such case reports extant but no formal study in panic disorder. The second type of study involves HLA typing in families. One family studied in this way had several members who suffered from panic disorder (Surman, Sheehan, Fuller, & Gallo, 1983). The HLA patterns were consistent with positing a genetic basis to the disorder.

Depression and Panic Disorder

The distinction between depression and panic disorder has generated a great deal of controversy in both clinical and research contexts. Because antidepressants—both tricyclics and MAOIs—can be used successfully to treat panic disorder, some investigators have suggested that it may be a variant of the larger group of depressive disorders. This is plying Occam's razor too assiduously. Although, generally speaking, the fewer the syndromes the better, drug actions should not be interpreted too loosely. Because a drug treats depression and is labeled an antidepressant does not mean that it cannot have other actions as well. For example, imipramine is used in some children to treat nocturnal enuresis, but this does not mean that these children are suffering primarily from a depressive disorder. Responses to various medications have to be set within a general clinical context and not used as criteria.

Several family studies of patients with panic disorder have failed to discover any increased incidence of major depressive disorder in their first-degree relatives, suggesting that genetic factors are not identical across the two conditions (Noyes, Clancy, Crowe, Hoenk, & Slymen, 1978). One study, however, suggested that some overlap did occur, as patients with depression plus one of the anxiety disorders (current or past panic disorder or generalized anxiety disorder) did have a greater frequency of depression among first-degree relatives than did those suffering from uncomplicated depression (Leckman, Merikangas, Pauls, Prusoff, & Weissman, 1983).

The dexamethasone suppression test has also been used to examine the relationship between panic and depression (Carroll, Feinberg, & Greden, 1981). Failure to suppress plasma cortisol concentrations after an oral dose of dexamethasone is more frequent in patients with "endogenous" or "biological" depression than in other groups of psychiatric patients and in normal controls. Patients with panic disorder suppress normally (Curtis, Cameron, & Nesse, 1982; Lieberman et al., 1983), but so do many patients with less severe forms of depression. Thus, this approach has not proved very fruitful.

The severity dimension is obviously important in this context. Studies should continue using biological variables believed to be abnormal in depression or panic and applying them to a wide range of patients. Unfortunately, few, if any, variables are available, and there seems little in the offing.

Induction of Panic

The induction of panic as a strategy has been very widely adopted, using a variety of chemical agents. The reliable and reproducible induction of a clinical phenomenon is often quite helpful in studying the pathological mechanisms associated with that disorder, though it is usually not much use in elucidating etiological processes. This point is not always clearly appreciated. Pathological mechanisms can be elucidated if information is available concerning the mode of action of an agent that reliably induces a clinical condition, or failing that, part of the condition, say a symptom cluster. The cause of the condition may still remain obscure unless the induction agent or some analogue of it can be found in a natural setting. For example, the induction of Parkinsonism by toxic agents is very informative concerning the biochemical mechanisms involved. If similar agents are found naturally, then the cause of the clinical conditions may become clearer.

Unfortunately, the actual pharmacological mechanisms involved in the mode of action of many of the agents used to induce anxiety are obscure. Lactate infusions, probably the most intensively studied of these agents, set in motion a complicated series of metabolic changes—themselves controversial—with little agreement among investigators about which ultimately provoke the panic attack. Consequently, little or nothing of utility is gleaned concerning the mechanisms of panic induction. Lactate infusions can only be used in an empirical way.

For this main reason much of the apparent wealth of material on biological aspects of panic disorders is only of secondary interest. Until the detailed pharmacology of the lactate ion, yohimbine, carbon dioxide, and caffeine has been worked out, the data that have accrued will tell us little about the mechanisms of panic attacks and nothing about the etiology of panic disorder. Nevertheless, some useful findings have emerged and will be outlined under individual drug headings. The various agents are summarized in Table 4.1.

TABLE 4.1 Psychopharmacological Models of Anxiety

Challenge	Antagonist	Effects[a]	Receptor	Site of action
Beta-carboline	Flumazenil Diazepam	↑ Cortisol ↑ Heart Rate ∅ MHPG	Benzodiazepine	Limbic
Yohimbine	Clonidine Diazepam	↑ MHPG (not blocked by D2)	Alpha$_2$	Locus coeruleus
Sodium lactate	Imipramine	↑ Adrenaline ∅ Cortisol ∅ Noradrenaline	?	?
Caffeine	—	↑ Adrenaline ∅ Noradrenaline	Adenosine Benzodiazepine	?
Carbon dioxide	? Beta-blocker	Panic symptoms	?	?
Isoproterenol	—	↑ Adrenaline ↑ Cortisol Panic symptoms	Beta-adrenergic	Peripheral sympathetic system

a ↑ = increase, ↓ = decrease, 0 = no change

Catecholamines

The earliest attempts to induce anxiety employed injections or infusions of catecholamines, long known to be released in anxiety and suspected of reinforcing the state (Kopin, 1984). As the catecholamines do not readily pass the blood-brain barrier, the legitimacy of such an approach is questionable.

An example of such an early study is that of Basowitz and his co-workers (Basowitz, Korchin, Oken, Goldstein, & Gussack, 1956), who interviewed 12 medical interns to establish any past history of stress and to list any specific reactions to it, such as palpitations, apprehension, tremor, or perspiration. Under appropriate double-blind circumstances, adrenaline was infused and its effects compared with those of saline in a cross-over design. The drug produced a distinct tachycardia and an increase in pulse pressure. Hand steadiness and persistence at a muscular task were impaired. The most common subjective experience was palpitations. Symptoms were also reported with saline but only half as frequently and usually when saline was the first treatment. Adrenaline produced symptoms generally akin to those described at the initial interview as occurring with stress. Emotionally labile subjects evidenced few cardiovascular changes but excess symptoms; rigid personalities developed marked physiological alterations but few symptoms. The latter observations suggest the importance of taking into account personality variables in biological studies. Well-validated personality inventories are available (such as the MMPI) and can always be included to advantage. Still, other measures of personality, such as coping strategies, locus of control, and cognitive styles may also be relevant.

Adrenaline, of course, is a general sympathomimetic. Some more recent studies have used isoprenaline (isoproterenol), a selective beta-agonist. Freedman, Ianni, Ettedgui, Pohl, and Rainey (1984) described panic attacks in five of eight panic disorder patients and one of nine control subjects during an isoprenaline infusion. However, after saline, three of eight patients but no controls reported panic. Heart rate changes were not pronounced. Lactate infusions were more likely to induce panic attacks, a finding replicated in a second study (Rainey et al., 1984). Because only one "dose" of each drug was used, it cannot be concluded that lactate provides a "better" model of panic than isoprenaline. Also, not only the frequency with which panics are induced but also their verisimilitude should be taken into consideration when evaluating the usefulness of an induction agent.

Another study examined the beta-adrenoceptor response to increasing intravenous doses of isoprenaline in eight panic patients and six normal controls (Nesse, Cameron, Curtis, McCann, & Huber-Smith, 1984). The patients had higher resting heart rates and elevated plasma concentrations of adrenaline, cortisol, and growth hormones compared with the controls. The patients' heart rate response to the infusions were decreased relative to the controls', suggesting that beta-adrenoceptor responses may actually be decreased in panic patients. If so, it would suggest a peripheral down-regulation of beta-receptors consequent on the repeated tides of catecholamines released during states of panic and anxiety. This is probably an epiphenomenon rather than an etiological factor.

Many of the catecholamine infusion studies suffer from problems of design, and many fail to address complex scientific or even philosophical problems that beset the relationship between the central and peripheral mechanisms of panic and anxiety. These problems include the mind-body relationship, Cartesian dualism, and the impossibility of reducing subjective reports to verifiable data. Noumena can never become phenomena. The whole topic of possible cognitive feedback loops in panic has been discussed by Tyrer (1976), who has pointed out the possibility that anxious and panicky patients have learned to associate the peripheral symptoms of anxiety with the central feelings, whereas normal subjects have not undergone such secondary conditioning.

Yohimbine

Attention has shifted from peripheral mechanisms in anxiety and panic to central ones, though noradrenergic pathways remain pivotal to the hypotheses. One of the leading theories supporting a biological basis of panic involves locus coeruleus activation (Redmond, 1979). The locus coeruleus is a small brain stem nucleus that supplies the majority of noradrenaline-mediated innervation in the primate brain, particularly in the cerebral cortex, hippocampus, cingulate gyrus, and amygdala. Afferents to this nucleus are believed to convey warnings of possible noxious consequences. Locus coeruleus efferents are postulated to be associated with motivation, learning, and memory, and also with the physiological aspects of anxiety via the hypothalamus. Noradrenaline projections to the cortex are very diffuse, and noradrenaline may subserve a neuromodulatory rather than a neurotransmitter function, acting by gearing up the effects of other neurotransmitters (Morrison, Molliver, Grzanna, & Coyle, 1981). If the locus coeruleus were induced to discharge at a high rate, the behavioral and symptomatic consequence might be a panic attack—or so the theory runs.

At low doses yohimbine blocks alpha$_2$-adrenoceptors, thereby enhancing the neural release of noradrenaline from the locus coeruleus projections. At higher doses it blocks alpha$_1$-adrenoceptors, producing an adrenolytic action.

A 20 mg dose had significant anxiogenic effects in eight normal volunteers (Charney, Heninger, & Sternberg, 1982). A 30-mg challenge in ten volunteers produced an additional increase in systolic blood pressure and autonomic symptoms such as piloerection and rhinorrhea. Plasma free MHPG concentrations were substantially increased. Both diazepam and clonidine antagonized yohimbine-induced anxiety, but only clonidine attenuated the increase in plasma MHPG, blood pressure, and autonomic symptoms (Charney, Heninger, & Redmond, 1983). Yohimbine can precipitate panic attacks in patients diagnosed as suffering from panic disorders (Uhde, Boulenger, Vittone, Siever, & Post, 1983). The effects of yohimbine were assessed in 39 drug-free patients with agoraphobia and panic attacks, as compared with 20 normal controls (Charney, Heninger, & Breier, 1984). Yohimbine (in 20-mg oral doses) was associated with greater self-ratings of anxiety, nervousness, palpitations, hot-and-cold flushes, restlessness, tremors, piloerection, and higher sitting systolic blood pressure in patients than in the normal subjects. MHPG plasma concentrations were higher in the patients, especially in those with frequent panic attacks.

Thus, yohimbine appears to be in effect a "panicogenic" compound. However, the relationship between noradrenergic activation, presumably of locus coeruleus projection pathways, and subsequent anxiety is not clear-cut. Again, as with the peripherally acting catecholamines, psychological factors, particularly cognitive ones, may be influential. Greater attention to the design of studies should control for such influences. Attempts should be made to trace the temporal relationships between cognitions, perceptions of physiological changes, and the onset of panic symptoms. Physiological monitoring of heart rate, electrodermal activity, and EEG might be very helpful. Proper saline controls are essential, preferably given on a separate occasion in a counterbalanced order. The time at which the yohimbine is added to the infusion should be known to neither patient nor investigator. Nor should the investigator know whether the subject is a patient or a control. These design considerations pertain to studies of other induction agents as well. Finally, more selective alpha$_2$-adrenoceptor antagonists would increase the precision of such studies.

Lactate and Carbon Dioxide

Following up on observations that patients with anxiety states have a less efficient exercise response than normal controls (see, for example, Holmgren & Strom, 1959), with greater rises in blood lactate, Pitts and McClure (1967) put forward the hypothesis that the lactate ion itself could produce anxiety attacks in susceptible persons. The research since then has been controversial, even contentious at times, but two main conclusions have emerged.

The first is that sodium lactate infusions provoke panic attacks in susceptible individuals diagnosed as having panic disorder but not in normal subjects (Shear, 1986). For example, in the largest series reported, approximately three-quarters of patients with panic disorder or agoraphobia with panic attacks developed panic during lactate infusions, compared with none of the normal controls (Liebowitz et al., 1984). Patients affirmed that panic attacks provoked by lactate resembled those experienced spontaneously. In other studies, however, 20% of normal subjects also experienced panic with lactate infusions.

The second finding is that the mechanism of action of lactate eludes discovery despite much experimentation and debate. The mechanism is not hypocalcemia (Grosz & Farmer, 1969), nor the induction of a metabolic alkalosis (Liebowitz et al., 1986). But several possibilities remain. Infusion of such a large volume (typically 10 ml per kg of body weight over 20 minutes) significantly stresses the cardiovascular system, increasing plasma volume, cardiac output, and stroke volume and inducing vasodilation. Consequently, it is conceivable that the perception of such changes precipitates a panic attack in patients but not in normal subjects, in a manner similar to that of the catecholamine infusions (see also Clark, 1986).

The fact that carbon dioxide production is also stimulated, resulting in a state of respiratory alkalosis, ties in with a series of other observations. Some clinicians have urged the importance of hyperventilation in the pathogenesis of panic and anxiety (Lum, 1981). During hyperventilation with room air, carbon dioxide is blown off, inducing a respiratory alkalosis. Indeed, hyperventilation attacks are treated by rebreathing air from a bag. Notwithstanding, hyperventilation does not reliably induce panic attacks in panic patients

(Gorman et al., 1984), though anxiety is often induced (Thyer, Papsdorf, & Wright, 1984). Surprisingly, inhaling 5% carbon dioxide (as a control for the physical exercise of hyperventilation) was much more effective. Replications of these findings have been communicated. Single-breath inhalation of 35% carbon dioxide has also been claimed to be anxiogenic (van den Hout & Griez, 1984; Griez, 1984), but expectancy effects cannot be excluded.

Elevated cerebral carbon dioxide is a stimulant of the locus coeruleus and also strongly stimulates respiration (Elam, Yoa, Thoren, & Svensson, 1981). Infused lactate may also produce a transient elevation of brain carbon dioxide levels and thereby induce locus coeruleus stimulation. Thus, the panicogenic effects of lactate, carbon dioxide, and yohimbine could have as their common denominator—at least in part—augmented activity of central noradrenergic pathways (Liebowitz et al., 1986). But even so the differences between panic patients and controls may not necessarily reflect differences in physiological sensitivity: cognitive factors cannot be ruled out but might be suspected if testing revealed different cognitive styles and content—for example, what a rapid heart connoted to an individual.

That cognitive factors are important in lactate-induced anxiety was emphasized in the small-scale study of van der Molen and his collaborators (van der Molen, van den Hout, Vroemen, Lousberg, & Griez, 1986). Lactate infusions were given to normal subjects in a double-blind, placebo-controlled cross-over study. One group of subjects was told that "the infusions might cause unpleasant bodily sensations similar to those experienced during periods of anxiety." The other subjects were informed that the infusions would evoke feelings of "pleasant tension," like those experienced during a sporting activity or while watching an exciting movie. Both groups were told the infusions were harmless. A single rating scale of "very anxious tension" to "very pleasant excitement" was used. The placebo infusions had no effect on either group; nor did the lactate infusion alter mood when given with instructions of pleasurable expectation. However, lactate induced marked feelings of anxiety when accompanied by the appropriate instructions.

Caffeine

Caffeine, a methylxanthine, is so well known and widely used that its anxiogenic properties have been largely overlooked. Case reports indicate that high doses of caffeine may produce symptoms of anxiety (Greden, 1974; MacCallum, 1979) such as insomnia, tremor (Wharrad, Birmingham, Mac-Donald, Inch, & Mead, 1985), palpitations, and diarrhea.

A preliminary survey comparing patients with panic disorder and normal controls showed that the patients had an increased sensitivity to caffeine (Boulenger & Uhde, 1982). Other evidence suggests that patients with anxiety disorders have increased caffeine sensitivity that leads to decreased consumption (Lee, Cameron, & Greden, 1985). At a high dose (72 mg, given orally), panic attacks were induced in two normal volunteers (Uhde et al., 1983), a finding of great relevance to the controversy about whether panic attacks and generalized anxiety are separate syndromes or panic attacks are a severe variant of anxiety.

In another study (Charney, Galloway, & Heninger, 1984), patients with panic disorder or agoraphobia with panic attacks were given 10 mg per kg of caffeine by mouth. Of 21 patients, 15 reported anxiety attacks after the caffeine dose that resembled their own panic attacks. Healthy controls reported significantly more anxiety symptoms following the dose, but no panic. MHPG levels were not consistently altered in either patients or controls.

Our own preliminary data involving the administration of caffeine base (250 mg and 500 mg) and placebo to groups of patients and controls suggests that some patients with generalized anxiety disorder may develop a panic attack after ingesting caffeine.

Caffeine and its related compounds interact weakly with the benzodiazepine receptor site (Boulenger, Patel, & Marangos, 1982). They also stimulate central noradrenergic activity (Berkowitz, Travers, & Spector, 1970). In caffeine-naive subjects they produce a dose-related increase in plasma noradrenaline (Robertson et al., 1978), although not in habitual caffeine users (Robertson et al., 1984). However, the most potent central effect is at the adenosine receptor site (Boulenger et al., 1982).

Thus, caffeine has a dual significance. In the clinical context, high and perhaps even average ingestion patterns of caffeine are associated with anxiety symptoms, probably to the point of precipitating panic. Enquiry should always be made into daily caffeine intake, not forgetting cola drinks. It is then worth advising the patient to curb his or her usage of caffeine-containing beverages, unless it is already low. On the research side, the greatest lacuna in our knowledge concerns the main biochemical action of caffeine. Sorting that out should become a high priority for fundamental anxiety research. Clinical research should further refine the parameters of the anxiety induction procedure, perhaps introducing cognitively defined stimuli to assess their interaction.

Benzodiazepine Inverse Agonists

The development of adrenaline- and yohimbine-induced models of anxiety stemmed from the well-known sympathomimetic concomitants of anxiety such as tachycardia and tremor. Another starting point has been the benzodiazepines and the discovery of specific high-affinity receptors in the brain of these and related drugs (Petersen, Jensen, Drejer, & Honore, 1986). It now seems that the benzodiazepines potentiate the inhibitory neurotransmitter gamma amino butyric acid (GABA) (Paul, Marangos, & Skolnick, 1981). It has been estimated that this transmitter is involved in 40% of all synapses, making it the most ubiquitous of all neurotransmitters. Any drugs potentiating GABA would have widespread inhibitory actions. The mechanism of the potentiation is unclear. Benzodiazepines do not act directly on GABA receptors but rather have their own receptors. The natural transmitter acting on benzodiazepine-binding receptors has not to date been identified with certainty, though several candidates have been suggested. Barbiturates do not bind to these receptors but have a less specific action on ionic mechanisms in synaptic membranes.

Because of this widespread inhibitory effect, benzodiazepines can alter the turnover of the neurotransmitters such as noradrenaline and 5-hydroxytryptamine. The main sites of action of the benzodiazepines are in the spinal cord, where muscle relaxant effects are mediated; the brain stem, perhaps accounting for its anticonvulsant properties; the cerebellum, causing ataxia; and the limbic and cortical areas involved in the organization of emotional experience and behavior.

In the search for endogenous substances binding to the benzodiazepine receptors with physiological effects, a class of beta-carboline compounds was studied. In animals, beta-carbolines antagonize the anticonvulsant actions of the benzodiazepines (Tenen & Hirsch, 1980; Cowen, Green, Nutt, & Martin, 1981). They also reduce the dose of a convulsant such as pentylenetetrazol, needed to induce convulsions, without producing convulsions themselves—a proconvulsant effect (Oakley & Jones, 1980). The sedative and antianxiety properties (as inferred from animal models) of benzodiazepines are antagonized by substituted beta-carbolines (Cowen et al., 1981; Peterson et al., 1986; Mendelson, Cain, Cook, Paul, & Skolnick, 1983). Beta-carbolines also possess intrinsic actions opposite in nature to the benzodiazepines. For example, they significantly increase sleep latency (Mendelson et al., 1983). These compounds have been termed *inverse agonists* or *contragonists*.

In primates, several beta-carbolines induce syndromes resembling anxiety. Following a large dose of drug (2.5 mg per kg of beta-carboline-3-carboxylic acid ethyl ester, beta-CCE), Rhesus monkeys rapidly became agitated and struggled in the restraining chair, their vocalization increased, and they urinated and defecated (Ninan et al., 1982). Their heart rate, blood pressure, plasma cortisol, and catecholamines were elevated. These effects were all blocked by prior administration of the benzodiazepine antagonist flumazenil (Ro 15—1788). More graded responses were obtained with lower doses (25 to 500 micrograms per kg) (Insel et al., 1984), with behavioral effects similar to those seen in monkeys facing threats such as the approach of an unfamiliar investigator.

One study in man used N-methyl-beta-3-carboxamide (FG 7142) (Dorow, Horowski, Paschelke, Amin, & Braestrup, 1983). Five healthy male volunteers received oral doses increasing from 100 to 200 mg and, in one case, to 400 mg. On two occasions (out of twelve) severe anxiety was observed, and in both instances the plasma concentration of FG 7142 was over 105 mg per ml. One volunteer reported severe anxiety with intense inner strain and excitation with an inability to speak. Flushes of the face and extremities were accompanied by a feeling of warmth. Blood pressure and pulse rate rose. Agitation increased, and the subject paced around the ward experiencing precordial pressure and palpitations. Muscle tension and reflexes increased. These effects peaked 1 hour after administration and lasted for 2 hours. The second volunteer was given 400 mg of FG 7142 after taking doses of up to 200 mg without incident. After 10 minutes, he developed facial flushes, tremor, and cold sweats. A stronger attack started 15 minutes later: he felt a sense of impending doom. Yet a third attack started, which was terminated by an intravenous benzodiazepine.

This group of compounds provides one of the most convincing models yet of the anxiety state and panic attack. It is, however, a little premature to regard this as a potential breakthrough. Further studies in humans are urgently needed, including careful dose effect studies. These might well throw light on whether everyone has a first threshold for the induction of generalized anxiety and a second for the induction of panic attacks. The ratio between the two might well vary greatly, so that some individuals when made anxious quickly developed panic attacks whereas others were much more resistant. Studies in patients would reveal whether they were a special subgroup with respect to anxiety and panic induction or merely at one end of a normal distribution. However, such a disposition might be a result of panic rather than a cause of it.

The pharmacological mechanism underlying the benzodiazepine agonists is understood better than any of the other anxiety induction agents. But it must be borne in mind that benzodiazepines and GABA are involved in a range of brain activities other than anxiety. Their anticonvulsant and muscle relaxant effects are well known, and, even in the emotional sphere, the benzodiazepines lessen a wide range of emotions other than anxiety—aggression and disgust among them. It may turn out that the beta-carbolines tell us more about the general effects of raising brain activity fairly nonspecifically than about the selective effects on the genesis of anxiety and panic. Nevertheless, the use of such pharmacological tools will be a welcome addition to the range of biological techniques available.

Reduction of Panic

The treatment of panic disorders is discussed elsewhere (see Chapters 6–12). However, the establishment of efficacy for a biological treatment of panic has major implications for research. Equally, an ability to block drug-induced experimental panics adds to our understanding. Various aspects can be separated: (1) the prevention of panic attacks, (2) the amelioration of panic attacks, (3) the lessening of anticipatory anxiety, and (4) the obviation of avoidance behavior.

The standard treatment for the prevention of panic attacks is the administration of an antidepressant, tricyclic, or monoamine oxidase inhibitor. Furthermore, patients treated with a tricyclic no longer panic when given a lactate infusion (Rifkin, Klein, Dillon, & Levitt, 1981). Phenelzine has an identical effect (Kelly, Mitchell-Beggs, & Sherman, 1971). These groups of antidepressants have in common the ability to down-regulate beta-receptors, and it is tempting to speculate that this results in desensitization to locus coeruleus outflow. Tricyclics are known in any case to decrease locus coeruleus firing (Nyback, Walters, Aghajanian, & Roth, 1975).

Clonidine also lessens locus coeruleus activity and has been shown to lessen panic attacks, at least in the short term (Liebowitz, Fyer, McGrath, & Klein, 1981; Hoehn-Saric, Merchant, Keyser, & Smith, 1981). However, yohimbine-induced panics are worsened by imipramine treatment (Holmberg & Gershon, 1961), an anomalous finding. But this is not a crucial stumbling block, as yohimbine is such a nonselective compound. Clonidine, as would be expected, blocks yohimbine-induced panics (Uhde et al., 1984).

Benzodiazepines can prevent panic attacks, provided high doses are given. The best-studied example is alprazolam (Lader & Davies, 1985), but clinical reports concerning diazepam and clonazepam also suggest efficacy. Benzodiazepines also lessen locus coeruleus activity by potentiating GABA-ergic inhibitory inputs.

This brief overview of treatment effects suggests that with few exceptions the literature agrees that drugs that prevent spontaneous panic attacks also attenuate drug-induced attacks. Behavioral treatments may also be effective, as shown in pilot studies (see, for example, Shear, 1986). Nonpharmacological mechanisms may also be effective in attenuating whatever physiological responses underlie the panic attack.

Anatomical Abnormalities

Anatomical anomalies, both central and peripheral, have been described in patients with panic disorders. The CNS findings were PET-scan abnormalities such as parahippocampal blood flow asymmetries, abnormally high brain metabolism, and abnormal sensitivity to hyperventilation in patients with panic disorder who are vulnerable to lactate-induced panic (Reiman, Raichle, Butler, Herscovitch, & Robins, 1984; Reiman et al., 1986). Again, as with so much biological research in this area, the implications of the data are not immediately apparent. It is certainly interesting that only patients whose panics were precipitated by lactate showed the anomaly. It is not clear whether the asymmetry reflects some fundamental abnormality or whether panic attacks produce secondary effects in the areas of the brain concerned with the control of autonomic functions.

The peripheral anomaly claimed to be associated with panic attacks and/or agoraphobia is mitral valve prolapse. This was first described nearly 25 years ago as a prolapse of the posterior leaflet of the mitral valve, identified during angiography, and related to the auscultatory phenomena of the late systolic click and murmur. It is common in some connective tissue diseases, particularly Marfan's syndrome. Mitral valve prolapse is now diagnosed by echocardiography, preferably using the newer two-dimensional techniques. Clinicians have associated it with atypical chest pain, palpitations, syncope, dyspnea, and neurotic symptoms. A whole series of complications have been cited, such as infective endocarditis, mitral valve failure, and platelet embolism. Cardiologists differ about the prognostic implications of mitral valve prolapse, some regarding it as a benign variant of normal, others as a harbinger of death (Oakley, 1984). A large epidemiological study in Framingham, Massachusetts, evaluated several thousand people using echocardiography. Mitral valve prolapse was detected in about 5% of the sample. Women showed a decline in prevalence from 17% in their 20s to 1% in their 80s. In men the prevalence remained between 2% and 4% throughout the various age groups. Only 5 out of 208 had a systolic click and murmur. Symptoms of chest pain, dyspnea, and syncope were no more common than in subjects without mitral valve prolapse. That high prevalences of mitral valve prolapse were claimed in patients with panic disorders reflects the inaccuracy of diagnosis using the earlier echocardiographic techniques. More recent studies have failed to show a prevalence of prolapse in panic disorder and agoraphobia higher than that in general population studies (for example, see Mavissakalian, Salerni, Thompson, & Michelson, 1983).

Conclusions

Two main explanatory schemata remain and complement each other (Gelder, 1986). Some instability or hypersensitivity of central noradrenergic mechanisms centering on locus coeruleus function would explain many data on both the induction and treatment of panic attacks. Further studies evaluating a range of biological functions in a range of anxious and panicky patients should prove productive.

The second approach is to elucidate the cognitive factors that appear to operate between the putative physiological abnormality, the perception of such activity, and the generation of a panic attack. The efficacy of nonpharmacological treatments needs assessment, and their mode of action needs dissecting.

But the most heuristic way forward is to combine the two approaches. Biological factors do not exclude psychological ones, and vice versa. Nor is it sensible to try to apportion the factors between the two domains. A more sophisticated and dynamic model is needed that emphasizes the interaction among all factors. If such a model could be developed it might pinpoint which factors interact in a multiplicative way to trigger the panic attack. Those factors would then be the most useful upon which to focus therapeutic effort, both pharmacological and behavioral.

The various techniques discussed in this chapter are continually being refined: made more sensitive, more artifact free, and less intrusive to the subject. But to make the most of these new and improved tools, we must examine our clinical and experimental schemata to ensure that we do not prejudge the issue and prejudice the outcome. In particular, we must regard diagnostic categories in psychiatry as a useful shorthand way of incorporating current research ideas into the clinic, and not as inviolate wisdom.

References

American Psychiatric Association. (1980). *Diagnostic and statistical manual of mental disorders* (3rd ed.). Washington, DC: Author.

American Psychiatric Association. (1987). *Diagnostic and statistical manual of mental disorders* (3rd ed., rev.). Washington, DC: Author.

Basowitz, H., Korchin, S. J., Oken, D., Goldstein, M. S., & Gussack, H. (1956). Anxiety and performance changes with a minimal dose of epinephrine. *Archives of Neurology and Psychiatry, 76,* 98–105.

Berkowitz, B. A., Travers, J. H., & Spector, S. (1970). Release of norepinephrine in the CNS by theophylline and caffeine. *European Journal of Pharmacology, 10,* 64–71.

Boulenger, J. -P., Patel, J., & Marangos, P. J. (1982). Effects of caffeine and theophylline on adenosine and benzodiazepine receptors in human brain. *Neuroscience Letters, 30,* 161–166.

Boulenger, J. -P., & Uhde, T. W. (1982). Caffeine consumption and anxiety: Preliminary results of a survey comparing patients with anxiety disorders and normal controls. *Psychopharmacology Bulletin, 18,* 53–57.

Carey, G., & Gottesman, I. I. (1981). Twin and family studies of anxiety, phobia, and obsessive disorders. In D. F. Klein & J. G. Rabkin (Eds.), *Anxiety: New research and changing concepts.* New York: Raven Press.

Carroll, B. J., Feinberg, M., & Greden, J. F. (1981). A specific laboratory test for the diagnosis of melancholia: Standardization, validation, and clinical utility. *Archives of General Psychiatry, 38,* 15–22.

Charney, D. S., Galloway, M. P., & Heninger, G. R. (1984). The effects of caffeine on plasma MHPG, subjective anxiety, autonomic symptoms and blood pressure in healthy humans. *Life Sciences, 35,* 135–144.

Charney, D. S., Heninger, G. R., & Breier, A. (1984). Noradrenergic function in panic anxiety: Effects of yohimbine in healthy subjects and patients with agoraphobia and panic disorder. *Archives of General Psychiatry, 41,* 751–763.

Charney, D. S., Heninger, G. R., Price, L. H., & Breier, A. (1986). Major depression and panic disorder: Diagnostic and neuro-biological relationships. *Psychopharmacology Bulletin, 22,* 503–511.

Charney, D. S., Heninger, G. R., & Redmond, D. E. (1983). Yohimbine induced anxiety and increased noradrenergic function in humans: Effects of diazepam and clonidine. *Life Sciences, 33,* 19–29.

Charney, D. S., Heninger, G. R., & Sternberg, D. E. (1982). Assessment of the alpha$_2$-adrenergic autoreceptor function in humans: Effects of oral yohimbine. *Life Sciences, 30,* 2033–2041.

Clark, D. M. (1986). A cognitive approach to panic. *Behaviour Research and Therapy, 24,* 461–470.

Cohen, A. S., Barlow, D. H., & Blanchard, E. B. (1985). Psychophysiology of relaxation-associated panic attacks. *Journal of Abnormal Psychology, 94,* 96–101.

Consensus Statement. (1987). Panic disorder. *British Journal of Psychiatry, 150,* 557–558.

Cowen, P., Green, A., Nutt, D., & Martin, I. (1981). Ethyl-beta-carboline-carboxylate lowers seizure threshold and antagonizes flurazepam-induced sedation in rats. *Nature, 290,* 54–55.

Crowe, R. R., Noyes, R., Jr., Pauls, D. L., & Slymen, D. (1983). A family study of panic disorder. *Archives of General Psychiatry, 40,* 1065–1069.

Curtis, G. C., Cameron, O. G., & Nesse, R. M. (1982). The dexamethasone suppression test in panic disorders and agoraphobia. *American Journal of Psychiatry, 139,* 1043–1046.

Dorow, R., Horowski, R., Paschelke, G., Amin, M., & Braestrup, C. (1983). Severe anxiety induced by FG 7142, a beta-carboline ligand for benzodiazepine receptors. *Lancet, 2,* 98–99.

Elam, M., Yoa, A. T. P., Thoren, P., & Svensson, T. H. (1981). Hypercapnia and hypoxia: Chemoreceptor-mediated control of locus coeruleus neurons and splanchnic, sympathetic nerves. *Brain Research, 222,* 373–381.

Freedman, R. R., Ianni, P., Ettedgui, E., Pohl, R., & Rainey, J. M. (1984). Psychophysiological factors in panic disorder. *Psychopathology, 17*(Suppl. 1), 66–73.

Freedman, R. R., Ianni, P., Ettedgui, E., & Puthezhath, N. (1985). Ambulatory monitoring of panic disorder. *Archives of General Psychiatry, 42,* 244–248.

Freud, S. (1961a). Obsessions and phobias. In J. Strachey (Ed.), *The standard edition of the complete works of Sigmund Freud* (Vol. 3). London: Hogarth Press.

Freud, S. (1961b). Studies on hysteria. In J. Strachey (Ed.), *Standard edition of the complete works of Sigmund Freud* (Vol. 3). London: Hogarth Press.

Freud, S. (1961c). Introductory lectures on psychoanalysis. In J. Strachey (Ed.), *Standard edition of the complete works of Sigmund Freud* (Vol. 15). London: Hogarth Press.

Gelder, M. G. (1986). Panic attacks: New approaches to an old problem. *British Journal of Psychiatry, 149,* 346–352.

Gorman, J. M., Askanazi, J., Leibowitz, M. R., Fyer, A. J., Stein, J., Kinney, J. M., & Klein, D. F. (1984). Response to hyperventilation in a group of patients with panic disorder. *American Journal of Psychiatry, 41*(7), 857–861.

Greden, J. F. (1974). Anxiety or caffeinism: A diagnostic dilemma. *American Journal of Psychiatry, 131,* 1089–1092.

Griez, E. (1984). Experimental models of anxiety: Problems and perspectives. *Acta Psychiatrica Belgica, 84,* 511–532.

Grosz, H. J., & Farmer, B. B. (1969). Blood lactate in the development of anxiety symptoms: A critical examination of Pitts and McClure's hypothesis and experimental study. *Archives of General Psychiatry, 21,* 611–619.

Herold, S., & Frackowiak, R. J. (1986). New methods in brain imaging. *Psychologial Medicine, 16,* 241–245.

Hoehn-Saric, R., Merchant, A. F., Keyser, M. L., & Smith, V. K. (1981). Effects of clonidine on anxiety disorders. *Archives of General Psychiatry, 38,* 1278–1282.

Holmberg, G., & Gershon, S. (1961). Autonomic and psychic effects of yohimbine hydrochloride. *Psychopharmacologia, 2,* 93–106.

Holmgren, A., & Strom, G. (1959). Blood lactate concentration in relation to absolute and relative work load in normal men, and in mitral stenosis, atrial septal defect and vasoregulatory asthenia. *Acta Medica Scandinavica, 163*, 185–193.

Insel, T. R., Ninan, P. T., Aloi, J., Jimerson, D. C., Skolnick, P., & Paul, S. M. (1984). A benzodiazepine receptor–mediated model of anxiety: Studies in nonhuman primates and clinical implications. *Archives of General Psychiatry, 41*, 741–750.

Jablensky, A. (1985). Approaches to the definition and classification of anxiety and related disorders in European psychiatry. In A. H. Tuma & J. D. Maser (Eds.), *Anxiety and the anxiety disorders,* (pp. 735–758). Hillsdale, NJ: Lawrence Erlbaum.

James, W. (1884). What is emotion? *Mind, 19*, 188–205.

Kelly, D. H. W., Mitchell-Beggs, N., & Sherman, J. (1971). Anxiety and the effects of sodium lactate assessed clinically and physiologically. *British Journal of Psychiatry, 119*, 129–141.

Klein, D. F. (1964). Delineation of two drug-responsive anxiety syndromes. *Psychopharmacologia, 5*, 397–408.

Ko, G. N., Elsworth, J. D., Roth, R. H., Rifkin, B. G., Leigh, H., & Redmond, D. E., Jr. (1983). Panic induced elevation of plasma MHPG levels in phobic-anxious patients. *Archives of General Psychiatry, 40*, 425–430.

Kopin, I. J. (1984). Avenues of investigation for the role of catecholamines in anxiety. *Psychopathology, 17*(Suppl. 1), 83–97.

Lader, M. H., & Davies, H. C. (Eds.). (1985). *Drug treatment of neurotic disorders: Focus on alprazolam.* Edinburgh: Churchill Livingstone.

Lader, M. H., & Mathews, A. M. (1968). A physiological model of phobic anxiety and desensitization. *Behaviour Research and Therapy, 6*, 411–421.

Lader, M. H., & Mathews, A. (1970). Physiological changes during spontaneous panic attacks. *Journal of Psychosomatic Research, 14*, 377–382.

Leckman, J. F., Merikangas, K. R., Pauls, D. L., Prusoff, B. A., & Weissman, M. M. (1983). Anxiety disorders and depression: Contradictions between family study data and DSM-III conventions. *American Journal of Psychiatry, 140*, 880–882.

Lee, M. A., Cameron, O. G., & Greden, J. F. (1985). Anxiety and caffeine consumption in people with anxiety disorders. *Psychiatric Research, 15*, 211–217.

Lieberman, J. A., Brenner, R., Lesser, M., Coccaro, E., Borenstein, M., & Kane, J. M. (1983). Dexamethasone suppression tests in patients with panic disorder. *American Journal of Psychiatry, 140*, 917–919.

Liebowitz, M. R., Fyer, A. J., Gorman, J. M., Dillon, D., Appelby, I. L., Levy, G., Anderson, S., Levitt, M., Palij, M., Davies, S. O., & Klein, D. F. (1984). Lactate provocation of panic attacks: I. Clinical and behavioral findings. *Archives of General Psychiatry, 41*, 764–770.

Liebowitz, M. R., Fyer, A. J., McGrath, P., & Klein, D. F. (1981). Clonidine treatment of panic disorder. *Psychopharmacology Bulletin, 17*, 122–123.

Liebowitz, M. R., Gorman, J. M., Fyer, A., Dillon, D., Levitt, M., & Klein, D. F. (1986). Possible mechanisms for lactate's induction of panic. *American Journal of Psychiatry, 143*, 495–502.

Lum, L. C. (1981). Hyperventilation and anxiety state. *Journal of the Royal Society of Medicine, 74*, 1–4.

MacCallum, W. A. G. (1979). Excess coffee and anxiety states. *International Journal of Social Psychiatry, 25*, 209–210.

Mavissakalian, M., Salerni, R., Thompson, M. E., & Michelson, L. (1983). Mitral valve prolapse and agoraphobia. *American Journal of Psychiatry, 140*, 1612–1614.

Mendelson, W. B., Cain, M., Cook, J. M., Paul, S. M., & Skolnick, P. (1983). A benzodiazepine receptor antagonist decreases sleep and reverses the hypnotic actions of flurazepam. *Science, 219*, 414–416.

Morrison, J. H., Molliver, M. E., Grzanna, R., & Coyle, J. T. (1981). The intra-cortical trajectory of the coeruleo-cortical projection in the rat: A tangentially organized cortical afferent. *Neuroscience, 6*, 139–158.

Nesse, R. M., Cameron, O. G., Curtis, G. C., McCann, D. S., & Huber-Smith, M. J. (1984). Adrenergic function in patients with panic anxiety. *Archives of General Psychiatry, 41*, 771–776.

Ninan, P. T., Insel, T. R., Cohen, R. M., Cook, J. M., Skolnick, P., & Paul, S. M. (1982). Benzodiazepine receptor–mediated experimental "anxiety" in primates. *Science, 218*, 1332–1334.

Noyes, R., Jr., Clancy, J., Crowe, R., Hoenk, P. R., & Slymen, D. J. (1978). The familial prevalence of anxiety neurosis. *Archives of General Psychiatry, 35*, 1057–1074.

Nutt, D. J. (1986). Increased central alpha$_2$-adrenoceptor sensitivity in panic disorder. *Psychopharmacology, 90*(2), 268–269.

Nyback, H. V., Walters, J. R., Aghajanian, G. K., & Roth, R. H. (1975). Tricyclic antidepressants: Effects on the firing rate of brain noradrenergic neurons. *European Journal of Pharmacology, 32*, 302–312.

Oakley, C. M. (1984). Mitral valve prolapse: Harbinger of death or variant of normal? *British Medical Journal, 288*, 1853–1854.

Oakley, N. R., & Jones, B. J. (1980). The proconvulsant and diazepam reversing effects of ethyl-beta-carboline-3-carboxylate. *European Journal of Pharmacology, 68*, 381–382.

Paul, S. M., Marangos, P. J., & Skolnick, P. (1981). The benzodiazepine-GABA-chloride-ionophore receptor complex: Common site of minor tranquilizer action. *Biological Psychiatry, 16*, 213–229.

Peterson, E. N., Jensen, L. H., Drejer, J., & Honore, T. (1986). New perspectives in benzodiazepine receptor pharmacology. *Pharmacopsychiatrica, 19*, 4–6.

Pitts, F. N., & McClure, J. N. (1967). Lactate metabolism in anxiety neurosis. *New England Journal of Medicine, 277*, 1329–1336.

Rainey, J. M., Pohl, R. B., Williams, M., Knitter, E., Freedman, R. R., & Ettedgui, E. (1984). A comparison of lactate and isoproterenol anxiety states. *Psychopathology, 17*,(Suppl. 1), 74–82.

Redmond, D. E. (1979). New and old evidence for the involvement of a brain norepinephrine system in anxiety. In W. E. Fann, I. Karacan, A. D. Pokorny, & R. L. Williams (Eds.), *Phenomenology and treatment of anxiety*. New York: SP Medical and Scientific Books.

Reiman, E. M., Raichle, M. E., Butler, R. K., Herscovitch, P., & Robins, E. (1984). A focal brain abnormality in panic disorder, a severe form of anxiety. *Nature, 310*, 683–685.

Reiman, E. M., Raichle, M. E., Robins, E., Butler, F. K., Herscovitch, P., Fox, P., & Perlmutter, J. (1986). The application of positron emission tomography to the study of panic disorder. *American Journal of Psychiatry, 14*, 469–477.

Rifkin, A., Klein, D. F., Dillon, D., & Levitt, M. (1981). Blockade by imipramine or desipramine of panic induced by sodium lactate. *American Journal of Psychiatry, 138*, 676–677.

Robertson, D., Frolich, J. C., Carr, R. K., Watson, J. T., Hollifield, J. W., Shand, D. G., & Oates, J. A. (1978). Effects of caffeine on plasma renin activity, catecholamines and blood pressure. *New England Journal of Medicine, 298*, 181–186.

Robertson, D., Hollister, A. S., Kincaid, D., Workman, R., Goldberg, M. R., Tung, C., & Smith, B. (1984). Caffeine and hypertension. *American Journal of Medicine*, 77, 54–60.

Shear, M. K. (1986). Pathophysiology of panic: A review of pharmacologic provocation tests and naturalistic monitoring data. *Journal of Clinical Psychiatry*, 47(Suppl.), 18–26.

Sheehan, D. V., & Sheehan, K. (1983). The classification of phobic disorders. *International Journal of Psychiatry*, 12, 243–266.

Slater, E., & Shields, J. (1969). Genetic aspects of anxiety. In M. H. Lader (Ed.), *Studies of anxiety* (pp. 62–71). London: Headley Bros.

Surman, O. S., Sheehan, D. V., Fuller, T. C., & Gallo, J. (1983). Panic disorder in genotypic HLA identical sibling pairs. *American Journal of Psychiatry*, 140, 237–238.

Taylor, C. B., Sheikh, J., Agras, W. S., Roth, W. T., Margraf, J., Ehlers, A., Maddock, R. J., & Gossard, D. (1986). Ambulatory heart rate changes in patients with panic attacks. *American Journal of Psychiatry*, 143, 478–482.

Tenen, S. S., & Hirsch, J. D. (1980). Beta-carboline-3-carboxylic acid ethyl ester antagonizes diazepam activity. *Nature*, 288, 609–610.

Thyer, B. A., Papsdorf, J. D., & Wright, P. (1984). Physiological and psychological effects of acute intentional hyperventilation. *Behaviour Research and Therapy*, 22, 587–590.

Torgersen, S. (1983). Genetic factors in anxiety disorders. *Archives of General Psychiatry*, 40, 1085–1089.

Tyrer, P. (1976). *The role of bodily feelings in anxiety*. London: Oxford University Press.

Tyrer, P., Lee, I., & Alexander, J. (1980). Awareness of cardiac function in anxious phobic and hypochondriacal patients. *Psychological Medicine*, 10, 171–174.

Uhde, T. W., Boulenger, J. -P., Vittone, B. J., & Post, R. (1984). Historical and modern concepts of anxiety: A focus on adrenergic function. In J.C. Ballenger (Ed.), *Biology of agoraphobia*. Washington, DC: American Psychiatric Press.

Uhde, T. W., Boulenger, J. -P., Vittone, B., Siever, L. J., & Post, R. M. (1983). Human anxiety and noradrenergic function: Preliminary studies with caffeine, clonidine and yohimbine. *Proceedings of the 7th World Congress of Psychiatry, Vienna*, 2, 693–698. New York: Plenum Press.

van den Hout, M. A., & Griez, E. (1984). Panic symptoms after inhalation of carbon dioxide. *British Journal of Psychiatry*, 144, 503–507.

van der Molen, G. M., van den Hout, M. A., Vroemen, J., Lousberg, H., & Griez, E. (1986). Cognitive determinants of lactate-induced anxiety. *Behaviour Research and Therapy*, 24, 677–680.

Vittone, B. J., & Uhde, I. W. (1985). Differential diagnosis and treatment of panic disorder: A medical model perspective. *Australian and New Zealand Journal of Psychiatry*, 19, 330–341.

Weissman, M. M., Myers, J. K., & Harding, P. S. (1978). Psychiatric disorders in a U. S. urban community: 1975–1976. *American Journal of Psychiatry*, 135, 459–462.

Wharrad, H. J., Birmingham, A. T., MacDonald, I. A., Inch, P. J., & Mead, J. L. (1985). The influence of fasting and of caffeine intake on finger tremor. *European Journal of Clinical Pharmacology*, 29, 37–43.

CHAPTER 5

Psychosocial Aspects of Panic Disorder

GEOFFREY L. THORPE AND JEFFREY E. HECKER

Recent changes in nomenclature have given prominence to agoraphobia and panic disorder among the anxiety disorders (American Psychiatric Association, 1980). In the most recent classification, the DSM-III-R (American Psychiatric Association, 1987), panic disorder subsumes agoraphobia, which itself has been the subject of an extensive professional literature in the last few decades. As a result, agoraphobia—with or without panic attacks—has been the focus of much of the theoretical and empirical work that is now also relevant to panic disorder.

In this chapter we shall review etiological models of these syndromes that concentrate on psychosocial aspects. These models all attempt to integrate the various clinical phenomena: panic attacks, agoraphobic avoidance, alarming thoughts, socially dependent behavior, and so forth. We shall proceed to an evaluation of research findings having some bearing on the models and conclude with a summary of clinical implications. But first some brief comments on the conditioning formulations of these disorders are in order.

Conditioning Models of Agoraphobia

Researchers interested in the efficacy of treatment procedures have established phobic avoidance as the chief treatment target in agoraphobia (Marks, 1981; Mathews, Gelder, & Johnston, 1981; Thorpe & Burns, 1983). A systematic program of exposure to feared situations typically reduces phobic avoidance and attenuates panic attacks. The success of exposure treatment seems to follow logically from an account of agoraphobia in conditioning terms, in which it is assumed that the client has been exposed to fear-conditioning trials and as a result has learned to fear and avoid public places and so forth. A parallel account of the treatment process proposes extinction of conditioned fear and avoidance as the chief therapeutic agent. Historically influential in this context has been the two-factor theory of Mowrer (1947; 1960). According to this view, fear is acquired by classical conditioning (the first factor) when an accidental noxious event occurs in the context of a hitherto innocuous stimulus situation. Because the situation subsequently elicits a conditioned fear response, the client is motivated to escape or avoid that situation. The instrumental learning of escape and avoidance responses constitutes the second factor of the model. These responses are presumed to explain the failure of the fear to extinguish naturally, because they curtail the necessary exposure to the conditioned stimulus.

Despite the potential appeal of a conditioning explanation of this kind, there are serious objections to two-factor theory on empirical grounds (Franks & Wilson, 1978). For one thing, classical conditioning procedures are not required to establish escape and avoidance in the laboratory (Hineline, 1977), defying predictions from the two-factor theory. Furthermore, several commentators have criticized the classical conditioning component of the model. For example, many people fail to develop a lasting fear despite exposure to extreme stress (for instance, in military combat); many people who *do* develop strong situational fears cannot recall having been traumatized in that situation; further, it has been notoriously difficult to establish conditioned fear reactions in human subjects in the laboratory (Rachman, 1977). Similarly, Mineka (1985) calls into question the assumed relevance of avoidance conditioning to phobias:

> What is so notoriously difficult to change in phobias is the intense and irrational subjective distress itself, whereas the laboratory analogues of the subjective distress component diminish quite rapidly in laboratory avoidance settings, without a comparable loss in avoidance response strength [p. 205].

The demonstrable success of exposure treatment for phobic avoidance is not sufficient evidence to support a conditioning model, because one cannot logically support a theory simply by demonstrating that treatments derived from it are effective (Marks, 1981).

Alternative conditioning formulations include the safety-signal perspective of Rachman (1984), who suggests that much agoraphobic behavior appears to be directed toward obtaining safety rather than toward avoiding specific noxious surroundings. Hallam (1978) has similarly argued against interpreting agoraphobia as a phobia, in that it is not notably characterized by avoidance of particular places. The commonly reported fluctuations in severity of agoraphobic fear also run counter to a straightforward stimulus-response formulation. (See Chapter 14 for a description of more recent conditioning formulations.)

Exposure in vivo remains the treatment of choice for agoraphobic avoidance, but its theoretical underpinnings remain open to question. Possibilities are extinction of conditioned fear and avoidance, habituation of anxiety responses, and the client's acquisition of effective coping skills of one kind or another (Marks, 1981). In this context influential writers such as Franks and Wilson (1978) have called attention to Bandura's (1977) social learning theory in general and his self-efficacy theory in particular as singularly helpful perspectives from which to approach agoraphobia and related disorders. Rather than assigning primacy to external conditioning events, Bandura argues that there is a continuous interplay among behavior, cognitive processes, and environmental events, each domain influencing the others. According to Bandura, changes in the client's expectations of his or her personal coping efficacy are central to the therapeutic process. These changes may be effected in principle by a variety of therapeutic procedures, but it is predicted that real-life behavior in the relevant situations affords the best opportunity for raising self-efficacy expectations. Hence, empirically, agoraphobia may be treated effectively by a systematic program of real-life exposure; theoretically, changes in expectations of personal efficacy in the problem situations form the principal therapeutic process.

Therapists are still left with the practical problem of dealing with panic disorder when there is no apparent situational fear or avoidance. Exposure to external situations cannot be practiced when there is no appropriate situation with which to confront the client. Attenuating the panic attacks themselves is the obvious treatment goal, but to design effective procedures theorists must first understand the etiology and maintenance of panic attacks. Such an understanding would be relevant to panic disorder with or without agoraphobic avoidance. Accounts of panic attacks in conditioning terms therefore deserve at least brief mention.

Conditioning Models of Panic

Mineka (1985) finds an appropriate animal analogue to panic attacks in the separation protest seen in human and nonhuman primate infants when they are taken away from a parent. Their behavior is characterized by "extremely high levels of vocalization, locomotion, and stereotypy" (p. 236). Responses include changes in heart rate, sleep patterns, and body temperature. Separation protest is viewed as a prototype for anxiety in general. A possible parallel to this process is the disturbed early relationships with parents described by some clients with panic disorder and given etiological significance by some authors (see "Early Separation and Fear of Abandonment"). The unpredictability and uncontrollability of such separations are notable features of experimental neurosis situations in general (Mineka & Kihlstrom, 1978).

Referring to Mineka's work, Baum (1986b) describes an animal model for panic attacks that lends some support to a safety-signal perspective on agoraphobia (Baum, 1986a; Rachman, 1984). The model derives from observations of the spontaneous behaviors of rats during flooding. In laboratory flooding procedures, animals are confronted with conditioned fear stimuli during experimental extinction while escape and avoidance responses are blocked or prevented. The spontaneous behaviors remarked on by Baum include abortive avoidance attempts, freezing, exploratory behavior, and grooming.

The more complex models to be reviewed below were mostly designed to explain agoraphobia. However, because we shall restrict our attention to the more broad-ranging accounts that seek to accommodate not only avoidance behavior but also panic attacks and various other features of agoraphobia, our conclusions should apply equally to panic disorder in general. We shall pay no further attention to simple conditioning views on the acquisition of phobic avoidance, because they have been adequately covered elsewhere (for example, in Emmelkamp, 1979; Thorpe & Burns, 1983).

Psychosocial Models of Agoraphobia

The Goldstein and Chambless Model

In an influential discussion of the etiology and maintenance of agoraphobia, Goldstein and Chambless (1978) proposed a distinction between "simple" and "complex" agoraphobia. Simple agoraphobia occurs in clients who become anxious in response to specific events such as a drug experience, a physical disorder such as inner ear problems, or a traumatic event such as a mugging. Treatment is directed at the specific situational fears, and may consist of a focused technique such as graded exposure in vivo. Complex agoraphobia refers to a syndrome in which the following features are present: (1) panic attacks, which lead to anticipatory fear and hence a fear-of-fear cycle; (2) low levels of self-sufficiency, independence, and assertiveness; (3) difficulties in appropriately attributing the source of distressing feelings; and (4) a background context of conflict, usually interpersonal, for the onset of symptoms.

The complex agoraphobia syndrome is addressed by Goldstein and Chambless. The four principal features just mentioned intereact to produce agoraphobic fear and avoidance. In the case of a married woman who feels unable to function independently, is reluctant to express her feelings openly, fails to recognize the source of her emotions, and is experiencing dissatisfaction with her marriage, panic attacks and agoraphobia may develop as follows. Her desire to leave the marriage immediately raises the threatening issue of living independently, so the client attempts to cope with the poor marriage (Goldstein, 1970; Wolpe, 1970). Lacking assertiveness skills or being inhibited by her anxieties about assertiveness, however, she is ineffective in persuading her husband to make the desired changes. She attempts to suppress her feelings of dissatisfaction but is unwittingly reminded of them in situations in which she feels physically trapped: in an elevator, at the beautician's, waiting in line at the supermarket checkout, or driving on a limited-access highway. Through semantic conditioning (Goldstein, 1970; Wolpe, 1969), feelings are aroused that resemble those created by being trapped in a bad marriage. The client is unable to trace these feelings to their source and is bewildered by having dysphoric feelings in apparently innocuous situations. She fears further episodes of this kind and learns to avoid the environments associated with them.

Agoraphobic avoidance, in turn, makes the prospect of independent living seem even less realistic or acceptable. The development of agoraphobia may serve to save the marriage, because (1) leaving the spouse is no longer a practical option, and (2) the spouse may feel compelled to help and support the affected person (see also A. A. Lazarus, 1966; Milton & Hafner, 1979).

Related etiological influences include possible "secondary gain" from receiving help from the spouse and others.

Similar Formulations

In their theories on the development of agoraphobia, other authors have suggested supplementary issues but have basically echoed the points made by Goldstein and Chambless (1978). Clarke and Wardman (1985), for example, discuss the wider issues that pose problems for individuals with agoraphobia in addition to the phobic fear and avoidance themselves: tensions in family relationships, reticence and nonassertiveness, dysphoric mood, obsessions, and even nightmares. Because Clarke and Wardman are themselves a therapist-client team, they are able to demonstrate the interaction of the various factors that maintain agoraphobia from a particularly illuminating perspective.

Fishman (1980) emphasizes fear of fear and describes the typical person with agoraphobia as presenting somatic symptoms such as "lightheadedness." Most commonly the client is passive-dependent, nonassertive, and emotionally inexpressive. Feeling trapped in an unsatisfactory life situation produces a dependence/independence conflict, and the sufferer fears abandonment and loss of control. The conflict gives rise to unpleasant thoughts and bodily sensations, which also arise in outside situations reminiscent of the conflict. Anticipatory fear of the unpleasant sensations leads to phobic avoidance. This is followed by self-blaming ruminations about personal inadequacy. Finally, these problems in turn may lead to a depressed mood.

The points about dependency, passivity, and unassertiveness, particularly as seen in women with panic disorder who have unsatisfactory marriages, raise the question of sex-role stereotyping and the different experiences of men and women in their development in our society. Fodor (1978) has argued that agoraphobia is itself a caricature of the traditional female role in a male-dominated society. The person with agoraphobia stays indoors while others go out and make an impact on the world, relies upon stronger people to make important decisions, shies away from affirming personal opinions and emotional reactions, and is expected to adopt a role of silence and stoicism in the face of unacceptable treatment by others. Cultural conditioning and modeling, therefore, encourage the development of agoraphobialike characteristics in women in general. Fishman (1980) accepts this argument and offers an extension of it. In a society in which women's roles are changing, an additional conflict ironically arises: the woman who feels she ought to be successful in a prestigious and demanding occupation outside the home, yet lacks self-confidence because of cultural conditioning, faces a conflict between feeling insecure in the business and professional world on the one hand and feeling guilty about adopting a traditional homemaker role on the other.

Comments on the Goldstein and Chambless Model

As a set of hypotheses about the origins and maintenance of panic attacks and agoraphobic avoidance, the Goldstein and Chambless model is intuitively appealing and matches the impressions of clinicians who have worked with clients with agoraphobia. Assigning prominence to the panic attacks and the fear-of-fear cycle is consonant with modern thinking and consistent with the notion of phobic avoidance as secondary to the onset of panic attacks. Whether individuals with agoraphobia have the postulated personality characteristics (unassertiveness, dependency, tendency to make unhelpful attributions) and whether they typically develop their problems against a background of interpersonal conflict are empirical issues. It has to be noted, however, that Goldstein and Chambless *define* complex agoraphobia in terms of these characteristics, so that they are present by definition in this formulation.

Issues that *are* matters for observation and experiment in the model include the following:

1. Is complex agoraphobia more common than simple agoraphobia?
2. Do these two disorders respond to different treatments (simple agoraphobia to focused techniques for situational fear reduction, complex agoraphobia to a more broad-spectrum approach)?
3. Does factor-analytic work support the view that the presence of panic attacks and avoidance of typical agoraphobic situations go hand in hand with marital difficulties, unassertiveness, and so forth?
4. Can individuals with agoraphobia be distinguished from those with social phobia—for example, in levels of self-sufficiency, assertiveness, attributional style, preexisting marital conflict, and so forth?
5. Can the development of complex agoraphobia be forecast in those people who have the requisite background but who are not yet avoiding specific situations?
6. Can an interactive theory of this type—postulating a causal chain of conflict, semantic conditioning, and misattribution—be adequately tested empirically?
7. Can clients become anxious without a panic attack occurring? (If so, this calls into question the fear-of-fear notion.)

Emmelkamp (1979) has argued that the conclusions of Goldstein and Chambless seem "unwarranted" (p. 64) because the data reported were gained retrospectively and that at a minimum, cross-validation by a different center would be desirable. Emmelkamp also noted that interpersonal conflict was not clearly defined. Goldstein and Chambless gave the impression that it was assumed to be causal by default, when agoraphobia appeared in the absence of obvious conditioning events.

The Integrative Model of Brehony and Geller

Seeking to explain the development and maintenance of agoraphobia, Brehony and Geller (1981) proposed a model based on a functional analysis of behavior and encompassing physiological, cognitive, behavioral, and interpersonal factors.

Social Learning Factors

The authors suggest that the agoraphobic client's social learning experiences have given rise to low assertiveness, low self-confidence, low tolerance of stress, and high dependency and approval-seeking behavior. Tension and anxiety are produced by the client's low tolerance of stress. A relatively high level of arousal sets the scene for a panic attack to appear in response to further stress. The experience of panic arouses the fear of another attack and the fear itself produces further fear. The client's general level of stress is in turn increased by the panic attacks. Reduced self-esteem and self-assurance result directly from a history of severe agoraphobic symptoms.

Situational Factors

Brehony and Geller note that several environmental contexts are typically avoided: being alone, far away from safety, or among groups of people (especially when the client is the focus of attention); feeling trapped; and being in novel situations in general. The authors interpret the avoidance of novelty in attributional terms: clients do not know whether to label the feelings aroused by a new situation as excitement or fear. New situations may also produce uncertainty about behaving appropriately or being able to control what happens. When fear is aroused by particular situations, clients notice the bodily sensations associated with it and may entertain worrisome thoughts about losing control. These thoughts in turn may produce stronger fear sensations, so that a combination of high sympathetic arousal and "catastrophic" cognitions results. Typically clients escape at this point, either by leaving the situation or by other devices, such as experiencing a dissociative episode. Avoidance of the situations associated with panic attacks ensues and is presumably maintained or reinforced by forestalling aversive stimuli. Such avoidance curtails clients' mobility, so social support is less available. At this point, clients begin to entertain the idea that they are becoming mentally ill; depressive thoughts and feelings follow.

Brehony and Geller point out that by the time a pattern of panic responses has developed, panic attacks may be triggered not only by particular situations but also by physiological and cognitive cues. Bodily sensations reminiscent of mounting anxiety, such as skin warmth or dampness, may actually produce a panic attack even when produced by physical exertion or by ambient temperature. Similarly, cognitions—specific worrisome thoughts about the alarming aspects of a planned outing—may themselves initiate a train of events that lead to panic.

Treatment Findings

Brehony and Geller reviewed the literature on the treatment of agoraphobia to evaluate the results for consistency with their model. They were dissatisfied with the reported research on several methodological grounds and concluded that the results were mixed. They agreed with other reviewers that exposure to phobia-relevant surroundings is an important element in treatment. In their view, important research challenges are (1) to identify etiological factors, (2) to explore treatments such as assertiveness training and reattributional methods, because of their potential for undermining the factors that maintain agoraphobia; and (3) to assess client functioning more thoroughly in treatment research.

Comments on the Brehony and Geller Model

Brehony and Geller argue that the scene is set for the development of agoraphobia by social learning experiences that give rise to problems with assertiveness, dependency, self-confidence, and the like. It must be shown, then, that such problems are present before the onset of panic attacks and agoraphobic avoidance but not before the onset of other common emotional disorders. Correlational studies have shown links between agoraphobia and certain personality characteristics; that information is not confirmatory, however, because Brehony and Geller relied upon those studies in developing their model. Those authors seem to argue that low self-esteem can precede *and* result from agoraphobia, so it is unclear whether initial problems in self-esteem are essential to the model. Similar points can be made about the attributional tendencies of individuals with agoraphobia. The model does point to the potential utility of assertiveness training and cognitive restructuring procedures that help relabel emotional responses. Research findings do support the efficacy of these techniques as part of the treatment approach to panic disorder, but those findings cannot, of course, verify the theory.

The Integrated Model of Mathews, Gelder, and Johnston

In an early chapter of their important book on agoraphobia, Mathews, Gelder, and Johnston (1981) reviewed the traditional theories and proposed an integrated model of their own. The authors summarized the principal findings that need to be considered as follows: (1) individuals with agoraphobia may display heritable traits of anxiety; (2) agoraphobia often develops in a context of general stress; (3) agoraphobia has many elements in common with generalized anxiety disorder; (4) persons with agoraphobia avoid specific situations, typically depend on other people for support, and tend to attribute the cause of their anxiety to their current external surroundings; and (5) avoidance behavior persists, even though it tends to fluctuate with a client's mood.

People who develop agoraphobia, then, may have certain familial predispositions. Parental over- and underprotection or family instability may lead to unduly dependent behavior later. Generalized background stress, together with the heritable anxiety traits, may produce the general anxiety that seems to be prodromal for agoraphobia. What determines the onset of agoraphobic avoidance (as opposed to the development of generalized anxiety disorder) is the experience of a panic attack while the client is away from home. The panic attack itself probably results from the combination of high general anxiety and anxiety-arousing external stimuli.

At this point two other factors are assumed to play a part but, as Mathews et al. note, this is speculative. First, a tendency toward dependence on other people rather than self-reliance in the face of challenges adds to the likelihood that agoraphobia will develop. This assumption is consistent, the authors point out, with Fodor's (1978) argument that women are often brought up to display dependent behavior, and with the observation that women predominate in agoraphobic but not in generalized anxiety disorder samples. Second, attributing the panic attack to some property of the immediate surroundings, as opposed to ascribing it to general stress, encourages the development of agoraphobia. This view is consistent with the observed correlation between phobic severity and the client's sense of an external locus of control.

Other factors operate to maintain agoraphobia once it has developed. Mathews et al. summarize these in two categories: (1) factors that discourage the client's efforts to get out and about, and (2) factors that positively encourage continued avoidance. The Mathews et al. model is illustrated graphically in Figure 5.1.

Comments on the Mathews, Gelder, and Johnston Model

The Mathews, Gelder, and Johnston model has elements in common with that of Goldstein and Chambless (1978): general background stress and dependent social behavior are assumed in both, for example. Mathews et al. suggest that panic attacks are a joint product of high anxiety and exposure to certain external stimuli, so that individuals with agoraphobia ascribe panic to their surroundings rather than to internal events. Although Mathews et al. acknowledge the contribution of the fear-of-fear cycle to panic attacks, their emphasis on external surroundings as a source of fear stands in contrast to the cognitive theories of panic disorder (Beck, 1988; Clark, 1986). In those theories it is assumed that clients ascribe panic to internal, somatic cues that can betoken serious medical danger. Issues for empirical resolution raised by this model include the following.

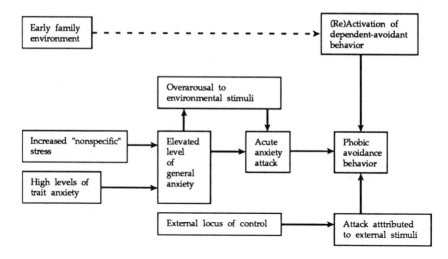

FIGURE 5.1 Hypothetical Flowchart Showing Factors Leading to the Onset of Agoraphobia. (Source: Mathews, A. M., Gelder, M. G., & Johnston, D. W. (1981) *Agoraphobia: Nature and Treatment.* New York: Guilford Press. Reprinted by permission.)

1. Do persons with agoraphobia have a history of parental over- or underprotectiveness or family instability, leading to their overdependence on other people?
2. Do they make faulty ascriptions concerning their bodily feelings?
3. Does an internal or an external locus of control predominate for these individuals?

Psychosocial Models of Panic Disorder

Stampler's Integrated Conceptual Model

Borrowing from other formulations, such as that of R. S. Lazarus (1966), Stampler (1982) sought to integrate psychophysiological, biochemical, and clinically observed aspects of panic disorder. Stampler felt that, although the initial panic attack might be preceded by "free-floating" chronic anxiety, the acute panic and the generalized anxiety were distinct phenomena (see also American Psychiatric Association, 1987). He also distinguished between factors responsible for the initial onset of panic attacks and those responsible for their continuation.

The initial panic attacks are not immediately precipitated by specific external stimulus events, but they do arise at a time of general stress for the individual. Most commonly, the stressors are changes in life circumstances, such as the development of marital conflict. The effects of this kind of stress may be compounded by social skills deficits, especially if the individual lacks a sense of self-sufficiency. The initial panic attack may be prompted by either psychological or somatic events, such as prolonged worrying about the social stress or physiological changes in the endocrine system. Cortical arousal increases, epinephrine is released, and, for largely unknown reasons, the receptor sites for epinephrine become hyperactive. This in turn produces symptoms of tachycardia, palpitations, respiratory difficulties, and so forth. Although panic attacks are self-limiting, the individual can contribute to the escalation of panic by his or her own appraisal of the sensations during an attack.

After the individual has experienced a series of panic attacks, the disorder may take on a life of its own, independent of the original precipitants. Prolonged rumination about the prospect of further attacks leads the individual to develop a fear of fear, after which he or she may become hypervigilant concerning fear sensations. A parallel fear of the inability to cope with an attack arises after the individual has experienced a sense of helplessness during previous attacks. In a manner consistent with Bandura's (1977) self-efficacy model, the victim's appraisal of his or her coping abilities as inadequate stimulates further anxiety. The individual may even come to avoid activities involving stress or exertion because they elicit sensations similar to those that precede panic attacks.

Stampler (1982) argues that this model allows the possibility of therapeutic intervention at three levels. An "antecedent-based" treatment approach aims at reducing the background stressors or conflicts. A range of methods including psychodynamic, cognitive-behavioral, and family systems therapy are useful here. A typical goal is to help the client cope with stress or conflict by developing problem-solving or assertive skills. A "response-based" approach seeks to dampen the hyperactive physiological responses. This may be achieved by pharmacological treatment or by behavioral interventions, such as relaxation training or flooding, that seek to produce habituation or extinction. A "mediation-based" focus leads to interventions designed to reduce the fear-of-fear cycle. Giving information and reassurance (for example, explaining to the client that panic attacks are not associated with impending psychosis) is helpful here, as are cognitive modification procedures that encourage coping self-statements and that may increase self-efficacy expectations.

Related Formulations

Jacob and Rapport (1984) have also put forward an account of panic in which a fear-of-fear cycle is fueled by current stressors and medical conditions, together with the development of self-preoccupation and the failure of situational fear to extinguish because of continued avoidance behavior. The authors focus particularly upon various medical conditions that may set the scene for panic disorder. These include "idiopathic postprandial hypoglycemia" and, perhaps more commonly, hyperventilation. Recent reviewers have noted that hyperventilation has long been considered important in explaining agoraphobia and panic attacks (Garssen & Rijken, 1986; Ley, 1987; Marshall, 1987). Such accounts typically include references to the initial elicitation of hyperventilation by life stressors; to the individual client's coping strategy and physiological response specificity; to anticipatory and attributional cognitive phenomena; to anxiety, with or without the development of avoidance behavior; and to the completion of a vicious circle, including the chief somatic and cognitive elements cited.

Comments on Stampler's Model

An advantage of an integrative model is that it encompasses physiological factors in panic as well as the hypothesized psychosocial antecedents. As a theory of the genesis and maintenance of panic attacks, it stands or falls on empirical questions such as these:

1. Do panics first arise in the context of stress and/or interpersonal conflict?
2. Are social skills deficits and low levels of self-sufficiency associated with panic disorder?
3. Can we demonstrate that clients make specific appraisals of early sensations of mounting anxiety that actually serve to increase panic in an upward spiral?

Questions about the processes posited by the theory are also of interest.

4. What is the mechanism by which troublesome thoughts or images concerning a stressful life situation actually produce physiological changes?
5. Can we assess the postulated hyperactivity of beta-adrenergic receptor sites independently of the clinical observation of panic attacks themselves?

Clark's Cognitive Model

Recent psychosocial formulations of panic disorder have addressed the important issue of the client's cognitive appraisal of somatic sensations. In the model described by Clark (1986), panic attacks are assumed to result from the "catastrophic misinterpretation" of certain bodily sensations, so that feelings commonly associated with anxiety (dizziness, palpitations, and so forth) are viewed by the client as dangerous signals of impending harm (such as a heart attack or a brain hemorrhage). This misinterpretation of bodily reactions as harbingers of danger would predictably lead to increased anxiety, in the familiar fear-of-fear pattern. The client comes to fear sensations that are themselves produced by fear, so that a vicious circle is established. In discussing a conditioning model of this pattern, Evans (1972) gave vivid illustrations of the phenomenon from case material. A woman who responded to stress by blushing began to dwell upon the embarrassment this could cause her, so that

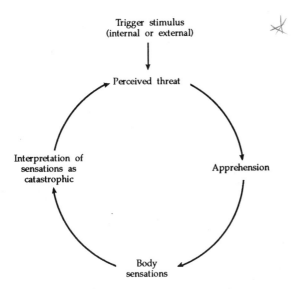

Trigger stimulus
(internal or external)

Perceived threat

Interpretation of
sensations as
catastrophic

Apprehension

Body
sensations

FIGURE 5.2 A Cognitive Model of Panic Attacks. (Reprinted with permission from *Behavior Research and Therapy*, 24:463, Clark, D. M., A cognitive approach to panic. Copyright 1986, Pergamon Journals Ltd.)

any sensation of warmth about her upper chest, neck, or face produced anxiety; this, of course, exacerbated the blushing. Similar patterns were seen in men who came to fear excessive perspiration or the possibility of vomiting in public.

Clark (1986) notes that panic may be produced in predisposed individuals by a variety of pharmacological agents (see Chapter 4 in this volume). Because individuals vary in their response to such provocation, it has been hypothesized that the agents might produce panic only when the elicited sensations are interpreted by the client in a certain way. If this is so, Clark argues, then it is immaterial whether the sensations are produced by drugs, by physical exercise, by warm or poorly ventilated surroundings, or by contact with stimuli that the client has learned to fear. The process is illustrated in Figure 5.2.

According to Clark, three patterns of events may precede a panic attack: (1) a period of heightened anxiety caused by the anticipation of an attack, (2) a period of heightened anxiety caused by other factors, such as a marital argument, and (3) in the absence of heightened anxiety, the interpretation of a certain bodily sensation in an anxiety-arousing way. The sensations that precede the third type of attack—apparently spontaneous attacks that seem to come "from out of the blue"—include those elicited by emotions such as anger, by quick shifts in bodily position leading to dizziness, and by physical exercise or coffee drinking. Clark's model applied to all three types of panic.

In a subsequent paper Clark (1988) made some additional points. The catastrophic misinterpretations that clients make appear to arise extremely quickly. This creates a methodological problem for the researcher, in that it is difficult to assess the cognitions suitably. Clark makes the intriguing suggestion that a *contextual priming* paradigm could be used, in which the client is provided with incomplete sentences, and his or her reaction time to recognizing possible concluding words is assessed. If the client automatically associates increased heart rate with imminent death, a sentence beginning "Jane's pulse quickened because she was . . ." would elicit faster reaction times to "dying" than to "eager." This line of argument also leads Clark to the conclusion that clients will misinterpret somatic feelings even when not anxious. If this is so, clients with panic disorder have an enduring trait in this regard. This trait may predate the first panic attack or develop later. Clark suggests that if a benign ascription of the first attack is made (by the client or by someone else), the trait of misinterpretation will not develop and future attacks will be forestalled.

Clark (1988) also elucidates some differences between his model and the fear-of-fear pattern. If panic results from a fear of fear, then a panic attack would ensue from any fear experience. This is not consistent with the evidence that clients with panic disorder may become anxious without an attack developing (it is well known, in any event, that panic disorder commonly subsumes moderate levels of generalized "background" anxiety). Further, in Clark's model a panic attack may be stimulated not only by early signs of fear, but also by similar sensations produced by exercise and the like.

In summary, Clark argues that panic attacks are caused by alarming appraisals of certain somatic sensations. The model is not incompatible with the evidence that biological factors play a role in panic disorder, as Clark points out. Those factors can influence the client's likelihood of entering the vicious circle depicted in Figure 5.2. There are three possibile biological explanations: (1) people with more frequent variations in bodily state (variations that are within a normal range and not medically significant) have more sensations to misinterpret and may therefore be more vulnerable; (2) people with certain physiological variants, such as inefficient neurotransmitter regulatory processes, may experience unusual sensations as a result (because these physiological events are assumed to be responses to stress, a perceived threat gives rise to the unusual sensations, which may then be overinterpreted); and (3) some of the physiological variants noted in (2) may be particularly likely to trigger panic if they involve surges of activity.

Comments on Clark's Model

Clark concludes his article by citing the central predictions of his model as follows:

> (1) Compared to other anxious patients and normal controls, patients who suffer from panic attacks will be more likely to interpret certain bodily sensations in a catastrophic fashion. . . . (2) Pharmacological agents which provoke panic (such as sodium lactate) do so only when the somatic sensations produced by the agent are interpreted in a catastrophic fashion, and the

panic-producing effects of these agents can be blocked by instructional manipulations. (3) Treatments which fail to change patients [sic] tendency to interpret bodily sensations in a catastrophic fashion will have higher rates of relapse than treatments which succeed in changing interpretations [Clark, 1986, p. 469].

Empirical questions raised by this model include the following.

1. What are the attributions of panic disorder clients compared to other groups?
2. Can drug provocation effects be blocked by instructions?
3. Do treatments that fail to change a client's interpretations lead to higher relapse rates?

These and similar questions are addressed in detail by Clark (1986) in a review of the relevant literature to date.

Beck's Cognitive Model

Beck (1985a; 1985b; 1988) has put forward a cognitive model of panic disorder that has its origins in his earlier work on emotional disorders in general (Beck, 1976). It has several elements in common with Clark's, and in fact these models were developed simultaneously but independently (Clark, 1988).

Discussing anxiety disorders in general, Beck (1985a) distinguishes between *predisposing* and *precipitating* factors. Predisposing factors include heredity, certain physical disorders that produce somatic effects resembling those of anxiety, traumatic experiences, ineffective coping abilities, and unhelpful thinking patterns. Examples of precipitating factors include physical disease, exposure to toxic substances, and various forms of external stress. Precipitating factors become significant when they impinge on the areas of vulnerability to which the client is predisposed. The negative role of cognition in anxiety disorders results in the client mistakenly interpreting certain events as dangerous.

Beck describes the chief characteristics of severe panic attacks thus:

1. The bodily reactions seem strange and unfamiliar to the client.
2. He or she has a sense of losing control of consciousness and behavior.
3. The chief experience is of depersonalization.
4. There is a sense of being overwhelmed by anxiety.
5. There is a feeling of faintness or weakness.

During an attack, the client is often convinced that he or she is dying. This belief produces further symptoms of anxiety, and a chain reaction begins. The attacks, though often described as if they arise haphazardly, are commonly triggered by understandable physiological changes, such as those produced by sudden alterations in ambient temperature. Alternatively, they may arise in response to an external threat or stressor. Beck notes that bereavements or other types of social loss may precipitate panic attacks. Regardless of the type of precipitant, it sets the scene for a series of "automatic thoughts" that focus on threat, danger, and harm. Commonly, a serious disease process is feared specifically.

In agoraphobia, of course, the client's panic attacks are associated with certain situations and locations. Beck (1985b) suggests that the agoraphobic client fears the same situations that would be dangerous for small children. Fear of being far from safety may arise after a noxious event is experienced or witnessed in public. Associations may develop between panic attacks and particular places, which are then avoided. These difficulties lead the client to seek out a particular companion or helper. Separation from the companion may itself become the chief phobic trigger. Noting that individuals with agoraphobia are sensitive to visual arrays with depth and parallax, Beck (1985b) makes the intriguing suggestion that there is a link between fears of boundless vistas or of architectural constrictions and fears of distance from or proximity to the safe companion.

Comments on Beck's Model

Questions raised by Clark's model apply equally to Beck's. Whether persons with agoraphobia are particularly troubled by large spaces or distance from support (an issue raised by Beck) has usually been interpreted as a conceptual, rather than an empirical, question. Despite the inclusion of a question on fear of "large open spaces" in the agoraphobia scale of the Marks and Mathews (1979) Fear Questionnaire, Marks (1970) has argued against including fear of open spaces in a definition of agoraphobia. He has suggested elsewhere that a syndrome in which the client fears a loss of physical support in spacious surroundings is best referred to as "space phobia," unrelated to agoraphobia (Marks & Bebbington, 1976). As for Beck's interesting speculations about the role of the "phobic companion," Rachman's (1984) safety-signal hypothesis seems relevant. An important empirical question is whether individuals with agoraphobia have specific fears concerning a relationship with a certain safe companion.

Review of Research Concerning the Models

Developmental Issues

Disorders in which panic attacks are prominent appear to run in families, but not all investigations successfully differentiate between biological and social learning factors. The data on life history, family context, and related issues often lead to uncertain conclusions because the information is typically anecdotal and retrospective (Stampler, 1982). Prospective studies may provide more accurate information, but they are typically more time consuming and costly. In both prospective and retrospective research, it is important to use appropriate control groups.

Level of Parental Protection

Some authors conclude that panic disorder and agoraphobia are suffered chiefly by people from close-knit, overprotective families, but the evidence is contradictory (Stampler, 1982). Forty-three percent of respondents reported that their mothers had been overanxious and overprotective in the National Survey of Agoraphobics in Great Britain (Thorpe & Burns, 1983). Eleven percent reported that their mothers were rejecting. Solyom, Silberfeld, and Solyom (1976) found that mothers of agoraphobic clients scored higher than the available normative sample on a maternal overprotection scale. It should be noted, however, that these data were collected after the client had developed agoraphobia. In any event, not all investigators have found evidence for maternal overprotection. Arrindell, Emmelkamp, Monsma, and Brilman (1983) found that the degree of parental overprotection, as assessed by subjects' self-report, did not significantly differentiate individuals with agoraphobia from a control sample or from persons with other phobias.

Childhood Fears

Separation anxiety in childhood and various childhood fears have been reported in the life history of agoraphobic clients (Stampler, 1982; Thorpe & Burns, 1983). Reviewing earlier work, Marks and Gelder (1965) commented that 50% of a sample of agoraphobic clients reported enuresis, fear, and night terrors as childhood problems. In a sample of respondents with a variety of phobias, 60% had phobias in childhood (Harper & Roth, 1962). (Of course, the significance of this finding would depend on the type of phobia, since several simple phobias typically arise in childhood.) About 37% of a sample of persons with agoraphobia reported a very unhappy or disrupted childhood (Shafar, 1976). In about a third of the cases bereavement had been an issue. Twenty-two percent of women (n = 786) in an agoraphobia correspondence club reported a history of school phobia (Berg, Marks, McGuire, & Lipsedge, 1974). This proportion was similar to that in a comparison group of people with neuroses other than phobia (n = 57). Past school phobia predicted an earlier onset of agoraphobia and greater severity of psychiatric symptoms other than agoraphobia. There was also evidence that the children of persons with agoraphobia show a greater prevalence of school phobia than would be expected (Berg, 1976). Women with school-phobic children were likely to have had school phobia themselves.

In a conflicting prospective study, children of persons with agoraphobia and of a matched group of normals were compared (Buglass, Clarke, Henderson, Kreitman, & Presley, 1977). There was no evidence of a greater prevalence of psychological problems in the children of the group with agoraphobia.

Eighteen percent of the children of parents with agoraphobia and 25% of the children of the control parents were phobic.

Early Separation and Fear of Abandonment

Empirical work on separation fears includes studies of animals as well as humans. Timmermans, Roder, and Hunting (1986) studied 12 monkeys, divided into experimental and control groups. Control subjects were raised by their parents in a group including other adult monkeys. The adults would habitually spread wood shavings on the floor by tearing up a paper bag into which the experimenters had put grain and wood chips. At one year the young monkeys were placed in a peer group. The other, experimental subjects were raised from birth in a peer group with an inanimate surrogate mother. The experimenter spread wood chips for the first year of the monkeys' lives. The results were as follows: at 1, 3, and 6 years of age the control group monkeys would approach and tear up a paper bag much as their parents had. The experimental monkeys consistently and unanimously avoided the bag, when tested either in groups or individually. Bag avoidance was maladaptive, since the only food source was placed on top of the bag. These findings suggest that fear or avoidance may arise when a subject is deprived of specific social learning experiences usually gained by means of parental modeling.

The authors of DSM-III-R describe separation anxiety disorder in childhood as a predisposing factor for the development of panic disorder. The origins of this idea are found in both psychoanalytic and biological theories. First, from a psychoanalytic perspective, Thyer, Nesse, Cameron, and Curtis (1985) summarize work relating the development of agoraphobia to a failure to achieve separation-individuation from the mother. Phobic symptoms occur when this symbiotic relationship is threatened symbolically or in actuality. Second, Klein (1981) argues that separation anxiety is an innate biological mechanism that is important in controlling attachment behavior. A form of separation anxiety is commonly observed in early stages of life in humans and other species and is in fact an adaptive mechanism that serves to restore protective attachment. In agoraphobia, the threshold for the release of this mechanism is assumed to be low. Thus, the separation anxiety mechanism becomes operative even when this type of response is no longer adaptive. Klein suggests that several factors might be related to this lowered threshold, including constitutional factors, endocrine imbalance, or an actual negative separation experience. It should be noted that although the separation anxiety hypothesis has been put forward to account for agoraphobia, it has not yet been shown to apply to panic disorder (Gittelman & Klein, 1984).

Support for the proposed relationship between separation anxiety and agoraphobia has been found in case reports and descriptive studies (see Thyer et al., 1985). When samples with agoraphobia are compared with suitable control populations, however, the relationship is less clear. Buglass et al. (1977) found no differences between 30 clients with agoraphobia and 30 general practice patients on scales designed to assess positive, negative, and ambivalent feelings toward parents. Similarly, Thyer et al. (1985) could find no differences between persons with agoraphobia and simple phobia on 14 questions related to childhood separation trauma. In a similar study, statistically significant differences were found on just 2 of the 14 questions (Thyer, Nesse, Curtis, & Cameron, 1986). The panic disorder subjects' responses on those two items, while suggesting a higher incidence of childhood separation problems, appear to be of limited clinical significance. For example, in response to the question "How scared were you when you started school?" the panic disorder clients' average response on a 5-point scale was 3.09, corresponding to the verbal description "some." Finally, in a study by Tennant, Hurry, and Bebbington (1982), no significant relationships were found between separation experiences occurring before the age of 5 and adult depression and anxiety states. Separation experiences after that age were associated more frequently with adult depression than with anxiety disorders.

Sex-role Factors

In view of the predominance of women in samples with agoraphobia, it is reasonable to call attention to the different developmental experiences of men and women in our culture (Fishman, 1980; Fodor, 1978). It is plausible and intuitively appealing to assume that women are generally brought up to adopt more fearful postures than men; hence, women would be more likely than men to develop anxiety disorders. However, Marks (in the foreword to Thorpe & Burns, 1983) has made the point that we would also expect disproportionate numbers of women in social phobia samples, based on the same argument. This does not appear to be the case: males are in fact seen more often in clinical samples of social phobia than females (American Psychiatric Association, 1987). This issue is important to the validation of the Goldstein and Chambless (1978) model and similar formulations.

In an interesting correlational study of the relationship between sex-role stereotyped behavior and agoraphobia, Chambless and Mason (1986) examined the responses of 334 females and 68 males with agoraphobia to a lengthy set of questionnaires on psychopathology and personality functioning. Few differences were found between male and female samples. This is consistent with the results of other studies (Mavissakalian, 1985). Clients' scores on a scale of femininity were generally unrelated to measures of psychopathology. Masculinity, however, was significantly and inversely related to psychopathology (that is, fear of negative evaluation, social avoidance, frequency of panic attacks, and phobic avoidance). These relationships were found for both men and women. In summary, stereotypically feminine traits were not associated with maladjustment, but lower levels of traits typically associated with masculinity (such as, activity and assertiveness) were related to psychopathology. These findings lend some support to the hypothesis that sex-role characteristics play a role in agoraphobia. No conclusions about the causal relationship between masculinity and psychopathology can be drawn, however, as the data were correlational.

Individual Differences and Personal Styles

Physiological Variants

Several physiological variants have been cited as predisposing persons to panic disorder and agoraphobia, and these are commonly invoked by the authors of the integrated models discussed earlier. Such variants include disturbances of lactate metabolism, mitral valve prolapse syndrome, and hyperventilation. Their explanatory role is a matter of some controversy (Marks, 1983). Asso and Beech (1975) have suggested that women may be particularly vulnerable to the acquisition of aversive responses a few days before the onset of menstruation. Occasionally women in their mid-50s report that chronic agoraphobia has disappeared practically overnight; this could be attributed to hormonal changes associated with menopause (Thorpe & Burns, 1983). Several biological mechanisms have been cited as interacting with attributional processes to produce panic attacks. These include hyperventilation (Ley, 1985; Salkovskis, Warwick, Clark, & Wessels, 1986); heart rate acceleration (Margraf, Ehlers, & Roth, 1987); and lactate metabolism (van der Molen, van den Hout, Vroemen, Lousberg, & Griez, 1986). Chapter 4 in this volume provides a commentary on some of these issues.

Attention to Somatic Cues

Evidence reviewed by Clark (1986) indicates that panic clients typically report that the onset of an attack is marked by a physical feeling of some kind. Reports that panic attacks occasionally first arise following experiences with illicit psychoactive drugs (Hollon, 1981) are not inconsistent with this observation. Authors of the integrative models of panic disorder described earlier have argued that panic attacks may be explained as the product of two factors: a bodily sensation of some kind (whether "normal" or "abnormal" in origin) followed by the client's misinterpretation or misattribution of that sensation. Salkovskis and Warwick (1986) have pointed out that a similar explanation can be offered for hypochondriasis, which they relabel as "health anxiety." However, the treatment implications are different in the case of hypochondriasis, because it may be construed as similar to an obsessive-compulsive disorder in which reassurance seeking and checking of bodily status represent avoidance behavior. Systematic exposure to the cues, with prevention of the avoidance responses, was therapeutic in two cases described in this report.

Fisher and Wilson (1985) tested the hypothesis that persons with agoraphobia would use internal cues more extensively than a control sample in gauging the intensity of their fears. Cue utilization was examined in two ways. First, a procedure was adopted to induce subjects to form a facial expression without being aware that they were doing so. After the subjects made the facial expression, they completed a self-report inventory of mood. Previous research had shown that subjects who use internal, rather than external, cues are more strongly influenced in their mood by facial expression. In the Fisher and Wilson study, no differences between individuals with and without agoraphobia were seen. Second, the rod-and-frame task was used to assess the use of internal and external cues (Witkin, Dyk, Paterson, Goodenough, & Karp, 1962). In this procedure the subject adjusts the angle of a rod until it appears to be vertical. As the rod is displayed against the background of a square frame having a nonvertical orientation, the researcher can determine to what extent the subject's response is dependent on the field or context of the frame's orientation, as opposed to internal cues, for vertical direction. Again, no group differences were observed. There is therefore no evidence from the Fisher and Wilson (1985) studies that individuals with and without agoraphobia differ on laboratory tasks evaluating the use of external or internal cues.

Despite these null findings, the role of somatic cues continues to deserve the attention of clinical researchers. It could be argued that Fisher and Wilson failed to identify the appropriate tasks for revealing group differences. Given the important role assigned to attention to somatic cues in the cognitive theories, it would be premature to abandon this line of inquiry.

Attributional Style

The Goldstein and Chambless (1978) hypothesis about agoraphobic clients' tendency to misattribute the source of emotional feelings is drawn from case material—and retrospectively at that (Emmelkamp, 1979)—so more data are required on this point. Ottaviani and Beck (1987) interviewed 30 clients with panic disorder without agoraphobia and observed that the first panic attack was precipitated by physical or psychosocial stress in all cases. All of the clients gave evidence of misattribution of their experiences. "Psychosocial stress" often referred to conflicts in relationships or to separations from significant people. Hence, a climate of conflict and a tendency to misattribute their experiences were common to these clients with panic disorder, consistent with the Goldstein and Chambless theory.

Fisher and Wilson (1985) examined the responses of a group with agoraphobia and a control group to a helplessness questionnaire. Their conclusions were that persons with agoraphobia, as compared to controls, made more internal attributions for negative events, and rated internal causes as more important and more consistently present. Subjects also completed an attributions questionnaire after observing videotaped scenes. Persons with agoraphobia were significantly more likely to rate the causes of fear as internal—that is, attributable to the person rather than to the circumstances—than were the control subjects.

Nevertheless, there is disagreement about the attributional style seen in panic disorder. Some of the information available on this topic has a bearing on the issue of perceived locus of control. In a recent review, Brodbeck and Michelson (1987) noted that, in contrast with the view of Fisher and Wilson (1985), some researchers conclude that individuals with agoraphobia describe an external locus of control. Emmelkamp (1982) has argued that persons with agoraphobia typically misattribute their panic attacks to dangerous external situations; as a result they adopt a policy of avoidance rather than of problem solving. Mathews, Gelder, and Johnston (1981) also cited external misattributions in agoraphobia. It has to be noted that there is a danger of conceptual confusion when both internal and external ascriptions of the source of a panic attack are viewed as incorrect attributions. It may be that the internal/external (locus of control) dimension may not be the best on which to focus. Approaches emphasizing catastrophizing attributional style and active versus passive problem solving may be more helpful.

As a result of their study, Brodbeck and Michelson (1987) concluded that individuals with agoraphobia display interpersonal problem-solving deficits, in that they tend to avoid challenging situations rather than attempt to resolve them. The deficits in question are specific to interpersonal issues, because the subjects with agoraphobia were able to organize a logical series of steps in solving anagrams and did not differ from control subjects in this respect. (Brodbeck and Michelson also pointed out that specific problem-solving treatment strategies have proven to be disappointing in the treatment of agoraphobia.) The authors also assessed attributional style, and interpreted the results as consistent with the Goldstein and Chambless (1978) view that individuals with agoraphobia have a "global, catastrophizing attributional style and interpersonal sensitivity" (Brodbeck & Michelson, 1987, p. 607).

Specific Cognitions

Beck, Laude, and Bohnert (1974) demonstrated that clients with generalized anxiety associated increases in fear with thoughts of danger or threat. Recent evidence indicates that clients with panic disorder are more likely than others to entertain thoughts about illness, death, and loss of control (Clark, 1986; Hibbert, 1984). It has also clearly been established that clients with panic disorder have thoughts of dying, becoming mentally ill, or losing control during panic attacks (Burns & Thorpe, 1977a, 1977b; Chambless, Caputo, Bright, & Gallagher, 1984). In a comparison of nonphobic clients with and without a history of panic attacks, Hibbert (1984) found that panic patients were significantly more likely than those without panic to report thoughts about possible illness, death, or loss of control. Beck (1988) refers to a study in progress in which eight panic disorder patients were able to induce a panic attack through voluntary hyperventilation. During a panic attack, these patients experienced vivid imagery and automatic thoughts reflecting fears of physical or mental disaster.

Recent correlational work by Mizes, Landolf-Fritsche, and Grossman-McKee (1987) indicates that persons with agoraphobia had scores on a test of irrational beliefs that were related to their total phobic severity. Many of the universal irrational beliefs cited by Ellis (1962) as related to psychopathology were endorsed by persons with agoraphobia, but a similar pattern was seen in the responses of persons with simple phobia as well. By comparing untreated and treated persons with agoraphobia with control subjects, McNally and Foa (1987) demonstrated that the untreated agoraphobic sample interpreted ambiguous stimuli—whether of internal or external origin—as threatening, whereas this tendency was clearly less marked in control subjects or in the treated sample.

Cognitive restructuring methods have also been shown to be of some benefit, at least when their effects are assessed a month or so after the termination of brief treatment programs (Emmelkamp & Mersch, 1982; Thorpe, Hecker, Cavallaro, & Kulberg, 1987). Together with relaxation training, these methods have proven beneficial for clients with panic disorder but without phobic avoidance (Barlow, Cohen et al., 1984; Waddell, Barlow, & O'Brien, 1984).

Self-Sufficiency, Independence, and Assertiveness

Buglass et al. (1977) found no premorbid difference in dependency between agoraphobic and nonagoraphobic samples. Individuals with agoraphobia do tend to score lower on measures of assertiveness (Chambless, Hunter, & Jackson, 1982; Fisher & Wilson, 1985; Thorpe, Freedman, & Lazar, 1985) and self-sufficiency (Thorpe & Burns, 1983) when compared with general adult normative data and with college students. Similarly, personality traits or styles of shyness, passivity, and dependency have been identified in clients with panic disorder (Stampler, 1982). In each case, it is unclear whether these personal characteristics are precursors or consequences of the anxiety disorder. It is difficult in principle to answer such questions from data that are almost inevitably correlational and retrospective.

Results of some studies are at least consistent with the hypotheses of Goldstein and Chambless (1978) and of Stampler (1982). Assertiveness training can be helpful to individuals with agoraphobia, for example, although panic attacks themselves have not been the focus of study (Cavallaro, 1987).

Marital and Interpersonal Conflict

At least three empirical questions emerge from the formulations of Goldstein and Chambless (1978) and others. First, do individuals with agoraphobia experience marital dissatisfaction? Second, does the quality of the marriage affect response to treatment? (Clients in dysfunctional relationships may be expected to improve less with treatments focused on phobic avoidance, because phobia removal might present a challenge to their strategy for coping in the relationship.) Third, does improvement in phobic symptoms have a negative impact upon clients' marriages? (If behavioral treatment reduces avoidance it might precipitate a crisis in the marriage, because the client's mechanism for coping with conflict—fearful avoidance—has been removed.) The latter two questions have been posed as hypotheses by Himadi, Cerny, Barlow, Cohen, and O'Brien (1986).

The notion of a relationship between marital factors and the development and/or maintenance of agoraphobia has a long history (see, for example, Webster, 1953), but the hypothesis that individuals with agoraphobia are dissatisfied in their marriages has not received strong support from empirical studies. Results of a national survey of persons with agoraphobia in Great Britain found nothing unusual about the marriages of the sample (Burns & Thorpe, 1977a, 1977b). Nonetheless, approximately one in five respondents did indicate that agoraphobia was putting a considerable strain on the marriage. In addition, a portion (37%) of the sample reported communication problems with their spouses regarding the agoraphobia.

Studies comparing agoraphobic individuals with appropriately matched control groups have tended to find no differences in marital satisfaction (Buglass et al., 1977; Fisher & Wilson, 1985). Fisher and Wilson examined the salience of marital conflicts for agoraphobic and control subjects by studying self-reported fear and anger as well as heart rate while subjects viewed a videotaped scene of marital conflict. Control subjects' self-ratings of fear and anger rose while viewing the argument, but agoraphobic subjects' fear ratings dropped and their anger rose only slightly as they observed the scene. Similarly, agoraphobic subjects' heart rate during the conflict scene fell below the controls' level, which increased as they observed the scene. These data suggest that the agoraphobic subjects were less troubled by the marital conflict scene, which seems inconsistent with the hypothesis concerning marital dysfunction. (It could be argued, however, that this observation supports the view that individuals with agoraphobia are so accustomed to marital conflict in their own homes that they have become inured to such material!)

Regarding whether the quality of the marriage affects response to treatment, empirical findings have been mixed. Hafner (1976, 1977, 1979; Milton & Hafner, 1979) has published a series of articles that provide some evidence that response to intensive in vivo exposure treatment was adversely affected by marital problems. Hafner (1977), for example, found that in four cases husbands became extremely jealous when their wife's agoraphobia improved. Consequently, those wives relapsed to their agoraphobic symptoms. Milton and Hafner (1979) found that those clients whose marriages were rated unsatisfactory before treatment improved less and were more likely to relapse than those with satisfactory marriages. Bland and Hallam (1981) reported similar findings. These studies have been criticized on a number of grounds, including the authors' failure to obtain an independent assessment of marital functioning and their use of inappropriate statistical procedures (Himadi et al., 1986). Furthermore, at least two studies have yielded results inconsistent with those of Hafner. Emmelkamp (1980) divided clients into groups scoring high and low on marital satisfaction scales prior to self-controlled in vivo exposure therapy. No significant group difference was found at posttest or 1-month follow-up. Similarly, Himadi et al. (1986) found treatment outcome to be independent of pretreatment marital adjustment in 42 agoraphobic women.

Finally, the question of whether behavioral treatment adversely affects marriages has been addressed in several studies. The results suggest that this phenomenon may occur, but only in a small percentage of persons with agoraphobia. Hand and Lamontagne (1976) provided clinical descriptions of seven cases (out of a total of twenty-one treated) in which couples experienced marital crises following the removal of the clients' agoraphobic symptoms by intensive group in vivo exposure. In two cases, for example, the clients developed orgasmic dysfunction after successful treatment. Interestingly, one of the clients described her marriage positively both before and after therapy. While caution must, of course, be exercised in generalizing from case reports, we can note that some empirical studies have reported the same phenomenon. Milton and Hafner (1979), for example, examined the relationship between marital satisfaction and in vivo exposure treatment using the Maudsley Marital Questionnaire (Crowe, 1978). They found that marriages were adversely affected by the clients' improvement in agoraphobic symptoms in nine out of fifteen couples. The results of this study provide only limited support for the hypothesis, however, as there was actually an improvement in marital harmony after treatment in six cases. Barlow, Mavissakalian, and Hay (1981) also found an inconsistent relationship between marital satisfaction and improvement in agoraphobia. Six agoraphobic women and their husbands participated in a group therapy program that employed exposure and cognitive restructuring. In two of the couples, marriages deteriorated as the client improved. In the other four there was a parallel relationship between phobia improvement and increases in marital satisfaction. Coincidental positive changes in both marital satisfaction and agoraphobia as a result of in vivo exposure treatment were also found by Cobb, McDonald, Marks, and Stern (1980) and by Himadi et al. (1986). Similarly, satisfaction with self and spouse (Bland & Hallam, 1981)—and spouse's psychological functioning (Himadi et al., 1986)—remained relatively stable over the course of exposure-based treatments.

Barlow, O'Brien, and Last (1984) suggested that differences in protocols for exposure treatment may account for some of the discrepancies in findings. Studies that have demonstrated the strongest negative effects of exposure in vivo on marital relationships have used time-limited intensive therapy. Hafner's (1977) clients received 12 hours of real-life exposure in 4 days of treatment over a 2-week period. It is perhaps not surprising that changes in long-standing behavioral patterns occurring over such a short period of time would negatively affect the spouse. Should those changes occur more gradually, the spouse might be able to adapt with greater ease (Barlow et al., 1984). It has also been suggested that the potentially negative influence of exposure treatment on marriages might be ameliorated if the spouse were involved in treatment.

Several studies have, in fact, examined the effects of including agoraphobic patients' spouses in treatment. Barlow et al. (1984) found an advantage to group treatment by cognitive restructuring and self-initiated exposure when spouses were included. It has been shown that a home treatment program that used spouses as therapists led to a significant decrease in agoraphobic symptoms (Mathews, Teasdale, Munby, Johnston, & Shaw, 1977). Recent investigations have focused on improving communication patterns in couples along with the treatment of agoraphobia. Arnow, Taylor, Agras, and Telch (1985) treated 24 females with partner-assisted exposure treatment, followed by either couples relaxation training or couples communication training. Communication training focused on helping couples to identify and change interaction styles that would interfere with efforts to overcome phobic avoidance. Posttest and 8-month follow-up assessments indicated a clear advantage to communication training. Attention to couples' communication patterns (specifically dealing with agoraphobic problems), therefore, appears to augment exposure treatment. This is consistent with epidemiological research that has found poor communication patterns in some agoraphobic couples (Burns & Thorpe, 1977a).

In summary, then, the bulk of the empirical data does not support the notion that marital dysfunction is crucial to the development and maintenance of agoraphobia. Agoraphobic persons as a group are not found to have particularly distressed marriages, though some clearly do. These observations seem inconsistent with the hypothesis of Goldstein and Chambless (1978) that agoraphobia may resolve a conflict between the desire to leave a marriage and the fear of being unable to survive alone. While some studies have found that clients in poor marriages improve less with treatment than do those with untroubled marriages, treatment does not appear to exacerbate marital problems in most cases. Exacerbation of marital problems appears to be most likely when treatment is intensive and takes place over a brief period. These findings should not be construed, however, to mean that clients' marital relationships should be ignored. Spouse involvement appears to facilitate improvement with exposure methods—the best results occurring when phobia-maintaining communication patterns are modified (Thorpe, Burns, Smith, & Blier, 1984). This is consistent with Stampler's (1982) recommendation of an antecedent-based focus for therapy.

Stressful Life Events

Stampler (1982) notes that the onset of panic attacks is often preceded by illness, interpersonal conflict, leaving home, bereavement, change in marital status, pregnancy, physical exertion, or witnessing an unpleasant event in public. He writes, "The events most commonly reported as the 'precipitating' causes of the panic attacks often involve some emotionally stressful change or occurrence in the individual's life" (p. 473). Many of the potentially stressful events that have been associated with the onset of panic attacks—such as pregnancy, thyroid problems, and hospitalization for surgery—involve endocrinal as well as environmental changes. In this context it is interesting to note that an assessment of functioning 8 years after successful behavioral treatment for agoraphobia, found that events associated with temporary setbacks or with relapse were invariably general stressors rather than specific conditioning events. Examples were the death of a relative or a pet, termination of the spouse's employment, and having a series of tests for cancer that proved negative (Burns, Thorpe, & Cavallaro, 1986). As we have noted earlier, the panic disorder clients of Ottaviani and Beck (1987) reported stress as the immediate precursor of their first panic attack. Most commonly, the stress resulted from marital conflict, separations, and the like.

Clinical and Research Implications

The integrative theories summarized in this chapter are broadly consistent with the available data. Two caveats are necessary, though. First, showing that a theory is consistent with the data does not verify the theory. Second, the theories were developed largely from the same research information that the theories were designed to explain! Difficulties in research on etiology include the correlational and retrospective nature of most data. The most revealing research strategy in this context is to attempt to disconfirm hypotheses. Some of the most interesting hypotheses are particularly difficult to test—for example, the notion that spontaneous thoughts directly cause feeling states of apparently sudden onset.

An important issue is the role of individual characteristics such as assertiveness deficits. Some authors (such as Goldstein & Chambless, 1978) argue that certain personal styles are vital to the etiology of panic disorder. Others might suggest that personal styles of this kind develop as a consequence of the problem. A closely related matter is the importance of treating problems such as social skills deficits and undue social dependency. Whether of central or peripheral importance, such problems deserve clinical attention. It remains unclear whether a treatment plan omitting these elements is adequately comprehensive in the long run.

Our review of research findings pertinent to the etiological models leads to mixed conclusions. There is little agreement about the importance of certain developmental experiences to the origins of panic disorder. Several case reports suggest the significance of early separation from parents, but controlled evaluations with suitable comparison groups show no convincing trend. The extensive literature on the interpersonal context of panic disorder and agoraphobia concludes uncertainly, not only about the prevalence of marital problems, but also, when they *are* present, about their etiological significance. The studies done with the most adequate controls suggest that marital problems are no more common in clients with panic disorder than in other clinical groups or, indeed, in the general population. As for the role of life stress in the development of these disorders, surveys show that general stressors, such as a change in occupational status or the death of a relative, are more commonly present than specific aversive events that would conform to a simple conditioning model of etiology.

The most conclusive information derives from studies of clients' cognitions, although there is some controversy about particular issues. Several studies indicate that panic disorder clients make unhelpful attributions concerning the source of their anxiety symptoms. Researchers disagree, however, about clients' perceptions of the locus of control. Some show that individuals with panic disorder attribute their panic attacks to external causes; others find evidence for a preoccupation with internal sources of fear. Recent research using the methodology of the experimental psychology of cognition suggests that stimulus ambiguity, rather than its internal or external origin, may be the crucial factor in clients' attributional processes. Impressive contributions by Clark (1986) and McCarthy (1987) have illustrated the potential for laboratory procedures such as contextual priming in assessing the cognitive fear structure of panic clients. Work of this kind could allow further links to be forged between empirical clinical research and the conceptual innovations of bioinformational theory (Lang, 1985).

The clinical implications of our review material clearly call for thorough, wide-ranging assessment. Clients with panic disorder may additionally be troubled by social skills problems, undue dependency on others, marital conflict, low self-esteem, difficulties in recognizing or differentiating emotional states, and unhelpful attributional styles. Such issues deserve clinical attention whether or not they are central to the development of panic disorder.

References

American Psychiatric Association. (1980). *Diagnostic and statistical manual of mental disorders* (3rd ed.). Washington, DC: Author.

American Psychiatric Association. (1987). *Diagnostic and statistical manual of mental disorders* (3rd ed., rev.). Washington, DC: Author.

Arnow, B. A., Taylor, C. B., Agras, W. S., & Telch, M. J. (1985). Enhancing agoraphobia treatment outcome by changing couple communication patterns. *Behavior Therapy, 16*, 452–467.

Arrindell, W. A., Emmelkamp, P. M. G., Monsma, A., & Brilman, E. (1983). The role of perceived parental rearing practices in the aetiology of phobic disorders: A controlled study. *British Journal of Psychiatry, 143*, 183–187.

Asso, D., & Beech, H. R. (1975). Susceptibility to the acquisition of a conditioned response in relation to the menstrual cycle. *Journal of Psychosomatic Research, 19*, 337–344.

Bandura, A. (1977). Self-efficacy: Toward a unifying theory of behavior change. *Psychological Review, 84*, 191–215.

Barlow, D. H., Cohen, A. S., Waddell, M. T., Vermilyea, B. B., Klosko, J. S., Blanchard, E. B., & Di Nardo, P. A. (1984). Panic and generalized anxiety disorders: Nature and treatment. *Behavior Therapy, 15*, 431–449.

Barlow, D. H., Mavissakalian, M., & Hay, L. R. (1981). Couples treatment of agoraphobia: Changes in marital satisfaction. *Behaviour Research and Therapy, 19*, 245–255.

Barlow, D. H., O'Brien, G. T., & Last, C. G. (1984). Couples treatment of agoraphobia. *Behavior Therapy, 15*, 41–58.

Baum, M. (1986a). An animal model for agoraphobia using a safety-signal analysis. *Behaviour Research and Therapy, 24*, 87–89.

Baum, M. (1986b). An animal model for situational panic attacks. *Behaviour Research and Therapy, 24*, 509–512.

Beck, A. T. (1976). *Cognitive therapy and the emotional disorders.* New York: International Universities Press.

Beck, A. T. (1985a). Generalized anxiety disorder and panic disorder. In A. T. Beck, G. Emery, & R. L. Greenberg (Eds.), *Anxiety disorders and phobias: A cognitive perspective* (pp. 82–114). New York: Basic Books.

Beck, A. T. (1985b). The agoraphobic syndrome. In A. T. Beck, G. Emery, & R. L. Greenberg (Eds.), *Anxiety disorders and phobias: A cognitive perspective* (pp. 133–145). New York: Basic Books.

Beck, A. T. (1988). Cognitive approaches to panic disorder: Theory and therapy. In S. Rachman & J. Maser (Eds.), *Panic: Psychological perspectives.* Hillsdale, NJ: Lawrence Erlbaum.

Beck, A. T., Laude, R., & Bohnert, M. (1974). Ideational components of anxiety neurosis. *Archives of General Psychiatry, 31*, 319–325.

Berg, I. (1976). School phobia in children of agoraphobic women. *British Journal of Psychiatry, 128*, 86–89.

Berg, I., Marks, I., McGuire, R., & Lipsedge, M. (1974). School phobia and agoraphobia. *Psychological Medicine, 4*, 428–434.

Bland, K., & Hallam, R. S. (1981). Relationship between response to graded exposure and marital satisfaction in agoraphobics. *Behaviour Research and Therapy, 19*, 335–338.

Brehony, K. A., & Geller, E. S. (1981). Agoraphobia: Appraisal of research and a proposal for an integrative model. In M. Hersen, R. M. Eisler, & P. M. Miller (Eds.), *Progress in behavior modification, Vol. 12.* New York: Academic Press.

Brodbeck, C., & Michelson, L. (1987). Problem-solving skills and attributional styles of agoraphobics. *Cognitive Therapy and Research, 11*, 593–610.

Buglass, D., Clarke, J., Henderson, A. S., Kreitman, N., & Presley, A. S. (1977). A study of agoraphobic housewives. *Psychological Medicine, 7*, 73–86.

Burns, L. E., & Thorpe, G. L. (1977a). Fears and clinical phobias: Epidemiological aspects and the National Survey of Agoraphobics. *The Journal of International Medical Research, 5*(Suppl. 1), 132–139.

Burns, L. E., & Thorpe, G. L. (1977b). The epidemiology of fears and phobias (with particular reference to the National Survey of Agoraphobics). *The Journal of International Medical Research, 5* (Suppl. 5), 1–7.

Burns, L. E., Thorpe, G. L., & Cavallaro, L. A. (1986). Agoraphobia 8 years after behavioral treatment: A follow-up study with interview, self-report, and behavioral data. *Behavior Therapy, 17*, 580–591.

Cavallaro, L. A. (1987). *Cognitive-behavioral assertiveness training with agoraphobics.* Unpublished doctoral dissertation, University of Maine.

Chambless, D. L., Caputo, G. C., Bright, P., & Gallagher, R. (1984). Assessment of fear-of-fear in agoraphobics: The Body Sensations Questionnaire and the Agoraphobic Cognitions Questionnaire. *Journal of Consulting and Clinical Psychology, 52,* 1090–1097.

Chambless, D. L., Hunter, K., & Jackson, A. (1982). Social anxiety and assertiveness: A comparison of the correlations in phobic and college student samples. *Behaviour Research and Therapy, 20,* 403–404.

Chambless, D. L., & Mason, J. (1986). Sex, sex-role stereotyping, and agoraphobia. *Behaviour Research and Therapy, 24,* 231–235.

Clark, D. M. (1986). A cognitive approach to panic. *Behaviour Research and Therapy, 24,* 461–470.

Clark, D. M. (1988). A cognitive model of panic attacks. In S. Rachman & J. Maser (Eds.), *Panic: Psychological perspectives.* Hillsdale, NJ: Lawrence Erlbaum.

Clarke, J. C., & Wardman, W. (1985). *Agoraphobia: A clinical and personal account.* Sydney: Pergamon.

Cobb, J., McDonald, R., Marks, I., & Stern, R. (1980). Marital versus exposure therapy: Psychological treatments of co-existing marital and phobic-obsessive problems. *Behavioural Analysis and Modification, 4,* 3–16.

Crowe, M. J. (1978). Conjoint marital therapy: A controlled outcome study. *Psychological Medicine, 9,* 623–636.

Ellis, A. (1962). *Reason and emotion in psychotherapy.* New York: Lyle Stuart.

Emmelkamp, P. M. G. (1979). The behavioral study of clinical phobias. In M. Hersen, R. Eisler, & P. M. Miller (Eds.), *Progress in behavior modification, Vol. 8* (pp. 55–125). New York: Academic Press.

Emmelkamp, P. M. G. (1980). Agoraphobics' interpersonal problems: Their role in the effects of exposure *in vivo* therapy. *Archives of General Psychiatry, 37,* 1303–1306.

Emmelkamp, P. M. G. (1982). *Phobic and obsessive compulsive disorders: Theory, research, and practice.* New York: Plenum.

Emmelkamp, P. M. G., & Mersch, P. P. (1982). Cognition and exposure *in vivo* in the treatment of agoraphobia: Short-term and delayed effects. *Cognitive Therapy and Research, 6,* 77–90.

Evans, I. M. (1972). A conditioning model of a common neurotic pattern: Fear of fear. *Psychotherapy: Theory, Research, and Practice, 9,* 238–241.

Fisher, L. M., & Wilson, G. T. (1985). A study of the psychology of agoraphobia. *Behaviour Research and Therapy, 23,* 97–107.

Fishman, S. (1980). *Agoraphobia: Multiform behavioral treatment.* New York: BMA Audiocassette Publications.

Fodor, I. G. (1978). *Phobias in women: Therapeutic Approaches.* New York: BMA Audiocassette Publications.

Franks, C. M., & Wilson, G. T. (Eds.). (1978). *Annual review of behavior therapy: Theory and practice, Vol. 5.* New York: Brunner/Mazel.

Garssen, B., & Rijken, H. (1986). Clinical aspects and treatment of the hyperventilation syndrome. *Behavioural Psychotherapy, 14,* 46–68.

Gittelman, R., & Klein, D. F. (1984). Relationship between separation anxiety and panic and agoraphobic disorders. *Psychopathology, 17*(Suppl. 1), 56–65.

Goldstein, A. J. (1970). Case conference: Some aspects of agoraphobia. *Journal of Behavior Therapy and Experimental Psychiatry, 1,* 305–313.

Goldstein, A. J., & Chambless, D. L. (1978). A reanalysis of agoraphobia. *Behavior Therapy, 9,* 47–59.

Hafner, R. J. (1976). Fresh symptom emergence after intensive behaviour therapy. *British Journal of Psychiatry, 129,* 378–383.

Hafner, R. J. (1977). The husbands of agoraphobic women and their influence on treatment outcome. *British Journal of Psychiatry, 131,* 289–294.

Hafner, R. J. (1979). Agoraphobic women married to abnormally jealous men. *British Journal of Medical Psychology, 52,* 99–104.

Hallam, R. S. (1978). Agoraphobia: A critical review of the concept. *British Journal of Psychiatry, 133,* 314–319.

Hand, I., & Lamontagne, Y. (1976). The exacerbation of interpersonal problems after rapid phobia-removal. *Psychotherapy: Theory, Research, and Practice, 13,* 405–411.

Harper, M., & Roth, M. (1962). Temporal lobe epilepsy and the phobic-anxiety-depersonalization syndrome. *Comprehensive Psychiatry, 3,* 129–151.

Hibbert, G. A. (1984). Ideational components of anxiety: Their origin and content. *British Journal of Psychiatry, 144,* 618–624.

Himadi, W. G., Cerny, J. A., Barlow, D. H., Cohen, S., & O'Brien, G. T. (1986). The relationship of marital adjustment to agoraphobia treatment outcome. *Behaviour Research and Therapy, 24,* 107–115.

Hineline, P. (1977). Negative reinforcement and avoidance. In W. K. Honig & J. E. R. Staddon (Eds.), *Handbook of operant behavior.* Englewood Cliffs, NJ: Prentice-Hall.

Hollon, S. D. (1981). Cognitive-behavioral treatment of drug-induced panic situational anxiety states. In G. Emery, S. D. Hollon, & R. C. Bedrosian (Eds.), *New directions in cognitive therapy: A casebook.* New York: Guilford Press.

Jacob, R. G., & Rapport, M. D. (1984). Panic disorder: Medical and psychological parameters. In S. M. Turner (Ed.), *Behavioral theories and treatment of anxiety* (pp. 187–237). New York: Plenum.

Klein, D. F. (1981). Anxiety reconceptualized. In D. F. Klein & J. Rabkin (Eds.), *Anxiety: New research and changing concepts.* New York: Raven Press.

Lang, P. J. (1985). The cognitive psychophysiology of emotion: Fear and anxiety. In A. H. Tuma & J. D. Maser (Eds.), *Anxiety and the anxiety disorders* (pp. 131–170). Hillsdale, NJ: Lawrence Erlbaum.

Lazarus, A. A. (1966). Broad-spectrum behaviour therapy and the treatment of agoraphobia. *Behaviour Research and Therapy, 4,* 95–97.

Lazarus, R. S. (1966). *Psychological stress and the coping process.* New York: McGraw-Hill.

Ley, R. (1985). Agoraphobia, the panic attack, and the hyperventilation syndrome. *Behaviour Research and Therapy, 23,* 79–81.

Ley, R. (1987). Panic disorder: A hyperventilation interpretation. In L. Michelson & L. M. Ascher (Eds.), *Anxiety and stress disorders: Cognitive-behavioral assessment and treatment* (pp. 191–212). New York: Guilford Press.

McCarthy, P. (1987, November). *Cognitive fear structure in agoraphobia, obsessive-compulsive disorder, and simple phobia.* Paper presented at the 21st Annual Meeting of the Association for the Advancement of Behavior Therapy, Boston.

McNally, R. J., & Foa, E. B. (1987). Cognition and agoraphobia: Bias in the interpretation of threat. *Cognitive Therapy and Research, 11,* 567–581.

Margraf, J., Ehlers, A., & Roth, W. T. (1987). Panic attack associated with perceived heart rate acceleration: A case report. *Behavior Therapy, 18,* 84–89.

Marks, I. M. (1970). Agoraphobic syndrome (phobic anxiety state). *Archives of General Psychiatry, 23,* 538–553.

Marks, I. M. (1981). *Cure and care of neurosis: Theory and practice of behavioral psychotherapy*. New York: Wiley.

Marks, I. M. (1983). Foreword. In G. L. Thorpe & L. E. Burns (Eds.), *The agoraphobic syndrome: Behavioural approaches to evaluation and treatment*. Chichester, UK: Wiley.

Marks, I. M., & Bebbington, P. (1976). Space phobia: Syndrome or agoraphobic variant? *British Medical Journal, 2*, 345–347.

Marks, I. M., & Gelder, M. G. (1965). A controlled retrospective study of behaviour therapy in phobic patients. *British Journal of Psychiatry, 111*, 571–573.

Marks, I. M., & Mathews, A. M. (1979). Brief standard self-rating for phobic patients. *Behaviour Research and Therapy, 17*, 263–267.

Marshall, J. R. (1987, October 15). Hyperventilation or panic disorder: What's in the name? *Hospital Practice*, 105–108, 111–118.

Mathews, A. M., Gelder, M. G., & Johnston, D. W. (1981). *Agoraphobia: Nature and treatment*. New York: Guilford Press.

Mathews, A. M., Teasdale, J., Munby, M., Johnston, D., & Shaw, P. (1977). A home-based treatment program for agoraphobia. *Behavior Therapy, 8*, 915–924.

Mavissakalian, M. (1985). Male and female agoraphobia: Are they different? *Behaviour Research and Therapy, 23*, 469–471.

Milton, F., & Hafner, J. (1979). The outcome of behavior therapy for agoraphobia in relation to marital adjustment. *Archives of General Psychiatry, 36*, 807–811.

Mineka, S. (1985). Animal models of anxiety-based disorders: Their usefulness and limitations. In A. H. Tuma & J. D. Maser (Eds.), *Anxiety and the anxiety disorders* (pp. 199–244). Hillsdale, NJ: Lawrence Erlbaum.

Mineka, S., & Kihlstrom, J. F. (1978). Unpredictable and uncontrollable events: A new perspective on experimental neurosis. *Journal of Abnormal Psychology, 87*, 256–271.

Mizes, J. S., Landolf-Fritsche, B., & Grossman-McKee, D. (1987). Patterns of distorted cognitions in phobic disorders: An investigation of clinically severe simple phobics, social phobics, and agoraphobics. *Cognitive Therapy and Research, 11*, 583–592.

Mowrer, O. H. (1947). On the dual nature of learning; A reinterpretation of "conditioning" and "problem-solving." *Harvard Educational Review, 17*, 102–148.

Mowrer, O. H. (1960). *Learning theory and behavior*. New York: Wiley.

Ottaviani, R., & Beck, A. T. (1987). Cognitive aspects of panic disorders. *Journal of Anxiety Disorders, 1*, 15–28.

Rachman, S. (1977). The conditioning theory of fear-acquisition: A critical examination. *Behaviour Research and Therapy, 15*, 375–387.

Rachman, S. (1984). Agoraphobia—A safety-signal perspective. *Behaviour Research and Therapy, 22*, 59–70.

Salkovskis, P. M., & Warwick, H. M. C. (1986). Morbid preoccupations, health anxiety and reassurance: A cognitive-behavioural approach to hypochondriasis. *Behaviour Research and Therapy, 24*, 597–602.

Salkovskis, P. M., Warwick, H. M. C., Clark, D. M., & Wessels, D. J. (1986). A demonstration of acute hyperventilation during naturally occurring panic attacks. *Behaviour Research and Therapy, 24*, 91–94.

Shafar, S. (1976). Aspects of phobic illness—A study of 90 personal cases. *British Journal of Medical Psychology, 49*, 221–236.

Solyom, L., Silberfeld, M., & Solyom, C. (1976). Maternal overprotection in the etiology of agoraphobia. *Canadian Psychiatric Association Journal, 21*, 109–113.

Stampler, F. M. (1982). Panic disorder: Description, conceptualization, and implications for treatment. *Clinical Psychology Review, 2*, 469–486.

Tennant, C., Hurry, J., & Bebbington, P. (1982). The relation of childhood separation experiences to adult depressive and anxiety states. *British Journal of Psychiatry, 141,* 475–482.

Thorpe, G. L., & Burns, L. E. (1983). *The agoraphobic syndrome: Behavioural approaches to evaluation and treatment.* Chichester, UK: Wiley.

Thorpe, G. L., Burns, L. E., Smith, P. J., & Blier, M. J. (1984). Agoraphobia: Research developments and clinical implications. In C. M. Franks (Ed.), *New developments in behavior therapy* (pp. 281–317). New York: Haworth.

Thorpe, G. L., Freedman, E. G., & Lazar, J. D. (1985). Assertiveness training and exposure *in vivo* for agoraphobics. *Behavioural Psychotherapy, 13,* 132–141.

Thorpe, G. L., Hecker, J. E., Cavallaro, L. A., & Kulberg, G. E. (1987). Insight versus rehearsal in cognitive-behavior therapy: A crossover study with sixteen phobics. *Behavioural Psychotherapy, 15,* 319–336.

Thyer, B. A., Nesse, R. M., Cameron, O. G., & Curtis, G. C. (1985). Agoraphobia: A test of the separation anxiety hypothesis. *Behaviour Research and Therapy, 23,* 75–78.

Thyer, B. A., Nesse, R. M., Curtis, G. C., & Cameron, O. G. (1986). Panic disorder: A test of the separation anxiety hypothesis. *Behaviour Research and Therapy, 24,* 209–211.

Timmermans, P. J. A., Roder, E. L., & Hunting, P. (1986). The effect of absence of the mother on the acquisition of phobic behaviour in Cynomolgus monkeys (Macaca Fascicularis). *Behaviour Research and Therapy, 24,* 67–72.

van der Molen, G. M., van den Hout, M. A., Vroemen, J., Louisberg, H., & Griez, E. (1986). Cognitive determinants of lactate-induced anxiety. *Behaviour Research and Therapy, 24,* 677–680.

Waddell, M. T., Barlow, D. H., & O'Brien, G. T. (1984). A preliminary investigation of cognitive and relaxation treatment of panic disorder: Effects of intense anxiety vs. "background" anxiety. *Behaviour Research and Therapy, 22,* 393–402.

Webster, A. S. (1953). The development of phobias in married women. *Psychological Monographs, 67* (Whole No. 367).

Witkin, H., Dyk, R., Paterson, H., Goodenough, D., & Karp, S. (1962). *Psychological differentiation.* New York: Wiley.

Wolpe, J. (1969). *The practice of behavior therapy.* New York: Pergamon Press.

Wolpe, J. (1970). Identifying the antecedents of an agoraphobic reaction: A transcript. *Journal of Behavior Therapy and Experimental Psychiatry, 1,* 299–304.

TREATMENT

PART 2

CHAPTER 6

The Pharmacologic Treatment of Panic Disorder and Agoraphobia

Abby J. Fyer, Diana Sandberg, and Donald F. Klein

Panic disorder, with or without agoraphobia, is a common and disabling illness. Therefore, the discovery of successful drug treatments has had a considerable impact on the lives of many individuals. A number of medications are now known to effectively block panic attacks. In this chapter we will first review the literature on pharmacologic panic blockade and then move on to clinical guidelines for medication use, management of common difficulties, and long-term outcome.

Treatment Overview

There are three phases in the evolution of panic disorder. The primary symptom is recurrent, unpredictable panic attacks. Repeated experience of these attacks leads to secondary worry, or anticipatory anxiety, about where and when the next one will occur. The final manisfestation is a phobic avoidance of situations in which help might be unavailable or escape difficult in case of an attack. Events and places associated with previous attacks are often avoided as well. Avoidance is intended to alleviate distress but is, of course, itself disabling.

Treatment addresses the same three phases. The initial goal is to block the panic attacks with medication. Once panic free, patients are encouraged to reenter their particular phobic situations to demonstrate to themselves that they will no longer panic. The regular absence of panic in spite of a return to normal activity in turn extinguishes anticipatory anxiety.

Treatment Studies: Literature Review

Imipramine

To date, six double-blind, placebo-controlled trials have established the antipanic efficacy of imipramine. Its antipanic effects were first noted and confirmed by Klein (Klein, 1964, 1967; Klein & Fink, 1962) in a series of studies of hospitalized phobic anxiety patients during the late 1960s. Subsequently, Klein and his colleagues (Klein, Zitrin, Woerner, & Ross, 1983; Zitrin, Klein, & Woerner, 1978; Zitrin, Klein, & Woerner, 1980; Zitrin, Klein, Woerner, & Ross,

1983) replicated and extended those findings in two large studies that compared imipramine and placebo in the context of various forms of psychotherapy.

The first of these (Zitrin et al., 1978; Zitrin et al., 1983) compared three treatments: imipramine plus behavior therapy, placebo plus behavior therapy, and imipramine plus supportive psychotherapy in patients classified as having agoraphobia with panic (N = 77), simple phobia (N = 81), or mixed phobia (N = 70). The mixed phobia group included patients with spontaneous panic attacks and circumscribed phobias. Imipramine was given on a fixed-schedule, flexible-dose basis with a maximum of 300 mg per day (the mean dose was 204 mg per day).

The great majority of patients in all groups showed moderate to marked global improvement (50% to 90%, depending on the rater). In both of the groups experiencing spontaneous panic attacks (agoraphobia and mixed phobia), imipramine was significantly superior to placebo. No difference was found between behavior therapy plus imipramine and supportive psychotherapy plus imipramine; both resulted in high improvement rates (70% to 96% depending on the rater). Patients with simple phobia showed no significant differences between imipramine and placebo or between behavior therapy and supportive therapy; patients in all three treatment groups improved considerably.

In the second study by this group, 76 women with agoraphobia were treated with a combination of group exposure in vivo and imipramine or placebo in a randomized double-blind design (Zitrin et al., 1980). The majority of patients in both groups showed marked to moderate improvement. However, imipramine was significantly superior to placebo on improvement measures for spontaneous panic, primary phobia, and global improvement. In addition, a greater proportion of imipramine patients showed marked improvement. For example, at 26 weeks the proportion of patients with marked global improvement was 62% for the exposure-plus-imipramine group and 29% for the exposure-plus-placebo group. The figures for marked improvement in spontaneous panic and primary phobia were 63% versus 27% and 78% versus 23%, respectively.

Three additional centers have now reported positive studies of the efficacy of imipramine for panic patients. The earliest (Ballenger, Sheehan, & Jacobson, 1977; Sheehan, Ballenger, & Jacobson, 1980) compared imipramine to both placebo and the monoamine oxidase (MAO) inhibitor phenelzine in the treatment of patients with a history of both recurrent panic attacks and multiple disabling phobias. All subjects also participated in weekly supportive group psychotherapy throughout the 12 weeks of the study. Both imipramine and phenelzine were significantly superior to placebo. Phenelzine was significantly superior to imipramine on scales for global, social disability, and work disability improvement. The proportion of patients markedly as compared to moderately improved was also greater on phenelzine.

The two more recently completed investigations were conducted by groups whose previous work had focused mainly on the behavioral treatment of agoraphobia (Marks et al., 1983; Mavissakalian & Michelson, 1986). Both contrasted imipramine versus placebo and therapist-aided exposure plus systematic self-directed exposure versus systematic self-directed exposure alone in 2-x-2 designs.

In the first study (Marks et al., 1983), 45 patients suffering from agoraphobia with panic attacks were treated for 28 weeks. Initial analyses of these data showed no imipramine effect and a slight advantage for the therapist-aided exposure condition. However, subsequent reanalyses found a significant advantage to imipramine over placebo (Raskin, 1983).

Mavissakalian and Michelson (1986) studied 62 patients with agoraphobia in a second trial of similar design but of shorter duration (12 weeks). Imipramine was used in doses of up to 200 mg per day (with mean daily doses of 80 in month 1, 125 in month 2, and 123 in month 3). All treatment groups showed significant improvements in all outcome measures over time. Imipramine was significantly superior to placebo with respect to global outcome, reduction of subjective distress during excursions, and two phobic measures. As discussed in detail under "Dosage," dosage of imipramine was an important variable. Fully 75 percent of patients on 150 mg per day or more of imipramine had no or minimal symptomatology during the last month of treatment, compared with 25% of patients on 125 mg per day or less of imipramine and 29% of those on placebo.

Continuing Controversies over Imipramine

The studies summarized here confirm the clinical efficacy of imipramine in the treatment of patients with panic attacks and multiple phobias. However, several important questions remain unanswered or are a subject of controversy in the literature.

One is whether patients who suffer recurrent panic attacks, uncomplicated by secondary phobias, will respond as well as those who have agoraphobia. The only controlled trial to address this issue was the 1983 study by Zitrin et al., which included a group of mixed phobia patients (spontaneous panic attacks plus circumscribed phobias). This group did as well or better than the agoraphobic patients on most outcome measures.

Two open trials also indicate a high degree of imipramine efficacy in panic patients having no significant phobic avoidance. Garakani, Zitrin, and Klein (1984) treated 10 panic disorder patients without agoraphobia with 50 to 300 mg per day of imipramine for 5 to 12 months. Panic attacks were completely blocked in all 8 patients who took imipramine for at least 3 weeks. In this study patients saw the doctor for approximately 15 minutes at each visit. There was no additional psychotherapy. Liebowitz et al. (1984) reported on the treatment of 43 panic disorder patients (17 without and 26 with agoraphobia) with imipramine or desipramine alone as part of a study of pre- and posttreatment panic response to sodium lactate infusion. Most (39, or 91%) became panic free. There were no significant differences between the two diagnostic groups on clinical outcome or rate of panic on sodium lactate reinfusion.

A large body of clinical experience supports these findings. However, controlled trials now in progress will provide a definitive answer to the question.

A second controversy involves the specific action by which imipramine produces improvement. One group of investigators (Klein, 1981; Zitrin, 1981) believes that imipramine has a direct panic-blocking effect. However, most controlled studies of imipramine have been done in the context of some form of psychotherapy. Other researchers have therefore suggested that the concomitant treatment (usually behavioral or supportive psychotherapy) explains the decrease in panic, anxiety, and phobia whereas imipramine either (1) exerts a nonspecific facilitatory effect (Telch, Tearnan, & Taylor, 1983) or (2) improves functioning by improving mood (Marks et al., 1983).

Several studies have attempted to separate the effects of imipramine and psychotherapeutic interventions on panic and avoidance (Garakani et al., 1984; Klein, Ross, & Cohen, 1987; Mavissakalian, Michelson, & Dealy, 1983; Telch, Agras, Taylor, Roth, & Gallen, 1985). However, methodologic issues or small sample size or both have limited interpretation of the data. Large controlled trials that report the frequency of panic attacks and the present outcome in terms of the percentage of patients recovered are greatly needed.

Studies by Garakani et al. (1984) and Mavissakalian et al. (1983) suggest that imipramine plus medical management alone is an effective treatment for many panic disorder patients. Marks (1981) has proposed that the differences between imipramine and placebo groups in various combined treatment studies are a result of imipramine's antidepressant action. It is common for agoraphobic patients, demoralized because of their limitations, to exhibit some depressive symptomatology. Concurrent depressive disorder also exists in some. Marks hypothesized that imipramine relieved depressive symptoms, allowing patients to make better use of psychotherapy. It was the psychotherapy (especially in vivo exposure to feared situations) that eliminated anxiety, panic attacks, and phobias. However, a later reanalysis of Marks's data found no relationship between imipramine-induced improvement and depression (Raskin, 1983).

Other investigators have also shown that agoraphobic patients' improvement while taking imipramine is independent of the presence or severity of preexisting depressive symptomatology (Mavissakalian & Michelson, 1986; Zitrin et al., 1983). Klein and Klein (1988) review aspects of psychopharmacologic treatment in more detail.

Clomipramine

Clomipramine is a tricyclic antidepressant not currently marketed in the United States but widely used in Europe, Canada, and South America for the treatment of depression and anxiety disorders. Two small controlled studies (Escobar & Landbloom, 1976; Karabanow, 1977) and a number of open trials (Beaumont, 1977; Carey, Hawkinson, Kornhaber, & Wellish, 1975; Colgan, 1975; Waxman, 1975) conducted during the 1970s suggest that clomipramine is an effective treatment for agoraphobia. However, interpretation of these results is limited by small sample size, comorbidity for other psychiatric disorders, and absence of both operationalized diagnostic criteria and specific panic attack assessments.

Recent open trials with patients who meet DSM-III criteria for panic disorder or agoraphobia with panic attacks support the earlier findings, however, and indicate that low-dose clomipramine may be an effective and well-tolerated antipanic agent. Gloger, Grunhaus, Birmacher, and Troudart (1981) treated 20 patients who met DSM-III criteria for panic disorder (N = 8) or agoraphobia with panic attacks (N = 12) with clomipramine doses of up to 100 mg per day for 8 weeks. Of the subjects in both diagnostic groups, 75% were asymptomatic at week 8. Another 15% had only mild symptoms. Grunhaus, Gloger, and Birmacher (1984) administered 25 to 150 mg per day of clomipramine to 20 subjects with panic disorder with or without agoraphobia. At 8 weeks, 17 (85%) of the 20 patients had "none or minimal symptoms." Caetano (1985) also reported positive results for the majority of 22 panic patients treated with doses of clomipramine at 10 to 50 mg per day. However, subjects in this trial were allowed to continue previously taken doses of benzodiazepines, whose amount and frequency were not specified.

Results of these trials are very promising; however, larger, placebo-controlled trials as well as comparative trials with imipramine and phenelzine are needed.

Other Tricyclics

Clinical experience and numerous case reports suggest that other tricyclic antidepressants may have antipanic effects similar to those of imipramine and clomipramine. However, controlled studies have not been reported.

Two investigators have described the systematic use of desipramine. Lydiard (1985) found desipramine to be an effective antipanic agent in a small open trial. Liebowitz et al. (1984), in a study of the effects of medication treatment on vulnerability to sodium lactate–induced panic, used desipramine as a second-choice drug for those patients who could not tolerate imipramine. Desipramine was as effective as imipramine, both clinically and in blocking lactate-induced panic. However, the mean dose of desipramine was higher than the mean dose of imipramine (271 versus 178 mg per day).

Monoamine Oxidase Inhibitors

Another class of drugs effective in blocking panic attacks is the monoamine oxidase (MAO) inhibitors. The most commonly used MAO inhibitor is the hydrazine derivative phenelzine. Other available MAO inhibitors are the hydrazine derivative isocarboxazid and the nonhydrazine tranylcypromine. Eutonyl is another MAO inhibitor that is approved in the United States only to treat hypertension but that is an effective antidepressant and antipanic agent in clinical experience.

These drugs were first developed as antidepressants. Early investigators, including West and Dally (1959) and Sargant and Dally (1962), noted that iproniazid especially helped "anxious" depressed patients. Later, Robinson, Nies, Ravaris, and Lamborn (1973) and Ravaris et al. (1976) observed that their nonendogenous depressed patients with prominent anxiety symptoms had significantly more improvement in anxiety symptoms on 60 mg of phenelzine per day than on placebo. These depressed patients, described in 1959 by West and Dally, were characterized by prominent anxiety and phobic features, emotional overreactivity, self-reproach, fatigue, initial insomnia, reverse diurnal variation, poor ECT response, and adequate premorbid personality.

This led several investigators, including Tyrer, Candy, and Kelly (1973); Lipsedge et al. (1973); Mountjoy and Roth (1974); and Solyom et al. (1973), to investigate the efficacy of MAO inhibitors in anxiety disorders. These studies are well summarized by Klein et al. (1980). They all showed either no difference between the MAO inhibitor and placebo or a suggestion of MAO inhibitor effectiveness for panic but not for avoidance. Reliance on these studies is problematic because of their low dosages, short treatment periods and use of mixed diagnostic groups (that is, social phobia and simple phobia patients were included in the sample). They also did not include adequate measures to differentiate the treatment response of the various components of the agoraphobic syndrome, including phobic avoidance, anticipatory anxiety, and panic attacks.

The first placebo-controlled, double-blind comparison of imipramine with phenelzine was undertaken in the mid-1970s (Ballenger et al., 1977; Sheehan et al., 1980). The study was a 12-week trial of 150 mg of imipramine versus 45 mg of phenelzine versus placebo in a sample of 57 agoraphobic patients. It showed marked benefits for both drugs compared with the placebo. Phenelzine produced more improvement than imipramine on disability and avoidance scales and had fewer side effects.

There continues to be a great deal of interest in the relationship between panic disorder and depression. Paykel, Rowan, Parker, and Bhat (1982) compared amitriptyline and phenelzine in depressed patients and found phenelzine superior for patients who also had an anxiety disorder.

Liebowitz et al. (1985) conducted a study of 120 patients meeting the criteria for atypical depression, which include the following:

1. Research Diagnostic Criteria (RDC) for major, minor, or intermittent depressive disorder
2. Maintenance of mood reactivity while depressed
3. Two of the following:
   a. Increased appetite or weight gain while depressed
   b. Oversleeping or spending more time in bed while depressed
   c. Severe fatigue to the point of a sensation of leaden paralysis or extreme heaviness of arms or legs while depressed
   d. Hypersensitivity to rejection as a trait throughout adulthood

Patients with or without a lifetime history of panic attacks were randomly assigned to treatment with imipramine (up to 300 mg per day) or phenelzine (up to 90 mg per day) or placebo. The first analysis strongly suggested that patients with atypical depression and a history of panic attacks responded more positively to phenelzine. Later work by Quitkin et al. (1988) did not support this finding.

Alprazolam

Recent studies suggest that the triazolobenzodiazepine alprazolam has an antipanic efficacy comparable to that of imipramine and phenelzine. Alprazolam's rapid onset of action and low side effect profile make it an appealing therapeutic agent. However, a frequent occurrence of relapse and withdrawal symptoms during discontinuation constitute a drawback to the use of this drug.

Alprazolam has been reported to be superior to placebo in the treatment of panic patients in three controlled trials. Chouinard, Annable, Fontaine, and Solyom (1982) studied 20 patients with DSM-III panic disorder in an 8-week trial. Eight of the 14 patients on active drug as compared to 1 of the 6 on placebo had a moderate to excellent response in 4 weeks. This study was limited by its small sample size and the lack of specific measures of occurrence of panic. However, its findings are confirmed and extended by preliminary results from a multicenter study initiated by The Upjohn Company (Ballenger, 1986). In it, 560 patients with panic disorder—with or without agoraphobia—were randomized under double-blind conditions to alprazolam or placebo and treated for 8 weeks. Fully 88% of alprazolam-treated patients, compared with only 38% of. those on placebo, were at least moderately improved at week 8. Alprazolam was significantly more effective than placebo in reducing panic attacks, phobic avoidance, and social and work disability.

In a 10-week, four-cell trial of 108 patients with panic disorder (with or without agoraphobia) conducted by Sheehan, Claycomb et al. (1984), alprazolam, imipramine, and phenelzine were comparable and significantly more effective than placebo in producing improvement. These data were presented but are not yet published in full, so a more detailed review of the findings is not possible at this time.

Four reported open trials also have had positive results. Alexander and Alexander (1986) reported on 27 retrospectively rated panic patients treated with alprazolam in a private practice setting for 4 to 14 weeks. Within the first week of treatment, 85% became panic free. Liebowitz et al. (1986) reported a 73% response rate in an open 12-week trial of alprazolam in 30 panic patients. Of the 22 "responders," 15 were panic free for the last 3 weeks of the study. The remaining 7 had occasional panics, which were less frequent or less intense or both than prior to treatment. Sheehan, Coleman et al. (1984) conducted a single-blind, 8-week comparison of alprazolam and the anti-inflammatory agent ibuprofen in 37 patients with panic disorder with agoraphobia. The alprazolam group showed a significantly greater global improvement and reduction of anticipatory anxiety as well as a trend toward greater panic reduction (which did not, however, reach significance). The studies by Liebowitz et al. (1986) and Sheehan, Coleman et al. (1984) also indicated that clinically effective treatment with alprazolam was able to block the panicogenic effects of sodium lactate infusion.

Though a number of trials are currently under way, only three published reports compare alprazolam to another established antipanic agent. Alprazolam was found to be as effective as either phenelzine or imipramine in the trial by Sheehan, Claycomb et al. (1984) summarized earlier. More detailed comparisons of imipramine and alprazolam are available from two more recent studies (Charney et al., 1986; Rizley, Khan, McNair, & Frankenthaler, 1986). Rizley et al. conducted a small 12-week, double-blind trial with a mixed group of patients: 13 having panic disorder (with and without phobic avoidance), 11 having agoraphobia with panic, and 2 having agoraphobia without panic. The mean daily doses of imipramine and alprazolam were 132.5 and 2.8 mg, respectively. End point effects of the two drugs were equivalent on phobia measures and on two out of three panic measures. However, doctors' ratings during the first 5 weeks judged alprazolam to be superior, suggesting an earlier onset of action. In addition, alprazolam-treated subjects reported significantly fewer side effects and a greater sense of global improvement. Interpretation of these data is subject to some reservation, because (1) the sample size was small, (2) the imipramine doses were modest, and (3) the 26 completers represent only 60% of the patients who entered the study. Data were reported for completers only. The authors state that they undertook an end point analysis (N = 35), but do not report its results in detail. They state that both types of analyses (completer and end point) yielded similar results except that there were fewer significant findings favoring alprazolam in the former.

The third study, reported by Charney et al. (1986), compared the efficacy of imipramine, alprazolam, and trazodone in 74 DSM-III panic disorder patients (panic disorder without agoraphobia). All subjects received an initial 3 weeks of placebo treatment. Those still ill were then assigned to 8 weeks on one of the three active drugs. Drug assignment was based on neurobiological characteristics of subjects (that is, a neurobiological profile derived from assessments such as response to yohimbine challenge and plasma MHPG levels). Patients, clinicians, and raters were aware of the drug assignments but not of the sequence of placebo and active treatment. Mean daily doses of imipramine, alprazolam, and trazodone at week 8 of active treatment were 141, 3.1, and 250 mg, respectively. Seventy percent (17 of 24) of the imipramine- and 56% (13 of 23) of the alprazolam-treated subjects were judged to be good or complete responders. Only 15% (4 of 27) of the trazodone-treated patients completed treatment and only 7% (2 of 27) were responders. The therapeutic effects of imipramine were not apparent until week 4, whereas the efficacy of alprazolam was apparent during the first week of active treatment.

Klein (1981) hypothesized that the anticipatory anxiety and phobic avoidance experienced by patients with panic disorder and agoraphobia are secondary complications of recurrent spontaneous panic. Since benzodiazepines are helpful for generalized anxiety, the introduction of alprazolam evoked great interest: it was hoped that one medication would be effective against both panic and anticipatory anxiety components of the illness. Contradicting this hypothesis, Liebowitz et al. (1986) reported that the major therapeutic effect of alprazolam for patients with agoraphobia was panic blockade. At the end of the trial, many responders still had at least a moderate level of phobic avoidance and anticipatory anxiety, even though they were panic free. However, Alexander and Alexander (1986) argue that alprazolam can treat both components but that higher doses are required to alleviate anticipatory anxiety than those needed to block panic attacks. The mean effective antipanic dose for their 27 patients was 2.2 mg per day, but the mean optimal dose (that which treated anticipatory anxiety as well) was 3.9. Given this dose range, 21 of the 23 subjects who had clinically significant phobic avoidance became asymptomatic on alprazolam without psychotherapeutic intervention.

Other Benzodiazepines

The antipanic efficacy of alprazolam has renewed researchers' interest in the possible usefulness of other benzodiazepines with this patient group. Clonazepam is a high-potency 1,4 benzodiazepine widely used in the treatment of minor motor epilepsy (Browne, 1978). It is of interest as a potential antipanic drug because, unlike other high potency-drugs in this family, it is an intermediate- to long-acting compound with an elimination half-life of 20 to 40 hours in humans. The longer half-life may allow less frequent dosing than alprazolam, which could easily result in improved patient compliance.

Fontaine and Chouinard (1984) first reported the antipanic efficacy of clonazepam. In this open clinical trial, 10 of 12 panic disorder patients treated with daily doses of 6 to 9 mg of clonazepam improved markedly. The remaining two continued to panic and required further treatment. Subsequently,

Spier, Tesar, Rosenbaum, and Woods (1986) reported a retrospective, uncontrolled trial of clonazepam in 50 patients with panic disorder (with or without agoraphobia). Response was defined as having at least a 2-week drug trial and a 2-level improvement on the clinician's global response scale. Of the 50 patients, 39 (78%) responded, 5 (10%) did not respond, and 7 (12%) dropped out. Of the 39 responders, 33 were rated "normal" or "borderline ill." Of all 50, 41 had failed or done poorly in previous treatment with an MAO inhibitor, a tricyclic antidepressant, or alprazolam.

Whether conventional benzodiazepines can block panic is of interest for both therapeutic and heuristic reasons. From the standpoint of treatment, the low side effect profile and more rapid onset of benzodiazepines make them easier to administer to panic patients than tricyclic antidepressants or MAO inhibitors. Long half-life, lower-potency compounds may also be more easily tapered. Heuristically, Klein (1981) has hypothesized that panic and generalized anxiety are qualitatively distinct. Considerable data from family, genetic, and biological studies support this distinction. If high enough doses of any benzodiazepine are able to treat both types of anxiety, some rethinking of current classifications may be necessary. However, currently unknown qualitative distinctions among benzodiazepines may account for differences in antipanic efficacy.

Results of the three published comparative trials using conventional benzodiazepines in panic patients are somewhat contradictory and as yet inconclusive. McNair and Kahn (1981) reported an 8-week comparison of moderate doses of chlordiazepoxide (Librium®) (with a mean of 55 mg per day) and imipramine (with a mean of 132 mg per day) in 26 patients with panic disorder with agoraphobia. Imipramine was significantly superior to chlordiazepoxide in reducing panic symptoms. There were no significant differences on measures of agoraphobia or self-report of global improvement between the drugs.

In contrast, Noyes et al. (1984) recently demonstrated that moderate doses of diazepam reduced the frequency and severity of panics but did not stop them over a 2-week period. Twenty subjects with panic disorder with or without agoraphobia were given diazepam and propranolol in a double-blind, crossover design. Each subject took each drug for 2 weeks. The median daily doses were 30 mg of diazepam (with a range of 5 to 40 mg) and 240 mg of propranolol (with a range of 80 to 320 mg). Diazepam reduced the average number of weekly panic attacks from 8.5 ($\pm$ 2.79) at baseline to 2.9 ($\pm$ 0.84) at week 2. At week 2 of propranolol, the number of weekly panics was not significantly different from the baseline. The number of panic-free subjects was not reported.

Somewhat equivocal results were reported by Dunner, Ishiki, Avery, Wilson, and Hyde (1986), who conducted a 6-week, double-blind, randomized trial comparing diazepam (in slightly higher doses), alprazolam, and placebo. Forty-eight patients with a diagnosis of panic disorder without agoraphobia (N = 16), panic disorder with agoraphobia (N = 16), or generalized anxiety disorder (N = 16) were studied. All subjects were experiencing "panic or anxiety attacks" at the start of the study. However, the frequency of these attacks for the generalized anxiety disorder group was not stated. Mean daily doses of diazepam and alprazolam during the last treatment week were 44 mg (with a range of 20 to 70) and 4 mg (with a range of 1 to 10), respectively. An end point analysis did not show a significant difference between drug groups for the frequency of panic attacks. However, significant differences between baseline and end point panic frequency were found for diazepam (from 3 to .6 per week) and alprazolam (from 4.5 to .8 per week) but not for placebo (from 5.9 to 4.3 per week). Neither the number of panic-free subjects nor the outcome by diagnostic group was presented.

Taken together, these data suggest that moderate daily doses of benzodiazepines may alleviate panic to some extent in some patients. Additional controlled trials of longer duration are needed. In particular, it would be of interest to know if conventional benzodiazepines block the panic attack itself or merely reduce the propensity to panic via a reduction of generalized anxiety.

Drug Discontinuation and Follow-up: Literature Review

Imipramine

Only three follow-up studies of imipramine treatment of panic disorder with or without agoraphobia are available, and their results are contradictory and inconclusive. Zitrin et al. (1983) and Klein et al. (1983) reported a relapse rate of 19% to 30% in patients who had been at least moderately improved after 6 months of treatment with imipramine plus behavioral or supportive psychotherapy and who were followed for 2 years after discontinuation of medication. Relapse was defined as the return of avoidance behavior. In contrast, Sheehan et al. (personal communication) found that over 70% of subjects treated for 6 months with imipramine or phenelzine relapsed after being taken off the drug. In this study, however, the definition of relapse was any return of unexpected anxiety or avoidance that led the patient to request that medication be prescribed again on at least two separate occasions.

Cohen, Monteiro, and Marks (1984) reported a 2-year follow-up of 40 of the 45 agoraphobic patients who had participated in a treatment study comparing imipramine versus placebo and therapist-aided exposure versus relaxation (Marks et al., 1983). A comprehensive criterion for relapse was not reported. The authors stated that at follow-up all groups remained significantly improved compared with pretreatment. There were no significant between-group differences with respect to clinical condition or degree of improvement. Significant placebo versus imipramine and relaxation versus exposure differences were not found. Mean scores on the severity of spontaneous panics were 1.1 for imipramine and 1.8 for placebo (8 = several a day and 0 = none) as compared to 3.1 and 3.3 at pretreatment. The number of patients panic free or relapsed is not stated. The history of further treatment was assessed by interviewing both subjects and their family doctors. No between-group differences were found. However, the authors did not state how many subjects reentered treatment.

Follow-up studies of other tricyclic antidepressants used in panic disorder have not been reported.

Monoamine Oxidase Inhibitors

Two follow-up studies of panic patients treated and discontinued from phenelzine have been reported. The study by Sheehan (personal communication) is discussed in the preceding section. A second study by Kelly, Guirguis, Frommer, Mitchell-Heggs, and Sargant (1970) retrospectively assessed outcome in a large sample of phobic anxiety patients treated with phenelzine. Of patients who had been well for at least one year on medication, 30% were able to taper off without recurrence. However, the length of follow-up is not stated. A second 30% relapsed during the tapering-off period. The remaining subjects were advised not to attempt tapering.

Alprazolam

Three systematic studies (Fyer et al., 1987; Mellman & Uhde, 1986; Pecknold & Swinson, 1986) and a number of case reports indicate that in many patients discontinuation of alprazolam is accompanied by a withdrawal syndrome or a recurrence of panic attacks or both.

Pecknold and Swinson (1986) compared discontinuation results in 197 panic disorder patients who participated in a comparative treatment trial of alprazolam and placebo. For 8 weeks, 58 patients had been treated with alprazolam; of these, 57% (33) completed the discontinuation. For the placebo, these figures were 49 patients, with 43% (21) completing discontinuation. Tapering was done at a rate of 1 mg every 3 days and generally lasted 4 weeks. During discontinuation, panic attacks returned to at least the baseline level of severity in the majority of patients in both groups. About a quarter of the alprazolam patients but only one of the placebo patients had a rebound effect (an increase of at least 50% over baseline levels and a change of at least three panic attacks).

Withdrawal symptoms were defined as those appearing during discontinuation that had not occurred prior to or during treatment. Typical benzodiazepine withdrawal symptoms were seen with mild to moderate severity in a small number of alprazolam-treated patients.

Mellman and Uhde (1986) reported on the double-blind gradual discontinuation of alprazolam in ten hospitalized patients (eight panic disorder, two bipolar). Assessments were made during tapering (withdrawal period) and at postwithdrawal. During the postwithdrawal period patients had returned to their usual pretreatment clinical condition. All subjects had greatly increased anxiety symptoms and plasma cortisol levels during withdrawal, compared with postwithdrawal.

Fyer et al. (1987) tapered 17 panic disorder patients from alprazolam at a rate of decrease of 10% of the starting dose every 3 days. Only 24% (4 of 17) of the patients were able to complete discontinuation at this rate (over 4 to 5 weeks). Another 24% (4 of 17) of the patients were able to complete the taper at a slightly slower rate (over 7 to 13 weeks). The remaining 9 subjects (52%) were either unwilling to discontinue or did so only with the use of an adjunctive medication (a tricyclic antidepressant). Of the 17 patients, 9 reported clinically significant new withdrawal symptoms during discontinuation. Panic attacks recurred or increased in 88% (15 of 17) of the patients. None of the subjects had seizures, delirium, or hallucinations. Clinically significant neurological or EEG changes were not seen.

Case reports of abrupt alprazolam discontinuation (Breier, Charney, & Nelson, 1984; Levy, 1984) indicate that seizures and delirium can occur after only 8 weeks of treatment. A severe withdrawal syndrome similar to that observed with conventional benzodiazepines has also been reported (Noyes et al., 1985). These findings indicate that patients using alprazolam must be strongly cautioned not to abruptly discontinue their medication.

The occurrence of a withdrawal syndrome during alprazolam discontinuation is consistent with its benzodiazepine structure. Observed withdrawal symptoms and onset are similar to those seen with other short-to-intermediate-elimination half-life benzodiazepines. The significance of panic recurrence during tapering is less clear; it could represent an interaction with the underlying illness. Anecdotal reports indicate that alprazolam withdrawal in depressed patients has been much easier.

Literature Review Summary

Imipramine, phenelzine, and alprazolam have been demonstrated to be effective antipanic agents in 70% to 90% of patients with panic disorder (with or without agoraphobia). Significant distinctions between these agents appear to be based on side effects, patient acceptability, and impact on comorbid disorders rather than on efficacy of panic blockade. Differences in drug effect on secondary anticipatory anxiety and avoidance have also been suggested.

Though controlled studies are not available, data from open trials suggest that the tricyclics desipramine and clomipramine, the MAO inhibitor tranylcypromine, and the high-potency benzodiazepine clonazepam may have similar efficacy.

Data on drug discontinuation and follow-up are incomplete and somewhat contradictory. Alprazolam discontinuation appears to be accompanied in many patients by panic recurrence and a mild to moderate benzodiazepine withdrawal syndrome. Withdrawal symptoms are transitory (1 to 4 weeks). The extent to which panic recurrence during tapering represents a persistent relapse requires further study.

Though controlled discontinuation studies of imipramine are in progress, data have not yet been reported. Follow-up studies and anecdotal evidence suggest that panic recurrence following imipramine tapering is both less frequent and (if it occurs) of later onset. Two of three follow-up studies indicate that over 50% of imipramine-treated patients remain well for 1 to 2 years after drug discontinuation. However, specific panic recurrence ratings were not reported. Insufficient data on the tapering of MAO inhibitors are available for any conclusions to be drawn. Further controlled (placebo) and comparative (between-drug) studies using operationalized and similar definitions of relapse and withdrawal are needed to clarify both the immediate effects of the drug taper and the long-term outcome in pharmacologically treated panic patients.

Clinical Treatment

The Medical Evaluation

As in all medical evaluation, the assessment of patients with probable panic disorder must be individualized. Because of the multiplicity of their physical symptoms, panic patients are often convinced that they have a serious physical illness. Many come to their psychiatric evaluation with an extensive medical workup in hand, but psychiatrists must use their clinical judgment in deciding how far to pursue a medical workup.

There are three major reasons to pursue medical testing: (1) to rule out other medical diagnoses masquerading as panic attacks, (2) to ensure that medication can be safely administered, and (3) to make sure concomitant illnesses are well cared for as part of good routine health care.

The major medical diagnosis to consider is hyperthyroidism, which can present with episodic anxiety or agitation. Hypothyroidism should also be ruled out, as panic attacks may begin during waning thyroid function. Every patient should have T_3, T_4, and TSH tests for thyroid function. If the patient does not respond to medication as expected, a TSH test and basal metabolic rate may be considered.

Another common cause of anxiety to rule out is caffeinism or the use of diet pills or other sympathomimetics. Rarer causes are paroxysmal atrial tachycardia and pheochromocytoma. For patients with prominent depersonalization, derealization, and faintness, temporal lobe epilepsy is a rare possibility. For these patients, as well as for those with unilateral symptoms, neurological consultation may be warranted.

Before beginning medication, we recommend that a physical examination, a complete blood count, and routine blood chemistries be done unless the patient has had a normal result within the past year. Many advise that patients beginning tricyclic drugs have an EKG, because the use of tricyclic antidepressants requires that individuals with preexisting bundle branch disease be monitored (Glassman & Bigger, 1981).

Persons with known medical illness or persons over 40 usually benefit from a discussion between the psychiatrist and the patient's internist. Narrow-angle glaucoma is also a contraindication for tricyclics, so many clinicians believe that persons with a positive family history for narrow-angle glaucoma should see an ophthalmologist prior to treatment.

Patients with a history of asthma should take MAO inhibitors with caution, since sympathomimetics are potentially harmful and may be necessary to treat an asthma attack. Similar awareness is required of individuals with any history of severe allergic reactions, as they may also unexpectedly require epinephrine treatment. Nevertheless, if the MAO inhibitor is the best therapy for the patient's condition and both the patient and his or her internist understand the treatment for adverse reaction, which includes intravenous phentolamine if necessary, the benefit is probably worth the minimal risk.

Establishing the Treatment

Most patients arrive at the psychiatrist's office frightened, confused, and misinformed about what is happening to them. Typically they already have had several medical evaluations (for instance, EKG; neurological; and ear, nose, and throat) and have been told that "there is nothing wrong." Because there is no tangible evidence of illness, family and friends can't understand what is going on and are often skeptical of and impatient with the patient's fears.

The first steps in the pharmacologic treatment of panic disorder are the following.

1. Acknowledging the patient's experience (this often includes educating the family as well and correcting their misperception of the patient's behavior as lazy, exploitative, or childish)
2. Explaining the three-stage development of the illness (spontaneous panic attacks, anticipatory anxiety, and phobic avoidance) and how the treatment will address it
3. Developing a descriptive language for the patient's symptoms to facilitate communication between doctor and patient

Developing an accurate terminology for the patient's symptoms is crucial for successful treatment. For example, the drug is expected to block panic attacks but not anticipatory anxiety. If the patient doesn't know the difference, or if the doctor misunderstands the description, the result will be incorrect assessments of progress and mistaken dosage adjustments. The best way to establish a common terminology is to begin from the patient's descriptions of specific episodes. The patient should be asked to give a detailed sequential account of the thoughts, feelings, and physical symptoms occurring during the anxiety episodes ("Can you tell me about your last attack? Where were you? What happened first?"). The doctor can then translate the phenomenological descriptions into psychiatric terminology and explain to the patient *in terms of the patient's own symptoms* what psychiatrists mean by panic attack, anticipatory anxiety, and phobia ("What happened to you in the elevator today is what we call a panic attack, because . . ."). Such examples can be referred to as treatment progresses, to illustrate changes in the patient's condition.

It is particularly important to be very explicit in describing what is meant by a panic attack. Some patients may call only their most severe episodes panic attacks. Milder attacks may be termed "anxiety" or "nervousness." Others freely use the term *panic* to describe almost any intense emotional experience, including temper tantrums and realistic fear.

Confusion about the distinction between panic and anticipatory anxiety is also common. A good approach is to have the patient recall a recent situation in which he or she expected to panic but didn't, comparing it to one in which panic did occur. Contrasting the characteristics of anticipatory anxiety with those of a true panic attack can be informative and once again used as an example to refer to during treatment.

Another useful strategy that facilitates both history taking and follow-up is to ask a family member or friend who lives with the patient to be present for at least part of the interview and to involve him or her in the treatment. Patients are often embarrassed or ashamed of their actions and may tend to underplay or "forget" them. This is particularly true of avoidant behavior.

The next task is to ensure the patient's compliance in taking the prescribed antipanic medication regularly. Most patients are extremely relieved when they find out that theirs is a common disorder that the doctor has frequently treated with great success. Many are further pleased to find out that a relatively simple regimen of daily medication will alleviate their distress. However, some panic patients have a number of fears about medication that evolve from the symptoms of their illness. An awareness of these fears is useful in getting the patient through the beginning phase of treatment, during which both symptoms and side effects are often present despite medication.

A common fear is that medication will in some way affect the ability to control oneself and one's environment. The fear of loss of control is often a central panic attack symptom; therefore, any threat to the patient's capacity for self-control is perceived as likely to either precipitate a panic attack or increase the possibility of loss of control during it. It is common for patients to avoid alcohol or nonprescription drugs or both on these grounds. Psychiatric medications are especially feared, because for many people they have acquired a reputation for sedating or changing one's personality or both. Medication may also damage the patient's self-esteem by emphasizing that he or she really is ill, not just emotionally troubled. In most cases empathy, reassurance, and clarification from the physician will enable a patient to take medication regularly and without undue anxiety. A patient has the most difficulty with medication when the physician is also ambivalent.

Severe cases of fear of medication may require added intervention. Strategies include (1) arranging for the patient to talk with another panic patient who takes medication; (2) arranging participation in a short-term educational support group with other patients who are also starting medication; and (3) beginning with relaxation, slow breathing, and support and then bringing up medication again once the patient is more trusting and feels somewhat better.

Finally, the physician should be as available as possible during the initial phases of medication treatment. We routinely provide 24-hour telephone coverage. In our experience, even though patients rarely call outside of normal working hours, they are greatly helped by knowing that they can. This support counteracts the panic-induced atmosphere of constant fearfulness and unpredictability in which most of these patients live. Many of them are also extremely vulnerable to separation anxiety; constant availability will increase trust.

Once the medication is started, somatic side effects can cause further difficulties. Frightening and apparently inexplicable physical sensations are a prominent feature of panic attacks. For many panic patients, then, any strange sensation becomes associated with the imminent possibility of panic. The significance of all physical symptoms may become so overrated that minor complaints are seen as evidence of impending death. The intensity of these responses can be contagious. If the physician does not have a clear assessment at the start of treatment of the patient's actual medical problems and the real medical complications that may arise from the medication, a vicious circle of new symptoms, fruitless medical evaluations, and ultimately unnecessary premature termination of treatment may ensue. This problem and strategies for its management are discussed later on in the section on treatment with imipramine.

Assessing the Drug Response

Because antipanic medications block panic attacks but usually have little direct effect on anticipatory anxiety or avoidance, patients frequently report little or no improvement during the initial phase of pharmacologic treatment. It is therefore important in assessing the drug's effect to inquire specifically at each contact about each component of the illness: panic attacks, anticipatory anxiety, and avoidance.

Anticipatory anxiety and the impairment caused by phobic behavior are often so overwhelming that the absence of panic attacks can be overlooked during a particular week. Further, since the occurrence of panic attacks is erratic, most patients derive no relief from a cessation of only a week or two. They remain on guard against the next episode, which they believe may occur at any moment.

An extremely helpful strategy is to have patients keep a daily diary of their anxiety symptoms throughout the course of treatment. Panic attacks, avoidance based on fear of panic, and the level of anticipatory anxiety are recorded on a daily basis. A review of the diary can guide medication dose changes by indicating the extent to which panic is blocked. A diary is also helpful in demonstrating to patients that, in spite of persistent anticipatory fears, they are no longer having panic attacks and can therefore safely reenter phobic situations.

The Dosage and Management of Specific Medications

The advantages, disadvantages, dosage, and side effects of each of the major medications used in Phase I of treatment—panic blockade—are shown in Table 6.1. More detail on side effect management is provided in Table 6.2. The use of the medications is described in detail in the sections on specific drugs that follow.

Imipramine

For most patients, the effective treatment of panic attacks requires 150 to 250 mg per day of imipramine. However, the range of effective doses is very wide (10 to 400 mg per day). In addition, panic patients tend to be both more sensitive to and more upset about the common side effects of tricyclic antidepressants. It is therefore best to start imipramine at a low dose and build slowly to a therapeutic range. We generally use a starting dose of 10 mg at bedtime and increase it at a rate of 10 mg every 1 to 2 days so that the patient reaches 50 mg per day by the end of the first week. Usually patients will have no or few difficulties on this slow regimen and can be switched over at this point to a more rapid rate of increase (25 mg every 2 to 4 days, up to 150 to 200 mg per day). Patients who continue to panic on 200 mg per day are raised 25 mg every 2 to 4 days (or 50 mg every 4 to 7 days) to 300 mg per day. The exact rate of increase depends on the patient's level of residual symptoms and side effects. Patients who continue to panic after 2 weeks on 300 mg per day and 6 weeks in all on imipramine should have an imipramine blood level test and an EKG. If the EKG is normal, the dose may be increased in 25-mg or 50-mg increments to 350 and then to 400 mg a day if necessary. The EKG should be repeated after 1 to 2 weeks on 350 mg a day if any further increase is anticipated. Guidelines for evaluation of imipramine effects on an EKG are discussed later in the section on the drug's side effects.

TABLE 6.1 Phase I—Panic Blockade: Major Antipanic Medications

Medication	Advantages	Disadvantages	Dosage	Side effects
Imipramine	• Well-studied antipanic agent • Once-daily dosage • Older, widely used drug with well-known side effect and safety profile	• 2-to-3-week delay in onset of action • 15% incidence of "hypersensitivity" necessitates slow dose changes	Begin at 10 mg daily, increase by 10 mg daily to 50 mg; then increase by 25 mg every 2 to 4 days until panic free or to 300 mg/day. May rise higher post EKG and blood level.	Dry mouth, constipation, orthostatic hypotension, tremor, sweating, flushing, urinary hesitancy, blurred vision, mania or hypomania in bipolar patients
Phenelzine	• Effective in atypical depression and social phobia • Possible more marked effect on phobic avoidance than other antipanic agents • Older drug with well-known side effects and safety profile	• Dietary restrictions • 2-to-3-week delay in onset of action • Possible severe side effect	Begin at 15 mg in A.M., increase by 15 mg each week or until panic free or to 60 mg. After 2 more weeks, if not panic free, increase to 75 mg for one week, then to 90 mg.	Dry mouth, constipation, orthostatic hypotension, urinary hesitancy, insomnia, sedation, anorgasmia, hypomania, elevated LFTS, edema, hypertensive reaction
Alprazolam	• Rapid onset of action • Low side effect profile • Possibly also helps anticipatory anxiety	• Possible withdrawal syndrome and recurrence of panic during discontinuation • Multiple daily doses required	Begin at 0.25 mg to 0.5 mg three times a day; raise 0.5 mg every 2 to 3 days until panic free. Average dose is 3 to 6 mg per day.	Sedation, loss of sexual desire, paradoxical excitation

Table 6.2 Side Effect Management

Side effect	Management
Dry mouth	Increase fluid intake; increase oral hygiene; try urecholine or sugarless gum
Constipation	Add bran to diet or as supplement; try stool softeners, high fluid intake, milk of magnesia to retain moisture in bowel
Orthostatic hypotension	Increase dietary salt; try salt tablets plus increased fluid intake, mineralocorticoids, low-dose amphetamines
Sexual dysfunction	Try urecholine or cyproheptadine (Periactin); decrease dose if possible; consider alternative antipanic medication
Urinary hesitancy	Decrease dose if possible; consider change to desipramine; try adjunctive urecholine after urological evaluation
Insomnia	Give all medication in morning; add benzodiazepine; add trazodone 50 mg hs if MAO inhibitor induced
Hypomania or mania	On tricyclic, discontinue medication, add low-dose neuroleptic; on MAO inhibitor, lower dose or discontinue if necessary, or use adjunctive clonazepam
Elevated liver function tests	Repeat test; lower dose and repeat; discontinue if persistent; change to a nonhydrazine MAO inhibitor
Edema	Use diuretics, support hose; may need to discontinue medication
Hypertensive reaction	Emergency room monitoring, chlorpromazine po or IM, intravenous phentolamine under direct M.D. supervision
Tremor, sweating, flushing	Give reassurance; try beta blocker for tricyclic antidepressant tremor
Hypersensitivity (imipramine), insomnia, agitation, sweating and flushing	Use lower starting dose, increasing in smaller increments and more slowly—do not try to "rush through" by raising dose quickly; induce sedation with benzodiazepine

There is some disagreement about the dose usually necessary for the treatment of panic attacks. Klein (1984) and Zitrin (1981) have stressed the importance of trying up to 300 mg a day. Mean daily doses in their clinical trials are 200 to 225 mg a day. In contrast, other investigators (Marks et al., 1983; Mavissakalian & Michelson, 1986; Sheehan et al., 1980) used maximum daily doses of 150 to 200 mg with means in a range of 125 to 160 mg per day.

The consistently better outcome reported by Klein and Zitrin (Klein et al., 1983; Zitrin et al., 1983) may reflect the use of higher doses in some patients. Supporting this is a report by Mavissakalian and Perel (1985). In a comparative study of imipramine and placebo in conjunction with behavioral treatments (Mavissakalian & Michelson, 1986), 76% of subjects whose mean dose of imipramine in the last month of the study was 150 mg or more had no or minimal symptoms at termination. Only 23% of the subjects on 125 mg per day or less of imipramine had a similarly good outcome.

The few studies correlating plasma imipramine levels and clinical outcome have had inconsistent results. Mavissakalian, Perel, and Michelson (1984) found a positive relationship between imipramine but not desipramine levels and clinical outcome in 15 agoraphobic patients treated with imipramine and behavior therapy. In contrast, Ballenger (1986) found no significant differences in the clinical outcome of two groups of panic disorder patients maintained at two different serum levels (100 to 150 ng [one billionth of a gram] per ml and 200 to 250 ng per ml) of imipramine plus its principal metabolite, desipramine. Furthermore, several case reports have suggested that effective antipanic treatment can be seen in conjunction with very low imipramine plasma levels. Pending further studies, there is no indication that routine plasma levels are useful in the treatment of panic disorder. In any case, the general strategy of starting low but pushing high if necessary should be explained in advance to the patient.

Special Issues in the Use of Imipramine for Panic Patients

Several difficulties can be encountered when starting panic disorder patients on imipramine. If correctly assessed, these difficulties are almost always transitory and do not interfere with a positive outcome. However, a mistaken interpretation of the patient's condition can lead to premature and/or unnecessary termination of treatment. These distinctions are important, because *inadequate dosage and premature termination of medication trials are probably the major causes of failure in tricyclic antidepressant treatment of panic patients*. Therefore, before describing the usual course of response we'll discuss these issues in some detail.

A small percentage of panic patients (about 15%) (Zitrin, 1981) have what is known as a "hypersensitivity" response to imipramine. This is characterized by insomnia, a sense of inner agitation, and feeling of "jumping out of one's skin." A number of patients also report flushing and sweating. This response usually occurs within 24 hours of reaching the critical dose. Its cause is not known, though some speculate that it may be related to the serotonergic system (Gorman et al., 1987). If a hypersensitivity response occurs, the dose of imipramine should be decreased until the syndrome is resolved. In some individuals, the lower dose will also be effective in blocking panic. Those who continue to panic should be given a small increase in dose after an interval of several days to a week. Often a habituationlike effect occurs, and patients are able to tolerate a dose to which they were previously hypersensitive. Further increases can be made at a similarly slow rate until panic is blocked.

A second group of patients will metabolize the drug very slowly and have a disproportionately high level of side effects to a given dose. This is relatively uncommon and is not specific to panic patients. Usually the side effect complaints are anticholinergic (dry mouth, sweating, constipation, urinary retention, and difficulty with visual accommodation). If this condition is suspected, the dose is reduced and confirming evidence obtained by checking the imipramine plasma level. If the patient cannot tolerate an effective anti-panic dose of imipramine, the usual approach is to switch to either a less anticholinergic tricyclic antidepressant (such as desipramine) or a monoamine oxidase inhibitor or alprazolam.

The third and most common difficulty is an anxious overreaction to the usual mildly uncomfortable side effects of imipramine. Patients who experience recurrent panic attacks often develop both hypochondriacal fears and an overawareness of somatic symptoms. In these patients a slight imipramine-induced tachycardia, which might be overlooked by another patient, appears as a symptom of impending heart failure. Any unusual sensation becomes intolerable, because it is associated with a panic attack and therefore with the fear of dying, losing control, or going crazy. This situation is, of course, exacerbated by the fact that with imipramine (and MAO inhibitors) patients experience side effects but little clinical improvement during the first 2 weeks of treatment.

Often the doctor's response to this type of patient unintentionally escalates the situation. This can happen in one of two ways. A common approach used by physicians is a scientifically appropriate dismissal of the clinical significance of the symptoms and a blanket assurance of eventual recovery. However, with many panic disorder patients this is unproductive, as it only serves to reinforce previous experiences of having their panic attacks pooh-poohed by medical doctors who told them mistakenly that "nothing was wrong." On the other hand, these patients can be so persistent and agitated that their hypochondriasis and fear become contagious. The doctor may find himself ordering a variety of tests to rule out conditions that were eliminated *before* the treatment started. This insecurity can be communicated to the patient, setting up a vicious circle of increased anxiety and frustration. Unnecessary discontinuation of medication often occurs at this point.

Effective management depends on the particular patient. One simple and extremely helpful procedure is to arrange for the patient to speak with others who have undergone the same treatment and have had a positive outcome. Most individuals find this enormously reassuring. Unlike the doctor, the fellow patient has no vested interest in promoting pill taking. Further, he or she understands what it is *really* like to be in this position. Some clinics and self-help groups routinely assign new patients either to a "partner" who is slightly further along in the program or to an educational support group whose members are at varying stages of treatment. In one case partners talked on the phone while taking their nightly medication, then checked with each other later to ensure that there were no ill effects.

Another technique is to use very low doses of alprazolam (.25 to .5 mg four times daily) or clonazepam (.25 to .5 mg twice a day) in conjunction with imipramine during the first 3 or 4 weeks of treatment. High-potency benzodiazepines have a rapid (4-to-7-day) onset of antipanic action. Relatively low doses of these drugs will often "take the edge off" panic and anticipatory anxiety. This in turn may make both the side effects and the fears of taking medication more tolerable. Once the imipramine takes effect, the benzodiazepine usually can be tapered off without difficulty.

The antipanic effect of imipramine usually starts during the third week on medication. Often the first sign is the patient's report of a partially aborted panic attack: "It seemed about to start but suddenly it just went away." Following this there is usually a gradual reduction in the frequency and intensity of episodes as the dose is increased. But because panic attacks tend to have an irregular pattern of occurrence (Uhde et al., 1985), during the later phases of treatment it is sometimes hard to tell whether a panic-free interval between visits is due to the drug or to the irregular rhythm of the illness. One approach is to have the patient test the drug effect by entering situations that in the past were almost always associated with panic attacks. However, some patients are extremely demoralized by recurrent attacks. Even a single panic attack may lead to persistent renewed anxiety or avoidance or both. In these cases it is probably better (provided side effects are not problematic) to use the alternative strategy of raising the medication slightly (10% to 15%) above the level at which the patient became panic free (for example, for a patient who became panic free at 150 mg, raise the dose to 175; for one who did so at 250, raise it to 275 or 300 mg).

Imipramine's Side Effects

The usual side effects of imipramine are a dry mouth and constipation. Other less common effects are increased sweating, orthostatic hypotension, slowness of visual accommodation (blurred vision), moderate weight gain, and cardiac conduction delays. Management of the dry mouth, constipation, and blurred vision is generally symptomatic. However, substitution of a less anticholinergic tricyclic antidepressant (such as desipramine) may also reduce these side effects. Increased sweating can be an embarrassing, uncomfortable, and difficult-to-control symptom. There is no specific antidote. Nortriptyline may be less likely to cause orthostatic hypotension than imipramine. Therefore, a trial of this drug may be merited in patients for whom this side effect is severe. Otherwise the management of orthostatic hypotension is similar to that discussed in detail later, in the section on MAO inhibitors. A small number of individuals develop a prolongation of PR and QRS intervals on their EKG. Clinically significant increases are rarely seen in patients who do not have preexisting conduction delays or other cardiac disease. Increases are usually dose dependent: discontinuation of imipramine (or any other tricyclic antidepressant) is usually recommended if PR or QRS prolongation is equal to or greater than 30% of the baseline value (Glassman & Bigger, 1981). (See Table 6.2 for more on side effect management.)

Clomipramine

Panic patients appear to have a particular sensitivity to clomipramine that is not seen in patients with depressive or obsessive-compulsive disorders. But the successful treatment of panic disorder may not require doses as high as those used for other disorders. Gloger et al. (1981) and Grunhaus et al. (1984) reported that 45% and 65% of their respective samples required 50 mg per day or less. The mean daily dose in the trial described by Caetano (1985) was 26.4 mg.

In addition, both Gloger and Caetano noted that a number of patients had exacerbations of panic symptoms during the first 2 weeks of treatment on doses of 25 mg a day or more. Caetano recommends a starting dose of 5 mg a day followed by slow, carefully monitored increases (increments of 10 mg or less are best). Antipanic efficacy was noted to begin in the second week of treatment.

Higher doses of clomipramine are often associated with multiple uncomfortable side effects (Insel et al., 1983; Rapoport & Ismond, 1982). However, the lower dosage required for panic patients may circumvent this difficulty. None of the three recent trials reported dropouts due to side effects, although specific side effect frequencies were not reported.

Monoamine Oxidase Inhibitors

Phenelzine is begun at 15 mg daily in the morning for 3 days, followed by 30 mg in the morning for 4 days, followed by 45 mg each morning for 1 week. The target symptom is the panic attack. If, at the end of a week on 45 mg, the patient continues to have panic attacks, the dose should be raised to 60 mg and held there for 2 weeks. Again, if the patient is not panic free, one can progress to 75 mg each morning and, if necessary, to 90 mg per day 1 week later. Our experience is that once a patient is panic free, support and encouragement are enough to get her or him to enter phobic situations, redevelop a sense of mastery, and rapidly become mobile and free of anticipatory anxiety. As with the tricyclics, the addition of a benzodiazepine may be useful in helping patients with high levels of residual anticipatory anxiety overcome their reluctance. However, there is an interaction between MAO inhibitors and benzodiazepines, so patients may become unusually sedated or apathetic.

Tranylcypromine is begun at 10 mg in the morning and may be raised if necessary by 10 mg per week to 60 mg a day. If the drug is tolerated well and the patient still does not respond, it may be raised to 80 mg a day.

Monoamine Oxidase Inhibitor's Side Effects

Common autonomic side effects of MAO inhibitors include a dry mouth, constipation, blurred vision, sweating, tremor, and palpitations (see Table 6.2). Urinary hesitancy occurs at higher doses and may progress to retention, especially if the patient has prostatic hypertrophy. A variety of sexual side effects may develop, including difficulty with erection or ejaculation, anorgasmia, and loss of desire. Cyproheptadine (Periactin®) (8 to 10 mg per day) and urecholine (75 to 100 mg per day) may be helpful in restoring sexual functioning.

A stimulant effect is often seen. This includes insomnia (for this reason the drug is given in the morning) but may progress to overtalkativeness, increased aggression, impaired judgment, hyperactivity, euphoria, irritability, and frank hypomania. Unlike the tricyclic-induced hypomania, phenelzine-induced hypomania rarely progresses to mania and may be treated by careful observation and dose reduction or, if necessary, discontinuation of the drug. Small doses of neuroleptic are rarely necessary. If insomnia is the only problem, we have found 50 mg of trazodone at bedtime to be safe and quite effective. Alternatively, a benzodiazepine could be added. Occasionally a patient is sedated rather than activated by phenelzine: this patient requires evening dosing.

Another, more troublesome side effect is orthostatic hypotension. A good practice is to ask patients whether they restrict their salt intake. In its milder forms this condition is easily controlled by adding salt to food or taking salt tablets. In patients without cardiac contraindication, fludrocortisone acetate, a mineralocorticoid, may effectively maintain blood pressure. Usual doses are .1 mg one to three times daily. In refractory cases of orthostatic hypotension, small doses of methylphenidate HCl or dextroamphetamine (2.5 mg per day to start) can be added safely and are highly effective (Feighner, Herbstein, & Damlouji, 1985).

Phenelzine can also induce pyridoxine (vitamin B6) deficiency (Stewart, Harrison, Quitkin, & Liebowitz, 1984). Some clinicians routinely add 150 to 300 mg a day of this vitamin to the regimen; others wait for the symptoms of pyridoxine deficiency to develop. Usual symptoms include numbness and electric shock sensations. Carpal tunnel syndrome is a rare complication. Doses of pyridoxine higher than 300 mg per day are not recommended, as they have been associated with neurotoxicity.

Peripheral edema is another rare but problematic side effect of phenelzine. Support hose and diuretics may be helpful, but in our experience this development may necessitate discontinuation of the drug.

A more serious but also rare side effect of the hydrazine derivative MAO inhibitors, including phenelzine, is hepatic toxicity. Iproniazid, the first MAO inhibitor investigated, was withdrawn from the market due to several cases of fatal hepatic necrosis. Occasionally patients on phenelzine develop elevated liver function tests. Decrease or discontinuation of the drug usually leads to fairly rapid normalization. However, if a hydrazine compound is given again, elevations will recur. Therefore, switching to the nonhydrazine tranylcypromine (Parnate®) is necessary. A 2-week drug-free period between them is mandatory to avoid hypertensive crisis.

Of course, the side effect of greatest concern with MAO inhibitors is the hypertensive crisis. This sudden rise in blood pressure is due to the inhibition of gut monoamine oxidase, which usually inactivates dietary tyramine. In order to avoid tyramine's pressor effect, foods containing tyramine must be

Table 6.3 Instructions to Patients on MAO Inhibitors*

1. Food and beverages to avoid
   - In particular, matured or aged cheeses such as blue, Swiss, cheddar, and American, as well as processed cheeses and spreads; (cottage, cream, or farmer's cheese is permissible)
   - Red wines (Chianti in particular) and Rose wines
   - Sherry, vermouth
   - Beer
   - Yeast or meat extracts used in making drinks, soups, sauces, or stews (for example, Marmite®, Bovril®).
   - Yogurt not made by a reliable manufacturer
   - Broad beans, fava beans, or Chinese pea pods
   - Banana skins and overripe bananas
   - Any meat, fish, poultry, or other protein food that is not fresh, freshly canned, or freshly frozen (including game meats, offal, lox, salami, sausage, corned beef, liver, and pâté)
   - Meat prepared with tenderizers
   - Pickled herring and pickled lox
   - Any food that previously produced unpleasant symptoms

2. Foods and beverages to be used in moderation, as they are occasionally associated with adverse reactions
   - Caffeinated beverages, such as coffee, tea, and cola
   - Chocolate
   - Alcoholic beverages of any kind[a]
   - Avocados
   - Soy sauce

3. Medications to avoid
   - Cold tablets or drops
   - Nasal decongestants (tablets or drops)
   - Hay fever medication
   - Sinus tablets
   - Weight-reducing preparations, pep pills
   - Antiappetite medicine
   - Asthma inhalants
   - Demerol
   - Other antidepressants
   - Epinephrine in local anesthesia (including dental)

4. Do not take any medicine, drugs, proprietary preparations (medicines bought without a prescription, including cough and cold cures), or any other medication whatsoever without consulting your doctor.

5. Follow these instructions (and carry this with you) all the time while taking MAO inhibitors and continue to do so for 2 weeks after stopping medication.

---

* This diet was developed by Jonathan W. Stewart, M.D. Used with permission.

[a] Distilled liquors (vodka, gin, rye, Scotch) will not produce a hypertensive reaction but will interact with phenelzine Nardil® to produce more rapid intoxication.

strictly avoided, as well as many medications (see Table 6.3 for dietary and drug restrictions). Cheese and pickled fish are the foods with the highest tyramine content, but any preserved, fermented, or aged protein can cause a reaction. Demerol is strictly contraindicated, though the mechanism of toxicity is not understood. Sympathomimetics are also traditionally forbidden, though as discussed, Feighner and other clinicians have reported their safe use. Patients should be given a wallet card stating they are on the drug and should be cautioned to inform all doctors *including their dentist*, as epinephrine (or norepinephrine) is often mixed with local anesthetics. It is actually not clear how toxic these agents are.

The hypertensive reaction is heralded by a severe throbbing, occipital headache, which may be associated with nausea, vomiting, stiff neck, and high blood pressure. The incidence of such paroxysmal headaches is about 2.1%. More rarely (.3 to .5%) this will progress to severe hypertension, chest pain, palpitations, and loss of consciousness. The incidence of progression to an intracranial bleed is very rare, with a fatality rate of less than 1 in 100,000 (Klein et al., 1980).

Many clinicians routinely give patients taking MAO inhibitors 100 mg of oral chlorpromazine to carry with them and use before proceeding to the emergency room in case of a severe headache or a known dietary error. The alpha-blocking properties of chlorpromazine will counteract the hypertension while the patient is in transit. The treatment of choice for hypertensive reactions is intravenous phentolamine, a pure alpha antagonist.

Alprazolam

Alprazolam is usually started at a dose of .25 or .5 mg three times a day and raised .5 mg every 2 to 3 days. With patients who are new to the drug, one strategy is to start with a .5 mg bedtime dose and begin the regular schedule the next day. Patients who experience a marked sedation effect from the first nighttime dose can be started on .25 mg each dose; those who do not can begin directly with .5 mg.

As is true of most psychiatric medications, the dose of alprazolam required to block panic attacks varies considerably, depending on the individual. Mean effective antipanic doses of alprazolam in reported clinical trials range from 2.2 mg per day (with a range of .25 to 6.9) (Alexander & Alexander, 1986) to 6.3 (with a range of 3 to 9 mg) (Sheehan, Coleman et al., 1984). In our experience, the majority of patients seem to need 3 to 6 mg a day to block their panic attacks. However, some patients do recover at lower doses (1 to 2 mg) (Alexander & Alexander, 1986; Chouinard et al., 1982), and others require over 6 mg a day (Ballenger, 1986; Sheehan, Coleman et al., 1984).

Because its half-life is relatively short (12 to 20 hours), alprazolam is generally taken on a three times daily schedule. However, even on this regimen some patients report a "wearing off" of therapeutic effect or a with-drawal-like syndrome or both in the hour or two before their next dose (Tesar

& Rosenbaum, 1986). Changing to four doses a day usually alleviates these symptoms. For a few individuals, more frequent dosing may be necessary.

Several reports corroborate the Rizley et al. (1986) finding that alprazolam has a more rapid onset of antipanic efficacy than is usually seen with antidepressant antipanic agents. Alexander and Alexander (1986) found that 85% of their patients (24 of 28) became panic free after 2 weeks on the drug. In the study by Liebowitz et al. (1986), 45% of the responders (10 of 22) reached their response level in the second week of treatment. Sheehan, Claycomb et al. (1984) and Chouinard et al. (1982) reported significant improvement during week 1 on the Physician's Global Rating and the Hamilton Anxiety Scale, respectively.

Though there is little systematic data as yet, tolerance to the antipanic effects of alprazolam does not appear to be a common problem. Clinical experience and reports from trials indicate that most responders appear to be controlled at the same or even lower doses over a 6-month-to-1-year period (Alexander & Alexander, 1986; Liebowitz et al., 1986).

The optimal length of alprazolam treatment for panic patients is not known. Based on our experience with other antipanic agents, we recommend an initial trial of 6 months. However, systematic studies are required to provide data-based guidelines in this area.

Alprazolam's Side Effects

Sedation is the most common side effect of alprazolam; it is managed by decreasing the dose, slowing the rate of increase, or both (see Table 6.2). In some patients, however, sedation and drowsiness have been reported to be so problematic as to prevent the increase of the dose to a therapeutically effective level. For example, Liebowitz et al. (1986) reported that four of eight nonresponders were unable to tolerate an increase in dose because of daytime sedation. Less frequent side effects include depressed mood and loss of sexual desire.

In a small number of patients alprazolam appears to have a paradoxical stimulant effect. Pecknold and Fleury (1986) reported two cases of alprazolam-induced mania in patients with panic disorder. They suggest that alprazolam-induced mania is related to a history of affective disorder, as two of the three cases fell into this category. A case of alprazolam-induced hypomania was also noted by Alexander and Alexander (1986). Another type of stimulant effect, paroxysmal excitement, has been observed in three cases reported by Strahan, Rosenthal, Kaswan, and Winston (1985).

Clonazepam

Clonazepam has only recently been used to treat panic disorder; therefore, dosage regimens are not well established. In most cases, clonazepam is begun in doses of .25 or .5 mg twice daily and raised by one pill every 2 to 3 days. There is a considerable discrepancy in the range of effective antipanic doses reported in the literature. Fontaine and Chouinard (1984) used 6 to 9 mg per day. Spier et al. (1986) reported an average dose of 1.9 mg per day. Many patients appear to recover on doses in the range of 1.5 to 3 mg per day. Since clonazepam is a benzodiazepine, whose discontinuation may be problematic, it is probably best to increase the dose at a slow rate above the range of 3 to 4 mg a day in order to maximize the patient's chance of being treated on the lowest effective dose.

The most common side effects of clonazepam appear to be drowsiness, nausea, and depression. Of the three, depression is the most troublesome. Spier et al. (1986) reported that 4 out of 50 patients became depressed during clonazepam treatment. Three of these had a history of depressive or dysthymic disorder. Anecdotal clinical reports corroborate this experience. Close monitoring for depressive symptomatology is recommended, as this side effect often goes unrecognized. Tesar and Rosenbaum (1986) have reported that drowsiness occurs in most patients transiently during the first 2 or 3 days of treatment, but that it resolves and does not recur on further dose increases.

Choosing an Antipanic Medication

Imipramine, phenelzine, and alprazolam are effective antipanic agents. Although in most cases controlled studies are not available, clinical experience suggests that other compounds in these families (such as desipramine, tranylcypromine, and clonazepam) also block panic. Each drug (tricyclic antidepressant, MAO inhibitor, and high-potency benzodiazepine) has advantages and disadvantages compared to the others. In choosing a medication, these factors are considered with respect to the particular patient's (1) medical history, (2) concomitant psychiatric disorder (current or past or both), (3) current severity of illness, and (4) attitude toward medication and medication side effects.

In most cases, a tricyclic antidepressant is our first choice. Tricyclic antidepressants have been marketed and widely used for depression, panic, and other disorders for a number of years. Their side effects and safety profile are well known. The once-daily dosage schedule is easy to follow; use of tricyclic antidepressants rarely interferes with daily functioning. Relapse and withdrawal syndrome during discontinuation are unusual. Although imipramine is the best-studied antipanic agent, we feel that for most patients desipramine is equally effective, and its lower sedative and anticholinergic effects may make it more acceptable. Patients for whom a tricyclic antidepressant would not be a first choice are those with medical contraindications (see Table 6.1) or a history of nonresponse or well-documented adverse side effects.

Because of its rapid onset of action, some physicians use alprazolam instead of imipramine or phenelzine for very anxious patients who they believe will not tolerate the delay in onset of action. We do not feel this is necessary. Most patients can tolerate the delay with supportive reassurance alone. For those who cannot we recommend an adjunctive use of doses of alprazolam (.25 to .5 four times daily) during the first 2 to 4 weeks of antidepressant treatment. Once the tricyclic antidepressant or MAO inhibitor takes effect, the alprazolam is gradually discontinued.

The choice between an MAO inhibitor and alprazolam depends on the clinician's evaluation of the specific situation and the relative acceptability of each medication to the patient (see Table 6.1). In most cases our strategy is to outline the advantages, disadvantages, effects on comorbid disorders (for example, depression or generalized social phobia), and side effects of each and make this decision in discussion with the patient. For patients with further concerns, we offer the opportunity to speak with others who have previously taken these drugs, and we provide references to relevant books and articles.

Most patients recover during their first medication trial. However, an important and often neglected point is that those who do not get better or who cannot tolerate the first medication will almost always recover on the second.

The Management of Secondary Symptoms: Anticipatory Anxiety and Avoidance

Over 70% of panic patients seen in clinical settings develop secondary phobias. Why some patients with recurrent panic attacks become avoidant while others do not remains one of the more intriguing questions in anxiety disorders research. Similarly, it is not known why the successful pharmacologic blockade of panic in some individuals is accompanied by a rapid return to normal activity whereas in others there is little apparent change in the level of anticipatory anxiety or phobic avoidance (Muskin & Fyer, 1981).

The theoretical premise of a pharmacologic approach to panic disorder is that patients develop anticipatory fear and avoidance not because they fear the avoided situation itself but because they are afraid of what will happen if they panic while there. From this it follows that the goal in treating secondary avoidance behavior is to get patients to go back "into the street," as Freud (1955) put it, and to prove to themselves that their panic will not recur. The clinician's task is to find the quickest way for each particular patient to accomplish this.

For many patients an explanation of the relationship between the panic attacks and phobias, assurance that the medication has blocked the panic, and encouragement to reenter avoided situations is sufficient to extinguish anticipatory anxiety and reestablish normal activity. Because it is not possible to predict the course of any particular patient, we routinely begin treatment with this strategy. If after being panic free for 8 to 12 weeks the patient has made no progress, a reevaluation is done and, if indicated, an additional treatment specifically directed at phobias and anticipatory anxiety is instituted. Reevaluation should also consider the possibility of (1) persistent unrecognized panic attacks, (2) undiagnosed atypical depression, and (3) existence of interpersonal or psychodynamic reasons for maintaining avoidant behavior. The management of phobic avoidance and anticipatory anxiety is summarized in Table 6.4.

Table 6.4 Phases II and III: Management of Phobic Avoidance and Anticipatory Anxiety

Situation	Management
Not panic free	• Carefully review diagnosis.
	• Be sure drug is at maximum tolerable dose.
	• If on tricyclic antidepressant or MAO inhibitor, consider adding low-dose alprazolam or clonazepam.
	• Change to another agent. Be sure to taper carefully and not to mix incompatible drugs.
Panic free, with high anticipatory anxiety	• Encourage entry into phobic situations; experience of doing so without panic will decrease anticipatory anxiety.
	• Add adjunctive benzodiazepine (if not using one).
	• Give relaxation training.
	• Use diary for clarification and education.
Panic free, with persistent phobic avoidance	• Give gentle encouragement to reenter phobic situations.
	• Add adjunctive benzodiazepine (if not using one).
	• Try exposure therapy (in vivo, imaginal desensitization, or programmed self-practice exposure).
	• Consider a change to phenelzine if unsuccessful.
	• Use diary for clarification and education.
	• Engage family support and direction.

There are three main types of treatment for avoidance in panic patients: behavioral therapy, supportive psychotherapy, and adjunctive medication. Behavioral therapy techniques developed for independent use (without medication) in the treatment of phobias are often used to treat avoidance in panic patients. These techniques can be divided according to two parameters, depending on whether the exposure is imaginal or in vivo (the real situation) and on whether it is graduated or sudden (flooding). In vivo techniques are further divided into those in which the therapist works with the patient in the situation (therapist-aided) and those in which the patient is given exposure assignments to carry out either alone or with a friend or family member between sessions (self-practice). Common to all these treatments is a structured approach and repeated scheduled entry (real or imagined) into the phobic situation. The therapist sets the pace in collaboration with the patient. The patient is encouraged to learn to tolerate anxiety and stay in the situation in spite of it. Often there is a focus on developing coping strategies to deal with anxiety.

In contrast, supportive psychotherapy provides patients with a realistic but nonjudgmental arena in which to discuss problems related to phobias as well as those in other areas of their life. The therapist is encouraging but does not set specific goals or deadlines. For example, if a patient who avoided trains were discussing the possibility of undertaking a business trip by train, the therapist might say, "You haven't had a panic in a very long time. In fact, the last time you went on a train you were fine. I understand that it's still frightening you. I think you will be okay, but if you don't feel you can do it this time, don't worry; another opportunity will arise."

There has been some controversy over whether behavioral treatments have a specific efficacy compared with supportive therapy for the treatment of phobias in panic patients. A number of studies have reported no difference between supportive or psychodynamic psychotherapy and imaginal desensitization. Klein et al. (1983) has argued that the specific effective ingredient in the psychotherapy of phobic panic patients is getting them into the situation. In vivo techniques force the patient to reenter situations more quickly. Therefore, in vivo exposure may look more effective than supportive or imaginal techniques in the short term, but gains may become equal over time. A comparison of results from the two studies of agoraphobic patients by Klein and his colleagues (Klein et al., 1983; Zitrin et al., 1983) described previously indicates that at 13 weeks group in vivo exposure was superior to supportive psychotherapy or imaginal desensitization with regard to reducing avoidance. However, at 26 weeks (after a 13-week hiatus in group exposure) there were no significant differences between the three, and the group exposure patients had suffered significant relapse.

A new and promising method is the use of programmed self-practice exposure (Mathews, Gelder, & Johnston, 1981). In this approach, the patient is given a programmed manual explaining the theory and practice of exposure. The therapist spends only a few initial sessions with the patient reviewing the material and helping him develop exposure hierarchies. Thereafter, the patient practices alone or with a family member or friend. Programmed self-practice has been found in some cases to be surprisingly effective, used either by itself or as an adjunct to medication or office-based supportive psychotherapy (Mathews et al., 1981). It is highly cost effective, as it provides an individualized exposure program for each patient without the cost of continual therapist visits. The behavioral approach to panic disorder has changed considerably since these early studies were done (see Chapter 7).

Benzodiazepines are sometimes used to decrease anticipatory anxiety. Their efficacy has not been studied; however, clinical experience suggests that benzodiazepines are an adjunct to rather than a substitute for exposure. The choice of benzodiazepine depends on patient and physician preference.

Patients Who Do Not Get Better

Panic-blocking drugs are usually well tolerated and extremely effective. In our experience well over 85% of patients can become panic free on medication. The remaining few will have a significant improvement. Treatment failures are commonly due not to the refractory nature of the illness but to the way the drug is administered or the basis on which outcome is assessed. Specifically, the most common causes of treatment failure are (1) insufficient dosage, (2) insufficient length of drug treatment, (3) misassessment of residual symptoms (such as the confusion of panic with anticipatory anxiety), and (4) misdiagnosis of concomitant psychiatric disorders (for instance, atypical depression or social phobia).

It is natural for patients to expect that a successful treatment will make them feel well again. But although medications block panic, they usually do not directly affect worry or avoidant behavior. Patients who have persistent anticipatory anxiety and phobias will often complain that the treatment does not work. An unsophisticated clinician often mistakenly concurs and discontinues the drug. Conversely, patients who minimize their symptoms may mislead the physician into believing that partially blocked panics are anticipatory anxiety.

One useful approach to clarifying these distinctions is to have the patient keep a diary of anxiety symptoms and the situations surrounding them over a period of 1 to 2 weeks. (A sample diary is included in the appendix to this book.) Careful review usually provides both a diagnosis and a persuasive context within which to explain the treatment plan to the patient. Bringing in family informants and having them help the patient practice exposure can be crucial.

Concomitant atypical depression that is nonresponsive to tricyclics or benzodiazepines is another cause of apparent treatment failure. The usual presentation is the inability to resume normal activity even though panics have been in remission for a long time. These patients may appear to be in a normal mood while with family, friends, or their doctor. However, when they are alone the depressed mood reasserts itself and the apathetic patient has no motivation. The treatment is to change to a monoamine oxidase inhibitor. If this is not possible, combining a more activating heterocyclic antidepressant with a high-potency benzodiazepine may be a viable alternative.

Many individuals suffer simultaneously from panic disorder and social phobia. Clinical experience suggests that imipramine and benzodiazepines have only a minimal effect on this disorder. However, pilot data (Liebowitz et al., 1985) suggest that phenelzine is often significantly helpful. Panic patients who continue to complain of severe situational anxiety after adequate treatment with imipramine or alprazolam should be reassessed for possible coexisting generalized social phobia. In certain cases a change to phenelzine may be merited.

Drug Discontinuation: Practical Aspects

Imipramine

Systematic studies of the optimal length of imipramine treatment for panic patients have not been carried out. However, several reports (Garakani et al., 1984; Zitrin, 1981; Zitrin et al., 1980) indicate that most patients may continue to improve for at least 6 months and in many cases for up to a year.

We recommend a minimum of 6 months' continuous treatment. Usually we begin a gradual discontinuation of imipramine at a point between 8 to 12 months on the drug, when patients have returned to, and shown assurance in, their normal level of activity. If a relapse occurs, the patient should be restarted on medication and the taper reattempted in another 6 months. Discontinuation of imipramine is usually done at a rate of 25 to 50 mg per day unless a more rapid taper is required for medical reasons. In some cases a more gradual reduction is used because it is psychologically more acceptable to the patient. Withdrawal symptoms are not usually seen during imipramine taper; however, in a small number of patients a transitory flulike syndrome (Dilsaver & Greden, 1984; Kramer, Klein, & Fink, 1961) accompanies the abrupt discontinuation of tricyclic antidepressants. If this occurs, the dose should be raised and a more gradual taper undertaken.

Monoamine Oxidase Inhibitors

As is the case for tricyclic antidepressants, the optimal length of treatment of panic patients with monoamine oxidase inhibitors is not known. Following the model set for imipramine, we generally maintain patients on medication for between 8 to 12 months and until they have been stable at a normal premorbid level of activity for several months. Responders are then discontinued at a pace psychologically acceptable to the particular patient. Nonresponders or patients discontinuing because of side effects may be tapered at 15 to 30 mg per day of phenelzine (or equivalent doses of another MAO inhibitor).

There is a *risk of hypertensive crisis for 2 weeks after discontinuation* of the drug, so the *diet must be continued* during this time. It should also be remembered that the *different MAO inhibitors are incompatible.* Therefore, to avoid a hypertensive crisis a 10-to-14-day washout period is required before switching from one to the other.

Alprazolam

Gradual alprazolam discontinuation is often accompanied in panic patients by both symptom recurrence and a benzodiazepine withdrawal syndrome. Abrupt cessation has been reported to be associated with seizures and delirium. Therefore, patients using this drug must be cautioned against decreasing the dose unless under a physician's supervision.

Because data on the optimal length of treatment are not yet available, we generally follow guidelines similar to those for imipramine and phenelzine. If a patient relapses during the first discontinuation, there are several alternatives. One is to readjust the dose until remission recurs, wait 3 to 6 months, and then reattempt the taper. Alternatively, a much slower taper might be tried after a shorter interval (such as 1 month). If a second attempt fails, the addition of a tricyclic antidepressant or a switch to an equivalent dose of clonazepam are useful alternatives. Clonazepam, which has a longer half-life, has been anecdotally reported to be less likely to be associated with relapse or withdrawal during taper (Herman, Brotman, & Rosenbaum, 1987) than alprazolam. If a tricyclic antidepressant is chosen, the patient should be maintained panic free on both drugs for 4 to 6 weeks. Once the panic blockade takes effect the alprazolam can usually be slowly tapered off without difficulty.

For nonresponders alprazolam can be tapered at a rate of .5 mg per day every 5 to 7 days. However, when there is no deadline for discontinuation we recommend a slower rate, tailored to the particular patient's psychological and physiological response. For example, one might begin at a rate of .25 mg per week. If after 1 week at the new lower dose panic, a benzodiazepine withdrawal symptom, or excessive anxiety occurs, we might allow the patient to continue at this level until symptoms resolve. The taper would then proceed, using a slower rate or smaller dose decrements or both. Further decreases may be made only after the patient has adjusted to and is well at the new lower dose. This empirically based method may not be suited to all patients, but has the advantage of alleviating anxiety about discontinuation by giving the patient considerable control over the process.

It is important, regardless of the rate of taper, to maintain a three or four times daily dosage schedule. Reducing dosage frequency may lead to "interdose rebound," which will aggravate discontinuation difficulties.

Clonazepam

There are no reported systematic studies of clonazepam discontinuation in panic patients. As it is a high-potency benzodiazepine, it is probable that abrupt discontinuation would be accompanied by a withdrawal syndrome and possibly a relapse or rebound similar to that seen with alprazolam. For this reason, discontinuation should be gradual (.5 mg every 4 to 7 days). It is hoped that the longer elimination half-life of clonazepam may reduce the occurrence and severity of withdrawal and relapse during discontinuation, as is seen in the case of conventional benzodiazepines. However, controlled studies are required to test these expectations.

Conclusion

The pharmacologic treatment of panic disorder is simple and effective. Several types of drugs have been shown to block panic attacks in 75% to 90% of patients. These include the tricyclic antidepressant imipramine, the mono-amine oxidase inhibitor phenelzine, and the triazolobenzodiazepine al-prazolam. Other medications in the same class as these drugs, though not as well studied, may also be useful. For most patients, the combination of medication, education about the illness, and supportive encouragement to reenter phobic situations constitutes adequate treatment. For others, adjunc-tive treatment (such as systematic exposure exercises) may be required. Treat-ment failures are most commonly due to an inadequate dosage, an insufficient medication trial, or the failure to diagnose a concomitant psychiatric disorder.

References

Alexander, P. E., & Alexander, D. D. (1986). Alprazolam treatment for panic disorder. *Journal of Clinical Psychiatry, 47*(6), 301–304.

Ballenger, J. (1986). Pharmacotherapy of the panic disorders. *Journal of Clinical Psychiatry, 47* (Suppl.), 27–31.

Ballenger, J. C., Sheehan, D. V., & Jacobson, G. (1977). Antidepressant treatment of severe phobic anxiety. In *Scientific Proceedings of the 130th Annual Meeting of the American Psychiatric Association,* Toronto (abstract).

Beaumont, G. (1977). A large open multicentre trial of clomipramine (Anafranil) in the management of phobic disorders. *Journal of International Medical Research, 5,* 116–123.

Breier, A., Charney, D. S., & Nelson, J. C. (1984). Seizures induced by abrupt discontin-uation of alprazolam. *American Journal of Psychiatry, 141*(12), 1606–1607.

Browne, T. R. (1978). Drug therapy: Clonazepam. *New England Journal of Medicine, 299,* 812–816.

Caetano, D. (1985). Treatment for panic disorders with clomipramine (Anafranil): An open study of 22 cases. Ciba-Geigy reprint. *J. Brasileiro de Psiquiatria, 34*(2), 125–132.

Carey, M. S., Hawkinson, R., Kornhaber, A., & Wellish, C. S. (1975). The use of clomipramine in phobic patients. Preliminary research report. *Current Therapeutic Research, 17,* 107–110.

Charney, D. S., Woods, S. W., Goodman, W. K., Rifkin, B., Kinch, M., Aiken, B., Quadrino, L. M., & Heninger, G. R. (1986). Drug treatment of panic disorder: The comparative efficacy of imipramine, alprazolam, and trazodone. *Journal of Clinical Psychiatry, 47*(12), 580–586.

Chouinard, G., Annable, L., Fontaine, R., & Solyom, L. (1982). Alprazolam in the treatment of generalized anxiety and panic disorders: A double-blind placebo-con-trolled study. *Psychopharmacology, 77,* 229–233.

Cohen, S. D., Monteiro, W., & Marks, I. M. (1984). Two-year follow-up of agoraphobics after exposure and imipramine. *British Journal of Psychiatry, 144,* 276–281.

Colgan, A. (1975). A pilot study of Anafranil in the treatment of phobic states. *Scottish Medical Journal, 20*(Suppl. 1), 55–60.

Dilsaver, S. C., & Greden, J. F. (1984). Antidepressant withdrawal phenomena. *Biological Psychiatry, 19*(2), 237–255.

Dunner, D. L., Ishiki, D., Avery, D. H., Wilson, L. G., & Hyde, T. S. (1986). Effect of alprazolam and diazepam on anxiety and panic attacks in panic disorder: A controlled study. *Journal of Clinical Psychiatry, 47*(9), 458–460.

Escobar, J. I., & Landbloom, R. P. (1976). Treatment of phobic neurosis with clomipramine: A controlled clinical trial. *Current Therapeutic Research, 20*(5), 680–685.

Feighner, J., Herbstein, J., & Damlouji, N. (1985). Combined MAOI, TCA and direct stimulant therapy of treatment resistant depression. *Journal of Clinical Psychiatry, 46*(6), 206–209.

Fontaine, R., & Chouinard, G. (1984). Antipanic effect of clonazepam (letter). *American Journal of Psychiatry, 141,* 149.

Freud, S. (1955). On infantile neurosis and other works. *The standard edition of the complete psychological works of Sigmund Freud,* (Vol. 17, pp. 165–166). London: Hogarth Press.

Fyer, A. J., Liebowitz, M. R., Gorman, J. M., Campeas, R., Levin, A., Davies, S. O., Goetz, D., & Klein, D. F. (1987). Discontinuation of alprazolam treatment in panic patients. *American Journal of Psychiatry, 144*(3), 303–308.

Garakani, H., Zitrin, C. M., & Klein, D. F. (1984). Treatment of panic disorder with imipramine alone. *American Journal of Psychiatry, 141*(3), 446–448.

Glassman, A. H., & Bigger, J. T. (1981). Cardiovascular effects of therapeutic doses of tricyclic antidepressants: A review. *Archives of General Psychiatry, 38,* 815–820.

Gloger, S., Grunhaus, L., Birmacher, B., & Troudart, T. (1981). Treatment of spontaneous panic attacks with clomipramine. *American Journal of Psychiatry, 138*(9), 1215–1217.

Gorman, J. M., Liebowitz, M. R., & Fyer, A. J. (1987). An open trial of fluoxetine in the treatment of panic attacks. *Journal of Clinical Psychopharmacology 7,* 329–332.

Grunhaus, L., Gloger, S., & Birmacher, B. (1984). Clomipramine treatment for panic attacks in patients with mitral valve prolapse. *Journal of Clinical Psychiatry, 45,* 25–27.

Herman, J. B., Brotman, A. W., & Rosenbaum, J. F. (1987). Rebound anxiety in panic disorder patients treated with shorter-acting benzodiazepines. *Journal of Clinical Psychiatry, 48*(Suppl.), 22–28.

Insel, T. R., Murphy, D. L., Cohen, R. M., Alterman, I., Kilts, C., & Linnoila, M. (1983). Obsessive-compulsive disorder. A double blind trial of clomipramine and clorgyline. *Archives of General Psychiatry, 40,* 605–612.

Karabanow, O. (1977). Double-blind controlled study in phobias and obsessions. *Journal of International Medical Research, 5*(Suppl. 5), 42–48.

Kelly, D., Guirguis, W., Frommer, E., Mitchell-Heggs, N., & Sargant, W. (1970). Treatment of phobic states with antidepressants: A retrospective study of 246 patients. *British Journal of Psychiatry, 116,* 387–398.

Klein, D. F. (1964). Delineation of two drug-responsive anxiety syndromes. *Psychopharmacologia, 5,* 397–408.

Klein, D. F. (1967). Importance of psychiatric diagnosis in prediction of clinical drug effects. *Archives of General Psychiatry, 16,* 118–126.

Klein, D. F. (1981). Anxiety reconceptualized. In D. F. Klein & J. Rabkin (Eds.), *Anxiety: New research and changing concepts.* New York: Raven Press.

Klein, D. F. (1984). Psychopharmacologic treatment of panic disorder. *Psychosomatics, 25*(10, Suppl.), 32–35.

Klein, D. F., & Fink, M. (1962). Psychiatric reaction patterns to imipramine. *American Journal of Psychiatry, 119,* 432–438.

Klein, D. F., Gittelman, R., Quitkin, F., & Rifkin, A. (1980). *Diagnosis and drug treatment of psychiatric disorders: Adults and children* (2nd ed.). Baltimore: Williams and Wilkins.

Klein, D. F., & Klein, H. M. (1988). Definition and psychopharmacology of spontaneous panic and phobia: A critical review. In P. Tyrer (Ed.), *Psychopharmacology of anxiety.* Oxford: Oxford University Press.

Klein, D. F., Ross, D. C., & Cohen, P. (1987). Panic and avoidance in agoraphobia. *Archives of General Psychiatry, 44,* 377–385.

Klein, D. F., Zitrin, C. M., Woerner, M. G., & Ross, D. C. (1983). Treatment of phobias. II. Behavior therapy and supportive psychotherapy: Are there any specific ingredients? *Archives of General Psychiatry, 40*(2), 139–145.

Kramer, J. C., Klein, D. F., & Fink, M. (1961). Withdrawal symptoms following discontinuation of imipramine therapy. *American Journal of Psychiatry, 118,* 549–550.

Levy, A. B. (1984). Delirium and seizures due to abrupt alprazolam withdrawal: Case report. *Journal of Clinical Psychiatry, 45,* 38–39.

Liebowitz, M. R., Fyer, A. J., Gorman, J. M., Campeas, R., Levin, A., Davies, S. R., Goetz, D., & Klein, D. F. (1986). Alprazolam in the treatment of panic disorders. *Journal of Clinical Psychopharmacology, 6*(1), 13–20.

Liebowitz, M. R., Fyer, A. J., Gorman, J. M., Dillon, D., Appleby, I. L., Levy, G., Anderson, S., Levitt, M., Palij, M., Davies, S. R., & Klein, D. F. (1984). Lactate provocation of panic attacks. I. Clinical and behavioral findings. *Archives of General Psychiatry, 41,* 764–770.

Liebowitz, M. R., Quitkin, F., Stewart, J. W., McGrath, P. J., Harrison, W., Rabkin, J., Tricamo, E., Markowitz, J. S., & Klein, D. F. (1985). Effect of panic attacks on the treatment of atypical depressives. *Psychopharmacology Bulletin, 21*(3), 558–561.

Lipsedge, J. S., Hajioff, J., Huggins, P., Napier, L., Pearce, J., Pike, D. J., & Rick, M. (1973). The management of severe agoraphobia: A comparison of iproniazid and systematic desensitization. *Psychopharmacologia, 32,* 67–80.

Lydiard, R. B. (1985, October). *Desipramine in panic disorder: An open fixed-dose study.* Paper presented at the meeting of the American Academy of Clinical Psychiatry, San Francisco, CA.

McNair, D. M., & Kahn, R. J. (1981). Imipramine compared with a benzodiazepine for agoraphobia. In D. F. Klein & J. Rabkin (Eds.). *Anxiety: New research and changing concepts.* New York: Raven Press.

Marks, I. M. (1981). Behavioral treatment plus drugs in anxiety syndromes. In D. F. Klein & J. Rabkin (Eds.), *Anxiety: New research and changing concepts.* New York: Raven Press.

Marks, I. M., Gray, S., Cohen, D., Hill, R., Mawson, D., Ramm, E., & Stern, R. S. (1983). Imipramine and brief therapist-aided exposure in agoraphobics having self-exposure homework. *Archives of General Psychiatry, 40,* 153–162.

Mathews, A. W., Gelder, M. G., & Johnston, D. W. (1981). *Agoraphobia: Nature and treatment.* New York: Guilford Press.

Mavissakalian, M., & Michelson, L. (1986). Agoraphobia: Relative and combined effectiveness of therapist-assisted in vivo exposure and imipramine. *Journal of Clinical Psychiatry, 47*(3), 117–122.

Mavissakalian, M., Michelson, L., & Dealy, R. S. (1983). Pharmacological treatment of agoraphobia: Imipramine versus imipramine with programmed practice. *British Journal of Psychiatry, 143,* 348–355.

Mavissakalian, M., & Perel, J. (1985). Imipramine in the treatment of agoraphobia: Dose-response relationships. *American Journal of Psychiatry, 142*(9), 1032–1036.

Mavissakalian, M., Perel, J. M., & Michelson, L. (1984). The relationship of plasma imipramine and N-desmethylimipramine to improvement in agoraphobia. *Journal of Clinical Psychopharmacology, 4*(1), 36–40.

Mellman, T. A., & Uhde, T. W. (1986). Withdrawal syndrome with gradual tapering of alprazolam. *American Journal of Psychiatry, 143*(11), 1464–1466.

Mountjoy, C. Q., & Roth, M. A. (1974). A controlled trial of phenelzine in anxiety, depression, and phobic neuroses. In Proceedings of the IX Congress of the Collegium International Neuropsychopharmacologium, *Excerpta Medica,* Amsterdam.

Muskin, P. R., & Fyer, A. J. (1981). Treatment of panic disorder. *Journal of Clinical Psychopharmacology, 1*(2), 81–90.

Noyes, R., Jr., Anderson, D. J., Clancy, J., Crowe, R. R., Slymen, D. J., Ghoneim, M. M., & Hinrichs, J. V. (1984). Diazepam and propranolol in panic disorder and agoraphobia. *Archives of General Psychiatry, 41,* 287–292.

Noyes, R., Jr., Clancy, J., Coryell, W. H., Crowe, R. R., Chaudhry, D. R., & Domingo, D. V. (1985). A withdrawal syndrome after abrupt discontinuation of alprazolam. *American Journal of Psychiatry, 142*(1), 114–116.

Paykel, E. S., Rowan, P. R., Parker, R. R., & Bhat, A. V. (1982). Response to phenelzine and amitriptyline in subtypes of outpatient depression. *Archives of General Psychiatry, 39,* 1041–1049.

Pecknold, J. C., & Fleury, D. (1986). Alprazolam-induced manic episode in two patients with panic disorder. *American Journal of Psychiatry, 143*(5), 652–653.

Pecknold, J. C., & Swinson, R. P. (1986). Taper withdrawal studies with panic disorder and agoraphobia. *Psychopharmacology Bulletin, 22*(1), 173–176.

Quitkin, F. M., Stewart, J. W., McGrath, P. J., Liebowitz, M. R., Harrison, W. M., Tricamo, E., Klein, D. F., Rabin, J. G., Markowitz, J. S., & Wager, S. G. (1988). Phenelzine versus imipramine in the treatment of probable atypical depression: Defining syndrome boundaries of selective MAOI responders. *American Journal of Psychiatry, 145*(3), 306–311.

Rapoport, J., & Ismond, D. R. (1982). Biological research in child psychiatry. *Journal of the American Academy of Child Psychiatry, 21*(6), 543–548.

Raskin, A. (1983, November). *The influence of depression on antipanic effects of antidepressant drugs.* Paper presented at Conference on Biological Considerations in the Etiology and Treatment of Panic Related Anxiety Disorders, Boston, MA.

Ravaris, C. L., Nies, A., Robinson, D. S., Ives, J. O., Lamborn, K. R., & Korson, L. (1976). A multiple dose, controlled study of phenelzine in depression-anxiety states. *Archives of General Psychiatry, 33,* 347–350.

Rizley, R., Kahn, R. J., McNair, D. M., & Frankenthaler, L. M. (1986). A comparison of alprazolam and imipramine in the treatment of agoraphobia and panic disorder. *Psychopharmacology Bulletin, 22*(1), 167–172.

Robinson, D. S., Nies, A., Ravaris, C. L., & Lamborn, K. R. (1973). The monoamine oxidase inhibitor, phenelzine, in the treatment of depressive-anxiety states: A controlled clinical trial. *Archives of General Psychiatry, 29,* 407–413.

Sargant, W., & Dally, P. J. (1962). Treatment of anxiety states by antidepressant drugs. *British Medical Journal, 1,* 6–9.

Sheehan, D. V., Ballenger, J., & Jacobson, G. (1980). Treatment of endogenous anxiety with phobic, hysterical, and hypochondriacal symptoms. *Archives of General Psychiatry, 37,* 51–59.

Sheehan, D. V., Claycomb, J. B., Surman, O. S. et al. (1984, May). The relative efficacy of alprazolam, phenelzine, and imipramine in treating panic attacks and phobias. In *Scientific Proceedings of the 137th Annual Meeting of the American Psychiatric Association,* Los Angeles (abstract).

Sheehan, D. V., Coleman, J. H., Greenblatt, D. J., Jones, K. J., Levine, P. H., Orsulak, P. J., Peterson, M., Schildkraut, J. J., Uzogara, E., & Watkins, D. (1984). Some biochemical correlates of panic attacks with agoraphobia and their response to a new treatment. *Journal of Clinical Psychopharmacology, 4*(2), 66–75.

Solyom, L., Heseltine, G. F. D., McClure, D. J., Solyom, C., Ledwidge, B., & Steinberg, G. (1973). Behaviour therapy versus drug therapy in the treatment of phobic neurosis. *Canadian Psychiatric Association Journal, 18,* 25–31.

Spier, S. A., Tesar, G. E., Rosenbaum, J. F., & Woods, S. W. (1986). Treatment of panic disorder and agoraphobia with clonazepam. *Journal of Clinical Psychiatry, 47*(5), 238–242.

Stewart, J., Harrison, W., Quitkin, F., & Liebowitz, M. R. (1984). Phenelzine-induced pyridoxine deficiency. *Journal of Clinical Psychopharmacology, 4*(4), 225–226.

Strahan, A., Rosenthal, J., Kaswan, M., & Winston, A. (1985). Three case reports of acute paroxysmal excitement associated with alprazolam treatment. *American Journal of Psychiatry, 142*(7), 859–861.

Telch, M. J., Agras, W. S., Taylor, C. B., Roth, W. T., & Gallen, C. C. (1985). Combined pharmacological and behavioral treatment for agoraphobia. *Behaviour Research and Therapy, 23,* 325–335.

Telch, M. J., Tearnan, B. H., & Taylor, C. B. (1983). Antidepressant medication in the treatment of agoraphobia: A critical review. *Behaviour Research and Therapy, 21,* 505–517.

Tesar, G. E., & Rosenbaum, J. F. (1986). Successful use of clonazepam in patients with treatment-resistant panic disorder. *Journal of Nervous and Mental Disease, 174*(8), 477–482.

Tyrer, P., Candy, J., & Kelly, D. A. (1973). A study of the clinical effects of phenelzine and placebo in the treatment of phobic anxiety. *Psychopharmacologia, 32,* 237–254.

Uhde, T. W., Boulenger, J.-P., Roye-Byrne, P. P., Geraci, M. F., Vittone, B. J., & Post, R. M. (1985). Longitudinal course of panic disorder: Clinical and biological considerations. *Progress in Neuro-Psychopharmacology and Biological Psychiatry, 9*(1), 39–51.

Waxman, D. (1975). An investigation into the use of Anafranil in phobic and obsessional disorders. *Scottish Medical Journal, 20* (Suppl. 1), 61–66.

West, E. D., & Dally, P. J. (1959). Effects of iproniazid in depressive syndromes. *British Medical Journal, 1,* 1491–1494.

Zitrin, C. M. (1981). Combined pharmacological and psychological treatment of phobias. In M. Mavissakalian & D. H. Barlow (Eds.), *Phobia: Psychological and pharmacological treatments.* New York: Guilford Press.

Zitrin, C. M., Klein, D. F., & Woerner, M. G. (1978). Behavior therapy, supportive psychotherapy, imipramine, and phobias. *Archives of General Psychiatry, 35,* 307–316.

Zitrin, C. M., Klein, D. F., & Woerner, M. G. (1980). Treatment of agoraphobia with group exposure in vivo and imipramine. *Archives of General Psychiatry, 37*(1), 63–72.

Zitrin, C. M., Klein, D. F., Woerner, M. G., & Ross, D. C. (1983). Treatment of phobias. I. Comparison of imipramine hydrochloride and placebo. *Archives of General Psychiatry, 40*(2), 125–138.

CHAPTER 7

The Cognitive-Behavioral Treatment of Panic Attacks and Agoraphobic Avoidance

RONALD M. RAPEE AND DAVID H. BARLOW

The treatment of panic disorder with agoraphobia has had a long and confusing history. Much of this confusion has been in the realm of definition and diagnosis, as panic disorder and agoraphobia have gone under a host of names through the years. At our current level of understanding, panic attacks and agoraphobic avoidance are seen as independent yet closely related anxiety factors. This view has helped guide the research for theoretical models as well as for the practical treatment of panic disorder. Although there is still a need for further research, we are currently at a point where the majority of sufferers from panic attacks and agoraphobia can expect marked improvement in their condition through the use of psychological techniques.

In this chapter we outline some of the recent theoretical and empirical developments in the cognitive-behavioral treatment of panic disorder with and without agoraphobia. Through most of the chapter we discuss separately the treatment of panic attacks and agoraphobic avoidance, based on the apparent theoretical advantage of viewing these as independent factors. We then go on to describe the treatment approach that is used in our clinic.

Theoretical Bases

In psychology and psychiatry a treatment is seldom developed on the basis of theoretical concepts of the etiology of a disorder. Successful treatments often emerge and are widely utilized before their mechanisms of action are understood (Barlow, Hayes, & Nelson, 1984). The success of the treatment of choice is often used as evidence to support various etiological theories or mechanism-of-change models. This has been the case particularly with agoraphobia and panic disorder, for which a variety of somewhat successful treatments, both psychological and pharmacological, have been used for many years while arguments about their mechanisms of action continue. For example, whereas most now agree that exposure is a crucial ingredient in psychological treatments for phobias, disagreement continues over whether the mechanism of action is based on habituation or extinction or is primarily cognitive, in that self-efficacy and emotional processing are facilitated (Barlow, 1988). Nevertheless, understanding the theoretical bases by which a treatment may work and understanding the factors responsible for the etiology of a disorder are of vital importance for several reasons. For one, identifying factors of importance in the cause or maintenance of a disorder may make it possible to modify and improve treatments. Understanding the mechanism of action of treatment may also contribute to theories of etiology and maintenance of the disorders. The following sections will describe briefly some of the factors thought to be important in the etiology and maintenance of panic attacks and agoraphobic avoidance, so the reader may more adequately place into a framework the later discussion of treatment mechanisms.

Panic Attacks

From the recent increase in research into the nature of panic attacks, a number of combined physiological/psychological interactionist models of panic have emerged (Barlow, 1986; Beck & Emery, 1985; Clark, 1986; Ley, 1985; Rapee, 1987; van den Hout & Griez, 1983). Although varying in certain details, these theories all stress the importance of the psychological response to a set of physiological sensations. A common theme is that panic attacks can be viewed as a fear reaction to a specific set of somatic sensations. In this way, panic attacks are seen almost as simple phobic responses, the phobic stimulus being an internal rather than an external cue. In one study supporting this position, Ehlers, Margraf, Roth, Taylor, and Birbaumer (1988) examined the response to false feedback of accelerations in heart rate in patients suffering from panic disorder with agoraphobia and in normal controls. These patients who believed that their heart rate had accelerated reported significantly greater anxiety than did the controls. One patient reported a panic attack triggered by the belief that her heart rate had accelerated (Margraf, Ehlers, & Roth, 1987).

The differences between various interactionist theories tend to be somewhat technical, chiefly reflecting the emphasis placed on the psychological versus the physiological aspects of the disorder. At one end of the spectrum, Ley (1985) emphasizes the physiological aspects, stating that a panic attack is merely the result of an episode of acute hyperventilation. Overbreathing results in a series of somatic sensations to which almost anyone would respond with fear. While a psychological reaction to the sensations is acknowledged, it is seen as an almost inevitable consequence of the sensations. At the opposite end of the spectrum, Beck and Emery (1985) strongly emphasize the psychological aspects of the panic attack. They believe the fear reaction to be the result of a set of catastrophic cognitions related to death, insanity, and loss of control. Although the physiological sensations are considered very real, they are presumed to be largely a result of attentional factors and exaggerations of normal physiological activity.

Barlow (1988) has developed a comprehensive model that places the panic attack in the context of the entire personality development of the individual. According to this model, which is based on emotion theory, initial panic attacks represent the misfiring of a coherent, tightly organized fear response (Lang, 1984) or perhaps an innate discrete emotion (Izard, 1977). This response occurs initially when the individual is under stress. While under stress some individuals are biologically vulnerable and respond with a more intense but diffuse physiological activation than others. These individuals then emit an unexpected, uncued fear response—perhaps because of similar response propositions shared by the specific fear response and the more diffuse stress response. Lang (1984) suggested that information relating to emotions is stored as a series of propositions in long-term memory, each related to a specific action or response. That is, such information is not stored as a series of objective representations of the environment but rather as a more flexible set of probabilities and interpretations. Another possibility is that the two responses share similar neurotransmitter systems. More likely, a combination of the above factors sparks the unexpected, uncued fear response. This fear response is the first "spontaneous" panic. Many individuals experience this response occasionally while under stress (see Norton, Dorward, & Cox, 1986; Rapee, Ancis, & Barlow, 1988). What determines whether panic disorder develops in a given individual experiencing an unexpected panic is his or her response to the initial panic attack or series of panic attacks. If the individual becomes apprehensively anxious over the possibility of the next attack and dreads its occurrence, a vicious circle will develop. Panic attacks will then occur more frequently (sparking off the chronic arousal associated with anxiety) and will be experienced far more intensely.

Perhaps a good summarizing model for the maintenance of panic disorder would go as follows: a panic attack begins (or is triggered) by one or a number of somatic sensations. These sensations may be (and probably are) caused in a number of ways. Some of the more common causes may be general sympathetic nervous system overactivity, hyperventilation, increased attention to normal sensations, physical activity, or drug ingestion. Noticing the somatic sensations, the individual responds with anxiety or fear. This fear response is characterized by a learned association between the somatic sensations and the fear proposition (in the sense of Peter Lang). This association includes meaning propositions relating to immediate danger (such as death, insanity, or loss of control). Between attacks, the individual with panic disorder generally anticipates the next attack with dread and in this way increases the probability of experiencing intense somatic sensations by increasing overall arousal. A major component of this anxiety is self-focused attention and a hypervigilance for sensations, which further increases arousal and the probability of perceiving sensations. A simplified diagrammatic representation of the maintenance of panic disorder is presented in Figure 7.1, based on earlier, more detailed models (for example, Barlow, 1988; Rapee, 1987).

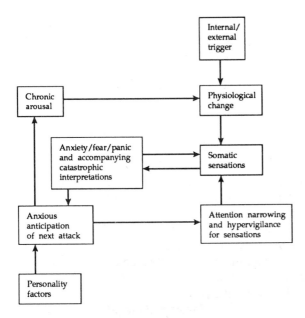

FIGURE 7.1 The Maintenance of Panic Disorder

Agoraphobic Avoidance

The development and maintenance of agoraphobic avoidance has received considerable attention for a number of years (Craske & Barlow, 1987). In terms of specific causal models, however, we are still far from an acceptable position. Much of the earlier work may not bear specifically on the problem of agoraphobic avoidance, as that work did not consider the relationship between avoidance and panic attacks. To separate the causal features specifically responsible for avoidance behavior from those involved with panic attacks, it becomes necessary to contrast groups of individuals suffering panic disorder with different levels of avoidance. This type of research is only beginning.

Over the years, a number of factors have been isolated that may contribute to the development of agoraphobic avoidance. Only those most pertinent to treatment will be discussed here. (See Chapter 5 for a more complete discussion.)

Some early writers focused on the importance of dependency as an underlying characteristic of persons with agoraphobia (for example, Andrews, 1966; Shafar, 1976). Childhood separation concerns have also been identified by some authors as important precursors to agoraphobia (for example, Bowlby, 1973; Klein, 1981). Evidence for a relationship between these two related concepts and agoraphobia has been equivocal, largely because of the difficulty in defining and measuring dependency and childhood separation fears (Barlow, 1988). The relationship of childhood separation anxiety to agoraphobia has perhaps been most widely studied (for instance, see

Raskin, Peeke, Dickman, & Pinsker, 1982; Gittelman & Klein, 1985; Klein, 1964). However, most controlled trials have found that childhood separation anxiety is not associated to a greater degree with panic disorder with agoraphobia than it is with other anxiety disorders (Berg, Marks, McGuire, & Lipsedge, 1974; Buglass, Clarke, Henderson, Kreitman, & Presley, 1977; Thyer, Nesse, Cameron, & Curtis, 1985; Thyer, Nesse, Curtis, & Cameron, 1986).

Studies of dependency as a more general characteristic have been commonly marred by poor definitions and measurement devices (Mathews, Gelder, & Johnston, 1981). As a result, early studies found both support (Shafar, 1976; Webster, 1953) and a lack of support (Buglass et al., 1977; Parker, 1979; Snaith, 1968) for a greater degree of dependency and a greater history of parental overprotection in individuals with agoraphobia compared with other disorders. More recent studies have used more specific criteria with some interesting results. Reich, Noyes, and Troughton (1987) administered structured questionnaires to ascertain personality disorders in 88 DSM-III-R panic disorder patients with varying amounts of agoraphobic avoidance. Patients with more extensive avoidance presented with more dependent personality disorders specifically and a greater number of other third-cluster (avoidant, compulsive, and passive-aggressive) personality disorders than panic patients with less agoraphobic avoidance. From a slightly different perspective, Rapee and Murrell (1988) found that panic disorder patients with extensive avoidance reported more social anxiety, less assertiveness, and less extraversion than patients with minimal avoidance. These researchers suggested that such a profile may be what earlier authors were alluding to in describing individuals with agoraphobia as "dependent." Other researchers have also reported a relationship between social phobic concerns and degree of agoraphobic avoidance (Chambless, 1985; Fisher & Wilson, 1985; Mathews et al., 1981; Rapee, Sanderson, & Barlow, in press; Thyer et al., 1985). Of course, whether these characteristics are causes or results of agoraphobic avoidance cannot be determined from currently available studies, because most are correlational. Agoraphobic avoidance can certainly lead to helplessness and dependency (Fisher & Wilson, 1985). Consistent with this suggestion, one study has found that when agoraphobia is successfully treated, personality disorder characteristics, especially dependent personality disorder, improved (Mavissakalian & Hamann, 1987). However, there is also some evidence that such characteristics may be at least partly independent of the avoidance behavior. Reich, Noyes, Hirschfeld, Coryell, and O'Gorman (1987) found that even recovered panic disorder patients (with or without agoraphobic avoidance) were more dependent and had less "emotional strength" than control subjects. The causal role and direction of these features must ultimately await prospective study.

Conflict in the marital relationship has also been highlighted as a specific cause of agoraphobia (Chambless & Goldstein, 1981; Milton & Hafner, 1979). However, controlled research has found no greater marital discord in agoraphobic patients compared to normal controls (Buglass et al., 1977; Fisher &

Wilson, 1985). Further, reports of separation-related stress at onset appear to be no different in panic disorder patients with different degrees of avoidance (Rapee & Murrell, 1988). Such data suggest that marital disharmony may not be a causal factor in agoraphobic avoidance. Attention to marital factors may facilitate treatment, however.

A number of researchers have noted the connection between agoraphobic avoidance and the experience of unexpected panic attacks (for example, Goldstein & Chambless, 1978; Klein, 1981). It has been suggested that the avoidant behavior of people with agoraphobia may be a result of anxiety about experiencing a panic attack (Barlow, 1988; Goldstein & Chambless, 1978). While some researchers have implied that avoidant behavior is an inevitable consequence of the experience of unexpected panic attacks, this cannot be the case because individuals with panic attacks demonstrate a wide range of avoidance, from virtually none to being almost totally housebound. Thus, in addition to the personality-oriented research discussed previously, some researchers have focused on the relationship between the panic attack and agoraphobic avoidance.

The simplest explanation would be that avoidant behavior is related to the frequency and severity of panic attacks: the more frequent and severe the panic attacks, the more the individual avoids. Recent research has not supported this suggestion, however. A number of studies have found no significant difference between the frequency of panic attacks experienced by panic disorder patients with minimal compared to extensive avoidance (Craske, Sanderson, & Barlow, 1987; Rapee & Murrell, 1988; Thyer et al., 1985). A similar lack of significant difference has been reported for the number and intensity of symptoms experienced during an attack (Barlow et al., 1985; Rapee & Murrell, 1988; Sanderson, Rapee, & Barlow, 1987b).

A more tenable model would suggest that avoidance is found in situations in which a panic attack is expected to occur or where a panic attack would be especially distressing. Indeed, Craske, Rapee, and Barlow (1988) found that panic disorder with agoraphobia patients reported a greater probability of experiencing a panic attack and a greater likelihood of discomfort and harm from physical sensations for those situations that they ultimately avoided compared with those they were willing to complete during a behavioral avoidance test. Similarly, Telch, Brouilard, and Telch (1987) found that patients with panic disorder with agoraphobia who avoid a particular situation report a greater expectancy of experiencing a panic attack in the situation and report more thoughts of fearful consequences of the panic attack than those who do not avoid the situation.

In the search for more general characteristics typifying patients with marked avoidance it has been suggested that attributional style is important. Specifically, it has been suggested that these patients are more likely to attribute the panic attack to external factors than are those with little avoidance (Mathews et al., 1981). Indeed, there is some evidence to suggest that patients with more extensive avoidance have a more external locus of control

(Emmelkamp & Cohen-Kettenis, 1975). Rapee and Murrell (1988) found that panic disorder patients with extensive avoidance were more likely than those with minimal avoidance to believe that attacks could be triggered and influenced by situational and cognitive events. Patients with minimal avoidance appeared more likely to believe that their panic attacks had a life of their own. In other words, it seems that panic disorder patients who perceive panic attacks as having no specific cause are unlikely to display avoidance behavior, whereas those who perceive a trigger for their attacks (whether real or inferred) will be more likely to avoid such an event.

That all these factors are causally important has yet to be demonstrated. Many fit with suggestions that extensive avoidance is associated with stereotypic female sex roles (as measured by sex role inventories rather than by biological sex) (Barlow, 1988; Chambless & Mason, 1986). While research into the nature of agoraphobic avoidance is far from complete, a picture is beginning to emerge. The panic disorder patient with extensive avoidance may have a personality characterized by a low sense of personal control and a tendency to be dependent on others. In the context of an unexpected panic attack, these traits may encourage the belief that the attack was caused by external factors (the situation) and that familiar places and specific people are likely to represent safety from such attacks (Rachman, 1984). The individual will thus avoid specific situations (associated with an attack) and seek out certain other situations (associated with safety) (Rapee & Murrell, 1988).

In summary, an interactionist model of panic disorder defines panic attacks as fear reactions to a specific set of somatic sensations. These sensations may be experienced normally by most individuals but exaggerated in the perception of panic disorder patients through highly focused attention. Alternatively, it may be that some panic disorder patients do in fact experience a high frequency and intensity of physical symptoms because of such factors as heightened arousal or hyperventilation. Once panic attacks are experienced, greater or lesser avoidance may emerge based on a variety of factors, not all of which are presently clear. It seems possible that certain personality characteristics predispose individuals to attribute their panic attacks to particular situations or events, leading them to avoid those perceived triggers. Individuals who do not perceive triggers for their actions will be less avoidant.

The Treatment of Panic Disorder

In this section we'll review the treatment techniques that have empirical support in the alleviation of panic attacks and agoraphobic avoidance. Whenever possible, theoretical connections between the models described previously and the treatment techniques will be highlighted. Experimental support for the theoretical bases will also be discussed briefly. This review should be considered to be illustrative rather than comprehensive.

An Evaluation of Cognitive-Behavioral Treatment Packages

Before discussing the active components of cognitive-behavioral treatment packages for panic disorder, it is necessary to ask whether such packages are effective. Evidence collected over the past 20 years has consistently shown that cognitive-behavioral techniques are of greater value in the treatment of panic disorder with agoraphobia than are various control conditions. Exposure in vivo, in particular, has been extensively investigated and is felt almost unanimously to be the treatment of choice for agoraphobic avoidance. The use of cognitive-behavioral techniques in the treatment of panic attacks is less widely accepted to date. Indeed, very little research has been carried out on the use of psychological techniques to alleviate panic attacks. One reason for this may be the view in some quarters that panic attacks are due solely to some type of central, "spontaneous" chemical discharge. Nevertheless, recent reviews have identified a growing literature supporting the value of cognitive-behavioral techniques in the treatment of unexpected panic attacks (Barlow, 1988; Clark, 1986; Craske, 1988; Rapee, 1987). Three groups have reported on the use of broad-based psychological treatment packages without medication for patients having panic disorder with mild agoraphobic avoidance (Barlow, Cohen et al., 1984; Beck, 1988; Gitlin et al., 1985).

In an uncontrolled trial, Gitlin et al. (1985) treated 11 subjects with panic disorder using a package that included education, abdominal breathing, and exposure. The results indicated that 10 of 11 patients were panic free following treatment and at an average of 5 months' follow-up. Interestingly, in a posttreatment interview most patients reported that education and reassurance about panic attacks (which may have altered their catastrophic cognitions) had been the most beneficial factor in the treatment package. Abdominal breathing was described as the next-most-beneficial factor.

Sokol-Kessler and Beck (1987; cited in Beck, 1988) reported the results of two studies investigating the effectiveness of a psychological treatment of panic attacks. The first was an open-ended trial that included 16 patients who completed a mean of 32 weeks of treatment and 1 year of posttreatment follow-up. Treatment included cognitive restructuring and exposure to somatic sensations through various exercises, such as climbing stairs and hyperventilation. All 16 patients reported zero panic attacks at posttreatment; this result was maintained at follow-up. In the second study, a further 7 patients given this same treatment for 12 weeks were compared with 16 patients given 8 weeks of brief weekly support. In the active therapy group, all 7 patients reported no panic attacks at posttreatment, which was significantly superior to the results for the supportive therapy group (in which the mean number of attacks after 8 weeks was 3.13).

The results reported by Barlow et al. (1984) were preliminary findings from a larger treatment study carried out at our clinic. This paper described five subjects suffering panic disorder with mild agoraphobic avoidance treated with a combination of muscle relaxation, electromyogram (EMG) biofeedback, and cognitive restructuring. They were compared with six panic disorder patients assigned to a waiting list control group. Results indicated a significantly greater reduction of panic attacks in the treatment group than in the control group.

The larger study is now complete. In this study four conditions were compared: (1) waiting list control, (2) applied relaxation, (3) cognitive restructuring and interoceptive exposure, and (4) combined treatment. All treatments involved 15 weekly sessions with an individual therapist. For the applied relaxation condition, subjects were taught progressive deep muscle relaxation along the lines advocated by Bernstein and Borkovec (1973) and were encouraged to apply those techniques to threatening situations. The cognitive restructuring condition was based largely on the work of Beck and Emery (1985). Patients in this condition were also encouraged to "hypothesis-test" their beliefs about specific situations by confronting them. Hypothesis testing was especially applied to beliefs about interoceptive stimuli. The fourth condition combined relaxation and cognitive restructuring. A detailed session-by-session description of the treatments can be found in Barlow and Cerny (1988).

At present, we have the results from 45 patients in the various treatment conditions compared to 17 patients in the waiting list group (Craske & Barlow, 1987). There were so few differences between the active treatment conditions with the numbers available that the data presented here are collapsed across conditions. The clinician's severity ratings dropped from 5.3 to 2.3 (on a 0-to-8 scale) for the treatment group compared to a minimal drop (5.5 to 4.8) for the waiting list condition. The most exciting results, however, can be found in the effect of treatment on panic attacks as measured by daily self-monitoring. The percentage of subjects reporting no posttreatment panic attacks was 83% in the treatment groups. Thus, panic attacks were almost entirely eliminated by using psychological treatment. In contrast, the proportion of subjects reporting no panic in the waiting list group was 36%. Further, results for 3- to 6-month follow-ups were available for 18 subjects. The results in terms of the percentage of patients reporting no panic as well as overall clinician's severity ratings were maintained at follow-up (see Figure 7.2).

Another study has just been completed at the Center for Stress and Anxiety Disorders in Albany, New York, in which the combined treatment and waiting list conditions described above were compared with treatment by either alprazolam or placebo (Klosko, Barlow, Tassinari, & Cerny, 1987). Fifteen patients from the cognitive-behavioral treatment group were compared with 15 from the waiting list control group, 16 from the alprazolam treatment group, and 11 from the placebo treatment group. Alprazolam was administered for 15 weeks with maximum doses in the range of 6 to 10 mg. Tapering began after 13 weeks with a goal of medication cessation by 15 weeks (posttreatment). However, 15 of the 16 subjects in the alprazolam condition refused to stop medication, so posttreatment assessment was conducted with all but one of the group members on active medication. At posttreatment assessment, 87% of the cognitive-behavioral treatment group were panic free

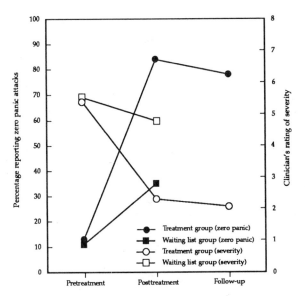

FIGURE 7.2 Effectiveness of Cognitive-Behavioral Treatment of Panic Disorder (Craske & Barlow, 1987)

compared to 50% of the alprazolam group, 36% of the placebo group, and 33% of the waiting list group. The data from other measures showed a similar pattern.

Thus, a growing body of evidence indicates that cognitive-behavioral techniques are very effective for the treatment of panic attacks as well as for agoraphobic avoidance. The effects of cognitive-behavioral treatment appear to be at least equivalent to those produced by drug treatment and appear more likely to be continued at follow-up. Having concluded that psychological treatment packages are of value in the treatment of panic disorder with agoraphobia, we can now look more specifically at the individual components of treatment.

Respiratory Control Techniques

A number of authors have stressed the importance of overbreathing in panic attacks (Lum, 1981; Ley, 1985; Bass, Kartsounis, & Lelliott, in press; Rapee, 1985b). The evidence is chiefly correlational at this time, and more refined studies are necessary to establish causal relationships. Nevertheless, several pieces of evidence seem relevant. First, the symptoms produced by hyperventilation are very similar to those associated with panic attacks: dizziness, breathlessness, faintness, choking, and paresthesia (Levinsky, 1983; Sanderson, Rapee, & Barlow, 1987b). While some authors attribute a broader range of sensations to hyperventilation, including hot flashes, nausea, sweating, trembling, and even anxiety (see Ley, 1985; Magarian, 1982), the latter symptoms probably reflect the anxious response to the more fundamental symptoms produced by overbreathing. There is some evidence that patients with panic disorder are more likely to report these hyperventilatory sensations than patients with other anxiety disorders (Hoehn-Saric, 1981; Rapee, 1985b; Sanderson et al., 1987b). This does not necessarily imply that panic disorder patients hyperventilate. Rather it may reflect an attentional bias in these patients (Sanderson et al., 1987b). That is, panic disorder patients may be more likely to report hyperventilatory symptoms, not because they experience them to a greater degree in any absolute sense, but because they are hypervigilant for such sensations (see Figure 7.1).

The major physiological effect of hyperventilation is a drop in the partial pressure of carbon dioxide (pCO_2) in the blood, which in turn results in a compensatory decrease in concentration of the bicarbonate ion. Some studies have demonstrated that patients with panic disorder have abnormally low pCO_2 and levels of biocarbonate at rest (Lum, 1976; Rapee, 1986; Gorman et al., 1986; Salkovskis, Jones, & Clark, 1986). At least one of these studies has found a significantly lower resting pCO_2 in patients with panic disorder than in patients with generalized anxiety disorder who had never experienced a panic attack (Rapee, 1986).

Finally, studies of hyperventilation in the laboratory suggest that some patients with panic disorder respond with considerable distress to a brief period of voluntary hyperventilation and rate this experience as being similar to their naturally occurring attacks (Garssen, van Veenendaal, & Bloemink, 1983; Rapee, 1986). It is these studies that, while providing some support for the hyperventilation theory of panic attacks, have most strongly indicated its limitations. Rapee (1986) found that panic disorder patients reported more distress after 90 seconds of voluntary hyperventilation than did patients with generalized anxiety disorder. However, not one of the panic disorder patients reported that they had actually had a "panic attack." Rather, they reported that while the experience was somatically very similar, they did not actually panic. In addition, only a proportion of patients requested to hyperventilate (50% to 75%, by clinical estimates) even report these sensations to be similar to their panic attacks in our clinic and other clinics (for instance, that of A. T. Beck, personal communication, June 1986). Thus, it appears that hyperventilation alone cannot explain panic attacks; other factors must be involved. This suggestion has found some support in findings that psychological characteristics can interact with the response to hyperventilation in normal subjects (Clark & Hemsley, 1982; Holloway & McNally, 1987). Clark and Hemsley found a positive correlation between the number of reported sensations following voluntary hyperventilation and neuroticism scores. Holloway and McNally found that the number and intensity of sensations, as well as the subjective anxiety produced by voluntary hyperventilation, were positively correlated with anxiety sensitivity (fear of the physical sensations of anxiety).

Other potentially important factors associated with the emotional response to somatic sensations will be discussed in the next section.

A distinction must be made between chronic and acute hyperventilation. Acute hyperventilation comprises brief episodes of overbreathing—whether it is causally involved in some or all panic attacks is still in question. However, there is little doubt that acute hyperventilation is associated with many panic attacks (Salkovskis, Warwick, Clark, & Wessels, 1986), at least as a consequence of the fear reaction (Barlow, 1988). Thus, respiratory control techniques are likely to be of benefit for most patients with panic disorder. Chronic hyperventilation is a long-term pattern of overbreathing to a mild degree. Such a pattern is likely to be found in only a small subset of panic disorder patients. In those cases, respiratory control may be especially helpful.

A number of case reports and empirical investigations have upheld the beneficial effects of breathing retraining on patients with panic disorder (Bonn, Readhead, & Timmons, 1984; Clark, Salkovskis, & Chalkley, 1985; Franklin, 1989; Lum, 1976; Rapee, 1985a; Salkovskis et al., 1986). Although there are subtle differences among breathing retraining techniques, they all share the major goal of trying to increase pCO_2, chiefly by reducing the amount (rate and depth) of respiration. Many of the patients in the studies just cited were selected for treatment based on symptom profiles that appeared hyperventilatory. In the one study involving a controlled comparison (Bonn et al., 1984), 12 individuals with panic disorder with agoraphobia were randomly allocated to treatment with either respiratory control training plus in vivo exposure or to in vivo exposure alone. The success of the manipulation was demonstrated at follow-up: the respiratory control group had a significantly lower respiratory rate compared to the in vivo–exposure-only group. There was a nonsignificant trend for the group taught respiratory control to report fewer panic attacks compared to the other group at posttreatment. At the 6-month follow-up, this difference between groups had become significant.

Most studies carried out to date have indicated that breathing retraining is of value in the treatment of panic attacks; nevertheless, these results could be attributed to other mechanisms. For example, the studies by Clark et al. (1985), Rapee (1985a), and Salkovskis et al. (1986) all included education and cognitive restructuring in their treatments. Although Salkovskis et al. did demonstrate that pCO_2 increased significantly during treatment and reached near-normal levels by posttreatment, this effect may have been associated with a reduction in overall arousal caused by some other treatment mechanism. It may be that breathing retraining produces a reduction in panic attacks through generally decreased arousal, as might any relaxation technique. Indeed, Öst (1988) has reported on the beneficial effects of "applied relaxation" in the reduction of panic attacks in seven patients. Results from our own center, also, are beginning to suggest that progressive muscle relaxation taught in an applied manner is beneficial in the alleviation of panic attacks. On the other hand, one multiple-baseline-design case study has indicated that breathing retraining may be more effective than a brief relaxation technique, isometric relaxation (Franklin, 1989). Obviously, systematic comparisons of breathing retraining with more traditional techniques are needed to separate the effects of various components of treatment.

Cognitive Restructuring

As mentioned previously, voluntary hyperventilation in the laboratory by patients with panic disorder results in somatic sensations but no marked sense of panic. For example, Rapee (1986) found that patients with panic disorder believed that 90 seconds of hyperventilation did not reproduce an actual panic because they felt they were safe and in control. Similar reports of an attenuated emotional response to lactate infusions have also been reported in panic disorder patients (Bonn, Harrison, & Rees, 1973; Pitts & McClure, 1967). Bonn et al. (1973) found that during infusions of sodium lactate 12 out of 20 patients reported that they "would have panicked but for your presence, doctor." These anecdotal reports suggest that beliefs and attributions, especially those related to safety and control, may be important in panic attacks.

A number of descriptive studies have found that panic disorder patients report more dramatic and catastrophic cognitions in response to somatic stimuli than do patients with other anxiety disorders (Beck, Laude, & Bohnert, 1974; Hibbert, 1984; Rapee, 1985b; Sanderson et al., 1987b). For example, Sanderson et al. found that panic disorder patients were significantly more likely to report fear of dying or going crazy and losing control during panic attacks than were patients with social phobia, obsessive-compulsive disorder, and simple phobia during their fear episodes. Similarly, panic patients have been found to report more belief that they were undergoing physical or psychological catastrophe (for example, heart attack, death, or insanity) while experiencing their symptoms than patients with generalized anxiety disorder (Hibbert, 1984; Rapee, 1985b). Thus, it seems that a tendency to activate dramatic beliefs regarding death, insanity, and loss of control in response to somatic symptoms is a fundamental characteristic of patients suffering from panic disorder. That such beliefs play a causal role in panic attacks is difficult to demonstrate. However, two recent studies have demonstrated that certain information can influence the intensity of laboratory-induced panic attacks in panic disorder patients, lending further support to the importance of cognitions in panic attacks.

In the first study (Rapee, Mattick, & Murrell, 1986), 16 patients with panic disorder received single-breath inhalations of a 50% CO_2/50% O_2 gas mixture. They were randomly allocated to two groups: an explanation group, which was given full information on the expected subjective and physiological effects of the inhalation, and a no-explanation group, which was given minimal information. The no-explanation group reported more subjective panic, greater similarity of the experience to a natural panic attack, and a greater proportion of catastrophic cognitions than the explanation group. These results demonstrated in a patient population that the provision of accurate information about the source of somatic sensations could attenuate the emotional response to those sensations.

In a second study, Sanderson, Rapee, and Barlow (1987a) administered continuous 15-minute inhalations of 5% CO_2 in air to 20 patients diagnosed as having panic disorder with agoraphobia. All patients were given identical instructions about what to expect from the inhalations. They were further told that a light in the room might or might not be illuminated. If the light were illuminated, they were informed, they would be able to control the amount of gas they received by using a dial (they were only to use it if absolutely necessary); if the light were not illuminated, they would have no control over the gas. In fact, both groups received the same amount of CO_2, because the dial was actually inoperative—in addition, no subject actually used the dial. The illusion-of-control group reported significantly fewer panic attacks, fewer and less intense symptoms, less anxiety, less similarity to a naturally occurring panic attack, and less catastrophic cognitions than did the no-control group. These results suggest that a sense of control over sensations can also attenuate the emotional response to the sensations.

The results of these studies in panic patients are supported by similar investigations using normal controls. Two studies have demonstrated that beliefs about the effects of CO_2 or lactate influence the emotional reaction to those substances (van den Hout & Griez, 1982; van der Molen, van den Hout, Vroemen, Louisberg, & Griez, 1986).

Evidence that cognitive factors affect the experience of panic suggests that cognitive restructuring may be of value in the treatment of this problem. Indeed, many clinicians suggest that cognitive alterations are very important in the treatment of panic attacks (Barlow, 1988; Beck & Emery, 1985; Clark, 1986; Clarke & Jackson, 1983; Wolpe, Lande, McNally, & Schotte, 1985). As mentioned earlier, some studies have combined education and cognitive restructuring with breathing retraining in the successful treatment of panic attacks (Clark et al., 1985; Rapee, 1985a; Salkovskis et al., 1986). However, controlled trials are not available to separate the effects of various treatment components, including cognitive restructuring. In our center, we are carrying out a study in which one group of panic disorder patients will receive only information and cognitive restructuring. The results, however, will be some time in coming.

Exposure-based Techniques

Exposure to feared stimuli has long been used as the foremost treatment for phobias of all types. When applied to panic disorder with agoraphobia, exposure traditionally has meant confrontation with feared external stimuli, with a goal of reducing avoidance behavior. However, more recently the focus has been extended to the reduction of panic attacks through exposure to interoceptive stimuli. Such a shift fits perfectly with the model presented earlier (Figure 7.1). If panic attacks involve a fear of somatic sensations, they can be treated by reducing that fear through exposure to the appropriate sensations (Barlow, 1986). Such interoceptive exposure is now advocated by many authors (see, for instance, Beck & Emery, 1985; Barlow, 1988; Griez & van den Hout, 1983), but controlled investigations are still rare.

The idea of using exposure to internal cues in the treatment of panic attacks is not new. Some authors have reported cases in which paradoxical intention has been used successfully in the alleviation of panic attacks (Gerz, 1966; Goldstein, 1978). Paradoxical intention asks the patient to attempt not to avoid, and in fact to increase, symptoms; and in this way it implies a strong component of exposure. The main clinical problem with paradoxical intention is that it relies on the natural occurrence of panic attacks, which may be infrequent and variable in some patients.

To conduct more systematic exposure to somatic sensations, therapists have attempted to discover the means by which such symptoms could be produced artificially. Over the years, many chemical means have been found, including infusions of adrenaline, sodium lactate, isoproterenol, and yohimbine; the ingestion of caffeine; and the inhalation of CO_2 mixed with air or oxygen in various amounts (see Barlow, 1988, for a review). Two of these methods, infusion of sodium lactate and inhalation of CO_2/O_2, have been used in the treatment of panic disorder with agoraphobia.

Bonn et al. (1973) reported the successful treatment of 33 patients with panic attacks using repeated infusions of sodium lactate. Unfortunately, the trial was uncontrolled and did not utilize a direct measure of panic attacks. Rather, successful outcome was inferred from measures of overall anxiety levels.

Wolpe (1958) reported on the successful use of repeated CO_2/O_2 inhalations in the treatment of severely anxious individuals, presumably with panic attacks. While the success of the technique probably had a lot to do with exposure to the somatic sensations produced by CO_2, Wolpe indicated that the mechanism of action was unknown and suggested that it might be due to postinhalation reactive relaxation. More recently, Griez and van den Hout (1983) reported a case study in which an individual suffering panic disorder with agoraphobia was given repeated inhalations of a 35% CO_2/65% O_2 gas mixture as well as being asked to intentionally and repeatedly hyperventilate and exercise. In the first week of treatment, interoceptive exposure alone resulted in a marked decrease in "fear of fear," but had little effect on phobic avoidance. The patient then practiced in vivo exposure over the next 3 weeks, and avoidant behavior decreased. This case study was extended by a controlled crossover comparison of the effects of CO_2/O_2 inhalations with those of propranolol (Griez & van den Hout, 1986). Fourteen patients suffering panic disorder with agoraphobia received 2 weeks' treatment with each technique in counterbalanced order. Gas inhalations produced a significant (50%) reduction in the frequency of panic attacks; propranolol produced nonsignificant

(38%) reduction. The difference between the two treatments was not significant.

While these data indicate that interoceptive exposure may be a valuable treatment technique in the alleviation of panic attacks, controlled evaluations of this component are still awaited. Some authors have suggested other methods for producing feared sensations that are more convenient for the clinician (Barlow, 1988; Beck & Emery, 1985; Craske, 1988): climbing flights of stairs, headshaking, taking a hot bath, spinning in a chair, and voluntary hyperventilation. These techniques will be discussed in more detail in the sample treatment protocol in the latter part of this chapter.

Exposure-based techniques have received widespread investigation and acceptance in their application to agoraphobic avoidance (Bandura, 1977; Marks, 1981; Mathews et al., 1981). A number of studies over the years have found cognitive-behavioral techniques featuring exposure as a major component to be superior to treatments without exposure (for instance, Emmelkamp, Kuipers, & Eggeraat, 1978). In fact, a recent study has demonstrated that exposure may be one of the essential ingredients in the successful treatment of agoraphobia (Michelson, Mavissakalian, Marchione, Dancu, & Greenwald, 1986). Consequently, few clinicians today would treat a patient with panic disorder with agoraphobia without including some degree of exposure to feared situations. Arguments over the last few years have centered not on whether exposure is necessary, but on the nature of that exposure and the value of additional procedures. Hence, we will briefly summarize some of the literature with this focus.

The Parameters of Exposure

One of the earliest areas of investigation was the value of imaginal as opposed to in vivo exposure in the treatment of panic disorder with agoraphobia. Wolpe's pioneering work on the use of systematic desensitization in the alleviation of phobic avoidance emphasized imaginal contact with the feared object or situation (Wolpe, 1958). This procedure was taken to its extreme by such researchers as Stampfl and Levis (1967), who used imaginal techniques to expose the patient to the worst possible scenario, sometimes involving quite horrific stimuli (imaginal flooding).

Imaginal techniques obviously have tremendous practical advantage over in vivo techniques. The therapist has control over the rate of exposure, the type of stimuli present, and even, to some extent, the patient's reactions. In addition, imaginal techniques allow exposure to stimuli that would be very difficult or even impossible to arrange in vivo. Unfortunately, most comparisons between imaginal and in vivo exposure in the treatment of panic disorder with agoraphobia have demonstrated a marked advantage to in vivo techniques (Jansson & Öst, 1982; Marks, 1981; Mathews et al., 1981).

Another issue that was the focus of much early work concerned the rate of exposure—that is, the rate at which patients were encouraged to face feared situations. The two ends of this spectrum are systematic desensitization and flooding. Systematic desensitization involves drawing up a hierarchy of feared situations and having the patient encounter them imaginally in a gradual, nonthreatening fashion. Flooding is rapid exposure to highly anxiety-provoking stimuli. Of course, there is a complete range in between (Marshall, Gauthier, & Gordon, 1979).

Marks, Boulougouris, and Marset (1971) found systematic desensitization to be less effective than imaginal flooding for agoraphobic patients. On the other hand, Gelder et al. (1973) reported no significant difference between systematic desensitization and imaginal flooding in a group of mixed phobic patients, though both treatments had significantly better results than a control condition. There seemed to be no differences in response to treatment between the agoraphobic and nonagoraphobic patients. However, a slight superiority for the flooding condition was seen on the behavioral avoidance test.

Another way of studying the rate-of-exposure issue is to manipulate anxiety levels in patients undergoing exposure treatment. This has been done using both instructions and tranquilizers. Hafner and Marks (1976) compared two groups of panic-disorder-with-agoraphobia patients undergoing in vivo exposure. One group received instructions designed to make them highly anxious; the other received instructions designed to make them calm. The manipulation was successful, based on self-report, but the two groups showed similar rates and degrees of improvement. In another study reported by Hafner and Marks (1976), two groups of agoraphobic patients received equivalent in vivo exposure. One group received small doses of diazepam immediately prior to the exposure; the other received a placebo. The diazepam group members rated themselves as less anxious than the placebo group during exposure, but there were no significant differences in treatment outcome. A different finding was reported by Chambless, Foa, Groves, and Goldstein (1979). These researchers compared imaginal flooding with and without the addition of Brevital® (a rapid, short-acting barbiturate) and found that the Brevital condition produced somewhat less improvement.

At present, the results of direct anxiety-manipulation-during-exposure studies are contradictory (Mathews et al., 1981). From a theoretical perspective, it could be expected that too little anxiety (in which no sensations occur) would not be beneficial in the long term, because patients would not be exposed to internal cues. However, assuming that anxiety sensations are experienced, the actual level of anxiety may not be of central importance. Practically, in terms of compliance, it is likely that patients will be less willing to attempt exposure assignments if anxiety levels are excessive.

A related consideration is the change in anxiety within the situation required for maximally effective exposure. Early learning theory models suggested that long periods of exposure, allowing complete habituation, would be more effective than shorter periods, which may allow sensitization (Eysenck, 1976). Indeed, a study by Stern and Marks (1973) found that a continuous 2-hour session of exposure was more effective than four half-hour sessions. However, reinforced practice, which encourages the patient to approach the situation only until undue anxiety arises, has been found to be effective in the treatment of panic disorder with agoraphobia (Agras, Leitenberg, & Barlow, 1968; Emmelkamp, 1982). In fact, Emmelkamp (1974) found this approach to be at least as effective as prolonged flooding in vivo at a 3-month follow-up. Two recent studies (DeSilva & Rachman, 1984; Rachman, Craske, Tallman, & Solyom, 1986) found that exposure in which agoraphobics were allowed to escape when their anxiety reached a specific high level was equally as effective as exposure in which they were encouraged to stay until their anxiety had dropped markedly.

The reasons for these discrepancies are not clear, but it does seem from the recent work that the earlier belief that patients had to stay in a situation until their anxiety dropped may not be warranted. More recent theories of the mechanisms of exposure suggest that the essential thing is for the individual to acquire information inconsistent with his or her earlier predictions (Foa & Kozak, 1986). In fact, more recent evidence shows that when the anxiety experienced by panic disorder patients in a situation is less than predicted, subsequent anticipatory anxiety will decrease (Rachman, Lopatka, & Levitt, 1988). Possibly what is necessary during exposure is simply to ensure that individuals stay long enough to disconfirm their earlier expectations of harm. A similar suggestion is that the critical ingredient is the establishment of a sense of control over emotional responding (Barlow, 1988). Exposure must therefore be long enough to promote a sense of control over runaway emotions such as panic attacks. The specific methods by which such factors as perceptions of control and predictions of harm can be assessed and modified—and their relation to exposure treatment—have still to be investigated.

The final variable in exposure treatment is the involvement of the therapist. At one extreme, the therapist has no involvement; treatment proceeds via literature and self-help manuals. At the other extreme, the therapist is very involved and participates in the exposure exercises.

At the minimal involvement end, Holden, O'Brien, Barlow, Stetson, and Infantino (1983) treated six women with severe agoraphobia using a self-help manual. The manual outlined instructions for in vivo exposure and cognitive restructuring. The results suggested that the self-help manual was not effective. Further, Holden et al. found that the same treatment administered by a therapist was highly effective. Different results were reported by Ghosh and Marks (1987). These researchers compared the effectiveness of an exposure-based treatment administered through a self-help manual (1.5 hours of therapist time), by the therapist (4.6 hours of therapist time), or by computer (4.7 hours of therapist time). All three groups improved substantially, with little difference among them. The main difference between these studies seems to have been the initial severity of the problem. Certainly, it seems that extensive involvement by the therapist in exposure exercises is not necessary for marked improvement (Barlow, 1988; Mathews et al., 1981). However, especially in the case of severe distress and disability, it seems that some therapist involvement is an advantage. In therapist-administered treatment, it is important to gradually reduce the therapist's involvement to help patients make their own exposure attempts and develop a sense of control and independence (Barlow, 1988).

Additional Treatment Components

One of the questions beginning to generate considerable research is whether exposure-based techniques are more effective when the spouse or a significant other is included in the treatment. There are two major reasons for assuming benefits. First, the spouse can learn to act as a therapist and can, in a sense, continue treatment and encourage the patient in the natural environment. Second, agoraphobic avoidance places a marked strain on the relationship. After living with the problem for a period of time, most relationships will adjust in various ways. Thus, changing the avoidance behavior will require readjustments in the relationship that may interfere with progress or cause relationship problems. Including the spouse in therapy can facilitate understanding and support. These factors may be particularly important for the long-term maintenance of treatment gains (Kleiner & Marshall, 1985). Some studies have found that patients with panic disorder with agoraphobia who had poorer marital adjustment were more likely to relapse than those with better marital adjustment (Bland & Hallam, 1981; Milton & Hafner, 1979).

To date, only a few studies have actually manipulated the presence of the spouse in treatment. Cobb, Mathews, Childs-Clarke, and Blowers (1984) treated 19 patients with panic disorder with agoraphobia who agreed to a treatment program that might include the spouse. Ten patients were treated without the spouse and nine with the spouse. Few differences in the degree of improvement emerged between the two groups, either at posttreatment assessment or at the 6-month follow-up. In this study, all therapist-assisted treatment was carried out in the patient's home. At the initial session and at all measurement sessions, the spouse was included. Therapists reported that spouses in the nonspouse group "showed an interest" in therapy. These factors may have increased the spouses' involvement in the treatment, in comparison to individual, clinic-based treatment.

Barlow, O'Brien, and Last (1984) reported on the treatment of 28 agoraphobic women; the husbands of 14 of them were included in therapy. Prior to treatment, the spouses of all 28 had agreed to participate. While both conditions resulted in improvement, the spouse-participation group improved significantly more on a number of measures. At a 2-year follow-up, differences between the groups had increased (Cerny, Barlow, Craske, & Himadi, 1987).

Finally, one study attempted to maximize the inclusion of the spouse by specifically teaching communication skills to the couples (Arnow, Taylor, Agras, & Telch, 1985). Following 4 weeks of standard exposure treatment, 24 couples were allocated randomly to groups taught either relaxation training or communication skills. The communication skills group improved significantly more than the relaxation group at both posttreatment assessment and 8-month follow-up.

It appears that including the partner in therapy has the advantage over standard exposure treatment. However, these results are not yet entirely clear (Cobb et al., 1984), and more research is needed to determine predictors of response to the inclusion of the partner.

Other additions to exposure may also offer some benefit. As research discussed earlier indicates, agoraphobic avoidance appears to be related to a number of personality characteristics, including dependency, unassertiveness, and social anxiety (Andrews, 1966; Chambless, 1985; Rapee & Murrell, 1988). It may be that specific attention to altering such traits could provide a valuable adjunct to exposure in vivo, especially for individuals with problems in those areas. Little systematic research has been conducted on these factors to date.

Emmelkamp (1980) found that assertive and unassertive agoraphobic patients benefited equally from exposure in vivo. In a more systematic study, Emmelkamp, van den Hout, and De Vries (1983) randomly assigned 21 "unassertive" patients having panic disorder with agoraphobia to one of three groups: exposure in vivo, assertiveness training, and a combination of the two. While assertiveness training had the largest impact on measures of assertiveness, it was the least effective treatment for phobic anxiety. The combined treatment was no more beneficial than the exposure-alone condition in its impact on phobic avoidance, suggesting that assertiveness training did not add to the effects of in vivo exposure.

Despite the negative findings in these two studies, there is room for considerable research in this area. The study by Emmelkamp et al. (1983) did show that assertiveness training specifically increased assertiveness. Thus, for certain patients, this technique might be a useful adjunct to exposure to promote more global improvement. In addition, the potential value of adding specific treatment for social anxiety has not been systematically investigated. Such adjuncts to in vivo exposure may be especially valuable for the difficult patient (see Chapter 12).

In summary, a number of components of the psychological treatment of panic disorder are of great theoretical importance. In most cases, empirical evidence confirming their importance is still awaited. The major components of treatment include the provision of accurate information and cognitive restructuring, breathing retraining, interoceptive exposure, and in vivo exposure. The provision of accurate information and cognitive restructuring are aimed at changing the belief that the somatic sensations experienced during anxiety episodes are harmful. Breathing retraining is aimed at reducing the tendency to hyperventilate, especially for that proportion of the panic disorder population who appear to have a major problem with this characteristic. Interoceptive exposure is aimed at reducing the more automatic information that the somatic sensations are harmful and at teaching the individual that such sensations can be experienced without fear. Finally, in vivo exposure is aimed at teaching the individual not to fear and avoid external situations.

A Sample Treatment Protocol

Having discussed the theoretical and empirical bases underlying the treatment techniques, we will now present an example of a protocol for the cognitive-behavioral treatment of panic disorder. The protocol will include treatment techniques for both panic attacks and agoraphobic avoidance, to be used for specific patients as appropriate. In addition, the protocol assumes group treatment and inclusion of the spouse or a significant other in treatment sessions. Naturally, if group treatment is not appropriate or if the spouse or significant other is not available, the protocol may be modified accordingly. This treatment protocol is based on the maximally effective treatment package currently in use at the Center for Stress and Anxiety Disorders of the State University of New York at Albany. An outline of the protocol is presented in Table 7.1. A more detailed description of our protocol for treating panic attacks, suitable for distribution to clients, is available from the center.

TABLE 7.1 Cognitive-behavioral Treatment of Panic Disorder with Agoraphobia: Outline of Sample Protocol

1. Diagnosis and accurate description of problems

2. Assessment of current level of functioning

3. Introduction of principles and nature of treatment

4. Cognitive restructuring—overestimation of probability

5. Cognitive restructuring—overestimation of consequence

6. Instruction for breathing retraining

7. Introduction of principles and practice of exposure in vivo

8. Extension of exposure to internal cues

9. Continued practice of exposure, utilizing cognitive and breathing skills—regular homework assignments

10. Additional skills: communication, assertiveness, social

11. Termination and discussion of maintenance

12. Posttreatment assessment

13. Follow-up or "booster" sessions

Client Selection

The treatment protocol discussed here is designed specifically for the treatment of patients with a primary diagnosis of panic disorder, with or without agoraphobic avoidance. In addition, patients with panic attacks or avoidance behavior who primarily present with another problem could benefit from the inclusion of aspects of this protocol in their treatment.

While there are no empirical data available on clients who are less likely to benefit from such a protocol, some clinical observations may be useful. Patients presenting with marked depression should probably make their depression the primary focus of treatment. The cognitive-behavioral treatment package described here requires considerable motivation and effort for success, and severe depression is likely to interfere with its effectiveness. Similarly, patients who appear to lack motivation for other reasons (such as, secondary gain) may also benefit little from cognitive-behavioral treatment. If there is a substance abuse problem, it should generally be dealt with before treating the panic disorder.

The influence of personality disorder on treatment outcome has not been systematically assessed, but clinical experience suggests that where a personality disorder is present, treatment is likely to be more difficult and may be of longer duration. Nevertheless, at least one study has demonstrated that the successful treatment of agoraphobia can also benefit coexisting personality disorders (Mavissakalian & Hamann, 1987).

Most clients who present to our clinic are already taking considerable medication. Our impression is that this in no way interferes with treatment. However, patients are discouraged from attempting to reduce medication dosages until later in treatment; they then reduce it only under strict supervision. Individual attempts to adjust medication dosages often have adverse effects.

Another factor in client selection is physical conditions, such as heart disease, respiratory disease, or pregnancy. Cognitive-behavioral therapy should be the treatment of choice for these individuals, as medication has a number of associated risks. Caution needs to be exercised, however, with the interoceptive exposure component, and it may be best to exclude the technique from treatment of these patients. If the technique is felt to be important, it should be conducted in consultation with the individual's physician, perhaps using a pulse meter to monitor heart rate throughout.

One final point worth making relates to "selling" treatment to patients. Most panic disorder patients will gladly accept cognitive-behavioral treatment, as many do not like to take medication. In addition, the ideas of cognitive-behavioral therapy make good sense; in fact, many patients have attempted similar techniques themselves. Some patients will present, however, with a strict biochemical view of their disorder. In this case, some effort should be made to convince them that, regardless of any neurotransmitters involved, what they think and do can also be vitally important. As long as such individuals view their panic attacks as random chemical fluctuations over which they have no control, cognitive-behavioral treatment will be compromised.

The Preliminary Assessment

While it is vital for research to have reliable and valid outcome measures, such measures should not be viewed as solely a researcher's tool. Clinicians should also use assessment devices, for a number of reasons.

1. In general, it is important for the clinician to know if the treatment is effective.
2. It is often useful to have some evidence to feed back to the patient to demonstrate progress.
3. It can be valuable to have data to show new patients, to increase their motivation and confidence.

Many types of measures are possible and available.

Physiological Measures

Overall, physiological measures are probably the least practical assessment tools for clinicians. Not only are they generally expensive and difficult to use in office practice, but a number of studies have questioned their reliability and validity. Some studies have demonstrated that physiological measures are not reliable when taken repeatedly as measures of change (Arena, Blanchard, Andrasik, Cotch, & Meyers, 1983). Further, Holden and Barlow (1986) found a lack of discriminant validity for heart rate measured in vivo as a measure of treatment outcome. Nevertheless, where physiological assessment is available, it could be useful as an additional measure. It could also be useful as a treatment adjunct—for example, to demonstrate to patients that their heart rates are not as high as they think and are still well within normal physiological limits. Measures of respiration, such as the assessment of pCO_2, or even respiratory rate could be of value for those patients who appear to chronically overbreathe. These measures can also be used as biofeedback tools while teaching breathing retraining.

Behavioral Measures

The individualized Behavioral Avoidance Test (BAT) for the assessment of treatment outcome is an important tool for the therapist. This form of assessment requires no expensive equipment and is relatively fast and simple. More importantly, it is designed to assess the most debilitating aspect of panic disorder for many patients: the avoidance behavior.

The first step in conducting a BAT is to develop a hierarchy of feared situations or events. The therapist, in conjunction with the patient, identifies a number of avoided situations or tasks that could be performed relatively easily if it were not for fear and avoidance. In our clinic we use ten items, for a good range of assessment. These items must be described in detail in order to avoid ambiguity. For example, they must specify the duration, the specific location (names of stores, streets, and so on), and whether the person is alone or accompanied. The items should then be arranged in increasing order of difficulty. A common belief among anxiety researchers is that BATs are only useful for panic disorder patients who display considerable avoidance. This is not necessarily so. Patients who report only limited avoidance may in fact fear and avoid many events—typically those that produce somatic sensations. Some common examples are aerobic exercise, blowing up balloons, fast fairground rides, and saunas. Alternatively, the person may endure high levels of anxiety in certain situations rather than avoid them.

Once the hierarchy has been developed, the BAT is carried out by instructing the patient to perform the tasks in order of increasing difficulty. It is particularly important that the items be attempted exactly as specified in the hierarchy, so that later assessments will allow valid comparisons. To speed the assessment, it is possible to sample items from the hierarchy. In our clinic, we select five items from the ten. When patients report back on their performance of the BAT, each item is scored on the following 3-point scale: 0-patient refuses the item (avoidance), 1-partial completion of the item (escape), and 2-successful completion of the item. An example of a list of items from one client in our program is presented in Figure 7.3. We refer to this list as the Fear and Avoidance Hierarchy and use it in additional ways, as we'll show.

The BAT may also be combined with either physiological or self-report anxiety measures. Any of the common physiological measures, especially heart rate and respiratory rate, can be taken during the performance of the items. In terms of self-report, it is useful to have subjects rate their maximum level of anxiety while performing the item on the 0-to-8 anxiety scale shown in Figure 7.3. For more detailed information on the use of the Behavioral Avoidance Test procedure, refer to Barlow (1988).

The Fear and Avoidance Hierarchy

In addition to its use in the BAT, the Fear and Avoidance Hierarchy can be used as an ongoing self-report measure. Each item can be rated by patients on a 0-to-8 scale, for both fear of the item and the extent to which they would avoid that item (see Figure 7.3). Administered regularly throughout treatment, it can give the therapist a feel for the rate of improvement and any remaining difficulties.

Name: _____   Date: _____

PHOBIAS: FEAR AND AVOIDANCE

Rate the degree to which you tend to *avoid* the situations listed below because of fear or unpleasant feelings associated with them. Also rate your level of anxiety in each situation.

—0———1———2———3———4———5———6———7———8—

Do not avoid situation— no anxiety	Hesitate to enter situation but rarely avoid it—slightly/ somewhat anxious	Sometimes avoid situation— definitely anxious	Usually avoid situation— markedly or very often anxious	Invariably avoid situation—very severe/ continual anxiety, near-panic

	Description	Avoidance (0–8)	Fear (0–8)
1. Worst situation	Attending Mass in a Catholic church.	8	8
2. Second-worst situation	Walking through Colonie Center alone.	8	8
3. Third-worst situation	Riding the escalator in the Boston Store (Mohawk Mall).	8	8
4. Fourth-worst situation	Shopping in the CVS for 10 minutes alone.	6	4
5. Fifth-worst situation	Climbing on the roof of your shop for 10 minutes alone.	6	5
6. Sixth-worst situation	Walking through the Mohawk Mall alone.	5	6
7. Seventh-worst situation	Waiting in line behind three people in the P & C Market.	3	5
8. Eighth-worst situation	Having coffee in the Broadway Lunch Diner, early morning.	3	3
9. Ninth-worst situation	Driving on Central Ave. past Colonie Center (not rush hour).	3	3
10. Tenth-worst situation	Shopping in P & C Market near home for 10 minutes alone.	1	3

FIGURE 7.3 Fear and Avoidance Hierarchy

Self-report Measures—Questionnaires

A large number of questionnaire measures are currently used in panic disorder and agoraphobia research. Questionnaires are probably the most useful outcome measures for the clinician, because they are simple to use, inexpensive, and take up little office time. Their value lies not only in outcome assessment but also in gathering information that may be missed during the initial interview. (See this book's appendix for more details on these and other measures.)

The Fear Questionnaire

This widely used measure appears to possess adequate psychometric properties (Marks & Mathews, 1979) and yields four main scores: main phobia rating, total phobia rating, anxiety/depression rating, and a global measure of phobic symptoms. In addition, three particularly useful subscores—agoraphobia, blood/injury phobia, and social phobia—are derived. This measure requires only brief administration time, and the agoraphobia subscale, because of its wide acceptance, allows comparison of the severity of agoraphobia to published standards. For example, Mavissakalian (1986a) provided data on the validity of the scale and suggested a cutoff point of 30 on the agoraphobia subscale for severe agoraphobia. Additional investigation (Mavissakalian, 1986b) suggests that a posttreatment score below 10 identifies an excellent clinical response to therapy.

The Mobility Inventory for Agoraphobia

This 27-item questionnaire was designed primarily to assess agoraphobic avoidance (Chambless, Caputo, Jasin, Gracely, & Williams, 1985). Instructions require ratings of the severity of avoidance when alone and when accompanied—a particularly useful feature, because these ratings are often very different. In addition, ratings of panic frequency during the last week are obtained. Adequate reliability and validity data are reported for this inventory, which discriminates patients with agoraphobia from those with other anxiety disorders (Craske, Rachman, & Tallman, 1986).

The Agoraphobia Cognitions Questionnaire and the Body Sensations Questionnaire

These companion questionnaires are designed to assess the cognitive and physiological aspects of anxiety and panic (Chambless, Caputo, Bright, & Gallagher, 1984). They are particularly useful in initial assessment and in evaluating progress in panic disorder with either limited or extensive avoidance. Both questionnaires possess sound psychometric properties, although Craske et al. (1986) report an inability of the Agoraphobia Cognitions Questionnaire to discriminate panic disorder from other anxiety disorders.

The Anxiety Sensitivity Index

This questionnaire measures sensitivity to and discomfort from a number of physical sensations commonly associated with anxiety (Reiss, Peterson, Gursky, & McNally, 1986). It appears to have good reliability and validity (Maller & Reiss, in press). Patients with panic disorder with agoraphobia have been found to score high on the scale and to lower their score significantly following successful treatment. This questionnaire has a slightly different emphasis than the Body Sensations Questionnaire, as it focuses specifically on discomfort stemming from those bodily sensations associated with anxiety.

Self-monitoring Diary Measures

In the treatment of panic attacks and agoraphobic avoidance, it is important that both therapist and patient be aware of the occurrence of panic attacks and the level of general mood states such as anxiety and depression. Research in behavioral assessment (for example, Barlow, 1981) has demonstrated that continual monitoring of behavioral and emotional events is more accurate and reliable than periodic recall of those events. Self-monitoring procedures simply require patients to record their moods and panic attacks, either at regular intervals or whenever they occur. The more frequent the recording, the more accurate the information. This must be weighed against the risks to compliance caused by overtaxing patients, however. Compliance with record keeping is an especially difficult problem; the patient will only be as reliable as the therapist. Regular checks and interest in the week's records shown by the therapist are important to maintaining the patient's motivation. In addition, it is important to explain the value of self-monitoring to the patient in terms of its feedback role for both therapist and patient.

At our clinic, we currently use two complementary monitoring forms for the assessment of panic attacks and mood. The Weekly Record of Anxiety and Depression (Figure 7.4) shows daily ratings, on a 0-to-8 scale, of general mood states. Patients are asked to rate their general anxiety and depression throughout the day. Anxiety is rated twice: as general, background anxiety, and as the maximum anxiety reached that day. In addition, patients are asked to monitor their overall feeling of pleasantness for the day. This measure is especially important later in treatment, when patients may experience a reduction in depression but little increase in positive mood. A record of any medication taken is important, because it has a major influence on mood. Finally, a measure of particular importance for panic disorder that has just been assigned an important diagnostic role in the DSM-III-R is the level of anxiety associated with the anticipation of the next panic attack.

The accompanying monitoring form is the Panic Attack Record (Figure 7.5), a pocket-size sheet to be carried with the patient at all times and completed immediately following a panic attack. This is a particularly useful device if used properly, because the information is just barely retrospective. In fact, we are beginning to find some discrepancies among the data collected

Name: _____   Week ending: _____

WEEKLY RECORD OF ANXIETY AND DEPRESSION

Each evening before you go to bed please rate your *average* level of anxiety (taking all things into consideration) throughout the day, the *maximum* level of anxiety that you experienced that day, your *average* level of depression throughout the day, and your average feeling of pleasantness throughout the day. Use the scale below. Next, please list the dosages and amounts of any medication you took. Finally, please rate, using the scale below, how worried or frightened you were, on the average, about the possibility of having a panic attack throughout the day.

Level of Anxiety/Depression/Pleasant Feeling

—— 0 —— 1 —— 2 —— 3 —— 4 —— 5 —— 6 —— 7 —— 8 ——

| None | Slight | Moderate | A lot | As much as you can imagine |

Date	Average anxiety	Maximum anxiety	Average depression	Average pleasant-ness	Medication type, dose, number (mg)	Fear of panic attack

FIGURE 7.4 Daily Monitoring Form for Mood, Medication, and Fear of Panic Attacks

using these forms and those given to us at the initial interview. The features to be recorded are clear and require little concentration, an advantage in the aftermath of a panic attack.

In addition to the self-monitoring of panic attacks and mood, various other aspects of behavior can and should be monitored throughout treatment. For individuals with considerable avoidance, daily activities can be recorded. Patients record each major task they perform outside their home each day, in some detail: the duration of the task, the time spent alone, and their level of anxiety. It is particularly important to do this monitoring once exposure practice begins, both as a reminder and as a record. Once the patients are taught breathing retraining or relaxation, it is important to keep a record, for

---

PANIC ATTACK RECORD

NAME: _____

DATE: _____   TIME: _____   DURATION: _____ (mins.)

WITH: SPOUSE ____   FRIEND ____   STRANGER ____   ALONE ____

STRESSFUL SITUATION: YES/NO   EXPECTED: YES/NO

MAXIMUM ANXIETY (CIRCLE)

——0——1——2——3——4——5——6——7——8——
 NONE   MODERATE   EXTREME

SENSATIONS (CHECK)

Pounding heart	____	Sweating	____	Hot/cold flashes	
Tight/painful chest	____	Choking	____	Fear of dying	____
Breathlessness	____	Nausea	____	Fear of going crazy	____
Dizziness	____	Unreality	____	Fear of losing	
Trembling	____	Numbness/tingling	____	control	____

FIGURE 7.5 Portable Monitoring Form to Record Panic Attacks (Phobia and Anxiety Disorders Clinic, SUNY, Albany, NY)

MONITORING OF COGNITIONS

For each panic attack or anxious event this week, please describe your beliefs.

Actual event (trigger)	Initial thought	Probability (0–100)	Consequence	Anxiety level (0–8)
Riding on a bus	I cannot get off.	50	My heart will pound.	6
	My heart will pound.	80	I will have a heart attack.	5
	I will have a heart attack.	0		2
Difficult examination	I will fail.	10	I will be expelled.	4
	I will be expelled.	1	I will never have a job.	2
	I will never have a job.	0		1

FIGURE 7.6 Monitoring and Practice Form for Cognitive Modification

at least a few weeks, of their practice. Improvement cannot occur without regular practice, and self-monitoring is one way of improving compliance. /

Finally, an especially important task is the monitoring of cognitions during anxiety-provoking events. The value of this form cannot be stressed enough, as cognitive restructuring is a particularly difficult concept for most patients. To train the patient adequately, the therapist must have a good record of the patient's thinking style. The form currently used in our clinic is presented in Figure 7.6, as it was filled out by one of our patients. In the first column, the individual records the actual event that triggered the emotion. It can be an external event ("an argument with my boss") or an internal event ("sudden dizziness"). The patient is encouraged to record the event objectively, without interpretation. Next, the patient records the immediate (usually irrational) thought. This must be recorded in some detail and should not be altered in any way. The individual should then use newly acquired skills to rate the rational probability of the feared situation occurring and, should it happen, the realistic consequence. Next, the person should rate his or her anxiety, given the realistic probability and the consequence. If anxiety is still high, the consequence should be rewritten in the "thought" column and subjected to appraisal of its realistic probability and consequence. This procedure should be continued until anxiety is minimal or the "bottom line" belief is reached.

The Treatment Package

Session 1

The initial treatment session is essentially an introductory one, to discuss the patient's problem and the treatment rationale. For therapists conducting individual treatment with a patient they have already assessed, the first part of the session will be unnecessary. However, if treatment is being conducted in a group, spending a brief time discussing each person's problem is of value in building group cohesion. Each patient should describe the specific details of his or her problem, such as the somatic sensations involved in attacks, the situations feared and avoided, the onset of the anxiety problem, and the effect on his or her life. Partners should describe their view of the problem and the effect it has had on their lives. Most group members enjoy this aspect of treatment, because they commonly have felt they were the only one with this type of problem. The therapist uses this session to set the tone, encouraging people to interact with each other and keeping the group on track, not letting the discussion drift too far from the immediate problem.

Once all group members have a feel for the others' problems, the therapist sets the stage for the discussion of treatment by spending some time describing the "scientific" model of panic disorder. This discussion is based on the model described earlier and obviously must be tailored to the level of the audience.

The use of a diagram such as that in Figure 7.1 may be helpful. Some of the points to cover are as follows.

1. Panic disorder involves a fear of experiencing a panic attack.
2. Some of the characteristic behavior seen in panic disorder is directed at seeking safety in case of a panic attack.
3. A panic attack is simply a set of physical sensations to which the individual responds with fear.
4. The causes of these physical sensations are various, but knowing the cause is not essential for treatment.
5. The original panic attack often occurs during a time of stress, but identifying that stress is likewise not essential for treatment.
6. People who suffer panic attacks are often generally "aroused" people.
7. This characteristic is a result of both genetic and early life factors.
8. Thus treatment has *some* limitation, but patients can learn to be as they were prior to the problem.
9. Agoraphobia and panic attacks are a major strain on a relationship, and relationships change as a result of the problem.
10. Thus, overcoming the problem will also mean changes in the relationship, which may be difficult.
11. Treatment involves learning skills to cope with and overcome the anxiety. This means a great deal of work. Failure to work on the problem will jeopardize improvement.

At this point, the therapist describes the treatment based on the model just presented. By explaining the aims and functions of each of the techniques, understanding and credibility is improved. Techniques will be taught that can help cope with and reduce panic attacks. Patients will then be encouraged to gradually face frightening situations. Spouses or partners are included to increase their understanding of the problem and treatment, to help deal with relationship issues raised by treatment, and to coach and aid the patient in the natural setting. Improvement does not stop when therapy ends. In fact, the treatment will teach skills that the person with panic disorder will need to practice for some time. The partner is especially valuable in this regard.

It is a good idea to assess treatment credibility either verbally or through an established questionnaire (Borkovec & Nau, 1972). Treatment credibility refers to how useful or valid patients believe the treatment to be, hence the extent to which they expect it to benefit them. Credibility is known to be a good predictor of treatment response (Jansson & Öst, 1982); thus, identifying individuals with low expectations of improvement gives the therapist an opportunity to work on and maximize this factor. The session should end with an emphasis on accurate monitoring.

Session 2

At the beginning of each session, the therapist reviews and encourages brief discussion of the previous week's work. The therapist inquires whether the group members thought about the information given in the previous week and discussed it with their partners and whether any questions have arisen. In this session it is particularly important to review the model of panic attacks presented in the previous week.

The major aim of session 2 is to introduce the principles of cognitive restructuring. This technique is used first as a specific intervention for panic attacks and second as a general technique to help reduce other problems associated with panic disorder—for instance, general anxiety, unassertiveness, and depression. The main point to make is that the way we interpret and think about an event or situation determines our emotional reaction to it. A number of excellent texts have appeared over the years outlining the principles and practice of cognitive techniques (see, for example, Beck, 1976; Beck & Emery, 1985; Ellis & Harper, 1975).

It is important to begin with one or more good examples, because the basic premise of cognitive restructuring—that the interpretation of an event can produce or at least influence the emotional reaction—is often difficult for patients to understand. Patients and partners are asked to generate examples from their own lives in which their interpretation of an event or situation influenced their emotion. An explanation along the following lines may then be used.

> People tend to believe that "situation X *made me* anxious." In fact, the situation does not invariably result in an emotion. Rather, it is the interpretation or the thoughts surrounding the event that result in the emotion. Thus, altering those interpretations or thoughts can change the resulting emotion. Anxious people have a tendency to think in certain stereotypic ways. These thought patterns tend to be very extreme and often result in extreme emotions such as anxiety and depression. A different way of thinking may result in more moderate nervousness or sadness. Cognitive restructuring is not the same as positive thinking. Positive thinking may encourage us to look at life through rose-colored glasses, which may be unrealistic. Cognitive restructuring encourages us to look at life in a realistic and rational manner. Thus, it may sometimes be realistic to experience sadness or anxiety. But it may not have to happen as frequently or intensely as it does for those of you currently experiencing those emotions.

In our clinic we divide the logical errors that anxious individuals make into two types: overestimations of probability and catastrophic estimations of consequence. Anxious individuals tend to overestimate the likelihood that an aversive event will occur, particularly to themselves (Butler & Mathews, 1983). In addition, having decided that the aversive event will most likely occur, the anxious individual tends to overdramatize the consequences of the aversive event. Dividing problem thoughts into these two categories facilitates training in cognitive restructuring.

Session 2 focuses on altering estimates of the likelihood of the feared event. Patients are encouraged to think of the last time they had a panic attack. Each is then asked to describe the first thoughts about aversive events that surfaced, at the start of the attack. The therapist discusses each one in turn and challenges the individual about the realistic probability that the feared aversive event would occur. Partners are encouraged to listen and learn so that they may apply the same technique in the natural environment. Common examples include triggers such as dizziness, a pounding heart, or feelings of unreality accompanied by thoughts such as "I am going to pass out," "I am having a heart attack," or "I am going to lose control."

For homework, patients are encouraged to record a number of high-anxiety episodes (including panic attacks) occurring during the coming week. They are asked to use the monitoring sheets (see Figure 7.6) to record the actual event that precipitated their increased anxiety (for example, "heart pounding"), as well as the immediate thought about a feared event (for example, "heart attack") that followed the precipitant. They then record the realistic probability of the feared event occurring. The precipitating event must be recorded purely objectively, without any interpretation or added emotion (that is, "pounding heart" rather than "pounding heart making me scared"). Similarly, the thought recorded must be a straightforward description of the feared event, with no added emotion. The group is told that at first it may be difficult to do such monitoring at the actual time of the precipitating event; at this stage, it is perfectly acceptable to analyze the probability of the feared event after the episode has passed. With practice, such rational thinking should become more automatic. The partner is encouraged to discuss the monitoring with the patient and to challenge the patient's beliefs if there is difficulty in identifying the initial thought or assessing the realistic probability of the feared event.

Session 3

Session 3 begins with a discussion of group members' ability to identify overestimations of probability of feared events. In turn, patients read one of their homework examples to the group. The other members are encouraged to discuss the example if there is any difficulty. Partners are questioned about whether they helped to discuss each example throughout the week. In particular, the therapist checks whether each patient was able to carry out the monitoring as specified. Any problems with monitoring are discussed in the group, since this is so important in promoting understanding of the technique. Once the homework has been reviewed, the second stage of cognitive restructuring is introduced. In this stage patients identify the assumed consequences of the event and their rational appraisal of them. This technique has been described by Beck and Emery (1985) as "decatastrophizing."

Once again, the most difficult aspect for patients to master is the identification of the aberrant belief. In some cases, patients may not want to admit to the group or to themselves that they are entertaining a particular belief. The partner can be helpful here, as the patient may have admitted certain beliefs to the partner. At this point, as always, couples should be encouraged to communicate with each other about how much involvement by the partner is comfortable. The idea is not to promote conflict but rather to use the partner to help identify beliefs that the patient may not be aware of or may not have stated. As always, beliefs connected with panic attacks are the primary focus. However, it is useful to point out that other emotional states are amenable to similar modification. The therapist asks the patients to think of their last major panic attack. Patients are then asked, in turn, to identify the worst thing they could envision happening. As each individual describes the most feared consequence imagined during a panic attack, the group and therapist challenge each belief by asking about the realistic probability of the event occurring and about the subsequent realistic consequence if it did. The words *so what* and *what if* are introduced at this point as a way of identifying subsequent consequences ("So what if you feel breathless?"). The group is reminded that anxious individuals often overestimate the negative consequences of events; that is, they catastrophize.

Having by this stage discussed both the overestimation of probability and the overestimation of consequence, patients are in a position to combine techniques to combat these tendencies. To do so, they are encouraged to use the monitoring forms. They are reminded that, at first, most cognitive restructuring will occur after the episode. With practice, however, the ability to challenge beliefs will become more automatic and will begin to occur during the actual episode. The partner may encourage the patient to engage in cognitive restructuring in these early stages.

Here is an example of cognitive restructuring from one of our treatment sessions.

Pt: On Thursday night I had to do my shopping, and I was just walking down the aisle when all of a sudden I began panicking.

Th: What do you mean by "panicking"—what sort of sensations were you actually feeling?

Pt: Well . . . lots of things—mainly I felt dizzy and faint and I had a weak feeling in my legs.

Th: Okay . . . so the actual event then, the objective thing that happened, was that you felt dizzy, faint, and had a weak feeling in your legs.

Pt: Yes.

Th: So that is what you would record in the first column. What was the first thought that flashed into your mind when you had those feelings?

Pt: I thought I was going to faint.

Th: How likely do you think you would be to actually faint?

Pt: Maybe 50%.

Th: You mean you have a one-in-two chance of fainting? Have you ever fainted during a panic attack before?

Pt: No.

Th: Have you ever seen anyone faint in a store before?

Pt: No.

Th: Have you ever heard from friends or relatives that they fainted in a store?

Pt: Yes . . . one of my friends fainted once in a restaurant.

Th: So putting all that together—that you have never fainted during a panic attack before, that you have never seen anyone faint in a store, and that you have only heard of one friend fainting once, do you really believe you had a one-in-two chance of fainting?

Pt: I guess not . . . I suppose maybe I had a 5% chance.

Th: Okay, so now let's imagine you did faint—what would happen to you?

Pt: That would be terrible.

Th: Why? What happened to your friend who fainted?

Pt: Well, not much, I guess. She only blacked out totally for a few seconds and then her boyfriend and the waiter helped her to a couch. She was fine in about 10 minutes.

Th: So what would happen to you if you fainted in a store?

Pt: I guess people would come to my aid and I would come around in a few minutes.

Th: So putting all that together . . . there is really a very small—5%—chance you would faint, and even if you did, nothing terrible would happen to you. I know it's difficult to do, but if you could tell yourself these things at the time you first noticed your symptoms, how anxious do you think you would become?

Pt: Oh . . . maybe a one or a two [on a 0-to-8 scale].

For homework, patients are instructed to record their beliefs and subsequent challenges on the monitoring forms for all panic attacks and any anxiety-provoking situations. They are encouraged to discuss each recording with their partner.

Session 4

Reviewing the previous week's homework is especially important in this session, because most patients will have made many errors in their cognitive restructuring. The problems are discussed in the group so that all members learn from the errors. In addition, the therapist may select some of the examples and redo the challenges as demonstrations to the group.

The remainder of session 4 is devoted to breathing retraining. The aims of the session are to explain that hyperventilation may be an important component of some panic attacks and to teach a technique to control hyperventilation.

Before the term *hyperventilation* is mentioned, all group members (including partners) are asked to intentionally overbreathe for a short period. The overbreathing is done before they have full information, so that they are more likely to be surprised by the effects. This will probably increase the impact of the exercise. The group is instructed to stand and take fast and deep breaths ("as if inflating a balloon") for up to 90 seconds. This period has been found to produce multiple symptoms and considerable anxiety for many patients with panic disorder (Rapee, 1986). The therapist demonstrates by taking three to four deep breaths and exhaling hard at around two to three times the normal rate. Once the group has begun overbreathing the therapist needs to encourage members to continue, because many of them will ease off after a few breaths. Once the 90 seconds is up, group members are instructed to sit, close their eyes, and breathe slowly and calmly. The therapist should count out a slow breathing rate by saying "in" and "out" until most symptoms have abated (around 1 minute).

This demonstration provides an excellent launching pad for a discussion of the role of hyperventilation in panic attacks. First, the group members discuss the symptoms they experienced. Patients are asked about the similarity of these symptoms to the ones they usually experience in a panic attack. They are cautioned that the experience may be somewhat different because they knew what was happening and were in a controlled environment. Partners are also encouraged to discuss their experience and may gain their first insight into what the patient has been experiencing for years.

Following the group discussion, the therapist spends a brief time describing the physiology of hyperventilation. Many patients will have heard the term *hyperventilation* previously but associate it with catastrophic consequences. A discussion of what actually occurs during hyperventilation will help modify this interpretation and should also increase credibility for the technique. It is important that therapists thoroughly understand the physiology of hyperventilation before discussing it with the group and answering questions. There are a number of good descriptions of hyperventilation, including Brown's (1953), Johnson's (1967), and Fried's (1987). Naturally, the discussion must be aimed at the level of the audience. A description that we use and that appears to be acceptable to most individuals with at least a moderate level of education is given here.

> The body needs oxygen to survive. Whenever a person inhales, oxygen is taken into the lungs, where it is picked up by the hemoglobin (the "oxygen-sticky" substance in the blood). The hemoglobin carries the oxygen around the body, where it is released for use by the body's cells. The cells use oxygen in their energy reactions and produce carbon dioxide (CO_2) as a by-product, which is in turn released back to the blood, transported to the lungs, and exhaled.
>
> Efficient control of the body's energy reactions depends on maintaining a specific balance between oxygen and CO_2. This balance is maintained chiefly through an appropriate rate and depth of breathing. Obviously, breathing "too much" will result in increased levels of oxygen (in the blood only) and decreased levels of CO_2; breathing too little will result in decreased levels of oxygen and increased levels of CO_2. The appropriate rate of breathing, at rest, is usually 10 to 14 breaths per minute.
>
> Hyperventilation is defined as a rate and depth of breathing that is too much for the body's needs at a particular point in time. Naturally, if the need for oxygen and the production of CO_2 both increase (such as during exercise), breathing should increase appropriately. Alternatively, if the need for oxygen

and production of CO_2 both decrease (such as during relaxation), breathing should decrease appropriately.

Although most of the body's mechanisms are controlled by "automatic" chemical and physical means (and breathing is no exception), breathing has an additional property of being able to come under voluntary control. For example, it is quite easy for us to hold our breath or speed up our breathing. Therefore, a number of "nonautomatic" factors such as emotion, stress, or habit can cause us to alter our breathing. These factors may be especially important in people who suffer panic attacks, causing them to tend to breathe too much.

Interestingly, though most of us probably assume that oxygen is the determining factor in our breathing, the body actually uses CO_2 as its "marker" for appropriate breathing. The most important effect of hyperventilation is to produce a marked drop in CO_2. This in turn produces a drop in the acid content of the blood, leading to what is known as alkaline blood. It is these two effects—a decrease in blood CO_2 content and an increase in blood alkalinity—that are responsible for most of the physical changes that occur during hyperventilation.

One of the most important changes produced by hyperventilation is a constriction or narrowing of certain blood vessels around the body. In particular, the blood going to the brain is somewhat decreased. Coupled with this tightening of blood vessels is the fact that the hemoglobin increases its "stickiness for oxygen." Thus, not only does less blood reach certain areas of the body, but the oxygen carried by this blood is less likely to be released to the tissues. Paradoxically, while overbreathing takes in more oxygen, we are actually receiving less oxygen in certain areas of our brain and body.

This results in two broad categories of symptoms: (1) centrally, some symptoms are produced by the slight reduction in oxygen to certain parts of the brain (including dizziness, lightheadedness, confusion, breathlessness, blurred vision, and feelings of unreality), and (2) peripherally, some symptoms are produced by the slight reduction in oxygen to certain parts of the body (including an increase in heartbeat to pump more blood around, numbness and tingling in the extremities, cold and clammy hands, and sometimes muscle stiffness). It is important to remember that the reductions in oxygen are slight and totally harmless. Overbreathing (possibly through a reduction in oxygen to certain parts of the brain) can itself produce a feeling of breathlessness, sometimes extending to feelings of choking or smothering, so that the person actually feels as if he or she were not getting enough air.

Hyperventilation is also responsible for a number of other effects. Overbreathing is hard physical work. Hence, the individual may feel hot, flushed, and sweaty. Prolonged periods of overbreathing will often result in exhaustion. In addition, people who overbreathe often tend to breathe from their chest rather than diaphragm. Their chest muscles, which are not made for breathing, tend to become tired and tense. Thus, they may experience chest tightness or even severe chest pains. Finally, many people who overbreathe tend to habitually sigh or yawn. These habits may contribute to the effects of hyperventilation, because yawns and sighs "dump" a large quantity of CO_2 very quickly. Therefore, when combating the problem, it is important to become aware of habitual sighing and yawning and to try to suppress those habits.

Hyperventilation may be very subtle and not at all obvious to the person or the observer. This is especially true if the individual has been slightly overbreathing for a long period of time. In this case, there can be a marked drop in CO_2 but, due to the body's compensation, relatively little change in alkalinity. Thus, symptoms will not be produced. But whenever CO_2 levels are kept low, the body's ability to cope with changes in CO_2 is reduced, so even a slight change in breathing such as a yawn can be enough to suddenly trigger symptoms. This may account for the sudden nature of many panic attacks and is one reason why many sufferers report, "I don't feel as if I am hyperventilating."

Probably the most important point to be made about hyperventilation is that it is not dangerous. Hyperventilation is part of the fight/flight response; its purpose is to protect the body from danger, not to be a danger. Thus, hyperventilation sends an automatic message to the brain to expect immediate danger and prepare to escape. If there is no obvious external danger, the sufferer may believe the danger to be internal. It is important to remember that far from being harmful, hyperventilation is part of a natural, biological response aimed at protecting the body from harm.

Following this discussion, the breathing retraining technique is taught. It is described as both a specific technique to slow breathing during panic attacks and a good general relaxation technique. Thus, partners are also encouraged to practice the technique, which they may find useful. The instructions that we use are as follows.

Because many of the symptoms associated with panic attacks are caused by overbreathing, the best way to overcome a panic attack is to slow your breathing. The exercise that we have found to be best has a meditational component and a breathing component. The meditational component helps you improve your ability to focus your attention. Focusing your attention is important, because it will help you slow your thoughts and concentrate on your breathing if you begin to panic. Controlling your breathing is a skill that takes considerable time and practice to master. Learning to slow your breathing involves several steps. First you must learn to focus on your breathing while you breathe slowly and normally. This is quite difficult for many people; you may find that when you first start to focus on and pace your breathing it begins to speed up. First learn to focus on your breathing and stay at a normal rate and depth—*then* you can begin to slow down.

The following exercise should be practiced for a minimum of 10 minutes, *twice every day*. At first the exercise may be quite difficult. With practice and perseverance, however, it will become easier. Once you are good at controlling your breathing, you should be able to do so anywhere and at any time—but, at first it is best to practice in a quiet, comfortable area. Sit in a comfortable chair and allow yourself a few seconds to calm down.

Meditational component: Basically this involves learning to focus your attention on counting and saying the word *relax* in time with your breathing. Start to count on your in-breaths. That is, when you breathe in, think "1" to yourself; as you breathe out, think "relax." Think "2" on your next breath in and "relax" on the breath out. Continue this up to around "10," and then go back to "1." Ideally, you should think of nothing but your breathing and the words "1, relax," and so on. This is very difficult for some people, and you may never be able to do it perfectly. When you begin, you may not get past "1" without other thoughts coming into your mind. This is perfectly natural. When this happens, do not get angry or give up; simply allow the thoughts to pass and bring your attention back to "1." You may have to practice this many times before you even reach "2." Keep practicing; you will eventually get better. With the meditational component, it is best to first practice in a situation that is not too difficult—for example, in a quiet room and a comfortable chair. Later—perhaps in a number of weeks to months—you may start to practice in more difficult situations, such as during the advertisements on television, on a bus, or while standing in line.

Breathing control component: The first step is to learn to breathe smoothly and normally while counting your breathing. Thus, at first, while you count "1 . . . relax," and so on for each breath, you should breathe at your usual rate and depth. Do not take in too much air and do not yet try to slow your breathing. Just breathe smoothly and easily, as you normally would. When you first begin to count your breaths, you may become breathless or a little dizzy and begin to speed your breathing. If this becomes unbearable, just stop for a short while, calm down, and begin again. While doing the breathing exercise, and in general, you should concentrate on taking slow, smooth breaths, right down to your stomach. If you are having trouble taking the air down to your stomach, try to push your stomach out just before you breathe in so that there is a space for the air to fill. Another method of making this easier is to place one hand on your chest and the other on your stomach while you are practicing the exercise. The idea is for both hands to rise equally, or for your stomach hand to rise more than your chest hand. If your chest hand is rising more than your stomach hand, you are breathing too much from your chest. It is important to take the usual amount of air down to your stomach; do not take in more air to fill the space. When you breathe out, you should not let the air come out too quickly but rather let it escape equally the whole time you are breathing out. Think of the air as oozing and escaping from your nose rather than being suddenly released.

Once you can focus on and count your breathing while still maintaining a smooth, even breath and without feeling dizzy, you can begin to slow your breathing. To do this, simply slow your counting and perhaps pause slightly at each end of the breath. Normal breathing is around 10 to 14 breaths per minute. Once you become very good at this exercise, you should be able to slow your breathing to 10 or less breaths per minute (3 seconds in, 3 seconds out).

It is most important that you practice regularly. If results are not immediate, do not despair; they do take time. It is important to remember that panic attack sensations are caused largely by overbreathing and are a natural response of the body. The breathing control technique can be used as soon as you notice these symptoms beginning to prevent the symptoms of the panic attack from developing. By controlling your breathing, you should be able to stop the symptoms within a few minutes. Nevertheless, there may be times when the symptoms are too strong or you are too anxious to stop the attack.

In such cases, it is important to use the cognitive skills that we have already discussed and will continue to work on in future weeks.

Having described the technique and answered any questions, the therapist asks the whole group to practice for 3 to 4 minutes as he or she directs by counting out loud at a moderate rate. The group members then discuss the experience and ask questions, after which the exercise is repeated. This time, group members are first asked to hyperventilate, using the same technique as before, for about 1 minute. They then use paced breathing to eliminate the symptoms.

Homework is to practice the paced breathing technique at least twice each day for 10 minutes each time. Additional short practice sessions are also encouraged. This first week's practice should focus purely on counting breaths and breathing from the diaphragm at the normal rate of breathing. Slowing the breathing rate should not be attempted until the individual can focus on his or her respiration without altering its rate. This may easily take a week or more. Use of the cognitive monitoring form should continue, along with practice in cognitive restructuring.

Session 5

As usual, the therapist reviews the previous week's homework. The cognitive restructuring attempts are discussed and any difficulties explored. The information about hyperventilation and breathing retraining is briefly reviewed, and group members are encouraged to discuss their reactions to it. The week's practice of breathing control is discussed, and problems are dealt with. Common problems are difficulty finding a time or place to practice, difficulty maintaining concentration for 10 minutes, and the focus on respiration being frightening and actually resulting in some hyperventilation. Because of the importance of the techniques taught up to this point, as much as 50% to 70% of the session should be devoted to homework review. It may be worthwhile to practice paced breathing following hyperventilation again in this session.

The remainder of session 5 is devoted to the principles of in vivo exposure. As with all the other techniques, it is vitally important that patients understand the principles and purpose of exposure before they begin. This is not usually difficult, because exposure is commonsensical; many patients will already have attempted a similar approach, though their success may have been limited. The following introduction may be used.

> The fundamental principle is that you must face the situations you fear to overcome the fear. Fear reduction happens partly because you learn that the feared situations are not really dangerous. Although cognitive restructuring and paced breathing can be used to control anxiety and speed the process, unfortunately it is necessary to experience anxiety in order to overcome anxiety. This task is made easier by approaching the fears in a gradual, paced fashion that you control yourself.

To explain the basis of exposure treatment, it is often helpful to use an example of a common fear, such as a simple phobia or performance fear. The following is one such example.

> Try to imagine a new teacher going in to teach her first class. This teacher is likely to be somewhat anxious even the day before the class. As the time approaches, her anxiety increases steadily until it could be as high as 4 on a 0-to-8 scale when she is standing outside the classroom door. As she opens the door and sees the class, her anxiety probably escalates to a 7 or even an 8. If she were to run away at that point, it would be even harder to go back the next time. But, if she continued in and began to teach, eventually she would realize that the situation was not so bad. This realization could be accelerated by using cognitive restructuring to realistically appraise the worst possible scenario. Even if she didn't do this, eventually her anxiety would begin to decrease. By the end of the class, her anxiety could be as low as 2 or 3. The next day she would probably be anxious again, but when she reached the door her anxiety would probably be only a 3. When she opened the door, her anxiety would escalate but probably less than on the previous day. In addition, once in the class, her anxiety level would probably decrease more rapidly. This pattern would continue, with fluctuations, each day until eventually the teacher faced the class with no anxiety. All fears and anxieties follow the same basic pattern, and this is the principle that we would like you to apply to your own. Naturally there will be individual variations, but if you confront the situations you fear in a gradual and regular manner, you will find a general decrease in the anxiety you experience in response to them.

The therapist could then give another example, using an agoraphobic fear. Because credibility and motivation are especially important, it is a good idea to try to preempt questions, the most common themes of which are described here. Some patients confront their fears almost daily as part of their work or a regular chore, without any fear reduction. This is a particularly intriguing phenomenon that may have something to do with both attitude and the degree of cognitive engagement. It should be stressed that engaging in exposure "because you have to" is likely to be very different from doing it "because you want to." For example, exposing yourself to a situation because it is part of your job is likely to lead to self-statements such as the following: "I'll grit my teeth and bear it, and if I survive, I'm lucky." This is very different from doing the same thing because you want to and because it is part of treatment—"survival" is then an accomplishment and cause for self-congratulation. Similarly, when performing a task as part of work you are not as likely to process information telling you that the situation is really safe. You are more likely to be concentrating on the work and generally trying to distract yourself. In addition, it is possible to "expose" yourself regularly and yet experience no decrease in anxiety levels because of subtle forms of avoidance. This may include cognitive avoidance (such as distraction or pretending you are not there) and subtle behaviors (such as leaning against a wall when you feel dizzy).

Another point that is useful to discuss is the difference between "good days" and "bad days." Patients will probably comment that on some days they can do virtually anything, whereas on others their whole life seems restricted. The therapist should first stress that everyone, even the nonanxious, has bad days. These are not caused by some mysterious increase in fear; they are simply days when the individual is feeling tired, stressed, or generally less able to cope because of various bodily changes. Patients need not attempt on their bad days what they have achieved on a good day. But they should do *something*. With practice, what they can do on bad days will eventually equal what they have done on good days.

A third and particularly important point to discuss is how to experience panic attacks. Many patients believe that the goal of gradual exposure is to learn to approach situations without experiencing a panic attack. But it is vital to experience panic attacks to learn to cope with them. The attacks should be reconceptualized, not as terrible, dangerous experiences but rather as harmless physiological sensations. In vivo exposure may be couched in terms of learning to experience physiological sensations without fear. Once this is mastered, the fundamental fear will be eliminated and exposure to feared situations easier.

The importance of regular, repeated practice cannot be stressed enough. And practice will not always proceed in a smooth fashion; there may be minor setbacks. As these are to be expected, practice should continue as soon as possible following a setback. Our patients are warned that if they stop practicing for a time, the fear is likely to reappear to some degree, though probably to a lesser degree than originally.

The partner's role in exposure in vivo is also discussed. Partners can be involved in many ways, and their precise role should be a matter for extensive discussion by the couple. "How much should I push?" is a question often asked by partners. Good communication is vital here, because each patient has different needs. The partner may be included in the actual exercise, accompanying the patient the first few times and then gradually fading out. While accompanying the patient, the partner may prompt cognitive restructuring. Even if he or she does not accompany the patient, the partner is encouraged to discuss the practice and the cognitive restructuring both before and after the practice. The partner can be a major source of encouragement, especially following setbacks. Finally, the partner may help organize the practice assignments. For each practice, a specific date and time should be arranged so that the patient cannot keep postponing. Partners can ensure that patients arrange feasible and regular practice assignments and that they do their practice as specified.

After the therapist airs all these issues, the group is given about 5 minutes for each couple to arrange the first in vivo exposure practice. The patient is instructed to select a situation that is practical and that can be practiced at least three times in the coming week. It should produce some degree of anxiety but not be beyond the patient's current abilities. A situation producing an anxiety level of 3 to 4 is often a good start. Once each couple has decided on the practice assignment, the patient should announce it to the group, to promote accountability and encourage group cohesion.

When carrying out this homework assignment, patients are asked to keep a record of their average and maximum anxiety during each practice, on the usual 0-to-8 scale. This record can be used as an indication of progress. In addition, many patients report that rating the anxiety on a numerical scale during exposure assignments helps to decatastrophize them and thereby lessens the anxiety. Practice with cognitive restructuring and paced breathing should also continue throughout the week, and these techniques should be used during the in vivo practice when applicable.

Session 6

The therapist reviews the week's homework in the usual manner. Discussion of the in vivo exposure exercises requires most of the session. Patients describe to the group, in detail, their practice during the week. In particular, they should specify the somatic sensations experienced, the duration of the task, their anxiety levels throughout the task, and any attempts they made to cope with or control their anxiety. Cognitive restructuring attempts may have been more difficult under these circumstances, so it may be useful for therapists to systematically discuss any such attempts. Partners are asked to describe their perspective and the role they played. Partners and other group members are prompted to provide generous encouragement to the patient. Patients are asked how satisfied they were with the attempt. This point is especially important, as some patients may be disappointed in their first attempt. The therapist stresses that any attempt, no matter how minimal, is valuable and emphasizes that improvement will take time and practice. This may be a good time to discuss the debilitating effects of depression and self-disparagement. One reason that records of avoidant behavior are helpful is that patients can look back and objectively see how much they have improved at times when they are feeling discouraged. The partner plays a very important role in helping with encouragement and motivation. Alternatively, some patients will have had extremely good experiences and will be feeling as if they are virtually cured. With these patients it is important to stress that overall improvement takes time. It is quite possible to have an especially good week followed by a minor setback. If a setback occurs, it should be seen not as a failure but as a learning opportunity. The therapist emphasizes that progress with exposure will be variable, and that there is a great deal to learn about coping with stress and anxiety.

Once the week's assignments have been discussed, the next step in exposure can be introduced: exposure to the physical sensations associated with panic attacks. The model of panic attacks is reviewed briefly to remind the group that a panic attack is simply bodily sensations to which an individual responds with fear. These sensations may be viewed as just another experience that the person may attempt to avoid. The fear of bodily sensations may be reduced by arranging exposure exercises in the same way as for external events. In other words, the sensations experienced in panic attacks may be produced intentionally in a gradually more intense fashion, so that the patient learns that these internal events are harmless and need not be feared.

Various methods of producing bodily sensations are discussed, and the group is encouraged to be as inventive as possible. Some ways in which somatic sensations can be produced easily are shaking the head from side to side with the eyes open, tensing all the muscles in the body, running in place or stepping on and off a chair to increase heart rate, spinning around to produce feelings of dizziness, or hyperventilating (see Barlow & Cerny, 1988, for a more detailed discussion). In addition, a number of external activities may also be used to produce internal sensations, including fast fairground rides, saunas, frightening movies, or exercise classes.

The group then practices some of the symptom induction techniques, to rate the degree of fear produced by each. Patients are asked to select the technique that most closely reproduces the bodily sensations that occur during their panic attacks. They then practice those techniques at a level that results in moderate anxiety for 5 to 10 minutes. During this practice, they should continually rate their anxiety level while their partner prompts decatastrophizing. The therapist moves around the group and helps any couples having difficulty. If any distress remains in the group following the interoceptive practices (exposure to internal bodily sensations associated with anxiety), the therapist can initiate 2 to 3 minutes of paced breathing.

Finally, 5 to 10 minutes is provided for the group members to arrange in vivo exposure practice for the coming week. In addition to the minimum of three practices in feared external situations, they should also decide on an interoceptive exercise to attempt daily. The group is reminded that paced breathing practice should continue, as it takes considerable effort to become skilled in this technique.

Further Sessions

The remaining treatment sessions are devoted to discussing homework assignments, monitoring progress, and discussing any problems that arise. Couples are encouraged to communicate about treatment progress and problems. They are encouraged to take increasing responsibility for devising their own solutions to treatment problems.

As in vivo exposure continues successfully, patients are likely to encounter situations that they feel are irrelevant to them. For example, they may identify a fear of flying but say that they will never have to fly anyway. Nevertheless, they should be encouraged to confront such fears. The rationale is that learning to overcome even "irrelevant" or minor fears will allow them to make choices in their lives rather than be controlled by their fears.

The focus of later sessions will vary depending on the specific needs of the group or individual. The application of cognitive techniques to general anxiety, anger, and depression may be very important. These mood states are strongly connected with panic attacks and agoraphobic avoidance and may also be partly responsible for maintenance of the problem. A second area of focus might be communication skills. While the importance of good communication is stressed throughout treatment, this may require additional attention. Panic disorder places a tremendous strain on relationships, which results in major adjustments. Any alteration in the problem requires readjustment. Open, honest communication is vital during this time. Secondary gain factors may also be involved in the maintenance of some phobic avoidance. This may be a particular problem for some patients who have developed a lifestyle to accommodate their panic attacks that provides them with inherent reinforcement. These patients will not improve with the usual procedures until these reinforcers have been challenged. Put simply, it requires tremendous effort and considerable distress to overcome panic disorder. If living with panic disorder is relatively comfortable, or is at least as comfortable as living without it, there will be little motivation to change. Social anxiety is commonly associated with panic disorder and is even more strongly associated with increasing agoraphobic avoidance (Rapee et al., in press). For some patients, specific cognitive and exposure treatment for problems with social phobia may result in a more generalized improvement. Additional problems that may have to be addressed include poor social skills, unassertiveness, and lack of job skills (see Chapter 12 for a fuller discussion).

The number of treatment sessions depends on the nature and progress of the group. In our clinic, groups for individuals suffering panic disorder with moderate-to-severe avoidance currently meet for 12 sessions over a period of 16 weeks. Individuals with less severe problems may require less treatment. We have one group for individuals suffering infrequent panic attacks and minimal avoidance that meets for only 8 sessions. The actual number of sessions can be left partly up to the group. In this case, however, the therapist should be aware that some individuals display marked dependency traits and may not want to stop group meetings. To facilitate separation, it is often useful to arrange biweekly meetings for the last two to three sessions.

The last session focuses on termination issues. A brief review of the information and skills covered in the program is a good starting point. It must be stressed that improvement does not cease just because formal group meetings no longer occur. The couple must take charge of the problem and keep practicing skills and confronting feared events. If experience with a particular situation stops for a time, anticipatory anxiety may recur to some degree. However, arranging gradual exposure again will soon reduce any emergent anxiety. Patients are warned that they will probably experience intense bodily sensations related to their panic attacks again at some point. This can occur for a number of reasons, including physical illness, stress, and challenging life events. They should understand that these are natural and expected occurrences. As long as they do not fear the sensations, they will not panic. At times it may be necessary to repeat the formal practice of skills and exposure.

It is a good idea to organize another group meeting at some later date, say in 3 to 6 months, to check on progress. Such a meeting should be organized at the time of the final session, to provide patients with a temporal goal. It is often a good idea to set tasks that must be completed by the follow-up session. If patients encounter minor difficulties, they should be encouraged to contact the therapist, who can discuss their problem over the telephone or arrange an occasional individual session. For those patients who encounter major difficulties or relapse, "booster" sessions are a useful addition. In these sessions the therapist reminds individuals of the skills they have learned and focuses on issues pertinent to the individual patient. In our experience, only a small proportion of individuals request such booster sessions. These sessions stress homework and intersession exercises to help foster independence. In addition, patients are only permitted to attend a maximum of 12 sessions, after which they must spend 3 months out of therapy before returning to the booster group a second time. Very few patients feel the need to attend more than one series of booster sessions. (See Chapter 12 for more information on the difficult patient.)

In summary, the fundamental purpose of treatment is to teach patients with panic disorder that the physical symptoms they experience are natural and adaptive, not harmful. Patients must learn that they do have control over their emotional reactions. It is important for this reason that patients play an active role in treatment. Successful treatment involves major changes in a number of attitudes and behaviors. For treatment to succeed, they must be willing to devote considerable time and energy to it and to accept some discomfort. Given these premises, the techniques described in the preceding section are likely to be effective in the treatment of panic disorder.

The Long-range View

Cognitive-behavioral treatments for panic disorder with or without avoidance are successful and are becoming more familiar to both patients and professionals. Nevertheless, a great deal of work remains to be done to improve these techniques. In particular, treatment for patients suffering from panic disorder with severe avoidance is difficult. Preliminary results from our center and others indicate that up to 80% of panic disorder patients with mild avoidance can be panic free following treatment. However, typically only 50% or fewer of panic disorder patients with moderate to severe avoidance display high-end state functioning at posttreatment assessment. There are two possible explanations. First, it is likely that patients with severe avoidance are less willing and able, for various reasons, to practice the techniques emphasized in treatment. To address this factor, future research needs to examine more closely the parameters underlying compliance, motivation, and maintenance of treatment gains and maladaptive behaviors. Second, it may be that the techniques currently in use are not effective for all aspects of panic disorder. If this is the case, particular emphasis should be placed on developing and testing models of the etiology and maintenance of this disorder. In particular, more research is needed on avoidance behavior. As mentioned earlier, dependency, social anxiety, and an insufficient sense of personal control may all be important factors. Such factors need to be defined and studied more explicitly.

The psychological treatment of panic attacks is still a relatively new area. Much empirical work is needed to establish the parameters of effective treatment. In addition, the emerging psychological/physiological models require refinement and empirical validation. The relationships between the theoretical factors and the specific components of treatment described in this chapter also require further study. For example, recently Barlow (1988) has outlined a new theoretical base for the treatment of emotional disorders based on emotion theory. This approach is described as "affective therapy." In this model, there are both essential targets for change and helpful but not essential targets for change (see Table 7.2). In the case of panic disorder, the primary purpose of in vivo exposure is to modify escape action tendencies associated with the emotion of fear. An action tendency is a behavior or set of behaviors inherently associated with an emotion. Other components of therapy would be aimed at increasing one's sense of control as well as decreasing the self-focused attention and self-preoccupation that allows anxiety to spiral to disruptive levels. This theory of treatment is outlined in detail in Barlow (1988).

TABLE 7.2 Components of Any Affective Therapy

A. Essential targets for change

   1. Action tendencies
   2. A sense of uncontrollability or unpredictability
   3. Self-focused attention

B. Helpful but not essential targets for change

   1. "Hot" apprehensive cognitions
   2. Hypervalent cognitive schemata and attention narrowing
   3. Coping skills and social support
   4. Elevated psychological responding and altered neurobiological functions

---

SOURCE: Barlow, D. H. (1988). *Anxiety and its disorders*, p. 318. New York: Guilford Press. Reprinted with permission.

In brief, while the cognitive-behavioral treatment of panic disorder is promising, much of the rationale for this treatment is still based on clinical folklore and intuition. Future research must anchor all these factors, both theoretically and empirically. In this way, we will be able to maximize their effectiveness and efficiency.

References

Agras, W. S., Leitenberg, H., & Barlow, D. H. (1968). Social reinforcement in the modification of agoraphobia. *Archives of General Psychiatry, 19*, 423–427.

Andrews, J. D. W. (1966). Psychotherapy of phobias. *Psychological Bulletin, 66*, 455–480.

Arena, J. G., Blanchard, E. B., Andrasik, F., Cotch, B. A., & Meyers, P. E. (1983). Reliability of psychophysiological assessment. *Behaviour Research and Therapy, 21*, 447–460.

Arnow, B. A., Taylor, C. B., Agras, W. S., & Telch, M. J. (1985). Enhancing agoraphobia treatment outcome by changing couple communication patterns. *Behavior Therapy, 16*, 452–467.

Bandura, A. (1977). *Social learning theory.* Englewood Cliffs, NJ: Prentice-Hall.

Barlow, D. H. (Ed.) (1981). *Behavioral assessment of adult disorders.* New York: Guilford Press.

Barlow, D. H. (1986). Behavioral conception and treatment of panic. *Psychopharmacology Bulletin, 22*, 802–806.

Barlow, D. H. (1988). *Anxiety and its disorders.* New York: Guilford Press.

Barlow, D. H., & Cerny, J. A. (1988). *Psychological treatment of panic.* New York: Guilford Press.

Barlow, D. H., Cohen, A. S., Waddell, M. T., Vermilyea, B. B., Klosko, J. S., Blanchard, E. B., & DiNardo, P. A. (1984). Panic and generalized anxiety disorders: Nature and treatment. *Behavior Therapy, 15*, 431–449.

Barlow, D. H., Hayes, S. C., & Nelson, R. O. (1984). *The scientist-practitioner: Research and accountability in clinical and educational settings.* New York: Pergamon Press.

Barlow, D. H., O'Brien, G. T., & Last, C. G. (1984). Couples treatment of agoraphobia. *Behavior Therapy, 15*, 41–58.

Barlow, D. H., Vermilyea, J., Blanchard, E. B., Vermilyea, B. B., DiNardo, P. A., & Cerny, J. A. (1985). The phenomenon of panic. *Journal of Abnormal Psychology, 94*, 320–328.

Bass, C., Kartsounis, L., & Lelliott, P. (in press). Hyperventilation and its relationship with anxiety and panic. *Integrative Psychiatry.*

Beck, A. T. (1976). *Cognitive therapy and the emotional disorders.* New York: Meridian.

Beck, A. T. (1988). Cognitive approaches to panic disorder: Theory and therapy. In S. Rachman & J. D. Maser (Eds.), *Panic: Psychological perspectives*, Hillsdale, NJ: Lawrence Erlbaum.

Beck, A. T., & Emery, G. (1985). *Anxiety disorders and phobias: A cognitive perspective.* New York: Basic Books.

Beck, A. T., Laude, R., & Bohnert, M. (1974). Ideational components of anxiety neurosis. *Archives of General Psychiatry, 31*, 319–325.

Berg, I., Marks, I., McGuire, R., & Lipsedge, M. (1974). School phobia and agoraphobia. *Psychological Medicine, 4*, 428–434.

Bernstein, D. A., & Borkovec, T. D. (1973). *Progressive relaxation training.* Champaign, IL: Research Press.

Bland, K., & Hallam, R. S. (1981). Relationship between response to exposure and marital satisfaction in agoraphobics. *Behaviour Research and Therapy, 19*, 335–338.

Bonn, J. A., Harrison, J., & Rees, L. (1973). Lactate infusion in the treatment of 'free-floating' anxiety. *Canadian Psychiatric Association Journal, 18*, 41–45.

Bonn, J. A., Readhead, C. P. A., & Timmons, B. H. (1984). Enhanced adaptive behavioural response in agoraphobic patients pretreated with breathing retraining. *The Lancet, 2*, 665–669.

Borkovec, T. D., & Nau, J. D. (1972). Credibility of analogue therapy rationales. *Journal of Behavior Therapy and Experimental Psychiatry, 3*, 257–260.

Bowlby, J. (1973). *Attachment and loss: Separation, anxiety, and anger: Vol. 2. Separation.* New York: Basic Books.

Brown, E. B., Jr. (1953). Physiological effects of hyperventilation. *Physiological Reviews, 33*, 445–471.

Buglass, D., Clarke, J., Henderson, A. S., Kreitman, N., & Presley, A. S. (1977). A study of agoraphobic housewives. *Psychological Medicine, 7*, 73–86.

Butler, G., & Mathews, A. (1983). Cognitive processes in anxiety. *Advances in Behavior Research and Therapy, 5*, 51–62.

Cerny, J. A., Barlow, D. H., Craske, M., & Himadi, W. G. (1987). Couples treatment of agoraphobia: A two-year follow-up. *Behavior Therapy, 18*, 401–415.

Chambless, D. L. (1985). The relationship of severity of agoraphobia to associated psychopathology. *Behaviour Research and Therapy, 23*, 305–310.

Chambless, D. L., Caputo, G. C., Bright, P., & Gallagher, R. (1984). Assessment of fear in agoraphobics: The Body Sensations Questionnaire and the Agoraphobic Cognitions Questionnaire. *Journal of Consulting and Clinical Psychology, 52*, 1090–1097.

Chambless, D. L., Caputo, G. C., Jasin, S. E., Gracely, E. J., & Williams, C. (1985). The Mobility Inventory for Agoraphobia. *Behaviour Research and Therapy, 23*, 35–44.

Chambless, D. L., Foa, E. B., Groves, G. A., & Goldstein, A. J. (1979). Flooding with Brevital in the treatment of agoraphobia: Counter-effective? *Behaviour Research and Therapy, 17*, 243–251.

Chambless, D. L., & Goldstein, A. J. (1981). Clinical treatment of agoraphobia. In M. Mavissakalian & D. H. Barlow (Eds.), *Phobia: Psychological and pharmacological treatment.* New York: Guilford Press.

Chambless, D. L., & Mason, J. (1986). Sex, sex role stereotyping, and agoraphobia. *Behaviour Research and Therapy, 24*, 231–235.

Clark, D. M. (1986). A cognitive approach to panic. *Behaviour Research and Therapy, 24*, 461–470.

Clark, D. M., & Hemsley, D. R. (1982). The effects of hyperventilation: Individual variability and its relation to personality. *Journal of Behavior Therapy and Experimental Psychiatry, 13*, 41–47.

Clark, D. M., Salkovskis, P. M., & Chalkley, A. J. (1985). Respiratory control as a treatment for panic attacks. *Journal of Behavior Therapy and Experimental Psychiatry, 16*, 23–30.

Clarke, J. C., & Jackson, J. A. (1983). *Hypnosis and behavior therapy: The treatment of anxiety and phobias.* New York: Springer.

Cobb, J. P., Mathews, A. M., Childs-Clarke, A., & Blowers, C. M. (1984). The spouse as co-therapist in the treatment of agoraphobia. *British Journal of Psychiatry, 144*, 282–287.

Craske, M. G. (1988). Cognitive-behavioral treatment of panic. In A. J. Frances & R. E. Hales, *American Psychiatric Press annual review of psychiatry* (Vol 7, pp. 121–137). Washington, DC: American Psychiatric Press.

Craske, M. G., & Barlow, D. H. (1987). *Behavioral treatment of panic: A controlled study.* Paper presented at the annual meeting of the Association for the Advancement of Behavior Therapy, Boston, MA.

Craske, M. G., Rachman, S. J., & Tallman, K. (1986). Mobility, cognitions and panic. *Journal of Psychopathology and Behavioral Assessment, 8*, 199–210.

Craske, M. G., Rapee, R. M., & Barlow, D. H. (1988). The significance of panic-expectancy for individual patterns of avoidance. *Behavior Therapy 19*, 577–592.

Craske, M. G., Sanderson, W. C., & Barlow, D. H. (1987). The relationship among panic, fear and avoidance. *Journal of Anxiety Disorders, 1*, 153–160.

DeSilva, P., & Rachman, S. (1984). Does escape behaviour strengthen agoraphobic avoidance? A preliminary study. *Behaviour Research and Therapy, 22*, 87–91.

Ehlers, A., Margraf, J., Roth, W. T., Taylor, C. B., & Birbaumer, N. (1988). Anxiety induced by false heart rate feedback in patients with panic disorder. *Behaviour Research and Therapy, 26*, 1–12.

Ellis, A., & Harper, R. A. (1975). *A new guide to rational living*. Englewood Cliffs, NJ: Prentice-Hall.

Emmelkamp, P. M. G. (1974). Self-observation versus flooding in the treatment of agoraphobia. *Behaviour Research and Therapy, 22*, 87–91.

Emmelkamp, P. M. G. (1980). Agoraphobics' interpersonal problems: Their role in the effects of exposure *in vivo* therapy. *Archives of General Psychiatry, 37*, 1303–1306.

Emmelkamp, P. M. G. (1982). *Phobic and obsessive-compulsive disorders: Theory research and practice*. New York: Plenum.

Emmelkamp, P. M. G., & Cohen-Kettenis, P. T. (1975). Relationship of locus of control to phobic anxiety and depression. *Psychological Reports, 36*, 390.

Emmelkamp, P. M. G., Kuipers, A. C. M., & Eggeraat, J. G. (1978). Cognitive modification versus prolonged exposure *in vivo*: A comparison with agoraphobics as subjects. *Behaviour Research and Therapy, 16*, 33–41.

Emmelkamp, P. M. G., van den Hout, A., & De Vries, K. (1983). Assertive training for agoraphobics. *Behaviour Research and Therapy, 21*, 63–68.

Eysenck, H. J. (1976). The learning theory model of neurosis: A new approach. *Behaviour Research and Therapy, 14*, 251–267.

Fisher, L. M., & Wilson, G. T. (1985). A study of the psychology of agoraphobia. *Behaviour Research and Therapy, 23*, 97–107.

Foa, E. B., & Kozak, M. J. (1986). Emotional processing of fear: Exposure to corrective information. *Psychological Bulletin, 99*, 20–35.

Franklin, J. A. (1989). A 6-year follow-up of the effectiveness of respiratory retraining, in-situ isometric relaxation, and cognitive modification in the treatment of agoraphobia. *Behavior Modification, 13* (2), 139–167.

Fried, R. (1987). *The hyperventilation syndrome: Research and clinical treatment*. Baltimore: Johns Hopkins University Press.

Garssen, B., van Veenendaal, W., & Bloemink, R. (1983). Agoraphobia and the hyperventilation syndrome. *Behaviour Research and Therapy, 21*, 643–649.

Gelder, M. G., Bancroft, J. H. J., Gath, D. H., Johnston, D. W., Mathews, A. M., & Shaw, P. M. (1973). Specific and nonspecific factors in behaviour therapy. *British Journal of Psychiatry, 123*, 445–462.

Gerz, H. O. (1966). Experience with the logotherapeutic technique of paradoxical intention in the treatment of phobic and obsessive-compulsive patients. *American Journal of Psychiatry, 123*, 548–553.

Ghosh, A., & Marks, I. M. (1987). Self-treatment of agoraphobia by exposure. *Behavior Therapy, 18*, 3–16.

Gitlin, B., Martin, J., Shear, M. K., Frances, A., Ball, G., & Josephson, S. (1985). Behavior therapy for panic disorder. *The Journal of Nervous and Mental Disease, 173*, 742–743.

Gittelman, R., & Klein, D. F. (1985). Childhood separation anxiety and adult agoraphobia. In A. H. Tuma & J. D. Maser (Eds.), *Anxiety and the anxiety disorders* (pp. 389–411). Hillsdale, NJ: Lawrence Erlbaum.

Goldstein, A. J. (1978). Case conference: The treatment of a case of agoraphobia by a multifaceted treatment program. *Journal of Behavior Therapy and Experimental Psychiatry, 9,* 45–51.

Goldstein, A. J., & Chambless, D. L. A. (1978). A reanalysis of agoraphobia. *Behavior Therapy, 9,* 47–59.

Gorman, J. M., Cohen, B. S., Liebowitz, M. R., Fyer, A. J., Ross, D., Davies, S. O., & Klein, D. F. (1986). Blood gas changes and hypophosphatemia in lactate induced panic. *Archives of General Psychiatry, 43,* 1067–1071.

Griez, E., & van den Hout, M. A. (1983). Treatment of phobophobia by exposure to CO_2 induced anxiety symptoms. *Journal of Nervous and Mental Disease, 171,* 506–508.

Griez, E., & van den Hout, M. A. (1986). CO_2 inhalation in the treatment of panic attacks. *Behaviour Research and Therapy, 24,* 145–150.

Hafner, J., & Marks, I. (1976). Exposure *in vivo* of agoraphobics: Contributions of diazepam, group exposure, and anxiety evocation. *Psychological Medicine, 6,* 71–88.

Hibbert, G. A. (1984). Ideational components of anxiety: Their origin and content. *British Journal of Psychiatry, 144,* 618–624.

Hoehn-Saric, R. (1981). Characteristics of chronic anxiety patients. In D. F. Klein & J. Rabkin (Eds.), *Anxiety: New research and changing concepts.* New York: Raven Press.

Holden, A. E., & Barlow, D. H. (1986). Heart rate and heart rate variability recorded *in vivo* in agoraphobics and nonphobics. *Behavior Therapy, 17,* 26–42.

Holden, A. E., Jr., O'Brien, G. T., Barlow, D. H., Stetson, D., & Infantino, A. (1983). Self-help manual for agoraphobia: A preliminary report of effectiveness. *Behavior Therapy, 14,* 545–556.

Holloway, W., & McNally, R. J. (1987). Effects of anxiety sensitivity on the response to hyperventilation. *Journal of Abnormal Psychology, 96,* 330–334.

Izard, C. E. (1977). *Human emotions.* New York: Plenum.

Jansson, L., & Öst, L. (1982). Behavioral treatments for agoraphobia: An evaluative review. *Clinical Psychology Review, 2,* 311–336.

Johnson, C. (1967). The physiology of hyperventilation. In T. P. Lowry (Ed.), *Hyperventilation and hysteria.* Springfield, IL: Charles C. Thomas.

Klein, D. F. (1964). Delineation of two drug-responsive anxiety syndromes. *Psychopharmacologia, 5,* 397–408.

Klein, D. F. (1981). Anxiety reconceptualized. In D. F. Klein & J. Rabkin (Eds.), *Anxiety: New research and changing concepts* (pp. 164–235). New York: Raven Press.

Kleiner, L., & Marshall, W. L. (1985). Relationship difficulties and agoraphobia. *Clinical Psychology Review, 5,* 581–595.

Klosko, J. S., Barlow, D. H., Tassinari, R. B., & Cerny, J. A. (1987). *Comparison of alprazolam and cognitive behavior therapy in the treatment of panic disorder: A preliminary report.* Paper presented at the annual convention of the Association for the Advancement of Behavior Therapy, Boston, MA.

Lang, P. J. (1984). Cognition in emotion: Concept and action. In C. Izard, J. Kagan, & R. Zajonc (Eds.), *Emotion, cognition, and behavior* (pp. 192–225). New York: Cambridge University Press.

Levinsky, N. E. (1983). Acidosis and alkalosis. In R. Petersdorf, E. Adams, E. Braunwald, K. Isselbacher, J. Martin, & J. Wilson (Eds.), *Principles of internal medicine.* New York: McGraw-Hill.

Ley, R. (1985). Blood, breath and fears: A hyperventilation theory of panic attacks and agoraphobia. *Clinical Psychology Review, 5,* 271–285.

Lum, L. C. (1976). The syndrome of habitual chronic hyperventilation. In O. W. Hill (Ed.), *Modern trends in psychosomatic medicine, Vol. 3.* London: Butterworth.

Lum, L. C. (1981). Hyperventilation and anxiety states. *Journal of the Royal Society of Medicine, 74,* 1–4.

Magarian, G. I. (1982). Hyperventilation syndromes: Infrequently recognized common expressions of anxiety and stress. *Medicine, 61,* 219–236.

Maller, R. G., & Reiss, S. (in press). A behavioral validation of the Anxiety Sensitivity Index. *Journal of Anxiety Disorders.*

Margraf, J., Ehlers, A., & Roth, W. T. (1987). Panic attacks associated with perceived heart rate acceleration: A case report. *Behavior Therapy, 18,* 84–89.

Marks, I. M. (1981). New developments in psychological treatments of phobias. In M. Mavissakalian & D. H. Barlow (Eds.), *Phobia: Psychological and pharmacological treatment.* New York: Guilford Press.

Marks, I. M., Boulougouris, J. C., & Marset, P. (1971). Flooding versus desensitization in the treatment of phobic patients: A cross-over study. *British Journal of Psychiatry, 119,* 353–375.

Marks, I. M., & Mathews, A. M. (1979). Brief standard self-rating for phobic patients. *Behaviour Research and Therapy, 17,* 263–267.

Marshall, W. L., Gauthier, J., & Gordon, A. (1979). The current status of flooding therapy. In M. Hersen, R. M. Eisler, & P. Miller (Eds.), *Progress in behavior therapy, Vol. 7.* New York: Academic Press.

Mathews, A. M., Gelder, M. G., & Johnston, D. W. (1981). *Agoraphobia: Nature and treatment.* New York: Guilford Press.

Mavissakalian, M. (1986a). The Fear Questionnaire: A validity study. *Behaviour Research and Therapy, 24,* 83–85.

Mavissakalian, M. (1986b). Clinically significant improvement in agoraphobia research. *Behaviour Research and Therapy, 24,* 369–370.

Mavissakalian, M., & Hamann, M. S. (1987). DSM-III personality disorder in agoraphobia. II. Changes with treatment. *Comprehensive Psychiatry, 28,* 356–361.

Michelson, L., Mavissakalian, M., Marchione, K., Dancu, C., & Greenwald, M. (1986). The role of self-directed *in vivo* exposure practice in cognitive, behavioral, and psychophysiological treatments of agoraphobia. *Behavior Therapy, 17,* 91–108.

Milton, F., & Hafner, J. (1979). The outcome of behavior therapy for agoraphobia in relation to marital adjustment. *Archives of General Psychiatry, 36,* 807–811.

Norton, G. R., Dorward, J., & Cox, B. J. (1986). Factors associated with panic attacks in nonclinical subjects. *Behavior Therapy, 17,* 239–252.

Öst, L. B. (1988). Applied relaxation vs. progressive relaxation in the treatment of panic disorder. *Behaviour Research and Therapy, 26,* 13–22.

Parker, G. (1979). Reported parental characteristics of agoraphobics and school phobics. *British Journal of Psychiatry, 135,* 555–560.

Pitts, F. N., Jr., & McClure, J. N., Jr. (1967). Lactate metabolism in anxiety neurosis. *New England Journal of Medicine, 277,* 1329–1336.

Rachman, S. (1984). Agoraphobia—A safety-signal perspective. *Behaviour Research and Therapy, 22,* 59–70.

Rachman, S., Craske, M., Tallman, K., & Solyom, C. (1986). Does escape behavior strengthen agoraphobic avoidance? A replication. *Behavior Therapy, 17,* 366–384.

Rachman, S. J., Lopatka, C., & Levitt, K. (1988). Experimental analyses of panic. II. Panic patients. *Behaviour Research and Therapy, 26,* 33–40.

Rapee, R. (1985a). A case of panic disorder treated with breathing retraining. *Journal of Behavior Therapy and Experimental Psychiatry, 16,* 63–65.

Rapee, R. (1985b). Distinctions between panic disorder and generalized anxiety disorder: Clinical presentation. *Australian and New Zealand Journal of Psychiatry, 19,* 227–232.

Rapee, R. (1986). Differential response to hyperventilation in panic disorder and generalized anxiety disorder. *Journal of Abnormal Psychology, 95,* 24–28.

Rapee, R. (1987). The psychological treatment of panic attacks: Theoretical conceptualization and review of evidence. *Clinical Psychology Review, 7,* 427–438.

Rapee, R. M., Ancis, J. R., & Barlow, D. H. (1988). Emotional reactions to physiological sensations: Panic disorder patients and nonclinical subjects. *Behaviour Research and Therapy, 26,* 265–269.

Rapee, R. M., & Barlow, D. H. (1988). Assessment of panic disorder. In P. McReynolds, S. C. Rosen, & G. Chelune (Eds.), *Advances in psychological assessment, Vol. 7.* New York: Plenum.

Rapee, R., Mattick, R., & Murrell, E. (1986). Cognitive mediation in the affective component of spontaneous panic attacks. *Journal of Behavior Therapy and Experimental Psychiatry, 17,* 245–253.

Rapee, R. M., & Murrell, E. (1988). Predictors of agoraphobic avoidance. *Journal of Anxiety Disorders, 2,* 203–218.

Rapee, R. M., Sanderson, W. C., & Barlow, D. H. (in press). Social phobia features across the DSM-III-R anxiety disorders. *Journal of Psychopathology and Behavioral Assessment.*

Raskin, M., Peeke, H. V. S., Dickman, W., & Pinsker, H. (1982). Panic and generalized anxiety disorders. *Archives of General Psychiatry, 39,* 687–689.

Reich, J., Noyes, R., Jr., Hirshfeld, R., Coryell, W., & O'Gorman, T. (1987). State and personality in depressed and panic patients. *American Journal of Psychiatry, 144,* 181–187.

Reich, J., Noyes, R., Jr., & Troughton, E. (1987). Dependent personality associated with phobic avoidance in patients with panic disorder. *American Journal of Psychiatry, 144,* 323–326.

Reiss, S., Peterson, R. A., Gursky, D. M., & McNally, R. J. (1986). Anxiety sensitivity, anxiety frequency, and the prediction of fearfulness. *Behaviour Research and Therapy, 24,* 1–8.

Salkovskis, P. M., Jones, D. R. O., & Clark, D. M. (1986). Respiratory control in the treatment of panic attacks: Replication and extension with concurrent measurement of behaviour and pCO_2. *British Journal of Psychiatry, 148,* 526–532.

Salkovskis, P. M., Warwick, H. M. C., Clark, D. M., & Wessels, D. J. (1986). A demonstration of acute hyperventilation during naturally occurring panic attacks. *Behaviour Research and Therapy, 24,* 91–94.

Sanderson, W. C., Rapee, R. M., & Barlow, D. H. (1987a). *The influence of perceived control on panic attacks induced via inhalation of 5.5% CO_2 enriched air.* Manuscript submitted for publication.

Sanderson, W. C., Rapee, R. M., & Barlow, D. H. (1987b). *The phenomenon of panic across the DSM-III-Revised anxiety disorder categories.* Paper presented at the 21st Annual Meeting of the Association for the Advancement of Behavior Therapy, Boston, MA.

Shafar, S. (1976). Aspects of phobic illness: A study of 90 personal cases. *British Journal of Medical Psychology, 49*, 221–236.

Snaith, R. P. (1968). A clinical investigation of phobias. *British Journal of Psychiatry, 114*, 673–697.

Stampfl, T. G., & Levis, D. S. (1967). Essentials of implosive therapy: A learning theory based psychodynamic behavioral therapy. *Journal of Abnormal Psychology, 72*, 496–503.

Stern, R., & Marks, I. M. (1973). Brief and prolonged flooding: A comparison in agoraphobic patients. *Archives of General Psychiatry, 28*, 270–276.

Telch, M. J., Brouilard, M., & Telch, C. F. (1987). *Role of cognitive appraisal in panic-related avoidance*. Manuscript submitted for publication.

Thyer, B. A., Nesse, R. M., Cameron, O. G., & Curtis, G. C. (1985). Agoraphobia: A test of the separation anxiety hypothesis. *Behaviour Research and Therapy, 23*, 75–78.

Thyer, B. A., Nesse, R. M., Curtis, G. C., & Cameron, O. G. (1986). Panic disorder: A test of the separation anxiety hypothesis. *Behaviour Research and Therapy, 24*, 209–211.

van den Hout, M. A., & Griez, E. (1982). Cognitive factors in carbon dioxide therapy. *Journal of Psychosomatic Research, 26*, 209–214.

van den Hout, M., & Griez, E. (1983). Some remarks on the nosology of anxiety states and panic disorders. *Acta Psychiatrica Belgica, 83*, 33–42.

van der Molen, G. M., van den Hout, M. A., Vroemen, J., Louisberg, H., & Griez, E. (1986). Cognitive determinants of lactate-induced anxiety. *Behaviour Research and Therapy, 24*, 677–680.

Webster, A. S. (1953). The development of phobias in married women. *Psychological Monographs, 67*, Whole No. 367.

Wolpe, J. (1958). *Psychotherapy by reciprocal inhibition*. Stanford, CA: Stanford University Press.

Wolpe, J., Lande, S. D., McNally, R. J., & Schotte, D. (1985). Differentiation between classically conditioned and cognitively based neurotic fears: Two pilot studies. *Journal of Behavior Therapy and Experimental Psychiatry, 16*, 287–293.

CHAPTER 8

Combining Pharmacotherapy and Behavioral Therapy for Panic Disorder and Agoraphobia

RICHARD P. SWINSON, KLAUS KUCH, AND MARTY M. ANTONY

Introduction

The treatment of psychiatric disorders has advanced to a point at which we have the choice of a number of different therapeutic methods for many of the problems that patients present. We are also able to produce positive changes for most of our patients. In the area of the anxiety disorders, there is ample evidence of the efficacy of a number of different therapies. Antidepressants and anxiolytics have been shown to reduce panic attacks and phobic avoidance (see, Chapter 6). Behavioral and cognitive therapies have similarly been shown to reduce the symptoms of and the disability produced by anxiety disorders (see Chapter 7).

The practitioner is thus in the enviable position of being able to offer patients a range of therapies but also in the difficult position of matching the best therapy to each individual patient. Because there are several different types of therapy available, it is tempting to use combinations of them, in an attempt to cover all the bases. In this chapter we will review the evidence for and against combining treatments of panic disorder and agoraphobia and will provide suggestions for effective clinical practice.

Models of Panic Disorder and Agoraphobia

There are currently two main schools of thought about the nature and treatment of panic disorder and agoraphobia. These are the biological school, typified by the work of Donald Klein (1981), and the behavioral school, advocated by Isaac Marks (1987) and others (see Chapter 7). Briefly stated, the biological view of the etiology of panic disorder is that panic attacks are spontaneous physical events that occur unpredictably in predisposed individuals. The behavioral school views the onset of the panic attacks as a more predictable event and as the culmination of an increase in anxiety. The biological view is that panic attacks are a different kind of anxiety than situational anxiety; the behavioral view is that panic attacks differ in quantitative, rather than qualitative, ways from other kinds of anxiety. It follows from these two perspectives that the presenting symptoms are treated quite differently by practitioners from each school. The biologically based treatments are designed to reduce the frequency of panic attacks; the behavioral treatments focus on reducing phobic avoidance and developing coping strategies to deal with panic attacks. The phobic avoidance that often follows initial panic attacks is interpreted by the biological school as the response of a terrified person seeking to stay in a relatively safe place. Marks's (1987) view of the relationship of panic attacks to the development of agoraphobia is in sharp contrast to these biological explanations. He considers the onset of panic attacks to be secondary to the development of phobic fears (p. 329). In his view, patients report the onset as originating in panic attacks because of their selective focusing on a particularly unpleasant event in the course of the evolution of their disorder.

From a considerable accumulation of data about treatment response (Klein, 1967; Zitrin, Klein, Woerner, & Ross, 1983), family history (Weissman, 1985), childhood separation disorder (Gittleman & Klein, 1985), lactate infusion (Liebowitz et al., 1986), and brain imaging techniques (Reiman et al., 1986), strong evidence emerges for a biological diathesis being implicated in panic disorder and the accompanying phobic states.

If it is accepted that the symptom that marks the onset of panic disorder and agoraphobia is the occurrence of unpredictable panic attacks then, as Klein has indicated, the rest of the syndrome can be logically predicted from the repeated experience of unpredictable anxiety. However, the majority of initial panic attacks do not appear to occur randomly, as would be expected if the diathesis were purely biological; rather, they occur in places such as crowded subways, tunnels, or shopping malls. Panic attacks occur very commonly in the general population, but most people who experience panic attacks do not go on to develop panic disorder (see Chapter 3). Norton, Dorward, and Cox (1986) reported that approximately 3% of a college population experienced panic attacks with a frequency sufficient to meet DSM-III criteria for the diagnosis of panic disorder. They also found that none of these subjects had sought treatment for their symptoms. It is somewhat difficult to interpret these findings, however, because of the high rate of panic attacks discovered in nonclinical populations.

Factors other than biological determine whether a person having panic attacks will go on to develop a full-blown anxiety disorder. Although it is not yet clear what those factors are, they include the experience of certain cognitive symptoms (Rachman, Levitt, & Lopatka, 1987) and an initial appraisal of the threat from the panic (Clark, 1986). If a person feels that her heart is beating quickly, she may be able to explain it to herself as being caused by recent exercise or an emotion that she expects to produce arousal. If, on the other hand, she has no ready explanation for the change in heart rate, she may become fearful that there is something physically wrong with her heart and that she is going to die. The two different sets of thoughts following the same physical event cause very different emotional responses. In cognitively based therapies the interpretation of such physical events becomes a major focus for change.

The Choice of Therapy

Logically, the choice of therapy should follow from research into etiology and treatment effectiveness. More commonly it follows personal preference, experience, and habit. As therapists we are not immune from selective perception about the efficacy of our chosen therapies. There is considerable evidence regarding the effectiveness of medication (Ballenger et al., 1988), respiratory training (Salkovskis, Jones, & Clark, 1986), in vivo exposure therapy on its own or with other interventions (Barlow & Waddell, 1985), and relaxation and cognitive techniques (Michelson, Mavissakalian, & Marchione, 1988) in the treatment of panic disorder and agoraphobia. These approaches are all addressed in detail elsewhere in this volume. As yet there is less research on combined therapies than on the efficacy of single therapies, and opinions on the efficacy of therapy are more likely to be based on clinical impressions than on empirical evidence.

At present, the limited nature of the research available prevents us from concluding that any one approach to therapy is better than another. There are advantages and disadvantages to both pharmacologic and behavioral approaches. The advantages of medication are that it is easy to deliver, can act quickly, and demands little effort from the patient, apart from compliance. The disadvantages include the unwillingness of some people to take anything "chemical," the side effects that often occur, the drop-out rate due to side effects, the possibility of long-term dependence, and the problems of discontinuation.

Behavioral therapy is frequently effective within a few sessions, and its effects tend to persist. Its disadvantages are that patients have to commit themselves to a program of structured practice over a period of weeks, that it demands a certain degree of fortitude in facing feared situations, and that in many regions there are no behaviorally oriented therapists. Behavior therapy can be administered by therapists with little training (Marks, Waters, & Lindley, 1985), but we are less convinced that behavioral assessment can be conducted adequately without a period of specialized training.

The controversy over which therapy is of the greatest benefit to patients has at times become quite heated (Klein, Ross, & Cohen, 1987; Lelliott & Marks, 1988). This disagreement has served to emphasize the dichotomy between psychological and pharmacological therapies. For those involved in the academic study of the problems of therapy, these debates are useful and lead to further research. However, for those who are trying to get clear guidelines for treatment, the opposing claims can be very confusing.

The arguments about etiology and therapy are often presented in a polarized manner that tends to detract from the complex interactions that occur in the biological and psychological realms when any treatment is given. We have evidence from many sources that biological and psychological factors interact in the cause and treatment of a wide variety of illnesses. It is accepted by most clinicians that psychological stress is implicated in the etiology of many physical illnesses, including hypertension (Schwartz, 1977) and asthma (Luparello, McFadden, Lyons, & Bleeker, 1971). It is not surprising, then, that a psychological illness with a biological basis might be affected by both psychological and biological treatments. For example, it has been shown that lactate-induced panic can disappear after a successful course of exposure therapy (Guttermacher & Nelles, 1984). Rather than an area in which the etiological factors are separate, it is very likely that in panic disorder we have a situation in which they are closely interrelated.

Klerman (1984) has identified five major ideological schools within psychiatry: (1) the biological (pharmacotherapy), (2) the psychoanalytical, (3) the social (community mental health), (4) the interpersonal (family and group therapists), and (5) the behavioral. To date, the biological and behavioral schools have had the greatest impact on the treatment of panic and related disorders. Practitioners in each of these schools recognize that they cannot treat all patients effectively, and tend to reserve other choices of therapy for their treatment failures. This does not allow the alternative therapy to appear in its best light: it continues the perception of the alternative therapy as less efficacious than the preferred therapy. Practitioners who do not adhere closely to either the biological or behavioral school are more likely to use a mixture of therapies, to use different criteria for evaluating outcome, and to be less concerned with the relative efficacy of the pure forms of either treatment.

In a study of the attitudes of practicing psychiatrists and psychiatric residents toward various modalities of treatment, it was found that the majority of practitioners were most confident of the efficacy of insight-oriented psychotherapy and medication; they were least confident of the utility of behavioral therapy (McCarley, Steinberg, Spears, & Essok-Vitale, 1987).

It has been found that most patients with panic disorder or agoraphobia are usually treated with medication (Evans, Oie, & Hoey, 1988). Only 6.8% of such patients referred to psychiatrists were given no medication; in contrast, 26% were given combinations of three or more drugs, and the remaining 67% were receiving one or two medications. General practitioners usually gave lower doses of drugs than the psychiatrists—often doses below the therapeutic range.

The Possible Outcome of Combining Therapies

There are three possible outcomes of the combination of behavioral and pharmacological therapy: positive effects, negative effects, and no additive effect (Klerman, 1986). These possibilities are discussed next.

Possible Positive Effects of Combined Therapies

1. *Drugs make compliance with psychological therapy more likely.* Patients come for treatment seeking relief from their distress. Treatments that offer quicker relief are more likely to be adhered to than are those that take more time and effort. Many patients present for treatment at a time when they feel their self-efficacy to be diminished (Bandura, Adams, Hardy, & Howells, 1980) and their coping strategies to be less successful than usual. In this state, they may believe that their attempts to change the way they feel and function will not be very successful. A treatment regime such as medication, which demands little effort from the patient and produces rapid relief of symptoms, may be very powerful in yielding change and adherence to the therapy (Pomerleau & Rodin, 1986). If the medication is combined with a psychological therapy, such as exposure in vivo, compliance with the exposure tasks may be increased by the combination of the two therapies.

2. *Psychological therapy enhances compliance with the drug treatment.* Support, encouragement, and education can foster positive attitudes in the patient and thus increase compliance with a drug regime. Behavioral therapy, like all psychological therapies, includes support and encouragement as well as specific behavioral techniques. Many of these specific techniques are based on education about the disorder and ways of coping. (It is not known at present whether the behavioral approach enhances compliance with medication regimes when compliance is not the specific goal of the behavioral therapy.)

3. *Psychological and drug treatments may act on different aspects of the disorder.* Some clinicians believe that panic attacks are biologically based and that avoidance is psychologically determined. If a biological treatment is used to control the panic attacks and a psychological approach taken to reverse the avoidance, it is possible that combined treatment will offer more than either of the treatments alone.

Possible Negative Effects of Combined Therapies

1. *Giving a patient a medication is in itself a complex act.* Although the physician prescribing the drug may view it as a simple and direct way to help, the patient may not wish to take medication and may feel that his or her self-efficacy is further reduced. Taking medication can be seen by the patient as a way of giving up responsibility for the change expected in therapy. If drug effects are the focus of the therapist/patient interaction, the therapeutic process can develop into a search for the "right medication," with little regard for other issues that patient or therapist may bring to the interaction.

2. *Drugs can produce state-dependent learning.* In state-dependent learning, something learned in one emotional or drug state may not transfer to a changed state. If a person learns through therapy a way of approaching a feared situation while in a calm, medicated state, those skills may not be as

accessible when the drug is removed. In clinical practice this does not appear to be a very powerful factor in determining the ultimate outcome of treatment.

3. *Drugs can reduce anxiety to a point at which exposure therapy no longer simulates real-life situations.* The most frequently used behavioral techniques are those based on exposure principles. It is usual at the beginning of such behavioral therapy for patients to feel increased distress as they confront the previously avoided situations. Investigations into the degree of fear necessary to evoke in a patient in exposure therapy have shown that intense negative emotion is not an essential component (Foa, Blau, Prout, & Latimer, 1977). However, if the patient gets a "free ride" due to anxiety reduction by medication, he or she may not learn to deal with anxiety when it occurs later and may fail to resolve the "fear of fear" that Chambless, Caputo, Bright, and Gallagher (1984) describe as central to the concept of agoraphobia.

4. *The drug may have a negative placebo effect by increasing dependency and allowing the patient to assume a passive role in therapy.* The symptomatic relief produced by the medication effects may lead the patient to feel that nothing more need be done in therapy and thus to discontinue a planned behavioral program. The patient may also attribute all positive change to the medication and feel that he or she could not have made any progress without it.

5. *Drugs usually are administered for a particular length of time, and the patient expects to discontinue the drug at some time.* Some disorders require that drugs be taken for life; diabetes mellitus and hypertension are examples. For most disorders, however, the goal is usually to discontinue medication or attempt gradual dose reductions eventually. Approximately 95% of the anxious patients seen in the Anxiety Disorders Clinic at Toronto General Hospital are taking or have taken benzodiazepine anxiolytics. Some biologically oriented psychiatrists are comfortable with continuing benzodiazepines indefinitely; however, clinicians working in the field of drug dependence are very concerned about the effects of chronic benzodiazepine administration.

Gradual withdrawal of benzodiazepines after treatment for more than 3 months implies a period of a few weeks of increased distress, even if the dose has been in the usual therapeutic range (Busto et al., 1986; Owen & Tyrer, 1983). It is difficult to determine whether this increased anxiety represents withdrawal symptoms, a relapse of the original disorder, or an exacerbation of the disorder by the discontinuation of the drug (Pecknold, Swinson, Kuch, & Lewis, 1988). To relieve the patient's symptoms, the physician may be tempted to increase the medication and attempt discontinuation at a later date. We will return to this point later.

So far we have assumed that the combination of therapies is given, or controlled, by one therapist. In clinical practice this may not be the case. It has already been noted that a high proportion of patients are receiving multiple medications. If these patients see a psychologist for their behavioral treatment and a physician for their medication, the ideal situation is for the patient, psychologist, and physician to work as a therapeutic triad (Chiles, Carlin, &

Beitman, 1984). Chiles et al. point out that, unless the participants in the triad communicate openly, problems can easily arise in uncoordinated combined therapy. This may occur, for example, if the behavioral therapist encourages the patient to approach a feared situation regardless of how anxious he or she feels, whereas the physician tells the patient not to enter a phobic situation unless the medication has removed his or her anxiety. The patient clearly can not follow both directives and is therefore placed in a conflict that may add to his or her anxiety. In an informal survey reported by Gray (1987), it was found that although agoraphobic patients were often taking two or more drugs, the psychologists treating the group were frequently unaware of the pharmacological treatment their patients were receiving elsewhere.

Methodological Issues in Combined Treatment Studies

When treatment studies are assessed it is essential to examine the way the studies were conducted as well as the results reported. Commonly, new therapies are tested with small numbers of patients in situations in which both patient and therapist are aware of what is being attempted. At times unexpected positive results occur from a new therapy or from an established therapy applied to a different disorder. For example, antidepressants have been known to be effective in relieving major affective disorder for many years. Through trial and error they have also been shown to be effective, to varying degrees, in panic disorder (Klein, 1981) and obsessive-compulsive disorder (Capstick & Seldrup, 1973). Although a trial-and-error approach is very useful in introducing new therapies, it is not adequate as a scientific assessment of the efficacy of a treatment. Clinicians often find themselves having to assess the value of new therapies from summary data, without access to the basic assumptions that the researchers brought to their studies. This is a problem in all research, not just in small, innovative studies.

The preferred scientific method is for research therapists to give up control over which patient gets which therapy and for what length of time. Other systems can lead to bias in terms of who is approached to enter a clinical trial—which leads in turn to a systematic bias in the initial patient sample.

To permit a useful scientific interpretation of the results found in treatment research, some minimal methodological requirements have to be met, including procedural and patient selection factors. Studies also have to be prospective rather than retrospective. That is, the patient entry criteria, the methods of assessment, the length of treatment, the precise conduct of the therapy, and the identification of who will conduct the assessments are all determined before treatment begins. In addition, it is necessary to control for the expectancy and nonspecific effects of therapy by using a comparison group. This group may receive no treatment, as in a waiting list control, or it may receive some attention but not the specific therapy that the experimental group receives. Patient assignment to the various therapy or control groups should be random.

The criteria by which patients are selected are of paramount importance. It is no longer sufficient to state that patients were chosen because they had excessive anxiety or phobic avoidance. With the introduction of the DSM-III (APA, 1980) and the later DSM-III-R and the separation of the anxiety disorders into various discrete categories, it has become necessary to use more reliable means of making accurate diagnoses. Several interview schedules are used routinely, including the Diagnostic Interview Schedule (Robins, Helzer, Croughan, & Ratcliff, 1981) and the Structured Clinical Interview Schedule for the DSM-III (Spitzer, Williams, & Gibbons, 1985). Specialized diagnostic schedules for use with anxiety disorders have been developed—for example, the Anxiety Disorders Interview Schedule (DiNardo et al., 1985). (These interviews are described in Chapter 2.)

When drugs are included in a treatment study, it is important to specify how long patients must be off any previous medication before the new treatment can begin. If patients are taken off benzodiazepines and included in a study using another benzodiazepine before the discontinuation effects from the original medication are over, patients assigned to the active drug treatment will improve much more quickly than would otherwise be expected.

The choice of an end point for a drug study is important as well. Frequently the final assessment is conducted while the patient is still taking medication. This is appropriate if the study is one of short-term efficacy; however, as noted previously, clinicians usually wish to discontinue drug treatment after the symptoms have improved. To compare the effects of pharmacological treatment with the effects of psychological therapy, it is more realistic to assess symptoms and disability after the drug is discontinued. The timing of this assessment will vary depending on the drug used. An arbitrary time period of 6 months after discontinuation is often used in research of this nature.

Recently, Elkin and her colleagues addressed the methodological issues in comparative studies of psychotherapy and pharmacotherapy (Elkin, Pilkonis, Docherty, & Sotsky, 1988a, 1988b). They pointed out that because the treatments are so different it is difficult to provide adequate controls for each one. But despite the difficulty, there are ways of attempting to control for the differences. In many studies comparing psychotherapy with pharmacotherapy it has been assumed that merely giving the patients tablets is sufficient to control for the effects of drug administration. It is now clear that many other factors are involved between a therapist and a patient when drugs are prescribed.

To make both parts of the therapy as effective and consistent as possible, recent studies are making use of therapy manuals (Elkin, Parloff, Hadley, & Autry, 1985). A major problem in comparative research is the strong tendency for the preferred therapy at a research setting to be found more efficacious than the comparison therapy (Weissman, 1979). Thus, researchers who primarily

	Active drug	Placebo drug
Active behavior therapy	Double active therapy	Active behavior therapy; placebo drug
Placebo behavior therapy	Active drug; placebo behavior therapy	Double placebo therapy

FIGURE 8.1 Design of Studies Involving Two Active Therapies

use medication are more likely to find that, in their hands, medication works better than behavioral therapy—and vice versa. Whatever the reasons for this phenomenon, it is important in combined studies to use therapists who are equally expert in all the therapies that are to be compared.

Up to this point we have been addressing the problems of studies comparing the effectiveness of pharmacological versus psychological therapy. When we consider the difficulties of evaluating the effects of combined therapies, these problems multiply. It is necessary to compare the combination with each of the factors of the combination delivered separately as well as with adequately selected controls. This is illustrated in Figure 8.1.

This design allows us to study the effects of two active therapies separately and combined versus placebo treatment. The design is quite powerful in controlling for the effects of attention as long as the placebos are well chosen. To make the design more powerful, and thus the findings more definite, it is necessary to add two more groups: active behavior therapy alone and active drug therapy alone. This would approximate the clinical situation more closely. The decision about the number of groups to use depends largely on statistical advice about the number of subjects needed in each cell for a sufficiently powerful statistical test, given the measures used. For example, if 20 subjects per cell are needed, 80 subjects are required for the 4-cell design and 120 subjects for the 6-cell design. The more complex the design the higher the numbers needed. Practical considerations following from this are the availability of appropriate patients, the time it will take to enroll them, and the cost of the study. When strict selection criteria are set for the entry of patients into the study, the ratio of those screened to those who meet the criteria and are willing to go through placebo-controlled treatment may be quite high. But as a consequence, the subjects in such a treatment study may not be typical of the patients seen in a particular setting. In our clinic the ratio of patients screened to those enrolled in studies has varied from 1 in 3 to 1 in 12.

Combinations of Drug and Behavioral Therapies

We have described the experimental requirements for achieving meaningful results that can provide a basis to examine research conducted in combined behavioral and drug treatment. The studies available so far fall into two groups. First, an older group of studies used brief pharmacotherapy to enhance the effects of behavioral therapy; second, a more recent group of studies used medications as a primary antianxiety treatment in addition to behavioral techniques.

The number of possible combinations of behavioral therapy and pharmacotherapy is enormous. Every available drug could, potentially, be combined with each variant of behavioral technique. But in fact, most of the behavioral studies have used a form of exposure therapy and the drugs employed have belonged to three main groups: the benzodiazepines, the tricyclic antidepressants, and the monoamine oxidase inhibitor antidepressants (MAOIs).

Brief Drug Enhancement of Behavior Therapy

The initial behavioral treatment of the phobic disorders was based on the premise that if a patient's anxiety level could be reduced prior to approaching the feared situation—and if it could be kept low during the approach—the patient would learn that the situation was not inherently frightening. This would allow the patient to approach the previously phobic situation more comfortably. The main proponent of this technique was Joseph Wolpe (1958), who based his treatment on the theory of reciprocal inhibition of anxiety. The method of systematic desensitization, which developed from reciprocal inhibition, involved teaching deep muscular relaxation as a method of decreasing anxiety prior to approaching the phobic situation. Exposure to the phobic stimulus was conducted first in imagination and then in real life. The results from this treatment were quite good, particularly when compared with previously available therapies (Davison, 1968; Paul, 1966).

Attempts to combine desensitization techniques with medication have been devoted mainly to the enhancement of the relaxation component of the therapy with anxiolytic drugs (Johnston & Gath, 1973; McCormick, 1973; Solyom et al., 1973; Yorkston, Sergeant, & Rachman, 1968). Other medications, such as muscle relaxants and inhalations of carbon dioxide, have also been used as counterconditioners of anxiety (Foa, Steketee, & Ascher, 1980). Because the intent is to enhance relaxation in the patient approaching a phobic stimulus, drug usage has been limited largely to the period immediately prior to or during exposure. There is little or no reason for a therapist to consider using medication-assisted imaginal systematic desensitization, in the light of current knowledge.

Whether or not medication increases the effectiveness of systematic desensitization, it is well established that prolonged in vivo exposure is much more powerful than graded imaginal techniques (Emmelkamp, 1982). Brief drug enhancement of flooding, or exposure therapy, has also been investigated. Flooding consists of approaching the feared object or situation as quickly as the person can tolerate. In graduated exposure, on the other hand, the patient is allowed to approach the phobic situation somewhat more slowly. Flooding is usually done in vivo rather than in imagination. The person is informed about the rationale for exposure and the theoretical reasons why anxiety decreases with prolonged exposure to the feared situation. Therapist-assisted sessions may be used initially; then the patient is encouraged to continue the sessions alone. This approach may be accompanied by written information designed for patients (Marks, 1978). Unfortunately, some patients find the prospect of approaching their most feared situation to be so frightening that they refuse to attempt the therapy. This refusal may be overcome by the therapist offering support and modeling (Bandura, Blanchard, & Ritter, 1969). If the patient is still unable to approach the phobic situation, it is reasonable to consider using medication briefly to facilitate the initial approach.

Many of the studies of medication-assisted exposure fail to meet minimum criteria for satisfactory research design, which precludes generalization of the findings (Johnston & Gath, 1973). A number of studies have assessed the effects of combined therapy in patients with simple phobia (Marks, Viswanathan, Lipsedge, & Gardner, 1972; Whitehead, Robinson, Blackwell, & Stutz, 1978). Flooding during the period when the blood level of a single dose of diazepam was decreasing was found to be more effective than flooding during peak drug levels; however, chronic administration of diazepam did not offer any advantages over placebo. Hafner and Marks (1976) investigated the effects of diazepam at peak blood level and during decreasing level in a group of 57 agoraphobic patients receiving exposure therapy. Although the diazepam patients were more comfortable than placebo patients during flooding sessions, there was no difference in outcome nor at follow-up between the three treatment groups. They also reported that group exposure was more effective than individual exposure, even though the group subjects reported more panic attacks during treatment. Similar negative drug effects were found in a study of the nonbenzodiazepine muscle relaxant drug Brevital® (Chambless, Foa, Groves, & Goldstein, 1979). In this case, the Brevital appeared to detract from the effectiveness of flooding.

From the limited literature available, there is no evidence for drug enhancement of exposure therapy effects during exposure sessions. The use of drugs also exposes patients to the risks of medication that may be dependency producing. Medication may, however, help some patients stay involved in therapy until their symptoms and distress are reduced and they are able to discontinue it.

Prolonged Antianxiety Medication plus Behavior Therapy

As noted earlier, it has been shown that a number of medications have antipanic and antiphobic effects (Ballenger et al., 1988; Klein et al., 1987). The hypothesis proposed by Klein, that panic attacks are the driving force behind the development of agoraphobia, leads to the use of antipanic medications to suppress or eliminate panic attacks so that patients can learn that avoidance is no longer necessary. The behavioral position is the opposite: if patients stop avoiding, panic attacks will decrease (Marks, 1987). Because there is evidence to support both points of view, it is logical to investigate whether combined therapy offers advantages over the use of each therapy separately. In the majority of the studies reported, either imipramine or phenelzine has been the antipanic agent. A few recent studies have used benzodiazepines.

Imipramine Studies

Having shown that imipramine alone had an effect on panic attacks and overall improvement (Klein, 1964), Klein and his colleagues investigated combining imipramine with various behavioral therapies for the treatment of agoraphobia (Klein, Zitrin, & Woerner, 1977; Zitrin, Klein, & Woerner, 1978, 1980; Zitrin, Klein, Woerner, & Ross, 1983). The behavioral methods they used varied and included imaginal systematic desensitization, therapist-aided exposure, exposure homework, and group exposure. In all the studies these techniques were compared with the effects of imipramine administration and sometimes with supportive psychotherapy.

All studies indicated that imipramine was effective in reducing the occurrence of panic and the severity of phobic avoidance. In a 1978 study by Zitrin et al. of 111 patients with various phobias, the subjects received imipramine and imaginal exposure, placebo and imaginal exposure, or imipramine and supportive psychotherapy. The patients in the behavioral therapy groups also received supportive psychotherapy throughout the course of the 26-week study. All three experimental groups improved, at least moderately, compared to their baseline measures. There were no significant differences between the imipramine/supportive psychotherapy group and the imipramine/imaginal exposure group. This is not surprising, because the effects of imaginal exposure on agoraphobia are fairly minimal. Imipramine subjects did better than those on placebo, confirming the earlier findings of a drug effect.

In Zitrin and colleagues' (1980) study, 76 female agoraphobic patients were treated with group exposure plus placebo or imipramine. All patients received the same behavioral treatment; consequently, it is not possible to draw any conclusions about the relative efficacy of drug versus behavioral treatment. Treatment lasted for 26 weeks with a 6-month follow-up. It is of note that for a 4-week period at the beginning of the trial, medication alone was used. This was done to avoid interference with the therapy from unwanted drug side effects. Although this appears reasonable, it may have biased the subjects in favor of the medication. Comparisons are given for the baseline symptoms of the two groups, but no comparison is reported for week 4, when the exposure therapy was introduced. It was found that both groups improved and that the imipramine/exposure group did significantly better than the placebo/exposure group on measures of global improvement, primary phobia, and spontaneous panic. However, it is also clear from the findings that 72% of the placebo/exposure group achieved at least moderate improvement on the investigators' assessment of spontaneous panic. The imipramine group achieved a 93% improvement on the same measure. The study supports the use of imipramine for agoraphobia, particularly if patients are depressed, but it also calls into question the absolute need for drug treatment of spontaneous panic attacks, because 72% of the placebo/exposure group showed a reduction in spontaneous panic attacks.

Two reports of the treatment of 218 phobic patients in 1983 (Klein, Zitrin, Woerner, & Ross) included data reported in the 1978 paper. These reports compared the effects of imipramine/imaginal exposure, placebo/imaginal exposure, and imipramine/supportive psychotherapy. There was no placebo/supportive psychotherapy group. A single-blind design was used in which the patients did not know whether they were receiving placebo or active drug but the investigators did. The method of delivering psychotherapy was modeled along traditional lines for insight or supportive psychotherapy and was not a good approximation of the usual practice of behavioral therapists. There was no drug-free follow-up assessment.

The design of this study makes it difficult to draw conclusions from it. All subjects received a mixture of therapies; there was no pure exposure group or true placebo group. The inclusion of a supportive psychotherapy group known to be receiving the investigators' preferred therapy, imipramine, raises the possibility that the group might have received biased positive ratings. This might explain, in part, why the supportive psychotherapy group did so well. In addition, if the patients in the supportive therapy group asked about confronting feared situations, they were encouraged to do so. It was found that those patients who experienced spontaneous panic did better with imipramine than with placebo.

No differences were found between imaginal exposure and supportive psychotherapy. Although the investigators dismiss criticism of their study, the inclusion of supportive psychotherapy with nonblinded drug therapy means that definitive conclusions about the relative efficacy of behavioral therapy and supportive psychotherapy in the context of drug treatment must be drawn from other studies. It does appear that the combination of imipramine and behavioral therapy might offer advantages in the reduction of panic attacks and possibly depression in agoraphobic patients.

Mavissakalian and Michelson have also investigated the usefulness of imipramine and exposure therapy to agoraphobia (Mavissakalian & Michelson, 1982, 1983, 1986; Mavissakalian, Michelson, & Dealy, 1983; Michelson & Mavissakalian, 1985; Michelson, Mavissakalian, & Marchione, 1985; Michelson, Mavissakalian, Marchione, Dancu, & Greenwald, 1986). They conducted three separate studies involving different combinations of exposure therapy, group discussion, imipramine, and placebo. The least complex study compared the effects of imipramine alone with imipramine plus programmed in vivo exposure practice (Mavissakalian et al., 1983). Eighteen agoraphobic patients received 12 weeks of treatment, with the combined group improving more than the imipramine group on measures of phobic avoidance, panic, and anxiety.

The second study, which was reported at various stages of completion, ultimately examined the effects of four treatment strategies on sixty-two agoraphobic patients (Mavissakalian & Michelson, 1986). The design was a 2-x-2 comparison of imipramine or placebo with either flooding or programmed practice. The medication condition was double blind. The therapy was delivered in 12 weekly sessions of 90 minutes each. All subjects received a standard explanation of the principles of exposure therapy and were encouraged to practice self-directed exposure and to keep a daily diary of their homework. There were multiple measures of disability and change, including a behavioral approach test consisting of an unaccompanied standardized walk. All four groups improved significantly over their baseline. In the control group, which received behavioral instruction alone, a third of the patients showed marked improvement. The group receiving imipramine and flooding improved the most on the agoraphobia scale. Flooding was found to have little advantage over programmed practice.

Further investigations by Michelson and his colleagues have evaluated ways of enhancing the effects of behavioral interventions on agoraphobia (Michelson et al., 1985; Michelson et al., 1986). They compared exposure therapy, relaxation training, and paradoxical intention (a cognitive technique). All subjects received exposure instructions and diaries. Exposure produced the most rapid change in avoidance and, together with relaxation training, produced higher end point functioning than did paradoxical intention. However, exposure had the highest drop-out rate, whereas paradoxical intention reduced panic attack frequency by the greatest amount. Studies such as this, which attempt to isolate the individual components of behavioral treatments, allow us to examine the differential effects of various techniques and will eventually allow construction of the most effective and efficient treatment package.

Not all studies have found that imipramine adds to the effectiveness of exposure therapy. Marks and his colleagues (Marks et al., 1983; Cohen, Monteiro, & Marks, 1984) treated 45 chronically agoraphobic patients with imipramine or placebo in a double-blind study. All subjects received systematic self-exposure homework. Half had therapist-assisted exposure and half had therapist-aided relaxation training. Medication was given for 26 weeks with a drug-free follow-up assessment after 2 years.

There were very few differences between the treatments, and all patient groups improved on all the measures of anxiety, panic, and agoraphobia.

Imipramine was not found to be superior to placebo. Exposure produced more rapid change than relaxation, but at the 1-year follow-up, differences were no longer evident. There were no positive or negative interactions between the drug and psychological treatments. The conclusion was that the beneficial effects of imipramine are largely owing to its antidepressant properties. Because the findings were at variance with other studies of imipramine effects, these data were reanalyzed by Raskin, Marks, and Sheehan (1983). They found that imipramine contributed to an initial improvement in anxiety ratings but that these effects were lost by follow-up time.

Many of the studies described here confounded the findings by including self-directed exposure instructions for all patients. It has been shown that this treatment can be very powerful in itself (Greist, Marks, Berlin, Gournay, & Noshirvani, 1980). To address this point, Telch, Agras, Taylor, Roth, and Gallen (1985) included a treatment phase in which all exposure to feared situations was forbidden. In their study, 37 agoraphobic patients were treated over 26 weeks. In the first 4 weeks, all subjects received antiexposure instructions together with imipramine or placebo. The rationale for avoiding exposure was to give the medication time to work before the patient considered confronting feared situations. After 4 weeks, one group received imipramine and intensive therapist-assisted group exposure for a total of 9 hours in 3 sessions. This was followed by homework exposure tasks accompanied by a partner. The no-exposure group was simply instructed to try to go into feared situations, but apart from that received no further exposure therapy. The placebo group got active group exposure therapy.

After 8 weeks of treatment the imipramine/exposure group had improved on all measures except heart rate during the exposure sessions. The placebo/exposure group was improved on all measures except heart rate, panic frequency, and depression. The imipramine/no exposure group improved in terms of mood, anticipatory anxiety, and the ability to complete a standard walk. They did not improve, however, in terms of phobic avoidance in everyday life or frequency of panic attacks. The placebo/exposure patients improved compared to the imipramine/no-exposure group on measures reflecting approach to feared situations.

When patients were instructed to enter feared situations without receiving structured exposure therapy, the imipramine/no-exposure group made rapid gains—but the combined therapy of imipramine and structured exposure was found to be the most effective by week 28. These findings are discussed in detail by Telch (1988). He suggests that imipramine may act through a reduction of the dysphoria experienced by many agoraphobic patients. This could have the effect of increasing the amount of time spent on exposure homework and could reduce the self-defeating negative cognitions that are part of depressed affect.

In summary, it appears that imipramine is not very effective in reducing the symptomatology of panic and agoraphobia if used alone. Imipramine can help overcome the initial depression and demoralization that some patients experience. The addition of imipramine to exposure therapy has not been shown to be of great advantage over exposure alone.

Other Antidepressants

Few of the other tricyclic antidepressants have been combined with behavioral therapy in controlled clinical studies. Johnson, Troyer, and Whitsett (1988) compared clomipramine versus placebo and in vivo exposure versus no exposure in a study of 60 agoraphobic women. Treatment sessions were conducted for 6 hours per week over 8 weeks. Clomipramine was found to reduce panic frequency and phobic avoidance. Exposure therapy also reduced phobic avoidance and anticipatory anxiety but had no effect on panic frequency. The combination of the therapies did not add anything to the change achieved by the active therapies used singly.

Imipramine was compared to the monoamine oxidase inhibitor phenelzine in a 12-week trial in which all patients also received supportive group therapy stressing approaching feared situations (Sheehan, Ballenger, & Jacobson, 1980). Patients received 150 mg of imipramine per day, 45 mg of phenelzine per day, or placebo. There was no control condition for the behavioral instruction. All groups had improved by week 12, with the drug groups improving more quickly and more completely than the placebo group. The drug-treated patients were less avoidant at the end of the study than the control patients, but no data were presented about the frequency of panic attacks in the various groups. Phenelzine was found to be significantly more effective than imipramine on the severity-of-avoidance scale.

In a study of mixed phobic patients Solyom, Solyom, Lapierre, Pecknold, and Morton (1981) found that exposure therapy alone was more effective than phenelzine alone. Exposure therapy, with or without phenelzine, produced the greatest positive change in phobic avoidance.

At present there are limited data on the combination of behavior therapy and antidepressants other than imipramine. The available data are consistent with the findings for imipramine.

Anxiolytics

Early studies of combined pharmacological and behavioral treatment focused mainly on the use of the benzodiazepine tranquilizers, but more recent studies have featured antidepressants as the drugs of choice. This was mainly because imipramine was found to reduce panic attacks, whereas opinion held that benzodiazepines were less effective in this regard. The finding that alprazolam is an effective antipanic and antiphobic agent (Ballenger et al., 1988), at least in the short term, has led to the comparison of benzodiazepines and behavioral therapy.

Barlow and his colleagues demonstrated that cognitively based behavioral treatments can reduce panic attacks in panic disorder patients (Barlow et al., 1984). They compared alprazolam, placebo, cognitive-behavioral therapy, and a waiting list control in 57 panic disorder patients (Klosko, Barlow, Tassinari, & Cerny, 1988). There was a concerted attempt to avoid exposure instructions during the 15 weekly sessions for the groups not receiving behavior therapy. The behavioral treatment was a combination of cognitive therapy, relaxation training, and exposure to external and internal anxiety cues. There was a posttreatment follow-up after 2 weeks, but the majority of the alprazolam patients did not discontinue medication.

Of the cognitive therapy patients, 87% were panic free by the end of the study compared with 50% of the alprazolam group, 36% of the placebo group, and 33% of the waiting list controls. The treatment groups fared better than the control group on a global assessment, but there were no statistically significant differences between alprazolam and placebo. The importance of this study is that it demonstrates that nonpharmacological methods can be very useful in controlling panic attacks. The ability of medications to control or eradicate panic attacks has been the main rationale for the use of medications in panic disorder. The findings from Barlow's group suggest that nonpharmacological methods may be equally effective in reducing panic attacks.

The effect of alprazolam and exposure therapy singly and combined is being investigated currently in a two-site study by Isaac Marks's group in London and by our group in Toronto. In a 2-x-2 design of alprazolam or placebo and exposure or relaxation without exposure instructions, we are treating approximately 150 severely agoraphobic patients in a 3-phase study. In the first 8 weeks patients receive medication and psychological therapy. During the next 8 weeks the medications are gradually withdrawn without further supervised behavioral therapy. The third phase is a medication-free follow-up to week 43 without behavioral therapy. This study should determine whether alprazolam or exposure therapy differ in their short-term and long-term ability to reduce panic attacks and phobic avoidance and whether a combination of the two is superior or inferior to either treatment delivered with a placebo version of the other. Because of the large number of additional subjects required, this study does not include the behavioral and pharmacologic treatments delivered alone.

The Relevance of Findings to Clinical Practice

The setting of a research study is clearly quite different from that of day-to-day clinical practice. The expectations of both the therapist and patient differ in the two circumstances and, although the researcher wishes to provide the best therapy for each patient, the constraints of the research protocol limit the decisions that can be made about the ongoing care of a particular patient. The research psychiatrist has to use his or her clinical skills in a context in which treatment options are limited and with the knowledge that a certain percentage of the patients are receiving placebo therapy.

The patient who agrees to enter a controlled comparison of a number of therapies knows, or should know, that the course of therapy is determined before the trial begins. While a certain percentage of patients drop out, it is remarkable how powerful attention from a clinician can be in keeping research subjects coming back for further sessions when it is fairly clear that they have not improved from the baseline evaluation. In a short-term trial this does not present much of a conflict for either the patient or the therapist. However, when studies extend over several months or years the research design has to ensure that the investigator pays attention to the clinical needs of his or her patients.

The opposite situation is typical of clinical practice. A clinician is free to treat each patient with any of the available therapies without going through a detailed baseline assessment of the precise nature or severity of the symptoms. The most frequently used information that clinicians rely on to prescribe, change, or discontinue treatment is the verbal self-report of the patient. This is the case in primary care and in the psychotherapies, including supportive psychotherapy administered with drug therapy. In behavioral practice, it is essential that the patient keep diaries of triggers of their symptoms before and during therapy to direct the course of therapy. Routine behavioral practice is therefore more closely akin to a single-subject experiment than are most other forms of psychotherapy.

In the clinical setting the patient wants to know what is wrong and usually wants relief as soon as possible. Because clinicians also wish to produce rapid relief of the problem, it is understandable that they may rely on methods that produce rapid change. The most rapid relief of anxiety is produced by the anxiolytic medications, and the benzodiazepines are the most frequently prescribed medications of all classes of drugs (Skegg, Doll, & Perry, 1977).

Few primary care physicians and psychiatrists are familiar enough with behavioral principles to use them in their practice. Psychologists, who are often well trained in behavioral principles, do not have the legal right to use medications. We therefore have a schism in the treatment of anxiety disorders, because the two proven effective forms of therapy are available through different groups of practitioners. Consequently, the therapy that an anxious patient gets will depend mainly on the professional training of the therapist rather than on a determination that the therapy is optimal for that patient. At an even more basic level the choice of treatment is dependent upon the recognition that the patient has a mental disorder. In a recent study (Borus, Howes, Devins, Rosenberg, & Livingston, 1988), only 14% of depressed patients in a primary care setting were identified as having a mental disorder. Of patients with anxiety disorders, 44% were recognized as suffering from a mental disorder, but only 17% were correctly diagnosed. If this level of recognition of cases is representative of clinical practice, treatment is most likely to be determined by patient complaint rather than by accurate diagnosis of the syndrome the patient presents.

We have seen that antidepressants and anxiolytics reduce or eliminate the main symptoms of panic or agoraphobia. Whether they do so by their anti-dysphoriant action or by some specific antipanic or antiphobic properties is beyond the scope of this chapter and is, for the most part, irrelevant in clinical practice. The drugs work for a high proportion of patients, and, in the case of the anxiolytics, they work quickly. We have also seen that behavioral therapy based on exposure principles is very effective in reducing phobic avoidance. When cognitive therapy is included, behavioral treatment also reduces panic attacks substantially.

Some of the differences between clinical and research practice have been pointed out earlier. One of the artificial aspects of treatment studies is that they are time limited, whereas clinical practice is, ultimately, outcome oriented. A prospective-treatment trial occurs for a predetermined number of weeks, with measures of pathology taken at baseline and again at various points throughout the trial. It is usual in pharmacological trials to repeat the measures for the last time at the end point of active treatment, when the subjects are still taking the drug. This is reasonable if the acute drug effect is the main subject of the investigation, but less so if long-term maintenance of treatment effects is critical.

In clinical practice the patient and the clinician often prefer to use the drug for a limited period of time and then to see if the patient can manage without further use of medication. This model of therapy is standard practice in the management of major depressive episodes. Even in schizophrenia, which is a chronic condition, there is often an attempt to institute drug "holidays" (Schatzberg & Cole, 1986). "Real-life" therapy demands that we investigate the efficacy of the techniques or drugs we use *after* they have been discontinued as well as during the active treatment phase.

The typical patient seeking treatment for panic disorder and agoraphobia is a woman who is given either a benzodiazepine or an antidepressant and some advice about self-exposure. This is the most frequently prescribed combination of therapies. From our own experience of seeing approximately 300 new anxiety disorder patients a year for the last 7 years, we know that roughly 95% of patients are taking, or have taken, benzodiazepines for their anxiety when we first see them. A much smaller percentage—15 to 20%—have taken antidepressants. Most of the latter are referred by psychiatrists rather than primary care physicians.

Apart from the efficacy issue, practitioners do what they have been trained to do or have become comfortable doing. Most North American psychiatrists are trained in programs that emphasize dynamic psychotherapy and biological treatments. McCarley et al. (1987) found, in a survey of 191 psychiatrists in California, that behavioral treatments were the least commonly used therapies even though they were considered effective for phobic disorders. Biological therapies were used very frequently and were considered effective for those disorders with a predominance of depression and anxiety symptoms. A study of the treatment of anxiety disorders in Australia garnered little consensus among psychiatrists (Andrews, Hadzi-Pavlovic, Christensen, & Mattick, 1987). Of those surveyed, 59% of the psychiatrists included supportive psychotherapy in their treatment plan for panic disorder; 56% included behavioral psychotherapy; 59% included benzodiazepines; and 39% included antidepressants. It is thus not unexpected that phobic patients receive the kind of treatment they do. Given the recent emphasis on the biological nature of panic disorder, the use of biological therapies is predictable.

The Effects of Discontinuing Therapies

Medication

Medication use is often accompanied by side effects and discontinuation effects. Discontinuation of the medications used to treat anxiety often produces a reoccurrence of the original symptoms (relapse) or the appearance of new symptoms (withdrawal). Recurring symptoms may return with greater intensity than before treatment (rebound).

Antidepressant Discontinuation

Withdrawal syndromes are usually thought of in connection with substances that can cause dependence, such as the benzodiazepines and ethanol. The tricyclic antidepressants and the monoamine oxidase inhibitors are also associated with discontinuation symptoms, however. Dilsaver and Greden (1984) have described the onset of gastrointestinal distress, anxiety, agitation, sleep disturbance, and the occurrence of mania after discontinuing tricyclic antidepressant medication. MAOI discontinuation may also be followed by these symptoms and, on rare occasion, by delirium and psychosis (Dilsaver, 1988). Clearly, antidepressant discontinuation is not without risk of discomfort to the patient, either from the onset of new symptoms or from the recurrence of early symptoms.

Benzodiazepine Discontinuation

The discontinuation syndromes that occur when benzodiazepines are stopped depend on many factors, including the specific drug, dose, length of time of administration, rate of discontinuation, use of concurrent treatments, patient's expectations, therapist's expectations, and the original condition being treated.

There have been many reviews of the dependency produced by benzodiazepines (Owen & Tyrer, 1983; Petursson & Lader, 1981; Swinson, Pecknold, & Kirby, 1987). The most complete review is an immense work by Woods and his colleagues (Woods, Katz, & Winger, 1987), who concluded that physiological benzodiazepine dependence does occur. It is more severe if the dose is high, though it can occur at low doses if the drug is administered for more than a few weeks. Withdrawal symptoms are more severe after the administration of shorter-acting benzodiazepines than the longer-acting group. The concomitant use of other dependency-producing drugs such as ethanol increases the risk of dependence.

Agoraphobia and panic disorder are chronic conditions; thus, if medications are to be part of their treatment they will probably be used for some months, if not years. At present, few of the benzodiazepines have been shown to be effective for the treatment of panic disorder. Alprazolam, a moderately long-acting benzodiazepine, has been demonstrated to have antipanic properties in short-term treatment by Ballenger et al. (1988). In this study, when alprazolam was discontinued over approximately 5 weeks, a significant proportion of the patients experienced an increase in their symptomatology (Pecknold et al., 1988). Twenty-seven percent had rebound panic attacks; that is, they were worse during taper than at the onset of treatment. Discontinuation symptoms affected 35% of the alprazolam-treated patients and none of the placebo patients. The symptoms resolved by the end of the second medication-free posttaper week. In this study almost every patient who began alprazolam treatment had discontinued it by the end of the taper phase. This contrasts with the findings in the study by Fyer and her colleagues (described in Chapter 6), in which few of their patients were able to discontinue medication in an open trial. The rate of discontinuation may be a determinant of stopping benzodiazepine medication; another variable, yet to be investigated, is the attitude of the clinician to stopping the drug.

If a patient is being treated by a physician who believes that the primary treatment of anxiety should be biological, and the patient suffers an increase in symptoms as the drug is withdrawn, the physician may tend to slow down the taper or to suggest a temporary increase in the dose. The message to the patient is that medication discontinuation produces the increase in discomfort and raising the drug dose causes the discomfort to diminish. This can lead to a very prolonged taper phase or to difficulty in discontinuing. At some point the therapist has to offer the patient the choice of continuing with a symptomatic taper or trying some other form of therapy.

The alternative therapy may be a switch to a longer-acting benzodiazepine (Fontaine, Chouinard, & Annable, 1984), the addition of a drug such as clonidine (Redmond, 1985), or the use of an active form of psychotherapy such as cognitive-behavioral therapy (Sanchez-Craig, Cappell, Busto, & Kay, 1987). The switch to an alternative benzodiazepine may make the discontinuation phase more comfortable, but it does not solve the problem of the reemergence of original symptoms (relapse). The same difficulty is encountered with the use of other drugs that dampen anxiety mechanisms during and immediately after the taper period. Sanchez-Craig and her colleagues compared the effects of abrupt placebo-replacement discontinuation of benzodiazepine with a slow taper when both groups received a cognitive-behavioral treatment package. As expected, the placebo-replacement subjects

were more symptomatic than the slow taper subjects, but the former was
more likely to be abstinent at 1-year follow-up than were the latter. The
researchers argued that there may be an advantage to patients experiencing
some distress during the taper. It seems more likely that experiencing symptoms of distress at the same time as being taught other techniques to deal with
the symptoms was probably the effective ingredient rather than the experience
of the distress per se. The experience of such distress during drug discontinuation might also increase the patients' resolve not to take medication in the
future.

Behavioral Therapy

Behavioral therapy is usually administered for a period of time agreed upon
before therapy begins. It is done with the explicit expectation that patients are
going to learn new ways of coping with their anxiety using skills acquired
during the therapy. It is quite clear at the beginning of therapy that it will end,
usually in a few weeks. As far as we are aware, there is no literature on the
effects of the discontinuation of behavioral therapy. It is, in fact, difficult to
conceive just what the discontinuation effects might be. Treatment is designed
to give the patient experience and confidence in using anxiety-relieving
techniques. These methods are usually learned well by the end of treatment
and are always available to the patient. Discontinuing therapy that is based
on the working through of relationships may well lead to difficulties. However, the brief nature of behavior therapy and its focus on tasks rather than
relationships usually means little difficulty in terminating treatment.

Follow-up data relating to the treatment of panic and agoraphobia indicate that those patients who have improved maintain their improvement over
the succeeding years (Emmelkamp & Kuipers, 1979; Munby & Johnson, 1980)
without the occurrence of symptom substitution.

Conclusion and Recommendations

A number of therapies are effective in the short term for panic disorder and
agoraphobia. The long-term efficacy of the biological therapies has not been
established yet. After the discontinuation of biological therapies there is a
significant chance of withdrawal symptoms and relapse. The discontinuation
of behavioral therapy does not lead to withdrawal symptoms, and long-term
follow-up shows that patients maintain improvement in general anxiety levels
and reduced phobic avoidance.

What should the clinician do when faced with a new patient who has
panic disorder and agoraphobia? From the data that we have reviewed we
conclude that the first step in treatment should be a trial of exposure-based
behavioral treatment. This may be relatively simple and restricted to an

onale and procedure of exposure therapy. Or it may be featuring therapist-assisted exposure with daily home-chniques is beyond the capabilities of the physician or nes to learn them.

that panic attacks have to be controlled by medication by can begin. The majority of panic attacks experienced onal rather than unexpected or "spontaneous" and are therefore amenable to behavioral intervention. Even if patients are experiencing a high proportion of unexpected panic attacks, they can still benefit from a trial of exposure therapy to deal with the phobic avoidance and the situational panics. Exposure to interoceptive cues can also reduce the fear of panic symptoms so that minor symptoms no longer trigger major attacks.

A few patients will not agree to behavioral treatment and will insist on symptomatic relief from medication. In our experience these patients are fewer in number than those who refuse medication. If medication is used to control the panic attacks, it should be made explicit how long that treatment will last. It is also important to propose the medication as part of a larger program and not as a sole treatment. The end point of successful therapy is when the patient is both medication free and able to cope with those attacks of anxiety that will occur in the future without resorting to escape or avoidance. Techniques that enhance the patient's self-efficacy offer more than those that leave the patient dependent on some external agent for continued comfort. Indicating at the beginning that the drug therapy will end is likely to reduce dependence and allow for easier discontinuation.

We know from Norton and his colleagues' (1986) research that panic attacks are common in the general population. We also know that the treatment of panic disorder and agoraphobia will help many patients improve, but that it is unlikely to be a "cure." Panic patients may well continue to experience attacks at times, and they need to acquire skills for dealing with those events.

The available research indicates that imipramine enhances the effect of behavioral treatment. If exposure therapy alone is not sufficient, or if the patient is so demoralized that he or she cannot take part in exposure therapy, the addition of imipramine is justified. If the patient has a major mood disorder in addition to panic disorder, it has to be treated—and treatment will usually be with a tricyclic antidepressant.

The use of benzodiazepine tranquilizers is much more debatable. They are more accepted by patients than the antidepressants because many find the side effects of the antidepressants intolerable. Alprazolam reduces panic attacks very rapidly and can be very helpful for those patients who are having a high frequency of attacks and who feel out of control. As with any other medication, it is important to set a time limit on the use of tranquilizers. The patient should also be prepared in advance for the discontinuation symptoms that may occur. These can be reduced by using low doses that are withdrawn slowly in a supportive but firm therapeutic setting.

Some practitioners suggest that if antipanic drugs are going to be used, they should be used in doses sufficient to reduce the panic frequency to zero. Evidence does not yet support this point. The skills that patients will need to cope with the withdrawal symptoms are the same ones they will need to deal with further anxiety symptoms, and can therefore be proposed as being of value for the long term.

At present, we do not have data to indicate whether the concomitant use of benzodiazepines and exposure therapy adds or detracts from the effect of either therapy used alone. These data will be available in the near future and will help us to design comprehensive treatment plans using all the therapeutic modalities at our disposal. The patient for whom combined therapy appears to be most suited is the one who has unexpected and situational panic attacks combined with significant phobic avoidance and who is unable or unwilling to go through exposure therapy alone. In our view, however, the therapy that should be tried first is exposure therapy, with combined therapy reserved for those who do not improve.

References

American Psychiatric Association. (1980). *Diagnostic and statistical manual of mental disorders*(3rd ed.). Washington, DC: Author.

Andrews, G., Hadzi-Pavlovic, D., Christensen, H., & Mattick, R. (1987). Views of practicing psychiatrists on the treatment of anxiety and somatoform disorders. *American Journal of Psychiatry, 144*, 1331–1334.

Ballenger, J. C., Burrows, G. R., DuPont, R. L., Lesser, I. M., Noyes, R., Pecknold, J. C., Rifkin, A., & Swinson, R. P. (1988). Alprazolam in panic disorder and agoraphobia: Results from a multicenter trial. Efficacy in short term treatment. *Archives of General Psychiatry, 45*, 413–422.

Bandura, A., Adams, N. E., Hardy, A. B., & Howells, G. N. (1980). Tests of the generality of self-efficacy theory. *Cognitive Therapy and Research, 4*, 39–66.

Bandura, A., Blanchard, E. B., & Ritter, B. (1969). The relative efficacy of desensitization and modeling approaches for inducing behavioral, affective and attitudinal changes. *Journal of Personality and Social Psychology, 13*, 173–179.

Barlow, D. H., Cohen, A. S., Waddell, M. T., Vermilyea, B. B., Klosko, J. S., Blanchard, E. B., & DiNardo, P. I. (1984). Panic and generalized anxiety disorders: Nature and treatment. *Behavior Therapy, 15*, 431–449.

Barlow, D. H., & Waddell, M. T. (1985). Agoraphobia. In D. H. Barlow (Ed.), *Clinical handbook of psychological disorders*. New York: Guilford Press.

Borus, J. F., Howes, M. J., Devins, N. P., Rosenberg, R., & Livingston, W. W. (1988). Primary health care providers' recognition and diagnosis of mental disorders in their patients. *General Hospital Psychiatry, 10*, 317–321.

Busto, U., Sellers, E. M., Naranjo, C. A., Cappel, H., Sanchez, C., & Sykora, K. (1986). Withdrawal reaction after long-term therapeutic use of benzodiazepines. *New England Journal of Medicine, 315*, 654–659.

Capstick, N., & Seldrup, J. (1973). Phenomenological aspects of obsessional patients treated with clomipramine. *British Journal of Psychiatry, 122*, 719–720.

Chambless, D. L., Caputo, G. C., Bright, P., & Gallagher, R. (1984). Fear of fear in agoraphobics. *Journal of Consulting and Clinical Psychology, 52,* 1090–1097.

Chambless, D. L., Foa, E. B., Groves, G. A., & Goldstein, A. J. (1979). Flooding with Brevital in the treatment of agoraphobia: Countereffective? *Behaviour Research and Therapy, 17,* 243–251.

Chiles, J. A., Carlin, A. S., & Beitman, B. D. (1984). A physician, a nonmedical therapist and a patient: The pharmacotherapy-psychotherapy triangle. In B. D. Beitman & G. L. Klerman (Eds.), *Combining psychotherapy and drug therapy in clinical practice.* New York: Spectrum.

Clark, D. (1986). A cognitive approach to panic. *Behaviour Research and Therapy, 24,* 461–470.

Cohen, S. D., Monteiro, W., & Marks, I. M. (1984). Two-year follow-up of agoraphobics after exposure and imipramine. *British Journal of Psychiatry, 144,* 276–281.

Davison, G. C. (1968). Systematic desensitization as a counterconditioning process. *Journal of Abnormal Psychology, 73,* 91–99.

Dilsaver, S. C. (1988). Monoamine oxidase inhibitor withdrawal phenomena: Symptoms and pathophysiology. *Acta Psychiatrica Scandinavica, 78,* 1–7.

Dilsaver, S. C., & Greden, J. F. (1984). Antidepressant withdrawal phenomena. *Biological Psychiatry, 19,* 237–256.

DiNardo, P. A., Barlow, D. H., Cerny, J., Vermilyea, B. B., Vermilyea, J. A., Himadi, W., & Waddell, M. (1985). *Anxiety Disorders Schedule—Revised (ADIS-R).* Albany, New York: Phobia and Anxiety Disorders Clinic, State University of New York at Albany.

Elkin, I., Parloff, M. B., Hadley, S. W., & Autry, J. H. (1985). NIMH Treatment of Depression Collaborative Research Program: Background and research plan. *Archives of General Psychiatry, 42,* 305–316.

Elkin, I., Pilkonis, P. A., Docherty, J. P., & Sotsky, S. M. (1988a). Conceptual and methodological issues in comparative studies of psychotherapy and pharmacotherapy: I. Active ingredients and mechanisms of change. *American Journal of Psychiatry, 145,* 909–917.

Elkin, I., Pilkonis, P. A., Docherty, J. P., & Sotsky, S. M. (1988b). Conceptual and methodological issues in comparative studies of psychotherapy and pharmacotherapy: II. Nature and timing of treatment effects. *American Journal of Psychiatry, 145,* 1070–1076.

Emmelkamp, P. M. G. (1982). Anxiety and fear. In A. S. Bellak, M. Hersen, & A. E. Kazdin (Eds.), *International handbook of behavior modification and therapy.* New York: Plenum.

Emmelkamp, P. M. G., & Kuipers, A. C. M. (1979). Agoraphobia: A follow-up study four years after treatment. *British Journal of Psychiatry, 134,* 352–355.

Evans, L., Oie, T. P. S., & Hoey, H. (1988). Prescribing patterns in agoraphobia with panic attacks. *Medical Journal of Australia, 148,* 74–77.

Foa, E. B., Blau, J. S., Prout, M., & Latimer, P. (1977). Is horror a necessary component of flooding (implosion)? *Behaviour Research and Therapy, 15,* 397–402.

Foa, E. B., Steketee, G. S., & Ascher, M. (1980). Systematic desensitization. In A. Goldstein & E. B. Foa (Eds.), *Handbook of behavioral interventions: A clinical guide.* New York: Wiley.

Fontaine, R., Chouinard, G., & Annable, L. (1984). Rebound anxiety in anxious patients after abrupt withdrawal of benzodiazepine treatment. *American Journal of Psychiatry, 141,* 848–852.

Gittleman, R., & Klein, D. F. (1985). Childhood separation anxiety and adult agoraphobia. In A. H. Tuma & J. D. Maser (Eds.), *Anxiety and the anxiety disorders*. Hillsdale, NJ: Lawrence Erlbaum.

Gray, J. A. (1987). Interactions between drugs and behavior therapy. In H. J. Eysenck & I. Martin (Eds.), *Theoretical foundations of behavior therapy*. New York: Plenum.

Greist, J. H., Marks, I. M., Berlin, F., Gournay, K., & Noshirvani, H. (1980). Avoidance versus confrontation of fear. *Behavior Therapy, 11*, 1–14.

Guttermacher, L. B., & Nelles, C. (1984). In vivo desensitization alteration of lactate-induced panic: A case study. *Behavior Therapy, 15*, 369–372.

Hafner, J., & Marks, I. (1976). Exposure in vivo of agoraphobics: Contributions of diazepam, group exposure and anxiety evocation. *Psychological Medicine, 6*, 71–88.

Johnson, D. G., Troyer, I. E., & Whitsett, S. F. (1988, May). *Clomipramine and exposure therapy in agoraphobia*. Paper presented at American Psychiatric Association Annual Conference, Montreal, Canada.

Johnston, D., & Gath, D. (1973). Arousal levels and attribution effects in diazepam-assisted flooding. *British Journal of Psychiatry, 122*, 463–466.

Klein, D. F. (1964). Delineation of two drug-responsive anxiety syndromes. *Psychopharmacologia, 5*, 397–408.

Klein, D. F. (1967). Importance of psychiatric diagnosis in prediction of clinical drug effects. *Archives of General Psychiatry, 16*, 118–126.

Klein, D. F. (1981). Anxiety reconceptualized. In D. F. Klein & J. Rabkin (Eds.), *Anxiety: New research and changing concepts*. New York: Raven Press.

Klein, D. F., Ross, D. C., & Cohen, P. (1987). Panic and avoidance in agoraphobia: Application of path analysis to treatment studies. *Archives of General Psychiatry, 44*, 377–384.

Klein, D. F., Zitrin, C. M., & Woerner, M. G. (1977). Imipramine and phobia. *Psychopharmacology Bulletin, 13*, 24–27.

Klein, D. F., Zitrin, C. M., Woerner, M. G., & Ross, D. C. (1983). Treatment of phobias. II. Behavior therapy and supportive psychotherapy: Are there any specific ingredients? *Archives of General Psychiatry, 40*, 139–145.

Klerman, G. L. (1984). Ideological conflicts in combined treatment. In B. D. Beitman & G. L. Klerman (Eds.), *Combining psychotherapy and drug therapy in clinical practice*. New York: Spectrum.

Klerman, G. L. (1986). Drugs and psychotherapy. In S. L. Garfield & A. E. Bergin (Eds.), *Handbook of psychotherapy and behavior change*. New York: Wiley.

Klosko, J. S., Barlow, D. H., Tassinari, R. B., & Cerny, J. A. (1988). Comparison of alprazolam and cognitive behavior therapy in the treatment of panic disorder: A preliminary report. In I. Hand & H.-U. Wittchen (Eds.), *Treatments of panic and phobias: Modes of application and variables affecting outcome*. Heidelberg: Springer.

Lelliott, P., & Marks, I. (1988). The cause and treatment of agoraphobia. *Archives of General Psychiatry, 45*, 388–389.

Liebowitz, M. R., Gorman, J. M., Fyer, A. J., Dillon, D., Levitt, M. M., & Klein, D. F. (1986). Possible mechanisms for lactate's induction of panic. *American Journal of Psychiatry, 143*, 495–502.

Luparello, T. J., McFadden, H. D., Lyons, H. A., & Bleeker, E. R. (1971). Psychological factors and bronchial asthma. *New York State Journal of Medicine, 71*, 2161–2165.

McCarley, T., Steinberg, A., Spears, M., & Essok-Vitale, S. (1987). Integrating biological and psychosocial therapies: A survey of psychiatric training, practice and attitudes. *Journal of Psychiatric Education, 11*, 43–53.

McCormick, W. O. (1973). Declining dose desensitization in the treatment of phobias. *Journal of the Canadian Psychiatric Association, 18,* 9–12.

Marks, I. M. (1978). *Living with fear.* New York: McGraw-Hill.

Marks, I. M. (1987). *Fears, phobias and rituals.* New York: Oxford University Press.

Marks, I. M., Gray, S., Cohen, C., Hill, R., Mawson, D., Ramm, E., & Stern, R. S. (1983). Imipramine and brief therapist-aided exposure in agoraphobics having self-exposure homework. *Archives of General Psychiatry, 40,* 153–162.

Marks, I. M., Viswanathan, R., Lipsedge, M. S., & Gardner, R. (1972). Enhanced relief of phobias by flooding during waning diazepam effect. *British Journal of Psychiatry, 121,* 493–505.

Marks, I. M., Waters, H., & Lindley, P. (1985). Nurse therapy in primary care. *British Medical Journal, 290,* 1181–1194.

Mavissakalian, M., & Michelson, L. (1982). Agoraphobia: Behavioral and pharmacological treatments, preliminary outcome and process findings. *Psychopharmacology Bulletin, 18,* 91–103.

Mavissakalian, M., & Michelson, L. (1983). Self-directed in vivo exposure practice in behavioral and pharmacological treatments of agoraphobia. *Behavior Therapy, 14,* 506–519.

Mavissakalian, M., & Michelson, L. (1986). Agoraphobia: Relative and combined effectiveness of therapist-assisted in vivo exposure and imipramine. *Journal of Clinical Psychiatry, 47,* 117–122.

Mavissakalian, M., Michelson, L., & Dealy, R. S. (1983). Pharmacological treatment of agoraphobia: Imipramine versus imipramine with programmed practice. *British Journal of Psychiatry, 143,* 348–355.

Michelson, L., & Mavissakalian, M. (1985). Psychophysiological outcome of behavioral and pharmacological treatments of agoraphobia. *Journal of Consulting and Clinical Psychology, 53,* 229–236.

Michelson, L., Mavissakalian, M., & Marchione, K. (1985). Cognitive and behavioral treatments of agoraphobia: Clinical, behavioral and psychophysiological outcomes. *Journal of Consulting and Clinical Psychology, 53,* 913–925.

Michelson, L., Mavissakalian, M., & Marchione, K. (1988). Cognitive, behavioral and psychological treatments of agoraphobia: A comparative outcome investigation. *Behavior Therapy, 19,* 97–120.

Michelson, L., Mavissakalian, M., Marchione, K., Dancu, C., & Greenwald, M. (1986). The role of self-directed in vivo exposure in cognitive, behavioral and psychophysiological treatments of agoraphobia. *Behavior Therapy, 17,* 91–108.

Munby, M., & Johnson, D. W. (1980). Agoraphobia: The long term follow-up of behavioural treatment. *British Journal of Psychiatry, 137,* 418–427.

Norton, G. R., Dorward, J., & Cox, B. J. (1986). Factors associated with panic attacks in non-clinical subjects. *Behavior Therapy, 17,* 239–252.

Owen, R. T., & Tyrer, P. (1983). Benzodiazepine dependence: A review of the evidence. *Drugs, 25,* 385–398.

Paul, G. L. (1966). *Insight versus desensitization in psychotherapy.* Stanford, CA: Stanford University Press.

Pecknold, J. C., Swinson, R. P., Kuch, K., & Lewis, C. P. (1988). Alprazolam in panic disorder and agoraphobia: Results from a multicenter trial. III. Discontinuation effects. *Archives of General Psychiatry, 45,* 429–436.

Petursson, H., & Lader, M. H. (1981). Benzodiazepine dependence. *British Journal of Addiction, 76*, 133–145.

Pomerleau, O. F., & Rodin, J. (1986). Behavioral medicine and health psychology. In S. L. Garfield & A. E. Bergin (Eds.), *Handbook of psychotherapy and behavior change*. New York: Wiley.

Rachman, S., Levitt, K., & Lopatka, C. (1987). Panic: The link between cognitions and bodily symptoms. *Behaviour Research and Therapy, 25*, 411–423.

Raskin, A., Marks, I. M., & Sheehan, D. V. (1983). The influence of depressed mood on the antipanic effects of antidepressant drugs. Unpublished data. Quoted by D. H. Barlow (1988) in *Anxiety and its disorders: The nature and treatment of anxiety and panic* (p. 433). New York: Guilford Press.

Redmond, D. E. (1985). Neurobiochemical basis for anxiety and anxiety disorders: Evidence from drugs which decrease human fear or anxiety. In A. H. Tuma & J. D. Maser (Eds.), *Anxiety and the anxiety disorders*. Hillsdale, NJ: Lawrence Erlbaum.

Reiman, E. M., Raichle, M. E., Robins, E., Butler, F. K., Herscovitch, P., Fox, P., & Perlmutter, J. (1986). The application of positron emission tomography to the study of panic disorder. *American Journal of Psychiatry, 143*, 469–476.

Robins, L. N., Helzer, J. E., Croughan, J., & Ratcliff, K. S. (1981). National Institute of Mental Health Diagnostic Interview Schedule: Its history, characteristics and validity. *Archives of General Psychiatry, 38*, 381–389.

Salkovskis, P. M., Jones, D. R. O., & Clark, D. M. (1986). Respiratory control in the treatment of panic attacks: Replication. *British Journal of Psychiatry, 148*, 526–532.

Sanchez-Craig, M., Cappell, H., Busto, U., & Kay, G. (1987). Cognitive-behavioural treatment for benzodiazepine dependence: A comparison of gradual versus abrupt cessation of drug intake. *British Journal of Addiction, 82*, 1317–1327.

Schatzberg, A. F., & Cole, J. O. (1986). *Manual of clinical psychopharmacology*. Washington, DC: American Psychiatric Press.

Schwartz, G. E. (1977). Psychosomatic disorders and biofeedback: A psychobiological model of dysregulation. In J. D. Maser & M. E. P. Seligman (Eds.), *Psychopathology: Experimental models*. San Francisco: Freeman.

Sheehan, D. V., Ballenger, J. C., & Jacobson, G. (1980). Treatment of endogenous anxiety with phobic, hysterical, and hypochondriacal symptoms. *Archives of General Psychiatry, 37*, 51–59.

Skegg, D. C. G., Doll, R., & Perry, J. (1977). Use of medicines in general practice. *British Medical Journal, 288*, 1379.

Solyom, C., Solyom, L., Lapierre, Y., Pecknold, J., & Morton, L. (1981). Phenelzine and exposure in the treatment of phobias. *Biological Psychiatry, 16*, 239–247.

Solyom, L., Heseltine, G. F. D., McClure, J. D., Solyom, C., Ledwidge, B., & Steinberg, G. (1973). Behaviour therapy versus drug therapy in the treatment of phobic neurosis. *Journal of the Canadian Psychiatric Association, 18*, 25–32.

Spitzer, R. L., Williams, J. B. W., & Gibbons, M. (1985). *Instruction manual for the Structured Clinical Interview for DSM-III*. New York: Biometrics Research Department, New York State Psychiatric Institute.

Swinson, R. P., Pecknold, J. C., & Kirby, M. E. (1987). Benzodiazepine dependence. *Journal of Affective Disorders, 3*, 109–118.

Telch, M. J. (1988). Combined pharmacological and psychological treatment. In C. G. Last & M. Hersen (Eds.), *Handbook of anxiety disorders*. New York: Pergamon Press.

Telch, M. J., Agras, W. S., Taylor, C. B., Roth, W. T., & Gallen, C. G. (1985). Combined pharmacological and behavioural treatment for agoraphobia. *Behaviour Research and Therapy*, 23, 325–335.

Weissman, M. M. (1979). The psychological treatment of depression: Evidence for the efficacy of psychotherapy alone, in comparison with, and in combination with, pharmacotherapy. *Archives of General Psychiatry*, 36, 1261–1269.

Weissman, M. M. (1985). The epidemiology of anxiety disorders: Rates, risks and family patterns. In A. H. Tuma & J. D. Maser (Eds.), *Anxiety and the anxiety disorders*. Hillsdale, NJ: Lawrence Erlbaum.

Whitehead, W. E., Robinson, A., Blackwell, B., & Stutz, R. M. (1978). Flooding treatment of phobias: Does chronic diazepam increase effectiveness? *Journal of Behavior Therapy and Experiential Psychiatry*, 9, 219–225.

Wolpe, J. (1958). *Psychotherapy by reciprocal inhibition*. Stanford, CA: Stanford University Press.

Woods, J. H., Katz, J. L., & Winger, G. (1987). Abuse liability of benzodiazepines. *Pharmacological Reviews*, 39, 251–419.

Yorkston, N., Sergeant, H., & Rachman, S. (1968). Methohexitone relaxation for desensitising agoraphobics. *Lancet*, 2, 651–653.

Zitrin, C. M., Klein, D. F., & Woerner, M. G. (1978). Behavior therapy, supportive psychotherapy, imipramine and phobias. *Archives of General Psychiatry*, 35, 307–316.

Zitrin, C. M., Klein, D. F., & Woerner, M. G. (1980). Treatment of agoraphobia with group exposure in vivo and imipramine. *Archives of General Psychiatry*, 37, 63–72.

Zitrin, C. M., Klein, D. F., Woerner, M. G., & Ross, D. C. (1983). Treatment of phobias. I. Comparison of imipramine hydrochloride and placebo. *Archives of General Psychiatry*, 40 (2), 125–138.

CHAPTER 9

The Psychodynamic Approach in the Treatment of Panic Disorder

M. KATHERINE SHEAR

Introduction

The past few decades have seen major advances in psychiatric research in the field of anxiety disorders. Neurobiologic studies have led to increased understanding of biological aspects of panic and phobic anxiety states, and have gone hand in hand with the development of effective psychopharmacologic treatments. New strategies for cognitive-behavioral treatments have also been developed and tested. During this period psychodynamic theories of anxiety have received less attention. There is as yet no formal body of prospective clinical research data relevant to the psychodynamic treatment of anxiety disorders. Nevertheless, a considerable amount of thoughtful theoretical material and careful clinical observation has accumulated relative to this topic. It is possible that a psychodynamic perspective can provide insights into questions as yet unanswered by current theoretical models. For example, what determines the time of onset of a panic disorder? What determines the timing of panic attacks during an illness episode? What is the relationship between personality traits and symptom formation? What determines the consequences of panic for an individual patient? In addition, psychodynamically based treatments may help in the management of treatment-resistant patients or provide protection against future panic vulnerability or both. Psychodynamic thinking can be used to guide supportive treatment strategies, including those that use cognitive-behavioral and/or medication treatment.

Psychodynamic treatment is a therapeutic approach that focuses primarily on the elucidation of underlying intrapsychic disturbances in treating symptoms and characterologically based maladaptive behaviors. According to psychoanalytic theory, behavior and mental experience are manifestations of interacting and opposing intrapsychic forces arising among the putative agents of a mental apparatus. These agents are the id, which encompasses instinctual drives; the ego, responsible for self-awareness, mental representations of others, and executive and inhibiting activities; and the superego, the agent of judgments related to conscience and ideals. Much of the activity of the psychic agencies occurs beyond conscious awareness. Preconscious activity is passively beyond awareness, whereas the unconscious field is actively repressed. Psychodynamic explanations emphasize the importance of unconscious determinants of thoughts, feelings, and behavior. Psychological symptoms are seen as having important unconscious mental origins. Anxiety plays a central role in psychoanalytic theory.

Childhood experiences influence the development and, ultimately, the adult configuration of the mental apparatus. Mature psychological structures bear the imprint of developmental vicissitudes. Constitutional and environmental factors interact to determine the type and quality of childhood experience, so each of these has its effect on adult psychological functioning. A particularly salient manifestation of the influence of past on present behavior is interpersonal relationships. The concept of "object relations" refers to internalized mental images of other people in relation to the self and is differentiated from actual interpersonal experiences. The quality and constancy of early relationships form the core object representations. These internalized representations dictate a set of predetermined expectations about the attitude and behaviors of others. Such expectations make important contributions to the quality of relationships with help givers and influence the potential effectiveness of any treatment relationship. The degree of stability of object representations determines responses to the loss of real relationships and vice versa. The presence of stable, satisfying object representations contributes to an ongoing sense of safety and protection against threat. Disturbances of object relations can shake the foundations of personal security and thus increase vulnerability to anxiety.

The psychodynamic therapist listens to a patient from a special perspective, tracking verbal productions and behaviors with a view to understanding how they represent symbolic transformations of underlying themes. The therapist pays attention to manifestations of psychosexual drives, identifies types of psychological defenses and the situations in which they appear, and characterizes the quality and content of object relations and self-representations. The special techniques used to elucidate these underlying issues include the therapist's maintenance of a state of free-floating attention and the encouragement of the patient to communicate thoughts without censoring (free association). In addition, the patient's specific expectations and assumptions about the therapist (transference) are a central focus of the treatment. The therapist's position of friendly neutrality facilitates the clear delineation of transference distortions. Clarification and interpretation of transference feelings can then be used as an effective therapeutic tool.

Psychodynamic treatment can be conducted in a brief, focused form known as brief psychodynamic psychotherapy; in a long-term, moderately intensive form known as exploratory psychotherapy; or in the long-term, frequent, highly intensive form that is psychoanalysis proper. Case reports in the literature document the effective treatment of patients with panic attacks using each of these forms (for example, Malan, 1976; Mann, 1973; McDougall, 1985; Sandler, 1988; Sifneos, 1972; and Silber, 1984). A psychodynamic approach to the treatment of panic focuses attention on four aspects of the therapy situation:

1. The psychological issues that may underlay panic vulnerability and/or trigger specific panic episodes
2. The particular psychological meaning of panic to a given patient
3. The presence and basis of associated life problems
4. The importance of the therapeutic relationship as a supportive context and potential therapeutic tool

The purpose of this chapter is to present psychodynamic thinking about anxiety and panic from a theoretical and clinical perspective. We will trace the historical progression of Freud's thinking about anxiety, as core elements of current psychoanalytic understanding of anxiety are still based on those ideas. A modern psychodynamic approach would use an integrated biopsychosocial model. An integrated model is particularly useful in allowing us to incorporate psychodynamically informed thinking with other currently available theoretical models and treatment strategies. In this chapter we will illustrate this approach by comparing and contrasting various aspects of psychodynamically based ideas about anxiety with biological and cognitive-behavioral theories. We will then suggest ways in which a psychodynamic approach can be used, alone or in combination with other strategies, to optimize effective treatment.

The Theoretical Background

Freud's Theory of Anxiety

Much of current psychoanalytic theory of anxiety is unchanged from Freud's original conceptions. Anxiety, defined as the mental reaction to anticipated dangers, was a central feature of Freud's clinical and metapsychological theory. Freud discussed anxiety in virtually all of his major theoretical papers, so his thinking about anxiety spanned the length of his career. A series of papers summarize his views: "On the Grounds for Detaching a Particular Syndrome from Neurasthenia Under the Description of Anxiety Neurosis" (Freud, 1895); "The Common Neurotic State" and "Anxiety," presented as part of the *Introductory Lectures on Psychoanalysis* (Freud, 1917); the seminal work *Inhibitions, Symptoms and Anxiety* (Freud, 1926); and "Anxiety and the Instinctual Life" as part of the *New Introductory Lectures* (Freud, 1933). In these works, Freud elaborates his ideas about anxiety, proposing a dimensional view that ranges in intensity from signal to traumatic levels. He presents a categorical conceptualization of the origin of anxiety, which can be physiological (for instance, arising from unreleased sexual tension), psychological (from a build-up of repudiated loving or longing feelings), or responsive to a real danger. Thus, Freud discusses biological, psychological, and social-environmental models of anxiety separately. Although the combination was in some ways implicit in his thinking, Freud himself did not write about situations in which anxiety might occur with subthreshold activation related to two or three of these situations. However, the model he proposed led others to postulate this possibility. A biopsychosocial model enables us to incorporate newer knowledge based on psychological and neurophysiological research while maintaining many of Freud's core ideas. The discussion that follows will attempt to demonstrate this.

In 1972 Alan Compton reviewed the development of Freud's theory of anxiety. He organized his papers according to five chronological phases in Freud's writing and traced four major themes: the physiological basis of anxiety, signal anxiety, normal anxiety, and neurotic anxiety. These themes provide a useful format within which to discuss the major elements of Freud's theory.

The Physical Basis of Anxiety

Freud's first ideas about anxiety (pre-1900) focused on explaining its somatic manifestations, which he believed resulted from an incomplete discharge of physiological excitation. By this he meant that certain experiences, such as trauma and sexual activity, were associated with neuronal excitation that required discharge by motor or verbal activity. If this discharge did not occur, the state of excitation persisted in the form of neurotic anxiety. In 1895, Freud published a description of a syndrome called "anxiety neurosis" that is nearly identical with present-day descriptions of panic disorder. He explained this condition as an "actual" neurosis, by which he meant there was an immediate, physiological basis. He later distinguished actual neurosis from psychoneurosis, in which a quantity of energy (undischarged excitation) was generated in connection with an unacceptable sexual *idea* and retained in memory. In both cases, the build-up of sexual excitement provided the energic basis and explained the origin of anxiety. However, in actual neurosis, the build-up occurred because of interrupted sexual activity, whereas in psychoneurosis excitement accumulated in relation to sexual thoughts that were blocked from expression by a psychologically based prohibition.

Viewed from a modern perspective, this early notion can be seen as a theory of a peripheral physiological origin of anxiety. In this respect, the theory fits with a similar hypothesis proposed recently by biologically oriented psychiatric researchers. The difference is that today's ideas about peripheral physiological activation center on causes such as autonomic hyperactivity or mitral valve prolapse rather than on blocked sexual release.

Similarly, Freud's belief that anxiety resulted from the physiological effects of disturbed sexual behavior is reflected in current cognitive-behavioral ideas in several ways. First, both schools share a hypothesis that behavioral disturbance can result in symptoms and a corollary that the cure is based on a behavioral intervention. Second, cognitive-behavioral therapists have noted that somatic activation caused by excitement, as well as other affects, can provoke anxiety. The difference is in the mechanism of provocation of anxiety, which is seen by such therapists as a conditioned response rather than a blocked instinctual pressure for tension release.

In 1900 Freud wrote his landmark work *The Interpretation of Dreams*. In it he maintained that the source of anxiety (the physical basis) was undischarged neuronal excitation, but added a new physiological mechanism. Now anxiety was derived from one of three possible sources: (1) disturbed somatic processes, especially those that led to difficulty breathing; (2) neurotic anxiety, in turn derived from excessive undischarged sexual excitation (actual neurosis); and (3) the affective aspect of repressed libido. Evidently Freud had noticed the central role of respiratory functioning in anxiety; nonetheless, this role was never fully elaborated in his theories.

The final theory of anxiety was presented in 1926 in *Inhibitions, Symptoms and Anxiety* and was accompanied by the introduction of the structural theory (the division of the mind into id, ego, and superego). Freud now abandoned his search for a physiological basis of anxiety and moved on to develop a fully psychological model. The generation of anxiety was seen as an ego function, activated in response to a perception of danger. Danger was defined as a situation of potential helplessness that could originate in either an internal (the id or superego) or external (the environment) threat. His interest in the relationship of anxiety to ego function enabled Freud to shift his focus away from physiological explanations. On the other hand, he seemed to remain concerned with understanding the mechanism of development of somatic symptoms, and he never abandoned the idea of anxiety as a discharge phenomenon, related to the accumulation of libidinal energies.

Although Freud did not say so directly, his ideas are consistent with a notion that the ego confers the quality of anxiety upon sensations of physiological arousal that: (1) accompany the perception of impending external physical or social danger, (2) arise physiologically (from "spontaneous" autonomic activation, drugs, or physical illness), or (3) occur in connection with other affective responses (such as excitement, anger, or frustration). The reader will recognize that these conditions are commonly accepted as triggers of anxiety by cognitive-behavioral or biological researchers. The perspective that remains unique to psychodynamic theory is that neurotic anxiety is generated when there is an activation of unconscious mental urges and prohibitions. Thus, there is a fourth possible trigger situation, in which a stimulus directly activates unconscious danger situations without an intermediary conscious perception.

The Concept of Signal Anxiety

Freud's preoccupation with the physical basis of anxiety led to his attempts to explain the origins of anxiety. The development of the concept of signal anxiety introduced other features of anxiety, for example, its function as a trigger of defensive behavior and the meaning of its modulation along a continuum of intensity.

Freud's earliest notion of anxiety as a signal of the emergence of repressed material was presented in *The Interpretation of Dreams*. He suggested that the "dream censor" responded to the anxiety signal by limiting the expression of unacceptable wishes. At this time Freud used a "topographical" model that explained all mental processes as occurring at one of three levels: unconscious, preconscious, or conscious. A wish belonging to the unconscious—and recognized as unacceptable by the preconscious—generated anxiety. Freud's first presentation of the idea of signal anxiety held that it occurred as a consequence of repression and served to warn of the reemergence of repressed material. The idea of a signal heralding the undisguised appearance of a forbidden repressed wish introduced the concept of intrapsychic conflict and represented the first psychodynamic explanation of anxiety. Freud suggested that the mind responded to the anxiety signal by altering the character of images and the focus of attention, to protect itself from the full emergence of forbidden urges.

From 1902 to 1914 Freud formulated his ideas about infantile sexuality and the developmental progression of libidinal urges through the oral, anal, phallic, and genital phases. His major contribution to anxiety theory during this period was the analysis of little Hans (Freud, 1909). This case provided a basis for discussing the psychodynamic origins of anxiety. The boy's fears were seen as related to longing, to aggressive wishes, and to a fear of punishment. Anxiety was identified as resulting from the perception of internal danger associated with drives or wishes. The role of conscience and guilt in producing anxiety were introduced. Freud's discussion of this case also introduced the important idea of symbolic transformation as a mechanism of phobia development.

In the 1917 chapter on anxiety Freud elaborated the idea of its signal function by asserting that anxiety led to the institution of defenses in situations in which dangerous drives were activated. When the generation of anxiety was limited to an aborted, unconscious, signal form, it triggered effective defenses. Freud argued that in this form anxiety was adaptive. Generation of the experience of anxiety, on the other hand, was seen as inexpedient, disorganizing, and likely to thwart effective defensive maneuvers.

Finally, in *Inhibitions, Symptoms and Anxiety*, Freud proposed a developmental concept to explain the intensity of anxiety. He suggested a progression from an infantile, predominantly somatic, inexpedient, fully expressed form to a mature, effective, and fleeting signal form. In other words, once generated, anxiety could be described within an intensity dimension. The intense, symptomatic form, with prominent somatic manifestations (traumatic anxiety), was viewed as ontogenetically primitive, whereas the signal form, predominantly cognitive and often unconscious, represented the developmentally advanced form. The two forms were considered to be on a continuum, with signal anxiety an attenuated version of traumatic or "automatic" anxiety. Signal anxiety triggered psychological defense mechanisms.

The capacity to develop signal anxiety was seen as related to ego maturation and to the development of permanent object cathexes. Freud held that in the adult, anxiety could either occur as a massive, overwhelming experience of helplessness or as a signal of anticipation of this state. The latter could be experienced in graded levels of intensity. The psychic content of signal anxiety was determined by unconscious danger situations that could be related to any of the phases of libidinal organization.

Normal Anxiety

In 1917, in a chapter of the *Introductory Lectures*, Freud added the idea of a realistic as well as a neurotic form of anxiety. This new concept of realistic anxiety heralded a shift to a more directly formulated psychological origin for anxiety and away from interest in identifying putative sources of undischarged nervous excitation. Freud wrote that realistic anxiety was derived from "ego" libido, though the concept of the ego was not yet well developed.

Realistic, or normal, anxiety occurred in response to the accurate perception of actual external danger. The capacity to generate normal anxiety was a manifestation of the self-preservative instinct, the ego's reaction to danger. Normal anxiety was a signal to take defensive action and was adaptive in that it stimulated problem solving. The intensity of this normal anxiety was always low enough to avert its painful and disorganizing consequences.

The Roots and Manifestations of Neurotic Anxiety

Neurotic anxiety was described in 1917 as the ego's reaction to internal (libidinal) demands perceived as dangerous. Clinically, three types of neurotic anxiety were delineated: (1) chronic, general, or free-floating apprehensiveness; (2) psychically bound anxiety attached to external objects or situations (phobias); and (3) anxiety with no discernable relation to danger (spontaneous anxiety attacks or anxiety accompanying hysterical symptoms).

Freud described neurotic anxiety in relation to infantile fears. The latter were defined by phylogenetic and ontogenetic fear situations that were considered universal and inborn. These included fears of the loss of mother, of the loss of mother's love, of castration, and of guilt. In normal development, a smooth progression through the predetermined psychosexual phases precluded the triggering of these infantile fears. In neurotics, however, this progression was impeded, leaving them vulnerable to anxiety in response to the activation of infantile fears.

In the *New Introductory Lectures*, written in the final phase of his career, Freud again outlined his theory of anxiety. He defined neurotic anxiety as based on internal fear situations related to realistic anxiety through their connection with infantile fears. During childhood, certain libidinal wishes are connected with realistic, threatening consequences and thus represent real dangers to the child. In the adult, neurotic anxiety and its associated symptoms are generated in response to the activation of unresolved infantile conflicts.

Summary

In summary, Freud's theory of anxiety was initially based on the idea that accumulated nervous excitation needed discharge. Anxiety was the result of this accumulation, when normal discharge channels were impeded. *The Interpretation of Dreams* marked the beginning of the development of Freud's psychodynamic theory, which was to constitute his major contribution to psychological thinking. In this work he introduced the relationship between anxiety and repressed wishes that would eventually develop into the signal theory of anxiety.

In the years that followed Freud developed his theory of infantile sexuality and elaborated a developmental progression of psychosexual wishes and fears. Freud postulated a continuing role for these early wishes and fears in adult mental life. He placed them in a hidden, primitive matrix—the unconscious mind—where psychic activity was nonverbal and governed by symbolic, autistic, associative rather than reality-based, logical rules. He argued that understanding the true meaning of human psychological events required the ability to recognize and symbolically decode manifestations of unconscious motivational states. Direct manifestations of unconscious processes were seen as constituting a potential threat. Forbidden material was prevented from emerging by a warning, called signal anxiety, that served to trigger the elaboration of defense mechanisms.

Through the years Freud's conceptual models shifted, as he deepened and elaborated his innovative theory of psychological processes. This development is reflected most clearly in the shift from the topographical model, with its explanatory principles rooted in ideas of energy transformation, to the structural theory, in which the interaction of different sides of the personality plays a much greater role. Although the two models were not incompatible, the structural model was far more complex psychologically and led to a shift in focus away from neurophysiological energetics. With this shift, the roots of anxiety were seen as more importantly psychological.

Contributions of Later Analysts

Psychoanalysts have continued to be interested in developing Freud's theory of anxiety, which is still believed to be incomplete. Specifically, whether anxiety is best viewed as a discharge phenomenon or as an ego phenomenon continues to be debated. Other areas of interest include the importance of cognition, meaning, communication, and object relations. The developmental progress of anxiety is also of considerable interest, and research is actively under way in this area. Emde (1985) summarizes and reviews this work.

The psychodynamic view of anxiety as outlined by Freud has been generally accepted with some additions to the types of instinctual drives and to the kinds of danger situations that can evoke anxiety. In particular, the role of aggressive drives in the generation of anxiety has been discussed. The development of self psychology has added fear of fusion, of loss of self-esteem, of humiliation, and of ego disintegration to the other internal fear situations.

Several analysts have become interested in child development and the relationship of human behavior to that of other animals. John Bowlby is a central contributor in both of these areas. Bowlby (1973, 1980) emphasizes the occurrence and importance of a primary instinct for attachment. He sees the preprogrammed reaction to the loss of a primary attachment figure as central to the development of anxiety. He distinguishes anxiety from fear, which is the response (also preprogrammed) to perceived danger. In other words, anxiety is related to the loss of safety, especially as safety is embodied by an interpersonal attachment. Fear is related to the appearance of external danger. Inborn cues of danger and of impending separation are modified during development by cultural and learned cues.

Infancy researchers—notably Spitz (1950), Benjamin (1961), Emde, Gaensbauer, and Harmon (1976), and Stern (1974)—have looked closely at the development and manifestation of early infantile fear states such as separation and stranger reactions. They have noted that the development of fear occurs in a biobehavioral context in which other related behaviors are also developing. These include attachment, exploratory, and affiliative behaviors. Specific types of fearfulness develop at different maturational stages and often herald the appearance of a biobehavioral shift at multiple levels of functioning. In this paradigm, early anxiety reactions are seen as precursors but not prototypes of adult anxiety. The notion of regression of adult behaviors to prototypical infantile states no longer holds. The vicissitudes of early experiences are still believed to influence later development, but the relationship between infantile fears and adult anxiety is no longer direct.

The Problem of Panic

In recent years the differentiation by psychopharmacologists (Klein, in particular) of panic from other anxiety states has again raised the possibility of two different types of anxiety. Psychoanalysts have returned to Freud's early descriptions of actual neurosis, finding there a description of spontaneous anxiety attacks that closely parallels the DSM-III. As we have seen, Freud attributed the origin of actual neurotic states to nonpsychological factors. However, this view was not well integrated into the body of his work, and some analysts have not concurred in this view. Instead, they have seen panic states as a failure of ego functioning in the face of overwhelming instinctual threat. Hence, the content of the anxiety is seen as unconscious but related to prohibited infantile wishes, not different from anxiety in other psychoneurotic states. In this view, panic is on a continuum of intensity and is not qualitatively different from anxiety.

On the other hand, it is clear that Freud's model provided a special place for "traumatic anxiety," defined as a state in which the ego is overwhelmed by a sense of helplessness in the face of immediate, catastrophic danger. Other forms of anxiety are conceived of as anticipatory to this state and as serving to signal the institution of defenses to ward off helplessness. This conception is more consistent with current ideas of panic as qualitatively different, though related, to other forms of anxiety. It is important to emphasize that there is a role for underlying psychological conflict in triggering a panic episode in either of these models.

An alternative way to conceptualize panic is discussed articulately by Cooper (1985). He reviews the neurobiological evidence that panic is not necessarily an indication of an underlying conflict or a primary disorder of self or object relations. If these occur, he points out, they may be secondary to the disorganizing effects of anxiety. Panic could be viewed instead as a manifestation of an ongoing biological dysregulation. Cooper suggests the analyst try to tease apart which manifestations of anxiety are related to an underlying biological disturbance and which are in fact disturbances of the intrapsychic world. He presents a case vignette to illustrate the usefulness of medication treatment for an anxious, depressed patient. He points out that in addition to the direct effects of the medication, such patients benefit from being given a model of symptom formation that does not hold them fully responsible for the dysphoria and affective intensity they experience. Clinical experience supports the observation that many patients flee treatment or suffer symptom exacerbation (or both) upon entry into a standard psychodynamic treatment.

In summary, the unique quality of Freud's ideas is related to his central focus on the vicissitudes of "instinctual" (sexual and aggressive) feelings. In this way, his theories of actual neurosis and psychoneurosis can be seen as similar. Differences are related to whether the psychological disturbance is viewed as behavioral (in the actual neuroses) or cognitive (in the psychoneuroses). Freud elaborated a view of mental life as centrally concerned with managing forces related to the modulation and satisfaction of sexual and aggressive urges. In his view, virtually all psychopathology could be explained by the mind's inability to manage this effectively. Later psychoanalysts have further developed Freud's ideas, in particular in the areas of object relations and self psychology, but this work has not changed the basic orientation of the model.

On the other hand, scientific advances have now revealed that neurophysiological regulatory disturbances play an important role in the etiology and pathogenesis of many psychiatric disorders. Symptoms such as panic can also be explained as manifestations of conditioning processes or of a somatic behavioral disturbance such as hyperventilation. It is clear that psychodynamic theories are often neither necessary nor sufficient to explain psychopathology. Nevertheless, there is also clear evidence that environmental stimuli influence neurophysiological reactivity and that the meaning of such stimuli often mediates their impact. Correction of persistent maladaptive behaviors or consistent distortions in the appraisal of life experiences—or both—promises to afford symptomatic relief through a process somewhat different from the direct amelioration of neurophysiological disturbance. Thus, in spite of major scientific advances in understanding the biological and cognitive-behavioral underpinnings of psychopathology, a psychodynamic perspective has considerable explanatory and therapeutic power and should not be completely abandoned. In the remainder of this chapter, we will discuss the usefulness of this perspective from a more practical, clinical viewpoint.

The Clinical Approach

An Overview of the Treatment Approach

Principles of psychodynamic treatment grew out of the theoretical ideas we have outlined. As noted, the perspective of the psychodynamic therapist stems from a particular interest in aspects of mental life centrally concerned with the development and management of instinctual forces, the patient's sense of self, and the quality and stability of object relations. A psychodynamic treatment is oriented toward ameliorating these aspects of psychopathology, just as a pharmacological approach is oriented toward ameliorating neurobiological disturbance and behavioral therapy is oriented toward alleviating symptoms rooted in pathological conditioned responses. A large available literature supports the usefulness of each of these approaches in the actual clinical management of anxiety. It is not yet clear when and if the different approaches should be used in combination. In the discussion that follows we will describe some of the existing case reports and suggest an integrated approach that is likely to be most beneficial to the panic patient.

As we have reviewed, psychodynamic theory predicts that anxiety is generated when unconscious danger situations are activated. Such situations include the threatened emergence of prohibited instinctual urges or the impending disruption of self or object representations. Activation of unconscious dangers may occur in response to consciously perceived internal psychological or physiological disturbances, or to an external physical or social threat. Alternatively, the link between the triggering stimulus and an unconscious danger situation may occur beyond awareness. In this case anxiety is experienced as arising "spontaneously." The psychodynamic therapist is interested in the common intrapsychic themes associated with both "triggered" and "spontaneous" panic states. It is important to note, as Cooper (1985) does, that this perspective does not necessarily mean that panic or other anxiety states

never originate *de novo* from neurophysiological discharge, or as a manifestation of a conditioning process without significant relation to an unconscious
danger. Rather, the psychodynamic therapist makes an effort to tease apart
those situations in which panic is triggered by physiological changes in the
brain and those in which it is triggered by the unconscious activation of
intrapsychic dangers.

The theory further predicts that the intensity of anxiety will be determined
by the degree to which the ego feels able to defend itself against a perceived
threat. Panic occurs when a sense of helplessness is coupled with a virtually
complete lack of accessible, adaptive coping strategies with which to manage
danger. It follows that the degree of helplessness will be related to both the
strength of coping capacities and the intensity and immediacy of a perceived
threat. The sudden activation of an intrapsychic conflict may trigger a sense
of desperation or panic if the activation occurs in the context of significantly
weakened coping capacity, or if the intensity of repressed urges means that
emergence into consciousness would constitute a substantial and immediate
threat. The goals of the psychodynamic therapist are to identify whether this
kind of situation is contributing significantly to the patient's symptomatology
and, if so, to develop a treatment plan designed to strengthen defenses and/or
weaken the intensity of impulses.

There is another advantage to psychodynamic thinking in the treatment
of a panic patient. As we have seen, the theory predicts that a given panic
episode may be triggered by the activation of unconscious material in a
vulnerable area. Clearly implicit in this idea is the expectation that an area of
psychological vulnerability is present. The psychodynamic therapist expects
this vulnerability to manifest itself in other areas of the patient's life that may
have a considerable role in interfering with adaptation. In some cases, panic
episodes may constitute the "ticket of admission" that allows the patient to
discuss disturbing life problems for which he or she would otherwise be
reluctant to seek help. In general, the psychodynamic psychotherapist will be
interested in placing the panic symptom in the context of the patient's life.
Treatment goals will include, but may not be limited to, symptom relief.

Even if psychological disturbances do not best explain the etiology of
panic, vulnerable psychological areas may be stressed by the occurrence of
panic episodes. For example, patients with a vulnerable sense of self develop
global self-doubts and fear of psychological decompensation after experiencing recurrent panic. Patients with conflicts in aggressivity fear the loss of
control of aggression. In this sense, panic may be seen as providing a window
into intrapsychic vulnerability and an opportunity to identify and treat important characterological disturbance. For any given patient a decision must
be made whether such treatment is indicated. This decision is based on the
therapist's assessment of the patient's general level of psychological functioning and on the patient's interest in participating in a treatment designed to
address identified problems. Although there are no formal studies document-
ing the usefulness of psychodynamic treatment in protecting against the

relapse of panic disorder, some available data suggests that personality disorders are present in a high proportion of panic disorder patients (Friedman, Shear, & Frances, 1985; Reich, 1988; Reich, Noyes, & Troughton, 1987). It is probable that the treatment of characterological disturbances increases adaptational flexibility and lowers the likelihood of symptom development during periods of life stress.

Another central defining characteristic of psychodynamic treatment is its focus on identifying the nature of the transference. The psychodynamic therapist assumes that the patient will enter a treatment situation with predetermined expectations about the attitude of the therapist. These expectations will influence the patient's behavior and experience of the therapeutic process. The therapist will decide how best to use the transference to facilitate treatment. In a psychodynamic treatment per se, transference material will be used as a tool to elucidate intrapsychic processes. In a supportive treatment, transference issues will help guide the therapist's approach in presenting advice and reassurance or in prescribing medication. For example, a dependent patient may need support in making decisions. A therapist who is aware of this dimension of the treatment will provide appropriate reassurance in response to the patient's efforts to be independent. The management of medication in a dependent patient may utilize transference attitudes to ensure compliance. With such a patient the therapist will enhance effectiveness by taking a firm, authoritative stand to convince the patient of the need for medication and a strong, protective stance to manage fears related to side effects. On the other hand, if the patient's transference reaction is characterized by distrust and a need to feel in control, the therapist will behave differently. For this patient, supportive treatment would focus on learning to use others' help more effectively. Medication management would be assisted by allowing the patient to participate actively in dosage decisions.

Choosing a Treatment Strategy

There is good empirical evidence that the symptomatic treatment of panic attacks can be accomplished effectively and efficiently by pharmacological or cognitive-behavioral treatments. Such evidence does not exist for psychodynamic treatment. This means that the choice of psychodynamic treatment as a first-line strategy should be made only with clear justification. In addition, a therapist choosing a psychodynamic approach without providing simultaneous direct, symptomatic treatment should closely track the patient's progress with a plan to initiate such treatment if necessary. Clinical experience and some case reports suggest that many patients do better in exploratory treatments once the panic symptoms are effectively under control.

On the other hand, case reports describe situations in which patients who met criteria for panic disorder responded well to brief psychodynamic therapy without medication. Mann (1973) reports a case of a housewife disabled by agoraphobic symptoms whose dependency and lack of assertiveness were seen as central to symptom formation. The report includes a detailed description of a brief therapy, heavily focused on transference interpretations, that produced virtual recovery. Sifneos (1972) also describes a psychodynamic treatment in some detail. The patient was a young mother, employed part-time as a fashion model. This patient complained of frigidity and agoraphobia. The treatment focused on feelings of guilt about sexual pleasure and in particular guilt related to her aggressive, competitive feelings toward her mother. Sifneos convincingly linked the agoraphobic symptoms with the frigidity. The treatment was successful, with remission maintained through a 7-year follow-up.

There are also case reports of patients whose recovery from panic states occurred in response to psychoanalytic work. An example is a treatment reported by Silber (1984). He describes a patient whose onset of panic episodes occurred during the course of an analysis. The episodes were analyzed and clearly represented responses to prohibited underlying impulses. For example, one of the panic attacks, triggered in the context of a stressful situation (the analyst's vacation) through symbolic association with environmental stimuli (being on a bus at a street whose number matched her father's age when he died of a heart attack) indicated activation of an unacceptable aggressive wish that the analyst would die as punishment for leaving her. The other panic episodes were associated with "many aspects of the patient's repressed past." Analysis of each episode led to relief of anxiety as well as personal growth associated with the strengthening of her ego functioning. Another patient, reported by Sandler (1988), was a 32-year-old woman who had anxiety attacks and depression in the context of planning her first pregnancy. The analysis revealed fears of passivity and murderous wishes toward rivals. Analytic work elucidating these frightening unconscious impulses as well as object relations disturbances led to substantial symptomatic relief. The author underscores her "view that the same unconscious fantasies and internal object relationships lie behind the patient's symptoms, character traits, and relationships, and can be discerned in the transference" (p. 326).

These cases illustrate the usefulness of a psychodynamic approach in ameliorating other psychological disturbances in patients with panic attacks. In each of them, panic symptoms were also relieved; however, in our experience many patients have a less favorable response to exploratory treatment alone. Some of them benefit from psychodynamic treatment by managing to cope with panic and anxiety symptoms while avoiding dealing directly with the symptoms in the treatment. These patients often report that they learned something about themselves but experienced no amelioration of panic symptoms as a result of the therapy. Another group experiences an exacerbation of panic and/or flees treatment if a structured, supportive, symptom-focused treatment is not initiated.

On initial contact patients are almost always preoccupied with panic and highly resistant to a discussion of psychological issues. Premature indications by the therapist of interest in exploring the psychological roots of episodes leads to a heightening of already strong resistance and may alienate the patient. There is a need for the therapist to focus on the experience of panic, to empathize, and to demonstrate actively his or her expertise in managing the symptoms directly. Patients in this phase of treatment often appear to be unpsychologically minded, uninterested in psychological issues, and "dumb" about identifying inner experience. They are compliant but don't hear much that is not action oriented and directly related to resolving the panic. They are rarely able to be reflective. Interestingly, this attitude often changes after the initial phase of treatment (that is, after the panic is dealt with effectively).

Another aspect of the patient's focus on panic is that current life problems are neglected. In fact, virtually all psychological work is abandoned in favor of a preoccupation with patients' efforts to make the panic episodes predictable and controllable and with fears of their inability to do this. Patients develop various hypotheses about what has caused the panic and what precipitates episodes. They institute behavioral patterns such as interpersonal clinging, situational avoidance, and sometimes compulsive rituals. The accompanying difficulty with everyday functioning and problem solving accentuates their sense of vulnerability, fears of loss of control, and personal deterioration. The best initial route into this vicious circle is panic management. However, once the panic is addressed, patients vary in their ability to put the rest of the pieces back together. Often they need further help. Moreover, in the context of the development of a panic disorder, a set of infantile fears and repudiated wishes that has been activated appears to be available to conscious awareness (either as a precipitant or in response to the initial panic). The panic disorder episode can thus be seen as an opportunity for self-exploration—the unlocking of a door to primitive, survival-oriented fears and urges. Many patients can make productive use of this opportunity. Doing so may enhance their overall life adjustment and reduce vulnerability to future episodes.

In summary, a psychodynamic approach to the treatment of panic has its assets and limitations. The main strength of this type of treatment is its focus on understanding each individual patient. In the initial phase of treatment, a psychodynamic approach encourages the therapist to be sensitive to establishing rapport with the patient. Panic attacks are usually experienced as frightening, seemingly irrational episodes in which loss of control is a prominent concern. Consultation with a psychiatrist may be seen as confirmation of the patient's worst fear (losing control and going crazy). Many panic patients have been told repeatedly that no physical illness is causing their symptoms. Because they continue to feel physically ill they decide they must be crazy, and they anticipate that a psychiatrist will confirm this humiliating fear. Because medical doctors have been unable to help them or to diagnose their problem clearly, patients may have little hope of obtaining relief of their physical symptoms from a psychiatrist. These fears may cause them to postpone seeking therapy for a long time. The psychodynamic therapist is likely to be sensitive to the meaning of panic and will plan interventions to help the patient feel understood. A psychodynamic formulation such as the one suggested by Perry, Cooper, and Michels (1987) will allow the therapist to predict the major types of transference and resistance issues. These issues will be important to any treatment approach chosen.

The therapist will also be aware of the need to provide a supportive treatment and will use varying techniques to accomplish this. For example, the therapist will need to decide when it is more useful to provide direct reassurance to a panic patient and when it is more supportive to encourage the patient to manage the symptoms independently (Wallace, 1983). Throughout the treatment, the psychodynamic therapist will explore the context in which panic occurs. The patient will thus be invited to discuss other aspects of his or her life, and crucial emotional issues will be brought to light. A psychodynamic therapy will easily incorporate and integrate treatment of these issues into the panic disorder treatment.

The major limitation of a standard psychodynamic treatment is the omission of a direct discussion with the patient of the diagnosis, a presentation of a model to explain the etiology and consequences of panic, and a direct explanation of the treatment plan. Instead, there is a more open-ended, indirect approach, with the therapist taking a more neutral position. Patients may not be able to tolerate this ambiguity, which may underscore their fears of being crazy or having serious and difficult psychological problems. Psychodynamic treatment thus may be most useful when instituted following direct symptomatic treatment in patients who have a characterological disturbance. Such an approach may improve the outcome for treatment-resistant patients (Muskin & Fyer, 1981) and may provide some protection against future episodes of illness.

References

Benjamin, J. D. (1961). Some developmental observations related to the theory of anxiety. *Journal of the American Psychoanalytic Association, 9,* 652–668.

Bowlby, J. (1973). *Attachment and loss: Vol. 2. Separation: Anxiety and anger.* New York: Basic Books.

Bowlby, J. (1980). *Loss: Sadness and depression.* New York: Basic Books.

Compton, A. (1972a). A study of the psychoanalytic theory of anxiety: I. The development of Freud's theory of anxiety. *Journal of the American Psychoanalytic Association, 20,* 3–44.

Compton, A. (1972b). A study of the psychoanalytic theory of anxiety: II. Developments in the theory of anxiety since 1926. *Journal of the American Psychoanalytic Association, 20,* 341–394.

Cooper, A. M. (1985). Will neurobiology influence psychoanalysis? *American Journal of Psychiatry, 142,* 1395–1402.

Emde, R. N. (1985). Early development and opportunities for research on anxiety. In A. H. Tuma & J. D. Mazer (Eds.), *Anxiety and the anxiety disorders.* Hillsdale, NJ: Lawrence Erlbaum.

Emde, R. N., Gaensbauer, T. J., & Harmon, R. J. (1976). Emotional expression in infancy: A biobehavioral study. *Psychological Issues, 10* (1, Monograph 37).

Freud, S. (1895). On the grounds for detaching a particular syndrome from neurasthenia under the description of anxiety neurosis. In J. Strachey (Ed.)(1961), *The standard edition of the complete psychological works of Sigmund Freud* (Vol. 3, pp. 85–116). London: Hogarth Press.

Freud, S. (1900). The interpretation of dreams. In J. Strachey (Ed.)(1961), *The standard edition of the complete psychological works of Sigmund Freud* (Vols. 4 & 5). London: Hogarth Press.

Freud, S. (1909). Analysis of a phobia in a five year old boy. In J. Strachey (Ed.)(1961), *The standard edition of the complete psychological works of Sigmund Freud* (Vol. 10, pp. 1–148). London: Hogarth Press.

Freud, S. (1917). Introductory lectures on psychoanalysis, Part III. General theory of the neuroses. In J. Strachey (Ed.)(1961), *The standard edition of the complete psychological works of Sigmund Freud* (Vol. 16, pp. 241–478). London: Hogarth Press.

Freud, S. (1926). Inhibitions, symptoms and anxiety. In J. Strachey (Ed.)(1961), *The standard edition of the complete psychological works of Sigmund Freud* (Vol. 20, pp. 75–175). London: Hogarth Press.

Freud, S. (1933). Anxiety and the instinctual life. In J. Strachey (Ed.)(1961), *The standard edition of the complete psychological works of Sigmund Freud* (Vol. 22, pp. 1–183). London: Hogarth Press.

Friedman, K., Shear, M. K., & Frances, A. (1985). DSM-III personality disorders in panic patients. *Journal of Personality Disorders, 2,* 132–136.

McDougall, J. (1985). *Theaters of the mind.* New York: Basic Books.

Malan, D. (1976). *The frontier of brief psychotherapy.* New York: Plenum.

Mann, J. (1973). *Time-limited psychotherapy.* Cambridge, MA: Harvard University Press.

Muskin, P., & Fyer, A. (1981). Treatment of panic disorder. *Journal of Clinical Psychopharmacology, 1,* 81–90.

Perry, S., Cooper, A. M., & Michels, R. (1987). The psychodynamic formulation: Its purpose, structure and clinical application. *American Journal of Psychiatry, 144,* 543–550.

Reich, J., Noyes, R., & Troughton, E. (1987). Dependent personality disorder associated with phobic avoidance in patients with panic disorder. *American Journal of Psychiatry, 144,* 323–326.

Reich, J. H. (1988). DSM-III personality disorders and the outcome of treated panic disorder. *American Journal of Psychiatry, 145,* 1149–1152.

Sandler, A. (1988). Aspects of the analysis of a neurotic patient. *British Journal of Psychoanalysis, 69,* 317–326.

Sifneos, P. E. (1972). *Short-term psychotherapy and emotional crisis.* Cambridge, MA: Harvard University Press.

Silber, A. (1984). Temporary disorganization facilitating recall and mastery: An analysis of a symptom. *Psychoanalytic Quarterly, 53,* 498–501.

Spitz, R. (1950). Anxiety in infancy: A study of its manifestations in the first year of life. *International Journal of Psychoanalysis, 31,* 138–143.

Stern, D. N. (1974). General issues in the study of fear. In M. Lewis & L. A. Rosenblum (Eds.), *The origins of fear.* New York: Wiley.

Wallace, E. R. (1983). *Dynamic psychiatry in theory and practice.* Philadelphia: Lea and Febiger.

CHAPTER 10

The Role of
the Primary Care Physician
in the Treatment of Panic Disorder

REJEAN FONTAINE

During the last 10 years we have witnessed major changes in our understanding of the diagnosis, pathophysiology, and treatment of panic disorder. In this chapter we will attempt a practical task: to review those changes that are relevant for the primary care physician. We begin with a historical review, which should provide sufficient background to understand the current approach to panic disorder. Then we describe the clinical presentation of panic attacks and panic disorder. Panic disorder is often compared to tuberculosis, as its treatment has become so straightforward that it is possible to induce a remission in most cases. Several treatment approaches and a sequential treatment will be described.

History

In the 19th century, several physicians described clinical entities in which anxiety attacks were present: the soldier's heart syndrome and Da Costa's syndrome are examples of these (Wheeler, White, Reed, & Cohen, 1950). However, Freud (1895, 1959) was the first to clearly describe the treatment of a patient who was having panic attacks, and he related it to the development of agoraphobia. Years later the same group of patients with panic attacks was described by Cohen (1949) under the heading of "neurocirculatory asthenia." These patients could not tolerate physical exercise. This finding is of clinical significance because patients seen today with panic disorder are often frightened by physical exercise.

With the development of modern psychiatry, several British psychiatrists (for example, Sargant, 1962) reported that panic attacks in "atypical depression" or agoraphobia were improved with monoamine oxidase (MAO) inhibitors. In the late 1950s and early 1960s, a major turning point was reached via the work of Klein (Klein, 1964, 1967; Klein & Fink, 1962), who showed that imipramine was an effective antipanic agent in agoraphobic patients having spontaneous panic attacks. This major contribution was not well known to clinicians in the 1960s and 1970s; they continued to emphasize traditional verbal therapies for these patients. Practitioners' thinking about the treatment of panic had been highly influenced by the British school of psychiatry; Marks (1969) had reported how effective behavior therapy (desensitization and exposure) was in the treatment of these patients.

However, during the 1970s, several other investigators replicated Klein's findings, which led to increasing controversy about the current classification of anxiety neurosis. With the publication of the DSM-III (American Psychiatric Association, 1980), anxiety neurosis was subdivided into panic disorder and generalized anxiety disorder. In terms of pharmacological strategies, patients with recurrent panic attacks were to be treated with imipramine or MAO inhibitors, whereas patients with diffuse anxiety (generalized anxiety disorder) were to be given psychotherapy and benzodiazepines (when necessary).

In the mid-1970s, biological psychiatry became more popular. The work of Pitts and McClure (1967) in relation to panic disorder was rediscovered. They had reported that a lactate infusion given to a patient with a history of panic attacks would induce a panic attack in most cases. To date several controlled studies have replicated these findings (reviewed by Shear, 1986). Lactate-induced panic provides a biological experimental model of panic disorder. During the 1980s, researchers became interested in further assessing the pathophysiology involved in panic and in developing other antipanic agents. Finally, a clear approach to the treatment of this condition has emerged.

Panic Attacks or Anxiety Episodes?

In daily practice, the clinician is often faced with patients who are acutely anxious and at times agitated. Whether they are seen in the emergency room or at the office, the issue of differential diagnosis becomes crucial. Is this a medical problem? Is this a drug-induced state? Are we facing a patient with a psychiatric disorder? Is this an anxious patient? The physician first ensures, by taking a detailed history, that no drug or medical disorder has induced an acute anxiety reaction (see Table 10.1).Then the physician rules out a state of agitation as part of another psychiatric disorder. A state of acute anxiety caused by drugs or by medical or psychiatric disorders should be treated appropriately. However, once these diagnoses have been excluded, the physician is left with the patient who has had an anxiety episode, a panic attack, or an acute hyperventilation syndrome (reviewed by Fleeming, 1986).

Spontaneous panic attacks are discrete phenomena involving psychic symptoms such as marked fear and apprehension and physical symptoms such as palpitations, dizziness, sweating, shaking, faintness, tingling in the extremities, and breathing difficulties. The spontaneous panic attack occurs abruptly, without warning and usually lasts less than 15 to 30 minutes. During this state of intense anxiety, patients are often unable to go on with what they were doing and may try to escape from the situation. The word *panic*, of course, implies a state of acute fearfulness and discomfort. Following the attack, victims are usually in a state of fatigue and impaired concentration. The clinician is often faced with patients who describe a spell of terror with numerous physical symptoms that have disappeared by the time they get to the emergency room. Indeed, in most cases the physician sees the patient once

TABLE 10.1 Drug and Medical Disorders That May Cause Acute Anxiety Reactions

Drugs

- Digitalis toxicity
- Aminophylline
- Bronchodilators
- Stimulants
- Hallucinogens
- Cocaine
- Caffeine
- Amphetamines

Medical Disorders

• Cardiovascular	• Paroxysmal atrial tachycardia
	• Angina
	• Arrythmias
• Metabolic	• Pheochromocytoma
	• Hypoglycemia
• Neurologic	• Temporal lobe epilepsy
	• Autonomic epilepsy
	• Acute labyrinthitis
	• Vestibular dysfunction
• Pulmonary	• Pneumothorax

the panic attack is over; nonetheless, the patient requires reassurance. Panic attacks are very common, occurring in over 20% of the population at some time. However, if they become recurrent, further assessment and treatment is warranted.

Most patients coming to the emergency room in the midst of a panic attack are acutely anxious and do not understand what is happening to them. The physician may use 5 to 10 mg of diazepam or 1 to 2 mg of lorazepam (either sublingually, intravenously, or intramuscularly) as an initial treatment. This reassures the patient that the physician is taking the condition seriously; it also allows the physician to take down the history of the attack and to exclude drug abuse and medical or other psychiatric disorders in the 10 or 15 minutes required for the medication to act or for the attack to cease spontaneously. If in the course of taking the history the physician learns that the patient has had previous attacks that lasted for more than an hour, the diazepam or lorazepam dose may be repeated after 30 minutes. In these cases, the "paper bag technique" may be contraindicated, as it is hypothesized that CO_2 inhalation may prolong attacks (Woods, Charney, Goodman, & Heninger, 1988); this requires further research. Patients with panic disorder are unusually sensitive to in-

TABLE 10.2 Psychiatric Disorders in Which Acute Anxiety Episodes or Panic Attacks May Appear

Anxiety Disorders

- Panic disorder
- Generalized anxiety disorder
- Post–traumatic stress disorder
- Obsessive-compulsive disorder
- Simple phobia
- Social phobia

Affective disorders

- Major depression
- Atypical depression
- Dysthymic disorders

Other disorders

- Borderline personality disorder
- Psychosis (schizoaffective, schizophrenia)

creased CO_2, probably because it causes hyperactivity of the noradrenergic neuronal functions.

The differential diagnosis becomes more complex when patients have recurrent panic attacks. It may take several visits and tests before the clinician can be comfortable with a diagnosis of panic disorder, because anxiety and panic attacks can be related to so many medical or psychiatric disorders (see Tables 10.1 and 10.2).

Over the years it has become accepted that the spontaneous panic attack, or unexpected panic attack, takes its own course: a sudden onset progressing to the panic stage within seconds to minutes. The panic stage usually lasts less than 15 to 30 minutes and recedes gradually, leaving the patient in a state of fatigue and impaired concentration that may then last for hours.

Spontaneous panic attacks differ from the situational panic attacks seen in patients suffering from phobic disorders or in patients whose well-being is threatened. The situational panic attack is related to specific circumstances or places and is often anticipated. As a rule it does not cause a very high level of anxiety, because avoidance behavior will terminate the episode. Thus, the situational panic attack is less circumscribed in time and has an ill-defined beginning and end, in contrast to the spontaneous panic attack (see Table 10.3). Both types of panic attack abate with high-potency benzodiazepines, whereas imipramine is more effective in controlling spontaneous panic attacks in patients with panic disorder (Klein, 1984).

A second form of anxiety is the anxiety episode, which can occur with or without immediate cause and usually means hours of inner tension, irritability, concentration difficulties, and physical symptoms. During the episode, the

TABLE 10.3 Characteristics of Spontaneous and Situational Panic Attacks

Characteristic	Spontaneous	Situational
Onset	abrupt	gradual
Duration	5–30 minutes	variable
Severity	+++	+
Impaired functioning	severe	moderate
Situation-specific?	no	yes
Improved by		
• Alprazolam or clonazepam	+++	+
• Imipramine	+++	?

patient is usually able to carry on activities but at a slower pace; the anxiety level reached is much lower than that of a spontaneous panic attack. However, these patients tend to come to the emergency room in a state of anxiety and complaining of breathing difficulties and at times paresthesias and muscle cramps. The anxiety episode often evolves into an acute hyperventilation syndrome as a result of major metabolic changes stemming from the breathing difficulties. At the emergency room, this patient is often given 10 mg of diazepam sublingually or intramuscularly; it is the fastest-acting benzodiazepine available because of its liposolubility, which allows rapid absorption and rapid crossing of the blood-brain barrier. In addition, the medical staff helps the patient slow down his or her breathing. These anxiety episodes can occur in several medical and psychiatric disorders but are often part of a long-lasting anxious condition such as generalized anxiety disorder (GAD).

Panic attacks, anxiety episodes, and the acute hyperventilation syndrome differ with respect to several variables, as previously described. However, their treatment at the emergency room or at the office is similar in the acute phase: support, reassurance, and at times a benzodiazepine. Long-term treatment varies according to the diagnosis. For generalized anxiety disorder the favored treatment is long-term psychotherapy with benzodiazepines prescribed when functioning is impaired. For panic disorder with avoidance behavior, the treatment is medication combined with desensitization. A state of remission will be induced in most cases of panic disorder within a year of treatment, and the relapse rate during the first 2 years following treatment is less than 30% (Lydiard & Ballenger, 1987).

Panic Disorder

A New Entity

Panic disorder is a new entity, recognized officially since the DSM-III was first published in 1980. With the DSM-III, anxiety neurosis was divided into panic disorder and generalized anxiety disorder for several reasons. First, the course of the untreated illness is different. In the former disorder, recurrent spontaneous panic attacks are characteristic; in the latter, we see mostly diffuse, free-floating anxiety. Second, the treatment is viewed as clearly different. For panic disorder, the emphasis is on blocking the panic attacks with medication. Antidepressants were the first-line treatment throughout the 1970s, but alprazolam or clonazepam have more recently become popular. Thereafter, desensitization, support, and other treatment strategies are used. For generalized anxiety disorder, a psychotherapeutic approach remains at the core of any treatment. Antianxiety drugs are used only when functioning is impaired or suffering becomes too intense (Freedman, 1980). This combination is the most effective treatment to date.

Panic disorder has been further studied and the diagnostic criteria updated in the DSM-III-R (American Psychiatric Association, 1987). In several studies, cardiac monitoring has been carried on for several days. These have shown similar findings: the heart rate increases abruptly by about 50% for a limited period of time during a spontaneous panic attack before going back to baseline (Freedman, Ianni, Ettedgui, & Puthezhath, 1985). This objective finding parallels patients' descriptions of their spontaneous panic attacks. (Heart rate is not well correlated with situational panic.) These studies have shown that spontaneous panic attacks can occur anywhere and at any time. If they occur during the night, they should not be confused with nightmares. Criticism of cardiac monitoring studies have mainly focused on the variability in the data. If we exclude situational panic attacks, however, there is a good correlation between the patients' descriptions of spontaneous panic attacks and a rapid increase of heart rate, which lasts for a short time in most cases.

Epidemiology

Spontaneous panic attacks occur in more than 20% of the population at some time and are features of several psychiatric and medical disorders, as described previously. However, conditions characterized by *recurrent* panic attacks are less common. We have limited epidemiological studies providing data on the lifetime prevalence of panic disorder. However, if we rely on the multicenter studies with sound methodology reported by Weissman and Merikangas (1986), we see that the lifetime prevalence for panic disorder is about 1%; if we include agoraphobia with panic attacks (stage 4 of the disorder), another 2% of the population is affected. The disorder occurs three to four times more often in women than in men. The implications of these studies are very important. First, the disorder tends to occur in late teens or early adulthood—a population that has many resources and that could be productive. Accordingly, the treatment of the disorder in the early months of its occurrence has become a priority in most centers. Second, panic disorder is a common disorder with several different stages, treatable with current approaches.

A Progressive Disorder

Most patients seen in our anxiety clinic over several years have described a state of diffuse mild anxiety with difficulties adjusting to problems in life during the months preceding the first spontaneous panic attacks (stage 1). Thus, there is a prodromal phase of diffuse anxiety and other vague symptoms. Later, patients experience recurrent spontaneous panic attacks (stage 2). As Klein, Ross, and Cohen (1987) have stated, the development of anticipatory anxiety then slowly develops (stage 3). Patients begin to avoid activities outside the home as they anticipate the next panic attack. Between spontaneous panic attacks these patients experience diffuse anticipatory anxiety. Approximately two-thirds of patients proceed to a phase characterized by avoidance behavior (stage 4). Spontaneous panic attacks are a paradigm of massive conditioning and lead patients to avoid places in which they have had intense attacks. Some patients avoid being alone in a car or an elevator; others avoid public places or using public transportation. Stage 4 of the illness begins with a circumscribed avoidance that progresses over several months and, following Klein's hypothesis, may lead to agoraphobia in the broad sense. The classic definition of agoraphobia applies to patients avoiding public places and public transportation, but in the DSM-III-R a much broader definition has been used, including the fear of being in situations in which no help is available or where escape would be difficult should there be a panic attack. We have described four stages of the illness that if untreated may lead to several social and familial complications, even within the first year of illness. In a more chronic course, several medical complications may develop (Noyes, Clancy, & Hoenk, 1980): for instance, premature death from suicide and cardiac disease is three times more common in these patients compared to controls. Moreover, drug and alcohol abuse is common, especially in men. These complications set in as the disorder progresses and often become more difficult to treat than the primary disorder itself.

Differential Diagnosis

The diagnostic approach is different for patients who present occasional panic attacks than for those with recurrent spontaneous panic attacks. In treating the latter, the clinician must take a long-term approach: it may take several months to exclude the physical or psychiatric illnesses listed in Tables 10.1 and 10.2. For instance, approximately one-third of depressed patients in their 20s or 30s experience spontaneous panic attacks. A psychotic breakdown may begin with recurrent panic states; not until months later will psychotic symptoms develop. With respect to medical disorders, it is not always simple to exclude pheochromocytoma, temporal lobe epilepsy, or angina. Overall, it is important that the clinician think of a probable diagnosis and come to a definite one only after excluding all the disorders in Tables 10.1 and 10.2.

Clinically Relevant Etiological Factors

The pathogenesis and etiological factors for panic disorder have been reviewed in detail in other chapters of this book. For the clinician it is important to remember that patients with panic disorder usually have family members with the same disorder. In fact, the morbidity risk for first-degree relatives is about 20%, ten times higher than the prevalence in the general population (Crowe, Noyes, Pauls, & Slymen, 1983).

For many years there has been an association between panic attacks and neurological disorder, the best examples being temporal lobe epilepsy and brain tumor. Our group (Beauclair & Fontaine, 1986) has described an increased incidence of epileptiform discharges on the baseline EEG of patients suffering from panic disorder. In fact, 27% of these patients have had epileptic discharges, which is ten times more than one would expect in a normal population. In this study we excluded all patients who had seizures in the past. Whether these findings will be replicated remains to be seen.

If patients with panic disorder and reduced seizure thresholds are treated with high-potency benzodiazepines such as alprazolam and clonazepam, they should be warned that abrupt discontinuation might lead to seizure. The same caution applies to antidepressants known to lower the seizure threshold.

Recent findings have shown that the brains of a subgroup of patients with recurrent panic attacks show some abnormalities (Reiman et al., 1986; Stewart, Devous, Rush, Lane, & Bonte, 1986). PET scan studies have shown increased blood flow perfusion as well as increased oxygen consumption between the attacks and a state of vasoconstriction during attacks. Also, magnetic resonance imaging studies have found an increased prevalence of atrophy of the anterior horn of the temporal lobe and focal lesions of the white matter in the medial part of the temporal lobe in panic patients (Fontaine, Breton, Dery, Tourgman, & Elie, 1988). A subgroup of panic patients may have neurological abnormalities. The role of these findings in the pathogenesis of the disorder is still unknown but is the subject of much study and speculation. (See Chapter 2 for a detailed description of the medical evaluation of panic disorder.)

Treatment Approaches

The Implications of a Better Understanding of Panic Disorder

During the past 10 years, we have seen a major change in the clinical presentation of panic disorder. We used to see patients in our anxiety clinic with a chronic illness, in which several complications had set in and considerable avoidance behavior was present. In recent years, most cases have had the disorder for less than a year and have fewer complications (Noyes et al., 1980). Also, we often see patients in stage 2 or 3 of the illness, which makes treatment simpler. For instance, for the chronic agoraphobic patients we saw 10 years ago, the medical treatment was the same but patients' motivation for desensitization was poor at times. Often we had to refer such patients to behavior therapists, having in mind a treatment duration of several months. Most patients we have seen during the last few years do not need to be referred for behavior therapy, as their avoidant behavior decreases with medication to block the panic attacks and desensitization instructions from the physician (see Table 10.4). Thus, the clinician sees a more treatable population nowadays, mostly because of the impact of the media on the general population. Many television programs and articles in newspapers or magazines have informed the population of the nature of this disorder and of the fact that it is treatable. The end result is that patients come for treatment earlier. It is also possible that there are fewer patients in the population left to treat.

TABLE 10.4 Steps in the Treatment of Panic Disorder

1. Blocking the panic attacks for 6 to 8 months
   a. Benzodiazepines: alprazolam or clonazepam
   b. Antidepressants: imipramine or phenelzine
2. Desensitization
   a. Spontaneous
   b. Therapist directed
   c. Systematic (behavior therapy)
3. Gradual cessation of medication
4. Follow-up period

Lifestyle Issues

It is very important that the clinician review the patient's living habits. Abuse of coffee is particularly relevant, as caffeine clearly increases anxiety levels and can often induce a panic state (Charney, Heninger, & Jatlow, 1985). The intake of regular coffee should be limited and the use of decaffeinated coffee recommended. Alcohol intake should be discussed directly in all cases. In addition, the physician should make sure that the patient has sufficient sleep, regular physical exercise, and some time to relax on a daily basis. Moreover, an assessment of life stressors and overwork is in order. These factors are important to discuss with patients who have recurrent panic attacks, as they are relevant both during treatment and for the prevention of relapses once medication is stopped.

Blocking Panic Attacks

Antidepressants

Two groups of drugs have become widely accepted as antipanic agents: the antidepressants imipramine and phenelzine (Pohl, Berchou, & Rainey, 1982) and the high-potency benzodiazepines alprazolam and clonazepam (Chouinard, Annable, Fontaine, & Solyom, 1982; Fontaine, 1985) (see Tables 10.5 and 10.6). In the United States, the classic treatment for blocking panic attacks is imipramine (Zitrin, Klein, & Woerner, 1978), given initially at a dose of 25 mg at bedtime or 10 mg three times a day. The dose is increased every three days to a mean dose of about 200 mg per day. However, panic disorder patients do not tolerate imipramine as well as depressed patients do. At the beginning of treatment, over one-third of the patients will get jittery or worsen (Aronson, 1987). Also, the range for the therapeutic dose is very wide: some patients respond to less than 100 mg per day, but others require over 300 mg per day for spontaneous attacks to be blocked.

Throughout the 1970s imipramine was poorly accepted by clinicians, especially because of its side effects: 30% to 50% of patients were unable to tolerate the drug. The most problematic side effect of imipramine is an amphetaminelike production of profound agitation and anticholinergic symptoms (dry mouth, constipation, orthostatic hypotension, and weight gain). The anticholinergic side effects are an important factor, because treat-

TABLE 10.5 A Stepcare Approach to the Pharmacological Treatment of Panic Disorder

1. Alprazolam or clonazepam
2. High-potency benzodiazepine + imipramine—if there is marked improvement, discontinue benzodiazepine gradually
3. High-potency benzodiazepine + phenelzine

TABLE 10.6 Comparison of Alprazolam and Clonazepam for the Treatment of Panic Disorder

	Alprazolam	*Clonazepam*
Half-life (hours)	12–15	24
Withdrawal reactions (rebound anxiety)	+++	+
Regimen	four times daily	twice daily or single dose
Dose	3–6 mg/day	2–4 mg/day

ment has to continue for at least 6 to 8 months. Some patients have had significant complications, such as a weight gain of up to 20 or 30 pounds. In addition, the therapeutic response to imipramine takes between 4 and 8 weeks (Klein, 1984).

The monoamine oxidase (MAO) inhibitor phenelzine has been found to provide effective antipanic therapy (Klein, 1984). Phenelzine has a robust antipanic effect within 4 to 6 weeks. However, MAO inhibitors require the adoption of a complex diet to avoid a hypertensive crisis. Alcohol as well as several types of medication acting on the central nervous system must be avoided. A hay fever tablet or cough syrup could cause an acute hypertensive crisis. This has made their use unpopular in North America. Furthermore, the dosage range is quite variable, and numerous side effects ranging from orthostatic hypotension to edema tend to occur, especially after a few months of treatment. Consequently, we recommend the use of MAO inhibitors only if the patient has not improved significantly with a high-potency benzodiazepine or imipramine (Table 10.5).

Alternatives to Antidepressants

Given the complications associated with both types of antidepressants, several researchers began to look for alternatives. Our group began a study of alprazolam versus placebo in the treatment of panic disorder in 1977, a time when benzodiazepines were rarely indicated for patients with a history of spontaneous panic attacks. To date, thousands of patients have been treated with alprazolam, which has proven to be an effective antipanic agent. Long-term studies have shown that its efficacy is maintained over several months. However, alprazolam's short duration of action means that patients have to take their medication at least three times a day to avoid between-dose rebound anxiety. Also, the discontinuation of alprazolam after several months of high doses can be very complicated (Fyer et al., 1987). This is probably related to its high potency combined with a short half-life and no active metabolites. Alprazolam is a triazolobenzodiazepine, and there is a poor cross-tolerance with the 1,4 benzodiazepine derivatives (diazepam, clorazepate, flurazepam) that are often used to provide a more gradual withdrawal when short-acting benzodiazepines such as alprazolam have been given for several months. The end result is a high frequency of rebound panic attacks on discontinuation of alprazolam. These can be mistaken for a relapse.

Because of these problems with alprazolam, in 1982 our group began investigating the use of clonazepam in treating panic disorder, first in open label trials and later in placebo controlled studies (Fontaine, 1985; Tesar et al., 1987). Clonazepam proved to be an effective antipanic agent at about half the dose required with alprazolam. Clonazepam is usually given at an initial dose of .5 mg at supper and bedtime, which is then increased by .5 mg every three days to 3 mg daily and readjusted upward or downward according to therapeutic response and side effects. Clonazepam has a long duration of action, so most patients may take it just once or twice a day. Moreover, the discontinuation of clonazepam following several months of treatment presents fewer difficulties than alprazolam. These benzodiazepines are compared in Table 10.6. Clonazepam is now recognized as an alternative to alprazolam. Both of these high-potency benzodiazepines have a rapid onset of action, which is especially important for patients who have developed phobic avoidance. The high-potency benzodiazepines cannot be used by patients with a history of alcohol or drug abuse, but they are compatible with any other medication and are not fatal in the event of an overdose, as are antidepressants. Imipramine differs from the benzodiazepines, as shown in Table 10.7.

The use of several other antipanic agents has been described in recent years. For instance, clomipramine was reported to be effective in several open clinical trials with methodological limitations (Liebowitz, Fyer, Gorman, &

TABLE 10.7 Comparison of the High-potency Benzodiazepines and Tricyclic Antidepressants

	Benzodiazepines (alprazolam or clonazepam)	Tricyclic antidepressants
Previous history of alcohol or drug abuse	–	– or +
Side effects	Minimal	Significant in over 30% of cases
Overdose	Sedation, sleep	Sleep, coma leading to death
Withdrawal syndrome upon drug cessation	+++	+

Klein, 1986). Other medications that have been reported to be antipanic agents include tryptophan, deprenyl, diazepam, carbamazepine, and valproic acid. However, placebo-controlled studies are needed before we can be certain of the efficacy of these medications and the extent to which they can block panic attacks.

Desensitization

Desensitization is not a new treatment. British psychiatrists in the 1950s were asking their patients to go back to the feared situation, just as Freud did in the early 20th century. Throughout the 1960s and 1970s, systematic desensitization in the office was popularized by behavioral therapists, but it was later shown that in vivo desensitization (or in vivo exposure) is more effective and more practical. Systematic desensitization asks patients to imagine the feared situation; in vivo desensitization requires that the patient actually enter the feared situation. After a few weeks of effective medicated blockade of their spontaneous panic attacks, patients are asked to draw up a hierarchy of avoided situations. They then enter situations of increasing difficulty, mastering their anxiety at each step. Patients should be told that they will be anxious while practicing exposure but that after about half an hour their anxiety level will begin to decrease as a result of the deconditioning. Patients are asked to remain in the situation even if their anxiety increases; they are reminded that spontaneous panic attacks will not complicate this procedure. Most patients can practice desensitization alone or with the help of relatives or friends at first. Some patients must be referred to a behavioral therapist, especially when chronic and systematized agoraphobia is present. In vivo desensitization in such cases may begin with the therapist accompanying the patient into the feared situations.

Over the years we have seen most patients take an active role in desensitization and carry out this crucial therapeutic task successfully while on medication. However, a subgroup seems to be more passive and shows less interest in this procedure. The primary care physician may need to refer such patients to behavioral therapists who can provide other coping strategies in addition to desensitization.

Family Meetings

Most physicians treating patients with this disorder will want to meet with the spouse or the whole family to discuss the nature of the disorder, its treatment, and the complications that have developed since its onset. Overall, these meetings are informative and speed up the treatment as well as help prevent relapses following cessation. We often see patients who are trapped in families with so much psychopathology or for whom marital dysfunction is so severe that the treatment of recurrent panic attacks is meaningless without concomitant counseling.

Relapse

Very few prospective studies of relapse are available with panic disorder patients who have been treated adequately with medication and desensitization. From the available reports, however, it would appear that fewer than one-third of patients with panic disorder will relapse during the first few years following treatment (Zitrin, Klein, Woerner, & Ross, 1983). A major question is How do you define a relapse? Zitrin and Klein have used a criterion of panic attacks sufficient to induce avoidant behavior that had disappeared during treatment. Other researchers define relapse as the recurrence of spontaneous panic attacks, whether major or minor. Between these two extremes, other researchers have defined relapse as a recurrence of spontaneous panic attacks leading to interference with functioning. We avoid a narrow definition in which avoidance has to take place, as we know that a substantial number of patients will not develop avoidance behavior. We also steer clear of an overinclusive definition of the relapse, as some patients will experience occasional panic attacks during follow-up. These are often transient phenomena with which the patient can cope without resuming treatment.

During the follow-up period, it is important to assess the extent of residual anxiety symptoms, the recurrence of panic attacks, and any complications that have not improved during the first year of treatment. More specialized treatment may be required for about 30% of patients during the first 2 years of follow-up. Some cases may benefit from a specialized form of psychotherapy, such as psychoanalysis, long-term cognitive therapy, or maintenance pharmacotherapy. Generally, panic patients should be followed for 1 to 2 years, and the physician should be prepared for a long-term approach.

Conclusion

In conclusion, several major changes have occurred in the understanding and treatment of panic disorder. Among the most significant is that patients now come for treatment earlier in the course of their illness, often during stage 2 or 3. Also, we have a clear understanding of the essential therapeutic ingredients of treatment: blocking panic attacks and desensitization. Making a differential diagnosis is now easier, as panic disorder has been well defined in the DSM-III and DSM-III-R. All of these developments offer hope for both patients and clinicians. Further work will be required to find means of preventing relapses and to better understand the pathogenesis of this disorder, which will lead to the development of more specific drug and behavioral treatments.

References

American Psychiatric Association. (1980). *Diagnostic and statistical manual of mental disorders* (3rd ed.). Washington, DC: Author.

American Psychiatric Association. (1987). *Diagnostic and statistical manual of mental disorders* (3rd ed., rev.). Washington, DC: Author.

Aronson, T. A. (1987). A naturalistic study of imipramine in panic disorder and agoraphobia. *American Journal of Psychiatry, 144,* 1014–1019.

Beauclair, L., & Fontaine, R. (1986). *Epileptiform abnormalities in panic disorder.* Paper presented at Canadian College of Neuropsychopharmacology, 9th Annual Scientific Meeting.

Charney, D. S., Heninger, G. R., & Jatlow, P. I. (1985). Increased anxiogenic effects of caffeine in panic disorders. *Archives of General Psychiatry, 42,* 233–243.

Chouinard, G., Annable, L., Fontaine, R., & Solyom, L. (1982). Alprazolam in the treatment of generalized anxiety and panic disorders: A double-blind placebo-controlled study. *Psychopharmacology, 77,* 229–233.

Cohen, M. (1949). Neurocirculatory asthenia. *Medical Clinics of North America, 33,* 1343–1364.

Crowe, R. R., Noyes, R., Pauls, D. L., & Slymen, D. (1983). A family study of panic disorder. *Archives of General Psychiatry, 40,* 1065–1069.

Fleeming, J. A. E. (1986). The assessment and management of panic disorder. *Emergency Care,* July-September, 47–63.

Fontaine, R. (1985). Clonazepam for panic disorders and agitation. *Psychosomatics, 26* (12, Suppl.), 135–185.

Fontaine, R., Breton, G., Dery, R., Tourgman, S., & Elie, R. (1988). *Neuroanatomical changes in panic disorder assessed with MRI.* Paper presented at the 43rd Annual Convention and Scientific Program, Society of Biological Psychiatry.

Freedman, A. M. (1980). Psychopharmacology and psychotherapy in the treatment of anxiety. *Pharmacopsychiatry, 13,* 277–289.

Freedman, R. R., Ianni, P., Ettedgui, E., & Puthezhath, N. (1985). Ambulatory monitoring of panic disorder. *Archives of General Psychiatry, 42,* 244–248.

Freud, S. (1895). On the grounds for detaching a particular syndrome from neurasthenia under the description of anxiety neurosis. In J. Strachey (Ed.) (1961), *Standard Edition of the Complete Psychological Works of Sigmund Freud* (Vol. 3, pp. 85–116). London: Hogarth Press.

Freud, S. (1959). Obsessions and phobias: Their physical mechanisms and their etiology. In J. Riviere (Trans.), *Collected Papers* (Vol. 1, pp. 128–137). New York: Basic Books.

Fyer, A. J., Liebowitz, M. R., Gorman, J. M., Campeas, R., Levin, A., Davies, S. O., Goetz, D., & Klein, D. F. (1987). Discontinuation of alprazolam treatment in panic patients. *American Journal of Psychiatry, 144,* 303–308.

Klein, D. F. (1964). Delineation of two drug-responsive anxiety syndromes. *Psychopharmacologia, 5,* 397–408.

Klein, D. F. (1967). Importance of psychiatric diagnosis in prediction of clinical drug effects. *Archives of General Psychiatry, 16,* 118–126.

Klein, D. F. (1984). Psychopharmacologic treatment of panic disorder. *Psychosomatics, 25*(10, Suppl.), 32–35.

Klein, D. F., & Fink, M. (1962). Psychiatric reaction patterns to imipramine. *American Journal of Psychiatry, 119,* 432–438.

Klein, D. F., Ross, D. C., & Cohen, P. (1987). Panic and avoidance in agoraphobia. *Archives of General Psychiatry, 44,* 377–384.

Liebowitz, M. R., Fyer, A. J., Gorman, J., & Klein, D. F. (1986). Recent developments in the understanding and pharmacotherapy of panic attacks. *Psychopharmacology Bulletin, 22*(3), 792–796.

Lydiard, R. B., & Ballenger, J. C. (1987). Antidepressants in panic disorder and agoraphobia. *Journal of Affective Disorders, 13,* 153–168.

Marks, I. M. (1969). *Fears and phobias.* New York: Academic Press.

Noyes, R., Clancy, J., & Hoenk, P. R. (1980). The prognosis of anxiety neurosis. *Archives of General Psychiatry, 37,* 173–178.

Pitts, F. N., & McClure, J. N. (1967). Lactate metabolism in anxiety neurosis. *New England Journal of Medicine, 25,* 1329–1336.

Pohl, R., Berchou, R., & Rainey, J. (1982). Tricyclic antidepressants and monoamine oxidase inhibitors in the treatment of agoraphobia. *Journal of Clinical Psychopharmacology, 2,* 399–407.

Reiman, E., Raichle, M. E., Robins, R., Butler, F. K., Herscovitch, P. F., & Perlmutter, J. (1986). The application of positron emission tomography to the study of panic disorder. *American Journal of Psychiatry, 143,* 469–477.

Sargant, W. (1962). The treatment of anxiety states and atypical depressions by the monoamine oxidase inhibitor drugs. *Journal of Neuropsychiatry, 3*(Suppl.), 96–103.

Shear, K. (1986). Pathophysiology of panic: A review of pharmacologic provocative tests and naturalistic monitoring data. *Journal of Clinical Psychiatry, 47*(6, Suppl.), 18–26.

Stewart, R. S., Devous, M. D., Rush, A. J., Lane, L., & Bonte, F. J. (1986). *Cerebral blood flow changes during sodium lactate induced panic attacks.* Paper presented at the 139th Annual Meeting of the American Psychiatric Association.

Tesar, G. E., Rosenbaum, J. F., Pollack, M. H., Herman, J. B., Sachs, G. S., Mahoney, E. M., Cohen, L. S., McNamara, M., & Goldstein, S. (1987). Clonazepam versus alprazolam in the treatment of panic disorder: Interim analysis of data from a prospective, double-blind, placebo-controlled trial. *Journal of Psychiatry, 48*(10, Suppl.), 16–20.

Weissman, M. M., & Merikangas, K. R. (1986). The epidemiology of anxiety and panic disorders: An update. *Journal of Clinical Psychiatry, 47*(6, Suppl.), 11–18.

Wheeler, E. O., White, P. D., Reed, E. W., & Cohen, M. E. (1950). Neurocirculatory asthenia (anxiety neurosis, effort syndrome, neurasthenia). A twenty-year follow-up study of one hundred and seventy-three patients. *Journal of the American Medical Association, 142,* 878–889.

Woods, S. W., Charney, D. S., Goodman, W. K., & Heninger, G. R. (1988). Carbon dioxide–induced anxiety. *Archives of General Psychiatry, 45,* 43–52.

Zitrin, C. M., Klein, D. F., & Woerner, M. G. (1978). Behavior therapy, supportive psychotherapy, imipramine and phobias. *Archives of General Psychiatry, 35,* 307–316.

Zitrin, C. M., Klein, D. F., Woerner, M. G., & Ross, D. C. (1983). Treatment of phobias. I. Comparison of imipramine hydrochloride and placebo. *Archives of General Psychiatry, 40*(2), 125–138.

CHAPTER 11

Treatment of the Difficult Case with Panic Disorder

DAVID V. SHEEHAN AND B. ASHOK RAJ

Introduction

Okay, you've studied the recent journals, attended a number of continuing medical education courses, and even picked up a few books on recent advances in the treatment of anxiety disorders. You've learned some interesting facts and are beginning to rethink some of your earlier ideas about anxiety disorders. It sounds so easy and straightforward when you listen to the "experts" and read their papers, full of optimistic words like "significant therapeutic effect." Yet here you are, faced with a case that is not responding the way the "experts" led you to expect. What do you do next? Come to think of it, do the "experts" ever find themselves in this refractory situation? You can't recall any discussion of that thorny dilemma. You feel lost, alone, misled, powerless—perhaps even a little embarrassed—as you search for what you might have done wrong.

If you have sometimes felt this way, this chapter is for you. *Of course* the "experts" have to deal with resistant cases regularly. Indeed, because of their special interest in the subject they see such cases more frequently than does the average clinician. One of the ways clinicians learn new treatment strategies is by referring such difficult cases to the expert and watching how he or she deals with them.

In a difficult situation like this, what you need is not an encyclopedic collection of new tricks but an organized strategy that you can impose on the situation again and again. Over time, the specific details may change, but the essential approach remains the same. With experience and advances in knowledge, you plug the leaks in the strategy so that its success is enhanced. As a busy clinician, you haven't much time before the patient returns complaining that he or she is as disabled as ever. You want a strategy that's clear and simple.

The Strategy

The problems you're encountering can lie in one of two stages (or both): diagnosis and treatment.

Diagnosis

Ask yourself the following questions to double-check your diagnosis.

1. Are you sure the patient has an anxiety disorder and not *some other psychiatric disorder*, such as major depressive illness, bipolar disorder, eating disorder, or alcohol or drug abuse?
2. Are you really sure the patient does not have *another medical illness*, perhaps Parkinson's disease, thyroid disease, multiple sclerosis, a brain tumor, complex partial seizures, heart disease, or an endocrinopathy?

Treatment

Treatment problems can be clustered into five groups. The problem could be with any one of the following.

1. *Drug treatment.* Frequently the dose is too low, the drug trial too short, or the dose excessive initially and then not increased appropriately. Perhaps you stayed with the same drug too long when it was only partially effective, and it is even less effective now. Perhaps the patient claims an immunity or "allergy" to all the psychotropics you'd like to try.

2. *Behavior therapy.* Is behavior therapy any different from psychotherapy? Isn't exposure therapy just as good in the office as it is in vivo? Are these curious rituals you see behaviorists doing really necessary, or are they better dismissed in favor of a good talk with the patient? Did you personally ensure that the in vivo exposure was done correctly? Did you explain it properly to the patient and his or her family? Do you really understand the essential ingredients in implementing behavior therapy?

3. *Psychotherapy.* You have been well trained in implementing psychotherapy. But in focusing on managing the medication and behavioral treatment, did you overlook some significant psychosocial factors that interfere with the patient's ability to make a full recovery? Perhaps recovery, for all its benefits, may present the patient with a new set of difficulties he or she feels ill equipped to deal with. Perhaps the patient has excessively inflated, unrealistic expectations about the outcome of treatment that have contributed to disappointment. Perhaps family relationships were shaken up by the patient's recovery, and both patient and family were more comfortable with the prior state of equilibrium.

4. *Long-term monitoring.* "I was doing fine for several months, and now I've developed an immunity to the medicine and relapsed. What can you do?" Did the patient gain weight, develop a tolerance to the drug, start exercising excessively, abuse another drug like marijuana, drink too much coffee, or have a recent illness? Could you have seen this relapse coming before it became full-blown? Is the patient slipping in just a few areas, and if so, where should you look for the regression and how?

5. *Patient education and compliance.* Has the patient decided to deviate from your treatment instructions and follow his or her aunt's ideas about the best approach? Were the illness, the treatments used, and the need for compliance discussed in detail with both patient and family? Over the months of treatment was adequate, direct, and concrete educational information given, so they were able to understand the condition as you do and see the need for compliance with your directions? Have you a good, open, two-way communication with them so that they feel you listen to, accept, and act on their reasonable concerns and negotiate with them as partners in the treatment team?

Guiding Principles

Panic disorder is chronic in the majority of cases, and its treatment is best approached as with any other chronic medical disease. Persistence in seeking the maximum benefit and patience in struggling with difficulties on the journey to that goal are the harbingers of success. When clinicians approach treatment of the panic disorder patient as the endocrinologist approaches treatment of the insulin-dependent diabetic, the results are gratifying. The endocrinologist knows it is not enough just to write a prescription for insulin to ensure success—"Here's a prescription for insulin, Mrs. Jones. I hear it's terrific for diabetes. Why don't you try it four times a day, and I'll see you in a month." That would be a prescription for failure. The successful endocrinologist spends considerable time evaluating the severity and complications of the diabetes; deciding on the best of several medical strategies and how to sequence them should initial interventions fail; educating the patient about the illness, the treatment approaches, and the need to manage weight, diet, exercise, and stress; involving the family; and planning a careful, long-term monitoring program to ensure that all improvements are maintained. In a word, the approach is multimodal. It is comprehensive and long-term. It requires persistence to keep the illness under control and patience to struggle with the many predictable setbacks and inconveniences along the way.

How to Identify the Problem

You identify the resistant problem area by reviewing several components of the case (shown in Table 11.1): the psychiatric diagnosis, the medical diagnosis, compliance, and progress in each of the dimensions of the disorder.

TABLE 11.1 Identifying the Problem Area in the Resistant Case

Review	Check by
Psychiatric diagnosis	Psychiatric history
Medical diagnosis	Medical history Laboratory findings
Compliance	Patient diary and education Family cooperation
Dimensions of the disorder (5+)	Finding the lagging dimension
Reasons for relapse after prior improvement	Discussing prescription practices
Medications used	Trying untried medications
Medication combinations	Trying combinations

Review the Psychiatric Diagnosis

Reconsider whether you have made the correct psychiatric diagnosis. Perhaps the patient has another primary psychiatric diagnosis and only appears to have the panic attacks typical of panic disorder. Is there a system for generating a diagnosis that can be replicated by another psychiatrist reviewing the same case? Indeed there is, and we recommend it strongly. Use the Structured Clinical Interview for the DSM-III-R (SCID) (Spitzer, Williams, & Gibbon, 1988). This interview asks questions in a structured sequence to generate a current and lifetime DSM-III-R diagnosis. It assesses to what extent the patient meets criteria for the various DSM-III-R axis 1 diagnoses. It is structured by diagnostic group; that is, there is an anxiety disorder group module, an affective disorder module, a substance abuse module, and so on. The entire SCID can be administered in 45 to 90 minutes, depending on the complexity of the case. You can confine your interview to the anxiety disorder module, which takes 10 to 20 minutes, but it is wiser to cover all the disorders systematically. Clinicians are sometimes surprised when they do the SCID to find that their patient now meets criteria for substance abuse or dependence (usually alcohol), or for major depressive disorder or bipolar disorder. Perhaps the patient did not respond to treatment because of a clandestine use of alcohol, taken partly as self-medication. Alcohol may interfere with the metabolism and therapeutic effect of the medication and with your ability to correctly adjust the dose. Or alcohol withdrawal symptoms may be masquerading as "panic attacks."

Some patients with agitated major depressive disorder may complain of "panic attacks." However, if you follow the wording of the SCID question to assess the presence of panic attacks, you will find that your patient's episode has not started suddenly and reached its full crescendo with at least four symptoms within 10 minutes of the start of the attack. Instead, the patient may have awakened early in the morning in a state of restless agitation, felt especially in the epigastrium. One of our patients said it felt "like having your foot on the accelerator and the brake, full blast, at the same time." This phenomenon can continue for a number of hours, typically has a diurnal variation, and is more typical of an affective disorder. Indeed, it is wise to suspect an affective disorder in anyone who has a continuous sense of agitation rather than spiky paroxysms of anxiety (generalized anxiety disorder notwithstanding). We have also had referred to us refractory cases of "anxiety disorder" that on closer scrutiny were revealed as rapid-cycling bipolar illness. In one such case the patient was in a state of restless hyperactivity, agitation, and anxiety for 1 week, followed by apathy and anhedonia for 2 weeks, in a cyclical pattern. She was unusually hyperactive during sleep and was not responding to tricyclics and benzodiazepines. When switched to carbamazepine, she improved.

Every serious clinician should get a copy of the SCID. The time you invest in studying it and using it in your practice, especially for refractory cases, will be well rewarded. If another psychiatric disorder is present, treat it first and then review the overall response thoroughly. A detailed decision-tree approach to the diagnosis and treatment of anxiety disorders is shown in Figure 11.1 (pp. 374–375).

Rule Out Medical Illness

Suppose you have satisfied yourself that your patient is not suffering from any other psychiatric disorder. Perhaps the patient is suffering from a medical illness whose symptoms mimic those of an anxiety disorder or seriously aggravate an anxiety disorder. We have published an approach to the medical evaluation of the anxious patient elsewhere (Raj & Sheehan, 1987, 1988). The approach we recommend is simple and follows the long-standing logic of clinical examinations in medical practice. First, take a careful medical history by reviewing symptoms in the patient's various systems (a systems review): note the patient's past medical illnesses, surgeries, hospitalizations, treatments, medication use, accidents, injuries, and allergies. Positive findings in the systems review suggest a need for physical examination and indicate where special attention needs to be focused during the exam. Abnormalities on physical examination (and by history) will then suggest a need and provide focus for a choice of laboratory evaluations to identify the medical illness more precisely. It makes little sense clinically or economically to plunge into a frenzy of laboratory testing before you have reviewed the medical history carefully.

Figure 11.2 (pp. 376–377) outlines a strategy for a medical evaluation of the anxious patient. It proceeds from history to physical examination to several escalating levels of sophistication (Levels 1–4) in choosing laboratory procedures for the major medical differential diagnoses of anxiety. The details may be debatable, may be modified by experience, and will change with time and increasing knowledge. The important point is to have a methodical system that you can remember easily and that works to solve your clinical problems.

What medical illnesses should you be looking for, particularly in this phase of review? The endocrinopathies first come to mind. Hyperthyroidism is suggested by increased appetite, weight loss, heat intolerance, fine tremor, a history of radiation to the neck, or a subtotal thyroidectomy. Hypothyroidism or myxedema, though not usually considered in the differential diagnosis of anxiety, can indeed present with an agitated depression associated with anxiety symptoms. Cushing's disease (and the administration of corticosteroids) can be associated with mood swings and anxiety symptoms. Hypocalcemia may be suggested by a history of carpopedal spasm or a positive Trousseau's sign. Postprandial anxiety attacks raise the possibility of hypoglycemia. Pheochromocytoma, in spite of its exotic appeal, is actually rare. Its presence is suggested by paroxysmal or sustained hypertension, severe headaches, flushing and sweating, café au lait spots, or neurofibromata.

Neurological causes of anxiety are another major group to consider. Several reports have shown that right temporal lobe seizures are associated with panic attacks. Complex partial seizures may resemble panic attacks in that they may occur suddenly without a precipitating event, may be paroxysmal, and may be accompanied by intense feelings of fear, terror, and unreality. Seizures may be associated with diaphoresis, flushing, hyperventilation, and tachycardia. The occurrence of semipurposeful motor or psychic behavior, hallucinations, altered states of consciousness, or progression into other seizure states suggests the possibility of a seizure disorder. When anxiety is refractory to or worsened by a psychotropic drug that can lower the seizure threshold, or is accompanied by impulse control problems, consider the possibility of a seizure disorder. This may be confirmed by a sleep-deprived EEG and may respond to an anticonvulsant rather than a conventional anxiolytic.

Parkinson's disease is often associated with anxiety or may present with anxiety and depression in the elderly. This anxiety may not respond particularly well to anxiolytics but frequently responds to antiparkinson agents such as L-DOPA. Other neurological disorders, such as multiple sclerosis and cerebral tumor, have presented with anxiety symptoms and, though they are a remote cause for anxiety, need to be considered in refractory cases.

A variety of cardiac disorders, including congestive cardiac failure, may be associated with anxiety. Some of these, particularly mitral valve prolapse, may be associated disorders rather than the cause of the anxiety disorder, in which case both diagnoses are used concurrently. The cardiac assessment of the anxious patient is outlined in Figure 11.2 and reviewed in detail elsewhere (Raj & Sheehan, 1987, 1988).

One of our patients was referred with "panic attacks" and acute shortness of breath and tachycardia, occurring mainly at night. These attacks started for

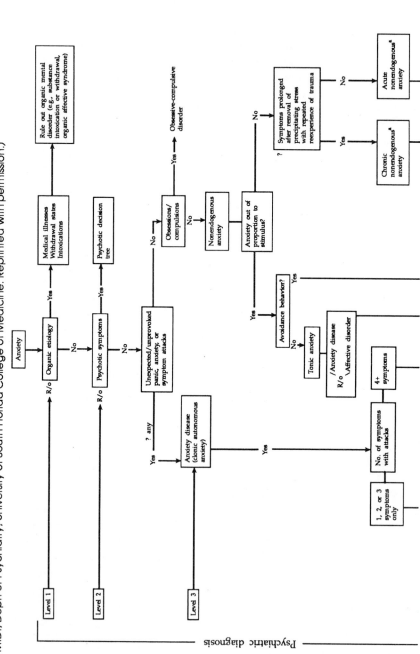

FIGURE 11.1 Decision-tree Approach to Diagnosing and Treating Anxiety Disorders (Copyright 1988 David V. Sheehan, M.D. & B. Ashok Raj, M.D., Dept. of Psychiatry, University of South Florida College of Medicine. Reprinted with permission.)

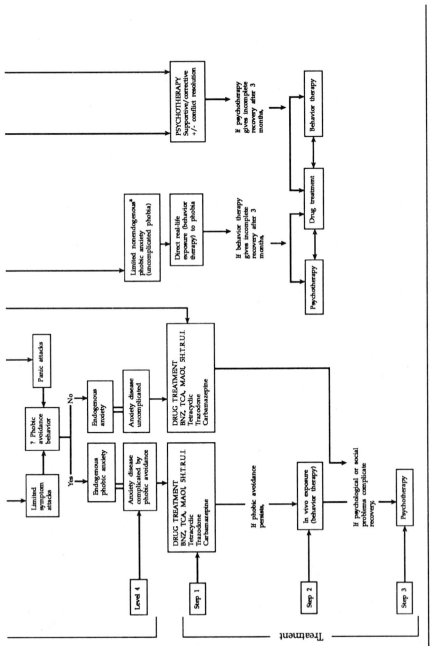

[a]Nonendogenous means occurring in the absence of any history of unexpected limited symptom attacks or unexpected anxiety attacks.

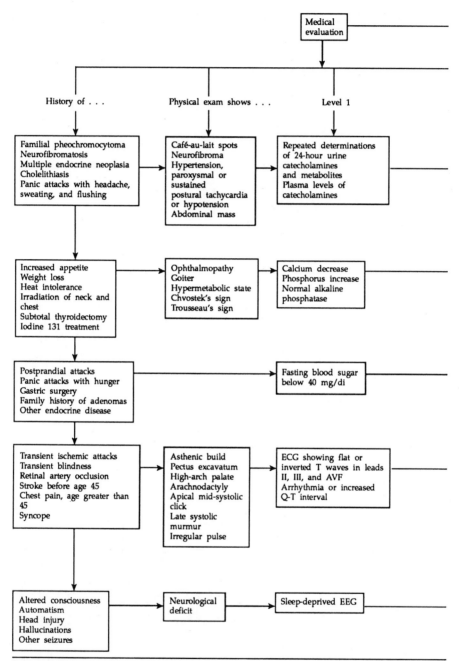

Medical
evaluation

History of . . .

Physical exam shows . . .

Level 1

Familial pheochromocytoma
Neurofibromatosis
Multiple endocrine neoplasia
Cholelithiasis
Panic attacks with headache,
sweating, and flushing

Café-au-lait spots
Neurofibroma
Hypertension,
paroxysmal or
sustained
postural tachycardia
or hypotension
Abdominal mass

Repeated determinations
of 24-hour urine
catecholamines
and metabolites
Plasma levels of
catecholamines

Increased appetite
Weight loss
Heat intolerance
Irradiation of neck and
chest
Subtotal thyroidectomy
Iodine 131 treatment

Ophthalmopathy
Goiter
Hypermetabolic state
Chvostek's sign
Trousseau's sign

Calcium decrease
Phosphorus increase
Normal alkaline
phosphatase

Postprandial attacks
Panic attacks with hunger
Gastric surgery
Family history of adenomas
Other endocrine disease

Fasting blood sugar
below 40 mg/di

Transient ischemic attacks
Transient blindness
Retinal artery occlusion
Stroke before age 45
Chest pain, age greater than
45
Syncope

Asthenic build
Pectus excavatum
High-arch palate
Arachnodactyly
Apical mid-systolic
click
Late systolic
murmur
Irregular pulse

ECG showing flat or
inverted T waves in leads
II, III, and AVF
Arrhythmia or increased
Q-T interval

Altered consciousness
Automatism
Head injury
Hallucinations
Other seizures

Neurological
deficit

Sleep-deprived EEG

[a]This is a scintographic imaging after injection of meta-iodobenzyl guanidine labeled with
iodine 131.

FIGURE 11.2 Decision Tree for Medical Evaluation of the Anxious Patient
(Copyright 1988 David V. Sheehan, M.D., & B. Ashok Raj, M.D., Dept. of Psychiatry,
University of South Florida College of Medicine. Reprinted with permission.)

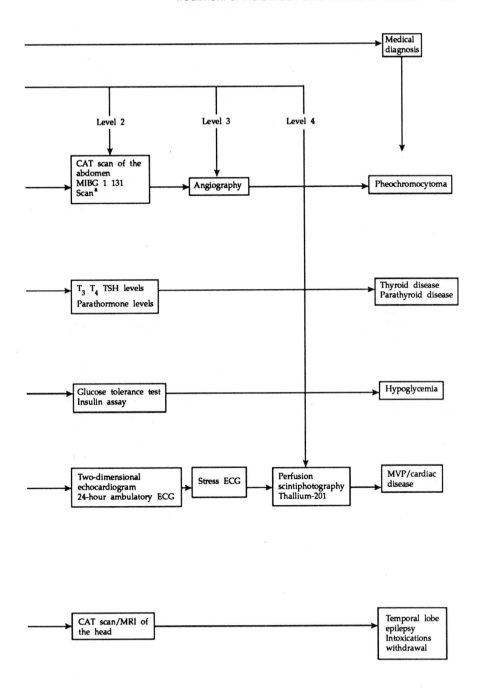

FIGURE 11.2 *(continued)*

the first time at age 70, without any prior psychiatric history. When referred, our patient was on 75 mg of a tricyclic, which had failed to help his symptoms and indeed appeared to have worsened them. A careful history suggested cardiac illness, which was further confirmed on physical examination. This prompted admission with continuous cardiac monitoring. The first-degree atrioventricular block noted on the ECG converted at 2:00 A.M. to third-degree atrioventricular block, at which point the patient awoke with a "panic attack." The tricyclic was stopped. The "panic attacks" stopped after the patient was treated with a pacemaker! Escalation of the dose of tricyclic in this case would have hastened disaster.

When such a medical illness is treated effectively, the psychiatric status is again reviewed; if anxiety is still present in spite of adequate control of the illness, it is necessary to treat the anxiety in its own right.

Review Compliance

At least four factors contribute to noncompliance: (1) inadequate preparation and education of the patient, the family, or the "significant other," (2) psychological factors in the patient, (3) side effects of treatment, and (4) medication phobia.

Preparation of the Patient

All too frequently patients are prescribed treatments too casually, with inadequate preparation. Patients' expectations of being fully informed participants in their treatment decisions have changed significantly in the past 20 years. Those whose involvement is encouraged in a truly collaborative way are more likely to comply with instruction and to strive to succeed in their treatment. A regrettable leftover from psychiatric treatment attitudes of the past is a critical posture toward patients, as if somehow they or their families were responsible for their problem and their treatment outcome. This attitude is clearly not conducive to motivating patients and their families to comply.

In concrete terms, we feel it necessary to spend an hour or more in the initial three sessions simply giving information about the illness and the treatment strategies to patients and their significant others, inviting questions, and encouraging a collaborative discussion of their views and concerns. They need to know that they have been heard fully and that their concerns are going to be addressed in the overall treatment strategy. Keep the information simple, clear, and as practical and concrete as possible. Listen to patients' feedback and incorporate it into your information package for future patients. Disregard what doesn't work. Always seek new ways that work better. The days of the passive psychiatrist, unresponsive to patients' legitimate requests for concrete answers and information, are over. We usually provide patients with reading material, printed directions, precise instructions on how to proceed, and a diary to track compliance and response.

Psychological Factors

Psychological factors in the patient also may contribute to noncompliance. Panic disorder has long been perceived as a self-inflicted or conflict-related problem, as a sign of weak willpower or personality inadequacy, or as an inferiority that one should be ashamed of rather than the genetically inherited metabolic disease that it appears to be. Many have been led to believe that simply "shaping up," making an effort of willpower and positive thinking, will bring reliable relief of symptoms. Coping without medication has been portrayed as desirable and possible. To make matters worse, many patients know that some of the effective medications have a significant withdrawal syndrome, and they are concerned that cooperating with this treatment will turn them into "drug addicts." Is it any surprise that patients and their families are often conflicted about taking medication? They may act this out in a variety of ways.

One common scenario finds them taking some medication but not the adequate dose or on the carefully timed schedule you had drawn up for them. The result is minimal improvement. On reviewing this with a patient, you find that she wanted to cooperate with you because you appeared interested in helping. But she also wanted to heed Aunt Millie's dismissal of medication for anxiety as "giving in," "showing no mind of her own," and indicating weakness. By taking half the dose you recommended, half as frequently, she left room to show Aunt Millie (and herself) that she still had some willpower, was making some effort of her own toward improvement, and was therefore not totally inadequate. The solution to this problem is to co-opt Aunt Millie (and those who influence Aunt Millie) and redirect their efforts toward a more constructive outcome. Finding the correct solution always means eliciting more information. The more information you have, the more likely you are to discover the solution.

Some patients present with a history of carelessness in following their physicians' directions. Question every patient about this. If they have done it in the past, chances are they will do it with you. You will need to take special steps with such a patient to remedy this situation. Involve a more compulsive significant other to ensure that directions are followed precisely. This is of particular concern with the intellectually limited patient. Such a patient may misunderstand clear instructions or may apply them injudiciously. Involving family, friends, or the visiting nurses' association to closely monitor such cases is obviously critical to a good outcome.

Side Effects

Realistically speaking, even the most cooperative and compulsive patients'compliance will be affected by the side effects of the treatment. Patients quite naturally dislike the sexual side effects of antidepressants, the weight gain frequently associated with hydrazine MAO inhibitors and tricyclics, and the anticholinergic side effects and early-phase anxiogenic effects associated with tricyclic antidepressants. They may feel restricted by a MAO inhibitor diet and may be concerned about the idea of others noticing they are sedated or that they have slowed or slurred speech on benzodiazepines. They may also be concerned about becoming "dependent" on the medication.

These concerns are best dealt with by giving them the facts about all the side effects they can expect, in a balanced way. It is not helpful to minimize the side effects or to pretend that a side effect that has occurred is not caused by medication. The physician shouldn't feel a need to defend the medication. Often when we readily acknowledge that the side effect reported is indeed caused by the medication and experienced by others, the patient expresses relief, having feared that it was a sign of something much more ominous. In this light, patients are often quite willing to tolerate side effects. We may need to clarify terms like *addiction, tolerance,* and *withdrawal* in such situations as well, to reassure patients with specific fears about these phenomena.

Medication Phobia

Medication phobias are common among panic disorder patients. Patients having frequent unexpected anxiety attacks are unlikely to make a satisfactory recovery without effective medication. Getting them over this phobia is therefore a critical step toward ensuring success. The issue needs to be approached delicately, however. On the one hand, your aim is unequivocally to get the patient to take the medication, and you must not waver from this goal. On the other hand, if you impose this directly on the patient from the beginning you will frequently fail to reach your goal. Let your patient know that you will be patient but gently persistent. Some come around in time of their own accord. Others need more discussion and family involvement and encouragement.

We often invite patients with medication phobia to attend medication groups, where they can watch other patients go through the process of medical treatment while they observe and have the opportunity to ask questions of the physician and the other patients. This is an educational group: an exchange of information about medication, side effects, successes, and failures among patients is encouraged. The frequent contact with others in various phases of recovery who are on medications, and the formal and informal exchange of information and experiences decreases their fears of medication over time and increases their willingness to take the medication as prescribed. Months of patience may be necessary before they agree to take the first tablet. Overzealous attempts to accelerate this process often backfire.

Other patients, fearful of dying after taking the medication, are invited to come to our offices in the morning, to take their tablet and sit around in the waiting area. Should their worst fear materialize, we are immediately available to "rescue" them and provide the necessary medical support. If two or more such patients can be scheduled to do this at the same time, it is even better. In the final analysis, getting them to do in vivo exposure—to actually swallow the tablet—is central to overcoming their fear. Once they have successfully done so three or four times, their medication fear has lessened considerably. Choosing a medication that provides quick relief—like a benzodiazepine—is preferable in this situation as a starting point, even if you feel sure the patient will eventually need an antidepressant. The initial unpleasant side effects of antidepressants and the slow onset of action threaten to worsen the medication phobia and frighten the patient out of treatment. Patients may also confuse symptoms of the illness with side effects of the medication and become even more medication phobic.

When other measures fail, a patient may feel more secure starting treatment in a comprehensive inpatient service (Pollard, Obermeier, & Cox, 1987). It is advisable to present the bad with the good in describing the medication to the patient and to "call the shots" accurately and realistically. When things materialize, however unpleasantly, as you predicted, it increases the patients' confidence in your knowledge and ability. They are then more likely to comply with your next instructions, knowing you didn't mislead them the last time.

Review Progress in Each of the Dimensions of the Disorder

Not all the dimensions of panic disorder respond to treatment in tandem. In fact, each dimension usually responds a little differently to each intervention and at a different rate over time. Your task at this stage is to find the lagging dimension and focus your efforts on it. How do you identify the lagging dimensions or measure the extent to which each of them is responding? By using rating scales. Every patient we see at each visit, including those not in our studies, completes a packet of rating scales to track his or her progress in as many areas as feasible over time. Most of these are patient-rated and can be completed while patients are in the waiting room in the half hour prior to their appointment. Anxious patients are particularly cooperative about this task, which is instructive and yields valuable information. We recommend it particularly when you are dealing with a refractory case.

What dimensions should you assess? We find that particular attention needs to be paid to (1) panic attacks or limited symptom attacks, (2) overall anxiety symptoms, (3) phobias, (4) associated depression, and (5) life changes, psychosocial stress, and social support.

Panic Attacks or Limited Symptom Attacks?

Limited symptom or panic attacks are the acute paroxysmal surges of symptoms of somatic and/or cognitive anxiety. The only reliable distinction that can be made between the two types is the number of symptoms per attack. If there are four or more symptoms in the attack, it is a panic attack by definition. If there are three or less, it is a limited symptom attack. Some limited symptom attacks occur even in the absence of cognitive anxiety and consist of somatic symptoms only.

With drug treatment the panic attacks disappear first, but some limited symptom attacks often remain. When following a patient, therefore, it is not enough to ask "Have your panic attacks stopped?" The patient may still be having regular limited symptom attacks that are reinforcing the phobic avoidance and undermining recovery. It is more important to focus your attention on getting rid of all the limited symptom attacks, especially the unexpected ones. When you have effectively blocked these, you have probably adjusted the medication correctly. The focus in the literature on the word *panic*—as in *panic disorder* and *panic attack*—has shifted treatment slightly off target. The clinician needs to make a conceptual shift from the word *panic* and regard the limited symptom attacks as the central target of treatment. Check the list of 13 symptoms in the DSM-III-R (American Psychiatric Association, 1987) under Panic Disorder. Ask the patient on follow-up, "Have any of these symptoms occurred suddenly and unexpectedly in attacks even if you did not feel very anxious at the time?" If the patient is continuing to have these unexpected limited symptom attacks, the medication is probably not adjusted correctly. If you feel that it is then it is time to consider switching to another medication.

Overall Anxiety Symptoms

A cluster of symptoms is typically found in panic disorder patients. As a patient improves, these should all clear up. It is useful to have a measure of the extent to which they have cleared up in response to treatment. If too many of these symptoms remain, especially in the absence of major provocation, the medications have probably not been adjusted correctly. Some of the symptoms are not listed in the DSM-III-R, so to assess this dimension we use the Sheehan Patient Rated Anxiety Scale (SPRAS)(Sheehan, 1986b). It is shown in Table 11.2.

In a study of over 50 panic disorder patients, the mean SPRAS (Part 1) score at the start of treatment was 58 (with a standard deviation of 21) (Sheehan, Raj, Soto, & Sheehan, 1988). The aim of treatment is to get this score at least below 20 and as close to 0 as possible. Tracking scores via this scale has been useful in tracing fluctuations in the patient's illness throughout long-term management. Checking the patient's responses on this scale closely may also reveal a pattern of symptoms or an isolated symptom that fails to respond when all others have. For example, in one alprazolam study two patients had responded well in all dimensions of their panic disorder, but both continued to have residual diarrhea. It became obvious eventually that no additional alprazolam adjustment would improve this symptom. The diarrhea cleared up in both patients when 50 mg of a tricyclic at bedtime was added to the alprazolam regimen. Even within a dimension, then, some symptoms may selectively respond better to one medication.

Phobias

Phobias are the situations, places, or things that the patient fears and avoids, usually as a complication of having unexpected anxiety attacks in these and related situations. First identify the situations. They usually fall into five clusters: an agoraphobia cluster, a social phobia cluster, a blood-injury-illness cluster, a loss-of-control cluster, and a miscellaneous simple phobia cluster (animals, flying, public speaking, and so on). Assess the extent of the fear *and* avoidance of each of the phobias. A patient may not actually avoid a particular situation but still fear it greatly. This dimension can be assessed using either the Marks-Mathews Fear Questionnaire (Marks & Mathews, 1979) or the Marks-Sheehan Phobia Scale (Sheehan, 1986a), which was designed with psychopharmacological studies in mind.

Our experience has been that patients only overcome their phobias some time after their other symptoms have improved and they have gained enough confidence to know theirs is not a transient improvement—that they can dare to try coping with these situations successfully. Encouraging them to face their milder, more recently acquired phobias first and to take a gradual approach to their long-standing phobias may make the process easier for them.

If a patient's limited symptom attacks and panic attacks are under control, yet phobic avoidance behavior persists, you need to focus your attention on more in vivo exposure behavior therapy rather than on the medication choice or dose adjustment. Tricyclic antidepressants have little antiphobic effect, whereas MAO inhibitors and benzodiazepines have more. These last two particularly facilitate in vivo exposure. However, if phobias are persisting, you need to explain to patients and their families or significant others how to do in vivo exposure effectively. Give patients concrete assignments to accomplish before the next visit. Patients should bring themselves into direct contact with the feared stimulus, maintain this direct contact for as long as possible at each exposure (preferably for more than 2 hours), avoid fleeing in response to the urge to do so, and practice this real-life exposure frequently. To the extent that they do so, they should experience extinction of their phobias. If they are doing this and still not succeeding, therapist-assisted exposure may help. If this doesn't help, focus particularly on maintaining the duration of each exposure session for up to 3 hours. If that is not helpful, consider a switch to an MAO inhibitor and repeat the exposure treatment.

Associated Depression

As many as 60% of panic disorder patients have some associated depressive symptoms at the time of evaluation. Some may even meet criteria for major depressive disorder in addition to panic disorder. Usually the depressive symptoms are a late complication of the unexpected anxiety attacks, however, coming on months or years after the first anxiety attack. Treatment with a benzodiazepine may greatly improve all the anxiety symptoms as well as block the panic and limited symptom attacks, and exposure treatment may extinguish much or all of the avoidant behavior. Yet some depressed mood or depressive symptoms may remain. Patients may be puzzled about why, in spite of their progress, they remain depressed for no apparent reason. If this

TABLE 11.2 Sheehan Patient Rated Anxiety Scale

INSTRUCTIONS: Below is a list of problems and complaints that people sometimes have. Part 1 asks about how you have felt during the past week; Part 2 asks about how you feel right now. Blacken only one circle for each problem, and do not skip any items.

PART 1—DURING THE PAST WEEK, HOW MUCH DID YOU SUFFER FROM . . .	Not At All	A Little	Moderately	Quite A Bit	Extremely
1. Difficulty in getting your breath, smothering, or overbreathing	O	O	O	O	O
2. Choking sensation or lump in throat	O	O	O	O	O
3. Skipping, racing, or pounding of your heart	O	O	O	O	O
4. Chest pain, pressure, or discomfort	O	O	O	O	O
5. Bouts of excessive sweating	O	O	O	O	O
6. Faintness, lightheadedness, or dizzy spells	O	O	O	O	O
7. Sensation of rubbery or "jelly" legs	O	O	O	O	O
8. Feeling off balance or unsteady like you might fall	O	O	O	O	O
9. Nausea or stomach problems	O	O	O	O	O
10. Feeling that things around you are strange, unreal, foggy, or detached from you	O	O	O	O	O
11. Feeling outside or detached from part or all of your body, or a floating feeling	O	O	O	O	O
12. Tingling or numbness in parts of your body	O	O	O	O	O
13. Hot flashes or cold chills	O	O	O	O	O
14. Shaking or trembling	O	O	O	O	O
15. Having a fear that you are dying or that something terrible is about to happen	O	O	O	O	O
16. Feeling you are losing control or going insane	O	O	O	O	O
17. SITUATIONAL ANXIETY ATTACK Sudden anxiety attacks with three or more of the symptoms listed above that occur when you are in or about to go into a situation that is likely, from your experience, to bring on an attack	O	O	O	O	O
18. UNEXPECTED ANXIETY ATTACK Sudden unexpected anxiety attacks with three or more symptoms (listed above) that occur with little or no provocation (i.e., when you are *not* in a situation that is likely, from your experience, to bring on an attack)	O	O	O	O	O
19. UNEXPECTED LIMITED SYMPTOM ATTACK Sudden unexpected spells with only one or two symptoms (listed above) that occur with little or no provocation (i.e., when you are *not* in a situation that is likely, from your experience, to bring on an attack)	O	O	O	O	O
20. ANTICIPATORY ANXIETY EPISODE Anxiety episodes that build up as you anticipate doing something that is likely, from your experience, to bring on anxiety that is more intense than most people experience in such situations	O	O	O	O	O
21. Avoiding situations because they frighten you	O	O	O	O	O
22. Being dependent on others	O	O	O	O	O
23. Tension and inability to relax	O	O	O	O	O
24. Anxiety, nervousness, restlessness	O	O	O	O	O
25. Spells of increased sensitivity to sound, light, or touch	O	O	O	O	O
26. Attacks of diarrhea	O	O	O	O	O
27. Worrying about your health too much	O	O	O	O	O
28. Feeling tired, weak, and exhausted easily	O	O	O	O	O

29. Headaches or pains in neck or head	○	○	○	○	○
30. Difficulty in falling asleep	○	○	○	○	○
31. Waking in the middle of the night, or restless sleep	○	○	○	○	○
32. Unexpected waves of depression occurring with little or no provocation	○	○	○	○	○
33. Emotions and moods going up and down a lot in response to changes around you	○	○	○	○	○
34. Recurrent and persistent ideas, thoughts, impulses, or images that are intrusive, unwanted, senseless, or repugnant	○	○	○	○	○
35. Having to repeat the same action in a ritual (e.g., checking, washing, counting repeatedly), when it's not really necessary	○	○	○	○	○

PART 2 —
RIGHT NOW, AT THIS MOMENT,
HOW MUCH LIKE THIS DO YOU FEEL?

	Not At All	A Little	Moderately	Quite A Bit	Extremely
1. Mouth drier than usual	○	○	○	○	○
2. Worried, preoccupied	○	○	○	○	○
3. Nervous, jittery, anxious, restless	○	○	○	○	○
4. Afraid, fearful	○	○	○	○	○
5. Tense, "uptight"	○	○	○	○	○
6. Shaky inside or out	○	○	○	○	○
7. Fluttery stomach	○	○	○	○	○
8. Warm all over	○	○	○	○	○
9. Sweaty palms	○	○	○	○	○
10. Rapid or heavy heart beat	○	○	○	○	○
11. Tremor of hands or legs	○	○	○	○	○

SOURCE: David V. Sheehan, M.D., Dept. of Psychiatry, University of South Florida College of Medicine. Reprinted with permission.

is the problem, consider using an antidepressant instead of a benzodiazepine. Of all the antidepressants, it appears as though the MAO inhibitors are particularly useful in eradicating depressive symptoms in panic disorder patients. If you do make a switch, keep them on the benzodiazepine (or most of it) until *after* the antidepressant has begun to work—that is, for more than 6 weeks—and only then, and very, very slowly, taper the benzodiazepine.

The depression dimension can be assessed using one of several depression rating scales. The Hamilton Depression Scale (Hamilton, 1967) or the Montgomery-Asberg Depression Rating Scale (Montgomery & Asberg, 1979) are clinician-rated scales, whereas the Zung Depression Scale (Zung, 1965) and the Beck Depression Inventory (the 21-item version) (Bech, Kastrup, & Rafaelsen, 1986) are patient-rated scales. We favor the patient-rated scales, particularly the Beck Depression Inventory.

Life Changes, Psychosocial Stress, and Social Support

We use two simple discan visual analog scales to crudely assess the extent of psychosocial stress and social support at each visit (see Table 11.3). The extent

TABLE 11.3

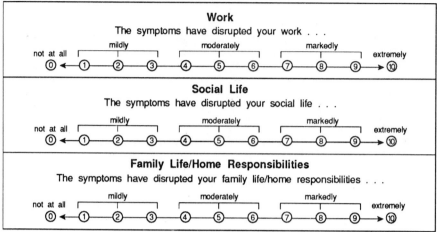

Disability Scales
Instructions—Please fill in *one* circle for each scale.

Stress and Social Support Scales

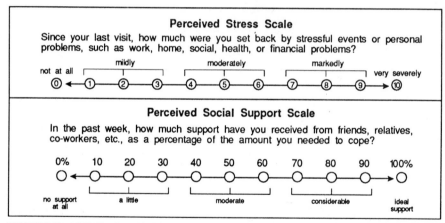

SOURCE: David V. Sheehan, M.D., Dept. of Psychiatry, University of South Florida College of Medicine. Reprinted with permission.

of life changes can be assessed using the Holmes-Rahe Social Readjustment Rating Scale (Holmes & Rahe, 1967). These instruments, of course, are not intended to substitute for a careful history to assess those stresses. Rather, we find that responses on these scales often alert us to probe deeper, even after patients assure us they have had no significant psychosocial problems since their last visit. When a patient is not responding as expected, and we find significant psychosocial stressors or a lack of social support, psychotherapeutic interventions are likely to be needed to attend to and minimize these difficulties. The family's role in, reactions to, and cooperation with treatment need to be assessed particularly carefully, as they often exert an inordinate influence on the outcome. The wise clinician pays particular attention to getting the family's full compliance with and encouragement of the patient to ensure a successful outcome.

Conclusion

Several dimensions in addition to those already mentioned are worth assessing in a patient resistant to treatment. However, such an assessment should at least begin by trying to identify whether one or all of those five dimensions are lagging in response to treatment. The more dimensions that lag simultaneously, the more likely it is that a medication failure is the problem. Identifying which dimension is not responding and by how much is an important first step in breaking down the problem of the resistant case into its smaller, more manageable components.

Relapse After Prior Improvement

Relapse is a particularly common problem, leading to requests for a second opinion. The majority of these cases can be rehabilitated by reviewing and correcting *prescribing practices*.

Often failure to respond is due to subtherapeutic doses of medication. Much time has to be spent with the patient in reviewing the regulation of doses and their timing and spacing and in monitoring complications. The starting dose of alprazolam is usually .5 mg three times daily. This may be increased by .5 mg every 2 days until side effects or significant benefits occur. It is not unusual for tolerance to occur after several weeks, with some reemergence of symptoms. Before switching to an alternative drug, check to see whether in addition to a loss of benefit the patient has also lost the side effects. If so, an increase in dosage is indicated. Several such increments may occur in the first few weeks of therapy before the patient reaches a final stable therapeutic level. Alprazolam has a half-life of 10 to 12 hours, but its effective therapeutic action is only 4 to 6 hours. So if the doses are spaced too far apart (that is, more than 6 hours apart), breakthrough of symptoms may occur between doses. Taking the drug with food slows absorption, reduces sedation, and prolongs the antipanic effect a little. If the roller coaster effect persists, with benefits alternating with some anxiety symptoms every 4 to 8 hours, a switch to clonazepam may be helpful. Clonazepam is structurally related to diazepam and is used in the treatment of myocolonic seizures. It has a longer half-life and a slightly longer duration of action (6 to 8 hours) than alprazolam. Fontaine (1985) used doses in the range of 6 to 9 mg per day; Spier, Tesar, Rosenbaum, and Woods (1986) suggested that doses as low as 2 to 3 mg a day are effective. Our experience is that 1 mg of alprazolam is approximately equivalent to .75 mg of clonazepam. During the course of therapy with alprazolam, patients may benefit from the addition of a tricyclic antidepressant if they have symptoms of depression or insomnia. This combination is well tolerated, usually with minimal increase in side effects (The Upjohn Company, 1985).

The side effects of tricyclic antidepressants in the early weeks are more disruptive relative to the benefits, which often leads to a premature discontinuation of medication. Educating the patient to expect this disruption and minimizing it by slow and small increments in dose will improve compliance. Another problem is inadequate dosage and length of treatment. It is not unusual to need a final dose of 250 to 300 mg of imipramine to obtain a stable, satisfactory antipanic effect, and it usually takes from 4 to 8 weeks to achieve this effect. The idea that stable benefit can be achieved consistently in less than 3 weeks is simply wishful thinking; it is a view that has contributed to many treatment failures.

The hydrazine monoamine oxidase inhibitors (MAOIs), particularly phenelzine, appear to be somewhat superior in the treatment of difficult cases (Sheehan, Ballenger, & Jacobson, 1980). Phenelzine is started in doses of 15 mg daily and increased by 15 mg weekly until a dose of 45 mg per day is reached. Beyond this, increments are made more slowly and, if need be, by half tablets, with frequent sphygmomanometer monitoring for postural hypotension. At therapeutic doses, common side effects are a dry mouth, constipation, sweating, delayed urination and orgasm, weight gain, and postural hypotension. The latter is the most likely to limit treatment. This problem may be minimized by paying attention to hydration, taking salt tablets, and drinking cola, tea, or coffee. The small amounts of tyramine in a normal meal will help lessen the hypotensive effect of the drug. Vitamin B6 in doses of 200 to 300 mg per day will decrease the electric shock effects and carpal tunnel syndrome that can occur as complications of long-term hydrazine MAO inhibitor use.

Drug Combinations

As an operating principle, it is better to use one medication correctly before attempting combinations. When you use a combination you risk the presence of both medications precluding your ability to correctly adjust the dose of either one to an optimal level. The side effects—particularly sedation—may cause concern that you cannot move the dose of either up without worsening them. This may immobilize you as the patient worsens. You can, of course, use such combinations with care. Practical experience has impressed on us that some patients really do fare better on a combination than they previously did on either drug alone.

When the combination is not working well enough—and this is usually the combination of a benzodiazepine and an antidepressant—slowly lower the doses of the benzodiazepine by .25 to .5 mg of alprazolam or its equivalent per week. If anxiety worsens at this slow withdrawal rate, treat it by increasing the antidepressant dose. Don't expect a therapeutic response to this increased dose of antidepressant for 5 to 7 days. If sedation returns, lower the benzodiazepine further until anxiety returns, and treat this by increasing the dose of antidepressant. Keep doing this until you have a better therapeutic response and a good balance between side effects and benefit. Lowering the benzodiazepine dose also lessens the side effects such as ataxia, confusion, and amnesia that are sometimes encountered.

Pharmacotherapy—Alternative Choices

When you establish that the patient is truly resistant to adequate doses and trials of benzodiazepines, tricyclic antidepressants, and monoamine oxidase inhibitors—singly and in combination—it is time to consider medications that have not been studied extensively but are reported in the literature to sometimes possess antipanic effects. New agents such as these typically should be used only by the specialist. Use of a less thoroughly evaluated treatment should also be discussed with the patient, and informed consent obtained.

Clonidine

Several lines of evidence suggest that the locus coeruleus, a noradrenergic positive nucleus, might be involved in the mediation of anxiety. Electrical or pharmacologic stimulation with piperoxine of the locus coeruleus induces behavior similar to that triggered by a natural threat. Inhibition by the alpha-2-adrenergic agonist clonidine reduces primates' response to threat (Redmond, 1979). Clonidine has also been shown to block symptoms of opiate withdrawal (Gold, Redmond, & Kleber, 1979). Liebowitz, Fyer, McGrath, and Klein (1981), in an 8-week open clinical trial of patients with panic disorder with or without agoraphobia, observed some antipanic efficacy for clonidine. Doses were started at .1 mg twice daily and increased by .1 mg a week until patients were panic free (or up to a limit of 1 mg a day). Of eleven patients, four had a good response at .2 to .5 mg a day, and four had a benefit that later wore off despite dosage increases to .7 or 1 mg a day in two of the subjects. The remaining three subjects had no benefit at the doses they were able to tolerate (.2 to .3 mg per day). Common bothersome side effects were drowsiness, sedation, fatigue, loss of motivation, and anergia. A 10 to 20 mmHg drop in blood pressure may also occur, leading to dizziness or weakness. Dry mouth, blurred vision, irritation, and loss of sexual interest (or impotence) were also reported.

Hoehn-Saric, Merchant, Keyser, and Smith (1981) treated nine patients with generalized anxiety disorder (GAD) and fourteen with panic disorder (PD) in a double-blind crossover design with clonidine and placebo over a 4-week period. Clonidine was better than a previous treatment for five patients (three PD, two GAD) and worse for four patients (three PD, one GAD)—to the point that drug treatment was discontinued. The remaining fourteen patients got a moderate anxiolytic response but less than they had with previous anxiolytic therapy. Anxiolytic effect begins in the first week, with additional gains in the second week. The therapeutic dosage range was from .2 to .5 mg per day. Side effects reported were as in the Liebowitz et al.

(1981) study, and were experienced in varying degrees by 95% of the patients by the second week. Sedation, dry mouth, and irritability decreased by the second week. In a follow-up phase no further reductions in anxiety were noted after 2 weeks, with a tendency for relapse after 3 to 4 months of treatment despite an increase in dosage.

Calcium Channel Blockers

Receptors signal the interior of their cells to perform certain functions by increasing the intracellular concentrations of second messengers like cyclic AMP and calcium ion. A small elevation of free calcium ion concentration within the cell is sufficient to stimulate some cellular processes. Intracellularly, calcium ions exert their action by forming a complex with an intracellular protein called calmodulin. This then activates many systems within the cell, acting alone or in combination with cyclic AMP. The intracellular action of calcium can be antagonized by calcium channel (entry) blockers. They may act in the following manner (Dubovsky, 1986).

1. By occupying the channel (lanthanam and cobalt)
2. By altering membrane permeability of the channel by working on calcium antagonist receptors that are functionally linked to the calcium channel (verapamil, nifedipine, and diltiazem)
3. By inhibiting mobilization of calcium from intracellular stores (dantrolene)
4. By interfering with the metabolism of the membrane receptor–stimulated phosphatidylinositol system (lithium)
5. By interfering with calmodulin or the calcium-calmodulin complex (phenothiazines, tricyclic antidepressants, and beta adrenergic blockers)

Thus, many psychiatric drugs have calcium channel–blocking properties, though it is unclear whether this has anything to do with their therapeutic effects. Goldstein (1985) reports on seven treatment-resistant patients with panic disorder, four of whom improved with either 80 mg of verapamil or 60 mg of diltiazem, both administered three times a day. Klein and Uhde (1988) report on a 16-week double-blind crossover study of verapamil in 11 patients with panic disorder. Doses of up to 480 mg a day were used. Four patients rated themselves as getting a marked benefit, three had a marginal response, and four were complete non-responders. The responders had a satisfactorily significant, if clinically modest, reduction in the number of panic attacks and the Zung Anxiety Scale, with no significant change in state anxiety as reflected by the Spielberger State-Trait Anxiety Scale, suggesting more improvement in somatic anxiety symptoms than in psychic anxiety. There was no significant improvement in agoraphobia during the study period. As expected, there was a mean reduction of diastolic blood pressure by 6.8 mmHg with no subjective complaints. ECG monitoring did not reveal a clinically significant (greater than .24 millisecond) increase in P—R intervals (Klein & Uhde, 1988).

Overall the data suggest some potential for benefit if this group of drugs is used with panic patients. Care should be taken to get baseline ECGs and to monitor blood pressure and pulse. When using calcium channel blockers as an adjunct to other psychotropics, the possibility of additive effects should be kept in mind, particularly the combination of bradycardia with lithium in older patients and the elevation of serum carbamazepine levels to a toxic range (MacPhee, McInnes, Thompson, & Brodie, 1986; Brodie & MacPhee, 1986). Metabolism of this group of drugs may be inhibited by cimetidine, leading to excessive plasma levels at usual therapeutic dosages. Valdiserri (1985) has reported a patient who appeared rigid and had parkinsonism while receiving lithium, diltiazem, and thiothixene. The rigidity continued despite sequentially stopping lithium and thiothixene. It remitted only after diltiazem was stopped.

Serotonin Reuptake Inhibitors

It has not been determined conclusively yet if a significant defect in the serotonergic system exists in panic disorder and, if so, whether it is overactivity or decreased activity that is responsible (Sheehan, Zak, Miller, & Fanous, 1988). Anatomically, serotonergic neurons that originate in the raphe nuclei in the brain stem have an inhibitory effect on the activity of several brain regions implicated in anxiety mediation, such as locus coeruleus, amygdala, and hippocampus (Eriksson, 1987; Wang & Aghajanian, 1977; Segal, 1975). Lactate infusion precipitates panic attacks in panic disorder patients. Lactate as well as pyruvate stimulate serotonin uptake in human platelets, so they may stimulate serotonin reuptake in central serotonergic neurons, thereby decreasing serotonergic activity. This in turn may induce anxiety by reducing the inhibitory serotonergic influence on the locus coeruleus (Lingjaerde, 1985). Plasma serotonin levels are lower in panic disorder patients with agoraphobia as compared to normal controls (Schneider et al., 1987).

Imipramine, monoamine oxidase inhibitors, and trazodone all have a significant effect on serotonin by increasing activity in the central nervous system. They also have some effect on noradrenaline, but to a lesser degree. Clomipramine, a potent 5HT reuptake blocker, has been shown to be effective in panic disorder (Gloger, Grunhaus, Birmacher, & Troudart, 1981). Zimelidine, which has been withdrawn from clinical use, is a potent inhibitor of central serotonin reuptake. Evans, Kenardy, Schneider, and Hory (1986), in a double-blind, placebo-controlled study of panic disorder, found it to be superior to imipramine and placebo. Overall, drugs that increase 5HT activity appear to exert antipanic effects (Sheehan, Zak et al., 1988). This is important because when it is necessary for the treatment-resistant patient, clomipramine may be obtained from sources outside the United States—or a trial of fluoxetine may help. Fluvoxamine and sertraline, potent new 5HT reuptake inhibitors, are undergoing trials in depressed patients; once approved for that indication, they may be tried with possible benefit in panic disorder also (Sheehan, Zak et al., 1988).

Special Problems

Panic Disorder in Pregnancy

A patient recently applied to one of our research studies for treatment with a recent history of dizzy spells, faintness, nausea, tachycardia, some weakness, hot flashes, and sweating spells. Unable to explain the source of these unexpected symptoms, she decided that she had panic disorder. A careful history revealed that her last menstrual period was 8 weeks earlier, though she had a history of menstrual irregularity. The pregnancy test called for in the research protocol confirmed that she was pregnant! She did not have panic disorder. Be forewarned.

Because panic disorder is commonly a disease of women during their childbearing years, many patients will have pregnancies during the course of their illness. The most troublesome scenario is when a panic disorder patient that you have treated effectively with medication calls to announce that she is about 8 to 10 weeks pregnant. She wants to know what to do now about the medication. She is most likely to be taking a benzodiazepine, and your first impulse may be to get her to stop abruptly. Don't: that may precipitate a seizure and perhaps even a miscarriage. Start lowering the dose slowly, at a rate no faster than .5 mg of alprazolam or its equivalent every 4 to 7 days. Schedule an appointment immediately and involve significant others in the decision and discussion. Carefully document what you are doing in the chart and document the patient's involvement in this process. In a situation like this, there are no easy answers. The physician needs to protect the best interests of the unborn child and mother and protect himself or herself legally. Spend time in an open, balanced, frank discussion of these issues with the patient. Nothing can be gained by frightening the patient or reprimanding her. Approximately 3% of all pregnancies result in an abnormal liveborn infant; of these, only about 3% are associated with known teratogenic exposure (Coustan & Carpentar, 1985). Even if a panic disorder patient takes no medication, this 3% risk still holds. It is not yet known whether panic disorder itself may be associated with complications to the pregnancy and fetus. It is also possible *but not documented* that some antipanic medications such as benzodiazepines, because of their effects on muscle, may decrease the normal rate of miscarriage, so that fetuses with abnormalities that would normally be miscarried by nature may survive to full term and inflate the number of abnormalities noted in this group at birth. Certainly, being on an antipanic drug is not an indication for a therapeutic abortion procedure, nor is it a routine indication for amniocentesis, as this procedure exposes the patient to new if minor risks. Even with drugs of known teratogenicity, such as thalidomide, abnormalities only occurred in 20% of those exposed for the critical 14-day danger period (Coustan & Carpentar, 1985).

"What are the realistic risks?" patients will ask. In the first and second trimester with benzodiazepines, there is some evidence of an increased risk of cleft lip and/or palate (Safra & Oakley, 1975; Saxen, 1975a, 1975b), inguinal hernia, pyloric stenosis, and congenital heart defects (Bracken & Holford, 1981). Second-trimester use has been associated with hemangiomas and cardiovascular defects (Bracken & Holford, 1981). In the last trimester and through delivery, two complications have been noted. At birth, the baby is often hypotonic and will then develop a withdrawal syndrome. If the child is born prematurely, it is at increased risk. For these reasons it is always advisable to have the mother off medication entirely (tapered slowly) in the last 2 months to minimize these complications to the baby. In the postpartum period, many antipanic drugs (especially benzodiazepines) are excreted in breast milk. Patients should therefore choose between breast feeding and their antipanic medication, but not attempt both.

Your function is to adopt a calm and helpful manner and to provide good sense and balance in your advice, not to alarm the patient. Protect yourself by keeping a detailed record of your discussions, your advice, the information imparted, the patient's choice, and your consultation calls, all reflecting your reasonable care.

Substance Abuse

Patients presenting with substance abuse may have underlying panic disorder, and patients presenting with panic disorder may have substance abuse complicating the clinical picture. Mullaney and Trippet (1979) found rates of panic symptoms as high as 60% in alcoholics, with about half of these showing diagnosable panic disorder. Aronson and Logue (1988) reported a 27% rate of secondary alcohol abuse and a 32% rate of secondary sedative abuse. An additional problem facing the clinician is the sorting out of withdrawal-related anxiety symptoms.

As a first step, a full substance use history must be taken from patients with anxiety disorder, as resistance to treatment may be due to this problem. During the physical examination, look for track marks, sweating, pupillary changes, enlarged liver, and laboratory evidence of abuse. Cocaine use has increased dramatically in recent years, and adverse psychological effects include depression (83%), anxiety (83%), and panic attacks (50%) (Watson & Gold, 1984). In fact, cocaine and other psychostimulants can precipitate panic disorder (Aronson, 1986). There is some evidence that tricyclic antidepressants, when combined with nonpharmacologic therapy, help decrease the craving for cocaine (Gawin & Kleber, 1986).

As a general rule, benzodiazepines should be avoided for this group, as it is more likely to abuse this drug. However, we have used it in several cases, and effective benzodiazepine therapy has led to anxiety control. Patients were then able to avoid further use of other substances. At times, the dependence and abuse may be severe enough to warrant inpatient detoxification and then treatment of the anxiety disorder. In the patient with strong evidence for primary substance abuse, success may depend on combining pharmacotherapy with concurrent enrollment in Alcoholics Anonymous, Narcotics Anonymous, group therapy, or treatment contracts that include random urine testing for drugs.

It is reported that panic disorder patients are sensitive to and may exacerbate their condition by the use of caffeine (Uhde, Boulenger, Jimerson, & Post, 1984), cannabis (Sheehan & Sheehan, 1982), or over-the-counter preparations containing phenylpropanolamine or psuedoephedrine (Gardner & Hall, 1982). With the treatment-resistant patient, it may be helpful to recommend abstinence from all these products.

Personality Disorder

The treatment of panic disorder may be complicated by personality disorders leading to a poor outcome caused by noncompliance with medication regimens, office visits, and behavioral recommendations. During the evaluation phase, then, it is useful to look for personality disorder. The clinician should keep in mind, however, that in some patients this is a state-dependent disorder related to the anxiety problem rather than a true trait disturbance. The most frequently seen disorders are passive-dependent, compulsive, and antisocial personalities. When personality disorder is present, certain strategies are helpful. Take a supportive stance, structure the treatment situation in great detail, and practice firm but consistent limit setting—for example, comment on missed visits and keep track of patterns of drug use.

Conclusion

Treating resistant cases of panic disorder is a rewarding challenge. The majority eventually respond well. As with any puzzle, the solution becomes clear when it is broken down into its smallest manageable components. Use a practical system to assess each dimension of the disorder, actively address all the difficulties that come into focus, and you are on your way to a satisfying solution to your patient's problem.

References

American Psychiatric Association. (1987). *Diagnostic and statistical manual of mental disorders* (3rd ed., rev.). Washington, DC: Author.

Aronson, T. A. (1986). Cocaine precipitation of panic disorder. *American Journal of Psychiatry, 143,* 643–645.

Aronson, T. A., & Logue, C. M. (1988). Phenomenology of panic attacks: A descriptive study of panic disorder patients' self reports. *Journal of Clinical Psychiatry, 49*(1), 8–13.

Bech, P., Kastrup, M., & Rafaelsen, O. J. (1986). Mini-compendium of rating scales for states of anxiety, depression, mania, schizophrenia with corresponding DSM-III syndromes. *Acta Psychiatrica Scandinavica, 73*(Suppl.), 1–37.

Bracken, M. B., & Holford, T. R. (1981). Exposure to prescribed drugs in pregnancy and association with congenital malformations. *Obstetrics and Gynecology, 58,* 336–344.

Brodie, M. J., & MacPhee, G. J. A. (1986). Carbamazepine neurotoxicity precipitated by diltiazem. *British Medical Journal, 292,* 1170–1171.

Coustan, D. R., & Carpentar, M. V. (1985). The use of medication in pregnancy. *Resident and Staff Physician, 31,* 64–70.

Dubovsky, S. L. (1986). Calcium antagonists: A new class of psychiatric drugs? *Psychiatric Annals, 16*(12), 724–728.

Eriksson, E. (1987). Brain neurotransmission in panic disorder. *Acta Psychiatrica Scandinavica, 76*(Suppl. 335), 31–37.

Evans, L., Kenardy, J., Schneider, P., & Hory, H. (1986). Effect of a selective serotonin uptake inhibitor in agoraphobia with panic attacks. A double blind comparison of zimelidine, imipramine and placebo. *Acta Psychiatrica Scandinavica, 73,* 49–53.

Fontaine, R. (1985). Clonazepam for panic disorders and agitation. *Psychosomatics, 26*(12)(Suppl.), 13–16.

Gardner, E. R., & Hall, R. C. W. (1982). Psychiatric symptoms produced by over the counter drugs. *Psychosomatics, 23,* 186–190.

Gawin, F. H., & Kleber, H. D. (1986). Pharmacologic treatments of cocaine abuse. *Psychiatric Clinics of North America, 9*(3)(Suppl.), 573–583.

Gloger, S., Grunhaus, L., Birmacher, B., & Troudart, T. (1981). Treatment of spontaneous panic attacks with clomipramine. *American Journal of Psychiatry, 138,* 1215–1217.

Gold, M. S., Redmond, D. E., & Kleber, H. D. (1979). Noradrenergic hyperactivity in opiate withdrawal supported by clonidine reversal of opiate withdrawal. *American Journal of Psychiatry, 136,* 100–102.

Goldstein, J. A. (1985). Calcium channel blockers in the treatment of panic disorder [letter]. *Journal of Clinical Psychiatry, 46*(12), 546.

Hamilton, M. (1967). Development of a rating scale for primary depressive illness. *British Journal of Social and Clinical Psychology, 6,* 278–296.

Hoehn-Saric, R., Merchant, A. F., Keyser, M. L., & Smith, V. K. (1981). Effects of clonidine on anxiety disorders. *Archives of General Psychiatry, 38,* 1278–1282.

Holmes, T. H., & Rahe, R. H. (1967). The social readjustment rating scale. *Journal of Psychosomatic Research, 11,* 213–218.

Klein, E., & Uhde, T. W. (1988). Controlled study of verapamil for treatment of panic disorder. *American Journal of Psychiatry, 145,* 431–434.

Liebowitz, M. R., Fyer, A. J., McGrath, P., & Klein, D. F. (1981). Clonidine treatment of panic disorder. *Psychopharmacology Bulletin, 17,* 122–123.

Lingjaerde, O. (1985). Lactate induced panic attacks: Possible involvement of serotonin reuptake stimulation. *Acta Psychiatrica Scandinavica, 72,* 206–208.

MacPhee, G. I. A., McInnes, G. T., Thompson, G. G., & Brodie, M. H. (1986). Verapamil potentiates carbamazepine neurotoxicity: A clinically important inhibitory interaction. *Lancet, 1,* 700–703.

Marks, I. M., & Mathews, A. M. (1979). Brief standard self-rating for phobic patients. *Behaviour Research and Therapy, 17,* 263–267.

Montgomery, S. A., & Asberg, M. (1979). A new depression rating scale designed to be sensitive to change. *British Journal of Psychiatry, 134,* 382–389.

Mullaney, J. A., & Trippet, C. J. (1979). Alcohol dependence and phobias: Clinical descriptions and relevance. *British Journal of Psychiatry, 135,* 565–573.

Pollard, A. C., Obermeier, H. J., & Cox, G. L. (1987). Inpatient treatment of complicated agoraphobia and panic disorder. *Hospital and Community Psychiatry, 38*(9), 951–958.

Raj, B. A., & Sheehan, D. V. (1987). Medical evaluation of panic attacks. *Journal of Clinical Psychiatry, 48,* 309–313.

Raj, B. A., & Sheehan, D. V. (1988). Medical evaluation of the anxious patient. *Psychiatric Annals, 18,* 176–181.

Redmond, D. E. (1979). New and old evidence for the involvement of a brain norepinephrine system in anxiety. In W. E. Faun, I. Karacan, A. D. Pokorny, & R. L. Williams (Eds.), *Phenomenology and treatment of anxiety* (pp. 153–203). New York: Spectrum.

Safra, J. F., & Oakley, G. P. (1975). Association between cleft lip with or without cleft palate and neonatal exposure to diazepam. *Lancet, 2,* 478–480.

Saxen, I. (1975a). Association between oral clefts and drugs taken during pregnancy. *International Journal of Epidemiology, 4,* 37–44.

Saxen, I. (1975b). Epidemiology of cleft lip and palate. *British Journal of Preventive and Social Medicine, 29,* 103–110.

Schneider, P., Evans, L., Ross-Lee, L., Wiltshire, B., Eadie, M., Kenardy, J., & Hoey, H. (1987). Plasma biogenic amine levels in agoraphobia with panic attacks. *Pharmacopsychiatry, 20,* 102–104.

Segal, M. (1975). Physiological and pharmacological evidence for a serotonergic projection to the hippocampus. *Brain Research, 94,* 115–131.

Sheehan, D. V. (1986a). *The anxiety disease.* New York: Bantam.

Sheehan, D. V. (1986b). *The Sheehan Patient Rated Anxiety Scale.* Tampa, FL: Research Division, University of South Florida Psychiatry Center.

Sheehan, D. V., Ballenger, J. C., & Jacobson, G. (1980). Treatment of endogenous anxiety with phobic, hysterical and hypochondriacal symptoms. *Archives of General Psychiatry, 37,* 51–59.

Sheehan, D. V., Raj, B. A., Soto, S., & Sheehan, K. H. (1988). *Is buspirone effective for panic disorder?* Manuscript submitted for publication.

Sheehan, D. V., & Sheehan, K. H. (1982). The classification of anxiety and hysterical states. II. Toward a more heuristic classification. *Journal of Clinical Psychopharmacology, 2,* 386–393.

Sheehan, D. V., Zak, J. P., Miller, J. A., & Fanous, B. S. L. (1988). Panic disorder: The potential role of serotonin reuptake inhibitors. *Journal of Clinical Psychiatry, 49*(6,Suppl.), 30–36.

Spier, S. A., Tesar, G. E., Rosenbaum, J. F., & Woods, S. W. (1986). Treatment of panic disorder and agoraphobia with clonazepam. *Journal of Clinical Psychiatry, 47,* 238–242.

Spitzer, R. L., Williams, J. B. W., & Gibbon, M. (1988). *Structured clinical interview for DSM-III-R*. New York: Biometrics Research Dept., New York State Psychiatric Institute.

Uhde, T. W., Boulenger, J.-P., Jimerson, D. C., & Post, R. M. (1984). Caffeine: Relationship to human anxiety, plasma MHPG and cortisol. *Psychopharmacology Bulletin, 20*, 426–430.

The Upjohn Company, Clinical Biopharmaceutics. (November, 1985). *A multicenter study to evaluate the pharmacokinetic and clinical interactions between alprazolam and imipramine*. (Protocol No. 0083). Kalamazoo, MI: Author.

Valdiserri, E. V. (1985). A possible interaction between lithium and diltiazem: Case report. *Journal of Clinical Psychiatry, 46*, 540–541.

Wang, R. Y., & Aghajanian, G. K. (1977). Inhibition of neurons in the amygdala by dorsal raphe stimulation: Mediation through a direct serotonergic pathway. *Brain Research, 120*, 85–102.

Watson, A. M., & Gold, M. S. (1984). Chronic cocaine abuse: Evidence for adverse effects on health and functioning. *Psychiatric Annals, 14*, 733–743.

Zung, W. W. K. (1965). A self rating depression scale. *Archives of General Psychiatry, 12*, 63–70.

CHAPTER 12

Psychological Approaches to the Difficult Patient

P. M. G. Emmelkamp and T. K. Bouman

Difficulties in treating patients with panic disorder (with or without agoraphobia) may originate in various sources. Some of the problems encountered by the therapist are caused by patient noncompliance. Other difficulties may emerge because the patient has other major problems in addition to panic disorder. The main consequence for therapy is slow or no progress. Our aim in this chapter is to make the therapist aware of some of the pitfalls that may complicate treatment. First, a general assessment strategy is discussed. Next, a number of potential difficulties are described, along with therapeutic interventions to supplement the typical cognitive-behavioral treatment of panic disorder. Because difficult patients often differ from the clear-cut textbook examples of panic disorder and agoraphobia, many case illustrations are provided as examples. In this chapter we cannot exhaust the problems the therapist may encounter in clinical practice, but we hope to alert practitioners to potential complications and to suggest at least a few solutions.

We particularly focus upon other anxiety and mood disorders, somatic abnormalities, hypochondriacal concerns, the abuse of medications, and deficient compliance, as well as relationship problems and personality disorders. The case descriptions are based on patients we have seen, so details have been changed to preserve anonymity.

Functional Analysis

The most important assessment approach in behavior therapy is the functional analysis of the problem behaviors. This implies a clear description of the components of the problem, including, if necessary, the relationship between patient and therapist. Generally, a diagnosis in terms of the DSM-III-R is of little use in making a functional analysis. A seemingly homogeneous problem such as panic disorder has different causes in different patients and may be maintained by a wide variety of factors. In clinical practice, patients often present more than one problem. They have not only panic disorder but also difficulty with depression, feelings of inferiority, or sexual problems. Emmelkamp (1982) distinguished two phases in the functional analysis: (1) macroanalysis and (2) microanalysis. Frequently different factors are involved in the development and the maintenance of a problem. Thus, clinicians should consider the current situation separately from the conditions at the time the problem developed.

Macroanalysis addresses the relationships among the various problems. The therapist tries to map out the different problems and to determine the functional relationships between them. The aim of macroanalysis is to place the various problems in a wider framework and to formulate hypotheses about how the problems are related. When patients describe problems with both panic disorder and depression, for example, it is very important to establish the functional relationship between the two: has depression been caused by the lack of reinforcers in the patient's limited lifestyle, or is agoraphobia the result of the depressed patient's lack of motivation and social withdrawal, or are the two problems unrelated? The answer to these questions determines which therapeutic interventions are most likely to be successful.

Microanalysis, on the other hand, deals with the (cognitive) behavioral analysis within one specific problem area. In the behavioral analysis, the therapist focuses on (1) the antecedent stimulus variables, (2) the organismic variables, (3) the overt maladaptive behavior, (4) the cognitive components, and (5) the consequences. For example, for a fear of panic attacks, the therapist examines the situations in which the patient becomes afraid (the discriminant stimuli, such as being on one's own in the street), the nature of the patient's behavior (for example, escape or avoidance), the physiological components (such as heart palpitations or trembling), the cognitive processes (such as irrational beliefs or the internal or external attribution of causes and self-statements), and the consequences of this behavior (for instance, anxiety reduction and occupational dysfunction). Environmental influences are also included (such as reinforcement of avoidance behavior by the family members). In short, the purpose of a microanalysis is to identify specific aspects of person/environment interactions presumed to be related to the anxiety and phobia. Each of the problem areas identified in the macroanalysis should be the focus of microanalysis.

It is often helpful to have the patient keep a structured diary to find out under what conditions the problem behavior occurs. The patient should fill in the diary throughout the day so that there will be no need to recall events. Inspection of the diary may reveal significant associations between anxiety and particular events. An important advantage of self-monitoring is that patients themselves begin to see connections they have not seen before. It is advisable to have patients rate their level of anxiety (for instance, on a scale of 0 to 10). Such a barometer gives more precise information than does simply monitoring the occurrence of anxiety. However, many patients find it difficult to keep a diary. Patients with fear of failure often experience the task as an assignment at which they might fail. Others are afraid that monitoring their feelings and thoughts might confront them with aspects of themselves that they find painful. A clear explanation of just what is expected of the patient and working through some examples together may be helpful. Further, it is recommended that the therapist design recording forms that are tailored to the needs of the patient and contain questions of specific interest to that patient.

Role-play rehearsal of situations that evoke anxiety can also reveal important information. One patient became anxious when discussing household issues with her husband. When rehearsing this situation in role-play it became evident to both therapist and patient that she was actually very angry but could not express those feelings to her husband. This resulted in a panic attack later on that evening. Having patients imagine a situation in which they became anxious may also be useful in finding connections between stimuli and feelings.

After the behavioral analysis is completed, the clinician integrates the results in a formulation of the case. A decision is then made about which problems to focus on first. For a more detailed discussion of behavioral analysis and treatment planning, the reader is referred to Emmelkamp (1982) and Turkat (1985).

The following case provides an example of a functional analysis of a complex case (Emmelkamp & Emmelkamp-Benner, 1983).

> Janet was a 28-year-old married woman with the following problems: (1) agoraphobia—she was completely housebound and afraid of going into the street alone, (2) sexual anxiety—she avoided sex with her husband as much as possible and was afraid of looking at her own body even when dressed, (3) social anxiety and unassertiveness, (4) marital distress, and (5) psychosomatic complaints such as headaches. Further questioning concerning the developmental history revealed that Janet had suffered from social anxiety for as long as she could remember. The first panic attack occurred in a social situation in which she felt that she was being watched. This eventually led to her agoraphobia, which became an excuse to avoid all kinds of social situations (like visiting her parents-in-law, who were constantly criticizing her). Her anxiety about sexuality appeared to be independent of the other problems; it was rooted in the fact that her elder sister was a prostitute, so that everything related to sexuality was negatively loaded for her from an early age. During sexual contact she, too, felt like a prostitute. Tension related to social anxiety also contributed to her headaches. The psychosomatic complaints appeared to be used to avoid having sex with her husband. If she said she had a headache, her husband no longer insisted, but she did not dare say directly that she did not feel like having sex. Janet's lack of social contacts and sexual interactions had led to considerable friction in her marriage. The relationship between the problem areas is depicted in Figure 12.1.

Based on this analysis, we decided to treat the social anxiety first with assertiveness training and exposure in vivo for social and agoraphobic situations. After that, sexual anxiety was treated by a graded in vivo exposure program, in which her husband's participation was required. At the end of the treatment program, social anxiety, sexual anxiety, and agoraphobic avoidance and panic attacks had disappeared almost completely. Interestingly, Janet's psychosomatic complaints and the relationship problems improved spontaneously, suggesting that the proposed functional analysis was indeed correct.

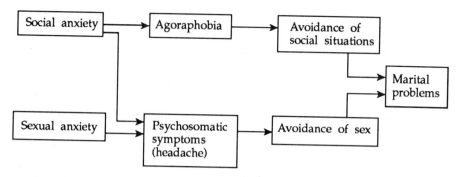

FIGURE 12.1 Hypothesized Relationships Among Problem Areas

The most important areas to examine in considering functional relationships are the following.

1. *Social relationships*. Several studies have found high levels of interpersonal conflict preceding the onset of panic disorder with agoraphobia (see, for example, Kleiner & Marshall, 1985; Last, Barlow, & O'Brien, 1984). However, as interpersonal problems are also common in the larger population, it may be that certain characteristics (especially dependent, socially anxious, and unassertive behavior) predispose people to react to these conflicts or to become involved in them (Kleiner & Marshall, 1985).

2. *Relationship with partner*. This issue will be dealt with extensively later in this chapter.

3. *Emotional processing of traumatic incidents*. In some cases panic and agoraphobia are related to an inadequate emotional processing of traumatic experiences. Examples of patients with post–traumatic stress disorder in combination with agoraphobia will be given in a later section. In these cases the therapist must determine whether treatment of the panic disorder will be impeded by the inadequate emotional processing.

4. *Cognitive style*. Locus-of-control orientation may be an important variable in the development of panic disorder. Persons with an external control orientation experiencing anxiety attacks in a stressful period are likely to misread the anxiety (and its accompanying physical symptoms) as caused by external situations (crowded areas, for instance) or to internal phenomena such as a severe illness (for example, a heart attack). Some may even interpret it as a sign of "going crazy." Treatment that focuses on changing this cognitive style (Beck, Emery, & Greenberg, 1985) may have an additional function in preventing posttreatment relapse.

5. *Medical history*. If the therapist has any doubt about medical complications or somatic conditions, it is necessary to obtain a medical evaluation. Sometimes such information has already been provided by the patient's general practitioner upon referral. If not, it is good to start by ruling out any somatic or anatomic reasons for the complaints by requesting a medical evaluation from the patient's physician. Such referrals should be properly

introduced and explained to prevent patients from erroneously inferring a somatic cause for their complaints. With the results of the medical evaluation in hand, patients may more easily be convinced of the role of cognitive and behavioral mechanisms in the onset and maintenance of their panic attacks. Medical evaluation is described in detail in Chapter 2.

Specific Difficulties and Complications

Additional Anxiety Disorders

Very often patients with panic disorder present with more than one anxiety problem. Some of these may be functionally related, such as social phobia resulting in agoraphobia. Others may be apparently unrelated and originate in different periods in the individual's development. Simple phobias (such as a dog phobia) often become evident during infancy or childhood, whereas social anxiety often emerges during adolescence and agoraphobia in early adulthood (Öst, 1987). Once again, the importance of the macro- and micro-analyses of the patient's problems is obvious.

Blood-Injury Phobia

In a number of cases panic disorder is associated with blood or injury phobias. Such cases deserve special attention because an unusual pattern of physiological responses has been reported. Instead of an increase in heart rate and respiration, as is typically seen in patients with phobia, those with blood phobia show bradycardia, a decrease in heart rate (Connolly, Hallam, & Marks, 1976) and a decrease in blood pressure when exposed to stimuli that are the focus of the blood-injury phobia. This somatic response may result in fainting (Öst, Sterner, & Lindahl, 1984). In the Öst et al. study, patients with blood phobia were shown a film of thoracic surgery involving large amounts of blood. The subjects displayed a biphasic response. The first phase consisted of an increase in heart rate and blood pressure, as is usually found in phobic subjects when confronted with the phobic stimulus. Then the subjects showed a sharp decrease *below* baseline in both heart rate and blood pressure. This may lead to fainting if escape from the situation is impossible. Despite the different physiological reactions, blood-injury phobia can also be treated by gradual in vivo exposure to feared situations. In the Thyrer, Himle, and Curtis (1985) study, 15 patients with blood phobia were gradually exposed to anxiety-evoking stimuli, including viewing horror and surgical movies, reviewing medical texts illustrated with pictures of trauma victims, receiving and administering repeated venipunctures and intramuscular injections, donating blood, and washing their hands in a small amount of blood. When a vasovagal faint occurred, subjects usually recovered rapidly when placed in a supine position. Graduated exposure was successful in most cases. The following case, of a 37-year-old female with both agoraphobia and blood-injury phobia, is typical.

Mary's agoraphobia developed 15 years previously, but her blood-injury phobia dated back to childhood. Her mother had frequently discussed serious illnesses and accidents, which regularly led to her brother's fainting. The first time it happened, Mary was led to believe that her brother was dead. Such typical statements by her mother as "because of you I will have a heart attack" resulted in Mary's further sensitization to all kinds of stimuli related to blood, illness, and death. Treatment consisted of gradual in vivo exposure to agoraphobic situations via homework assignments. After showing good progress, a relapse occurred. Just prior to the relapse, Mary's husband had an accident resulting in a clearly visible head wound. It was decided then to extend treatment to the blood-injury phobia. Mary and her therapist constructed a hierarchy of feared situations, including walking through the hospital area, reading about serious illnesses, reading obituaries, buying injection needles, watching medical programs on TV, sitting in the waiting room of an emergency unit, watching "bloody" movies, and visiting a blood donor bank. Nearly thirty items were included in the hierarchy. Treatment consisted of gradual exposure to these situations accompanied by the therapist in case Mary fainted (which actually never occurred). Treatment for her agoraphobia and blood-injury phobia took 21 sessions in all. At the end of treatment she had improved remarkably, with respect to both her agoraphobia and her blood-injury phobia.

Post–Traumatic Stress Disorder

In a number of cases agoraphobia and panic is associated with post–traumatic stress disorder (PTSD), which may complicate treatment. Two examples will illustrate this.

John was a patient with agoraphobia who was also extremely afraid of dying. When treated by prolonged in vivo exposure his anxiety did not decrease, partly due to his decision to escape the exposure situation when he felt he could not tolerate the anxiety. A further analysis revealed that his agoraphobic fears were related to a traumatic experience in the war when his father was shot. The standard exposure may not have been successful because stimuli related to the traumatic incident were avoided, or at best dealt with unsystematically. Such stimuli included cemeteries, a gun shop, and policemen or soldiers. The patient became sensitized to these situations, possibly due to a lack of systematic exposure.

In the next case, panic disorder with agoraphobia developed in a sexually victimized woman who had denied her traumatic experiences for many years. Only in the course of treatment did the nature, impact, and consequences of her trauma become apparent.

Sylvia was 35 years old when referred for treatment of her agoraphobia and panic attacks. Treatment started with in vivo exposure, but after 30 sessions progress was still meager and both Sylvia and her therapist were concerned about the limited improvement. In a reevaluation of the case, Sylvia admitted that other things bothered her that she was unable to talk about. It took several sessions before she was able to reveal that she had been raped at 18 by an older man and had been sexually abused by her father. At this stage, she remembered for the first time that her first anxiety attack occurred in a room with "dirty old men." Treatment was then directed toward the emotional processing of the rape experiences by using prolonged imaginal exposure to the traumatic situations that she recalled. The aim of this procedure was to gradually break down cognitive avoidance of those memories to achieve habituation of the negative emotions associated with them. It took many sessions before Sylvia's anxiety associated with the traumatic experiences was reduced. Although this resulted in a reduction in her nightmares, there was no reduction in agoraphobic avoidance. However, at this stage only six in vivo exposure sessions were needed before she was able to overcome her avoidance. She could then walk through the city, visit the village where her father lived, travel by bus, shop in crowded malls, and engage in many other previously avoided behaviors without anxiety.

In both of these cases, treatment of panic disorder with agoraphobia failed because the anxiety was related in part to previous unresolved traumatic experiences. Other patients evince a relationship between some unresolved grief and their phobia. It is important to determine whether unresolved grief leads to the phobia or is relatively independent of it. When the former appears to be the case, grief therapy—prolonged exposure to distressing stimuli related to the loss—(Ramsay, 1979) may be considered. There are now a number of studies demonstrating the effects of behavioral procedures for PTSD sufferers, but controlled studies are lacking (Steketee & Foa, 1987; Emmelkamp, 1990).

Social Anxiety, Social Phobia, and Unassertiveness

Occasional distress in social situations (that is, social anxiety) is familiar to most people; its essential characteristic is the fear of scrutiny by other people. Relatively few individuals feel hindered by this distress to the extent that they qualify for a diagnosis of social phobia, which is distinguished from social anxiety by the intensity of the fear and by avoidance of fear-evoking situations (Scholing & Emmelkamp, 1990). Although social anxiety or phobia is often related to unassertiveness, this is not always true; however, assertiveness is an important social skill contributing to healthy interpersonal relations.

A significant proportion of panic disorder patients are also socially anxious or phobic (Arrindell & Emmelkamp, 1987) or have difficulty being assertive. In some cases these problems improve as a result of treatment for panic disorder, but in others these problems have to be dealt with more directly. When social anxiety is related to a lack of social skills, an appropriate goal of therapy is to assist patients to acquire adequate skills. For example, when patients are unassertive, assertiveness training may be included in the treatment program. The aim of such training is to equip the patient with skills that will facilitate better interpersonal relations and increase resistance to relapse after treatment ends. Social skills training or assertiveness training may be given either in groups or individually. The format chosen will depend on the characteristics of the individual patient and the availability of group therapy. When patients are too anxious to benefit from treatment conducted in groups or when they have extreme skills deficits, the best option is to start with individual training and to switch to a group when the patient is ready. Individual assertiveness or social skills training may have the advantage of providing a more comprehensive program adapted to the individual needs of the patient.

The need for assertiveness or social skills training is indicated when the patient's anxiety is at least partly due to a lack of interpersonal skills. When social anxiety is not due to a lack of skills, other approaches may be more appropriate, such as exposure procedures and/or cognitive therapy (Emmelkamp, Mersch, Vissia, & van der Helm, 1985). Cognitive methods are also indicated when nonassertive behavior is a result of irrational beliefs or fear of the consequences of assertive behavior. For a more detailed discussion of the management of social phobia, the reader is referred to Scholing and Emmelkamp (1990).

Assertiveness training programs often emphasize training people to say "no," to the neglect of other behaviors. For some patients, learning to recognize and discriminate among their emotions and to express those emotions more adequately may also be important treatment targets. Therapists should be aware that assertive behavior is not always rewarded and may even be punished by partners, relatives, and friends. Patients may find that they were more highly valued when they were self-denying, submissive, and passive than when they are practicing their newly learned assertive behaviors. In such cases it may be worthwhile to include the partner in the therapy. There is now a growing body of evidence suggesting that communication training with an emphasis on assertiveness is helpful for couples in conflict (Emmelkamp, van der Helm, MacGillavry, & van Zanten, 1984; Emmelkamp, van Linden van der Heuvell et al., 1988). In couple treatment, the therapist may teach the patient appropriately assertive behavior and work with the partner to shape more effective responses, such as empathic listening skills.

Another important approach in assertiveness training, especially for patients having a strong interdependent relationship with their parents, is to teach patients how to handle conflict and express their feelings in those relationships. Family conflicts may be a significant factor maintaining anxiety problems (Everaerd, Emmelkamp, & Rijken, 1973; Kleiner & Marshall, 1985), and increased assertive skills may help the patient to deal with these conflicts more adequately.

Little research has been done on the effectiveness of assertiveness training for patients with panic disorder. Emmelkamp, van den Hout, and De Vries (1983) contrasted (1) assertiveness training, (2) in vivo exposure, and (3) a combination of assertiveness training and in vivo exposure in patients having panic disorder with agoraphobia and a low level of assertiveness. Exposure had more impact on measures of phobic avoidance and anxiety, but assertiveness training had more impact on measures of assertiveness. The results of this study indicate that both forms of treatment have something to offer panic disorder patients with low levels of assertiveness. In another study (Emmelkamp, 1980), assertive and unassertive patients with agoraphobia were found to benefit equally from in vivo exposure. Taken together, these data indicate that the most efficient strategy is to start with in vivo exposure and proceed to assertiveness training if necessary.

In some cases, patients are unable to differentiate among various emotions. For example, they actually may be very angry but experience their feelings as anxiety rather than as anger.

> In treating Jenny it became more and more apparent that her panic complaints were triggered by a large number of situations and circumstances, most of them interpersonal in nature. Nearly all of her days began quite well but worsened in the course of the afternoon. Jenny could not understand why. Somatically preoccupied as she was, she ascribed this phenomenon to the consumption of coffee or to a deficient intake of fluids. Closer scrutiny revealed that she particularly feared her husband's arrival home, which led to conflicts between him and the children. Disagreement between herself and her husband about how to handle these conflicts only increased Jenny's tension. Because she could not cope with interpersonal conflict and distress, she often experienced a lot of tension in interactions with family members. On several occasions her discomfort increased to result in a panic attack while she was at a family gathering. These attacks proved to be a powerful instrument to manipulate her social (family) environment.

In this case interpersonal conflicts caused an increase in tension over time. Goldstein and Chambless (1978) have pointed to the important role of interpersonal conflicts in the maintenance of agoraphobia. In patients with previous panic experiences, somatic arousal caused by interpersonal discord may be interpreted as the first signs of the feared panic attack. Once this vicious circle of fear, bodily symptoms, and misinterpretation has set in, it easily accelerates to a panic attack.

When patients have difficulty coping with their anger, emotional expression training may be of help. In this approach, patients are systematically trained to express their feelings more directly. In addition, rational-emotive therapy may be used when patients have the irrational belief that they must never be angry. Some patients are afraid of any sign of conflict or aggression and go to extreme lengths to avoid such exposure. For these cases, systematic exposure to situations involving conflict or aggression may be a worthwhile therapeutic strategy. This can be done either imaginally or in vivo by means of role-play. In the latter case, the therapist should carefully explain the "as if" character of the situation. If the patient fails to see that the therapist is role-playing, it can result in the premature termination of treatment.

Relationship Problems

A number of therapists have suggested that interpersonal, particularly marital, difficulties play an important part in the development and maintenance of patients' phobic symptoms (Emmelkamp, 1982; Goldstein & Chambless, 1978; Hafner, 1982). The partners of phobic patients have been described as impeding or reversing the positive effects of treatment or as developing psychiatric symptoms themselves if the patient changes. Furthermore, it has been suggested that a change in phobic symptoms through treatment may have a negative impact on the patient's marriage (see, for example, Hafner, 1982). On the basis of such clinical observations, it has been claimed that a system-theoretic interactional approach is needed to understand the etiology and maintenance of agoraphobia (Hafner, 1982).

Arrindell and Emmelkamp (1985) investigated whether partners of agoraphobic patients had psychological problems themselves. Partners of 32 females with agoraphobia were compared with the partners of nonphobic psychiatric subjects and nonpatient normal controls on a large number of variables. This study indicated that the partners of agoraphobic patients could not be characterized as more defensive than those of nonphobic psychiatric or normal controls. Further, no evidence was found that partners of agoraphobic patients were more neurotic, more socially anxious, or more obsessive than partners of controls.

A number of studies addressed the question of whether the marital relationship of agoraphobic patients is qualitatively different from that of control couples, as has been suggested by a number of authors. Previous research in this area is discussed in Chapters 5 and 7. More recently, Arrindell and Emmelkamp (1986) investigated whether the marriages of agoraphobic patients differed from those of controls. Thirty female agoraphobic patients and their partners filled in a number of questionnaires, including the Maudsley Marital Questionnaire and a communication questionnaire measuring intimate communication, destructive communication, discongruent communication, and avoidance of communication. Three control groups also participated in this study: (1) nonphobic psychiatric controls and their partners, (2) maritally distressed females and their partners, and (3) nondistressed females and their partners. The results revealed that agoraphobic patients and their spouses were more comparable to happily married subjects in terms of intimacy (that is, in marital and sexual adjustment and in satisfaction and quality of communication), while nonphobic psychiatric patients were more comparable to maritally distressed couples.

A third question, addressed in a number of studies, was the impact of the quality of the marital relationship on the outcome of behavior therapy. Some previous studies in this area had found a significant impact of relationship problems of agoraphobic patients on the outcome of behavioral treatment (Emmelkamp & van der Hout, 1983; Hudson, 1974; Milton & Hafner, 1979; Monteiro, Marks & Ramm, 1985; Bland & Hallam, 1981), but others found no relationship between initial marital ratings and improvement (Cobb, Mathews, Childs-Clarke, & Blowers, 1984; Emmelkamp, 1980; Himadi, Cerny, Barlow, Cohen, & O'Brien, 1986). The studies that evaluated the impact of marital quality on the outcome of in vivo exposure are hampered by a number of methodological problems. In previous studies the decision to classify couples as either maritally satisfied or maritally dissatisfied was based on an arbitrary criterion rather than on an externally validated cutoff score. Unfortunately, this makes it possibile to classify couples erroneously.

Acknowledging the limitations of previous studies, Arrindell, Emmelkamp, and Sanderman (1986) used a better criterion for distinguishing satisfied from dissatisfied marriages (a Maudsley Marital Questionnaire score over 20). In this study, patients were treated by means of prolonged in vivo exposure .

Results indicated that independent observers' marital rating and marital self-ratings on the Maudsley Marital Questionnaire predicted treatment failure neither at posttest nor at follow-up. Contrary to the expectations of the system-theorists, agoraphobic patients' marriage quality and sexual relationship did not deteriorate as a result of the patients' improvement. The partners also rated their marriage and sexual relationship as unaffected by improvement in the problems.

Although the "relationship hypothesis" of agoraphobia is still very popular among clinicians, little experimental evidence supports this conceptualization. Certainly, however, a reasonable proportion of patients will have relationship problems that may need to be dealt with to overcome the anxiety problems. Anxiety and marital difficulties may be related in a number of ways (Emmelkamp, 1982) that deserve close scrutiny by the therapist in treatment planning.

When anxiety and relationship problems are unrelated, there is no reason to treat the relationship problems first, unless the patient requests this. When the development of the panic disorder is clearly connected to relationship problems, however, treatment should deal with those problems. If both partners acknowledge the marital problems, this will cause no major trouble. However, when one—or both—denies the marital conflict, therapy may best proceed by having the partner "assist" in the treatment of the patient (Hafner, 1982). In some cases relationship difficulties may have played a part in the development of panic disorder but are no longer present. The main focus of the treatment is then the panic disorder.

In other cases, the panic disorder developed for reasons unrelated to marital distress, but the disorder has placed a heavy burden on the relationship, leading to marital distress. Treatment directed toward overcoming the anxiety disorder eventually may lead to increased marital satisfaction.

Relationship factors may also play a part in maintaining the problem. A spouse who gains in some way from the partner's problems may resist improvement in the patient. Some spouses fear changes in the relationship pattern, which may produce overt resistance or more subtle obstructionism. A number of patients in a study by Kleiner, Marshall, and Spevack (1987) reported encountering marked resistance and contempt from their partners and relatives because of their increased assertiveness and independent behavior. When a relationship pattern developed while the patient was dependent on the spouse, the possibility of change may make the spouse quite anxious. Even when spouses desire improvement of the phobic complaints, they may be responsive to the phobic behavior, thus reinforcing it.

Clearly, the relationship between marital conflict and panic and phobic behavior is often complex. It is necessary to determine the functional relationship (if any) between these areas before focusing on either or both of them as treatment targets.

Keep in mind that a lack of reported arguments or marital distress does not necessarily mean that relationship factors are not involved. To evaluate the part played by relationship behaviors in causing and/or maintaining panic disorder, the therapist must evaluate multiple aspects of marital functioning.

The interviews the therapist holds with the patient are often most informative with respect to a functional analysis. General questions such as "Are you satisfied with your marriage?" may be of little use because many patients, even those most maritally distressed, may answer in the affirmative. Questions must therefore be more specific. It is often useful to have the patient relate the development of the problem, especially the first panic attacks and episodes of severe anxiety. As the patient reports the first occurrence of the problem, the therapist has to determine whether marital conflict was involved. Detailed information about the current role of the patient's partner is also needed: the question to ask is how the partner responds to (or provokes) phobic behavior.

Although it is important that the patient be as specific as possible, eliciting this type of detailed information can be a laborious process requiring considerable tact and interviewing skill. If the patient is reluctant to provide this information, the therapist should not apply too much pressure, especially in the first sessions. It is more important to build a sound therapeutic relationship. It may be best to choose between two alternatives: either leaving the subject for the time being with the option of returning to it, or inviting the patient's partner in for further assessment. Although the latter strategy has several advantages, it might be too threatening for some patients (and their partners). One advantage of seeing the partner (either alone or together with the patient) is to have another opportunity to gather information about the connection between relationship factors and the anxiety problem. Perhaps even more important, the conjoint interview provides observational data that may add to the information provided by the spouse.

When the functional analysis reveals that anxiety is controlled in part by relationship factors, the question remains whether marital therapy is the best option. Even if the analysis shows these problems to be causally related, there is no reason to expect that treatment of relationship problems will lead to improvement of the anxiety. As there are no tested guidelines for when to begin with either marital therapy or treatment of the anxiety, the therapist must decide on the basis of available information and clinical intuition. Usually it is not a question of offering one therapy to the exclusion of the other, but rather of what to focus on first. Generally, the therapeutic intervention—or the sequencing of therapeutic interventions—should be chosen on the basis of what will provide the speediest improvement.

When a decision is made to work with both parties, further information is needed to decide which type of marital treatment is most suitable. It makes little sense to treat phobic patients with canned procedures (for example, communication and problem-solving training or contingency contracting) unless the analysis indicates that these approaches are necessary.

In some cases the partner may be invited to act as cotherapist. Several studies have investigated whether this approach could enhance the effectiveness of in vivo exposure. Cobb et al. (1984) found that spouse-aided exposure therapy was no more effective than exposure conducted with the patient alone. In contrast, Barlow, O'Brien, and Last (1984) found a clear superiority for the spouse-aided exposure condition when compared to a nonspouse group on measures of agoraphobia. Involving the spouse as a cotherapist may be less feasible when there is so much animosity between the partners that homework exercises are likely to lead to further arguments and increased tension. In these instances, it is quite likely that involving the spouse in treatment may exacerbate rather than alleviate the problems.

The effects of treatment focusing on the relationship rather than on the phobia were investigated by Cobb, McDonald, Marks, and Stern (1980). Subjects were agoraphobic and obsessive-compulsive patients who also manifested marital discord. In vivo exposure was contrasted with marital therapy; results indicated that the former led to improvements in both the phobic or obsessive-compulsive problems and the marital relationship, while marital therapy affected only the marital relationship. More recently Arnow, Taylor, Agras, and Telch (1985) investigated the effects of communication training on agoraphobic patients. Communication training enhanced the improvement in phobic symptoms gained via exposure therapy but did not affect marital satisfaction. This is not surprising, because the training focused on communications about the phobia rather than on other relationship problems. Furthermore, only a limited number of the patients was maritally distressed.

If treatment is going to focus on the relationship, it must be made clear to the couple. The therapist must describe what is involved in marital treatment and explain how it may differ from the treatment the patient initially requested. If the patient and/or the spouse are reluctant to engage in marital therapy, it is therapeutically wiser to refocus treatment on the anxiety problems than to "sell" the treatment to the couple. One might reasonably question the feasibility of marital therapy for an unmotivated couple. It could be argued that there is little danger in starting marital therapy, regardless of the couple's commitment to it, because if it does not work one can still treat the phobic problems directly. Unfortunately, failure of marital therapy can have negative consequences for both partners, eventually resulting in their dropping out of treatment. And these considerations apply in the context of other interpersonal relationships as well.

Depression

When depression is associated with panic disorder, a careful history should be taken to investigate whether the anxiety is primary or secondary to the depression, or whether the problems are unrelated. Most patients are able to discriminate between these emotional states and to use different words for their description. Although some behaviors, such as the avoidance of situations and people, are shared by anxiety and depression, the motivation for the behaviors differs. Anxious individuals are avoidant because of an anticipated threat, anxious expectations, fear of having a panic attack, and so on. Depressed persons, on the other hand, may become avoidant because of their general lack of motivation or because of the excessive guilt or shame characteristic of this emotional state. Therefore it is worthwhile to distinguish the two conditions by their cognitive (or motivational) components.

The next step is to trace the temporal relationship between panic attacks and depressed mood—that is, to answer the question "Which came first?" or "Which led to which?" Many of our patients are quite capable of delineating the relationship between the two. Often patients with panic disorder lead a very restricted life, resulting in a depressed mood that can be considered secondary to the anxiety disorder. In these cases the depression often lifts after treatment of the panic disorder and agoraphobia, and no further measures dealing with the depressive symptoms are necessary. In some patients the (originally secondary) depression evolves to become the major complaint after the patient has become disabled by anxiety. The functional analysis may then indicate starting with treatment of the depression, to mobilize the patient.

When depression is primary, a lack of initiative may easily be mistaken for agoraphobic avoidance. When depression impedes progress in the treatment of the panic disorder, other interventions are indicated. In depression certain cognitive patterns or schemata are activated (Beck, Rush, Shaw, & Emery, 1979) that structure patients' interpretations of themselves, their situation, and the world as a whole. In these cases cognitive treatment approaches, aiming to identify and change the patient's assumptions and cognitive schemata that support stereotypical negative thinking, may give full relief. For more details on this challenging approach, the reader is referred to the work of Beck and colleagues (see, for example, Beck et al., 1979).

Behavioral approaches for depression have been found to be as effective as cognitive therapy (Emmelkamp, 1986). In cognitively less amenable patients, behavioral approaches to depression are the treatment of choice to increase positive reinforcement and reduce depression before actual treatment of the panic disorder. Typically, nonphobic activities that the patient has enjoyed in the past but does not currently engage in are given as homework assignments. Apparently easy activities are chosen first; more difficult tasks are assigned in later sessions.

When exposure procedures are applied with depressed patients, it is especially important that patients monitor their daily activities and their progress. Furthermore, patients should be encouraged to set realistic goals that are concrete and attainable and to rate their progress in meeting those goals. It may be helpful to provide external reinforcement and to have patients self-administer reinforcement contingent on the accomplishment of behavioral goals.

Personality Characteristics and Personality Disorders

Patients with agoraphobia have been described as typically overdependent, socially anxious, unassertive, passive, anxious, and highly neurotic (Foa, Steketee, & Young, 1984; Tearnan, Telch, & Keefe, 1984). Chambless (1982) characterized the typical agoraphobic patient as a female housewife who ". . . is probably anxious, depressed, unassertive, and low in self-esteem. A rather extroverted person, compared to other neurotics, she regrets her social isolation, yet is fearful of many others. She is highly worried about her physical health, reporting profuse specific and vague somatic symptoms" (p. 14). As noted by Foa et al. (1984), however, most studies in this area have serious flaws, which precludes firm conclusions with respect to the existence of and the characteristics of the "agoraphobic personality."

Prompted by the lack of a coherent picture of the personality of agoraphobic patients, Arrindell and Emmelkamp (1987) compared agoraphobic patients with nonphobic psychiatric patients and normal controls on a number of personality measures. The results did not support the notion that agoraphobic patients as a group are generally more affectionally dependent than controls. On the other hand, there were clear-cut differences among the groups on interpersonal difficulties (social anxiety and social inadequacy). Agoraphobic patients were found to be less extroverted and less sociable; they showed a greater tendency to isolate themselves from others. In the absence of a longitudinal design, the etiological significance of these findings remains unclear. In this context, it should be noted that a number of agoraphobic patients were active, sociable, and outgoing before their symptoms began. By the time they are assessed, however, they may evince many "traits" mistakenly assumed to have existed premorbidly (Tearnan et al., 1984).

Reich, Noyes, and Throughton (1987) commented on the prevalence of dependent personality disorder associated with phobic avoidance in patients with panic disorder. Dependent, histrionic, and avoidant personality disorders were more prevalent among agoraphobic subjects than among those with panic disorder without agoraphobia. In the course of behavioral treatment the histrionic and dependent characteristics have been found to diminish (Mavissakalian & Hamann, 1986). The next case may illustrate this.

> Ted, a 42-year-old administrator, had developed agoraphobia after a panic attack during a trip to work on the bus 10 years prior to treatment. Gradually he became afraid of crossing bridges leading away from his safe territory. He

nearly always used his car, but as he also feared freeways and motorways (where there was no possibility of turning around), he had to take elaborate detours between home and work. He did not dare go to unknown places on his own, so his wife had to accompany him. He was clearly lacking in self-sufficiency. He once remarked that the therapist showed more faith in him than he did in himself. After some time in behavior therapy, Ted began to be reluctant to follow directions for homework assignments. The therapist labeled this an attempt to become more independent and self-determined. After this phase, Ted gradually showed more determination in facing new situations. He took more initiative and depended less on the therapist's praise. Several months after termination of treatment, the therapist received a postcard from Ted sent from a neighboring country.

In cases such as these, the subtle aspects of the therapeutic relationship are very important. At times if there is a conflict or disagreement in therapy, it may be wiser for the therapist to lose, on purpose or not. This may enhance the patient's feeling of self-esteem in a number of areas related to the goals of therapy. Particularly for a patient who is very dependent, it may be encouraging to feel "one up" instead of constantly feeling "one down." Often the therapist is perceived as a powerful, omniscient person devoid of any pathology. Conflicts and disagreements with patients may be difficult, of course, because of the uncertainty they introduce to the therapeutic relationship. On the other hand, they offer the therapist an opportunity to provide a model for resolving conflicts, given an awareness of his or her own weak spots.

In quite a number of patients specific personality traits, rather than personality disorders, play a pathogenetic role with regard to anxiety complaints. These traits are manifested by a specific lifestyle and provide a continual source of stress and tension, which may result in panic attacks. A frequently encountered personality characteristic is perfectionism and fear of failure. Individuals with this trait adopt very high standards for themselves and expend great effort on their tasks at home and at work. Test anxiety in students is a specific example. The general mechanism is avoidance of failure at considerable cost (typically, tremendous stress and overwork), often because the consequences of failure are grossly and unrealistically overestimated. The motivation for perfectionism may be internal (high personal standards) or external (fear of criticism or dismissal). In the latter case assertiveness training may be an important component of treatment. Unrealistically high personal standards can be more rationally molded with the use of rational-emotive therapy. The next case serves as an illustration.

A few months after starting his new job, Jim, a 35-year-old former law student, experienced a full-blown panic attack. Jim's anxiety was overwhelming; he feared he might become "insane" and "be locked away in a mental institution." In his first job in a law firm, he wanted to prove to himself that he could easily cope with the work, being intelligent and socially skillful. He admitted, though, that he was afraid of a negative evaluation by his employer, even though there was no particular reason for concern. Jim dreaded board meetings because there was a good deal of competition and confrontation among the staff. Early in therapy it became apparent that Jim always wanted to be in control and that he became very distressed when he felt he was losing his grip on his emotions. When he had his first panic attack he was caught completely off balance and reported sick for some months. The therapist first taught him to cope with panic attacks by prescribing breathing exercises and correcting his catastrophic misinterpretations of the panic symptoms. Jim was a very compliant patient who meticulously practiced the treatment procedures. Then the actual source of the daily stresses was attacked by applying ratio-nal-emotive therapy. Irrational beliefs about failure and his approach to his job were explored. Jim began to recognize the high demands he made on himself and gradually managed to adopt a more realistic attitude.

In this case, as in many others, it was important to look for the source of tension and stress. The patient's perfectionist traits could be held respon-sible for increased arousal while on the job. After the cognitive interven-tion, Jim changed his way of performing his job and consequently felt less tense.

Somatic Complications

In the previous sections we have described some of the problems encountered when panic disorder is complicated by other psychological or relationship factors. Still other patients suffer from a somatic complication. It may be causally related to the anxiety disorders or may complicate the treatment or increase the degree of disability. Mitral valve prolapse, thyroid dysfunction (Matuzas, Al-Sadir, Uhlenhuth, & Glass, 1987), cardiac problems (Beitman, DeRosear, Basha, Flaker, & Corcoran, 1987), and Menière's disease are often considered important pathogenetic factors in panic attacks. Somatic compli-cations may cause patients to worry excessively about their health and the possibility of a catastrophic outcome. (Chapter 2 describes medical factors in panic disorder in detail.)

The symptoms caused by some medical problems closely resemble the bodily sensations experienced during episodes of anxiety and panic. It is important to disentangle the symptoms of a health problem from the symp-toms of anxiety. The aim of the psychological treatment of panic disorders should be to eliminate undue anxiety caused by a misinterpretation of harm-less bodily processes. Thus, for example, when a patient is able to distinguish between symptoms of hyperthyroidism and those of anxiety, he or she may be less anxious.

The first step is to obtain a detailed account of the patient's experience with the somatic disorder and the subtle signs and symptoms associated with it. Next, the patient should learn to discriminate between these symptoms and those of anxiety and panic. Some of the following examples may illustrate this point.

Fainting

Many patients with panic disorder are afraid of fainting, but few actually faint. In cases in which there is a history of fainting, a careful analysis must be carried out before treatment planning.

> Margie was a 28-year-old unmarried female referred to our department for treatment of agoraphobia. She avoided crowded areas or buildings because she was afraid of fainting. She fainted for the first time at the age of 13, when visiting a crowded cathedral. Since then she had fainted regularly in public places such as restaurants, churches, and museums, which led her to avoid those places. Detailed questioning revealed that fainting seemed to be related to her menstrual period, as she only fainted during her period. She also had never fainted during a period when she was using oral contraceptives. Fainting was always accompanied by stomach pain, dizziness, and ringing in the ears. She did not faint in phobic situations between periods. She was referred to a gynecologist for her menstrual problems. Behavioral treatment consisted of a few exposure sessions in restaurants and churches *between* her periods. As expected, Margie did not faint during exposure, and anxiety decreased rapidly.

This case nicely illustrates the disentangling of anxiety from more somatic origins of seemingly similar phenomena. Practicing in less fainting-prone weeks helped Margie discriminate between the bodily signs of anxiety and those of fainting. Once she understood and was convinced of their origin, anxiety subsided.

Many female panic patients experience an increase in panic attack frequency in the week prior to their menstrual period. This may be caused in part by a progesterone-induced decrease in pCO_2. The same phenomenon has been reported in pregnant women (George, Ladenheim, & Nutt, 1987).

Thyroid Dysfunction

> A 24-year-old student, Alice, manifested agoraphobic avoidance for 2 years. The problem began after she experienced anxiety when driving a car. She had no panic attacks, but agoraphobic symptoms gradually spread to other areas of her daily life, such as shopping in crowded supermarkets, walking alone in the street, and, in the end, visiting other people. In the intake interview, she reported having had thyroid surgery to treat hyperthyroidism 18 months previously. After surgery she had received medication to stabilize her thyroid function. At the time of the intake interview, Alice's thyroid function was within normal range, according to her doctor. Treatment was planned according to the graduated in vivo exposure paradigm. A hierarchy of feared situations was constructed and homework assignments consisted of exposure to those situations, especially to supermarkets. There was a promising start, but after several assignments Alice reported that the anxiety did not subside as she had hoped. She remained tense and anxious much of the time. This caused her to have less faith in the treatment and to blame the therapist. After a few more sessions she decided to terminate therapy. At the final session she

reported that laboratory results reported to her by her doctor indicated that her thyroid function had been abnormal for some time. Now she could attribute her high tension level to this somatic cause. Nevertheless, she still terminated therapy. Some months later her therapist met her in the street. Alice reported additional gains after her thyroid function was normalized: she had used the exposure principles and the rationale given by her therapist to achieve this reduction in avoidance.

Presentation of agoraphobia with panic attacks in patients with thyroid hyperfunction has been described by Matuzas et al. (1987). Although they were unable to demonstrate a direct causal connection, the authors speculated that the syndromes might share a common etiology. Although no recent panic attacks were present she did mention situationally triggered periods of anxiety. The main puzzle was what factor caused her heightened level of arousal (which Alice often labeled "anxiety"). Part of the anxiety was triggered by the agoraphobic situations, but thyroid hyperfunction also had a significant effect. Presumably, during the course of therapy, as the latter grew stronger the effect of the exposure assignments diminished. An important lesson to learn from this case is to have thyroid function closely monitored, particularly when the patient does not make the progress typically seen in therapy. The interesting point here is that although Alice gradually lost faith in the exposure paradigm presented by her therapist, she resumed practicing on a self-initiated basis once her thyroid functions were normalized. This may have been partly a result of the therapist's explanation of the two-factor cause of her anxiety. Consequently, more adequate understanding of bodily symptoms may be fruitful, even in the face of a true organic cause.

Pseudoepileptic Seizures

Gilda, a 40-year-old housewife, complained of infrequent but impressive attacks of hyperventilation, causing what she called an "epileptic seizure." The last attack made her very reluctant to leave home for almost a year for fear of a recurrence. An extensive neurological examination, as well as hyperventilation provocation, gave no reason to suspect an organic cause (other than hyperventilation) for her "seizures." Her family doctor referred to her as a histrionic and difficult patient who tried to get attention via her bodily complaints. While alone at home, she drank a good deal of coffee. When the therapist told her that caffeine could play a role in provoking panic attacks, she immediately changed to decaffeinated coffee, which brought about a decrease in symptom severity. The fear of a nocturnal seizure had also made her anxious about going to bed. To be sure to sleep, Gilda used to drink a bottle of wine every night. The next day she felt guilty over this misconduct. Therapy started with a focus on coping with panic attacks and the fear of having a "seizure." Breathing exercises were prescribed and the instruction to abstain from caffeine was given. This had moderate success, and the intensity of the feared symptoms gradually decreased.

Edlund, Swann, and Clothier (1987) describe a number of patients with panic attacks who displayed a variety of slight EEG abnormalities. It remains uncertain, however, whether those abnormalities are causative or unrelated to panic attacks.

Undiagnosed Somatic Dysfunction

Barbara, a 55-year-old housewife, had been agoraphobic for the past 15 years. Her fear of leaving home on her own was related to feelings of choking and being short of breath. Both her physician and her behavior therapist believed mild hyperventilation to be the cause. In addition, lung emphysema played a role in the maintenance of these complaints. Behavioral treatment of the avoidance was of little avail; even after a long period of exposure her choking sensations did not disappear. This discouraged her from practicing, although she seemed convinced of the need to do so. Eventually therapy was discontinued. About 2 years later Barbara phoned the therapist to inform him that a long-standing upper airway obstruction had been diagnosed and surgically repaired. As a consequence, most of her choking sensations had disappeared and she felt more free to go out.

In this case an undiagnosed upper airway obstruction was responsible for the breathing complaints. Because this patient used to complain a great deal about various somatic ailments, many professionals had been less attentive to her organically based complaints.

Caffeine Use

Caffeine (Charney, Heninger, & Jatlow, 1985) is considered to be an important provocative agent in panic disorder. The symptoms of caffeinism—restlessness, nervousness, excitement, insomnia, flushed face, diuresis, gastrointestinal complaints, cardiac arrhythmia, and psychomotor agitation—closely resemble those of panic attacks. Patients who have experienced panic attacks before may readily interpret these symptoms as the first signs of an imminent attack. This misinterpretation in turn feeds the positively accelerating feedback loop common in panic attacks (Ley, 1987; Clark, 1986).

The clinician should therefore not hesitate to inquire about the daily consumption of this product. Many patients are surprised to hear about the undesirable effects of the caffeine in coffee and cola drinks, considering it to be a harmless substance. To convince patients of caffeine's power, a simple behavioral experiment can be very helpful. One week the patient should drink more coffee than usual and the next completely abstain from caffeine. The results are interesting for both patient and therapist. If there is no difference in anxiety levels between the two weeks, the possibility of a caffeine-induced effect can probably be ruled out. If anxiety worsens while drinking more coffee than usual, not much is needed to convince the patient that abstinence or reduction is therapeutic. Although abstention from caffeine may be only a small part of the treatment, it demonstrates the importance of looking for alternative explanations for the patient's anxiety. In this way the therapist is modeling adequate coping behavior: "Don't stick to only one explanation; look for more realistic alternatives as well."

Conclusion

These cases demonstrate the influence of somatic complications in panic disorder and agoraphobia. Whether diagnosed or undiagnosed, somatic factors contributing to symptomatology or interfering with treatment should be considered by the therapist. In cases of uncertainty, the clinician should not hesitate to request a thorough medical evaluation. The nature of the evaluation should be explained in detail, lest patients get the impression that their complaints are considered to be organically caused. The challenge is to navigate between uncertainty about physical causes on the one hand and the risk of the patient's developing a somatic fixation on the other.

Hypochondriacal Concerns

The somatic complications mentioned in the previous cases were clearly demonstrable. On the bases of their anatomic and functional consequences, the clinician and patient were able to ascribe at least some of the symptoms to a somatic problem. Many panic disorder patients, however, worry a great deal about their health in general in the absence of any somatic abnormality. They are obsessionally alert to bodily sensations and tend to interpret them in a catastrophic manner—for example, assuming that chest pain leads to a heart attack or headache leads to an apoplectic stroke. Before the clinician relabels the symptoms as the result of anxiety rather than of somatic dysfunction, a thorough medical examination should exclude the possibility of somatic dysfunction. The next case may serve as a demonstration.

> Charles, a 33-year-old unemployed custodian, suffered from an incapacitating fear of dying from a heart attack after experiencing a panic attack on the job several years previously. He attributed his symptoms to imminent heart failure and missed work due to this "illness." Although his doctor assured him that his heart was healthy, he doubted this, claiming that misdiagnoses do happen. He spent his days at home on sick leave, worrying about what might happen to him. In subsequent weeks he did not dare leave home; he sat in front of his television set and worried all day long. This built up tension and anxiety further and brought on several other panic attacks, which he dreaded because they seemed to come from out of the blue. Before the problem developed he had enjoyed sports and kept in good shape. Now he avoided excessive physical effort for fear of triggering a cardiac arrest. Gradually he became reluctant to leave his home on foot or by bicycle. Only his car was considered safe enough, as it could bring him home quickly. Thus, as a result of panic attacks and cardiac concerns, he developed agoraphobia as well.

An interesting point in this patient's case was the apparent discrepancy between his strategy of trying to relax by watching television and the panicky feelings he often experienced at those times. He reasoned that he might expect to have these feelings while under stress, but should not have them in such a nonstressful situation. Some television programs, however, are intended to produce states of bodily arousal. Here we can see a clear example of interoceptive conditioning (Goldstein & Chambless, 1978) and misinterpretation of the basically harmless phenomena of physical arousal. Thus, the actual phobic stimulus was the bodily arousal itself. Charles's original, acute panic attack followed a period of hard physical work. He dreaded similar somatic symptoms in the months following the panic attack, and generalized his concerns and fears from specific panic symptoms to any symptom of arousal whatsoever—any bodily phenomenon beyond the normal range. Charles also developed the habit of taking his pulse to check his cardiac functioning. Any heart rate acceleration provoked an increase in anxiety and worry, leading in turn to a positive feedback loop (Ley, 1985) of anxiety-induced arousal and catastrophic misinterpretation.

The first step in treatment was to identify the panic attacks as being brought about by hyperventilation. Clark's approach (1986) was followed, in which hyperventilation provocation is used to assess and demonstrate the similarity between the patient's symptoms and the consequences of hyperventilation. Charles immediately recognized the symptoms, and eagerly accepted the rationale given for his complaints. Breathing exercises given as a homework assignment were practiced meticulously, leading to a decrease in the frequency and severity of his bodily symptoms and subsequently to a reduction in his anxiety. Charles discovered that sitting and waiting for things to happen only aggravated his complaints, and that he should concentrate on other aspects of his life. When he was bothered by anxiety-provoking thoughts, he learned to repeat to himself that though his complaints might be disturbing they were basically innocent symptoms of hyperventilation. This intervention allowed his worrying behavior to diminish gradually, and he was able to leave the house without too much anxiety.

In this case the approach was to emphasize that the thoughts themselves caused the anxiety. Therefore, the patient was instructed to manage these disturbing thoughts by replacing them with more comforting and rational thoughts. Consequently, no debates took place about the validity of the medical diagnosis. The therapist stressed the importance of preventing an accumulation of disease-phobic thoughts by repeating the coping statements. This cognitive experiment worked, so the patient convinced himself of its effect. It should be noted that the agoraphobic avoidance was not treated directly. As soon as Charles learned to cope with his undesired somatic phenomena, he started to go out again.

Some patients request many consecutive referrals to medical specialists when the source of the problem is not understood. An apparent lack of demonstrable external cause for panic attacks and related complaints tends to confuse physician as well as patient. It is therefore understandable that many therapists have tried to find biological explanations for these symptoms. Closer scrutiny, however, reveals that patients frequently indulge in behaviors aimed at checking their bodily processes such as heart rate, breathing, and sweating. In this way they constantly provide fuel for their worrying and misinterpretations. In many cases patients are reluctant or even ashamed to admit that they are so preoccupied with their bodies. This should alert the behavior therapist to search actively for a variety of eliciting behaviors and cognitions that make panic attacks appear as if they "come from out of the blue."

Salkovskis and Warwick (1986) present a behavioral redefinition of hypochondriasis in which they describe how reassurance produces an immediate but transient reduction in anxiety and then a desire for more reassurance. In fact, habitual "doctor shopping" results in a long-term worsening of the symptoms and in an increase (or at least in a stable high level) of anxiety. The authors suggest an approach similar to that used in the cognitive-behavioral treatment of obsessive-compulsive disorder. The therapist encourages the patient to engage in activities that will result in exposure to the feared bodily sensations; at the same time, the reassurance seeking is eliminated (response prevention). In our own experience with this type of patient, it is important to discuss the results of their repeated reassurance seeking. Most patients will describe an absence of any prolonged reduction in anxiety, while their desire for more medical attention increases. After describing how reassurance seeking makes the problem worse, the therapist outlines the exposure and response prevention strategy to produce a reduction of fear. An oral or written contract is arranged in which the patient practices other anxiety management techniques and agrees not to seek reassurance in the ways that have been used in the past: checking with family members, friends, or medical staff; checking pulse rate; and so on. The involvement of those who have been reassurance givers in the past may be very important to ensure the success of the response prevention procedure.

The Intellectually Limited Patient

Intellectually limited individuals can be among the most challenging patients. It is frequently difficult to carry out an adequate functional analysis of their complaints because of the incomplete or inaccurate information they may provide. In such cases, it makes sense to involve significant others in the environment—partner, family, or friends—in both assessment and treatment. In the actual therapy, cognitive and imaginal procedures as well as homework assignments may be more difficult to apply with such patients. Often intensive therapist-assisted in vivo exposure is necessary—or significant others may be called on to assist with the homework assignments. Natural positive reinforcement (such as work or recreational activities) can be very helpful in maintaining the improvements gained. After therapy has ended, booster sessions may be required to help the patient integrate newly acquired skills in his or her daily life.

Problems with Medications Prescribed for Anxiety

Many medical practitioners prescribe minor tranquilizers or tricyclic antidepressants in treating anxiety problems. But drug discontinuation can have various negative effects: relapse, withdrawal, or rebound symptoms (see Chapters 6 and 8). In light of these problems, we feel these drugs should be prescribed cautiously. Given that cognitive-behavioral treatment may be more effective than alprazolam (Barlow, 1987), the automatic prescription of alprazolam or other minor tranquilizers no longer seems to be justified.

The simultaneous use of drugs during behavioral treatment may also provide specific problems, as illustrated by the next case.

> A 45-year-old housewife, Emily, was referred for the treatment of agoraphobia without panic attacks. She managed to follow the exposure assignments and reported a steady improvement. However, she was unable to discontinue her medication, diazepam. Detailed inquiry revealed that Emily tended to take her medication before each of her exposure assignments. In this way, she consolidated a contingency between the anxiety-reducing effect of diazepam and her practice. The therapist decided to break this contingency by emphasizing that the pill should be taken at a fixed time of day, independent of the exposure assignments. Thus, Emily would not be bothered by withdrawal symptoms while profiting from the exposure treatment. Eventually, the contingency between the medication and the practice was broken. Finally, the medication was gradually withdrawn.

Some behavior therapists consider anxiolytic medication and behavior therapy to be an undesirable combination. These medications may prevent the patient from experiencing the reduction in anxiety according to the exposure paradigm. Some patients will also increase the daily dose as practice becomes more difficult. One way to counter these problems is to forbid the use of anxiolytic medication during exposure therapy. Another is to allow the patient to take one dose during a new, more anxiety-provoking exercise (Mathews, Gelder, & Johnston, 1981). Some patients are reluctant to give up their medication before they have seen any progress via behavior therapy. They do not want to lose a treatment they have found to be helpful without having something to substitute. The fear of withdrawal symptoms is often prominent. Many patients have tried to stop taking medication in the past, only to find themselves with more anxiety and bodily symptoms than they expected. A first step, as Emily's case demonstrates, is to break the contingency between the use of medication and entering feared situations or coping with panic attacks. This encourages the consolidation of adequate coping behavior and makes the medication seem less necessary to the patient. When helping patients reduce and terminate medication, it is important to explain the experiences they may have during withdrawal, so they can appropriately label the symptoms they may encounter. It is, of course, important in this stage of treatment to work closely with the physician who has prescribed the medication.

Problems with Alcohol

Chambless, Cherney, Caputo, and Reinstein (1987), in a recent review, concluded that 23% to 44% of inpatient alcoholics have one or more anxiety disorders. Generally the onset of these disorders preceded the alcohol abuse. In view of these figures and the fact that alcohol abuse is very common in Western society, the therapist should inquire in detail about recent and past alcohol consumption. Some patients are helped by tracking their daily use of alcohol and medication in the diaries they keep during treatment. Even if the patient does not drink heavily, the therapist should be alert to the selective use of alcohol for anxiety reduction in the face of anxiety-provoking situations. It is obvious that selective drinking prevents patients from learning alternative and more adequate methods of coping with anticipatory anxiety. Patients who use alcohol for its anxiety-reducing effects are often unaware that large amounts of alcohol in fact induce anxiety. Hangovers and other side effects produce bodily symptoms and mood changes that increase anxiety: sweating, trembling, nausea, palpitations, lightheadedness, and the like may easily be misinterpreted as the first sign of a panic attack or anxiety episode.

When alcohol abuse has become a significant problem, the therapist has to decide whether this problem should be treated first, possibly in a specialized program. For this treatment to be successful, it may be necessary to include concurrent interventions for the reduction of anxiety. Close contact and consultation with the alcohol clinic should be maintained in these cases.

Poor Compliance with Treatment

Poor compliance with treatment may be related to a number of factors that should be investigated in a functional analysis of behavior. Many of these problems have already been discussed. A more detailed description of compliance-enhancing procedures may be found in Meichenbaum and Turk (1987). Specific measures that may be used to facilitate treatment adherence are listed in Table 12.1.

First, it is important that patients understand the reason that specific treatment tasks are prescribed. If they do not understand the rationale, they cannot be expected to perform these tasks enthusiastically. A major problem is the difficulty some patients have in finding the necessary time to do homework assignments. In a few cases assertiveness training may be required so that the patient can arrange the necessary practice time with the assistance

TABLE 12.1 Measures to Facilitate Compliance

- Establish a collaborative relationship

- Use behavioral diaries

- Present a clear treatment rationale

- Have patients describe the treatment rationale in their own words

- Give specific instructions in writing

- Use homework sheets

- Set specific subgoals

- Use specific behavioral contracts

- Reinforce progress

- Attribute progress to the patient's rather than the therapist's efforts

- Enlist the help of significant others

- Inform the patient of the possibility of relapse

of family members. With type A patients, who are characterized by extremes of competitiveness, achievement striving, and time urgency, the problem may be twofold: (1) the exercises do not have a high priority in their busy schedule of other "obligations," and (2) they want to see results at once and are less motivated when they don't. These irrational attitudes may be dealt with by cognitive techniques.

At times poor compliance and the eventual failure of therapy may be due to a hidden agenda of the patient's.

> Fran sought treatment for her incapacitating agoraphobia, which prevented her from leaving her house alone. Apart from being a homemaker, she had no other major activities. She was 25 years old and had been married for several years without having children. She wanted to adopt a baby, but her husband refused. Communication on this subject was difficult, as both were people of few words. Nevertheless, Fran was very motivated to engage in behavior therapy and started enthusiastically. She gradually progressed to the point at which she went shopping alone in the neighborhood. In the course of treatment, her wish to adopt a child was voiced more strongly and her husband again strongly stated his opposition. This caused a major relapse; Fran refused to do any homework assignments. The disagreement about adoption escalated and became the main focus for the couple. At this stage, Fran admitted that she started behavior therapy in the first place hoping that it would convince her husband to agree to an adoption. This hidden agenda obviously played a crucial role in the patient's motivation for treatment. Fran

and her husband decided they did not wish to continue any form of individual treatment or marital counseling.

This case illustrates the importance of establishing the actual motivation for treatment; some patients, like Fran, are very reluctant to acknowledge the motivating factors. In such cases, it may be worthwhile spending several sessions on establishing the major factors providing motivation for therapy. Again, a macroanalysis of the complaints may be very helpful in this stage.

The following case illustrates how secondary gain may also be an important factor.

> David, a 29-year-old civil servant with an outdoor job, had his first panic attack several months before he was referred to our facility. At the time of the first attack, which occurred at home, he consulted a physician. The physician was initially quite alarmed by the symptoms, according to David, and then made a diagnosis of hyperventilation. From that moment on, David dreaded the next occurrence of a panic attack. Prior to the attack he had been under occupational and domestic stress. At the time of intake panic attacks, fear of illness, and agoraphobia were his most prominent complaints. The initial treatment consisted of breathing exercises to counter the hyperventilation. This brought rapid relief of his symptoms. David went back to work, but had a severe relapse after several days of work, during which the weather happened to be extremely bad. He reported sick again and acknowledged a fear of having a heart attack to the therapist. This session revealed that he resented his work because it was dull and had limited future prospects. He also admitted to drinking an above-average amount of beer and eating rich food to "feel better." He was particularly bothered by the fact that even while watching television he occasionally experienced panicky feelings. The paradox of apparent relaxation and panic made him even more concerned about his cardiac functioning, and his mood became more depressed. The therapist then pointed to his inconsistent behavior pattern: fearing a heart attack while at the same time indulging in a lifestyle that actually might provoke one: no physical exercise, drinking too much, smoking too much, and eating greasy food. This alarmed David to such an extent that he suddenly became willing to adopt the activity schedule the therapist had suggested. As a consequence his mood improved, he felt better physically, and his worrying decreased. On the other hand, he also became more dissatisfied with his job, blaming himself for not acquiring more education when he was younger. After consultation with his physician and an occupational psychologist, David decided to improve his job prospects by pursuing additional education. He was more satisfied with life and received encouragement from his wife and significant others.

It appeared that this patient's panic attacks and subsequent problems were related to dissatisfaction with his job. After he went on sick leave, he had very limited motivation to return to work—despite his claim to be ashamed about being at home while his colleagues took over his job. His lack of job mobility (owing to his lack of education and to poor labor market circumstances) left him feeling trapped. After the relief of his manifest symptoms, there was in fact no reason for him to go back to work. If he had been considered unfit to perform his job, after some time on sick leave he would have received a social security benefit of about 75% of his original salary. Therefore the consequences of remaining "sick" were considerable but not dramatic; he would no doubt have been able to earn additional money by doing odd jobs. Several sessions were spent discussing his job prospects and how he might influence them. He proved to have a rather immature view of ideal jobs, preferring occupations he considered to be adventurous, such as being a policeman or a private investigator. A good deal of work was necessary to help him develop more realistic expectations. This case underscores that the patient's economic situation may also be an important maintaining factor in the problem.

Conclusion and Future Directions

As has been emphasized throughout this chapter, a functional analysis of the problem behaviors is an essential condition with difficult patients. Research in the area of panic disorders has focused thus far on the "average" patient. In writing this chapter we had to speculate well beyond available empirical data. Unfortunately, controlled studies with respect to the functional behavioral analysis and treatment of difficult patients are lacking. At present the clinician has to make decisions based on little more than hunches, extrapolating from clinical experience and detailed observation of behavior and its relation to the environment. A great deal of additional research is needed on how best to deal with patients presenting multiple problems. For most difficult cases, a plan in which various problems are tackled sequentially will be the most fruitful. The therapist should begin with the intervention that is likely to show the most rapid results, to boost the patient's motivation and hope.

Arranging the conditions for relapse prevention is an important task at the end of therapy. One approach is to relabel relapses during treatment as positive opportunities to practice the techniques the patient has acquired. In a few cases, symptom prescription—which asks patients to try to produce and confront their feared or avoided situations in real life—may be effective in fearful patients who improve during therapy but who are reluctant to relinquish the safety of contact with the therapist. Dependent patients, in particular, perceive the termination of therapy as threatening and try to find a way to continue by displaying numerous relapses. Emphasizing self-efficacy and gradually minimizing the role of the therapist is also a fruitful strategy.

Relapse prevention is, in fact, one of the most important topics for future research. Although cognitive therapy has not proven to be very effective in altering the phobic avoidance seen in some panic disorder patients (Emmelkamp, 1986), it may be very worthwhile for other targets. For example, in a study by Emmelkamp, Brilman, Kuipers, and Mersch (1986), cognitive therapy led to significant changes in irrational beliefs, whereas in vivo exposure did not. Further, Emmelkamp and Mersch (1982) found that cognitive therapy led to a significant improvement at follow-up on measures of depression, assertiveness, and locus of control, whereas in vivo exposure did not. A number of researchers have also found cognitive interventions to be effective in reducing panic attacks. (See Chapter 7 for more details.) Cognitive coping skills may also be prophylactic in preventing future relapse.

Another strategy that may help prevent relapse is teaching problem-solving skills. Kleiner et al. (1987) developed a problem-solving skills program for patients with panic disorder with agoraphobia. The main goals of this program were to increase the patient's awareness of ongoing interpersonal problems, to develop an awareness of the effects of those problems on the phobia, and to teach basic skills (including assertiveness skills) to deal with those problems. Patients who had received in vivo exposure and patients who had received treatment combining in vivo exposure with problem-solving improved significantly after 12 treatment sessions. Subjects in the in vivo exposure–alone condition either failed to show further gains at follow-up or relapsed, whereas the group receiving training in problem solving showed further improvement at 6-month follow-up. Interestingly, the latter also showed a significant shift in locus of control toward more internal control. Jannoun, Munby, Catalan, and Gelder (1980) investigated the effectiveness of a problem-solving treatment involving couples' discussion of life stresses and problems. In it, in vivo exposure was superior to the problem-solving treatment, but one of the two therapists involved obtained unexpectedly good results with problem solving. However, in a subsequent study (Cullington, Butler, Hibbert, & Gelder, 1984), the favorable results of problem solving were not replicated. Taking together the results of Kleiner et al. (1987) and the studies of the Oxford group (Gelder and colleagues), it seems that problem solving has something to offer when added to in vivo exposure. When exposure is left out of the treatment program, however, problem solving has not been shown to be an effective treatment for agoraphobia.

References

Arnow, B. A., Taylor, C. B., Agras, W. S., & Telch, M. J. (1985). Enhancing agoraphobia treatment outcome by changing couple communication patterns. *Behavior Therapy, 16,* 452–467.

Arrindell, W. A., & Emmelkamp, P. M. G. (1985). Psychological profile of the spouse of the female agoraphobic patient: Personality and symptoms. *British Journal of Psychiatry, 146,* 405–414.

Arrindell, W. A., & Emmelkamp, P. M. G. (1986). Marital adjustment, intimacy and needs in female agoraphobics and their partners: A controlled study. *British Journal of Psychiatry, 149,* 592–602.

Arrindell, W. A., & Emmelkamp, P. M. G. (1987). Psychological states and traits in female agoraphobics: A controlled study. *Journal of Psychopathology and Behavioral Assessment, 9,* 237–253.

Arrindell, W. A., Emmelkamp, P. M. G., & Sanderman, R. (1986). Marital quality and general life adjustment in relation to treatment outcome in agoraphobia. *Advances in Behaviour Research and Therapy, 8,* 139–185.

Barlow, D. H. (1987, October). *Treatment of panic disorder.* Paper presented at the Symposium on Treatment of Panic and Phobias, Schloss Ringberg, West Germany.

Barlow, D. H., O'Brien, G. T., & Last, C. G. (1984). Couples treatment of agoraphobia. *Behavior Therapy, 15,* 41–58.

Beck, A. T., Emery, G., & Greenberg, R. L. (1985). *Anxiety disorders and phobias: A cognitive perspective.* New York: Basic Books.

Beck, A. T., Rush, A. J., Shaw, B. F., & Emery, G. (1979). *Cognitive therapy of depression.* New York: Wiley.

Beitman, B. D., DeRosear, L., Basha, I., Flaker, G., & Corcoran, C. (1987). Panic disorder in cardiology patients with atypical or non-anginal chest pain. *Journal of Anxiety Disorders, 1,* 277–282.

Bland, K., & Hallam, R. S. (1981). Relationship between response to graded exposure and marital satisfaction in agoraphobics. *Behaviour Research and Therapy, 19,* 335–338.

Chambless, D. L. (1982). Characteristics of agoraphobics. In D. L. Chambless & A. J. Goldstein (Eds.), *Agoraphobia: Multiple perspectives on theory and treatment.* New York: Wiley.

Chambless, D. L., Cherney, J., Caputo, G. C., & Reinstein, B. J. G. (1987). Anxiety disorders and alcoholism. *Journal of Anxiety Disorders, 1,* 29–40.

Charney, D. S., Heninger, G. R., & Jatlow, P. I. (1985). Increased anxiogenic effects of caffeine in panic disorders. *Archives of General Psychiatry, 42,* 233–243.

Clark, D. M. (1986). A cognitive approach to panic. *Behaviour Research and Therapy, 24,* 461–470.

Cobb, J., McDonald, R., Marks, I., & Stern, R. (1980). Marital versus exposure therapy: Psychological treatments of co-existing marital and phobic-obsessive problems. *Behavioural Analysis and Modification, 4,* 4–16.

Cobb, J. P., Mathews, A. M., Childs-Clarke, A., & Blowers, C. M. (1984). The spouse as co-therapist in the treatment of agoraphobia. *British Journal of Psychiatry, 144,* 282–287.

Connolly, J., Hallam, R. S., & Marks, I. M. (1976). Selective association of fainting with blood-injury-illness fear. *Behavior Therapy, 7,* 8–13.

Cullington, A., Butler, G., Hibbert, G., & Gelder, M. (1984). Problem-solving: Not a treatment for agoraphobia. *Behavior Therapy, 15,* 280–286.

Edlund, M. J., Swann, A. C., & Clothier, J. (1987). Patients with panic attacks and abnormal EEG results. *American Journal of Psychiatry, 144,* 508–509.

Emmelkamp, P. M. G. (1980). Agoraphobics' interpersonal problems: Their role in the effects of exposure *in vivo* therapy. *Archives of General Psychiatry, 37,* 1303–1306.

Emmelkamp, P. M. G. (1982). *Phobic and obsessive-compulsive disorders: Theory, research and practice.* New York: Plenum.

Emmelkamp, P. M. G. (1986). Behavior therapy with adults. In S. Garfield & A. Bergin (Eds.), *Handbook of psychotherapy and behavior change.* New York: Wiley.

Emmelkamp, P. M. G. (1990). Anxiety disorders. In A. S. Bellack, M. Hersen, & A. Kazdin (Eds.), *International handbook of behavior modification and therapy,* (2nd ed.). New York: Plenum.

Emmelkamp, P. M. G., Brilman, E., Kuipers, H., & Mersch, P. P. (1986). The treatment of agoraphobia: A comparison of self-instructional training, rational emotive therapy and exposure *in vivo. Behavior Modification, 10,* 37–53.

Emmelkamp, P. M. G., & Emmelkamp-Benner, A. (1983). Anxiety-based disorders. In M. Hersen (Ed.), *Outpatient behavior therapy*. New York: Grune & Stratton.

Emmelkamp, P. M. G., & Mersch, P. P. (1982). Cognition and exposure *in vivo* in the treatment of agoraphobia: Short-term and delayed effects. *Cognitive Therapy and Research, 6*, 77–90.

Emmelkamp, P. M. G., Mersch, P. P., Vissia, E., & van der Helm, M. (1985). Social phobia: A comparative evaluation of cognitive and behavioral interventions. *Behaviour Research and Therapy, 23*, 365–369.

Emmelkamp, P. M. G., van der Helm, M., MacGillavry, D., & van Zanten, B. (1984). Marital therapy with clinically distressed couples: A comparative evaluation of system-theoretic contingency contracting and communication skills approaches. In K. Hahlweg & N. Jacobson (Eds.), *Marital interaction analysis and modification*. New York: Guilford Press.

Emmelkamp, P. M. G., & van der Hout, A. (1983). Failure in treating agoraphobia. In E. B. Foa & P. M. G. Emmelkamp (Eds.), *Failures in behavior therapy*. New York: Wiley.

Emmelkamp, P. M. G., van der Hout, A., & De Vries, K. (1983). Assertive training for agoraphobics. *Behaviour Research and Therapy, 21*, 63–68.

Emmelkamp, P. M. G., van Linden van der Heuvell, C., Rüphan, M., Sanderman, R., Scholing, A., & Stroink, F. (1988). Cognitive and behavioral interventions: A comparative evaluation with clinically distressed couples. *Journal of Family Psychology, 1*, 365–377.

Everaerd, W. T. A. M., Emmelkamp, P. M. G., & Rijken, H. M. (1973). A comparison of flooding and successive approximation in the treatment of agoraphobia. *Behaviour Research and Therapy, 11*, 105–117.

Foa, E. B., Steketee, G., & Young, M. C. (1984). Agoraphobia: Phenomenological aspects, associated characteristics, and theoretical considerations. *Clinical Psychology Review, 4*, 431–457.

Fyer, A. J. (1987, October). *Effects of drug-discontinuation studies in panic disorder and agoraphobia*. Paper presented at the Symposium on Treatment of Panic and Phobias, Schloss Ringberg, West Germany.

George, D. T., Ladenheim, J. A., & Nutt, D. J. (1987). Effects of pregnancy on panic attacks. *American Journal of Psychiatry, 144*, 1078–1079.

Goldstein, A. J., & Chambless, D. (1978). A reanalysis of agoraphobia. *Behavior Therapy, 9*, 47–59.

Hafner, R. J. (1982). The marital context of the agoraphobic syndrome. In D. L. Chambless & A. J. Goldstein (Eds.), *Agoraphobia: Multiple perspectives on theory and treatment*. New York: Wiley.

Himadi, W. G., Cerny, J. A., Barlow, D. H., Cohen, S., & O'Brien, G. T. (1986). The relationship of marital adjustment to agoraphobia treatment outcome. *Behaviour Research and Therapy, 24*, 107–115.

Hudson, B. (1974). The families of agoraphobics treated by behaviour therapy. *British Journal of Social Work, 4*, 51–59.

Jannoun, L., Munby, M., Catalan, J., & Gelder, M. (1980). A home-based treatment program for agoraphobia—Replication and controlled evaluation. *Behavior Therapy, 11*, 294–305.

Kleiner, L., & Marshall, W. L. (1985). Relationship difficulties and agoraphobia. *Clinical Psychology Review, 5*, 581–595.

Kleiner, L., Marshall, W. L., & Spevack, M. (1987). Training in problem-solving and exposure treatment for agoraphobics with panic attacks. *Journal of Anxiety Disorders, 1*, 219–238.

Last, C. G., Barlow, D. H., & O'Brien, G. T. (1984). Precipitants of agoraphobia: Role of stressful life events. *Psychological Reports, 54*, 567–570.

Ley, R. (1985). Agoraphobia, the panic attack and the hyperventilation syndrome. *Behaviour Research and Therapy, 23*, 79–81.

Ley, R. (1987). Panic disorder: A hyperventilation interpretation. In L. Michelson & M. L. Ascher (Eds.), *Anxiety and stress disorders*. New York: Guilford Press.

Mathews, A. M., Gelder, M. G., & Johnston, D. W. (1981). *Agoraphobia: Nature and treatment*. London: Tavistock.

Matuzas, W., Al-Sadir, J., Uhlenhuth, E. H., & Glass, R. M. (1987). Mitral valve prolapse and thyroid abormalities in patients with panic attacks. *American Journal of Psychiatry, 144*, 493–496.

Mavissakalian, M., & Hamann, M. S. (1986). DSM-III personality disorder in agoraphobia. *Comprehensive Psychiatry, 27*, 471–479.

Meichenbaum, D., & Turk, D. C. (1987). *Facilitating treatment adherence*. New York: Plenum.

Milton, F., & Hafner, J. (1979) The outcome of behavior therapy for agoraphobia in relation to marital adjustment. *Archives of General Psychiatry, 36*, 807–811.

Monteiro, W., Marks, I. M., & Ramm, E. (1985). Marital adjustment and treatment outcome in agoraphobia. *British Journal of Psychiatry, 149*, 383–390.

Öst, L. G. (1987). Age of onset in different phobias. *Journal of Abnormal Psychology, 96*, 223–229.

Öst, L. G., Sterner, U., & Lindahl, I. L. (1984). Psychological responses in blood phobics. *Behaviour Research and Therapy, 22*, 109–117.

Ramsay, R. W. (1979). Bereavement: A behavioral treatment of pathological grief. In P. O. Sjöden, S. Bates, & W. S. Dockens (Eds.), *Trends in behavior therapy*. New York: Academic Press.

Reich, J., Noyes, R., Jr., & Throughton, E. (1987). Dependent personality disorder associated with phobia avoidance in patients with panic attacks. *American Journal of Psychiatry, 144*, 323–326.

Salkovskis, P. M., & Warwick, H. M. C. (1986). Morbid preoccupations, health anxiety and reassurance: A cognitive-behavioural approach to hypochondriasis. *Behaviour Research and Therapy, 24*, 597–602.

Scholing, H. A., & Emmelkamp, P. M. G. (1990). Social phobia: Nature and treatment. In H. Leitenberg (Ed.), *Handbook of social anxiety*. New York: Plenum.

Steketee, G., & Foa, E. B. (1987). Rape victims: Post-traumatic stress responses and their treatment: A review of the literature. *Journal of Anxiety Disorders, 1*, 69–86.

Tearnan, B. H., Telch, M. J., & Keefe, I. (1984). Etiology and onset of agoraphobia: A critical review. *Comprehensive Psychiatry, 25*, 51–62.

Thyrer, B. A., Himle, J., & Curtis, G. C. (1985). Blood-injury-illness phobia: A review. *Journal of Clinical Psychology, 41*, 451–459.

Turkat, I. D. (1985). *Behavioral case formulation*. New York: Plenum.

FUTURE DIRECTIONS IN RESEARCH, ASSESSMENT, AND TREATMENT

PART 3

Anxiety Disorders: A Review of Neurotransmitter Systems and New Directions in Research

GEORGE N. M. GURGUIS AND THOMAS W. UHDE

Introduction

The last two decades have witnessed a deluge of studies investigating the biological underpinnings of anxiety. Several factors appear to have contributed to this phenomenon. First is the growing trend in North American psychiatry toward adopting a psychobiological philosophy in the conceptualization of psychiatric disorders. This philosophy depends mainly on a descriptive or phenomenological approach to identifying and classifying psychiatric syndromes, and on the use of biological or somatic methods for both treatment and investigation of underlying biological correlates of these syndromes. This "neo-Kraepelinian" trend has led to understanding some forms of pathological anxiety as separate diagnostic entities. Within a psychodynamic framework, anxiety had often been viewed as a common denominator for all psychiatric disorders rather than an entity in its own right.

Second, the work of Klein (1964, 1981), demonstrating the efficacy of imipramine in the treatment of a group of patients with severe episodes of anxiety and agoraphobia, and proposing the existence of two qualitatively different types of anxiety disorders (generalized anxiety disorder versus panic disorder) with differential drug responsiveness, lent momentum to the current investigation of the biology of anxiety. Klein's adoption of the method developed by Pitts and McClure (1967)—for inducing anxiety through the use of lactate infusion—has stimulated the use of pharmacologic challenge paradigms for the experimental induction of anxiety and the study of different pathophysiological variables under controlled experimental conditions.

Third, new techniques such as gas chromatography mass spectrometry, high-pressure liquid chromatography, radioenzymatic assays for the measurement of different neurotransmitters and their metabolites, radioimmunoassays with high sensitivity and specificity for the measurement of very low levels of different hormones, radioreceptor binding assays, and cyclic AMP assays to evaluate functioning on a cellular level have become available to a broader population of investigators and have made hypotheses that could not be tested in the past amenable to laboratory testing and experimental verification.

Nonetheless, research into the biology of anxiety is also decades old. Somatic symptoms have long been recognized as an integral part of the phenomenon of anxiety. In fact, in the late 19th century James (1884, 1890) focused on the biological aspects of human emotion, particularly fear and rage. James assumed a direct linkage between peripheral bodily changes and human emotion. In fact, he viewed alterations in bodily sensations *as* the emotion. He even introduced the concept that some individuals might be unusually sensitive to their own internal physiological cues. This concept has recently been suggested as a partial model to explain the apparent vulnerability of agoraphobic patients to "spontaneous" and chemically induced panic attacks. James's hypothesis stimulated much interest in the autonomic nervous system and the neurobiology of emotion. In the early 20th century, Cannon (1928, 1929) demonstrated that emotional stimuli may induce adrenal gland secretion. However, he subsequently reported that although the exogenous administration of epinephrine produced palpitations and chest discomfort, there was no simultaneous experience of fear, as would have been predicted by the James-Lange theory of human emotion.

These and other findings led Cannon to shift his attention to the study of the brain and related systems that might be involved in the neurobiology of fear, anxiety, arousal, and other human emotions. On the basis of a series of studies in the cat, Cannon eventually proposed that thalamic discharges simultaneously produced both an emotion, including fear, and alterations in the autonomic and peripheral nervous systems. Cannon's experiments using stress paradigms (such as exposing cats held on their backs to barking dogs, without incurring physical injury) also pioneered and inspired the later trend that prevailed in the 1950s and 1960s of research into the neurobiology and neuroendocrinology of stress. For reviews see Mason (1968), Rose (1980), and Seyle (1950).

Despite the wealth of information that has accumulated in the field of anxiety research, definitive conclusions about the nature of anxiety have yet to be reached. Advances in the field of anxiety research have been delayed in part because investigators have failed to take into account all dimensions of the anxiety experience, including its cognitive, psychological, and somatic manifestations.

Although it is remote from the clinical domain, one example of an integrated research approach that attempts to address multiple dimensions of anxiety is the classical work of Kandel (1983). Using a classical conditioning paradigm in the sea snail Aplysia as a model to parallel the anticipatory dimension of anxiety in humans, Kandel showed that an augmented form of presynaptic facilitation accounted for the associative component of conditioning. The work shows a direct connection between environmental/psychological factors and the induction and establishment of biological substrates that mediate the responses of the organism. However, the situation is much more complex in human research. A multivariate analysis of different somatic, psychic, and cognitive aspects of anxiety, and their pathophysiological correlates, might help to clarify different underlying biological substrates of anxiety.

Finally, though it is arguable that real insights into the nature of anxiety await answers to questions such as those mentioned earlier, scientific enquiry is reductive by nature. For example, objective testing of the James-Lange theory proposed in 1890—that anxiety was secondary to bodily changes—was only possible with the availability of peripheral beta blockers. Adequate peripheral beta blockade, though it helped with the somatic component of anxiety, had little impact on the psychological component. Scientific enquiry works by breaking down research questions into their primary components. As facts are established, new hypotheses are proposed that require new investigations to either confirm, reject, or modify the hypothesis under study. There is, therefore, a natural cycle to the scientific method. Within the context of this cycle, this chapter will systematically review different neurotransmitter systems and their possible role in the pathophysiology of anxiety. As we review each system, we shall underscore recent developments and point out directions for future research.

Neurotransmitter Systems Implicated in Anxiety— General Considerations

It is conceivable that any neurotransmitter system could be involved in the pathophysiology of anxiety. Even though studies investigating the role of some neurotransmitter systems (such as the cholinergic system or histaminergic system) have not yielded results sufficient to encourage further exploration, the role of other systems (like the noradrenergic system) has been extensively studied and still attracts considerable attention. In addition, information regarding some neurotransmitters—for example, the peptidergic system—is just emerging and will require considerable research to determine whether it might be relevant to the neurobiology of anxiety.

The anatomic distribution of the neurotransmitter systems varies. Some (like the GABA-ergic system or adenosinergic system) are widely distributed throughout the brain and tend to have a widespread inhibitory effect. Others (like the noradrenergic and dopaminergic systems) have clusters of cell bodies from which stem well-defined tracks that carry their neurotransmitter to specific brain regions. These latter systems tend to have a specific inhibitory or stimulatory role. Identification of a neurotransmitter depends on several criteria. A neurotransmitter is synthesized by special enzymes found only in the neuron and stored in vesicles that travel down the axons and become located near their terminals. A neurotransmitter is released as a result of a firing of the presynaptic neuron to stimulate specific sensitive receptors located on the postsynaptic neuron. Release of the neurotransmitter is dependent on the firing rate of the presynaptic neuron. Ending of impulse transmission depends, to a great extent, on reuptake of the neurotransmitter by the presynaptic neuron and stimulation of presynaptic autoreceptors, which results in the inhibition of further release of the neurotransmitter. A small proportion of the neurotransmitter released is metabolized intra- or extra-neuronally by specific enzymes. Neurotransmitters have a high micromolar or nanomolar affinity to specific receptor sites located on the presynaptic or postsynaptic neurons, hence stimulating postsynaptic neurons at low concentrations and presynaptic autoreceptors at still lower concentrations. Finally, stimulation of these receptors results in either the generation of an impulse on the postsynaptic neuron or, in the case of neurohormonal transduction, in the release of a hormone. Often different types of receptors exist in the same system and respond to the same neurotransmitter, though with different end results (for example, alpha$_1$-and alpha$_2$-noradrenergic receptors). This differential response at the receptor level allows the same neurotransmitter to have different effects and circumvents the need for more neurotransmitters. Finally, neurotransmitter-receptor interaction results in the activation of second messengers (for instance, cAMP) that precipitate a chain of reactions at the cellular level.

Considering these steps in the neuronal transmission process, it is likely that an abnormality could exist at the level of one or more of these steps. For example, in the case of noradrenergic neurons, there could be an increase in the neuronal firing rate and/or a dysfunction at the level of presynaptic inhibitory alpha$_2$-receptors that in turn increases the firing rate. Also, dynamic adaptational mechanisms occur as a result of an established pathologic process (for instance, down-regulation of a receptor population in the face of an excessively available neurotransmitter, and vice versa). Hence, it is important to keep such possibilities in mind whenever an abnormality is found. Furthermore, in view of interactions between different neurotransmitter systems, it is likely that adaptational changes could occur in one system in response to an abnormality in another system.

Search for a neurophysiologic basis of anxiety was, for a period of time, simplistic in terms of attempting to implicate one system or another. Researchers are becoming increasingly aware of the possible interactions and balances that exist among various neurotransmitter systems and the implications of those interactions for research strategies and their findings.

The Gamma-Amino-Butyric Acid (GABA) System

Basic Science Aspects

Several compounds have been identified as inhibitory neurotransmitters—for example, amino acid glycine and beta-alanine. GABA, however, has been identified as the most widely distributed. It is synthesized in GABA-ergic neurons from glutamic acid by glutamic acid decarboxylase enzyme and stored in vesicles near their terminals, to be released on neuronal firing. Following discharge into the synaptic cleft, GABA is soon metabolized by GABA-transaminase. GABA-ergic neurons are interneurons; they are involved in almost 30% of synaptic transmission in the brain. They exercise their inhibitory effects through the opening of chloride channels, thereby inducing hyperpolarization of pre- and/or postsynaptic neurons. GABA-receptors are classified into two types: $GABA_A$ and $GABA_B$. $GABA_A$-receptors are bicuculline sensitive and chloride coupled, whereas $GABA_B$-receptors are bicuculline insensitive and calcium coupled. GABA-receptors form an oligomeric receptor complex with the benzodiazepine receptor and chloride channel. The nature of the interaction between GABA-receptors and benzodiazepine receptors is intricate and incompletely understood. Benzodiazepines enhance the binding of GABA and GABA-mimetics to their recognition sites. Alternatively, GABA-agonists enhance the binding of benzodiazepines to their receptors. Possible explanatory mechanisms involve the induction of conformational changes in the GABA-benzodiazepine receptor complex that increases their affinity to their respective ligands. However, this is not always the case. For example, benzodiazepines do not enhance the effects of GABA on peripheral neurons. GABA-mimetics do not cross the blood-brain barrier; hence, their clinical utility is limited.

Benzodiazepines and Their Receptors

The successful synthesis and introduction of the first benzodiazepine, chlordiazepoxide, into the market as an anxiolytic in 1960 was followed over the years by the synthesis of several chemically related derivatives with essentially similar effects but different potencies and pharmacokinetic properties (Greenblatt, Shader, & Abernethy, 1983a, 1983b). Initially attempts to uncover their underlying mechanism of action were directed toward exploring their effect on other known classical neurotransmitter systems. However, the mechanism of action of these compounds was only to be elucidated by the identification and characterization of stereospecific, saturable, and reversible binding sites, using nanomolar concentrations of ^{3}H-diazepam. Benzodiazepine receptors are found both centrally—in the brain—and peripherally—for example, in liver and kidney tissue. Peripheral benzodiazepine binding sites have different binding characteristics than do central benzodiazepine receptors. Their physiological significance is unclear. However, peripheral benzodiazepine binding sites also exist on central glial cells. Central benzodiazepine receptors are further classified into a high-affinity type I and a low- affinity type II, based on binding to the triazolapyridazine CL 218872, and on other thermal characteristics (Gee & Yamamura, 1983). However, binding of benzodiazepines is equal for both types. Benzodiazepine receptors are found mainly in the cerebral cortex, cerebellar cortex, amygdala, hippocampus, and dentate gyrus. Type I receptors are found to constitute 100% of benzodiazepine receptors in the cerebellum, but only 40% in the hippocampus. Yet, evidence about which type mediates the anxiolytic effect has been inconsistent. Using receptor-binding methodologies and displacement experiments, a high correlation was found between the affinity of different benzodiazepine derivatives and their therapeutic potency.

The discovery of naturally occurring binding sites for artificially synthesized compounds led researchers to speculate about the existence of naturally occurring ligands. Several compounds (for instance, inosine and melatonin) have been identified as candidates. However, the role of these compounds has not yet been clarified. Benzodiazepine receptor ligands are classified as follows.

1. Agonists (such as diazepam)—compounds that possess the typical benzodiazepine actions of sedative effects, muscle relaxant effects, anticonflict effects, and antiseizure effects
2. Partial agonists (such as triazolapyridazines)
3. Antagonists—compounds capable of displacing agonists from their binding sites that have no effect of their own (such as RO-15-1788)
4. True antagonists, or inverse agonists—compounds that induce effects opposite to those of benzodiazepines, such as seizures and anxiety (for example, beta-carboline)

For reviews of these ligands see Haefley (1983), Paul and Skolnick (1981), and Ticku (1983).

Studies on the Role of Benzodiazepines in Anxiety

These compounds are of particular interest from a research viewpoint in terms of their potential use as a neurobiological model of anxiety. Robertson, Martin, and Candy (1978) reported lower benzodiazepine receptor density in Maudsley reactive rats (rats selectively bred for emotionality and used as a genetic model of anxiety). Stress was also reported to increase cortical benzodiazepine binding. In a recent report, Insel et al. (1984) used beta-carbolines to induce anxiety in primates. Using doses of between 50 and 500 mg per kg of B-CCE, dose-dependent activation and increases in blood pressure, heart rate, and cortisol were observed in adult rhesus monkeys. Diazepam blocked these responses, whereas clonidine did not prevent behavioral activation but had a significant effect on blood pressure and heart rate and prevented an increase in cortisol. Propranolol did not prevent behavioral activation or cortisol elevation, though it did reverse heart rate elevations. B-CCE failed to induce an elevation in MHPG levels. The absence of increases in MHPG in Insel's study, despite behavioral and cardiovascular activation, suggests that the mechanism of induction of anxiety by B-CCE may not necessarily involve the noradrenergic system. On the other hand, this study rekindles earlier interest in the relationship between benzodiazepines and other classical neurotransmitter systems—for example, the noradrenergic and serotonergic systems. Earlier studies showed decreased norepinephrine (NE) turnover after an acute challenge with oxazepam. Also, in view of their anticonflict effects, a relationship could exist between benzodiazepines and the serotonergic system involved in punishment behavior (Wise, Berger, & Stein, 1973). Following six doses of oxazepam, tolerance developed in terms of norepinephrine turnover rate in mid- and hindbrain regions, but serotonin levels continued to be reduced.

Studies from our group conducted on a nervous line of pointer dogs (another genetic animal model of anxiety) have shown that neither diazepam nor the benzodiazepine antagonist RO15-1788 had an anxiolytic effect on behavior, as measured by the Human Interaction Test scores (Uhde, 1986). This is in agreement with the later results reported by Klein, Marangos, Montgomery, Bacher, and Uhde (1987), who found no differences in the density of benzodiazepine receptors—as measured by ^{3}H-beta-CCE in the frontal cortex, cerebellum, and hippocampus—between the nervous and the normal line of pointer dogs.

Neuroendocrine research strategies should be another potentially useful area for exploring benzodiazepine-mediated anxiety, in terms of benzodiazepine's effect on different hormones as well as their interaction with other neurotransmitter systems. Koulo, Lammintausta, Kanges, and Dahlstrom (1979) and Koulo, Aaltonen, and Kanto (1982) have demonstrated that diazepam administration induces stimulation of growth hormone secretion. They furthermore demonstrated that the effect was partly mediated via dopaminergic—but not serotonergic—mechanisms. Shur, Petursson, Checkley, and Lader (1983) showed that the growth hormone response developed tolerance to continued diazepam administration. However, no hypersensitivity could be demonstrated following the discontinuation of diazepam. On the other hand, diazepam had no significant effect on prolactin or thyroid-stimulating hormone (Ajlouni & El-Khateeb, 1980). It is noteworthy that such neuroendocrine strategies have not been exhausted in the study of anxiety disorders, despite their potential.

Alprazolam

In view of the current knowledge of the basic science aspect of benzodiazepines and benzodiazepine receptors, there is a potential that new benzodiazepines may be synthesized with high affinity to the receptors and milder side effect profiles as well as benzodiazepine derivatives with differential affinity to one type of benzodiazepine receptor or the other. The relatively new benzodiazepine alprazolam is a current example. Alprazolam is one of the very few benzodiazepines that have been proven effective in the treatment of panic disorder. This fact would suggest that panic disorder is qualitatively no different from generalized anxiety disorders. Alprazolam differs from other benzodiazepines in having an extra triazol ring in its structure. Pharmacologic studies have shown it to have an affinity for benzodiazepine receptors that is approximately ten times that of diazepam. Its efficacy at low dosage and its low side effects profile has allowed therapeutically effective doses unachievable with other benzodiazepines due to their side effects.

Another topic of debate is the claimed antidepressant effect of alprazolam. It is worth noting that most of the studies supporting this claim were conducted on depressed outpatient populations, which are likely to include patients with reactive depression. These studies reflect, in part, the long-standing phenomenological dispute over the relationship and overlap between anxiety and depression. A review of the literature reveals that the response to alprazolam is probably secondary to alprazolam's effect on the anxiety subscales in the depression rating scales. Core depressive symptoms, such as anhedonia, weight loss and/or appetite loss, and early morning mood worsening have proven to be relatively unresponsive to treatment with alprazolam. It is important, therefore, to phenomenologically discriminate between the disinhibited behavior seen at times in patients treated with benzodiazepines and a genuine antidepressant effect. An earlier study by Schatzberg and Cole (1978) showed that benzodiazepines are not effective in alleviating depression. It has been suggested that the antidepressant effects of alprazolam are a result of its triazol ring, but thus far there are no studies to support this suggestion. It is not known whether alprazolam affects serotonin or norephinephrine uptake, an effect that is shared by most antidepressants. Also, unlike antidepressants, alprazolam did not alter central presynaptic alpha$_2$-adrenergic receptor function in rats chronically treated (for 14 days) with alprazolam (Senkowski, Gurguis, Spengler, & Smith, 1986).

In Senkowski and colleagues' study, neither ^{3}H-clonidine-specific binding to alpha$_2$-receptors in different rat brain areas nor clonidine-induced inhibition of ^{3}H-norephinephrine release from hippocampal slices was changed. In a study by Sethy and Hodges (1982), alprazolam did not alter the density of beta-adrenergic receptors in normal rats. However, it prevented an increase in beta-adrenergic receptors in chronically reserpinized rats (an animal model of drug-induced depression). This effect was seen with electroconvulsive treatment, but was not seen with diazepam. However, doses of alprazolam and diazepam administered in this experiment were not biologically equivalent. The link between benzodiazepines and other neurotransmitter systems such as the noradrenergic system has long been recognized (Taylor & Laverty, 1969). Despite its well-proven efficacy in treating panic disorder, caution regarding alprazolam's claimed antidepressant effect is justifiable until future studies settle this issue.

The Adenosinergic System

Basic Science Aspects

Criteria required to identify a neurotransmitter are set strictly to avoid misidentifying compounds as neurotransmitters. Nonetheless, it is known that some compounds like adenosine that do not meet those rigorous criteria significantly affect neurotransmission. This fact has led to the development of the concept of neuromodulation. A neuromodulatory substance possesses some but not all the criteria for classical neurotransmitters and also regulates the release of other neurotransmitters. An example is adenosine and the adenosinergic system. The adenosinergic system is one of the widely distributed inhibitory systems in the CNS. Although it possesses some of the characteristics of classical neurotransmitter systems (for example, specific receptor sites and high-affinity uptake sites), it lacks a well-defined anatomical distribution and storage mechanism (Marangos & Boulenger, 1985). Several mechanisms are implicated in the synthesis of adenosine, yet the exact mechanism is unclear. Adenosine is released on neuronal firing and is inactivated by the enzyme adenosine deaminase into inosine; a good portion is taken up by high-affinity reuptake sites. The availability of ^{3}H-adenosine congeners that are resistant to the effect of adenosine deaminase, as well as the use of adenosine deaminase inhibitors, have allowed the identification and characterization of cell surface adenosine receptor sites that are highly stereospecific, saturable, and reversible. Adenosine receptors are subclassified into A_1 (inhibitory) and A_2 (stimulatory) receptor subtypes, with markedly different affinities (.4 versus 4 nM, respectively).

Xanthines are adenosine antagonists of both receptor subtypes. Antagonism by xanthines is seen at concentration levels far below those required for the inhibition of the phosphodiesterase enzyme. High-affinity adenosine reuptake sites have also been characterized using binding methodologies. Dipyridamole is a potent inhibitor of adenosine reuptake. Adenosine receptors are distributed mainly in the cerebellum, hippocampus, and superior colliculus. However, reuptake sites are not evenly codistributed with the receptors; they are mainly found in the superior colliculus and the nucleus tractus solitarius. Adenosine exerts its neuromodulatory effect on other neurotransmitters through the blockade of neuronal calcium influx, thereby inhibiting the release of other neurotransmitters (such as norepinephrine, dopamine, serotonin, acetylcholine, and GABA). Hence, the relevance of the adenosinergic system to the pathophysiology of anxiety has become an area of increasing interest in anxiety research. (See reviews of this area by Marangos and Boulenger (1985), Patel and Marangos (1984), Phillis and Wu (1981), Snyder (1985), and Uhde (1988)).

Studies on the Role of the Adenosinergic System in Anxiety

Animal studies have shown that the adenosine analogues cyclohexyladenosine (CHA) and 2-chloradenosine significantly decrease the number of movements and mean exploratory distance per move in mice (Crawley, Patel, & Marangos, 1981). Similar effects were seen using adenosine reuptake blockers (Crawley, Patel, & Marangos, 1983). On the other hand, Snyder, Katim, Annau, Bruns, and Daly (1981) demonstrated that adenosine antagonist xanthines stimulated locomotor activity in mice in a manner that correlated with their potencies in blocking adenosine receptors. Using Maudsley reactive rats as a genetic model of anxiety, Marangos and associates (Marangos, Insel, Montgomery, & Tamborska, 1987) demonstrated that the number of cerebellar adenosine receptors was increased by 15% to 30% in the reactive strain compared with the nonreactive strain. It was suggested that, like the benzodiazepine receptors, a variety of chronic stress paradigms results in increases in the number of adenosine receptors (Boulenger, Bierer, & Uhde, 1985). Work from our group, using nervous pointer dogs and the drug ^{3}H-CHA, showed that adenosine receptors were increased in the hippocampus of the nervous dogs compared with the normal purebred dogs. There was also an increase in the cerebellar reuptake sites using ^{3}H-dipyridamole (Klein et al., 1987).

Human Research Studies (Caffeine)

Caffeine is one of the most widely consumed psychoactive drugs. It has long been recognized for its stimulant and anxiogenic effects. Caffeinism, whose symptoms are similar to those of anxiety, has been observed in patients who consumed more than 500 mg per day of caffeine (Greden, 1974; Uhde, 1988). Greden and associates (Greden, Fontaine, Lubetsky, & Chamberlin, 1978; Greden, Proctor, & Victor, 1981) also reported that high caffeine consumption was significantly associated with depression and state-trait anxiety in psychiatric patients. Boulenger and Uhde (1982) were the first to report on the daily consumption and effects of caffeine in a group of patients with well-defined psychiatric conditions (that is, panic disorder and generalized anxiety disorder). In this study Boulenger and Uhde found a nonsignificant trend whereby anxiety disorder patients consumed lower amounts of caffeine. The significant finding reported in this study was the high correlation between daily caffeine consumption and scores of trait anxiety within the patient group ($r = .90$, $p < .0001$) but not the normal volunteer group.

A later report by Boulenger and co-workers (Boulenger, Uhde, Wolff, & Post, 1984) showed that a higher number of patients with panic disorder than normal controls had discontinued caffeine intake due to untoward side effects. In a challenge paradigm, Uhde, Boulenger, Jimerson, and Post (1984) demonstrated that caffeine induced anxiety in normal volunteers in a dose-related fashion. In this study there was no significant increase in MHPG levels. Two of eight normal subjects (Uhde, 1988) experienced unequivocal panic attacks at the 720-mg dose. They also had a significant increase in cortisol compared with the six subjects who did not develop panic attacks. In this same study (Boulenger, Salem, Marangos, & Uhde, 1987) there was a linear correlation between the Zung anxiety scores and plasma caffeine levels. This occurred even though significant anxiety resulted only at a dose of 720 mg and despite the absence of significant changes in plasma adenosine levels. Using a 480-mg dose of caffeine in panic disorder patients and normal controls, the NIMH research team (Boulenger et al., 1985; Uhde, 1988; Uhde, Boulenger, Jimerson et al., 1984) reported no change in MHPG levels despite a trend toward a mild increase in peripheral norepinephrine levels and despite the fact that 9 of 24 panic disorder patients, compared with none of the normal controls, had panic attacks. In this study, there was a significant increase in blood lactate levels in the panicking patients compared with the nonpanicking patients. There was also a significant increase in plasma glucose and cortisol levels. Similar results were reported by the Yale group (Charney, Heninger, & Jatlow, 1985), except that they reported an equal increase of plasma cortisol levels in patients and normal controls. Finally, Uhde, Bierer, and Post (1985) reported that caffeine induces escape from dexamethasone suppression. This result suggests that dietary habits should be considered when interpreting the dexamethasone suppression test. For example, panic disorder patients avoid caffeine intake, but schizophrenic patients are known to consume excessive amounts of it.

These findings implicate the adenosinergic system in the pathophysiology of anxiety. Yet the exact mechanism through which caffeine-induced anxiety is mediated is not well understood. Among the positive findings of this pharmacologic model are the absence of change in MHPG level and increases in cortisol and blood lactate levels. Several analogies can be drawn between the benzodiazepine model and the adenosinergic model. Both systems are widespread in different brain areas and lack a well-defined anatomical circuitry. Also, both systems inhibit the release of classical neurotransmitters. Finally, in both systems there is an increase in cortisol levels in the absence of changes in MHPG. Benzodiazepines act by opening chloride channels, resulting in a hyperpolarized state of pre- or postsynaptic neurons, thereby reducing their responsivity to incoming stimuli. Adenosine, on the other hand, prevents calcium ion efflux into the neuron and hence inhibits neuronal firing. In this context, Klein and Uhde (1988) showed that verapamil hydrochloride, a calcium channel blocker, had a significant but clinically modest effect on anxiety symptoms and decreased the occurrence of panic attacks. These results need to be replicated on a larger scale. The comparison of verapamil's therapeutic efficacy with that of other drugs with established efficacy in the treatment of anxiety disorders appears to be a promising line of investigation. Adenosine agonists that are metabolically stable (that is, resistant to the effect of adenosine deaminase) and that can cross the blood-brain barrier are not currently available for therapeutic application in humans, even though—hypothetically—they could be effective in the treatment of anxiety. On the other hand, the notion of using adenosine reuptake blockers that could increase the level of adenosine at synaptic sites seems just as tempting. It is of interest that a blockade of only 20% of reuptake sites is sufficient to cause a 50% increase in adenosine levels. Dipyridamole, a peripheral vasodilator whose effect has a particular predilection for coronary arteries, is known also for its effect as an adenosine uptake blocker. Although dipyridamole may not cross the blood-brain barrier (Berne, Rubio, & Curnish, 1974), it could conceivably have an antianxiety effect through peripheral blockade of reuptake sites, with a resultant excess of or increase in adenosine levels. Our group is currently studying the possible antianxiety effects of dipyridamole.

The role of the adenosinergic modulatory system in the pathophysiology of anxiety poses several hypotheses that should be explored more fully. For example, chronic low caffeine ingestion is known to induce upregulation of adenosine receptors. It would be interesting to investigate whether panic disorder patients develop a tolerance to the effect of chronic caffeine ingestion or continue to experience anxiety in response to caffeine. It would also be interesting to apply acute caffeine challenge paradigms to find out if anxiety disorder patients react differently after adequate treatment than before treatment. Such a posttreatment design would explore the role of the adenosinergic system at the interaction level with other antianxiety drugs with known central mechanisms. Several aspects of this system remain to be worked out in the domain of basic science before more advanced clinical research is feasible. For example, peripheral adenosinergic receptors have been identified in fatty tissues and in the seminiferous tubules. However, neither of these are conveniently available for the application of receptor-binding methodology, as is the case with other neurotransmitter systems. Reuptake binding sites have been identified on red blood cells, though reuptake sites are not likely to be responsive to a variety of compounds. Adenosine receptors could exist on lymphocytes, but preliminary investigation has been negative. Furthermore, the anticipated discovery of tritiated agonist or antagonist ligands with a high affinity for a specific receptor subtype will considerably advance this area of research.

The Dopaminergic System

Basic Science Aspects

The dopaminergic system is one of the classical neurotransmitter systems that has well-defined clusters of neurons with projections to other dopamine-rich areas in the brain. The majority of dopaminergic neuron cell bodies are localized in the ventral tegmental area (Dahlström & Fuxe, 1964). Projections from those areas are divided into three subsystems: the mesostriatal system, with projections to the caudate and putamen; the mesolimbic system, with projections to the septum, olfactory tubercle, accumbens, amygdala, and piriform cortex; and the mesocortical system, with projections to the limbic cortex, entorhinal, cingulate, and prefrontal areas. Two other subsystems, the tuberinfundibular and tuberohypophyseal systems, regulate hypothalamic-pituitary secretory functions (such as prolactin and growth hormone secretion). While the mesostriatal system is relevant to the study of motor movement disorders, the mesolimbic, mesocortical, tuberoinfundibular, and tuberohypophyseal systems are more relevant to the study of psychiatric disorders.

Dopaminergic receptors are classified into two subtypes, D_1 and D_2, on the basis of whether they stimulate or inhibit adenylate cyclase activity.

Agonist stimulation of D_2-receptors results in an inhibition of adenylate cyclase activity. The regulation of different dopaminergic receptor subtypes is complex. D_2-receptor subtypes exist exclusively in the tuberohypophyseal and tuberoinfundibular systems. The latter system, along with the meso-cortical system, lacks autoreceptors, which are important for the development of dopamine receptor supersensitivity. Neuroleptics of the phenothiazine and thioxanthine groups have equally high affinities for D_1- and D_2-receptors, whereas butyrophenones have a high affinity for D_2 and a very weak affinity for D_1-receptors.

Dopamine is synthesized along the same metabolic chain of reactions that results in the formation of norepinephrine and epinephrine. Dopamine possesses an equal affinity for D_1 and D_2. While dihydroxyphenylacetic acid (DOPAC) tissue content levels reflect intraneuronal metabolism, homovanillic acid (HVA) is the final metabolite of dopamine. Several techniques have been employed to ensure measurements of HVA levels that can be interpreted in a meaningful way. Probenecid has been employed to block the efflux of mono-amine metabolites from the CSF to the plasma. HVA from peripheral tissues contributes 40% to 65% of total plasma HVA levels. Sternberg and associates (Sternberg, Heninger, & Roth, 1983) recommended the use of debresquin, a monoamine oxidase inhibitor that does not cross the blood-brain barrier, to block peripheral dopamine metabolism from contributing to the total plasma levels. With this technique, it has been suggested that 62% to 87% of plasma HVA levels is derived from the brain. For reviews of this topic, see Cooper, Bloom, and Roth (1986) and Creese (1987).

Studies on the Role of the Dopaminergic System in Anxiety

While the dopaminergic system has been strongly implicated in the patho-physiology of schizophrenic disorders, and circumstantial evidence exists implicating the dopaminergic system in major depressive disorders, very few investigators have explored its possible role in anxiety disorders. Most of the available data are derived from animal studies, using stress paradigms or pharmacologic manipulations. Stress studies using foot shock, immobiliza-tion, swimming, and psychosocial stress have found an increase in brain dopamine release and HVA levels (Bliss & Ailion, 1971). Although it is known that increased motor activity is associated with increased dopamine release and turnover rates, this study argues that similar increases occur in the absence of increased movement (such as during psychosocial stress). This study did not specify which brain areas were assayed for dopamine, though it is likely to have been the whole brain. However, another study, by Lidbrink, Corrodi, Fuxe, and Olson (1972), showed that immobilization stress decreased dopa-mine turnover in the neostriatum and median eminence. This agrees with the results of Corrodi, Fuxe, Lidbrink, and Olson (1971), who reported decreases in neostriatum, forebrain, and median eminence. Stress-induced decrease in dopamine turnover was intensified by pretreatment with barbiturates or meprobamate. Yet Lidbrink et al. reported that median eminence dopamine terminals reacted to barbiturates differently from telencephalic dopamine terminals, in that they showed an increase in dopamine turnover. Goldberg and Salama (1970) showed that revolving drum stress decreased dopamine turnover in mice. On the other hand, Thierry, Javoy, Glowinski, and Kety (1968) showed that electric foot shocks had no effect on dopamine in the brain stem, mesencephalon, and striatum. However, later data showed an acceleration of dopamine utilization in the nucleus accumbens but not in the striatum or the tuberculum olfactorium. Finally, Roth and Tam (1985) showed that the anxiogenic beta-carboline FG 7142 induced a dose-dependent increase in DOPAC in the prefrontal cortex but not in the cingulate cortex, whereas there was a decrease in DOPAC levels in the striatum and olfactory tubercle. Recent studies by Deutch, Tam, and Roth (1985) and Herman et al. (1982) showed that foot shock stress increased DOPAC concentration in some but not other dopamine-rich areas. These studies underscore the fact that within the dopaminergic system dopamine levels, turnover rate, and metabolite concentration may vary between subsystems, depending on the nature of the stressor or paradigm used.

A preliminary study from our group directly measured plasma HVA levels in 15 patients with panic disorder and 9 normal controls using a single morning plasma sample. This study showed that though HVA levels in panic disorder patients were no different from levels in normal controls, the distribution of HVA level was bimodal. Patients with a history of more frequent panic attacks and high Spielberger anxiety scores had significantly higher HVA levels than those with a lower incidence of panic attacks and lower anxiety scores. There are obvious limitations to this preliminary study; nonetheless, the findings are intriguing and deserve further investigation.

Indirect evidence of a probable increase in central dopaminergic function in panic disorder is deduced from neuroendocrine studies. In examining thyroid-stimulating hormone (TSH) response to thyroid-stimulating hormone releasing factor (TRH) in panic disorder patients, our unit (Roy-Byrne, Uhde, Sack, Linnoila, & Post, 1986) found blunted TSH responses in panic disorder patients compared to normal controls. Increased hypophyseal dopamine was hypothesized as one of the factors causing blunted TSH response to TRH (Besses, Burrow, Spaulding, Donabedian, & Pechinski, 1975). Among the other factors involved is an increased serotonergic activity. Gold, Goodwin, Wehr, and Rebar (1977) found a significant negative correlation between TSH response and CSF-5HIAA in depression. Further evidence implicating increased dopaminergic functions in anxiety disorders stems from the finding by Roy-Byrne, Uhde, Sack et al. (1986) of a blunted prolactin response. However, this study suggested that prolactin response and TSH response are two separate phenomena. Dopamine is known to suppress prolactin secretion, and neuroleptics, which act as D_2-receptor antagonists, cause increased secretion of prolactin. Caution is warranted in interpreting such findings, and further controlled studies are needed.

Psychopharmacologic studies provide evidence of decreased dopaminergic functions as opposed to increased function. If increased dopaminergic function is implicated in the pathophysiology of anxiety, it would be expected that neuroleptics would be beneficial in treatment. Klein and associates, in their earlier reports and later reviews (Klein, 1964, 1981; Klein, Rabkin, & Gorman, 1985) pointed out that treatment with neuroleptics resulted in a worsening of the condition of panic disorder patients. Several studies have shown that benzodiazepines were superior to small doses of neuroleptics and placebo. However, other studies have shown equal efficacy or superiority of neuroleptics to benzodiazepines. These studies are difficult to interpret in a meaningful manner, because diagnostic issues, dosage, and length of treatment trial are so variable. Fear of the development of tardive dyskinesia and the availability of other treatment modalities with proven clinical efficacy have discouraged further pursuit of this line of research.

Recently buspirone HCl, a drug with moderate agonist affinity to brain D_2-dopamine receptors in addition to other complex effects, has proven to be of help in generalized anxiety disorder, though its efficacy in panic disorders requires further exploration.

Studies on the effect of antidepressants on dopaminergic function have shown that repeated imipramine administration enhances d-amphetamine-induced locomotor hyperactivity. These results indicate that repeated, but not acute, doses of antidepressants increase responses mediated by dopamine receptors—in other words, dopamine up-regulation (Maj, 1984).

The role of the dopaminergic system in anxiety disorders is still an open field for future research. The use of peripheral challenge paradigms such as L-Dopa infusions and acute central pharmacologic challenge paradigms (for example, small doses of receptor-specific neuroleptics along with the measurement of endocrine responses and neurotransmitter metabolite levels) could provide valuable insights into the role of the dopaminergic system in anxiety disorders.

The Serotonergic System

Basic Science Aspects

The distribution of the serotonergic neurons in the brain is rather more diffuse and widespread than the dopaminergic system. Most serotonergic neurons exist in areas designated as B_1-B_9 by Dahlström and Fuxe (1964). Neurons originating from caudal nuclei descend to supply the medulla and spinal cord; those originating from more rostral nuclei (B_7-B_9, the raphe) form ascending tracts to supply the septal areas, hippocampus, hypothalamus preoptic area, and cerebral cortex. Serotonergic neurons have also been identified in the locus coeruleus and area postrema. Serotonergic receptors are subclassified into $5HT_1$ and $5HT_2$. $5HT_1$-receptors are further divided into $5HT_{1A'}$, $5HT_{1B'}$, and $5HT_{1C}$. Stimulation of $5HT_1$-receptors results in the activation of adenylate cyclase and induces hypotensive effects, whereas stimulation of $5HT_2$-receptors results in an increased phosphoinositol turnover excitation of neuronal firing and contraction of vascular smooth muscle. $5HT_{1B}$-receptors are believed to be presynaptic autoreceptors, the stimulation of which results in decreased neuronal firing. Reuptake binding sites have been characterized using the prototype tricyclic ^{3}H-imipramine (Rehavi, Paul, Skolnick, & Goodwin, 1980). A similar site has been found on platelet membranes (Paul, Rehavi, Skolnick, Ballenger, & Goodwin, 1981; Paul, Rehavi, Skolnick, & Goodwin, 1980).

Tryptophan is taken into the brain by an active carrier process that depends on plasma tryptophan levels and also on the levels of other neural amino acids that can compete with tryptophan in this carrier process. Tryptophan is transformed into hydroxytryptophan by tryptophan hydroxylase, which is the rate-limiting enzyme. Hydroxytryptophan is then transformed into serotonin (5-hydroxytryptamine) by the enzyme decarboxylase. Although serotonin in the brain acts as a neurotransmitter and is localized in certain brain regions, it is widespread throughout the body and exists at high concentrations in the mast cells, platelets, and intestinal chromaffin cells. Serotonin is metabolized by monoamine oxidase into 5-hydroxyindoleacetic acid (5H1AA). For a review of this, see Cooper et al. (1986) and Perotka (1987).

Studies on the Role of the Serotonergic System in Anxiety

Involvement of the serotonergic system in panic disorders is inferred from several observations. Tricyclic antidepressants with proven efficacy in treating panic disorder act, in part, as serotonin uptake inhibitors. Studies cited earlier by Paul and Rehavi have shown that imipramine binds to serotonin uptake sites. Second, the recently developed anxiolytic buspirone has been shown to be a $5HT_{1A}$ antagonist and its microiontophoretic application to the dorsal raphe neurons causes their inhibition (Van der Maelen & Wilderman, 1984). Third, the therapeutic efficacy of benzodiazepines may not be related to decreased norepinephrine turnover, which shows adaptation to the repeated administration of benzodiazepines; rather, it may be related to decreased serotonin turnover, which remains low. In this regard animal studies also have shown that, in a conflict paradigm, benzodiazepines, para-chloro-phenyl-alanine (a serotonin synthesis inhibitor), and destruction of serotonergic pathways all increase animal behavior that is suppressed by punishment, while serotonin agonists and electrical stimulation of the raphe act as proconflict agents and suppress punished behavior (Geller & Blum, 1970; Stein, 1981, 1983; Stein, Wise, & Belluzzi, 1975).

Despite this evidence, the role of the serotonergic system in anxiety has only recently been studied. Lewis and associates (Lewis, Noyes, Coryell, & Clancy, 1985) reported a significant decrease in both B_{max} and K_d (reflecting the number of binding sites and affinity) in agoraphobic patients with panic attacks. In that study, a subpopulation of agoraphobics with a concurrent or past history of depression tended to have higher B_{max} and K_d values. There was also an association between B_{max} and the age at onset of illness. However, more recent studies from our group (Uhde, Berrettini, Roy-Byrne, Boulenger, & Post, 1987) and elsewhere have failed to replicate these findings (Innis, Charney, & Heninger, 1987). Possible variations in assay method, circadian, circannual, and drug status might have contributed to the different findings. Contradictory reports on ^{3}H-imipramine binding sites in panic disorder patients are in contrast with a rather general consensus among several studies reporting fewer imipramine binding sites in depressed patients (Briley, Langer, Raisman, Sechter, & Zarifian, 1980; Paul, Rehavi, Skolnick, Ballenger, & Goodman, 1981; Raisman, Sechter, Briley, Zarifian, & Langer, 1981; Wagner et al., 1985).

Peripheral loading with l-tryptophan is another research strategy for studying serotonergic function in panic disorder. In a study by Charney and associates (Charney & Heninger, 1986b), the ability of tryptophan to increase prolactin did not differ between patients and healthy controls. Furthermore, alprazolam treatment had no effect on prolactin response.

A third research strategy, which combines an acute central challenge paradigm using an agent having receptor-specific effects with the measurement of endocrine responses, has been adopted recently. A metabolite of the antidepressant trazodone, m-chlorophenylpiperazine (mCPP), acts as an agonist at the $5HT_1$-receptor site and decreases 5H1AA brain levels. Again, intravenous administration of .1 mg per kg mCPP to panic disorder patients and healthy volunteers produced similar psychological (anxiety) and endocrinological (prolactin, growth hormone, and cortisol) responses (Charney, Woods, Goodman, & Heninger, 1987). A study by Klein, Zohar, Geraci, Murphy, and Uhde (1987) comparing the effect of mCPP and caffeine to placebo in panic disorder patients showed that both drugs induced similar increases in anxiety. However, mCPP caused greater increases in prolactin response compared with caffeine. The lack of a control group in this study is a major limitation. However, an oral dose of .5 mg per kg has previously been shown not to be associated with remarkable behavioral effects in normal volunteers (Mueller, Murphy, & Sunderland, 1985). In this regard, the use of an intravenous dose of .1 ml per kg in the study by Charney et al. might have exceeded the levels needed to discriminate between normal subjects and panic disorder patients.

Psychopharmacologic evidence does implicate the serotonergic system in the pathophysiology of obsessive-compulsive disorder. Clomipramine, an antidepressant with specific effects on the blockade of serotonin uptake, has been reported superior to other pharmacologic treatment modalities (for a review see Insel & Murphy, 1981). Clomipramine was superior to clorgyline in alleviating obsessive-compulsive symptoms (Insel et al., 1983) and in improvement correlated with plasma clomipramine levels, but not in level of metabolites. Prasad (1984) showed that zimelidine, a serotonin uptake inhibitor, also was superior to imipramine. Thoren, Asberg, Bertilsson et al. (1980) and Thoren, Asberg, Cronholm, Jornestedt, and Traskman (1980) also showed that clomipramine but not nortriptyline was superior to placebo in interview-based ratings of obsessive-compulsive symptoms. Higher CSF levels of 5H1AA predicted favorable treatment response and the amelioration of obsessive-compulsive symptoms, also correlated with a reduction of CSF 5H1AA levels and negatively correlated with plasma clomipramine concentrations. Recently, a study by Mellman and Uhde (1987) reported an overlap in the symptomatology of obsessive-compulsive disorder and panic disorder in a subgroup of patients.

Judging from this review, the role played by the serotonergic system is not fully understood. Several steps in the regulatory functions of this system remain to be clarified. Plasma tryptophan levels, circadian variations, or variations in dietary habits and the impact of those changes on brain serotonin levels have not been examined. Also, the nature of the tryptophan transport process into the brain and the activity of the tryptophan hydroxylase enzyme are other systems that could be a target for investigation. The use of psychopharmacologic agents to study release, uptake, and metabolism of serotonin could be other strategies (for instance, using fenfluramine in an acute challenge paradigm combined with the measurement of endocrine responses). Another target for investigation would be different serotonin receptors, either for measurement or in terms of their coupling with second messengers and hormonal responses. Although they are static measures, plasma and CSF 5H1AA baseline levels have not been determined. In sum, the serotonergic system seems to be an open area for future research.

The Noradrenergic System

Of the neurotransmitter systems discovered so far, the noradrenergic system has been most extensively studied and most heavily implicated in the pathophysiology of anxiety. Hypotheses proposed in this regard have stimulated an immense number of studies. For a review, see Redmond (1987).

Basic Science Aspects

Neuroanatomy

Noradrenergic neuronal pathways stem from a cluster of cell bodies that form the nucleus locus coeruleus, or area A6. The nucleus locus coeruleus is located bilaterally in the pontine gray at the level of the fourth ventricle, extending between the dorsal tegmental nucleus and motor nucleus of the trigeminal nerve. It is made up of approximately 1500 cell bodies, and its name refers to their characteristic bluish coloration. Cell bodies of the locus coeruleus mainly supply the ipsilateral side of the brain with a very small number of neurons that cross to the contralateral side. The anatomical characteristics of the locus coeruleus are remarkably consistent across species. Cell bodies of noradrenergic neurons from the locus coeruleus send efferents through the dorsal bundle, medial forebrain bundle, and other tracts to supply the cerebral cortex, cerebellar cortex, thalamic and hypothalamic nuclei, olfactory bulb, and other limbic structures including the cingulate gyrus, hippocampus, amygdala, and septal nuclei. Descending tracts from caudal parts of the locus coeruleus carry afferents to the brain stem and spinal cord.

Much less is known about the afferent supply to the locus coeruleus from other brain regions. The locus coeruleus receives input from the spinal cord dorsal horns carrying pain sensation, cortical areas, raphe nuclei, reticular formation, and the contralateral locus coeruleus. Other afferent supplies have been shown to come from the nucleus paraganta cellularis and nucleus prepositus hypoglossi (Pieribone, Aston-Jones, & Bohn, 1988). Finally, another cluster of noradrenergic neurons exists outside the locus coeruleus in the lateral tegmental area, the functional nature of which is unclear.

Stimulation of the locus coeruleus system and its projections produces behavior-specific effects on a range of responses: from an enhanced sense of well-being and increased alertness to fear. Yet the behavioral specificity of the system is a matter of debate, and some argue for more generalized nonspecific stimulatory responses. For a review, see Clark (1979) or Foote, Bloom, and Aston-Jones (1983).

Noradrenergic receptors are classified into alpha-receptors and beta-receptors. Each type is further subclassified into alpha$_1$- and alpha$_2$-receptors and beta$_1$- and beta$_2$-receptors. Brain beta-adrenoreceptors are mainly of the beta$_1$-receptor subtype, whereas beta$_2$-receptors seem to be mainly distributed on glial and vascular tissue. Beta$_1$-receptors are distributed mainly in the cerebral cortex and cerebellar cortex, besides other limbic structures, the hypothalamus and pineal gland. Beta receptors are coupled to adenylate cyclase; their stimulation results in an increase in cAMP levels. Whereas alpha$_1$-adrenoreceptors are mainly postsynaptic, alpha$_2$-adrenoreceptors are both presynaptically and, to a lesser extent, postsynaptically located. Presynaptic alpha$_2$-adrenoreceptors are autoreceptors, stimulation of which results in the inhibition of further norepinephrine release. The existence of postsynaptic alpha$_2$-receptors is deduced from neuroendocrine studies showing hormonal secretory responses to alpha$_2$-receptor agonists or antagonists. Alpha-adrenoreceptor stimulation results in an increase of inositol triphosphate. Alpha-adrenoreceptors are distributed in the cerebral cortex, limbic structures, hypothalamus, and brain stem. Adrenergic receptors follow the same regulatory mechanisms as do other receptors; that is, they up-regulate (develop supersensitivity) with a decrease in synaptic norepinephrine (NE) levels and down-regulate in the presence of excess NE levels at the synaptic cleft.

Reuptake of NE is the main mechanism through which the neurotransmission process is brought to an end. NE reuptake is an energy-requiring process. Brain NE reuptake sites have been characterized using ^{3}H-desipramine binding methodologies. Tricyclic antidepressants block the reuptake of peripheral and central NE.

Neurochemistry

Norepinephrine is synthesized from tyrosine through a chain of reactions in which tyrosine-beta-hydroxylase is the rate-limiting enzyme. Epinephrine is further synthesized from norepinephrine through the action of phenyl-ethan-olamine-N-methyl transferase (PNMT). Several factors, including neuronal firing rate, NE levels, and turnover rate, affect the activity of tyrosine-beta-hydroxylase enzyme. NE is stored in vesicles near the nerve ending, to be released on neuronal firing. Glucocorticoids have been shown to affect noradrenergic functions at the level of enzymatic synthesis, as well as reuptake sites and receptor regulation. Norepinephrine and epinephrine are metabolized intraneuronally by MAO (type A) and extraneuronally by the much less substrate-specific catecholamine-O-methyl-transferase (COMT) enzyme. 3-Methoxy-4-hydroxy-phenylglycol (MHPG) and vanillylmandelic acid (VMA) are the end metabolites of NE and epinephrine. For reviews, see Cedarbaum and Aghajanian (1977), Cooper et al. (1986), Janowsky and Sulser (1987), and Redmond (1979).

The preceding brief review of the noradrenergic system indicates several sites whose role in anxiety could be investigated. They are as follows.

1. Tyrosine plasma levels and uptake into the neural tissue
2. Regulation of synthetic enzymes, specifically tyrosine hydroxylase and PNMT
3. Norepinephrine storage in the neurons
4. Rate of NE and E release and the role of alpha$_2$-adrenoreceptor
5. Reuptake function
6. Postsynaptic alpha$_1$- and beta$_1$-adrenoreceptor function as reflected through direct measurement and neuroendocrine strategies
7. MAO and COMT enzyme activity, metabolite levels, and turnover rate
8. Agonist-receptor coupling and effects on cAMP production or phosphoinositol

Clinical Studies on the Role of the Noradrenergic System in Anxiety

A series of experiments on primates by Redmond and his associates has shown an association between the activation of locus coeruleus activity and fearful behavior (for a review, see Redmond, 1979). As a result, clinical studies have set out to test the hypothesis of increased noradrenergic function in human anxiety.

Plasma NE levels basically reflect peripheral sympathetic functions; epinephrine (E) levels, on the other hand, are a measure of adrenomedullary activity. Early studies by Frankenhauser, Dunn, and Lundberg (1976), using a stress paradigm in normal subjects, showed that plasma NE and E levels reflect the intensity of subjective reaction to stress. They also showed that there was a sex difference (Frankenhauser, 1971; Frankenhauser et al., 1976). Kopin (1984) pointed out that NE and E secretions vary in response to a variety of activating contexts (anxiety, anger, sexual arousal, and so on). Other studies have demonstrated that there is an excess secretion of E in situations in which subjects felt helpless; excess NE levels were associated with aggressive feelings. Baseline NE and E levels need to be examined for different categories of anxiety disorder based on the current nomenclature or diagnostic criteria. There are some indications of higher baseline NE and E levels, though these need further confirmation (Nesse, Cameron, Curtis, McCann, & Huber-Smith, 1984; Uhde, 1988).

The significance of MHPG plasma level and the extent to which it reflects central noradrenergic activity is controversial. Elsworth, Redmond, and Roth (1982) showed correlations between MHPG levels in brain areas, CSF, and plasma. Maas, Hattox, Greene, and Landis (1979) showed that 60% of plasma MHPG is contributed by the brain. Other studies, by Jimerson, Ballenger, Lake, Post, and Goodwin (1981) and Post et al. (1981), have shown that plasma MHPG levels correlate with CSF MHPG levels. Uhde, Boulenger, Jimerson et al. (1984) demonstrated that, in normal subjects who were about to participate in an anxiety-provoking procedure, plasma MHPG levels correlated with self-rated measures of anxiety ($r = .59$, $p < .05$). Ballenger et al. (1984) found significantly higher plasma MHPG in panic disorder patients compared with normal controls. Similar results were reported by Ko et al. (1983). Despite the correlations with the severity of self-rated state anxiety, recent studies by Uhde, Joffe, Jimerson, and Post (1987) and Gurguis and Uhde (1988) found no differences in resting plasma MHPG baseline levels between panic patients and normal controls. These results agree with those reported by Nesse et al. (1984) and Charney and Heninger (1985a, 1985b), but they are at odds with results reported by Edlund, Swann, and Davis (1987), who found significantly lower MHPG levels in panic patients compared with normal controls. It is possible that Edlund's results are due to the afternoon sampling time compared with the morning sampling time of other studies. Plasma catecholamine levels are known to show circadian variations.

Finally, while the 24-hour urinary NE/E levels reflect mainly peripheral sympathetic activity in humans, 24-hour urinary MHPG levels are hard to interpret in terms of peripheral versus central contribution, and caution should be exercised in interpreting any finding. For a review, see Kopin (1984).

We are not aware of studies investigating 24-hour urinary catecholamine levels in anxiety disorders.

There are few studies of baseline levels and activities of peripheral enzymes involved in the synthesis or degradation of catecholamines in anxiety disorders. Mathew, Ho, Kralik, Taylor, and Claghorn (1980) found a negative correlation between red blood cell COMT and trait-anxiety measures in a group of anxious patients compared with controls. Shulman, Griffith, and Diewold (1978) reported increased red blood cell COMT in anxiety states compared with controls and patients with other psychiatric diagnoses. Ballenger et al. (1981) reported a negative correlation between trait-anxiety measures and CSF dopamine-beta-hydroxylase (DBH) levels in normal volunteers. However, in the Mathew and associates study, serum DBH did not correlate with anxiety measures, but correlated negatively with both plasma NE levels and RBC COMT activity. Later, Mathew, Stolk, Peter, and Cooper (1984) reported no association between serum DBH activity and scores of Taylor manifest anxiety; also, DBH failed to reflect state changes in anxiety. These studies are preliminary and need to be replicated with different categories of anxiety disorders, carefully chosen, with clear diagnostic criteria.

Noradrenergic Psychopharmacologic Challenge Paradigms

As early as the beginning of this century the notion that anxiety is due to excess catecholamines enticed researchers to administer epinephrine or NE and measure behavioral responses. These techniques prompted what is currently known as a psychopharmacologic challenge paradigm (Uhde & Tancer, 1988). Studies that administered epinephrine produced what was described as a "cold" feeling. Peripherally administered E or NE does not cross the blood-brain barrier. Peripherally administered catecholamines have little impact on mood. A naturalistic experiment that supports this conclusion can be seen in patients with pheochromocytoma (Starkman, Cameron, Nesse, & Zelnick, 1985). Despite peripheral increases in NE/E levels, there were no anxiety symptoms significant enough to warrant a DSM-III diagnosis. In a study comparing three groups of patients (with pheochromocytoma, hypertension, and panic disorder) (Starkman, Cameron, Nesse, & Zelnick, 1987), epinephrine correlated with somatic symptoms, but NE correlated with anxiety only in hypertensives and panic disorder patients. This result most likely reflects peripheral sympathetic nervous system activation. In a recent study by Nesse et al. (1984) using an acute challenge of isoproterenol (a beta-adrenergic receptor agonist), patients with panic disorder had markedly elevated resting heart rate, plasma E levels, cortisol, and growth hormone, and mildly elevated NE levels. Interestingly, there was a decrease in heart rate response to isoproterenol. These results do not support a hypothesis of increased beta-receptor functions in panic disorder, but rather suggest decreased peripheral receptor function, probably in response to increased peripheral catecholamine levels.

More recently, investigators have been using compounds with high specificity in terms of their site of action. Clonidine, an alpha2-receptor agonist that decreases locus coeruleus activity, and yohimbine, an alpha2-receptor antagonist that increases locus coeruleus activity, have been employed recently to test noradrenergic functions in anxiety.

Clonidine acts as a central alpha2-adrenergic agonist, though it also has an affinity for histaminergic receptors. Given that alpha2-autoreceptors can be stimulated at much lower concentrations than postsynaptic adrenergic receptors, clonidine selectively stimulates alpha2-receptors at low doses. Behaviorally, clonidine induces sedation and sleepiness. Uhde et al. (1981) reported that clonidine lacked analgesic effects in normal volunteers but had noteworthy antianxiety effects in depressed patients. Acute intravenous administration of clonidine results in a decrease in blood pressure, cardiac rate, plasma NE, and MHPG levels. Growth hormone secretion is increased in response to clonidine's effect on postsynaptic alpha2-adrenoreceptors. In a study by Uhde, Vittone, Siever, Kaye, and Post (1986), the growth hormone response to clonidine was blunted in panic disorder patients compared with normal controls. Similar results have been reported by Charney and Heninger (1986a) in terms of growth hormone response. A blunted growth hormone response to clonidine also has been reported in depressed patients (Siever & Uhde, 1984) and in obsessive-compulsive disorder (Siever et al., 1983). As proposed earlier by Uhde et al., this suggests that the blunted growth hormone response might be a trait marker for a heterogeneous group of tricyclic-responsive diseases. In Siever and Uhde's study (1984), clonidine's induced decrease in cortisol was significantly higher in depressed patients than in controls. In a recent report by Stein and Uhde (1987), depressed patients showed a trend toward a greater fall in cortisol levels compared with panic disorder patients, but this was attributed to their higher levels of cortisol at baseline.

Yohimbine, on the other hand, is an alpha2-adrenoreceptor antagonist. On administration, yohimbine increases behavioral measures of anxiety in both humans and primates, causing increases in heart rate and blood pressure. Yohimbine increases both NE turnover rate and plasma MHPG. Endocrine effects include decreases in growth hormone, thyrotropin hormone, and stimulation of prolactin in monkeys (Goldberg & Robertson, 1983). Given these properties, yohimbine offers a good pharmacologic model for the induction of anxiety. Yohimbine has been found to increase anxiety scores in healthy volunteers (Charney, Heninger, & Redmond, 1983; Uhde, Boulenger, Post et al., 1984). In the Charney and associates study, both clonidine and diazepam reversed yohimbine-induced anxiety, but only clonidine attenuated increases in MHPG, BP, and autonomic symptoms. In this study, panic disorder patients had significantly higher anxiety scores and higher sitting systolic blood pressure counts; higher MHPG plasma levels were limited to the subgroup of patients who experienced more than 2.5 panic attacks per week. In a more recent study by our group (Gurguis & Uhde, 1988), yohimbine produced main drug effects as indicated by increases in Spielberger anxiety scores, norepinephrine, and cortisol, and by a trend toward increased diastolic blood pressure. However, panic disorder patients had significant increases only in anxiety and cortisol after baseline correction.

Receptor-binding studies have proven another useful approach to the study of some psychiatric and medical conditions. Receptor studies examine the size or number of the receptor population and the affinity for the receptor of the drug used in the experiment. Oftentimes no changes in the affinity of the receptor take place, but increases (up-regulation) or decreases (down-regulation) are observed in the receptor population in response to a variety of treatments. Because central receptors are not currently amenable to measurement in humans, contemporary studies have relied on analogous receptor populations in peripheral tissues (platelets, lymphocytes, or fibroblasts). Alpha$_2$-receptors have been identified on platelet membranes and beta-receptors have been identified on lymphocytes and neutrophils. Some argue that the platelet receptor model is close to the actual neuronal receptor system, as both have a neural ectodermal origin and similar enzyme systems. Monoamine uptake sites and alpha$_2$-receptors have shown characteristics similar to those in the mammalian brain (García-Sevilla, Hollingsworth, & Smith, 1981). A variety of antidepressants has been shown to induce down-regulation of alpha$_2$-receptors, in both brain and blood platelets (García-Sevilla, Zis, Zelnick, & Smith, 1981; Smith, García-Sevilla, & Hollingsworth, 1981). In depressed patients, platelet alpha$_2$-receptors were found to be significantly higher in number, using ^{3}H-clonidine as a ligand (García-Sevilla, Hollingsworth et al., 1981). Tricyclic antidepressant treatment led to a significant decrease in receptor number (García-Sevilla, Zis, Hollingsworth, Greden, & Smith, 1981). In another study (Cameron, Smith, Hollingsworth, Nesse, & Curtis, 1984), which compared depressed patients and patients with panic disorder with normal controls, there was no difference in ^{3}H-clonidine binding between panic disorder patients and normal controls, though it was lower than in depressed patients. On the other hand, yohimbine binding was lower in panic disorder patients compared with depressed patients and normal controls. Treatment with antidepressants caused further lowering of platelet alpha$_2$-receptors as measured by both clonidine and yohimbine, in conjunction with increased catecholamine levels in patients with panic attacks. Such findings are rather difficult to interpret. Apparently both the increase in plasma catecholamines and the decrease in the number of platelet alpha$_2$-receptors are a direct effect of the antidepressant treatment. Whether they are causally related to treatment response is unclear, though there was a close temporal relationship between the observed changes and improvement in anxiety scores. It must be noted that [^{3}H]-dihydroergocryptine binding to platelet membranes was significantly higher in patients with panic disorder than normal controls, whereas prostaglandin E1 (PGE1)-stimulated cyclic AMP production was significantly lower (Uhde, Roy-Byrne, Vittone, Boulenger, & Post, 1985). These results need to be replicated. Also, the significance of lower yohimbine, but not clonidine, binding in panic disorder patients needs further exploration, as both have a high affinity for alpha$_2$-adrenoreceptors.

Beta-adrenergic receptors have been identified on lymphocytes and granulocytes. Characterization of these receptors shows that they are of the beta$_2$-receptor subtype. Physiological studies have shown a reciprocal relationship between plasma catecholamine levels, urinary epinephrine and NE levels, and lymphocyte receptor density. On the other hand, beta receptor density correlated significantly with the cardiac sensitivity to isoproterenol. Hence, it appears that peripheral beta-receptors could be used as a parameter for the measurement of peripheral physiological functions. Several studies have examined changes in beta-receptor density, affinity, and functions in depression. Recently, Mann and colleagues (Mann et al., 1985; Mann et al., 1986) reported that beta-receptor-mediated cAMP levels were lower in depressed patients in the absence of any differences in the receptor affinity. In the 1985 study, Mann and colleagues found no difference in lymphocytic beta-receptor density or affinity between depressed patients and normal controls. However, when further subclassified into agitated versus retarded, only agitated depressed patients had lower beta-adrenergic responsivity. Other studies, nevertheless, reported lower beta-receptor density in depressed patients in the absence of changes in receptor affinity (Carstens et al., 1987). Reduced beta-receptor function had also been reported earlier by Extein, Tallman, Smith, and Goodwin (1979).

Studies that have used the beta-adrenoreceptor lymphocyte model suffer from a variety of methodological shortcomings (Davies & Lefkowitz, 1980), including the use of a single concentration of the ligand, the reporting of results per cell count (which introduces a high degree of variability), and the use of crude lymphocytic preparations.

The study of beta-receptor functions in patients with anxiety disorder is important from the point of view of reflecting peripheral sympathetic functions. Various symptoms of panic attacks are consistent with beta-receptor sensitivity. However, Nesse et al. (1984) found that beta-receptor responses to isoproterenol infusion did not differ between panic disorder patients and normal controls. Furthermore, slowing of heart rate responses suggested a decrease in beta-receptor function in the context of increased peripheral catecholamine levels. These results need to be replicated. Isoproterenol-stimulated cAMP levels might be another approach to test such a hypothesis. It would be interesting to test beta-receptor function during either naturally occurring or pharmacologically induced panic attacks, as beta-receptors have been shown to up- and down-regulate in response to a variety of physiological stimuli and pharmacological agents in a short period of time.

The Interaction Between the Noradrenergic System and the Hypothalamic-Pituitary-Adrenocortical Axis

An extensive literature exists on the interaction between the hypothalamic-pituitary-adrenocortical (HPA) axis and both the central noradrenergic system and the peripheral sympathetic system, a review of which is beyond the scope of this chapter. We will merely summarize the main outline of this interaction and its implications for the field of anxiety research.

Ganon (1977) showed that NE inhibits the release of the adrenocorticotrophic hormone (ACTH). Other studies found that hypothalamic epinephrine inhibits ACTH release (Mezey, Kiss, Skirboll, Goldstein, & Axelrod, 1984; Roth et al., 1981). Conversely, beta-adrenoreceptors are known to be present on pituitary cells. Isoproterenol and epinephrine have been shown to stimulate, while propranolol inhibits, ACTH release. Prazosin, an alpha$_1$-receptor blocker, inhibits epinephrine-induced ACTH, while clonidine, an alpha$_2$-receptor agonist, inhibits NE-induced ACTH release. It is likely that NE/E possess an inhibitory effect on release at the hypothalamic level and a stimulatory effect at the level of the pituitary. It was also demonstrated that high concentrations of catecholamines selectively diminish the sensitivity of CRF-stimulated ACTH release to the suppressive effect of dexamethasone.

Corticotropin-releasing factor (CRF) increases the activity of noradrenergic neurons of the locus coeruleus, augments sympathetic nervous system activity, and induces behavioral changes comparable to those in an animal model of anxiety. Glucocorticoids block the reuptake of catecholamines into non-neuronal tissues (reuptake 2) and induce increases in granulocytic beta-adrenoreceptor density and adenylate cyclase activity. Finally, a decrease in the activity of dopamine-beta-hydroxylase and phenylethanolamine N-methyl transferase (the enzyme responsible for epinephrine synthesis) has been found following removal of the pituitary; activity was restored by dexamethasone and ACTH.

The relevance of the HPA axis to anxiety is indicated in the extensive literature that exists on adrenocortical responses to a variety of stress models. Also, cortisol has been shown to increase in some, but not all, clinical models of fear and anxiety in both animals and humans. For example, cortisol increases have been documented in pharmacologically induced panic attacks in humans using caffeine and yohimbine. Yet no consistent increase in cortisol has been observed in patients exposed to phobic stimuli using flooding techniques, despite extreme degrees of manifest anxiety and self-reported anxiety in those patients (Curtis, Buxton, Lippman, Nesse, & Writh, 1976; Curtis, Nesse, Buxton, & Lippman, 1978). However, in a later study using this same experimental design, Nesse et al. (1985) reported significant increases in cortisol along with epinephrine and norepinephrine. These latter discrepant findings raise the possibility that the initial methods might have masked a rise in cortisol. In contrast to the extensive literature on the 24-hour cortisol secretory pattern in depressed patients, no analogous studies exist for patients with panic disorder. Baseline plasma cortisol levels, as reported in the context of other studies, have been shown in selective studies to be higher in panic patients than in normal controls (Nesse et al., 1984; Roy-Byrne, Uhde, Sack et al., 1986). In a recent study (Goldstein, Halbreich, Asnis, Edincott, & Alvir, 1987) using continual-sampling techniques, afternoon plasma cortisol levels in panic disorder patients were found to be almost identical to those of depressed patients. On the other hand, urinary-free cortisol levels in patients with panic disorder and generalized anxiety disorder were no different from those of normal controls (Uhde, Joffe et al., 1987; Rosenbaum et al.,1983).

Challenging the HPA axis with dexamethasone has shown that 40% to 60% of depressed patients do not suppress plasma cortisol levels. In contrast, the rate of nonsuppression in panic disorder patients has been found in most studies to be similar to that seen in normal controls (Curtis, Cameron, & Nesse, 1982; Sheehan et al., 1983; Roy-Byrne, Bierer, & Uhde, 1985). The corticotro-pin-releasing factor stimulation test is another challenge paradigm to test HPA function. Like depressed patients (Gold et al., 1984), panic disorder patients were shown to have a blunted ACTH response to CRF (Roy-Byrne, Uhde, Post et al., 1986). In this latter study, there was a high baseline plasma cortisol level in panic disorder patients. This suggests that the blunted ACTH response was a physiologically appropriate response to feedback inhibition. However, it is not clear if the hypercortisolemia was sustained around the 24 hours or if it was a stress response to the experimental procedure itself. Should the hypercortisolemia be part of a pathophysiological process rather than stress induced, the blunted ACTH response to CRF would reflect derangement at or above the level of the hypothalamus. Chronobiological studies might help clarify the afternoon hypercortisolemia that has been reported. Finally, these challenge paradigms (DST or CRF stimulation tests) might help differentiate among diagnostic categories of anxiety disorder—or show that they share a common pathophysiology.

Conclusion

Research into the pathophysiology of anxiety has flourished over the past two decades. However, no clear understanding of the neurobiological nature of anxiety has been achieved. We are beginning to understand that panic disorder runs a chronic-intermittent course, with marked individual variation in the frequency and distribution of panic attacks. A good percentage of patients with panic disorder have histories suggestive of separation anxiety. Dependent personality traits have been reported in agoraphobics, though it remains unclear whether specific personality disorders or traits are tightly linked to this condition as opposed to other nonpsychotic or Axis I psychiatric disorders. Stressful life events also precede the onset of panic attacks in a subpopulation of patients with panic disorder. Finally, even though adequate biological treatments are available, a high relapse rate is seen after discontinuation of treatment. Thus, an ultimate cure is not so far available, and extensive research into the molecular bases of anxiety will be required to both improve currently available pharmacotherapies and ultimately develop treatments that can correct the underlying pathology. Although there are several phenomenological categories of anxiety disorder, it is not clearly known if they can be differentiated with biological parameters. Although we know from epidemiologic studies that anxiety disorders are far more widespread than would be thought from the clinical data, only a small number of patients seek help. Do they represent a specific subgroup that differs from the rest of the population? Although most studies have included a "normal" control population, very few have reported any psychological measures in these controls or examined the likelihood of correlations between biological findings and psychological measures. Some of the negative results reported in biological studies might be a result of the fact that patients and normal controls represent a continuum on a normal distribution curve. In contrast, when there is little or no overlap in biological indices between panic disorder patients and normal controls, one might reasonably suspect that this represents a qualitative difference in the mechanisms that mediate the response under study. However, significant quantitative differences reported on some biological parameters do not necessarily indicate qualitative differences, and a parsimonious approach dictates that this be understood.

Several areas of research are still open for study. The role of some neurotransmitter systems has not been extensively studied. Recent advances in molecular biology should make those techniques available for use in anxiety research. This seems to be one of the areas in which new pharmacologic therapies might be developed should our understanding of processes on a cellular level improve. However, the serendipitous nature of science ensures the possibility of future surprises.

References

Ajlouni, K., & El-Khateeb, M. (1980). Effect of glucose on growth hormone, prolactin and thyroid stimulating hormone response to diazepam in normal subjects. *Hormone Research, 13*, 160–164.

Ballenger, J., Peterson, G., Laraia, M., Jucek, A., Lake, C., Jimerson, D., Cox, D., Trockman, C., & Wilkinson, C. (1984). A study of plasma catecholamines in agoraphobia and the relationship of serum tricyclic levels to treatment. In J. C. Ballenger (Ed.), *Biology of Agoraphobia* (pp. 27–64). Washington, DC: American Psychiatric Press.

Ballenger, J. C., Post, R. M., Jimerson, D. C., Lake, C. R., Lerner, P., Bunney, W. E., Jr., & Goodwin, F. K. (1981). Cerebrospinal fluid (CSF)-noradrenergic correlations with anxiety in normals. *Scientific Proceedings of the Annual Meeting of the American Psychiatric Association, 134*, (Abstract No. 96), 235.

Berne, R. M., Rubio, R., & Curnish, R. R. (1974). Release of adenosine from the ischaemic brain. Effect of cerebral vascular resistance and incorporation into cerebral adenine nucleotides. *Circulation Research, 35*, 262–271.

Besses, G. S., Burrow, G. N., Spaulding, S. W., Donabedian, R. K., & Pechinski, T. (1975). Dopamine infusion acutely inhibits TSH and prolactin response to TRH. *Journal of Clinical Endocrinology and Metabolism, 41*, 985–988.

Bliss, E. L., & Ailion, J. (1971). Relationship of stress and activity to brain dopamine and homovanillic acid. *Life Sciences, 10,* 1161–1169.

Boulenger, J.-P., Bierer, L. M., & Uhde, T. W. (1985). Anxiogenic effects of caffeine in normal controls and patients with panic disorder. *Biological Psychiatry, 20,* 454–456.

Boulenger, J.-P., Salem, N., Jr., Marangos, P. J., & Uhde, T. W. (1987). Plasma adenosine levels: Measurement in humans and relationship to the anxiogenic effects of caffeine. *Psychiatry Research, 21,* 247–255.

Boulenger, J.-P., & Uhde, T. W. (1982). Caffeine consumption and anxiety: Preliminary results of a survey comparing patients with anxiety disorders and normal controls. *Psychopharmacology Bulletin, 18,* 53–57.

Boulenger, J.-P., Uhde, T. W., Wolff, E. A., III, & Post, R. M. (1984). Increased sensitivity to caffeine in patients with panic disorder: Preliminary evidence. *Archives of General Psychiatry, 41,* 1067–1071.

Briley, M. S., Langer, S. Z., Raisman, R., Sechter, D., & Zarifian, E. (1980). Tritiated imipramine binding sites are decreased in platelets of untreated depressed patients. *Science, 209,* 303–305.

Cameron, O. G., Smith, C. B., Hollingsworth, P. J., Nesse, R. M., & Curtis, G. C. (1984). Platelet alpha$_2$-adrenergic receptor binding and plasma catecholamines: Before and during imipramine treatment in patients with panic anxiety. *Archives of General Psychiatry, 41,* 1144–1148.

Cannon, W. B. (1928). Neural organization for emotional expression in feelings and emotions. In M. L. Regmert (Ed.), *The Wittenberg Symposium.* Worcester, MA: Clark University Press.

Cannon, W. B. (1929). *Bodily changes in pain, hunger, fear and rage.* New York: Appleton-Century-Crofts.

Carstens, M. E., Engelbrecht, A. H., Russell, V. A., Aalbers, C., Gagiano, C. A., Chalton, D. O., & Taljaard, J. J. F. (1987). Beta-adrenoreceptors on lymphocytes of patients with major depressive disorder. *Psychiatry Research, 20,* 239–248.

Cedarbaum, J. M., & Aghajanian, G. K. (1977). Catecholamine receptors on locus coeruleus neurons: Pharmacological characterization. *European Journal of Pharmacology, 44,* 375–385.

Charney, D. S., & Heninger, G. R. (1985a). Noradrenergic function and the mechanism of action of antianxiety treatment. I. The effect of long-term alprazolam treatment. *Archives of General Psychiatry, 42,* 458–468.

Charney, D. S., & Heninger, G. R. (1985b). Noradrenergic function and the mechanism of action of antianxiety treatment. II. The effect of long-term imipramine treatment. *Archives of General Psychiatry, 42,* 473–481.

Charney, D. S., & Heninger, G. R. (1986a). Abnormal regulation of noradrenergic function in panic disorder: Effects of clonidine in healthy subjects and patients with agoraphobia and panic disorder. *Archives of General Psychiatry, 43,* 1042–1054.

Charney, D. S., & Heninger, G. R. (1986b). Serotonin function in panic disorder: The effect of intravenous tryptophan in healthy subjects and patients with panic disorder before and during alprazolam treatment. *Archives of General Psychiatry, 43,* 1059–1065.

Charney, D. S., Heninger, G. R., & Jatlow, P. I. (1985). Increased anxiogenic effects of caffeine in panic disorders. *Archives of General Psychiatry, 42,* 233–243.

Charney, D. S., Heninger, G. R., & Redmond, D. E., Jr. (1983). Yohimbine-induced anxiety and increased noradrenergic function in humans: Effects of diazepam and clonidine. *Life Sciences, 33,* 19–29.

Charney, D. S., Woods, S. W., Goodman, W. K., & Heninger, G. R. (1987). Serotonin function in anxiety. II. Effects of the serotonin agonist mCPP in panic disorder patients and healthy subjects. *Psychopharmacology, 92,* 14–24.

Clark, T. K. (1979). The locus coeruleus in behavior regulation: Evidence for behavioral-specific versus general involvement. *Behavioral and Neural Biology, 25,* 271–300.

Cooper, J. R., Bloom, F. E., & Roth, R. H. (1986). *The biochemical basis of neuropharmacology* (5th ed.). New York/Oxford: Oxford University Press.

Corrodi, H., Fuxe, K., Lidbrink, P., & Olson, L. (1971). Minor tranquilizers, stress, and central catecholamine neurons. *Brain Research, 29,* 1–16.

Crawley, J. N., Patel, J., & Marangos, P. J. (1981). Behavioral characterization of two long-lasting adenosine analogs: Sedative properties and interaction with diazepam. *Life Sciences, 29,* 2623–2630.

Crawley, J. N., Patel, J., & Marangos, P. J. (1983). Adenosine uptake inhibitors potentiate the sedative effects of adenosine. *Neuroscience Letters, 36,* 169–174.

Creese, I. (1987). Biochemical properties of CNS dopamine receptors. In H. Y. Meltzer (Ed.), *Psychopharmacology: The third generation of progress* (pp. 257–264). New York: Raven Press.

Curtis, G. C., Buxton, M., Lippman, D., Nesse, R., & Writh, J. (1976). Flooding *in vivo* during the circadian phase of minimal cortisol secretion: Anxiety and therapeutic success without adrenal cortical activation. *Biological Psychiatry, 11,* 101–107.

Curtis, G. C., Cameron, O. G., & Nesse, R. M. (1982). The dexamethasone suppression test in panic disorder and agoraphobia. *American Journal of Psychiatry, 139,* 1043–1046.

Curtis, G. C., Nesse, R. M., Buxton, M., & Lippman, D. (1978). Anxiety and plasma cortisol at the crest of the circadian cycle: Reappraisal of a classical hypothesis. *Psychosomatic Medicine, 40,* 368–378.

Dahlström, A., & Fuxe, K. (1964). Evidence for the existence of monoamine-containing neurons in the central nervous system. I. Demonstration of monoamines in the cell bodies on brain stem neurons. *Acta Physiologica Scandinavica, 62*(Suppl. 232), 1–55.

Davies, A. O., & Lefkowitz, R. J. (1980). Corticosteriod-induced differential regulation of beta-adrenergic receptors in circulating human polymorphonuclear leukocytes and mononuclear leukocytes. *Journal of Clinical Endocrinology and Metabolism, 51,* 599–605.

Deutch, A. Y., Tam, S. Y., & Roth, R. H. (1985). Footshock and conditioned stress increases 3,4-dihydroxyphenylacetic acid (DOPAC) in the ventral tegmental area but not substantia nigra. *Brain Research, 333,* 143–146.

Edlund, M. J., Swann, A. C., & Davis, C. M. (1987). Plasma MHPG in untreated panic disorder. *Biological Psychiatry, 22,* 1488–1491.

Elsworth, J. D., Redmond, D. E., Jr., & Roth, R. H. (1982). Plasma and cerebrospinal fluid 3-methoxy-4-hydroxyphenylethylene glycol (MHPG) as indices of brain norepinephrine metabolism in primates. *Brain Research, 235,* 115–124.

Extein, I., Tallman, J., Smith, C. C., & Goodwin, F. K. (1979). Changes in lymphocyte beta-adrenergic receptors in depression and mania. *Psychiatry Research, 1,* 191–197.

Foote, S. L., Bloom, S. L., & Aston-Jones, G. (1983). Nucleus locus coeruleus: New evidence of anatomical and physiological specificity. *Physiological Reviews, 63,* 844–914.

Frankenhauser, M. L. (1971). Behavior and circulating catecholamines. *Brain Research, 31,* 241–262.

Frankenhauser, M. L., Dunn, E., & Lundberg, U. (1976). Sex differences in sympathetic-adrenal medullary reactions induced by different stressors. *Psychopharmacology, 47,* 1–5.

Ganon, W. F. (1977). Neurotransmitters involved in ACTH secretion: Catecholamines. In D. T. Krieger & W. F. Ganon (Eds.), *ACTH and related peptides: Structure, regulation and action.* Annals of the New York Academy of Sciences, *297,* 509–517.

García-Sevilla, J. A., Hollingsworth, P. J., & Smith, C. B. (1981). Alpha$_2$-adrenoreceptors on human platelets: Selective labeling by [^{3}-H]-clonidine and [^{3}H]-yohimbine and competitive inhibition by antidepressant drugs. *European Journal of Pharmacology, 74,* 329–341.

García-Sevilla, J. A., Zis, A. P., Hollingsworth, P. J., Greden, J. F., & Smith, C. B. (1981). Platelet alpha$_2$-adrenergic receptors in major depressive disorder: Binding of tritiated clonidine before and after tricyclic antidepressant drug treatment. *Archives of General Psychiatry, 38,* 1327–1333.

García-Sevilla, J. A., Zis, A. P., Zelnick, T. C., & Smith, C. B. (1981). Tricyclic antidepressant drug treatment decreases alpha$_2$-adrenoreceptors on human platelet membranes. *European Journal of Pharmacology, 69,* 121–123.

Gee, K. W., & Yamamura, H. I. (1983). Benzodiazepine receptor heterogeneity: A consequence of multiple conformational states of a single receptor or multiple population of structurally distinct macromolecules? In E. Usdin, P. Skolnick, J. F. Tallman, Jr., D. Greenblatt, & S. M. Paul (Eds.), *Pharmacology of benzodiazepines* (pp. 93–108). Basel, Switzerland: Verlag Chemie.

Geller, I., & Blum, K. (1970). The effects of 5HT on parachlorophenylalanine (PCPA) attenuation of "conflict" behavior. *European Journal of Pharmacology, 9,* 319–324.

Gold, P. W., Chrousos, G., Kellner, C., Post, R., Roy, A., Avgerinos, P., Schulte, H., Oldfield, E., & Loriaux, D. L. (1984). Psychiatric implications of basic and clinical studies with corticotropin-releasing factor. *American Journal of Psychiatry, 141,* 619–627.

Gold, P. W., Goodwin, F. K., Wehr, T., & Rebar, R. (1977). Pituitary thyrotropin response to thyrotropin-releasing hormone in affective illness: Relationship to spinal fluid amine metabolites. *American Journal of Psychiatry, 134,* 1028–1031.

Goldberg, M. E., & Salama, A. I. (1970). Relationship of brain dopamine to stress-induced changes in seizure susceptibility. *European Journal of Pharmacology, 10,* 333–338.

Goldberg, M. R., & Robertson, D. (1983). Yohimbine: A pharmacological probe for study of the alpha$_2$-adrenoreceptor. *Pharmacological Reviews, 35,* 143–180.

Goldstein, S., Halbreich, U., Asnis, G., Edincott, J., & Alvir, J. (1987). The hypothalamic-pituitary-adrenal system in panic disorder. *American Journal of Psychiatry, 144,* 1320–1323.

Greden, J. F. (1974). Anxiety or caffeinism: A diagnostic dilemma. *American Journal of Psychiatry, 131,* 1089–1092.

Greden, J. F., Fontaine, P., Lubetsky, M., & Chamberlin, K. (1978). Anxiety and depression associated with caffeinism among psychiatric inpatients. *American Journal of Psychiatry, 135,* 963–966.

Greden, J. F., Proctor, A., & Victor, B. (1981). Caffeinism associated with greater use of other psychotropic agents. *Comprehensive Psychiatry, 22,* 565–571.

Greenblatt, D. J., Shader, R. I., & Abernethy, D. R. (1983a). Drug therapy: Current status of benzodiazepines. I. *New England Journal of Medicine, 309,* 354–358.

Greenblatt, D. J., Shader, R. I., & Abernethy, D. R. (1983b). Drug therapy: Current status of benzodiazepines. II. *New England Journal of Medicine 309*, 410–416.

Gurguis, G., & Uhde, T. W. (1988). *Baseline plasma MHPG, HVA and 5-HIAA levels in panic disorder patients: Relationship to HPA function.* Paper presented at the meeting of the Society of Biological Psychiatry, Montreal, Canada.

Haefley, W. (1983). The biological basis of benzodiazepine actions. *Journal of Psychoactive Drugs, 15*, 19–39.

Herman, S. P., Guilonneau, D., Dantzer, R., Scatton, B., Semerdjian-Rieuquier, L., & Le Moal, M. (1982). Differential effects of inescapable footshocks and of stimuli previously paired with inescapable footshocks on dopamine turnover in cortical and limbic areas of the rat. *Life Sciences, 30*, 2207–2214.

Innis, R. B., Charney, D. S., & Heninger, G. R. (1987). Differential ^{3}H-imipramine platelet binding in patients with panic disorder and depression. *Psychiatry Research, 21*, 33–41.

Insel, T. R., & Murphy, D. L. (1981). The psychopharmacological treatment of obsessive compulsive disorder: A review. *Journal of Clinical Psychopharmacology, 1*, 304–311.

Insel, T. R., Murphy, D. L., Cohen, R. M., Alterman, I., Kilts, C., & Linnoila, M. (1983). Obsessive compulsive disorder: A double-blind trial of clomipramine and clorgyline. *Archives of General Psychiatry, 40*, 605–612.

Insel, T. R., Ninan, P. T., Aloi, J., Jimerson, D. C., Skolnick, P., & Paul, S. M. (1984). A benzodiazepine receptor-mediated model of anxiety: studies in nonhuman primates and clinical implications. *Archives of General Psychiatry, 41*, 741–750.

James, W. (1884). *Mind, 9*, 188–205.

James, W. (1890). *The principles of psychology.* New York: Holt, Rinehart & Winston.

Janowsky, A., & Sulser, F. (1987). Alpha and beta adrenoreceptors in the brain. In H. Y. Meltzer (Ed.), *Psychopharmacology: The third generation of progress* (pp. 249–256). New York: Raven Press.

Jimerson, D. C., Ballenger, J. C., Lake, C. R., Post, R. M., & Goodwin, F. K. (1981). Plasma and CSF MHPG in normals. *Psychopharmacology Bulletin, 17*, 86–87.

Kandel, E. R. (1983). From metapsychology to molecular biology: Explorations into the nature of anxiety. *American Journal of Psychiatry, 140*, 1277–1293.

Klein, D. F. (1964). Delineation of two drug-responsive anxiety syndromes. *Psychopharmacologia, 5*, 397–408.

Klein, D. F. (1981). Anxiety reconceptualized. In D. F. Klein & J. Rabkin (Eds.), *Anxiety: New research and changing concepts* (pp. 235–263). New York: Raven Press.

Klein, D. F., Rabkin, J. G., & Gorman, J. M. (1985). Etiological and pathophysiological inferences from the pharmacological treatment of anxiety. In A. H. Tuma & J. D. Maser (Eds.), *Anxiety and the anxiety disorders* (pp. 501–532). Hillsdale, NJ: Lawrence Erlbaum.

Klein, E., Marangos, P. J., Montgomery, P., Bacher, J., & Uhde, T. W. (1987). Adenosine receptor alteration in nervous pointer dogs: A preliminary report. *Clinical Neuropharmacology, 10*, 462–469.

Klein, E., & Uhde, T. W. (1988). Controlled study of verapamil for treatment of panic disorder. *American Journal of Psychiatry, 145*, 431–434.

Klein, E., Zohar, J., Geraci, M. F., Murphy, D. L., & Uhde, T. W. (1987). *Anxiogenic effects of mCPP in patients with panic disorder: Comparison to caffeine's anxiogenic effects.* Unpublished manuscript.

Ko, G. N., Elsworth, J. D., Roth, R. H., Rifkin, B. G., Leigh, H., & Redmond, D. E., Jr. (1983). Panic induced elevation of plasma MHPG levels in phobic-anxious patients. *Archives of General Psychiatry, 40,* 425–430.

Kopin, I. J. (1984). Avenues of investigation for the role of catecholamines in anxiety. *Psychopathology, 17,* 88–97.

Koulo, M., Aaltonen, L., & Kanto, J. (1982). The effect of oral flunitrazepam on secretion of human growth hormone. *Acta Pharmacologica et Toxiocologica, 50,* 316–317.

Koulo, M., Lammintausta, R., Kanges, L., & Dahlstrom, S. (1979). Effect of methysergide, pimozide and sodium valproate on the diazepam-stimulated growth hormone secretion in man. *Journal of Clinical Endocrinology and Metabolism, 48,* 119–122.

Lewis, D. A., Noyes, R., Jr., Coryell, W., & Clancy, J. (1985). Tritiated imipramine binding in patients with agoraphobia. *Psychiatry Research, 16,* 1–9.

Lidbrink, P., Corrodi, H., Fuxe, K., & Olson, L. (1972). Barbiturates and meprobamate: Decreases in catecholamine turnover of central dopamine and noradrenaline neuronal systems and the influence of immobilization stress. *Brain Research, 45,* 507–524.

Maas, J. W., Hattox, S. E., Greene, N. M., & Landis, D. H. (1979). 3-Methoxy-4-hydroxy phenylethylene glycol production by human brain *in vivo. Science, 205,* 1025–1027.

Maj, J. (1984). Mechanism of action of antidepressant drugs given repeatedly: Changes in responses mediated by noradrenaline (alpha1) and dopamine receptors (pp. 137–143). MacMillan Press.

Mann, J. J., Brown, R. P., Halper, J. P., Sweeney, J. A., Kocsis, J. H., Stokes, P. E., & Bilezikian, J. P. (1985). Reduced sensitivity of lymphocyte beta-adrenergic receptors in patients with endogenous depression and psychomotor agitation. *New England Journal of Medicine, 313,* 715–719.

Mann, J. J., Brown, R. P., Sweeney, J. A., Stokes, P. E., Kocsis, J. H., McBride, P. A., & Willner, P. J. (1986 December). *State dependent dysregulation of beta-adrenergic responsivity in endogenous depression.* Paper presented at the American College of Neuropsychopharmacology Meeting, Washington, DC.

Marangos, P. J., & Boulenger, J.-P. (1985). Basic and clinical aspects of adenosinergic neuromodulation. *Neuroscience and Biobehavioral Reviews, 9,* 421–430.

Marangos, P. J., Insel, T. R., Montgomery, P., & Tamborska, E. (1987). Brain adenosine receptors in Maudsley reactive and non-reactive rats. *Brain Research, 421,* 69–74.

Mason, J. W. (1968). A review of psychoendocrine research on the sympathetic-adrenal medullary system. *Psychosomatic Medicine, 30,* 631–653.

Mathew, J. F., Stolk, J. M., Peter, O. H., & Cooper, T. B. (1984). Serum dopamine-beta-hydroxylase activity in depression and anxiety. *Biological Psychiatry, 19,* 557–570.

Mathew, R. J., Ho, B. T., Kralik, P., Taylor, D., & Claghorn, J. L. (1980). MAO, DBH and COMT: The effect of anxiety. *Journal of Clinical Psychiatry, 41,* 25–28.

Mellman, T. A., & Uhde, T. W. (1987). Obsessive-compulsive symptoms in panic disorder. *American Journal of Psychiatry, 144,* 1573–1576.

Mezey, E., Kiss, J. Z., Skirboll, L. R., Goldstein, M., & Axelrod, J. (1984). Increase of corticotropin-releasing factor staining in rat paraventricular nucleus neurons by depletion of hypothalamic adrenaline. *Nature, 310,* 140–141.

Mueller, E. A., Murphy, D. L., & Sunderland, T. (1985). Neuroendocrine effects of m-chlorophenylpiperazine, a serotonin agonist in humans. *Journal of Clinical Endocrinology and Metabolism, 61,* 1–6.

Nesse, R. M., Cameron, O. G., Curtis, G. C., McCann, D. S., & Huber-Smith, M. J. (1984). Adrenergic functions in patients with panic anxiety. *Archives of General Psychiatry, 41*, 771–776.

Nesse, R. M., Curtis, G. C., Thyer, B. A., McCann, D. S., Huber-Smith, M., & Knopf, R. F. (1985). Endocrine and cardiovascular responses during phobic anxiety. *Psychosomatics, 47*, 320–332.

Patel, J., & Marangos, P. J. (1984). Adenosine: Its action and sites of action in the CNS. In P. Marangos, I. Campbell, & R. Cohen (Eds.), *Brain receptor methodologies, Part B* (pp. 297–325). New York: Academic Press.

Paul, S. M., Rehavi, M., Rice, K. C., Ittah, Y., & Skolnick, P. (1980). Does high affinity [^{3}H] imipramine binding label serotonin reuptake sites in brain and platelet? *Life Science, 28*, 2753–2760.

Paul, S. M., Rehavi, M., Skolnick, P., Ballenger, J. C., & Goodwin, F. K. (1981). Depressed patients have decreased binding of tritiated imipramine to platelet serotonin "transporter." *Archives of General Psychiatry, 38*, 1315–1317.

Paul, S. M., Rehavi, M., Skolnick, P., & Goodwin, F. K. (1980). Demonstration of specific "high affinity" binding sites for [^{3}H] imipramine on human platelets. *Life Sciences, 26*, 953–959.

Paul, S. M., & Skolnick, P. (1981). Benzodiazepine receptors and psychopathological states: Towards a neurobiology of anxiety. In D. F. Klein & J. Rabkin (Eds.), *Anxiety: New research and changing concepts.* New York: Raven Press.

Perotka, S. (1987). Serotonin receptors. In H. Y. Meltzer (Ed.), *Psychopharmacology: The third generation of progress* (pp. 303–311). New York: Raven Press.

Phillis, J. W., & Wu, P. H. (1981). The role of adenosine and its nucleotides in central synaptic transmission. *Progress in Neurobiology, 16*, 184–239.

Pieribone, V. A., Aston-Jones, G., & Bohn, M. C. (1988). Adrenergic and non-adrenergic neurons in the C1 and C3 areas project to locus coeruleus: A fluorescent double labeling study. *Neuroscience Letters, 85*, 297–303.

Pitts, F. N., Jr., & McClure, J. N., Jr. (1967). Lactate metabolism in anxiety neurosis. *New England Journal of Medicine, 277*, 1329–1336.

Post, R. M., Jimerson, D. C., Ballenger, J. C., Goodwin, F. K., Lake, C. R., Uhde, T. W., & Bunney, W. E., Jr. (1981). Amine research: Relationship of norepinephrine and its metabolites to mood in normal volunteers and depressed patients. In C. Perris, G. Struwe, & B. Jansson (Eds.), *Biological psychiatry, 1981* (pp. 561–564). Amsterdam: Elsevier.

Prasad, A. (1984). A double-blind study of imipramine versus zimelidine in treatment of obsessive-compulsive neurosis. *Pharmacopsychiatry, 17*, 61–62.

Raisman, R., Sechter, D., Briley, M. S., Zarifian, E., & Langer, S. Z. (1981). High-affinity ^{3}H-imipramine binding in platelets from untreated and treated depressed patients compared to healthy volunteers. *Psychopharmacology, 75*, 368–371.

Redmond, D. E., Jr. (1979). New and old evidence for the involvement of a brain norepinephrine system in anxiety. In W. E. Fann, I. Karakan, A. D. Porkorny, & R. L. Williams (Eds.), *Phenomenology and treatment of anxiety* (pp. 153–203). New York: Spectrum.

Redmond, D. E., Jr. (1987). Studies of the nucleus locus coeruleus in monkeys and hypotheses for neuropsychopharmacology. In H. Y. Meltzer (Ed.), *Psychopharmacology: A third generation of progress* (pp. 967–975). New York: Raven Press.

Rehavi, M., Paul, S. M., Skolnick, P., & Goodwin, F. K. (1980). Demonstration of specific high affinity binding sites for [^{3}] imipramine in human brain. *Life Sciences, 26,* 2273–2279.

Robertson, H. A., Martin, J. L., & Candy, J. M. (1978). Differences in the benzodiazepine receptor binding in Maudsley reactive and Maudsley non-reactive rats. *European Journal of Pharmacology, 50,* 455–457.

Rose, R. M. (1980). Endocrine responses to stressful psychological events. *Psychiatric Clinics of North America, 3,* 251–276.

Rosenbaum, A. H., Schatzberg, A. F., Jost, F. A., III, Cross, P. D., Wells, L. A., Jiang, N. S., & Maruta, T. (1983). Urinary free cortisol levels in anxiety. *Psychosomatics, 24,* 835–837.

Roth, K. A., Katz, R. J., Sibel, M., Mefford, I. N., Barchas, J. D., & Carroll, B. J. (1981). Central epinergic inhibition of corticosterone release in rat. *Life Sciences, 28*(21), 2389–2394.

Roth, R. H., & Tam, S. Y. (1985). Selective increase in dopamine metabolism in the prefrontal cortex by the anxiogenic beta-carboline FG7142. *Biochemical Pharmacology, 34,* 1595–1598.

Roy-Byrne, P. P., Bierer, L. M., & Uhde, T. W. (1985). The dexamethasone suppression test in panic disorder: Comparison with normal controls. *Biological Psychiatry, 20,* 1237–1240.

Roy-Byrne, P. P., Uhde, T. W., Post, R. M., Gallucci, W., Chrousos, G. H., & Gold, P. W. (1986). The corticotropin-releasing hormone stimulation test in patients with panic disorder. *American Journal of Psychiatry, 143,* 896–899.

Roy-Byrne, P. P., Uhde, T. W., Sack, D., Linnoila, M., & Post, R. M. (1986). Plasma HVA and anxiety in patients with panic disorder. *Biological Psychiatry, 21,* 849–853.

Schatzberg, A. F., & Cole, J. O. (1978). Benzodiazepines in depressive disorders. *Archives of General Psychiatry, 35,* 1359–1365.

Senkowski, C. K., Gurguis, G., Spengler, R. N., & Smith, C. B. (1986). *Presynaptic alpha2-adrenergic receptor function after chronic alprazolam treatment.* Paper presented at the meeting of the American Society for Pharmacology and Experiential Therapeutics.

Sethy, V. H., & Hodges, D. H., Jr. (1982). Role of beta-adrenergic receptors in the antidepressant activity of alprazolam. *Research Communications in Chemical Pathology and Pharmacology, 36,* 329–332.

Seyle, H. (1950). *Stress: The physiology and pathology of exposure to stress.* Montreal: Acta.

Sheehan, D. V., Claycomb, J. B., Surman, O. S., Baer, L., Coleman, J., & Gelles, L. (1983). Panic attacks and the dexamethasone suppression test. *American Journal of Psychiatry, 140,* 1063–1064.

Shulman, R., Griffith, J., & Diewold, P. (1978). Catechol-o-methyl transferase activity in patients with depressive illness and anxiety states. *British Journal of Psychiatry, 132,* 133–138.

Shur, E., Petursson, H., Checkley, S., & Lader, M. (1983). Long-term benzodiazepine administration blunts growth hormone response to diazepam. *Archives of General Psychiatry, 40,* 1105–1108.

Siever, L. J., Insel, T. R., Jimerson, D. C., Lake, C. R., Uhde, T. W., Aloi, J., & Murphy, D. L. (1983). Growth hormone response to clonidine in obsessive-compulsive patients. *British Journal of Psychiatry, 142,* 184–187.

Siever, L. J., & Uhde, T. W. (1984). New studies and perspectives on the non-adrenergic receptor system in depression: Effects of the alpha2-adrenergic agonist clonidine. *Biological Psychiatry, 19,* 131–156.

Smith, C. B., García-Sevilla, J. A., & Hollingsworth, P. J. (1981). Alpha2-adrenoreceptors in rat brain are decreased after long-term tricyclic antidepressant drug treatment. *Brain Research, 210,* 413–418.

Snyder, S. H. (1985). Adenosine as a neuromodulator. *Annual Review of Neuroscience, 8,* 103–124.

Snyder, S. H., Katim, J. J., Annau, Z., Bruns, R. F., & Daly, J. W. (1981). Adenosine receptors and behavioral actions of methylxanthines. *Proceeding of the National Academy of Sciences of the United States of America, 78,* 3260–3264.

Starkman, M. N., Cameron, O. G., Nesse, R. M., & Zelnick, T. C. (1985). A study of anxiety in patients with pheochromocytoma. *Archives of Internal Medicine, 145,* 248–252.

Starkman, M. N., Cameron, O. G., Nesse, R. M., & Zelnick, T. C. (1987). *Catecholamine levels and symptoms of anxiety.* Paper presented at the Annual Meeting of the Society of Biological Psychiatry (Abstract No. 112).

Stein, L. (1981). Behavioral pharmacology of benzodiazepines. In D. F. Klein, & J. Rabkin (Eds.), *Anxiety: New research and changing concepts* (pp. 201–213). New York: Raven Press.

Stein, L. (1983). Benzodiazepines and behavioral disinhibition. In E. Usdin, P. Skolnick, J. F. Tallman, Jr., D. Greenblatt, & S. M. Paul (Eds.), *Pharmacology of benzodiazepines* (pp. 383–390). Basel, Switzerland: Verlag Chemie.

Stein, L., Wise, C. D., & Belluzzi, J. D. (1975). Effects of benzodiazepines on central serotonergic mechanisms. In E. Costa, & P. Greengard (Eds.), *Mechanism of action of benzodiazepines* (pp. 29–44). New York: Raven Press.

Stein, M. B., & Uhde, T. W. (1988). The cortisol response to clonidine in panic disorder: Comparison with depressed patients and normal controls. *Biological Psychiatry, 24,* 320–330.

Sternberg, D. E., Heninger, G. R., & Roth, R. H. (1983). Plasma homovanillic acid as an index of brain dopamine metabolism: Enhancement with debriquin. *Life Sciences, 32,* 2447–2452.

Taylor, K. M., & Laverty, R. (1969). The effect of chlordiazepoxide, diazepam, and nitrazepam on catecholamine metabolism in regions of the rat brain. *European Journal of Pharmacology, 8,* 296–301.

Thierry, M. A., Javoy, F., Glowinski, J., & Kety, S. S. (1968). Effects of stress on the metabolism of norepinephrine, dopamine and serotonin in the central nervous system of the rat. I. Modification of norephinephrine turnover. *Journal of Pharmacology and Experimental Therapeutics, 163,* 163–171.

Thoren, P., Asberg, M., Bertilsson, L., Mellstrom, B., Sjoqvist, F., & Traskman, L. (1980). Clomipramine treatment of obsessive-compulsive disorder. II. Biochemical aspects. *Archives of General Psychiatry, 37,* 1289–1294.

Thoren, P., Asberg, M., Cronholm, B., Jornestedt, L., & Traskman, L. (1980). Clomipramine treatment of obsessive-compulsive disorder. I. A controlled clinical trial. *Archives of General Psychiatry, 37,* 1281–1285.

Ticku, M. K. (1983). Benzodiazepine-GABA receptor-ionophore complex. *Neuropharmacology, 22,* 1459–1470.

Uhde, T. W. (1986, December). *Animal models of anxiety.* Paper presented at the American College of Neuropsychopharmacology Meeting, Washington, DC.

Uhde, T. W. (1988). Caffeine-induced panic: A modern tool for an ancient drug. In J. C. Ballenger (Ed.), *Neurobiological aspects of panic disorder*. New York: Alan R. Liss.

Uhde, T. W., Berrettini, W. H., Roy-Byrne, P. P., Boulenger, J.-P., & Post, R. M. (1987). Platelet [^{3}H] imipramine binding in patients with panic disorder. *Biological Psychiatry, 22*, 52–58.

Uhde, T. W., Bierer, L. M., & Post, R. M. (1985). Caffeine-induced escape from dexamethasone suppression. *Archives of General Psychiatry, 42*, 737–738.

Uhde, T. W., Boulenger, J.-P., Jimerson, D. C., & Post, R. M. (1984). Caffeine: Relationship to human anxiety, plasma MHPG and cortisol. *Psychopharmacology Bulletin, 20*, 426–430.

Uhde, T. W., Boulenger, J.-P., Post, R. M., Siever, L. J., Vittone, B. J., Jimerson, D. C., & Roy-Byrne, P. P. (1984). Fear and anxiety: Relationship to noradrenergic function. *Psychopathology, 17*, 8–23.

Uhde, T. W., Joffe, R. T., Jimerson, D. C., & Post, R. M. (1988). Normal urinary free cortisol and plasma MHPG in panic disorder: Clinical and theoretical implications. *Biological Psychiatry, 23*, 565–585.

Uhde, T. W., Post, R. M, Siever, L., Buchsbaum, M. S., Jimerson, D. C., Silberman, E. K., Murphy, D. L., & Bunney, W. E., Jr. (1981). Clonidine: Effects on mood, anxiety and pain. *Psychopharmacology Bulletin, 17*, 125–126.

Uhde, T. W., Roy-Byrne, P. P., Vittone, B. J., Boulenger, J.-P., & Post, R. M. (1985). Phenomenology and neurobiology of panic disorder. In A. H. Tuma & J. D. Maser (Eds.), *Anxiety and the anxiety disorders* (pp. 557–576). Hillsdale, NJ: Lawrence Erlbaum.

Uhde, T. W., & Tancer, M. E. (1988). Chemical models of panic: A review and critique. In P. Tyrer (Ed.), *Psychopharmacology of anxiety* (pp. 110–131). London: Oxford University Press.

Uhde, T. W., Vittone, B. J., Siever, L. J., Kaye, W. H., & Post, R. M. (1986). Blunted growth hormone response to clonidine in panic disorder patients. *Biological Psychiatry, 21*, 1077–1081.

Van der Maelen, C. P., & Wilderman, R. C. (1984). Iontophoretic and systemic administration of the non-benzodiazepine anxiolytic drug buspirone causes inhibition of serotonergic dorsal raphe neurons in rats. *Federation Proceedings, 43*, 947.

Wagner, A., Aberg-Wistedt, A., Asberg, M., Ekquist, B., Martensson, B., & Montero, D. (1985). Lower ^{3}H-imipramine binding in platelets from untreated depressed patients compared to healthy controls. *Psychiatry Research, 16*, 131–139.

Wise, D. C., Berger, B. D., & Stein, L. (1973). Evidence of alpha-noradrenergic reward receptors and serotonergic punishment receptors in rat brain. *Biological Psychiatry, 6*, 3–21.

CHAPTER 14

A
Forward Look:
Psychosocial Perspectives

RICHARD HALLAM

The most casual observer of the recent flood of articles and books on panic disorder could not fail to get the impression that a new era of research into anxiety problems has begun. The impetus has come from a recognition of the importance of panic episodes in the development of anxiety complaints—a recognition rooted in biological hypotheses and fed by the promise of new pharmacologic remedies. The current research effort will undoubtedly take us farther than we have traveled before, whether the direction be biological, psychosocial, or more realistically, both. In this chapter we'll comment on and critique the principal methodological approaches of psychosocial research on panic. The object is not to review the empirical evidence for different psychosocial perspectives on panic but rather to point to potentially fruitful lines of enquiry.

It seems wise to begin a forward look by taking note of the growing points from which current developments have proceeded. We will therefore open with a brief historical account of the concept of panic episodes and of the American Psychiatric Association's adoption of panic disorder as a type of anxiety disorder in its *Diagnostic and Statistical Manual of Mental Disorders* (DSM-III and DSM-III-R) (APA, 1980, 1987). The classification of psychological problems and their scientific investigation go hand-in-hand, so the adequacy of psychiatric diagnostic criteria as a foundation for psychosocial research deserves extensive discussion. For example, psychiatric taxonomies define disorders that are assumed to differ in some important way. However, what is "important" depends on one's theoretical perspective, and some psychosocial anxiety theorists would not accept that panic disorder represents a qualitatively different type of anxiety complaint. It is one thing, they might argue, to concede that panic complaints have distinctive antecedents and phenomenology and another to argue that these are of theoretical significance and to demand a separate causal explanation for panic. The view taken on this issue determines whether research carried out using a different taxonomic framework (for example, one that considers panic and anxiety to be on the same dimension) has any relevance to the explanation of panic complaints defined according to the APA criteria.

In this chapter we will be confined in the main to research conducted within the contemporary North American psychiatric nosology. The term *panic-anxiety* will be used to refer to a cluster of complaints that have been extracted from checklists and structured interviews by factor analytic techniques and that bear an obvious similarity to the DSM-III-R definition of panic disorder (Hallam, 1985). Naming a cluster of statistically associated complaints is not equivalent, however, to naming a disorder. In the former case, it should not be assumed that the cluster is the external manifestation of an essential underlying process. Statistical associations can arise on the basis of processes that hold little theoretical interest. The cluster is therefore a point of departure for further taxonomic efforts and not an end in itself.

Notwithstanding all the cautions of scientific researchers, the clinical reality and etiological significance of panic episodes would probably find widespread agreement among practitioners. Panic episodes often seem to signal the onset of a family of problems that become gradually more debilitating (Breier, Charney, & Heninger, 1986; Uhde et al., 1985). This condition is associated with the fearful avoidance of public places and dependence on substances that have a calming effect (Bibb & Chambless, 1986; Stockwell, Smail, Hodgson, & Canter, 1983). It is on this presentation of complaints and their clinical course that we wish to take a psychosocial perspective. Of course the clinical picture, which probably presents somewhat differently in medical and psychiatric contexts (Katon, Vitaliano, Russo, Jones, & Anderson, 1987), is rarely observed in its early stages of development. The later presentation represents an accretion of processes such as the client's attempts to understand the causes of anomalous sensations; labeling of the problem by the client and others; the results, successful or otherwise, of coping efforts; and the interaction of the problem with family and work relationships. The matured cluster of complaints represents a complex interaction of psychological and social processes occurring over many years. From a psychosocial perspective, this cluster is multifactorial in terms of both the number of systems involved (biological, psychological, social) and the number of possible explanations of the final common pathway: panic-anxiety. So it is probably unreasonable to seek an account of the severity of the presenting complaints by means of just a few interrelated processes. An alternative model of severity would see this as the cumulative effect of a variety of predisposing traits, social disadvantages, and current existential circumstances. These might include inherited traits, tendency to depressed mood, and satisfaction with work or personal relationships.

In light of these considerations, there are a multiplicity of psychosocial perspectives on different "clinical features" of the psychiatrically defined condition. Causes and consequences of particular features—such as the coping strategy of staying at home—are difficult to disentangle from preexisting personality predispositions, from patterns of marital interaction, and from the theorist's stereotypic views of the female role (Hallam, 1983). What makes panic-anxiety so interesting are "panic attacks" appearing seemingly from out of the blue in persons who may regard themselves as lacking neurotic traits and who cannot understand what has happened to them. It is this illnesslike feature that is so enticing to the biomedical researcher. Moreover, as noted above, the importance of the panic episode is suggested by the fact that it may herald a disabling condition. I will therefore put most emphasis on panic episodes in this chapter and only briefly touch on the ensuing impact on mobility, marital relationships, and related factors that are dealt with elsewhere in this book (see Chapters 5, 7, and 12).

There are good reasons for adopting the hypothesis that there are no sharp discontinuities between infrequent, mild paniclike phenomena and panic disorder. Norton and his colleagues have documented the high prevalence of panic episodes in the general population. Approximately 35% of extension course students had experienced one or more panic attacks, cued or uncued, within the previous year (Norton, Harrison, Hauch, & Rhodes, 1985). As these authors note, the similarity between people who panic infrequently and psychiatrically diagnosed subjects makes them an excellent subject pool in which to study panic attack mechanisms. One might add that these subjects are less likely to be influenced by possibly extraneous factors contributing to severity and psychiatric status. For example, individuals who panic and are also unhappy in their relationships or who are subject to depressed moods are more likely to seek psychiatric help.

A satisfactory structure for a chapter of this kind is difficult to devise. Following our discussion of classification issues, we will discuss methods of investigating (1) distal antecedents (that is, events antedating the initial panic episode), (2) proximal antecedents (that is, events occurring within minutes or days of an episode or accounting for longer-term temporal fluctuations), and (3) general psychosocial correlates of panic complaints such as social class and personality. We will conclude by commenting on psychosocial models of panic.

Recent History and Current Status of the Panic Concept

In the last 20 years there has been a major realignment of psychiatric thinking about the classification of anxiety disorders. The outmoded concept of anxiety neurosis, defined negatively as "nonelicited" (generalized and free-floating) anxiety has been replaced by a positive conception of nonelicited anxiety in the form of the panic attack. Klein (1964, 1981) was the prime mover in this shift of opinion. He argued that panic attacks were a type of anxiety that responded to antidepressant medication, and that this type of anxiety was mediated by a discrete biological mechanism. According to this view, some elicited anxieties such as fears of public places were said to arise as secondary consequences of unpredictably occurring panic attacks. Moreover, some forms of generalized anxiety complaint were conceptualized as a response to the threat of a panic attack ("fear of fear") rather than to the threat posed by an external danger or other external cause. As is well known, this conceptualization has led to the incorporation of panic disorder into the DSM-III and DSM-III-R.

The impetus that the concept of panic has given to anxiety research has not resulted entirely from biological hypotheses of the origins of panic attacks, however. Clinical and statistical descriptions of anxiety complaints have also helped single out the importance of panic episodes and their association with fears of public places (Arrindell, 1980; Goldstein & Chambless, 1978; Hallam, 1978). If, as now seems likely, the history of some anxiety complaints begins with an episode (or series of episodes) of panic or paniclike phenomena, developing into more severe and generalized distress, then we have good reason to pay more attention to panic. The promise of a satisfactory biological account of panic is so far unfulfilled (Margraf, Ehlers, & Roth, 1986), and we have no good reason for discounting the possibility that psychosocial models will ultimately provide the most convincing explanation of panic-anxiety and its clinical course.

However, given the intellectual origins of the panic disorder concept, it is not surprising that biomedical and clinical descriptive investigations have led the field in the recent surge of research activity. Apart from long-standing research into the treatment of fears of public places (Emmelkamp, 1982; Mathews, Gelder, & Johnston, 1981), it is not inaccurate to characterize research into psychosocial aspects of panic as clinging to the coattails of this larger biomedical effort. A computer search of the literature over the last 30 months using the keyword *panic* produced 241 articles. The proportion of articles devoted to biological aspects, pharmacotherapy, psychiatric diagnosis, and clinical description was 88%; 8% covered primarily psychosocial factors, 3% psychological therapies, and 1% methodological issues. Bearing in mind this minority representation and the psychiatric origins of the panic disorder concept, this forward look at psychosocial research could well be more wide-ranging and speculative than its biological counterpart. There is every indication that this imbalance in the type of research conducted will soon be rectified. The coming shift is most evident in research on the contextual determinants of provoked panic, in the monitoring of naturally provoked panics, and in the personality and cognitive characteristics of people disposed to panic.

Already it is apparent that the definition of panic has run into some difficulty. The panic phenomenon has shown signs of rampant and uncontrolled growth, necessitating some trimming and remodeling of the concept. If given free rein, it would lead us to see panic in all corners of medicine and psychiatry and in a sizeable proportion of the population as well. Defined simply as a "sudden rush of intense fear or anxiety or feeling of impending doom," panic is extremely common in a range of anxiety and depressive disorders (Barlow et al., 1985). In a large proportion of Barlow's subjects, DSM-III criteria for panic disorder were also met. The danger of defining panic too loosely has already led to strategies for its delimitation. Barlow and his colleagues suggest excluding panic episodes cued by external objects or situations. This tactic may be too severe, however, if uncued episodes later give rise to the avoidance of external cues to which they have become associated. Another tactic, used by the DSM-III, is to exclude from panic disorder any case in which panic episodes are associated with another primary medical or psychiatric disorder. If followed too rigorously, this strategy would cast out of consideration cases in which the interaction between panic complaints and other medical or psychological factors was of interest in its own right and would confound comparisons between psychiatric disorders. Another way of expanding or restricting the definition of panic disorder is to adjust the frequency criterion for panic episodes or for the number of somatic symptoms required to be reported. It is worth noting that none of these solutions to the problem of defining panic has been devised on sound theoretical grounds; all seem to have arisen on the basis of technical and methodological convenience. Researchers such as Rachman, Lopatka, and Levitt (1988) see no reason to employ diagnostic criteria and define panic in relation to an arbitrary point on a 0-to-100 self-report anxiety scale.

More problematic are those examples of panic phenomena in which clients have difficulty in describing the cognitive and emotional aspects of their experiences (Jones, 1984). Uhde and his colleagues (1985) have described subjects—all male—who had panic episodes but no associated anxiety complaints or fears of public places. They tended to have been referred by family physicians who were interested in the research or to have been self-referred. In another sample of subjects experiencing panic attacks (Breier et al., 1986), only one reported that his first understanding of the episodes was as a panic attack; 15 subjects understood it as some form of "anxiety" or "nervousness" and 41 did not regard it as a form of anxiety but still conceived of it as a potent life-threatening event. Katon et al. (1987) noted that patients who met diagnostic criteria for panic disorder or met these criteria in all respects except frequency of occurrence (classified as "simple panic") often misinterpreted their complaints as being due to a physical illness. These patients focused on the somatic symptom and regarded their nervousness as secondary.

Once the decision is made to include episodic presentations of somatic distress within the class of panic phenomena, the field is immediately and enormously expanded. Beitman and associates (1987) note that changes to the DSM-III now permit recognition of a nonfearful panic disorder. That is, some individuals experience discomfort rather than apprehension or fear during the episode and express no fears of dying, going crazy, or doing something uncontrolled. They are remarkably similar in other respects to panic disorder subjects who *are* fearful. In a second study by Katon et al. (1987), 195 patients at a primary care clinic were asked questions designed to elicit primarily somatic presentations of panic episodes. The DSM-III definition of panic disorder was used, without excluding agoraphobia or major depression. Simple panic was defined as a case in which the subject had four or more autonomic symptoms of a panic attack but did not have a period of at least three panic attacks in three weeks (required for DSM-III panic disorder). The lifetime prevalence of simple panic in this subpopulation was estimated as 18.4% and of panic disorder as 20.5%. The current prevalence of simple panic plus panic disorder was 22% (at least one panic attack during the previous month). Katon notes that physicians are likely to be misled by somatic presentations of panic and regard them as physical disorders. Discerning medical specialists are in fact discovering that considerable numbers of their patients fulfill the criteria for panic disorder (Coyle & Sterman, 1986; Mukerji et al., 1987). The most common somatic presentations are cardiac symptoms (chest pain, tachycardia), neurologic symptoms (headache, dizziness, vertigo, syncope), and gastrointestinal symptoms (epigastric distress) (Katon, 1984).

Comments on Clinical Presentation and Classification Issues

There are several impressions to take away from these clinical observations and surveys. The first is that panic episodes are embarrassingly commonplace if defined loosely. The idea that all of them or some arbitrary subsection of them share an underlying pathology or common psychological mechanism (except one that is very generally formulated) therefore does not impress one as convincing. This should not worry the empirical researcher seeking to validate a particular concept of panic. The empirical consequences of using different definitions of panic can be explored, and eventually it is likely that theory and classification will evolve a complementary partnership.

A second impression is that the manner of presentation varies considerably, from the purely somatic to the predominantly psychological. It would be profitable to investigate this continuum from a variety of psychosocial perspectives (causal attribution, lay models of distress and illness, coping resources, class, educational level, and so on).

Third, an implicit dualism can be observed in some of the literature, as if panic disorder is required to be an unequivocal "psychiatric" disorder whereas some presentations of anxiety are really "organic disorders" producing anxiety symptoms (Lesser & Rubin, 1986; MacKenzie & Popkin, 1983). In fact there is no one-to-one relationship between organic factors such as pheochromocytoma and complaints of anxiety (Starkman, Zelnick, Nesse, & Cameron, 1985). A combination of medical and psychological factors could well be the norm in panic disorder. In view of the considerable overlap between physical illness and psychological problems (Eastwood & Trevelyan, 1972) and some evidence that anxiety complaints may portend later physical morbidity (Coryell, Noyes, & House, 1986; Noyes, Clancy, Hoenk, & Slymen, 1980), this dualistic tendency may be a sign of researchers' unwillingness to develop an integrated biopsychosocial model of panic. Yet the intimate relationship between psychological processes and bodily systems such as respiration and balance is evident from many sources. For example, an increase in respiration rate can occur in response to psychological stimulation, and psychological strategies can reduce spinning sensations arising from stimulation of the vestibular sense organs (Baloh, Lyerly, Yee, & Honrubia, 1984). These facts require a psychophysiological explanation; an either/or, medical-versus-psychiatric perception of our subject matter cannot do it justice. The implication of this comment is that greater theoretical efforts should be made to conceptualize the interaction of somatic and psychological factors, an attitude more characteristic of psychosocial researchers than of biological theorists.

Finally, the creation of a new diagnostic entity that cuts across medicine and psychiatry could lead to profound changes in professional practice. The very existence of such a diagnosis might stimulate collaboration. Furthermore, the economic implications of detecting and treating panic are considerable. It is possible that through early intervention some of the socially disabling consequences such as avoidance of public places, substance abuse, and unnecessary medical investigation could be prevented. A preventive program of this kind would require physicians, psychiatrists, and psychologists to work in closer partnership. As part of such a program, it would be desirable to develop reliable and easy-to-follow guidelines and behavioral tests for the detection of panic phenomena, especially in medical settings. However, the definitional needs of scientific researchers in this field are slightly different from those of clinicians, and it is to this issue we turn.

Description, Classification, and Panic Research

Most research on panic-anxiety complaints has been conducted from a natural science standpoint, though contributions from social scientists have not been absent. The culturally relative nature of Western clinical descriptions becomes obvious when similar phenomena are studied in non-Western peoples (Good & Kleinman, 1985; Kleinman, 1987). Natural science researchers work under the not unreasonable assumption that there are some universal underlying natural processes waiting to be discovered. In this endeavour, the adoption of psychiatric criteria for defining psychological distress may be unduly limiting. Psychiatric taxonomies are devised for a variety of reasons, among which scientific research requirements are not the most pressing. For example, the conventional nature of some definitions, though vital to impose order on a variable universe (and essential for epidemiological and other kinds of investigation) may not be appropriate for all research questions. The fact that complaints look similar or different on the surface is no guarantee that these superficial characteristics correspond to underlying natural processes. In medicine there are numerous examples of similar complaints (such as headache) that have different mediating mechanisms—as well as of different complaints that have the same cause (such as syphilis). As Boyle (1988) has recently pointed out (in connection with a different putative disorder), the normal scientific procedure is to infer a scientific construct from a pattern of observations and then to attempt to validate the construct by predicting new properties and/or relationships between them under controlled conditions.

The observations that led Klein (1981) to postulate the panic disorder construct included a different pharmacologic response in cases of panic and anticipatory anxiety. In addition, comparisons were drawn between panic and observations on distress produced by maternal separation. Unfortunately, Klein's hypotheses have not been well supported (Margraf et al., 1986), which leaves us in the position of either producing new scientific constructs to make sense of the evidence or abandoning the notion that panic phenomena form a meaningful pattern for which it is worth seeking a unitary explanation.

In practice, many researchers have assumed the validity of the panic disorder concept. Observations have been made not to test a construct but to confirm the validity of the concept by showing that panic disorder differs from other putative anxiety disorders. Having invented panic disorder, it is difficult to uninvent it. For example, descriptive studies have been more concerned with the reliability of panic diagnoses than with their validity (Wittchen & Semler, 1986). If we go only on clinical observations and their reliability there is indeed little to choose between, say, the clinical syndrome of agoraphobia that Marks (1987a) champions as a separate entity and panic disorder, which subsumes most of the features of agoraphobia. Instead, theoretical reasons should be provided to help us choose one construct rather than another. The evidence Marks presents for agoraphobia as a distinct syndrome consists of arbitrarily selected clinical observations (Marks, 1987a, 1987b). He asserts that panic attacks occurring in the absence of phobic avoidance have no distinct etiology and that they lie on a continuum with tonic tension. This is not sufficient to convince us that the features of agoraphobia can be explained by a set of processes that differ in an important way from processes underlying other putative anxiety disorders. We know, for instance, that "pure panic disorder" often develops into agoraphobia, and there is scant descriptive evidence of a statistical kind for making his diagnostic distinction. In other words, Marks's insistence on separating "pure" panic disorder from agoraphobia needs to be justified with stronger arguments and evidence.

In criticizing these contemporary attempts to construe anxiety complaints we are not suggesting there is a right and a wrong way to proceed in research on panic. As with other medical or psychological problems, we are required to make sense of correlated observations in a number of different assessment domains: self-report, overt behavior, physiology, pathology, and others. It is well recognized that correlations between measures in these domains are often low. If there are indeed pathophysiological processes operating in panic disorder, they are unlikely to show a one-to-one correlation with measures of a panic construct derived from self-report. Already it can be seen that too great a reliance on the self-report of "panicking" may result in failure to observe similar episodic somatic phenomena.

It can be argued that the term *anxiety* (or *panic*) is not the name of a "feeling" with universal validity but a lay construct with multiple referents (Hallam, 1985). If this is the case, we should not expect to find reliable relationships between self-report and other variables, even in the same individual. There are likely to be wide individual differences, with some people using anxiety labels casually, others with considerable restraint. The developmental antecedents of the learning of lay anxiety constructs can of course be studied systematically (Lewis & Michelson, 1983), and this research may reveal findings of relevance to panic disorder. What the child learns in communicating about emotion is in part a set of social conventions—what it is "normal" to be anxious about, how this anxiety is conventionally expressed, how much dependency on others is legitimate given personal resources and task complexity, how much effort is expected of the sufferer in overcoming difficulties, and so forth. Thus, the regularities we observe in the use of terms like *panic* or *anxiety* not only reflect universal natural processes but also represent the regularity of local social practices. For this reason, the psychosocial investigation of panic disorder cannot be divorced from prescriptive and normative social processes.

While idioms of distress and the social practices in which they are embedded are interesting in their own right, clinicians might wish to view panic in more purely behavioral or physiological terms (assuming that complaints of panic are not entirely reducible to linguistic and social-cognitive processes). At this early stage of research it seems essential to keep an open mind about whether a definition of panic phenomena in more behavioral or physiological terms would prove most useful. One phenomenon pointing in this direction is an episode of anomalous somatic sensation occurring in the absence of nameless apprehension and fear—or of a social context that renders it intelligible. The clinician presented with a somatically focused complaint might find the following behavioral signs significant in exploring the form (rather than the content) of complaint that conforms to the panic disorder pattern.

1. An avoidance of certain places
2. A temporal pattern of discomfort or distress resembling episodic panic attacks
3. An immediate response to alcohol (or other substance with comparable pharmacologic effect) of improvement in discomfort
4. Deterioration with provocation tests (overbreathing, chair rotation, caffeine)
5. Complaint elicitation or worsening with fantasy evocation and prompting of thought content and symptom sensations.

This list is, of course, no more than a set of clinical guidelines.

As empirical findings accumulate from ambulatory and laboratory provocation studies, a clearer understanding of the antecedents of panic complaints will emerge. Such work may result in a model that emphasizes behavioral and physiological processes. If, on the other hand, the linguistic-cognitive domain proves to be the one that best differentiates panic sufferers from nonsufferers, a classification linking complaints of panic to cognitive and personality processes may prove to have greater heuristic value.

Distal Antecedents of Panic

Early Antecedents

It is striking that the first panic episode can occur in persons who do not regard themselves in any way prone to nervousness or anxiety (Hallam, 1985). These self-perceptions do not imply, of course, an absence of life stressors. Goldstein and Chambless (1978) suggest that their agoraphobic subjects were unskilled in recognizing subtle distinctions in feeling states and in connecting feelings to interpersonal events. Consequently, methods of data collection that rely on self-observation (especially of past events) may be ill suited to the panic population. Relevant events may be inaccessible because they have been forgotten—alternatively, their significance may never have been recognized in the first place. Biological theorists will seize on this as a last-ditch attempt on the part of psychosocial researchers to save their perspective, but in fact this is a plausible position to take and one that can be tested by behavioral and functional analysis if data is gathered at the time. As has been shown by laboratory studies (Mathews & Eysenck, 1987), anxious subjects are not necessarily aware of the influence of threatening stimuli on their behavior.

It is therefore with some caution that one must evaluate retrospective studies of the distal antecedents of panic. Considerable effort has been devoted to testing Klein's hypothesis that childhood separation and anxiety are related to adult panic disorder. The early antecedents of panic disorder and generalized anxiety disorder (Raskin, Peeke, Dickman, & Pinkster, 1982; Torgersen, 1986) or panic disorder and simple phobias (Thyer, Nesse, Curtis, & Cameron, 1986) have been compared. The existence of a specific association between early separation and panic disorder has not been supported. However, it might be expected that childhood separation or loss, real or threatened, would generally predispose individuals to adult psychiatric problems. For example, Berg, Marks, McGuire, and Lipsedge (1974) found that school phobia predicted an earlier onset of phobic avoidance and a greater severity of other complaints.

Several surveys of psychiatric patients diagnosed as having panic disorder (with or without phobic avoidance) have revealed lifetime histories of problem drinking or clinical depression, often beginning before the first panic episode (Bibb & Chambless, 1986; Breier et al., 1986; Uhde et al., 1985). In clinical populations these features of the life history could be indications of psychiatric problems (that is, of the severity of psychological disturbance) of which panic is just one expression.

As noted earlier, the validity of the retrospective method is suspect when the subject's memory is the sole source of information. For example, childhood perceptions of family events and actual happenings may be irrecoverable, and a variety of circumstances may act to moderate the effect of particular events. Retrospective studies should perhaps be regarded as suggestive and then followed up by prospective investigations. Greater subtlety of hypothesis testing in this area might be achieved by retrodicting on the basis of, say, panic-related cognitions, the class of sensitizing developmental experience to which the subject might be expected to have been exposed. Fears of loss of control, embarrassment, fatal illness, and insanity are likely to have different early antecedents. Data of this kind are required to test certain learning theory formulations discussed in the following pages.

The lack of prospective studies is understandable in the light of their expense and duration and the recency of interest in panic. A question of crucial significance is whether and in what way people who panic are predisposed to do so. There is a clear familial risk for offspring of adults diagnosed as having panic disorder (Crowe, Pauls, Slymen, & Noyes, 1980), but the mode of transmission—genetic and environmental—is not so clear. The problem is to know what to look for in childhood experience. Buglass, Clarke, Henderson, Kreitman, & Presley (1977) interviewed married women who feared public places and a group of matched control subjects to find out whether their children expressed common childhood difficulties. There was no difference in the frequency of problems (including fears) between the groups. However, it would have been more desirable to interview the children themselves and put them through a more thorough clinical and laboratory examination that included their responses to threat and stressors. A longitudinal study of children of panic sufferers is feasible and should not be too expensive to mount. These subjects could be followed from late childhood to find out whether patterns of parent/child interactions, personality characteristics, fears, or developmental experiences were predictive of the onset of panic episodes and related behavior.

Antecedents of Initial Episodes

Another line of inquiry is the investigation of events precipitating the first panic episode. These studies have been carried out both casually and with greater refinement (Finlay-Jones & Brown, 1981; Roy-Byrne, Geraci, & Uhde, 1986). Life events research ought to tell us whether (1) panic episodes come from out of the blue (in the manner of a physical affliction); (2) panic disorder, in contrast to other disorders, is precipitated by a certain type of event; and (3) within the class of panic precipitants there is a meaningful, or merely general, relationship between the event and the panic episode. The consensual view is that stress events can be identified in the majority of cases and that usually they are in the nature of a threat rather than a loss. The period intervening between onset and the life event interview in these studies is usually rather long, though Faravelli (1985) managed to find 23 cases within 4 months of their onset. Compared to normal subjects, his panic subjects showed an excess of events in the 2 months preceding onset, especially the serious illness or death of close relatives. These events could be regarded as losses, threats, or both. Roy-Byrne and his colleagues (1986) observed that, overall, their subjects with panic disorder did *not* have a greater number of life events (except, interestingly enough, personal health events), but they tended to report more distress and to interpret events as uncontrollable, undesirable, and causing low self-esteem. (The comparison group subjects were employees of a clinic.) These retrospective reflections are from sufferers in the patient role, and it is uncertain how they would compare with subjects' interpretations of events made at the time of occurrence.

There is likewise some doubt that the onset of panic disorder can always be dated with precision. Only a minority describe their initial episode as severe—and therefore presumably as memorable. Even then it is possible that milder episodic sensory disturbances, which may not seem obviously related or may go unnoticed, have preceded it. The events that appear to precipitate panic may in fact have more to do with the decision to seek help. Moreover, it cannot be assumed that a person is capable of or willing to report on the events—often anticipatory—to which he or she is responding. It is difficult for a skilled therapist to identify key events in a client's present situation, let alone in the past. The identification of events with an objective reference may provide some clues, but given the wide scope for interpretation, retrospective studies of precipitants are unlikely to tell us much about psychosocial causal mechanisms. Last, Barlow, and O'Brien (1984) classify the precipitating events of birth of a child, miscarriage, hysterectomy, and drug reaction as endocrinal and physiological reactions (which they are), but this may not be their most relevant characteristic. Because of these problems in interpretation, testing specific predictions will be more useful than a general fishing expedition for triggering events.

Notably absent from these studies is a precise description of the circumstances in which the first episode occurred, although some researchers have attended to this (Thorpe & Burns, 1983). Abandoning the view that panic is either primarily endogenous or a nonspecific response to stressors, these missing details may conceal much of interest. For example, physical or psychological entrapment or visuospatial and movement cues could be of as much significance as life stressors (Hallam, 1985; MacNab, Nieuwenhuijse, Jansweyer, & Kuiper, 1978).

Proximal Antecedents of Panic

The irrational nature of panic-anxiety is one of its striking characteristics and a stimulus to biological theorizing. The study of clients' diaries reveals that certain triggers obvious to the therapist are not apparent to the client, though he or she can be educated to recognize the importance of such factors as physical entrapment, interoceptive cues, and catastrophic cognitions. There still remain many panic episodes whose origin is inexplicable. "Good" and "bad" days (or longer-term fluctuations) are also puzzling. It is reasonable to expect that empirical investigation of the events that covary with self-reports will provide some answers to these puzzles.

Biological theorists can hope that panic will covary with physiological measures. Psychosocial researchers are more inclined to complex psychophysiological models (see, for example, Margraf et al., 1986). The principal methods of investigation are naturalistic monitoring and controlled provocation. Experimental control is easier to achieve in the laboratory, but naturalistic studies have greater ecological validity. It must be admitted that the cueing and maintenance of apparently uncued panic attacks is far more complex than in the case of the more well researched small animal fears. A safe long-term prediction is that future models will have to take many variables into account. Because panic can be such a traumatic experience, it provides fertile ground for subsequent intero- and exteroceptive conditioning, avoidance learning, and semantic elaboration.

What is stored in long-term memory, according to Lang (1985), is an associative network of information about the emotion-provoking situation. Information from multiple sources is said to be linked in this network. Lang suggests that the network can be triggered as a whole if enough of this information is available when a subject attends to the environment. In some cases, attention will be drawn to the environment when emotion-relevant information is actively being processed; if so, less stimulus information may be required to activate the whole network. For example, when visceral information is processed, as in the case of physical exercise or general excitement, relatively little additional emotion-relevant input may be needed to trigger a complaint of anxiety. This hypothetical account accords well with clinical observations of complaint elicitation. Lang's description of the properties of fear memories helps to explain the nonspecific and variable manner in which complaints are expressed.

Naturalistic Studies

Preliminary studies of the temporal pattern of panic episodes have so far failed to find one (Freedman, Ianni, Ettedgui, & Puthezhath, 1985; Uhde et al., 1985), but these studies have lacked the methodological refinement to answer the question definitively. Twenty-four-hour monitoring has produced evidence of a clustering of episodes between 1:30 A.M. and 3:30 A.M., waking subjects from sleep (Taylor et al., 1986). Some evidence of cycling should perhaps be expected if panic is associated with endogenous processes. Covariation of panic episodes with physiological parameters such as heart rate is of central interest, but analysis of the causal sequence of events raises a chicken-and-egg problem. Once a panic episode—and therefore the opportunity for interoceptive conditioning—has occurred, a person may pay greater attention to somatic cues and notice them prior to panicking. Anticipation of panic can mediate autonomic activity, and these sensations may be noticed before the full-blown panic. It is therefore difficult to know what causal significance can be drawn from the finding that sensory experiences precede episodes (Hibbert, 1984; Ley, 1985).

While interviewing clinical subjects, Ley observed rapid respiration, shallow thoracic breathing, and sighing in the majority. Somatic sensations, assumed to be related to hyperventilation, were reported *before* panic attacks. Without denying the signficance of these triggers, one can still ask what events were related to changes in respiration. The sequence of events, whatever their ultimate causal priority, does of course have therapeutic implications. The positive feedback loop postulated by Ley (1985) and others (Lum, 1981), involving fearful interpretations of the sensory consequences of low levels of CO_2 in the blood, can be interrupted by the correction of misattributions and breathing retraining (Clark, Salkovskis, & Chalkley, 1985).

Reporting their ambulatory monitoring study, Taylor et al. (1986) described sudden increases of heart rate (unassociated with physical activity) as "unique physiological events," but they pointed out there are several possible interpretations of their data. These heart rate changes were observed in about two-thirds of self-reported panic attacks (and presumably occurred without reports of panic), so the correlation is a loose one. Basal heart rate and other measures tend to be similar in individuals with panic disorder and control subjects (Shear, 1986), but Shear speculates that patients with panic disorder may have more variable rates related to an inability to maintain parasympathetic dominance. Once more, the safest prediction to make about prospects in this area is that endogenous physiological factors and psychological processes will be found to interact in a complex manner.

The frequency of panic attacks in the natural environment is associated with several measures of psychological disturbance, such as unassertiveness and neuroticism (Chambless, 1985). In nonclinical populations, panicking is associated with trait measures of anxiety and depression (Norton, Dorward, & Cox, 1986). These correlational data are difficult to interpret, but it could be argued that dysphoric mood and other nonspecific factors (such as disappointments or failure to assert oneself) lower the threshold of response to more specific kinds of precipitant. Relapse after therapy is associated with depressed mood, for example (Mathews et al., 1981). There is an infinite variety of triggers for panic (Marks, 1970), including the absence of safety cues and motivational influences. Some triggers are idiosyncratic and relate to the nature of associated fears (for example, panic may be less likely in darkness if blushing is an autonomic symptom and the subject fears embarrassment). One way to deal with this variety and multiplicity of precipitating factors is to adopt an intensive single-case approach. Another tactic would be to select less severely distressed subjects whose panic episodes occurred less frequently with more obvious precipitants. Naturalistic monitoring could be combined with the planned introduction of psychosocial or physiological stressors.

Rapee, Ancis, and Barlow (1988) examined the correlations between questionnaire measures of naturally occurring somatic sensations and self-reported response to stressors and uncued panic episodes. Almost 90% of a nonclinical population reported having experienced (for no apparent reason) some of the somatic sensations described in the DSM-III-R. Nonclinical subjects who had experienced at least one uncued panic attack did not differ from nonpanicking subjects in the number, intensity, or duration of sensations, but there were some signs of greater emotional responsivity in the former group. However, somatic reactivity and emotional reactions (worrisome thoughts about sensations) were far more common in a separate group of clinical subjects who complained of panic attacks. Recalling the chicken-and-egg problem, the authors conclude that "further research is needed to determine whether uncued panic attacks are a result of or result in increased apprehension over physiological sensations" (p. 269).

Provocation Studies

Panic episodes can be provoked in a controlled situation by (1) physiological stressors (such as overbreathing or exercise), (2) chemical stimulation (such as hormones, caffeine, or lactate), (3) thoughts and fantasies, and (4) controlled in vivo exposure. There is now a considerable literature, too large to review, in which these methods have been employed (see Ehlers, Margraf, & Roth, 1986, for pharmacologic studies, and Chapter 4 in this book). Research has been motivated by a search for a biological mechanism, by attempts to evaluate behavior therapy, and lately by an intrinsic interest in manipulating the psychosocial context.

It is now evident, as it was evident before when the effects of infusing sympathomimetic agents were investigated (Breggin, 1964), that there is an interaction between chemical provocation and psychological variables. Illustrating the importance of expectation, it was found that clinical subjects were more likely to panic and express catastrophic beliefs if they had no explanation of the effects of a 50% CO_2/O_2 mixture (Rapee, Mattick, & Murrell, 1986). In a double-blind study of normal subjects, expectations of "anxious tension" produced a greater subjective response than an expectation of "pleasant excitement" when sodium lactate was infused (van der Molen, van den Hout, Vroeman, Louisberg, & Griez, 1986). Sodium lactate potentiated this effect, as there was very little response to a placebo glucose solution.

Provocation by infusion of sodium lactate was originally studied to test biological hypotheses (Pitts & McClure, 1967). Now that the influence (but not the sufficiency) of the psychological context has been demonstrated, it must be taken into account in the design of future biological studies. Double-blind procedures and control of demand effects are essential. However, provocation by chemical and physiological stressors does not necessarily provide the most appropriate method to further the investigation of psychosocial influence. Alternatives are available in the form of fantasy and thought, methods that have arisen out of an interest in cognitive processes in panic-anxiety. False feedback of bodily processes is another form of provocation. Subjects with panic disorder who perceived a falsely contrived abrupt increase in heart rate became more anxious and physiologically aroused (Ehlers, Margraf, Roth, Barr-Taylor, & Birbaumer, 1988). Another promising approach is an in vivo test such as walking a prescribed route while physiological processes and self-observations are monitored (Michelson & Mavissakalian, 1985). This method could be used to test the effect of different types of instruction (for instance, body focusing versus outward focusing, or coping instructions). Controlled provocation of this type is less artificial, and physiological recording is becoming easier to perform with advances in techniques of ambulatory monitoring.

Rachman and his colleagues have devised some ingenious but simple experiments to study panic episodes in a standard environment: an enclosed space (Rachman, 1988; Rachman et al., 1988). They looked at aspects of their subjects' psychological state that predicted the occurrence of panic in the test environment and also examined the consequences of panicking on subsequent exposure and self-report. These are some of the first direct studies of the "fear-of-fear" phenomenon. Expected panics and disconfirmed panic expectations were followed by a decline in predicted and reported panic, substantiating clinical impressions of the circumstances in which exposure is effective. These authors also compared the cognitions of claustrophobic with panic subjects and discovered a high proportion of "noncognitive" panics in the latter but not in the former. A noncognitive panic is defined as an episode unaccompanied by the endorsement of fearful beliefs, such as a fear of passing out. Further research into the antecedents of noncognitive panic is likely to illuminate new mechanisms of panic production.

Judging by this sample of recent provocation studies, there is every reason to believe that we will now make rapid progress in understanding the proximal factors that predispose persons to panic. The importance of these studies lies in the clues they provide to the maintenance of panic and by implication to new therapeutic interventions. (Factors that provoke panic do not necessarily inform us about the acquisition of panic disorder.)

The possibilities for the manipulation of fantasy material and environmental stimulation have hardly been explored. Imaginative exceptions are found in the work of Fisher and Wilson (1985) and Lang (1985). Prior to exposure to controlled stimulus material, subjects could be prepared cognitively or physiologically to study the interaction between individual and environmental variables. Traditional response measures could be extended to include facial expressions and posture recorded on videotape. In guided fantasy or hypnotic procedures, features of the provoking situation could be systematically suggested or withdrawn and the effect noted. Similarly, in controlled environments the effects of pictorial stimuli (in which visuospatial cues are varied) could be assessed.

In all likelihood, the complaint of panic has multiple antecedents, so the results of provocation may be unpredictable. Provocation studies may, however, assist researchers in developing a more refined typology of panic.

General Psychosocial Correlates of Panic

We'll consider first demographic and then personality variables, selecting just a few studies that point out interesting directions for research. Interpretation of the social correlates of panic-anxiety is no simple matter, but psychological and biological models cannot afford to ignore them. Findings in this area could help to stimulate and validate theoretical notions. In clinical practice, the social and cultural aspects of a case help in the formulation, but because these factors usually cannot be manipulated they constrain rather than determine management. For this reason they may have received less attention in theory construction.

One exception to this neglect in the clinical literature of the sociocultural context is the relationship between fears of public places and the perceived role of women in society (Fodor, 1974; Hallam, 1983), but this topic has been pursued parallel to, rather than intersecting, other areas of research. Exploration of the social milieu and sociohistorical trends of the type conducted by de Swaan (1981) on agoraphobia could help us see more clearly the links between gender and the manner in which problems are presented. Moreover, by taking a wider perspective we can avoid relying solely on clinical features for hypothesis generation, a tendency that may obscure empirical and conceptual links between apparently separate problem areas. For example, a link between panic disorder and alcohol dependence is suggested by epidemiological and demographic data (Hallam, 1985).

Fundamental to understanding the psychosocial correlates of mental health is a decision about the level of generality at which relationships are sought. For example, age and social class correlates of neuroticism tell us little about panic-anxiety in particular. However, given the multifactorial determination of complaint, examination of single factors such as class leaves the data open to a host of competing interpretations. A hope—or plea—for the longer term is that the gulf between clinical/psychiatric and social science disciplines will be bridged to enrich theory and clarify empirical findings. A good example here is the analysis of everyday discourse about emotion (Lutz, 1988), which should help clarify sex differences in the prevalence of anxiety complaints.

A methodological issue in research of this kind is whether to adopt the psychiatric categorization of anxiety complaints. The theoretical significance of distinguishing between generalized anxiety and panic-anxiety (or in DSM-III-R terms, generalized anxiety disorder and panic disorder) is still uncertain, even though there are some differences in their clinical presentation (Anderson, Noyes, & Crowe, 1984; Barlow, Cohen, Waddell, & Vermilyea, 1984). A further complication is the overlap between somatization and panic-anxiety dimensions (King, Margraf, Ehlers, & Maddock, 1986). Arrindell (1980) also found that somatization items loaded the panic-anxiety factor. Factorial analysis of the Hopkins Symptom Checklist (and its later versions) has not provided evidence of more than one anxiety dimension (Hallam, 1985), but other studies have obtained separate factors of a lifelong traitlike disposition to report anxiety and a cluster of complaints with sudden onset characterized by situational phobias, panic episodes, and somatic symptoms (Arrindell, 1980; Roth, Garside, & Gurney, 1965). The classification of anxiety complaints is therefore unresolved, and psychosocial research cannot proceed as though the "anxiety disorders" provided a sound starting point. It is natural for researchers to want to share their findings with clinicians who adopt the currently accepted nosology. However, until psychiatric diagnostic concepts are properly validated (and have a reasonable life expectancy), clinical concepts suited to the research objectives derived from alternative methodologies may prove to be more useful.

Another consideration is the extent to which conclusions from studies of clinical subjects can be generalized to nonclinical populations. The method of comparing different clinical groups equates for clinical status per se, but the influence of factors that lead subjects to seek help is not thereby removed from the data. It need not be assumed that these factors are similar for different psychological problems. For these reasons the insights into panic-anxiety afforded by general population surveys are likely to be of greater interest.

Demographic Characteristics

Of the psychological problems satisfying psychiatric criteria, anxiety disorders are the most common, excluding substance abuse broadly conceived (Robins et al., 1984). Simple phobias and fears of public places are more prevalent than panic disorder. Six-month prevalence rates range from .6% to 1.1% for panic disorder, 2.7% to 3.6% for agoraphobia, and 4.1% to 4.7% for simple phobia, using the DSM-III criteria (Wittchen, 1986). In a survey carried out in Munich, Wittchen found that the lifetime prevalence of at least one panic attack was 9.3%, and that about half of this group satisfied the DSM-III criteria for panic disorder. Complaints of generalized anxiety and panic are more prevalent in women than in men (Weissman, 1985). The sex ratio is approximately 2:1 for panic and at least 3:1 for fears of public places. In contrast, the sex ratio for social anxieties is approximately equal (Marks, 1987a). These data represent a challenge to both biological and psychosocial theorists. For example, how might cognitive theorists account for this differential pattern?

The occurrence of panic attacks is associated with high rates of consultation at outpatient (ambulatory) services, whether the episodes are the primary or a secondary problem (Boyd, 1986). In fact, individuals with panic attacks consult more than any other group, although Boyd found that the favored facility varied between medical or psychiatric depending on the geographical site of the survey. A high utilization of medical facilities could be explained by the following features of panic-anxiety: (1) the somatic focus of many of the complaints, (2) a belief that the cause is medical, (3) an absence of obvious psychological triggering factors, and (4) the difficulty that physicians experience in excluding physical causes. Minor, contributory physical dysfunctions may indeed be present, even though referral is largely determined by a somatopsychic response. The high rate of consultation and the real risk of misdiagnosis underline the importance of studying psychosocial aspects of complaint and health service utilization.

Broad cultural and personality factors are also likely to influence the mode of presentation. One view is that the expression of distress in the anxiety idiom depends on a developed vocabulary of emotion terms (Leff, 1977, 1981). In the absence of a vocabulary of this type, complaints are expressed in a "less sophisticated" somatic form. Leff argues that a historical progression from somatic to psychological expressions can be traced in English-language culture. As would be expected from this assumption, somatic expressions of anxiety (common in panic-anxiety) and somatization complaints have been found to be associated with educational level, social class, and age (Crandell & Dohrenwend, 1967; Derogatis, Lipman, Covi, & Rickels, 1971; Hollingshead & Redlich, 1958). Crandell and Dohrenwend observed that educational level was related to psychophysiological complaints but not to psychological expressions of distress (for example "nervous," "worried"). It is interesting to read in reports of community surveys of 25 or 30 years ago that somatic expressions were clearly linked to class and psychological sophistication. For example, members of Class V "are unable to understand that these troubles are not physical illnesses" (Hollingshead & Redlich, 1958, p. 340) or that "only in psychologically sophisticated circles is a psychogenic contribution to discomfort recognized" (Langner & Michael, 1963, p. 407). Judging from these quotations, perhaps there has been some genuine change in our degree of self-understanding. Derogatis and his colleagues (1971) found clear evidence that within anxious outpatients somatization was strongly class-related and that anxiety complaints were somewhat less so. Other complaint clusters, such as depression, were not significantly related to class. Once again, data such as these cry out for interpretation. The effort to provide one may throw light on the psychological-somatic dimension within the spectrum of panic-anxiety complaints.

Recent surveys of the demographic correlates of panic disorder have produced conflicting results. Reporting on the Epidemiological Catchment Area Survey, Weissman (1985) stated that there was *no* strong relationship between panic disorder and race, education, or age. In contrast, rates of agoraphobia were higher in women, the less educated, and non-Whites. Similarly, Chambless (1985) found that phobic avoidance—but not frequency of panic attacks—was associated with socioeconomic status. However, in a community survey reported by Von Korff, Eaton, and Keyl (1985), subjects satisfying panic disorder criteria were more likely to be female, to be separated or divorced, and to have less than a high school education. Katon et al. (1987), on the other hand, did not find demographic correlates of panic disorder in a sample of primary care patients.

Some interesting questions in this area are whether there are differences in the demographic correlates of generalized anxiety disorder and panic disorder with or without phobic avoidance of public places; whether the association with class and other factors varies geographically; and whether the explanation of these data lies in social constructions of distress, coping style or resources, health status, or other variables. It is interesting to speculate that the "hysterical defenses" said to be characteristic of agoraphobic subjects (Goldstein & Chambless, 1978) are related to their social class or educational level.

Personality Characteristics and Coping Styles

This topic has been reviewed by Chambless (1982), who was understandably cautious in her conclusions in view of the quality of much of this research. Correlational studies have recently centered on the characteristics of panic disorder subjects with or without phobic avoidance. The cognitive characteristics that differentiate individuals with panic disorder from other clinical subjects or normal controls have also been studied.

Avoidance

Phobic avoidance typically develops some time after the first panic episodes have been experienced. Although there is doubt about dating the precise onset of these episodes, a period of 8 years from onset to avoidance is typical (Thyer & Himle, 1985). Phobic avoidance is therefore, in one sense, a sign of severity. It is worth noting that not all fears of public places develop following panic episodes, and that panic can in any case develop into other types of phobia (Wittchen, 1986). As noted earlier, phobic avoidance is associated with socioeconomic status. Roth et al. (1965) observed that it was more common in older, married women and in those subjects who were more depressed and had more frequent panic attacks. Recent research has not confirmed that avoidance is associated with the degree of subjective distress and severity of mood disturbance (Chambless, 1985; Costello, 1982; Thyer & Himle, 1985).

The importance of mobility for most people means that fearful subjects are likely to travel and tolerate distress if they can, especially if their livelihood depends on it and they enjoy the company of others. In a survey of individuals with agoraphobia, Marks and Herst (1970) found that those who worked rather than staying at home described their previous personality as independent, sociable, and extroverted. Fewer of them were married; when married, they had fewer young children. Otherwise their fears were no less severe, and they were, in fact, more afraid of being alone. Consistent with the tendency to introversion of those with avoidance were findings by Vitaliano et al. (1987) that the more phobic of his panic disorder subjects were *less* likely to use social support as a method of coping and that they engaged in more wishful thinking.

The bulk of the evidence supports the position that avoidance in panic-anxiety is not the escape/avoidance component of a phobia of public places but a strategy employed to minimize subjective distress in a more general sense (Hallam, 1978). In other words, though escape to a safe place during a panic episode is an unequivocal sign of fear, the tendency to stay at home or carry on regardless in public reflects a more general cognitive or behavioral style. The choice of this style appears to be influenced by pragmatic and personality factors. This conclusion needs to be substantiated and may require modification in the light of a finding by Ganellen, Matuzas, Uhlenhuth, Glass, and Easton (1986) that avoiders expressed more anxious and intrusive thoughts relating to danger. Studies of the personality and coping style of nonfearful panic disorder subjects would complement this research, and it would be interesting to know both how much avoidance these subjects demonstrate and how it is interpreted. Studies of subjects whose behavior and verbal accounts are desynchronous should be especially revealing of the processes of cognitive-behavioral interaction.

Cognitive Styles

The importance of the cognitive attributes of individuals with panic disorder is evident from many sources, and in some psychological models these attributes are fundamental. Roy-Byrne and his colleagues (1986) observed that in their life events study there was little difference between panic disorder subjects and controls in the number of objective life events. However, the former group placed more threatening interpretations upon the events and therefore suffered greater subjective distress. Fisher and Wilson (1985) gave subjects with fears of public places a variety of self-report and psychophysiological tests and concluded that they had a cognitive/attributional problem rather than abnormal physiological characteristics. Consistent with that view, anxious subjects tend to interpret *ambiguous* events as threatening (Butler & Mathews, 1983; McNally & Foa, 1987). McNally and Foa also tested agoraphobic subjects with *unambiguous* situations and found that their threatening interpretations were not of a general nature but were specific to internally arousing events, thereby lending support to the fear-of-fear hypothesis.

Research on attributional bias and coping style is gathering speed and may eventually lead to a new taxonomy of anxiety complaints. However, it still remains to be established whether the cognitive characteristics of anxious individuals are the cause, an accompaniment, or the consequence of anxiety complaints. The answer to this question is fundamental to their significance and role in theoretical explanations.

Theoretical Issues

An attraction of the panic concept is that it abstracts from a sea of diverse clinical features a phenomenon that seems to require a unitary explanation. At the same time, it helps to draw these features together into a meaningful pattern. It appears from the literature that a search is on for a process that underlies the acute escalation of distress characteristic of panic. Is this search justified? Assuming that panic disorder has a relatively discrete pathophysiological basis, it certainly is. As Teasdale (1988) has soberly perceived, most of the psychological features of panic can be explained as secondary consequences of sudden arousal states caused by a primary physical dysfunction.

Psychological models of panic, though integrating many processes, do not really question the assumption that all panic episodes share some unique attributes that can be explained in reasonably simple terms. Parsimony is a good scientific principle; complexity can always be (and almost always is) introduced later. Even so, it is worth considering where complexity is likely to come in. First, panic disorder may follow a series of stages. The causes of the initial episodes may be distinct from the factors responsible for maintaining them later on. Second, panic may be a final common pathway for etiological processes that bear little resemblance to each other. Within the general rubric of a positive feedback model, the events interacting in this way could be quite variable. Third, as noted earlier, a hybrid biopsychosocial model is likely to emerge as closer to the truth than either a biological or a psychological model. For example, Clark (1986) has referred to a homeostatic adjustment to chronic hyperventilation that adds complexity to the role of faulty breathing patterns in the generation of panic.

Another reason for doubting that panic is a simple phenomenon is the fact that its identification is heavily dependent on self-report. If "panic" and "anxiety" are multireferential lay terms whose function is primarily conceptual and communicative (Hallam, 1985), it follows that the antecedents of reports of panic need not share a great deal in common from one context to the next. However, if anxiety is conceptualized as a primary emotion whose referent is the perception of a feeling, then panic is more likely to be seen as a unitary phenomenon—for example, as "intense" or "spiraling" anxiety.

Having dealt with these introductory points concerning general theoretical assumptions, we should now discuss two issues that are important in future developments and illustrate how they are currently being handled by panic theorists. Inevitably, we will neglect some perspectives that, because of lack of space, we cannot include. However, other authors have already produced admirable reviews and critiques in these areas. For example, see Lang (1985) on information processing; Mineka (1985) on animal learning models; and, Teasdale (1988) on cognitive models.

One issue is how trait anxiety (and by implication generalized anxiety disorder) is related to panic disorder. One possibility is that panic disorder lies on a severity continuum with trait anxiety and generalized anxiety disorder. Another is that trait anxiety predisposes individuals toward panic disorder but is not necessarily a causal factor. A third is that all anxiety complaints have some common causes but that each type of complaint has distinctive antecedents. For example, panic has been conceptualized as a phobia of interoceptive stimuli (van den Hout & Griez, 1986). Apart from trying to understand how interoceptive stimuli acquire this cueing function, we would not in this view need to explain panic as a special *type* of anxiety. Of course, if panic is not a unitary phenomenon, some examples of it may be intense forms of general anxiety and others phobiclike.

A second issue is how to explain the initial episodes of panic. These are puzzling because the problem can arise unexpectedly, in the absence of any obvious triggering factor. Psychological models have yet to put forward a credible alternative to a biological etiology.

Panic and Trait Anxiety

This issue has been most thoroughly discussed and investigated by Mathews and Eysenck (1987), whose model is founded on extensive experimental data. They suggest that there is a continuum from everyday reports of anxiety to high trait anxiety, generalized anxiety, and panic. The common basis of this continuum is said to be a predisposition to perceive threat. Trait anxiety is conceptualized as a highly heritable and stable characteristic that predisposes one to clinical anxiety (Eysenck & Mathews, 1987). Clinical anxiety complaints are assumed to arise through an interaction between trait anxiety and environmental stress, though factors specific to panic disorder and generalized anxiety disorder can be introduced to explain differences in their features. For example, panic can be explained as a spiraling process involving a positive feedback interaction between tonic levels of arousal and phasic responses to stimuli (Lader & Mathews, 1968). An impressive set of experiments supports the thesis that individuals high in trait anxiety allocate cognitive processing resources to threatening stimuli when threatening and neutral stimuli are presented concurrently. This bias is assumed to be preattentive and therefore capable of operating outside of conscious awareness.

The experimental evidence has been obtained in studies of subjects known to be complaining of anxiety. Therefore, evidence is lacking that a cognitive bias predisposes subjects to clinical anxieties. The inference that high trait anxiety predisposes them to generalized anxiety disorder and panic disorder has strong face validity but is so far untested. In this connection, trait anxiety need not be conceptualized as an inherited characteristic; even if the trait is acquired in early development, its importance as a predisposing factor could be established. However, if trait anxiety is learned (and after all, threat is not inherent in the environment and may be quite specific, even in the case of biologically prepared stimuli) (Marks, 1987a), it would be expected that a bias to perceive danger would alert subjects to specific cues rather than threats in general. Threat is normatively defined—it is what most people most of the time regard as "threatening." It is therefore difficult to ascertain exactly what a predisposition to a perceived threat amounts to. From the perspective that threat is a normative concept, it would make sense to explore how infants learn to use threat and anxiety concepts (Lewis & Michelson, 1983) and come to apply them habitually. This approach may provide insights into the complementary process of the underemployment of threat perception in circumstances in which there is physiological or behavioral evidence of a defensive process.

In conflict with the assumption that trait anxiety predisposes to panic-anxiety is the uncomfortable fact that at least some individuals with panic disorder (admittedly, on their own self-report) do not consider that they have always been "nervous" or "worrying" types. One of the puzzling features of panic-anxiety is that the initial episodes often come from out of the blue, as an experience alien to the self. Mathews and Eysenck (1987) can accommodate this observation by emphasizing the importance of life stress in interaction with trait anxiety—even stating that trait anxiety is unnecessary if stress is severe. They also suggest that clinical anxiety is more likely to occur when the nature of the life stress and the content of danger schemata are congruent. One must assume in this case that, prior to the anxiety complaint, danger schemata are in some sense active (and that attention is allocated to the relevant threat cues) but that anxiety is not reported. This is perhaps true of individuals who adopt an anxiety-repressive cognitive style (Eysenck & Mathews, 1987). A speculative hypothesis to account for "spontaneous" panic in these subjects is a process of "flipping-over" between repressive and sensitized modes of defense when threat exceeds a certain level.

In conclusion, an analysis of the relationship between trait anxiety and panic throws out many interesting possibilities, but a close examination undermines any simple hypothesis. Eysenck and Mathews (1987) note evidence that trait anxiety is multidimensional; if this is the case, a reductive explanation of trait anxiety will be harder to achieve. This in turn would mean that its heuristic value in the clinical field will diminish. It seems that the only satisfactory way to test the hypothesis that trait anxiety is related to panic-anxiety is to conduct a longitudinal predictive study—for example, one of at-risk individuals, as suggested earlier. On the face of it, the proposal that anxiety complaints are associated with knowledge structures in long-term memory that result in selective processing of information does not point to any distinctive anxiety process. The same description could apply to hungry or lusty individuals. It is necessary to show that danger schemata respond differently to other kinds of schemata (for which there is now some evidence) (Mogg, Mathews, & Weinman, 1987).

The Etiology of Initial Panics

Researchers have observed that panic is not commonly associated with traumatic events at its onset. Stressful life events seem to bear an indirect relationship to panic rather than provide the basis for traumatic aversive conditioning. The panic or its real or imagined consequences may be perceived as traumatic, but this is beside the point. It is partly because of their failure to square these observations with a traumatic aversive conditioning model of etiology that learning theory formulations have been viewed as inadequate. However, alternative models derived from conditioning theory have also been proposed.

Cognitive Approaches

Some cognitive theorists believe that a panic attack is the result of a positive feedback relationship between a bodily sensation, its perception as threatening, and subsequent threat-mediated responses (Clark, 1986). The sensory events that potentially initiate this cycle are conceptualized as quite variable. They include "symptoms" of anxiety itself, depersonalization experiences, tachycardia, dizziness, mental confusion, the effects of hyperventilation, and many more. These sensory events presumably do have diverse causes, so the question of how the initial episodes are triggered is only of subsidiary interest. The model hinges on threat cognitions, so their etiology takes pride of place in the formulation. While it is understandable that panic attacks could give rise to catastrophic beliefs, evidence is required that threat cognitions predispose persons to panic, as the theoretical model demands. As Teasdale (1988) comments, evidence from the laboratory that the manipulation of the cognitive state of panic subjects influences panic frequency or severity does not prove that spontaneous panic episodes are cued by threat cognitions or originate in the manner suggested. A possible response to this objection is that the stressful events initiating anomalous perceptual experiences simultaneously activate threat cognitions. But this line of argument still leaves unexplained the fact that life stress produces panic in some people but not in others. A further challenge for the model is to account for the existence of noncognitive panics (Rachman et al., 1988) or nonfearful panic disorder.

A research solution to the problem of establishing the causal efficacy of cognitions is hard to find. Longitudinal study of at-risk subjects, as proposed earlier, may help to establish the importance of prior cognitive characteristics. This assumes the availability of an independent measure of the predisposition to perceive threat. Panic subjects who are in remission but show long-term fluctuations in their condition could also usefully be studied.

Behavioral Approaches

A rather different theoretical perspective emphasizes features of the environment and behavioral responses to them. Taking up the argument for a conditioning model, Davey (1987, 1989) points out that a broad range of unconditioned aversive events other than pain has been overlooked. Events that naturally elicit fright and defensive reactions in a number of species include looming shadows, loud sudden noises, and staring eyes. Visuospatial cues of enclosure may also be naturally aversive for humans (MacNab et al., 1978). Besides these innate elicitors of fear, responsiveness to the environment may be altered in a general way by common physical disorders. This alteration can include diminished adaptation to sensory change and therefore an enhanced response to innate fear elicitors. For example, physical disorders that disturb the normal sense of equilibrium appear to lead to fears of public places and fears of loss of support (Marks, 1987a; Pratt & McKenzie, 1958). Marks describes "space phobia" as a pseudoagoraphobic syndrome, but the inability to integrate multisensory information to achieve a sense of balance may lie on a continuum with the normal and act as a general predisposing factor. Indeed, this idea can be traced back to Benedikt (1870). Deficits in the equilibrial sense reduce a person's capacity to negotiate the environment whether, on foot or in transport. Sloping terrain, sudden bodily movement, darkness, heights, and patterned visual input may lead to disorientation and unpleasant bodily sensations.

The etiological significance of disequilibrium is suggested by a finding that the complaint of dizziness (in an ear, nose, and throat medical setting) is associated with high scores on scales of phobic and somatic anxiety (Hallam & Stephens, 1985). Although a proportion of the subjects in this study were clinically assessed as suffering from imbalance or vertigo, there was no correlation between psychopathology scales and behavioral tests of balance. The importance of vestibular malfunction in panic-anxiety is therefore unclear at this stage.

Another disorder that may alter responsiveness to the environment is migraine. The prevalence of migraine is high in agoraphobic subjects: 27% (Buglass et al., 1977) or 25% (Thorpe & Burns, 1983). Sensitivity to bright lights, sounds, and certain visual movements is increased during migraine episodes, which may last for days or even weeks. These prevalence figures, though more than double the population average, require confirmation.

Like many other somatic factors in panic disorder, migraine and balance disorders can manifest themselves episodically and, in the absence of correct attributions, their sensory effects are likely to be perceived as inexplicable and frightening. Insofar as these disorders give rise to anomalous sensations that may be frightening, they may be regarded by cognitive theorists as playing the same role as any other physical disorder. But in addition, their sensory consequences may be intrinsically unpleasant (for example, nausea) or elicit defensive reactions (for instance, to a loss of support).

A more strictly behavioral account of the fear-of-fear process can also be offered (Hallam, 1985). This model is an application of Mandler's (1975) concept of interruption. It assumes that defensive reactions, notably escape, are first triggered by circumstances that are innately arousing (bright lights, close proximity of strangers, confinement, and so on). If escape from the situation is blocked, interruption of this prepotent and reflexive response leads to an increase in physiological arousal. If there are no alternatives, the potentiated escape reaction remains blocked, leading to a further escalation of arousal. This theory is consistent with the very high importance assigned to entrapment and ease of escape by agoraphobic subjects (Thorpe & Burns, 1983). This model of panic escalation would fail as a general account, however, if nonfearful panic disorder subjects do not demonstrate any behavioral signs of a lowered threshold for escape during panic episodes.

Finally, some new speculative applications of conditioning theory have been put forward by Hallam (1985) and by Davey (1987, 1989). Traditionally, phobias and other anxiety complaints have been assumed to develop through traumatic or incremental excitatory conditioning. However, other possibilities explain sudden changes in response strength. For example, excitation may result from a release of inhibition. In aversive learning situations that give rise to learned inhibition—for instance, when signals of unconditioned stimulus (UCS) omission are available—conditioned response (CR) strength is known to fluctuate in response to changes in inhibitory processes. Mastery and/or tolerance of aversive situations may be acquired gradually, so the process of acquiring an inhibitory CR may not be memorable. Disinhibitory events, such as novel information about the UCS or about the adequacy of coping skills, could produce a rather abrupt change in conditioned responding such that an "inexplicable" excitatory response is released. This event may be experienced as panic or may form the substrate for the cognitive elaboration of threat. To test the validity of this notion, it would be necessary to know the process through which mastery was acquired, the subjects' conceptualizations of the aversive situation, any past events that may have sensitized a subject to the aversive situation, and the detailed circumstances of panic elicitation. Information of this sort has been collected on aircrew who developed flying anxieties (Aitken, Lister, & Main, 1981).

A somewhat different account has been derived from studies of UCS reevaluation (Dickenson, 1987). Davey (1987) has pointed out that recent cognitive conceptions of the conditioning process may have considerably more to offer than the older contiguity-based concepts of conditioning. In humans especially, Davey argues, response strength is determined by knowledge of and evaluation of events in the conditioning situation (possibly socially or verbally transmitted), self-observation, and processes of response attribution. In studies in animals using the technique of postconditioning stimulus reevaluation, the value of the UCS is altered so that it becomes, for example, more or less aversive. This procedure immediately affects the strength of the CR, supporting the view that learning is mediated by a CS-UCS association and demonstrating that response strength can be influenced in the absence of direct exposure to CS-UCS event contingencies. Reevaluation of the UCS provides one explanation, according to Davey, for the fact that phobic persons might be unable to account for the onset of their fears in traumatic terms. Thus, a prelearned innocuous association between two events might be transformed if the second event were reevaluated negatively, creating a fear response to the first. This mechanism and others mentioned by Davey, such as response attribution, may be helpful in understanding day-to-day fluctuations of anxiety complaints or spontaneous remission.

Summary

In this chapter, we have considered and pointed out only those issues we view as important for future research in this area. No conclusions can be drawn at this point, but a summary of the issues may be helpful.

1.   There are several difficulties in delimiting the phenomena of panic episodes and the features associated with the panic-anxiety cluster of complaints. It seems unlikely that all panic episodes have a similar etiology or that the panic process (which many believe involves positive feedback) is predominantly either exogeneously or endogenously caused. Panic phenomena seem to call for a complex interactive explanation.

2.   Little is known about the developmental antecedents of panic. Two factors that may obscure those antecedents are the inability of individuals who panic to report on the relevant psychosocial events and the inherent complexity of those events.

3.   The triggering factors for day-to-day variations in panic-anxiety complaints may have arisen as secondary conditioned elicitors or through semantic interpretation of primary episodes. Therefore, the investigation of day-to-day variation in panic-anxiety may have more implications for therapy than for identifying the etiology of the initial panics.

4.   Studies of variation in the presentation of panic-anxiety—historically, culturally, geographically, or by socioeconomic class, gender, and age—may be a useful way to explore the phenomenon. Social class appears to be related to the degree of somatization of complaints as well as to phobic avoidance.

5.   The personality and cognitive style of individuals who panic are likely to be significant determinants of the chronicity, severity, and type of complaints. Investigations in this area may lead to a new typology of clinical phenomena.

6.   Several outstanding theoretical issues relate to the generality or specificity of the predisposition to panic. Some theorists see the initial panic episodes as the manifestation of a general trait of fearfulness; others see them as phobic reactions to specific interoceptive cues. It seems likely that fruitful investigation will shun unitary views in favor of the unfortunately tedious complexity of psychological phenomena. This implies that a variety of etiological factors should be considered as acting together to produce the clinical phenomena; for example, sensitizing experiences in early development, physical disorders producing anomalous sensations, physiologically arousing circumstances of many kinds (innate elicitors, conflict, and so forth), and individual coping strategies. Despite differences of opinion, most theorists agree that the escalation of panic into an acutely distressing episode entails a positive feedback interaction between elements in the total personal/environmental complex.

References

Aitken, R. C. B., Lister, J. A., & Main, C. J. (1981). Identification of features associated with flying phobias in aircrew. *British Journal of Psychiatry, 139,* 38–42.

American Psychiatric Association. (1980). *Diagnostic and statistical manual of mental disorders* (3rd ed.). Washington, DC: Author.

American Psychiatric Association. (1987). *Diagnostic and statistical manual of mental disorders* (3rd ed., rev.). Washington, DC: Author.

Anderson, D. J., Noyes, R., & Crowe, R. (1984). A comparison of panic disorder and generalized anxiety disorder. *American Journal of Psychiatry, 141,* 572–575.

Arrindell, W. A. (1980). Dimensional structure and psychopathology correlates of the Fear Survey Schedule (FSS III) in a phobic population: A factorial definition of agoraphobia. *Behaviour Research and Therapy, 18,* 229–242.

Baloh, R. W., Lyerly, K., Yee, R. D., & Honrubia, V. (1984). Voluntary control of the human vestibular-ocular reflex. *Acta Otolaryngologica, 97,* 1–6.

Barlow, D. H., Cohen, A. S., Waddell, M J., & Vermilyea, B. B. (1984). Panic and generalized anxiety disorders: Nature and treatment. *Behavior Therapy, 15,* 431–449.

Barlow, D. H., Vermilyea, J., Blanchard, E. B., Vermilyea, B. B., DiNardo, P. A., & Cerny, J. A. (1985). The phenomenon of panic. *Journal of Abnormal Psychology, 94,* 320–328.

Beitman, B. D., Basha, I., Flaker, G., Derosea, L., Mukerji, V., & Lamberti, J. (1987). Non-fearful panic disorder: Panic attacks without fear. *Behaviour Research and Therapy, 25,* 487–492.

Benedikt, V. (1870). Über Platschwindel. *Algemeine Weiner Medizinische Zeitung, 15,* 488.

Berg, I., Marks, I. M., McGuire, R., & Lipsedge, M. (1974). School phobia and agoraphobia. *Psychological Medicine, 4,* 428–434.

Bibb, J. L., & Chambless, D. L. (1986). Alcohol use and abuse among diagnosed agoraphobics. *Behaviour Research and Therapy, 24,* 49–58.

Boyd, J. H. (1986). Use of mental health services for the treatment of panic disorder. *American Journal of Psychiatry, 143,* 1869–1874.

Boyle, M. (1988). *Schizophrenia: A scientific delusion?* Unpublished doctoral thesis, North East London Polytechnic.

Breggin, P. R. (1964). The psychophysiology of anxiety. *Journal of Nervous and Mental Disease, 139,* 558–568.

Breier, A., Charney, D. S., & Heninger, G. R. (1986). Agoraphobia with panic attacks: Development, diagnostic stability, and course of illness. *Archives of General Psychiatry, 43,* 1029–1036.

Buglass, D., Clarke, J., Henderson, A. S., Kreitman, N., & Presley, A. S. (1977). A study of agoraphobic housewives. *Psychological Medicine, 7,* 73–86.

Butler, G., & Mathews, A. (1983). Cognitive processes in anxiety. *Advances in Behaviour Research & Therapy 5,* 51–62.

Chambless, D. L. (1982). Characteristics of agoraphobics. In D. L. Chambless & A. J. Goldstein (Eds.), *Agoraphobia: Multiple perspectives on theory and treatment.* New York: Wiley.

Chambless, D. L. (1985). The relationship of severity of agoraphobia to associated psychopathology. *Behaviour Research and Therapy, 23,* 305–310.

Clark, D. M. (1986). A cognitive approach to panic. *Behaviour Research & Therapy, 24,* 461–470.

Clark, D. M., Salkovskis, P. M., & Chalkley, A. J. (1985). Respiratory control as a treatment for panic attacks. *Journal of Behavior Therapy & Experimental Psychiatry, 16,* 23–30.

Coryell, W., Noyes, R., & House, J. D. (1986). Mortality among outpatients with anxiety disorders. *American Journal of Psychiatry, 143,* 508–510.

Costello, C. G. (1982). Fears and phobias in women. A community study. *Journal of Abnormal Psychology, 91,* 280–286.

Coyle, P. K., & Sterman, A. B. (1986). Focal neurologic symptoms in panic attacks. *American Journal of Psychiatry, 143,* 648–649.

Crandell, D. L., & Dohrenwend, B. P. (1967). Some relations among psychiatric symptoms, organic illness, and social class. *American Journal of Psychiatry, 123,* 1527–1538.

Crowe, R. R., Pauls, D. L., Slymen, D. J., & Noyes, R. (1980). A family study of anxiety neurosis. *Archives of General Psychiatry, 37,* 77–79.

Davey, G. C. L. (1987). *A contemporary model of human Pavlovian conditioning: The role of UCS revaluation and its implications for the psychopathology of clinical fears.* Unpublished manuscript, City University, London.

Davey, G. C. L. (1989). Integrating contemporary models of animal and human conditioning: Implications for behaviour therapy. In P. Emmelkamp, P. Everaard, W. F. Kraaymaar, & M. Van Sohn (Eds.), *Theory and practice in behavior therapy.* Amsterdam, Netherlands: Swets.

Derogatis, L. R., Lipman, R. S., Covi, L., & Rickels, K. (1971). Neurotic symptom dimensions as perceived by psychiatrists and patients of various social classes. *Archives of General Psychiatry, 24,* 454–464.

de Swann, A. (1981). The politics of agoraphobia: On changes in emotional and relational management. *Theory and Society, 10,* 359–385.

Dickenson, A. (1987). Animal conditioning and learning theory. In H. J. Eysenck & I. Martin (Eds.), *Theoretical foundations of behavior therapy.* New York: Plenum.

Eastwood, M. R., & Trevelyan, M. H. (1972). The relationship between physical and psychiatric disorder. *Psychological Medicine, 2,* 363–372.

Ehlers, A., Margraf, J., & Roth, W. T. (1986). Experimental induction of panic attacks. In I. Hand & H.-U. Wittchen (Eds.), *Panic and phobias.* Berlin: Springer.

Ehlers, A., Margraf, J., Roth, W. T., Barr-Taylor, C., & Birbaumer, N. (1988). Anxiety induced by false heart rate feedback in patients with panic disorder. *Behaviour Research and Therapy, 26,* 1–11.

Emmelkamp, P. M. G. (1982). *Phobic and obsessive compulsive disorders: Theory, research and practice.* New York: Plenum.

Eysenck, M. W., & Mathews, A. (1987). Trait anxiety and cognition. In H. J. Eysenck & I. Martin (Eds.), *Theoretical foundations of behavior therapy* (pp. 197–216). New York:Plenum.

Faravelli, C. (1985). Life events preceding the onset of panic disorder. *Journal of Affective Disorders, 9,* 103–105.

Finlay-Jones, R., & Brown, G. W. (1981). Types of stressful life events and the onset of anxiety and depressive disorders. *Psychological Medicine, 11,* 803–815.

Fisher, L. M., & Wilson, G. T. (1985). A study of the psychology of agoraphobia. *Behaviour Research and Therapy, 23,* 97–107.

Fodor, I. G. (1974). The phobic syndrome in women. In V. Franks & V. Burtle (Eds.), *Women in therapy.* New York: Brunner/Mazel.

Freedman, R. R., Ianni, P., Ettedgui, E., & Puthezhath, N. (1985). Ambulatory monitoring of panic disorder. *Archives of General Psychiatry, 42,* 244–250.

Ganellen, R. J., Matuzas, W., Uhlenhuth, E. H., Glass, R., & Easton, C. R. (1986). Panic disorder, agoraphobia, and anxiety relevant cognitive style. *Journal of Affective Disorders, 11,* 219–225.

Goldstein, A. J., & Chambless, D. L. (1978). A reanalysis of agoraphobia. *Behavior Therapy, 9,* 47–59.

Good, B., & Kleinman, A. (1985). Culture and anxiety: Cross-cultural evidence for the patterning of anxiety disorders. In A. H. Tuma & J. D. Maser (Eds.), *Anxiety and the anxiety disorders.* Hillsdale, NJ: Lawrence Erlbaum.

Hallam, R. S. (1978). Agoraphobia: A critical review of the concept. *British Journal of Psychiatry, 133,* 314–319.

Hallam, R. S. (1983). Agoraphobia: Deconstructing a clinical syndrome. *Bulletin of the British Psychological Society, 36,* 337–340.

Hallam, R. S. (1985). *Anxiety: Psychological perspectives on panic and agoraphobia.* London: Academic Press.

Hallam, R. S., & Stephens, S. D. G. (1985). Vestibular disorder and emotional distress. *Journal of Psychosomatic Research, 29,* 407–413.

Hibbert, G. A. (1984). Ideational components of anxiety. *British Journal of Psychiatry, 144,* 618–624.

Hollingshead, A., & Redlich, F. (1958). *Social class and mental illness.* New York: Wiley.

Jones, B. A. (1984). Panic attacks with panic masked by alexithymia. *Psychosomatics, 25,* 885–889.

Katon, W. (1984). Panic disorder and somaticization: Review of 55 cases. *American Journal of Medicine, 77,* 101–106.

Katon, W., Vitaliano, P. P., Russo, J., Jones, M., & Anderson, K. (1987). Panic disorder: Spectrum of severity and somatization. *Journal of Nervous and Mental Disease, 175,* 12–19.

King, R., Margraf, J., Ehlers, A., & Maddock, R. (1986). Panic disorder—Overlap with symptoms of somatisation disorder in panic and phobias. In I. Hand & H.-U. Wittchen (Eds.), *Panic and phobias.* Berlin: Springer.

Klein, D. F. (1964). Delineation of two drug-responsive anxiety syndromes. *Psychopharmacologia, 5,* 397–408.

Klein, D. F. (1981). Anxiety reconceptualized. In D. F. Klein & J. Rabkin (Eds.), *Anxiety: New research and changing concepts.* New York: Raven Press.

Kleinman, A. (1987). Anthropology and psychiatry: The role of culture in cross-cultural research on illness. *British Journal of Psychiatry, 151,* 447–454.

Lader, M., & Mathews, A. M. (1968). A physiological model of phobic anxiety and desensitisation. *Behaviour Research and Therapy, 6,* 411–421.

Lang, P. J. (1985). The cognitive psychophysiology of emotion: Fear and anxiety. In A. H. Tuma & J. D. Maser (Eds.), *Anxiety and the anxiety disorders.* Hillsdale, NJ: Lawrence Erlbaum.

Langner, T. S., & Michael, S. T. (1963). *Life stress and mental health.* London: Free Press of Glencoe.

Last, C. G., Barlow, D., & O'Brien, G. T. (1984). Precipitants of agoraphobia: Role of stressful life-events. *Psychological Reports, 54,* 567–570.

Leff, J. P. (1977). The cross-cultural study of emotion. *Culture, Medicine & Psychiatry, 1,* 317–350.

Leff, J. (1981). *Psychiatry around the globe: A transcultural view.* New York: Marcel Dekker.

Lesser, I. M., & Rubin, R. T. (1986). Diagnostic considerations in panic disorders. *Journal of Clinical Psychiatry, 47,*(6, Suppl.), 4–10.

Lewis, M., & Michelson, L. (1983). *Children's emotions and moods: Developmental theory and measurement.* New York: Plenum.

Ley, R. (1985). Agoraphobia, the panic attack, and the hyperventilation syndrome. *Behaviour Research & Therapy, 23,* 79–81.

Lum, L. C. (1981). Hyperventilation and anxiety state. *Journal of the Royal Society of Medicine, 74,* 1–4.

Lutz, C. (1988, March). *Emotion and discourse.* Paper presented at a conference titled Accounts of human nature. Windsor, UK.

Mackenzie, T. B., & Popkin, M. K. (1983). Organic anxiety syndrome. *American Journal of Psychiatry, 140,* 342–344.

MacNab, B. I. E., Nieuwenhuijse, B., Jansweyer, W. N. H., & Kuiper, A. (1978). Height-distance ratio as a predictor of perceived openness-enclosure of space and emotional responses in normal and phobic subjects. *Nederlands Tijdschrift voor de Psychologie, 33,* 375–388.

McNally, R. J., & Foa, E. B. (1987). Cognition and agoraphobia: Bias in the interpretation of threat. *Cognitive Therapy and Research, 11,* 567–581.

Mandler, G. (1975). *Mind and emotion.* New York: Wiley.

Margraf, J., Ehlers, A., & Roth, W. T. (1986). Panic attacks: Theoretical models and empirical evidence. In I. Hand & H.-U. Wittchen (Eds.), *Panic and phobias.* Berlin: Springer.

Marks, I. M. (1970). Agoraphobic syndrome (Phobic anxiety state). *Archives of General Psychiatry, 23,* 538–553.

Marks, I. M. (1987a). *Fears, phobias, and rituals.* Oxford: Oxford University Press.

Marks, I. M. (1987b). Behavioral aspects of panic disorder. *American Journal of Psychiatry, 144,* 1160–1165.

Marks, I. M., & Herst, E. R. (1970). A survey of 1200 agoraphobics in Britain. *Social Psychiatry, 5,* 16–24.

Mathews, A., & Eysenck, A. W. (1987). Clinical anxiety and cognition. In H. J. Eysenck & I. Martin (Eds.), *Theoretical foundations of behavior therapy* (pp. 217–234). New York: Plenum.

Mathews, A., Gelder, M. G., & Johnston, D. W. (1981). *Agoraphobia: Nature and treatment.* London: Tavistock.

Michelson, L., & Mavissakalian, M. (1985). Psychophysiological outcome of behavioral and pharmacological treatments of agoraphobia. *Journal of Consulting and Clinical Psychology, 53,* 229–236.

Mineka, S. (1985). Animal models of anxiety-based disorders: Their usefulness and limitations. In A. H. Tuma & J. D. Maser (Eds.), *Anxiety and the anxiety disorders.* Hillsdale, NJ: Lawrence Erlbaum.

Mogg, K., Mathews, A., & Weinman, J. (1987). Memory bias in clinical anxiety. *Journal of Abnormal Psychology, 96,* 94–98.

Mukerji, V., Beitman, B. D., Alpert, M. A., Lamberti, J. W., DeRosear, L., & Basha, I. M. (1987). Panic disorder: A frequent occurrence in patients with chest pains and normal coronary arteries. *Angiology, 38,* 236–240.

Norton, G. R., Dorward, J., & Cox, B. J. (1986). Factors associated with panic attacks in non-clinical subjects. *Behavior Therapy, 17,* 239–253.

Norton, G. R., Harrison, B., Hauch, J., & Rhodes, L. (1985). Characteristics of people with infrequent panic attacks. *Journal of Abnormal Psychology, 94,* 216–221.

Noyes, R., Clancy, J., Hoenk, P. R., & Slymen, D. J. (1980). The prognosis of anxiety neurosis. *Archives of General Psychiatry, 37,* 173–178.

Pitts, F. N., & McClure, J. N. (1967). Lactate metabolism in anxiety neurosis. *New England Journal of Medicine, 277,* 1329–1336.

Pratt, R. T. C., & McKenzie, W. (1958). Anxiety states following vestibular disorders. *Lancet, 2,* 347–349.

Rachman, S. (1988). Panics and their consequences: Review and prospect. In S. Rachman & J. Maser (Eds.), *Panic: Psychological perspectives.* Hillsdale, NJ: Lawrence Erlbaum.

Rachman, S., Lopatka, C., & Levitt, K. (1988). Experimental analysis of panic II—Panic patients. *Behaviour Research and Therapy, 26,* 33–40.

Rapee, R., Ancis, J. R., & Barlow, D. H. (1988). Emotional reactions to physiological sensations: Panic disorder patients and non-clinical subjects. *Behaviour Research & Therapy, 26,* 265–269.

Rapee, R., Mattick, R., & Murrell, E. (1986). Cognitive mediation in the affective component of spontaneous panic attacks. *Journal of Behavior Therapy and Experimental Psychiatry, 17,* 245–253.

Raskin, M., Peeke, H. V. S., Dickman, W., & Pinkster, H. (1982). Panic and generalized anxiety disorders: Developmental antecedents and precipitants. *Archives of General Psychiatry, 39,* 687–689.

Robins, C. N., Helzer, J. E., Weissman, J. E., Orvaschel, H. M., Gruenberg, E., Burke, J. D., & Regier, D. A. (1984). Lifetime prevalence of specific psychiatric disorders in three sites. *Archives of General Psychiatry, 41,* 949–959.

Roth, M., Garside, R. F., & Gurney, C. (1965). Clinical and statistical enquiries into the classification of anxiety states and depressive disorders. In *Proceedings of Leeds Symposium of Behavioural Disorders.* London: May & Baker.

Roy-Byrne, P. P., Geraci, M., & Uhde, T. W. (1986). Life events and the onset of panic disorder. *American Journal of Psychiatry, 143,* 1424–1427.

Shear, M. K. (1986). Pathophysiology of panic: A review of pharmacologic provocation tests and naturalistic monitoring data. *Journal of Clinical Psychiatry, 47*(6, Suppl.), 18–26.

Starkman, M. N., Zelnick, T. C., Nesse, R. M., & Cameron, O. G. (1985). Anxiety in patients with pheochromocytomas. *Archives of Internal Medicine, 145,* 248–252.

Stockwell, T., Smail, P., Hodgson, R., & Canter, S. (1983). Alcohol dependence and phobic anxiety states II: A retrospective study. *British Journal of Psychiatry, 144,* 58–63.

Taylor, C. B., Sheikh, J., Agras, W. S., Roth, W. T., Margraf, J., Ehlers, A., Maddock, R. J., & Gossard, D. (1986). Ambulatory heart rate changes in patients with panic attacks. *American Journal of Psychiatry, 143,* 478–482.

Teasdale, J. (1988). Cognitive models and treatment for panic: A critical evaluation. In S. Rachman & J. Maser (Eds.), *Panic: Psychological perspectives* (pp. 189–203). Hillsdale, NJ: Lawrence Erlbaum.

Thorpe, G., & Burns, L. E. (1983). *The agoraphobic syndrome.* Chichester, UK: Wiley.

Thyer, B. A., & Himle, J. (1985). Temporal relationship between panic attack onset and phobic avoidance in agoraphobia. *Behaviour Research & Therapy, 23,* 607–608.

Thyer, B. A., Nesse, R. M., Curtis, G. C., & Cameron, D. G. (1986). Panic disorder: A test of the separation anxiety hypothesis. *Behaviour Research & Therapy, 24,* 209–211.

Torgersen, S. (1986). Childhood and family characteristics in panic and generalized anxiety disorders. *American Journal of Psychiatry, 143,* 630–632.

Uhde, T. W., Boulenger, J.-P., Roy-Byrne, P. P., Geraci, M. F., Vittone, B. J., & Post, R. M. (1985). Longitudinal course of panic disorder: Clinical and biological considerations. *Progress in Neuro-Pharmacology & Biological Psychiatry, 9,* 39–51.

van den Hout, M. A., & Griez, E. (1986). Experimental panic: Biobehavioral notes on empirical findings. In I. Hand & H.-U. Wittchen (Eds.), *Panic and phobias.* Berlin: Springer.

van der Molen, G. M., van den Hout, M. A., Vroeman, J., Louisberg, H., & Griez, E. (1986). Cognitive determinants of lactate-induced anxiety. *Behaviour Research & Therapy, 24,* 677–680.

Vitaliano, P. P., Katon, W., Russo, J., Masuro, R. D., Anderson, K., & Jones, M. (1987). Coping as an index of illness behavior in panic disorder. *Journal of Nervous and Mental Disease, 175,* 78–84.

Von Korff, M. A., Eaton, M. R., & Keyl, P. M. (1985). The epidemiology of panic attacks and panic disorder: Results of three community surveys. *American Journal of Epidemiology, 122,* 970–981.

Weissman, I. M. (1985). The epidemiology of anxiety disorders: Rates, risks, and familial patterns. In A. H. Tuma & J. D. Maser (Eds.), *Anxiety and the anxiety disorders* (pp. 275–296). Hillsdale, NJ: Lawrence Erlbaum.

Wittchen, H.-U. (1986). Epidemiology of panic attacks and panic disorders. In I. Hand & H.-U. Wittchen (Eds.), *Panic and phobias.* Berlin: Springer.

Wittchen, H.-U., & Semler, G. (1986). Diagnostic reliability of anxiety disorders. In I. Hand & H.-U. Wittchen (Eds.), *Panic and phobias.* Berlin: Springer.

CHAPTER 15

A Final Word:
Pragmatic Considerations
for the Practitioner

JOHN R. WALKER, COLIN A. ROSS, AND G. RON NORTON

There has clearly been a tremendous amount of exciting work done on panic disorder and agoraphobia in the past decade or so. The work summarized in the previous chapters has led to dramatic changes in our understanding and treatment of panic disorder and agoraphobia. In this chapter we would like to highlight several additional assessment and treatment issues that are of particular concern to the practitioner.

Assessment

Panic Attacks

Although the panic attack is given central importance in the development of panic disorder and agoraphobia, surprisingly little work has been done on the phenomenology of panic attacks. Hallam, in Chapter 14, points out that the definition of panic attack adopted in the DSM-III-R is rather arbitrary, based on a collective clinical judgment rather than on systematic research. Furthermore, he emphasizes that the terms *anxiety* and *panic*, as used in everyday language, do not have a universal meaning shared by all individuals and cultures. Even when the clinician provides a specific definition for the term *panic attack*, different patients may use the definition in idiosyncratic ways (Barlow, 1988). In our experience and that of others (such as Basoglu, Marks, Senqun, & Lax, 1988), patients have difficulty discriminating panic attacks from intense anxiety. Some patients, for example, describe very intense episodes of anxiety early in treatment as well as very mild episodes of anxiety (which may be quite normal experiences) later in treatment as "panic attacks." Other patients use the term *panic* to describe relatively moderate levels of anxiety early in treatment, but learn during treatment to apply a more stringent definition. Consequently, simple measures of the presence or frequency of panic attacks may omit a great deal of important information.

Much of the early research on panic disorder relied on retrospective reports of the frequency of panic attacks as a major dependent measure. Subsequently, many researchers have found that retrospective reports may not be reliable indicators of frequency. Patients typically report higher frequencies of panic attacks when this information is collected retrospectively (in interviews or questionnaires) rather than prospectively, (in panic diaries, for example) (Turner, Biedel, & Jacob, 1988). At the time of the initial assessment patients are typically experiencing a great deal of distress and wish to impress the clinician with the seriousness of their problem. They may tend to describe their more severe episodes of anxiety rather than the most typical, to ensure that they receive help. Too, their recall may be clearest for very aversive and highly salient events.

In addition to these problems with retrospective reports, the frequency and intensity of panic attacks are highly responsive to changes in life events—decreasing with expectations of help or reductions in life stress and increasing with stressful life events. For example, we often find that individuals report a decrease in the frequency of their panic attacks once they have had an intake interview and been accepted into treatment. They seem to obtain considerable relief from the expectation of assistance. Others have reported similar findings. For example, Coryell and Noyes (1988) found that approximately 25% of the patients in two double-blind studies of pharmacologic treatment showed "marked improvement" on clinician ratings following 8 weeks of placebo and the type of brief supportive psychotherapy that routinely accompanies pharmacotherapy. Patients with the most marked improvement tended to be those who showed less severe anxiety and distress at the start of treatment.

The difficulty with changing definitions may be handled best through repeated discussions with the patient and with the use of good assessment instruments.

A Package of Measures for Initial Clinical Assessment

A package of convenient self-report measures for the clinician treating panic disorder is shown in Table 15.1. Most of these assessment measures are described in some detail by Jacob and Lilienfeld in Chapter 2. Naturally, the package used in a particular setting will depend on the nature of the treatment provided and the preferences of the clinician or researcher. New measures will become available in time, and additional information on the psychometric properties of existing measures will influence which ones are used most widely. Most of the measures listed in Table 15.1 have good reliability and validity and have been shown to be stable over time (Michelson & Mavissakalian, 1983).

Another type of self-report measure is recommended by Barlow (1988) and others: panic diaries, structured to provide summary measures of the frequency, duration, and intensity of panic attacks. These researchers believe diaries are the most appropriate measure of panic attacks for clinical and research applications (see Chapter 7 and the Appendix). Diary measures of panic attacks are invaluable in gathering the detailed information necessary for planning and evaluating the outcome of treatment. In addition, diary recording in itself may be therapeutic. Many patients report a decline in anxiety after a few days of diary recording, when panic attacks begin to be seen as understandable and related to environmental events rather than as random and unpredictable.

TABLE 15.1 Example of a Self-report Measure Package for the Clinical Assessment of Panic Disorder

Measures of the nature and frequency of panic attacks

- Panic Attack Questionnaire (Norton; see Appendix)
- Agoraphobic Cognitions Questionnaire and Body Sensations Questionnaire (Chambless, Caputo, Bright, & Gallagher, 1984; see Appendix)

Diary measures of panic attacks

- Panic Attack Record (Rapee and Barlow; see Chapter 7)
- Panic Attack Diary (Walker, Rowan, Eldridge, & Holborn; see Appendix)

Measures of phobic avoidance

- Fear Questionnaire (Marks & Mathews, 1979; see Appendix)
- If agoraphobic—Mobility Inventory for Agoraphobia (Chambless, Caputo, Jasin, Gracely, & Williams, 1985; see Appendix)
- Fear and Avoidance Hierarchy (Rapee & Barlow; see Chapter 7)

Measures of depression, anxiety, and related psychopathology

- Beck Depression Inventory (Beck, Ward, Mendelsohn, Mock, & Erbaugh, 1961)
- Symptom Checklist—90 (SCL—90) (Derogatis, 1977)
- Measures of caffeine and alcohol consumption

General measure of disability

- Disability Scale (Sheehan; see Chapter 11)

A final area warranting clinical emphasis (and further investigation) is the assessment of the disability produced by panic disorder and agoraphobia. Common examples of disability are loss of employment, absenteeism, disruption of marital and family functioning, and curtailed social activities. Although this has not been an area of extensive research, it may be that the disability produced by panic disorder is relatively stable, as is the avoidance aspect of the problem. The disability scale described by Sheehan and Raj in Chapter 11 is an easy-to-administer measure that could be used in clinical and research applications alike.

Treatment

Common Themes

The chapters describing pharmacologic and cognitive-behavioral treatments provide evidence that panic disorder can be effectively treated using techniques from either approach. Both approaches, when appropriately used, are able to produce dramatic improvements in approximately 80% of patients who do not experience extensive avoidance. When avoidance is extensive or when the patient has other major psychopathology in addition to panic disorder, the success rates are substantially reduced.

Interestingly, though pharmacologic and cognitive-behavioral treatments differ greatly they also share several themes. The first is their emphasis on a careful, broad-based assessment of psychological and medical disorders. An accurate description of the anxiety problem and any related psychiatric or medical disorders is crucial in developing an optimal treatment plan.

A second common theme is the emphasis both place on educating the patient about the nature of panic disorder and the goals of the treatment program. This achieves several ends. First, the educational phase allows therapist and patient to develop a common language for describing panic attacks and other emotional experiences, thus helping the patient discriminate more effectively between them. The educational phase also helps the patient better understand the disorder. This may be particularly useful for those who are convinced they are seriously ill or "going crazy." Finally, education is likely to improve compliance. For example, if patients are aware that they might experience temporary side effects or setbacks they may be more willing to continue treatment rather than abandon or change the program when these occur.

A third shared theme is the value both methods assign to placing the problem within the broader context of the patient's life circumstances. The patient's personal and interpersonal problems, attitudes toward treatment, support systems, and coping abilities must all be considered when planning treatment. By the time many patients receive treatment for panic disorder, they may have developed extensive anticipatory anxiety and avoidance behaviors. They may also have developed a sense of despair or helplessness about their problem. Their relationships with significant others may also have changed. These additional problems and the person's ability to cope with them must be understood and dealt with if there is to be a positive outcome to treatment.

Which Treatment Should Be Offered to the Patient?

Research comparing pharmacological and cognitive-behavioral treatment is not yet extensive enough to allow us to decide which approach is more effective—in general or for a specific patient. Studies comparing the two approaches individually and in combination (outlined briefly by Swinson, Kuch, and Antony in Chapter 8) frequently use less than optimal forms of one of the treatments or less than optimal combinations. Swinson et al. suggest that the evidence currently available does not support routinely combining treatments, and we would strongly agree with this conclusion. On the other hand, if progress in the first treatment is limited, it is a reasonable clinical strategy to add the alternative treatment or to switch the patient to the alternative treatment after discontinuing the first.

Currently, the treatment offered to a particular patient depends more on the training of the practitioner than on the characteristics of the patient. The patient's own preferences may be given little consideration. As part of the process of obtaining informed consent for treatment, the practitioner should provide the patient with information about the various treatments available and the advantages and disadvantages of each. The major advantages and disadvantages of each treatment, from our perspective, are shown in Table 15.2. These points are open to interpretation and will change as new information becomes available.

Evidence is strong for the efficacy of both approaches, though additional work is required to determine how each affects various aspects of the problem (panic attacks, avoidance, mood, and resulting disability). Accessibility of treatment is a major factor; at this point pharmacologic treatment is much more accessible, particularly when provided by a primary care physician who consults with a specialist in psychiatry when needed.

Many of the disadvantages of pharmacologic treatment are related to the side effects of drugs and to relapse after discontinuation of treatment. Many patients and primary care providers expect that treatment will not have to be continued indefinitely. However, currently available research suggests that when treatment is discontinued the rate of relapse is quite high, particularly with the benzodiazepines and MAO inhibitors. There is also evidence that some patients have difficulty discontinuing the use of benzodiazepines. It is possible that clonazepam, with its longer half-life, will produce fewer withdrawal effects than benzodiazepines such as alprazolam, though this possibility must be investigated empirically. There is little systematic evidence on the rate of relapse over the months and years following discontinuation of tricyclic antidepressants such as imipramine, though clinicians report fewer problems with this class of drugs than with the benzodiazepines or MAO inhibitors (see Chapter 7 for more details).

Panic disorder is frequently seen in women of childbearing age, and research on the safety of pharmacologic treatment during pregnancy and lactation is limited (for more details, see Kerns, 1986; Robinson, Stewart, & Flak, 1986; Sheehan & Raj, Chapter 11). Patients should be informed routinely about this situation.

In many ways, the advantages and disadvantages of pharmacologic treatment are reversed for cognitive-behavioral treatment. There is more research on the long-term effectiveness of the latter, particularly for agoraphobic avoidance, and the research suggests good maintenance of treatment effects for follow-up periods of 5 years and beyond. Research on the impact of treatment on panic attacks also suggests good results 1 year after the treatment has ended, though research in this area is more recent and therefore covers more limited follow-up periods. In addition, a major advantage of using cognitive-behavioral therapy is that there is little evidence of undesirable treatment side

TABLE 15.2 Advantages and Disadvantages of Pharmacologic and Cognitive-Behavioral Treatments for Panic Disorder

Pharmacologic Treatment

Advantages

- Established efficacy
- Accessibility through primary care physicians
- Relatively low expense
- Less active patient participation requirements
- Easy integration with medical treatment
- Antidepressant effectiveness for depression also

Disadvantages

- Limited research on long-term outcome
- High relapse rate at treatment termination (with benzodiazepines and MAOIs)
- Difficulties in discontinuing benzodiazepines for some patients
- Risk of chemical dependency in patients with history of alcohol or drug problems
- Limited evidence regarding safety during pregnancy
- Side effect problems for some patients, leading at times to dropping out or lower-than-optimal dosage levels
- Reluctance of some patients to take pills in general
- MAO inhibitors' special diet requirements and incompatibility with some other medical treatments, such as general anesthetics

Cognitive-Behavioral Treatment

Advantages

- Established efficacy
- More research on long-term effectiveness (for agoraphobia)
- Good maintenance of gains after treatment
- Time-limited nature, which may reduce cost in the long run
- Easy integration with other psychological treatment
- Little evidence of negative side effects

Disadvantages

- Limited accessibility
- Higher demands on patients' time and effort
- Higher initial expense
- Possible increased anxiety, initially
- Possible difficulties in integrating medical assessment and treatment
- Problems in participation for patients with intellectual or language limitations

effects and that it may be easier to integrate treatment for other psychosocial problems (such as lack of assertiveness, dependency, or marital problems) with this treatment than with pharmacologic treatment.

On the disadvantage side, cognitive-behavioral treatment is definitely less accessible, as fewer practitioners are familiar with the treatment. It may also be more expensive initially, though this may be balanced in the long run by the time-limited nature of the treatment and good maintenance of gains. The treatment requires a greater time commitment and harder work by the patient and some willingness to tolerate increased anxiety—initially, at least.

A major factor affecting patients' decisions to enter and remain in therapy is their belief in the appropriateness and efficacy of the treatment. The few available surveys of patients (Norton, Allen, & Hilton, 1983) and the lay public (Norton, Allen, & Walker, 1985) suggest that both groups prefer exposure-based therapy to pharmacologic treatment for agoraphobia. These studies are preliminary, however, and more research on treatment preferences and personal variables would be helpful to the clinician. At this point, patients' preferences for one or the other approach should be considered in treatment planning, and they should be assisted in obtaining access to an alternative treatment that they prefer.

An important concern (and area for future research) is Which treatment will be most effective for which patient? This question was stated in a comprehensive way by Paul (1969): "What treatment, by whom, is most effective for this individual with that specific problem, under which set of circumstances, and how does it come about?" (p. 44). Norton, DiNardo, and Barlow (1983) reviewed some of the initial research in this area and have provided suggestions for future research.

A related issue is the assessment and treatment of special populations with panic disorder. Among the special groups that have been considered in recent years are adolescents (Barlow & Seidner, 1983; Last & Strauss, 1989), individuals presenting in cardiology clinics (Beitman et. al., 1988; Mukerji, Beitman, Alpert, Hewett, & Basha, 1987), individuals with dizziness or balance problems as a major component of their panic attacks (Jacob & Lilienfeld, Chapter 2), patients with chemical dependency (Norton, Malan, Cairns, Wozney, & Broughton, 1989), and patients with somatization (Noyes, Reich, Clancy, & O'Gorman, 1986). It is possible that these groups and others may require special adjustments in treatment approach.

Although many patients treated with pharmacotherapy or cognitive-behavioral techniques show improvement by the end of treatment, many also have some remaining disability. The specific nature of the residual disability has been largely ignored, but must be studied to improve our approaches to treating it. As suggested by Rapee and Barlow in Chapter 7, different treatments or components of treatment may be required for different aspects of the problem and should be emphasized in different phases of treatment. Relapse following successful treatment is a related problem. It will be important to study factors related to relapse (Rachman, 1989); the work on relapse prevention in addictive behavior (Marlatt & Gordon, 1985) may provide a useful model initially.

Challenges for Pharmacologic Treatment

Improving the Long-term Outcome of Treatment

Each of the broad areas of treatment clearly has major issues that remain to be addressed. A major issue in pharmacologic treatment is the long-term outcome. Fyer, Sandberg, and Klein (Chapter 6) recommend that treatment with antidepressants continue for at least 6 months to reduce the likelihood of relapse. Zitrin, Klein, Woerner, and Ross (1983) reported a 19% to 30% relapse rate during a 2-year follow-up period after treatment with imipramine and supportive psychotherapy or behavior therapy; Sheehan has indicated a relapse rate of 70% following 6 months of treatment with imipramine or phenelzine (quoted by Fyer, Sandberg, and Klein in Chapter 6).

There is an even greater concern with the high rate of relapse and withdrawal symptoms during gradual termination of benzodiazepines. Pecknold, Swinson, Kuch, and Lewis (1988), in a study described in Chapter 8, found that 27% of patients tapered off alprazolam over 5 weeks had rebound panic attacks—panic attacks more frequent than at the onset of treatment. Discontinuation symptoms (symptoms not seen before treatment) affected 35% of the alprazolam-treated group and no subjects in the placebo-treated control group. Upon discontinuation of treatment, subjects in the alprazolam group were similar to the placebo control group on most measures. Fyer and her colleagues (Chapter 6) report some difficulty persuading patients to discontinue treatment with alprazolam, but Swinson and his associates (Chapter 8) have found that in spite of the difficulties some patients encounter, most can be assisted to discontinue. There is some hope that slower withdrawal schedules, longer-acting benzodiazepines such as clonazepam, and additional cognitive-behavioral treatment (see Chapter 8), will result in fewer problems with withdrawal and rebound effects.

It is important for discontinuation symptoms, rebound, and relapse following treatment to be thoroughly studied so these factors may be considered when planning treatment and the patient appropriately informed. To date only a few studies exist, with variable results, to guide decision making.

New drugs are constantly being evaluated for their efficacy in treating panic disorder. Presumably new agents will be developed that will be even more effective or have fewer negative side effects.

Challenges for Cognitive-Behavioral Treatment

Improving the Accessibility of Treatment

A major problem for the proponents of cognitive-behavioral treatment is the limited accessibility of treatment for the average individual with panic disorder. Albee (1979) has argued, in an analysis of human resources in the provision of mental health services, that there will never be enough providers (in the North American context, at least) to help all those suffering from serious mental health problems. Therefore we must develop alternative methods of service delivery and, more importantly, preventive approaches if we are to provide adequate assistance to the public at large. (See "Early Intervention and Prevention" in the pages that follow.)

Self-help and Mutual Aid Approaches

An innovative solution to the problem of high demand and scarce treatment resources is the movement toward self-help and mutual aid. The American Psychological Association Task Force on Self-Help Therapies (1978; quoted in Rosen, 1987) noted that well-evaluated self-help programs "are able to reach large numbers of individuals on an extremely cost-efficient basis. These programs can help individuals to maintain their autonomy and individuality by decreasing reliance upon professionals. Self-help programs can also serve important educational and preventive functions" (p. 49).

Self-help comes in many forms, featuring various amounts of therapist involvement. Variations range from bibliotherapy, in which individuals select and use therapeutic or educational materials independently, to the use of structured self-help materials under the supervision of trained therapists. With each increment in the amount of therapist involvement, the cost of the program increases and accessibility decreases.

Mutual aid groups are a common variant of self-help. In these groups, individuals with a common problem (such as agoraphobia, grief, or chemical dependency) band together to provide mutual support, education, and assistance in coping with the problem. A number of groups focusing on the needs of individuals with panic disorder and agoraphobia are active in North America and Europe. They often provide educational materials, information about treatment resources, and self-help therapy groups to interested members of the public. The Phobic Society of America, for example, publishes a brief treatment manual for use in understanding and overcoming panic attacks and phobic avoidance (Wilson, 1987).

Self-help manuals may provide inexpensive, accessible, and immediate assistance for individuals interested in a self-help treatment approach, and they might be useful as an adjunct to more traditional psychological and pharmacologic treatments. A stepped approach to treatment is a potentially cost-effective method of service delivery. It introduces one program after another, beginning with the simplest and least costly intervention (for example, a self-help manual). The intensity of intervention is increased depending on an individual's performance. The object is to provide the optimal level of professional support and program structure to enable each individual to reach his or her treatment goals (Black & Threlfall, 1986).

There are clear indications that practitioners are ready to use self-help materials. Starker (1988), for example, reported that 88% of a sample of practicing psychologists routinely prescribed self-help books, and 93% rated them as "often" or "sometimes" helpful. This suggests that well-evaluated self-help materials might enhance the effectiveness or efficiency of treatment provided by trained therapists. Although many of the self-help manuals currently available focus on psychological approaches, books are also available that present biological models and emphasize pharmacologic treatment (Gold, 1989; Sheehan, 1986).

Unfortunately, little research has evaluated self-administered treatment for panic disorder. One of the earliest studies of minimal therapist involvement in the treatment of panic disorder was described by Mathews, Gelder, and Johnston (1981). Patients were provided with a behavioral treatment manual, initially used with the therapist's supervision. Subsequently, the manual was used more independently, with the assistance of a spouse or treatment partner. Mathews et al. reported that 3.5 hours of therapist time were sufficient to produce a marked improvement in agoraphobic avoidance. The magnitude of improvement was comparable to that reported in similar treatments involving more clinician time.

Holden, O'Brien, Barlow, Stetson, and Infantino (1983) evaluated a self-treatment manual in a multiple-baseline-across-subjects design. Six patients with severe agoraphobic avoidance showed no improvement with a self-treatment manual but moderate improvement with therapist-administered treatment. However, the patients selected for this study appeared to be more severely impaired than typical clinical samples, in that they were unable to attend a clinic for treatment. The degree of improvement with therapist-administered treatment was also more limited than that usually reported in clinical samples. This suggests that self-help manuals may be of limited utility in cases of severe phobic avoidance; however, little is known about the characteristics of individuals who successfully use a self-help approach for panic disorder.

In a larger group-comparison study, Ghosh and Marks (1987; Ghosh, Marks, & Carr, 1988) found that patients having panic disorder with agoraphobia showed a marked and equivalent reduction in agoraphobic avoidance when a behavior therapy program was administered by a psychiatrist (3.1 hours of clinician time), a computer program (1.2 hours of clinician time), or a self-help treatment manual (0 hours of clinician time). The treatment program involved graduated exposure to feared situations in extensive practice sessions. This was a striking demonstration of the potential utility of self-help materials in the treatment of panic disorder with agoraphobia.

More extensive evaluation of the effectiveness of self-administered treatment manuals and mutual aid groups is an important priority for increasing the accessibility of cognitive-behavioral treatment.

Identifying the Effective Components of Treatment

Another important challenge for the proponents of cognitive-behavioral treatment is to identify the effective components of what are typically multicomponent treatments and to determine the most effective ways to combine them. The most recently proposed cognitive-behavioral treatments for panic disorder (described by Rapee & Barlow in Chapter 7) include components such as education about panic attacks, cognitive restructuring, breathing retraining, exposure to internal cues related to panic attacks, self-paced exposure to avoided situations, and assistance with other life problems. To date there has been little research on the effectiveness of each of these components. In addition, which components should be stressed most strongly may depend on a detailed assessment of the individual's anxiety problem. For example, one might expect to take a different approach with a patient who has difficulty with hyperventilation during panic attacks than with one who has primarily gastrointestinal symptoms. Norton, DiNardo, and Barlow (1983) advocated research to consider which of Lang's (1978) three dimensions of anxiety (cognitive/subjective, physiological, and behavioral) is most affected in a particular individual and to evaluate whether interventions focused on the most affected dimension(s) have the greatest impact.

Rapee and Barlow point out in Chapter 7 that to develop the most effective treatments it is helpful to have a good understanding of the mechanism of action of all currently available treatments. Unfortunately, research on the mechanisms of action has lagged behind that on treatment outcome.

Early Intervention and Prevention

Early intervention—particularly primary prevention—has been advocated as an alternative to a focus on treating established disorders. Early-intervention programs often use approaches similar to those of currently available treatment to aid the affected individual before the problem becomes serious or disabling. One of the most likely places to provide early intervention is the primary health care setting. To date little or nothing has been published about efforts to intervene early in these settings, but it is clear that there is a considerable unmet need. Drug companies are making efforts to educate primary care physicians about the pharmacologic treatment of panic disorder by providing educational materials developed for this audience (McGlynn & Metcalf, 1989), but little has been done to provide information about alternative cognitive-behavioral treatments. In our experience, primary care service providers are very receptive to nonpharmacologic approaches, but limited numbers of trained individuals to provide treatment is a major problem. Given the high prevalence of panic disorder and the limited resources available, it is unlikely that even early intervention will be able to address the needs for treatment of panic disorder in the community.

Primary prevention is an alternative that has been shown to be feasible in other areas of health care. Experience in public health indicates that effective preventive interventions are often quite different in form from effective treatments (Winett, King, & Altman, 1989). They are developed most readily when we have a good knowledge of the factors that lead to the development of the disorder. However, it may not be reasonable to delay research on preventive approaches until we have a thorough understanding of the development of panic disorder, because effective public health preventive interventions have also been developed on the basis of "hunches," when a thorough understanding of a disorder was not available.

Considerable conceptual work has been done on preventive approaches in mental health in general (Albee, 1984; Winett et al., 1989), but there has been little empirical work in the area of anxiety disorders. An exception is the work on post–traumatic stress disorder (Steketee & Foa, 1987), for which there are identifiable risk factors and access to populations clearly at risk (for instance, rape victims and victims of violence). Some possibilities for preventive approaches to panic disorder could be considered based on our present knowledge and models of the development of panic disorder and agoraphobia. Work on the cognitive aspects of panic disorder, for example, suggests that misinterpretations of experiences of intense anxiety may be an important developmental factor (Ottaviani & Beck, 1987; Thorpe & Hecker, Chapter 5). Although our educational system is taking on more and more responsibility for preparing young people for important life experiences, little preparation is provided for the experiences of anxiety and depression that are a normal part of life. It would be interesting to follow the long-term impact of a preventive educational program with young people who are at risk. Courses on stress management are increasingly available in the workplace, and it would be helpful to evaluate more thoroughly the long-term effects of those programs in helping individuals cope with stress and anxiety. Barlow (1988) argues that earlier stress reactions may sensitize the individual to later experiences of more intense anxiety. Dusenbury and Albee (1988) suggest focusing on traumatic experiences, stress, coping and appraisal, self-esteem, and social support in research on the prevention of anxiety disorders. Work on family patterns and the genetic aspects of panic disorder (reviewed by Lader in Chapter 4) indicates that children of parents with panic disorder are at increased risk for developing it themselves. This would be an interesting and accessible group for research on risk factors and preventive approaches.

Research: The Role of the Practitioner

Although many of the advances in the assessment and treatment of panic disorder have occurred in large research centers around the world, the practitioner continues to play an important role in the development of new knowledge. The research designs used in large centers often require the accumulation of large numbers of subjects with relatively homogeneous problems. This may result in the exclusion of individuals with milder or less typical forms of the disorder. Both psychiatry and psychology have a long tradition of accumulating knowledge based on the intensive study of small numbers of cases by practitioners working in the field. This approach is particularly well established in the field of behavioral analysis (Barlow, Hayes, & Nelson, 1984; Hawkins, 1989). In fact Barlow (1984), in the first issue of his tenure as editor of *Behavior Therapy*, emphasized the importance of the practitioner in the development of new knowledge and initiated a special section of that prestigious journal for the purpose. Psychiatry journals are also receptive to collections of case studies of individuals that illustrate important points in the understanding, assessment, or treatment of a disorder. Practitioners working outside of large centers may be more likely to encounter and focus on unusual presentations of anxiety problems, early or less severe forms of the disorder (Ross, Walker, Norton, & Neufeld, 1988), or panic disorder associated with other health problems.

In fact, many of the most promising developments in our understanding and treatment of panic disorder have been based on the astute observations of experienced clinicians. The important contributions of Klein (1964) and Beck (1976), for example, began with clinical observations. Similarly, recent interest in the role of hyperventilation in panic attacks (Lum, 1981) and the large proportion of individuals with anxiety problems seen in cardiac clinics (Beitman et al., 1987) resulted from clinical observation.

Just as the last decade has been an exciting one for research in panic disorder, it is likely that the next will produce a great deal of new knowledge. The practitioner has an important role to play in this enterprise, whether by bringing forth interesting clinical observations or by providing detailed accounts of assessment and treatment that point out both the strengths and weaknesses of our current approaches.

References

Albee, G. W. (1979). Psychiatry's human resources: 20 years later. *Hospital and Community Psychiatry, 30,* 783–786.

Albee, G. W. (1984). Prologue: A model for classifying prevention programs. In J. M. Joffe, G. W. Albee, & L. D. Kelly (Eds.), *Reading in primary prevention of psychopathology: Basic concepts.* Hanover, NH: University Press of New England.

Barlow, D. H. (1984). Editorial. *Behavior Therapy, 15,* 1–2.

Barlow, D. H. (1988). *Anxiety and its disorders.* New York: Guilford Press.

Barlow, D. H., Hayes, S. C., & Nelson, R. O. (1984). *The scientist-practitioner: Research and accountability in clinical and educational settings.* New York: Pergamon Press.

Barlow, D. H. & Seidner, A. L. (1983). Treatment of adolescent agoraphobics: Effects on parent-adolescent relations. *Behaviour Research and Therapy, 21,* 519–527.

Basoglu, M., Marks, I. M., Sengun, S., & Lax, J. (Sept. 1988). *Phenomenological aspects of panic and anxiety.* Poster presented at World Congress of Behaviour Therapy, Edinburgh, Scotland.

Beck, A. T. (1976). *Cognitive therapy and the emotional disorders.* New York: International Universities Press.

Beck, A. T., Ward, C. H., Mendelsohn, M., Mock, J., & Erbaugh, J. (1961). An inventory for measuring depression. *Archives of General Psychiatry, 4,* 561–571.

Beitman, B. D., Basha, I., Flaker, G., DeRosear, L., Mukerji, V., & Lamberti, J. (1987). Non-fearful panic disorder: Panic attacks without fear. *Behaviour Research and Therapy, 25*, 487–492.

Beitman, B. D., Basha, I. M., Trombka, L. H., Jayaratna, M. A., Russel, B. D., & Tarr, S. K. (1988). Alprazolam in the treatment of cardiology patients with atypical chest pain and panic disorder. *Journal of Clinical Psychopharmacology, 8*, 127–130.

Black, D. R., & Threlfall, W. E. (1986). A stepped approach to weight control: A minimal intervention and a bibliotherapy problem-solving program. *Behaviour Therapy, 17*, 144–157.

Chambless, D. L., Caputo, G. C., Bright, P., & Gallagher, R. (1984). Assessment of fear of fear in agoraphobics: The Body Sensations Questionnaire and the Agoraphobic Cognitions Questionnaire. *Journal of Consulting and Clinical Psychology, 52*, 1090–1097.

Chambless, D. L., Caputo, G. C., Jasin, S. E., Gracely, E. J., & Williams, C. (1985). The Mobility Inventory for Agoraphobia. *Behaviour Research and Therapy, 23*, 35–44.

Coryell, W. & Noyes, R. (1988). Placebo response in panic disorder. *American Journal of Psychiatry, 145*, 1138–1140.

Derogatis, L. R. (1977). *SCL-90 administration, scoring and procedures manual—I.* Baltimore, MD: Johns Hopkins University Press.

Dusenbury, L., & Albee, G. W. (1988). Primary prevention of anxiety disorders. In C G. Last & M. Hersen, *Handbook of anxiety disorders.* Oxford: Pergamon Press.

Ghosh, A., & Marks, I. M. (1987). Self-treatment of agoraphobia by exposure. *Behaviour Therapy, 18*, 3–16.

Ghosh, A., Marks, I. M., & Carr, A. C. (1988). Therapist contact and outcome of self-exposure treatment for phobias: A controlled study. *British Journal of Psychiatry, 152*, 234–238.

Gold, M. S. (1989). *The good news about panic, anxiety and phobias: Cures, treatments and solutions in the new age of biopsychiatry.* New York: Villard Books.

Hawkins, R. P. (1989). Developing potent behavior-change technologies: An invitation to cognitive behavior therapists. *The Behavior Therapist, 12*, 126–131.

Holden, A. E., O'Brien, G. T., Barlow, D. H., Stetson, D., & Infantino, A. (1983). Self-help manual for agoraphobia: A preliminary report of effectiveness. *Behavior Therapy, 14*, 545–556.

Kerns, L. L. (1986). Treatment of mental disorders in pregnancy: A review of psychotropic drug risks and benefits. *Journal of Nervous and Mental Disease, 174*, 652–659.

Klein, D. F. (1964). Delineation of two drug-responsive anxiety syndromes. *Psychopharmacologia, 5*, 397–408.

Lang, P. J. (1978). Anxiety: Toward a psychological definition. In H. S. Akiskal & W. L. Webb (Eds.), *Psychiatric diagnosis: Exploration of biological criteria.* New York: Spectrum.

Last, C. G., & Strauss, C. C. (1989). Panic disorder in children and adolescents. *Journal of Anxiety Disorders, 3*, 87–95.

Lum, L. C. (1981). Hyperventilation and the anxiety state. *Journal of the Royal Society of Medicine, 74*, 1–4.

McGlynn, T. J., & Metcalf, H. L. (1989). *Diagnosis and treatment of anxiety disorders: A physician's handbook.* Washington, DC: American Psychiatric Press.

Marks, I. M., & Mathews, A. M. (1979). Brief standard self-rating for phobic patients. *Behaviour Research and Therapy, 17*, 263–267.

Marlatt, G. A., & Gordon, J. R. (Eds.) (1985). *Relapse prevention*. New York: Guilford Press.

Mathews, A. M., Gelder, M. G., & Johnston, D. W. (1981). *Agoraphobia: Nature and Treatment*. New York: Guilford Press.

Michelson, L. & Mavissakalian, M. (1983). Temporal stability of self-report measures in agoraphobia research. *Behaviour Research and Therapy, 21*, 695–698.

Mukerji, V., Beitman, B. D., Alpert, M. A., Hewett, J. E., & Basha, I. M. (1987). Panic attack symptoms in patients with chest pain and angiographically normal coronary arteries. *Journal of Anxiety Disorders, 1*, 41–46.

Norton, G. R., Allen, G. E., & Hilton, J. (1983). The social validity of treatments for agoraphobia. *Behaviour Research and Therapy, 21*, 393–399.

Norton, G. R., Allen, G. E., & Walker, J. R. (1985). Predicting treatment preferences for agoraphobia. *Behaviour Research and Therapy, 23*, 699–701.

Norton, G. R., DiNardo, P. A., & Barlow, D. (1983). Predicting phobics' response to therapy: A consideration of subjective physiological and behavioural measures. *Canadian Psychology, 24*, 50–58.

Norton, G. R., Malan, J., Cairns, S., Wozney, K., & Broughton, R. (1989). Factors influencing drinking behavior in alcoholic panickers. *Behaviour Research and Therapy, 27*, 167–171.

Noyes, R., Reich, J., Clancy, J., & O'Gorman, T. W. (1986). Reduction in hypochondriasis with treatment of panic disorder. *British Journal of Psychiatry, 149*, 631–635.

Ottaviani, R., & Beck, A. T. (1987). Cognitive aspects of panic disorders. *Journal of Anxiety Disorders, 1*, 15–28.

Paul, G. L. (1969). Behavior modification research: Design and tactics. In C. M. Franks (Ed.), *Behavior therapy: Appraisal and status*. New York: McGraw-Hill.

Pecknold, J. C., Swinson, R. P., Kuch, K., & Lewis, C. P. (1988). Alprazolam in panic disorder and agoraphobia: Results from a multicenter trial. III. Discontinuation effects. *Archives of General Psychiatry, 45*, 429–436.

Rachman, S. (1989). The return of fear: Review and prospect. *Clinical Psychology Review, 9*, 147–168.

Robinson, G., Stewart, D., & Flak, E. (1986). The rational use of psychotropic drugs in pregnancy and postpartum. *Canadian Journal of Psychiatry, 31*, 183–190.

Rosen, G. M. (1987). Self-help treatment books and the commercialization of psychotherapy. *American Psychologist, 42*, 46–51.

Ross, C. A., Walker, J. R., Norton, G. R., & Neufeld, K. (1988). Management of anxiety and panic attacks in immediate care facilities. *General Hospital Psychiatry, 10*, 129–131.

Sheehan, D. V. (1986). *The anxiety disease*. New York: Bantam Books.

Starker, S. (1988). Self-help treatment books: The rest of the story. *American Psychologist, 43*, 599–600.

Steketee, G., & Foa, E. B. (1987). Rape victims: Post–traumatic stress responses and their treatment: A review of the literature. *Journal of Anxiety Disorders, 1*, 69–86.

Turner, S. M., Beidel, D. C., & Jacob, R. G. (1988). Assessment of panic. In S. Rachman & J. Maser (Eds.), *Panic: Psychological perspectives*. Hillsdale, NJ: Lawrence Erlbaum.

Wilson, R. R. (1987). *Breaking the panic cycle: Self-help for people with phobias*. Rockville, MD: Phobic Society of America.

Winett, R. A., King, A. C., & Altman, D. G. (1989). *Health psychology and public health: An integrative approach*. New York: Pergamon Press.

Zitrin, C. M., Klein, D. F., Woerner, M. G., & Ross, D. C. (1983). Treatment of phobias. I. Comparison of imipramine hydrochloride and placebo. *Archives of General Psychiatry, 40,* 125–138.

Appendix

Compiled by John R. Walker

Introduction

A number of instruments and forms that the practitioner may find helpful in the assessment and treatment of panic disorder are described in the pages that follow. These are only a few of the measures available; the reader is referred to Chapters 2, 7, and 11 for descriptions and examples of alternative measures. We would like to thank the authors and publishers who gave us permission to reproduce their forms.

Panic Attack Questionnaire

BACKGROUND:
The Panic Attack Questionnaire provides a retrospective description of the symptoms and thoughts typically experienced during a panic attack and gives an indication of the frequency of attacks, duration of the problem, whether attacks are expected or unexpected, lifestyle change or avoidance, characteristics of attacks, and family history of attacks. Although this instrument was developed for use in research, it would also be suitable for clinical use, before or after a clinical interview. The version reprinted here is a revised version of an earlier DSM-III version prepared by Norton, Dorward, and Cox in 1986 to incorporate the changes of the DSM-III-R and to reflect more recent research experience.

PRIMARY REFERENCE:
Norton, G. R., Dorward, J., & Cox, B. J. (1986). Factors associated with panic attacks in nonclinical subjects. *Behavior Therapy, 17,* 239–252.

AVAILABILITY:
Dr. G. Ron Norton, Department of Psychology, University of Winnipeg, 515 Portage Ave., Winnipeg, Manitoba, Canada R3B 2E9. This instrument is reprinted with permission of the author.

_____ Panic Attack Questionnaire (DSM-III-R Version) _____

Please provide the following information:

ID Code   _____

Age   _____

Sex   _____

Occupation   _____

Educational Level_____

Marital Status (please check one):

_____ Single (never married)

_____ Cohabiting

_____ Married

_____ Separated

_____ Divorced

_____ Widowed

Panic Attack Questionnaire (DSM-III-R Version)

A panic attack is the sudden onset of intense apprehension, fear, or terror, often associated with feelings of impending doom. Some of the symptoms experienced during a panic attack are dizziness, shortness of breath, chest pain or discomfort, and trembling or shaking.

If you have experienced one or more panic attacks in the *past year*, please answer *all* of the remaining questions. If you *have not* had a panic attack in the *past year*, please skip to question 23.

1. In the past year, approximately how many panic attacks have you had?

   1   2   3   4   5   6   7   8   9   10   11 or more

2. In the past 4 weeks, how many panic attacks have you had?

   0   1   2   3   4   5   6   7   8   9   10 or more

3. What is the greatest number of panic attacks you have had during any 4-week period in your life?

   0   1   2   3   4   5   6   7   8   9   10 or more

4. For how many months or years (approximately) have you been experiencing panic attacks?

   _____ years   _____ months

5. How long ago was your worst attack?

   _____ years   _____ months   _____ weeks   _____ days

6. Have you ever had a panic attack that was unexpected ("from out of the blue")?

   _____ no   _____ yes

7. If you answered "yes" to question number 6, please indicate the proportion of your panic attacks that are unexpected.

   _____ all   _____ most   _____ some   _____ few   _____ none

8. If you recall your first panic attack, please describe briefly the circumstances surrounding the attack (e.g., where you were, what you were doing).

   _____

   _____

9. How disturbing or distressing are your panic attacks?

not at all	mildly	moderately	very	extremely
0	1	2	3	4

10. To what degree have your panic attacks restricted or changed your lifestyle (e.g., activities you engage in, places you go)?

not at all	some	moderately	quite a bit	extremely
0	1	2	3	4

11. Do you avoid certain situations due to fear of having a panic attack?

    _____ no   _____ yes

12. If you answered "yes" to question number 11, please indicate situations you avoid.

---

13. Please indicate how severely you experienced each of the following symptoms *during your most recent panic attacks* and *during your most severe attack*.

not at all	mildly	moderately	severely	very severely
0	1	2	3	4

	most recent	most severe
a. Shortness of breath or smothering sensation	0 1 2 3 4	0 1 2 3 4
b. Dizziness, unsteady feelings, or faintness	0 1 2 3 4	0 1 2 3 4
c. Racing or pounding heart	0 1 2 3 4	0 1 2 3 4
d. Trembling or shaking	0 1 2 3 4	0 1 2 3 4
e. Sweating	0 1 2 3 4	0 1 2 3 4
f. Choking	0 1 2 3 4	0 1 2 3 4
g. Nausea or abdominal distress	0 1 2 3 4	0 1 2 3 4
h. Feelings that things are not real	0 1 2 3 4	0 1 2 3 4
i. Numbness or tingling sensations	0 1 2 3 4	0 1 2 3 4
j. Hot flashes or chills	0 1 2 3 4	0 1 2 3 4
k. Chest pains or discomfort	0 1 2 3 4	0 1 2 3 4
l. Fear of dying	0 1 2 3 4	0 1 2 3 4
m. Fear of going crazy or losing control	0 1 2 3 4	0 1 2 3 4
n. Visual difficulties (blurring, tunnel vision)	0 1 2 3 4	0 1 2 3 4
o. Hearing difficulties (e.g., difficulty hearing, ringing in ears)	0 1 2 3 4	0 1 2 3 4
p. Difficulty concentrating	0 1 2 3 4	0 1 2 3 4
q. Desire to escape from scene of attack	0 1 2 3 4	0 1 2 3 4
r. Thoughts or images that you cannot get rid of	0 1 2 3 4	0 1 2 3 4
s. Difficulty speaking	0 1 2 3 4	0 1 2 3 4
t. Feelings of embarrassment	0 1 2 3 4	0 1 2 3 4

14. When a panic attack occurs, *generally* what is the time period between the onset of the attack and when the panic is the most intense?
    a. just a few minutes (less than 10 minutes)
    b. 10 to 30 minutes
    c. 30 minutes to an hour
    d. several hours
    e. more than a day

15. Have *any* of your attacks developed suddenly and increased to peak intensity within 10 minutes of your noticing the first symptom?

    _____ no   _____ yes

16. How long, *on the average*, does a panic attack last (from start to finish)?
    a. just a few minutes (less than 10 minutes)
    b. 10 to 30 minutes
    c. 30 minutes to an hour
    d. several hours
    e. more than a day

17. How anxious does the thought of future panic attacks make you?
    a. not at all
    b. mildly
    c. moderately
    d. very
    e. extremely

18. How serious (either psychologically or medically) do you think your panic attacks are?

not at all		moderately		extremely
0	1	2	3	4

19. To what extent have you considered seeking treatment for your panic attacks?
    a. I have never considered seeking treatment.
    b. I have thought about seeking treatment, but not seriously.
    c. I have seriously thought about seeking treatment, but doubt I will actually do so.
    d. I have seriously thought about seeking treatment and intend to do so in the future.
    e. I have asked for treatment in the past (or I am currently receiving treatment) specifically for panic attacks.

20. Have you ever been told there is a medical reason for your attacks?

    _____ no _____ yes   If yes, what were you told? _____

    _____

21. During an attack, have you ever lost control or done something uncontrolled that you later regretted?

    _____ no _____ yes   If yes, explain. _____

    _____

22. Please describe where you were and what you were doing when you experienced your last three panic attacks (if you've had three or more) and indicate if the panic attack was expected in each situation.

		expected	unexpected
a.	_____	_____	_____
b.	_____	_____	_____
c.	_____	_____	_____

23. To the best of your knowledge, have any of the following members of your family experienced panic attacks?

	age	yes	no	don't know	not applicable
Mother	____	____	____	____	____
Father	____	____	____	____	____
Sister(s)	____	____	____	____	____
Brother(s)	____	____	____	____	____
Daughter(s)	____	____	____	____	____
Son(s)	____	____	____	____	____

Agoraphobic Cognitions Questionnaire
_____ and Body Sensations Questionnaire _____

BACKGROUND:

These two questionnaires are described in some detail in Chapters 2 and 7. They were designed to assist in the clinical and research assessment of "fear of fear" in individuals with agoraphobia. The respondent is asked to rate his or her thoughts and bodily sensations when nervous or frightened. The authors present information on the reliability and validity of the scales in the primary reference following. Because the instructions do not specify that clients focus on experiences during panic attacks, it is not clear how specific the ratings are for panic attacks. Some thoughts—particularly thoughts about dying—that individuals commonly report during panic attacks are not specifically sampled by the Agoraphobic Cognitions Questionnaire, as Ottaviani and Beck pointed out in 1987.

PRIMARY REFERENCE:

Chambless, D. L., Caputo, G. C., Bright, P., & Gallagher, R. (1984). Assessment of fear of fear in agoraphobics: The Body Sensations Questionnaire and the Agoraphobic Cognitions Questionnaire. *Journal of Consulting and Clinical Psychology, 52,* 1090–1097.

AVAILABILITY:

Dr. Dianne L. Chambless, Department of Psychology, Asbury Building, The American University, Washington, DC 20016-8062. These instruments are reprinted with permission of the authors.

REFERENCES:

Ottaviani, R., & Beck, A. T. (1987). Cognitive aspects of panic disorders. *Journal of Anxiety Disorders, 1,* 15–28.

Agoraphobic Cognitions Questionnaire _____

Below are some thoughts or ideas that may pass through your mind when you are nervous or frightened. Indicate how often each thought occurs when you are nervous. Rate each one from 1 to 5, using the scale below.

1 = Thought never occurs.
2 = Thought rarely occurs.
3 = Thought occurs half the time when I am nervous.
4 = Thought usually occurs.
5 = Thought always occurs when I am nervous.

_____ I am going to throw up.

_____ I am going to pass out.

_____ I must have a brain tumor.

_____ I will have a heart attack.

_____ I will choke to death.

_____ I am going to act foolishly.

_____ I am going blind.

_____ I will not be able to control myself.

_____ I will hurt someone.

_____ I am going to have a stroke.

_____ I am going to go crazy.

_____ I am going to scream.

_____ I am going to babble or talk funny.

_____ I will be paralyzed by fear.

Other ideas, not listed (please describe and rate).

_____ _____

_____ _____

_____ _____

Body Sensations Questionnaire

Below is a list of specific body sensations that may occur when you are nervous or in a feared situation. Please mark down how afraid you are of these feelings. Use the 5-point scale shown here. Please rate all items.

1 = I am not frightened or worried by this sensation.
2 = I am somewhat frightened by this sensation.
3 = I am moderately frightened by this sensation.
4 = I am very frightened by this sensation.
5 = I am extremely frightened by this sensation.

_____ 1. Heart palpitations

_____ 2. Pressure or heavy feeling in chest

_____ 3. Numbness in arms or legs

_____ 4. Tingling in the fingertips

_____ 5. Numbness in another part of your body

_____ 6. Shortness of breath

_____ 7. Dizziness

_____ 8. Blurred or distorted vision

_____ 9. Nausea

_____ 10. "Butterflies" in the stomach

_____ 11. A knot in the stomach

_____ 12. A lump in the throat

_____ 13. Wobbly or rubber legs

_____ 14. Sweating

_____ 15. A dry throat

_____ 16. Disorientation and confusion

_____ 17. Disconnectedness from the body; or feeling only partly present

_____ 18. Other (please describe):

_____

_____

Panic Attack Diary

BACKGROUND:
As noted in Chapter 15, diary measures may provide a more accurate indication of the frequency and characteristics of panic attacks than retrospective measures. The Panic Attack Diary is lengthier than the Panic Attack Record described by Rapee and Barlow in Chapter 7, but it has the advantage of including clinically important information about the order in which symptoms were experienced, activities and thoughts before and after the attack, and coping strategies used to deal with the attack. Patients are instructed to complete the Panic Attack Diary as soon as possible after a panic attack has occurred. The diary is used for research and in the cognitive-behavioral treatment of panic disorder. In treatment contexts, the therapist and patient typically review the diaries to examine the situations and thoughts that provoke panic attacks and the coping strategies used to deal with them.

AVAILABILITY:
Dr. John R. Walker, M4—St. Boniface General Hospital, 409 Tache Ave., Winnipeg, Manitoba, Canada R2H 2A6. Developed by John Walker, Vivienne Rowan, Gloria Eldridge, and Steve Holborn. This instrument is reprinted with permission of the authors.

Panic Attack Diary

INITIALS: _____ DAY: _____ DATE: _____

A panic attack is a sudden, unexpected onset of intense apprehension, fear, or terror. Fill in the form immediately after your panic attack ends.

Please circle the numbers of the bodily sensations or symptoms that occurred during your attack.

1. shortness of breath or smothering sensations
2. choking
3. palpitations or accelerated heartrate
4. chest pain or discomfort
5. sweating
6. faintness
7. dizziness, lightheadedness, or unsteady feelings
8. nausea or abdominal distress
9. feeling that you or your surroundings are strange or unreal
10. numbness or tingling sensations
11. flushes (hot flashes) or chills
12. trembling or shaking
13. fear of dying
14. fear of going crazy or doing something uncontrolled
15. desire to flee or escape
16. difficulty thinking

other symptoms:

17. _____

18. _____

List in order the numbers of the first three symptoms that you experienced:

_____   _____   _____

Did you expect that you might panic in this situation?   yes _____   no _____

| Panic attack | | Where were you? | With whom? | What were you doing before the panic attack? | What were you thinking before the panic attack? |
Start time	Finish time				

What did you do after the panic attack?	What were you thinking after the panic attack?	Did you change your plans?	What did people around you do?

COMMENTS: _____

_____

_____

0	1	2	3	4	5	6	7	8
not at all		slightly		moderately		very		extremely

Choose a number from the scale above to indicate how frightening or distressing your

symptoms were.   _____

Did you do anything to control or stop your panic attack?   _____   If yes, describe
fully what you did.

_____

_____

How effective was it?   _____

_____

Fear Questionnaire

BACKGROUND:

The Fear Questionnaire (described in Chapters 2 and 7) is the most widely used self-report measure of phobic avoidance in both clinical and research applications. In addition to a total phobia score, it provides subscale scores for agoraphobia, social phobia, and blood-injury phobia as well as ratings of the main phobia and global phobic symptoms and a composite anxiety-depression score. Some normative data are available for nonclinical populations (Mizes & Crawford, 1986), and the questionnaire has good reliability and validity (Marks & Mathews, 1979; Mavissakalian, 1986a; Michelson & Mavissakalian, 1983). In addition, three major studies have considered what constitutes a clinically significant degree of improvement on the Fear Questionnaire (Jacobson, Wilson, & Tupper, 1988; Mavissakalian, 1986b; Trull, Nietzel, & Main, 1988). Given this information, it is possible to compare the results among the different studies and clinical settings that use this measure. A number of other areas of phobic avoidance may have theoretical significance, but they are not sampled by this measure (for instance, avoidance of interpersonal conflict, expressions of anger, physical activity, sexual activity, and other activities that produce bodily arousal). The Mobility Inventory, described later in this appendix, includes more situations that are typically avoided.

PRIMARY REFERENCE:

Marks, I. M., & Mathews, A. M. (1979). Brief standard self-rating for phobic patients. *Behaviour Research and Therapy, 17,* 263–267, Pergamon Journals Ltd.

AVAILABILITY:

Journal article. This instrument is reprinted with permission of the authors and Pergamon Journals Ltd.

REFERENCES:

Jacobson, N. S., Wilson, L., & Tupper, C. The clinical significance of treatment gains resulting from exposure-based interventions for agoraphobia: A reanalysis of outcome data. *Behavior Therapy, 19*(4), 539–554.

Mavissakalian, M. (1986a). The fear questionnaire: A validity study. *Behaviour Research and Therapy, 24,* 83–85.

Mavissakalian, M. (1986b). Clinically significant improvement in agoraphobia research. *Behaviour Research and Therapy, 24,* 369–370.

Michelson, L., & Mavissakalian, M. (1983). Temporal stability of self-report measures in agoraphobia research. *Behaviour Research and Therapy, 21,* 695–698.

Mizes, J. S., & Crawford, J. (1986). Normative values on the Marks and Mathews Fear Questionnaire: A comparison as a function of age and sex. *Journal of Psychopathology and Behavioral Assessment, 8,* 253–262.

Trull, T. J., Nietzel, M. T., & Main, A. (1988). The use of meta-analysis to assess the clinical significance of behavior therapy for agoraphobia. *Behavior Therapy, 19*(4), 527–538.

Fear Questionnaire

Choose a number from the scale below to indicate how much you would avoid each of the situations listed under it because of fear or other unpleasant feelings. Write the number in the blank opposite each situation.

0	1	2	3	4	5	6	7	8
Would not avoid it		Slightly avoid it		Definitely avoid it		Markedly avoid it		Always avoid it

1. Main phobia you want treated (describe in your own words):

_____ _____

2. Injections or minor surgery _____

3. Eating or drinking with other people _____

4. Hospitals _____

5. Traveling alone by bus _____

6. Walking alone in busy streets _____

7. Being watched or stared at _____

8. Going into crowded shops _____

9. Talking to people in authority _____

10. The sight of blood _____

11. Being criticized _____

12. Traveling alone far from home _____

13. Thought of injury or illness _____

14. Speaking or acting to an audience _____

15. Large open spaces _____

16. Going to the dentist _____

17. Other situations (describe) _____

_____

_____	_____	_____	_____	_____
Tot.	Ag.	B-I.	Soc.	M.F.

Now choose a number from the scale below to show how much you are troubled by
each problem listed under it, and write the number in the blank.

0	1	2	3	4	5	6	7	8
Hardly at all		Slightly troublesome		Definitely troublesome		Markedly troublesome		Very severely troublesome

18. Feeling miserable or depressed   _____

19. Feeling irritable or angry   _____

20. Feeling tense or panicky   _____

21. Having upsetting thoughts come into your mind   _____

22. Feeling you or your surroundings are strange
    or unreal   _____

23. Other feelings (describe)

_____   _____

_____   _____

Total _____

How would you rate the present state of your phobic symptoms on the scale below?
Please circle one number.

0	1	2	3	4	5	6	7	8
No phobias present		Slightly disturbing/ not really disabling		Definitely disturbing/ disabling		Markedly disturbing/ disabling		Very severely disturbing/ disabling

The Mobility Inventory for Agoraphobia

BACKGROUND:

This instrument was developed to provide a more comprehensive self-report measure of the types of situations typically avoided by individuals with agoraphobia. Although the Fear Questionnaire, described earlier, is widely used to assess agoraphobic avoidance, it has a limited range of items (5) on the agoraphobia subscale. The Mobility Inventory provides ratings of a much broader range of situations (27). It also provides separate scales for avoidance when accompanied (Avoidance Accompanied, AAC) or alone (Avoidance Alone, AAL)—a very important distinction that is not considered in the Fear Questionnaire. Information on reliability and validity of the subscales of the measure is provided in the primary reference. The psychometric characteristics of this scale are described in detail in Chapter 2. Because this measure covers a wide range of typical situations, it is particularly useful in clinical treatment planning and evaluation.

PRIMARY REFERENCE:

Chambless, D. L., Caputo, G. C., Jasin, S. E., Gracely, E. J., & Williams, C. (1985). The Mobility Inventory for Agoraphobia. *Behaviour Research and Therapy, 23,* 35–44, Pergamon Journals Ltd.

AVAILABILITY:

Journal article or Dr. Dianne L. Chambless, Department of Psychology, Asbury Building, The American University, Washington, DC 20016-8062. This instrument is reprinted with permission of the authors and Pergamon Journals Ltd.

___ The Mobility Inventory for Agoraphobia (MI) ___

NAME: _____   DATE: _____

Please indicate the degree to which you avoid the following places or situations because of discomfort or anxiety. Rate your amount of avoidance both when with a trusted companion and when alone, using the following scale.

    1 = never avoid
    2 = rarely avoid
    3 = avoid about half the time
    4 = avoid most of the time
    5 = always avoid

You may use numbers halfway between those listed (for example, 3 1/2 or 4 1/2) when you think it is appropriate. Write your score in the blanks for each situation or place under both conditions: when accompanied and when alone. Leave blank any situations that do not apply to you.

Places	Accompanied	Alone
Theaters	_____	_____
Supermarkets	_____	_____
Classrooms	_____	_____
Department stores	_____	_____
Restaurants	_____	_____
Museums	_____	_____
Elevators	_____	_____
Auditoriums or stadiums	_____	_____
Parking garages	_____	_____
High places	_____	_____
How high? _____		
Enclosed spaces (e.g., tunnels)	_____	_____
Open spaces A. Outside (e.g., fields, wide streets, courtyards)	_____	_____
B. Inside (e.g., large rooms, lobbies)	_____	_____

Riding in . . .

Buses   _____   _____

Trains   _____   _____

Subways   _____   _____

Airplanes   _____   _____

Boats   _____   _____

Driving or riding in a car

A. At any time   _____   _____

B. On expressways   _____   _____

Situations . . .

Standing in lines   _____   _____

Crossing bridges   _____   _____

At parties or social gatherings   _____   _____

Walking on the street   _____   _____

Staying at home alone   _____NA_____   _____

Being far away from home   _____   _____

Other (specify)   _____   _____

We define a panic attack as (1) a high level of anxiety accompanied by (2) strong body reactions (heart palpitations, sweating, muscle tremors, dizziness, nausea) with (3) the temporary loss of the ability to plan, think, or reason and (4) the intense desire to escape or flee the situation. (Note: this is different from high anxiety or fear alone.)

Please indicate the total number of panic attacks you have had in the last 7 days. _____

Symptom Questionnaire

BACKGROUND:

This questionnaire was developed to assess the symptoms of panic attacks; it includes all the major somatic symptoms given in the DSM-III-R, plus a number of items designed to investigate symptoms related to vestibular dysfunction, a particular interest of Jacob and his co-workers. The respondent completes the items twice, describing symptoms when very anxious (having a panic attack) and when not anxious. The psychometric properties of this instrument are described in Chapter 2.

PRIMARY REFERENCE:

Jacob, R. G., & Beidel, D. C. (1988). *The Symptom Questionnaire.* Manuscript in preparation.

AVAILABILITY:

Dr. Rolf Jacob, Department of Psychiatry, University of Pittsburgh, Western Psychiatric Institute and Clinic, 3811 O'Hara St., Pittsburgh, PA 15213, U.S.A. This instrument is reprinted with permission of the authors.

Symptom Questionnaire

This questionnaire is designed for people who have problems with recurrent anxiety or "panic" attacks. Side 1 asks how often you have certain specific symptoms, feelings or experiences *during* panic attacks. Side 2 asks how often you experience the same symptoms when you are *not* having a panic attack. If you do not have a problem with anxiety or panic attacks, only fill out Side 2 and write "NA" across page 1.

If you have any extra comments (such as a particular symptom not being asked for or difficulties answering certain questions), please make a note of it in the space below after you have completed the questionnaire.

See next page for the questionnaire.

_____ Symptom Questionnaire (Version P): Side 1 _____

Below is a list of body sensations you may experience when you are very anxious (having a panic attack). Please indicate how commonly you experience the symptoms below _when you are very anxious_ (having a panic attack).

	Never or hardly ever	Sometimes	Often	Very often or almost constantly
1. Lightheadedness	1	2	3	4
2. Trembling, shaking	1	2	3	4
3. Heart palpitations	1	2	3	4
4. Feeling as if you might be fainting	1	2	3	4
5. Feeling as if you might be falling (without losing consciousness)	1	2	3	4
6. Hot and cold flashes	1	2	3	4
7. Dry mouth	1	2	3	4
8. Tendency to fall or lose balance	1	2	3	4
9. Pressure or a heavy feeling in your chest	1	2	3	4
10. Nausea	1	2	3	4
11. Blurred vision	1	2	3	4
12. Dizziness	1	2	3	4
13. Numbness in arms, hands, legs, or face	1	2	3	4
14. Feeling a knot in your stomach	1	2	3	4
15. Feeling as if the room is spinning around you	1	2	3	4
16. Wobbly or rubbery legs	1	2	3	4
17. Sweating	1	2	3	4
18. Spinning sensations in head	1	2	3	4
19. Loss of consciousness, blacking out	1	2	3	4
20. Feeling disconnected from your body or unreal	1	2	3	4
21. Lump in your throat	1	2	3	4
22. Feeling disoriented and confused	1	2	3	4
23. Veering to the left or right	1	2	3	4

Symptom Questionnaire (Version P): Side 2

Please indicate how commonly you experience the symptoms below when you are *not* anxious (that is, *between* panic attacks).

	Never or hardly ever	Sometimes	Often	Very often or almost constantly
1. Lightheadedness	1	2	3	4
2. Trembling, shaking	1	2	3	4
3. Heart palpitations	1	2	3	4
4. Feeling as if you might be fainting	1	2	3	4
5. Feeling as if you might be falling (without losing consciousness)	1	2	3	4
6. Hot and cold flashes	1	2	3	4
7. Dry mouth	1	2	3	4
8. Tendency to fall or lose balance	1	2	3	4
9. Pressure or a heavy feeling in your chest	1	2	3	4
10. Nausea	1	2	3	4
11. Blurred vision	1	2	3	4
12. Dizziness	1	2	3	4
13. Numbness in arms, hands, legs, or face	1	2	3	4
14. Feeling a knot in your stomach	1	2	3	4
15. Feeling as if the room is spinning around you	1	2	3	4
16. Wobbly or rubbery legs	1	2	3	4
17. Sweating	1	2	3	4
18. Spinning sensations in head	1	2	3	4
19. Loss of consciousness, blacking out	1	2	3	4
20. Feeling disconnected from your body or unreal	1	2	3	4
21. Lump in your throat	1	2	3	4
22. Feeling disoriented and confused	1	2	3	4
23. Veering to the left or right	1	2	3	4

543

Situational Characteristics Questionnaire

BACKGROUND:

This questionnaire was developed for research purposes by Jacob and his co-workers. Its items are designed to investigate the vestibular problems that seem to accompany agoraphobia in some individuals. Other items sample the phenomenon of "space phobia" described by Marks and Bebbington (1976). The characteristics of this instrument are described in Chapter 2.

PRIMARY REFERENCE:

Jacob, R. G., Lilienfeld, S. O., Furman, J., Durrant, J., & Turner, S. M. (1989). Panic disorder with vestibular dysfunction: Further clinical observations and description of space and motion phobic stimuli. *Journal of Anxiety Disorders, 3*, 117–130.

AVAILABILITY:

Dr. Rolf Jacob, Department of Psychiatry, University of Pittsburgh, Western Psychiatric Institute and Clinic, 3811 O'Hara St., Pittsburgh, PA 15213, U.S.A. This instrument is reprinted with permission of the authors.

REFERENCES:

Marks, I. M., & Bebbington, P. (1976). Space phobia: Syndrome or agoraphobic variant? *British Medical Journal, 2*, 345–347.

Situational Characteristics Questionnaire

PART I

Below are some situations that may elicit discomfort or anxiety in you. We are interested in whether certain characteristics of the situation bother you in comparison with other characteristics of the same situation.

Specifically, please mark

3—if you are *very much* bothered by the characteristic
2—if you are *moderately* bothered by the characteristic
1—if you are *mildly* bothered by the characteristic
0—if you are *not* bothered by the characteristic

You can also mark the space *between* numbers if your discomfort seems greater than that indicated by one particular number but less than the next higher number (i.e., in between "moderately" and "very much," in between "mildly" and "moderately," or in between "mildly" and "not bothered"). If you rate all characteristics of a particular situation as "3" (very much bothered) but one is even worse than another, please underline the characteristic that bothers you the most.

RIDING AS A PASSENGER IN A CAR

1. Uphill	0___1___2___3	
Downhill	0___1___2___3	
2. Bumpy roads	0___1___2___3	
Smooth roads	0___1___2___3	
3. Straight roads	0___1___2___3	
Winding roads	0___1___2___3	
4. Wide highways	0___1___2___3	
Narrow roads	0___1___2___3	
5. Limited access roads		
(freeways, turnpikes)	0___1___2___3	
Unlimited access roads	0___1___2___3	
6. Front seat	0___1___2___3	
Back seat	0___1___2___3	
7. Changing speed (braking or		
accelerating)	0___1___2___3	
Steady speed	0___1___2___3	
8. Reading	0___1___2___3	
Looking out window	0___1___2___3	

BUSES

9. Standing on platform	0___1___2___3	
Sitting	0___1___2___3	
10. Aisle seat	0___1___2___3	
Window seat	0___1___2___3	
11. Standing still	0___1___2___3	
Moving	0___1___2___3	
12. Crowded	0___1___2___3	
Empty	0___1___2___3	

SUPERMARKETS

13. Crowded   0____1____2____3
    Empty   0____1____2____3
14. Near exit   0____1____2____3
    Far from exit   0____1____2____3
15. Looking at end of aisle
    while walking straight
    down the aisle   0____1____2____3
    Looking at items on shelf
    while walking straight
    down the aisle   0____1____2____3

LARGE FIELDS OR SQUARES

16. Open, i.e., without
    nearby boundaries
    (trees, fences, hedges)   0____1____2____3
    Enclosed, i.e., with
    nearby boundaries   0____1____2____3
17. Edge of field   0____1____2____3
    Middle of field   0____1____2____3

TUNNELS

18. Straight   0____1____2____3
    Curved   0____1____2____3
19. Looking at end of tunnel   0____1____2____3
    Looking at lights on
    side of tunnel   0____1____2____3

MOVIE THEATERS

20. Sitting in middle of row   0____1____2____3
    Sitting on aisle   0____1____2____3
21. Sitting far in front   0____1____2____3
    Sitting far in back   0____1____2____3
22. Wide screen   0____1____2____3
    Narrow screen   0____1____2____3

AIRPLANES

23. Changing altitude   0____1____2____3
    Flying at steady altitude   0____1____2____3
24. Landing   0____1____2____3
    Taking off   0____1____2____3
25. Smooth ride   0____1____2____3
    Turbulence   0____1____2____3
26. Window seat   0____1____2____3
    Aisle seat   0____1____2____3
    Middle seat   0____1____2____3

ELEVATORS

27. Stationary	0	1	2	3
Moving	0	1	2	3
28. Crowded	0	1	2	3
Empty	0	1	2	3
29. Going up	0	1	2	3
Going down	0	1	2	3
30. Standard	0	1	2	3
Glass	0	1	2	3
31. Starting	0	1	2	3
Moving at steady speed	0	1	2	3
Stopping	0	1	2	3

ESCALATORS

32. Going up	0	1	2	3
Going down	0	1	2	3

PART II

Are you bothered by any of the following? Use the scale to show how much.

3—very much
2—moderately
1—mildly
0—not at all

33. Aerobic exercise	0	1	2	3
34. Rolling over in bed	0	1	2	3
35. Closing your eyes in the shower	0	1	2	3
36. Looking up at tall buildings	0	1	2	3
37. Leaning far back in a chair	0	1	2	3
38. Reading a newspaper close to your face	0	1	2	3
39. Riding on roller coasters	0	1	2	3
40. Dancing	0	1	2	3
41. Does your discomfort increase as the day progresses (i.e., later in the day)	0	1	2	3

Goal Sheet

BACKGROUND:

In planning cognitive-behavioral treatment, it is important to establish the patient's life goals. Working to improve functioning in areas related to the individual's goals makes it more likely that the behavior change will be maintained by reinforcement in the natural environment. For example, if a person with agoraphobia wishes to return to work or school following a period of disability, work toward the goal of regaining employment is likely to be reinforced by factors such as an increase in income, family approval, and enjoyable interpersonal contacts. In turn, this reinforcement is likely to have a positive influence on work directed toward decreasing phobic avoidance. In our setting, we encourage patients to become involved in regular activities related to their goals (such as work, educational, or social activities) that will also help them engage in the in vivo exposure that will help reduce phobic avoidance. Clarity about goals helps provide a direction to the treatment and is likely to help both the therapist and patient identify sources of support for continued work.

The goal sheet is used at the beginning of therapy and reviewed regularly over its course. The Steps to Reach Goal form is used when needed throughout therapy, to break goals down into smaller steps.

AVAILABILITY:

Dr. John R. Walker, M4—St. Boniface General Hospital, 409 Tache Ave., Winnipeg, Manitoba, Canada R2H 2A6. These instruments are reprinted with permission of the author.

Goal Sheet

NAME: _____ DATE: _____

In planning treatment it is helpful to know about your goals in life: not only your goals for treatment but also your goals for other areas of your life—your work life and your home life, for example. Life goals may be quite general, but medium- and short-term goals should be as specific as possible.

		Importance (A,B,C)	Difficulty
Life goals:			
1.	_____	____	
2.	_____	____	
3.	_____	____	
4.	_____	____	
Medium-term goals (1 year):			(1–6)
1.	_____	____	____
2.	_____	____	____
3.	_____	____	____
4.	_____	____	____
5.	_____	____	____
6.	_____	____	____
Short-term goals (3 months):			(1–10)
1.	_____	____	____
2.	_____	____	____
3.	_____	____	____
4.	_____	____	____
5.	_____	____	____
6.	_____	____	____
7.	_____	____	____
8.	_____	____	____
9.	_____	____	____
10.	_____	____	____

After you have listed your goals, rank each one according to the following.

1. How important is it in your life? Grade your goals A, B, or C in decreasing importance and mark the column on the right.
2. How difficult is it? Rank your goals from 1 (most difficult) to 10 (least difficult) in the far right column. Rank short-term goals first (1–10), then medium-term goals (1–6).

Steps to Reach Goal

NAME: _____ DATE: _____

GOAL: _____

STEPS:

1. _____
   _____

2. _____
   _____

3. _____
   _____

4. _____
   _____

5. _____
   _____

6. _____
   _____

7. _____
   _____

8. _____
   _____

9. _____
   _____

10. _____
   _____

Homework Sheet

BACKGROUND:

This form was developed for use in cognitive-behavioral treatment. Homework assignments are an important aspect of many cognitive-behavioral treatments and are widely used to promote the in vivo exposure that is so important in overcoming phobic avoidance. In our experience we have found better compliance with homework assignments and better follow-up by the therapist when homework planned at the end of a session is recorded in written form. Typically, specific homework assignments are established in discussion between therapist and patient and written out by the patient at the end of the session. The therapist helps the patient to set specific goals for homework that are not excessively difficult. The form is taken home by the patient, who returns for the next session with the form completed. Early in the next session homework assignments are reviewed and plans are made for follow-up homework assignments as required.

AVAILABILITY:

The form was developed by Vivienne Rowan, Gloria Eldridge, and John Walker. Available from Dr. John R. Walker, M4—St. Boniface General Hospital, 409 Tache Ave., Winnipeg, Manitoba, Canada R2H 2A6. This instrument is reprinted with permission of the authors.

—————— Daily Assignment Log ——————

DATE: _____ to _____

Please write out your assignments as specifically as possible in the space below. Try to say exactly what you plan to do.

If possible, circle the box for the day or days on which you plan to do each assignment.

Check off the box of the day on which you do the assignment.

Use the blank space below and the space on the back of the form as needed to describe how the assignments went, how you felt about them afterward, and how you might do even better next time.

Assignments	Sun.	Mon.	Tues.	Wed.	Thurs.	Fri.	Sat.
1. _____ _____ _____							
2. _____ _____ _____							
3. _____ _____ _____							
4. _____ _____ _____							
5. _____ _____ _____							

Author Index

Because of space considerations, only the names of principal authors are listed in this index.

Subject Index